Exploring Moral Problems

Exploring Moral Problems

An Introductory Anthology

Edited by

STEVEN M. CAHN AND
ANDREW T. FORCEHIMES

New York Oxford
OXFORD UNIVERSITY PRESS

Oxford University Press is a department of the University of Oxford. It furthers the University's objective of excellence in research, scholarship, and education by publishing worldwide. Oxford is a registered trade mark of Oxford University Press in the UK and certain other countries.

Published in the United States of America by Oxford University Press
198 Madison Avenue, New York, NY 10016, United States of America.

For titles covered by Section 112 of the US Higher Education Opportunity Act, please visit www.oup.com/us/he for the latest information about pricing and alternate formats.

Library of Congress Cataloging-in-Publication Data

Names: Cahn, Steven M., editor.
Title: Exploring moral problems / edited by Steven M. Cahn and Andrew T. Forcehimes.
Description: 1st Edition. | New York : Oxford University Press, 2017.
Identifiers: LCCN 2017026457 (print) | LCCN 2017032184 (ebook) | ISBN 9780190670313 (ebook) | ISBN 9780190670290 (pbk.)
Subjects: LCSH: Ethical problems.
Classification: LCC BJ1031 (ebook) | LCC BJ1031 .E97 2017 (print) | DDC 170—dc23
LC record available at https://lccn.loc.gov/2017026457

Printing number: 9 8 7 6 5 4 3 2 1

Printed by LSC Communications, Inc.
United States of America

Contents

Preface ix

PART I INTRODUCTION 1

Andrew T. Forcehimes *Ethical Theories and Their Application 2*

PART II INTRODUCTORY READINGS 49

A. Challenges to Ethical Theory 50

Mary Midgley *Moral Isolationism 50*

James Rachels *Egoism and Moral Scepticism 57*

Steven M. Cahn *God and Morality 69*

B. Varieties of Ethical Theory 72

Thomas Hobbes *Leviathan 72*

Immanuel Kant *Groundwork for the Metaphysics of Morals 82*

John Stuart Mill *Utilitarianism 95*

Julia Driver *Virtue Ethics 107*

Virginia Held *The Ethics of Care 110*

John Finnis *Natural Law 124*

C. Good Lives 130

Richard Taylor *The Meaning of Life 130*

Susan Wolf *Meaning of Life 141*

Christine Vitrano *Meaningful Lives 146*

PART III THE LIMITS OF LAW 150

A. Free Speech 151

John Stuart Mill *On Liberty 151*

Miles Unterreiner *Limiting Free Speech 164*

Charles R. Lawrence III *Regulating Racist Speech on Campus 170*

Martin P. Golding *Campus Speech Restrictions 177*

B. Prostitution 183

Elizabeth Anderson *Value and the Gift of Sexuality 183*

Martha C. Nussbaum *Taking Money for Bodily Services 187*

Debra Satz *Markets in Women's Sexual Labor 203*

C. Organ Sales 212

Sarah McGrath *Organ Procurement, Altruism, and Autonomy 212*

Simon Rippon *The Harm of a Live Donor Organ Market 217*

Luke Semrau *A Reply to Rippon 224*

D. Pornography 227

Helen E. Longino *Pornography, Oppression, and Freedom 227*

Joel Feinberg *The Case against Pornography: An Assessment 238*

E. Drug Legalization 244

Douglas Husak *Three Points about Drug Decriminalization 244*

George Sher *On the Decriminalization of Drugs 251*

F. Gun Control 258

Samuel C. Wheeler III *Arms as Insurance 258*

David DeGrazia *Handguns, Moral Rights, and Physical Security 264*

PART IV ULTIMATE HARMS 278

A. Terrorism 279

Michael Walzer *Terrorism 279*

Lionel K. McPherson *Is Terrorism Distinctively Wrong? 285*

B. Torture 291

Henry Shue *Torture 291*

Alan M. Dershowitz *The Ticking Time-Bomb Terrorist 303*

Jessica Wolfendale *Training Torturers 307*

C. Capital Punishment 317

Walter Berns *The Morality of Capital Punishment 317*

Stephen Nathanson *The Death Penalty as a Symbolic Issue 322*

PART V JUSTICE 330

A. Distributive Justice 331

John Rawls *A Theory of Justice 331*

Robert Nozick *The Entitlement Theory 338*

B. Immigration 349

David Miller *Immigration: The Case for Limits 349*

Michael Huemer *Is There a Right to Immigrate? 364*

C. Injustice 381

Kwame Anthony Appiah *Racisms 381*

Ann E. Cudd and Leslie E. Jones *Sexism 388*

Iris Marion Young *Five Faces of Oppression 398*

D. Reparations 413

Bernard R. Boxill *The Morality of Reparation 413*

Chandran Kukathas *Reparations and the Problem of Agency 422*

E. Affirmative Action 433

Steven M. Cahn *Two Concepts of Affirmative Action 433*

Karen Hanson *Facing Facts and Responsibilities 444*

Laurence Thomas *What Good Am I? 450*

Celia Wolf-Devine *Proportional Representation 457*

PART VI SEX 465

A. Sex and Consent 466

Sarah Conly *Seduction, Rape, and Coercion 466*

Scott A. Anderson *Sex under Pressure 483*

B. Sexual Harassment 493

N. Ann Davis *Sexual Harassment in the University 493*

Margaret Crouch *Sexual Harassment in Public Places 504*

PART VII THE FAMILY 509

A. Marriage 510

Elizabeth Brake *Minimal Marriage 510*

Ralph Wedgwood *Is Civil Marriage Illiberal? 520*

Bonnie Steinbock *Adultery 533*

B. Parents and Children 539

Jane English *What Do Grown Children Owe Their Parents? 539*

Joseph Kupfer *Can Parents and Children Be Friends? 546*

Simon Keller *Four Theories of Filial Duty 553*

PART VIII THE LIMITS OF LIFE 566

A. Abortion 567

Judith Jarvis Thomson *A Defense of Abortion 567*

Mary Anne Warren *On the Moral and Legal Status of Abortion 584*

Don Marquis *An Argument That Abortion Is Wrong 600*

Amy Berg *Abortion and Miscarriage 607*

B. Genetic Choices 616

Laura M. Purdy *Can Having Children Be Immoral? 616*

Simo Vehmas *Parents and Genetic Information 625*

Julian Savulescu *Procreative Beneficence 630*

Michael J. Sandel *The Case against Perfection 640*

C. Euthanasia 653

James Rachels *Active and Passive Euthanasia 653*

Philippa Foot *Killing and Letting Die 660*

PART IX OBLIGATIONS TO OTHERS 669

A. World Hunger 670

Peter Singer *Famine, Affluence, and Morality 670*

Travis Timmerman *A Reply to Singer 681*

B. Animals 686

Peter Singer *Equality for Animals 686*

Bonnie Steinbock *Speciesism and the Idea of Equality 704*

Tom Regan *The Case for Animal Rights 712*

Mary Anne Warren *Speaking of Animal Rights 722*

C. The Environment 733

Elliott Sober *Philosophical Problems for Environmentalism 733*

John Broome *The Ethics of Climate Change 751*

APPENDIX: PUZZLES TO PONDER 759

A. Judith Jarvis Thomson *The Trolley Problem 760*

B. Steven M. Cahn *The Altruism Puzzle 763*

C. Derek Parfit *The Non-Identity Problem 764*

D. Steven M. Cahn *The Divestiture Puzzle 765*

Glossary 767

Preface

During the late 1960s, American philosophers, spurred by debate over the morality of the Vietnam War, broadened their approach to the field of ethics. Until that time, their focus had been on exploring the meaning and justification of moral judgments and assessing the strengths and weaknesses of various moral theories. But once the war was deemed an appropriate subject for moral inquiry, so were other pressing issues, such as abortion, euthanasia, and world hunger. Since then, the range of subjects given philosophical attention has increased dramatically every decade, as new technologies and new social challenges continually give rise to new moral perplexities.

Like the related Oxford University Press books, *Exploring Philosophy* (fifth edition), *Exploring Ethics* (fourth edition), and *Exploring Philosophy of Religion* (second edition), *Exploring Moral Problems* is marked most notably by three characteristics. First, its clear structure provides a helpful guide to the subject. Second, many selections have been edited to sharpen focus and increase accessibility. Third, the contents reflect the importance to contemporary philosophy of work authored by women, much of which has not been given its due in other anthologies.

Our thanks to executive editor Robert Miller, for his support and guidance; to associate editor Alyssa Palazzo and editorial assistant Sydney Keen, who have helped us in so many ways; to manuscript editor Marianne Paul, for her conscientiousness; and to the staff of Oxford University Press, for generous assistance throughout production.

We have been guided in part by suggestions from reviewers chosen by the Press and we wish to acknowledge them individually:

Justin Capes, *East Tennessee State University*
Charles E. Cardwell, *Pellissippi State Community College*
Patrick Fleming, *James Madison University*
Hans Pedersen, *Indiana University of Pennsylvania*
Aeon J. Skoble, *Bridgewater State University*
Todd Stewart, *Illinois State University.*

A final note. Some of the materials throughout the book were written when the custom was to use the noun "man" and the pronoun "he" to refer to all persons, regardless of gender, and we have retained the authors' original wording. Now we turn to problems of moral philosophy.

PART I

Introduction

Ethical Theories and Their Application

Andrew T. Forcehimes

§1. *Introduction*

Your life consists of a series of actions. You do mundane things. You brush your teeth and buy cups of coffee. You do momentous things. You fall in love and have a child. Mundane or momentous, you have no doubt thought about whether what you did is, in point of fact, what you ought to have done. Think, for example, about something you did that you deeply regret. (Take a moment to actually do this.) When thinking about this regrettable action, you are, inevitably, having two very different kinds of thoughts. You are thinking about what happened. You are having *descriptive* thoughts about what was the case. But, insofar as what you did was regrettable, you are also thinking about what should have happened. You are thus also having *normative* thoughts about what ought to have been the case (but wasn't) or what you were required to do (but didn't). Here—in the normative domain—is where ethics resides.

Although you've confronted ethical questions, chances are your answers have not formed a consistent set. Return to your regret. You think that you ought to have acted otherwise. This is a verdict about your action. Now if I asked you why you reached this verdict, you could probably point to certain facts that made the act one you ought to have refrained from performing. Perhaps you harmed someone, broke a promise, were untrue to yourself, or the like. If you are able to say what you ought to do and why you ought to do it, then you have the beginning of an ethical theory. But a mere beginning is insufficient. If you are to stand any chance of thinking about your life in a consistent and coherent fashion, then what you need is a *systematic* account of what you ought to do and why you ought to do it. You, in other words, need an ethical theory.

This introduction will prepare you for the intense ethical inquiry that takes place in this volume. Ethical inquiry, roughly, proceeds in two broad steps. First, we start with easy ethical cases—ones that we have high confidence that we are getting right—to help us build a theory. Second, we then use this theory to help us work out what to do in the hard cases—ones that we, pre-theoretically, are unsure about. The readings in this volume concern this second step: They deal with the hard cases, like abortion, terrorism, world hunger, and so forth. This introduction concerns the first step. We will first look at what any ethical theory tries to accomplish, then we will survey the dominant positions.

Being familiar with the process of theory construction as well as having the ability to recognize popular extant theories will prove an invaluable resource as you read through this volume. In trying to defend a position on a particular topic, most authors, usually only implicitly, rely on their preferred ethical theory. Your ability to recognize their reasoning as stemming from a particular theory will thus not only make their position more readily intelligible, but also make it easier to locate potential weaknesses. Relying on a particular theory entails that one inherits the problems that come with the theory. So, by being aware of the general objections faced by a theory, you will be able to quickly see the problems that beset specific applications of it.

A final remark before we begin. Ethics, as you shall see, is a trying endeavor. Like all areas of philosophy, the ideas can be complicated and abstract. And like all areas of philosophy, it is often unclear just which theory we should, in the end, believe. Ethics is intellectually taxing. But unlike most other areas of philosophy, we cannot comfortably take the time to sort out our thoughts. Right now, we are living. We have to act. And what we do matters. Ethics is thus taxing in an additional, special way. When we get things wrong, we do not just hold false beliefs. We live disastrous lives. When we are plagued by doubt, we do not just confront the discomfort of uncertainty. Our casting about in the dark might turn out to be deeply morally regrettable. That thought haunts me. And it should, I believe, haunt you too.

Let's thus turn, with some urgency, to figuring out the thing to do.

2. *What Is an Ethical Theory?*

Ethical theories have two main aims. The first is *enumerative*: identify those acts that we ought (or ought not) to perform. The second is *explanatory*: provide an account as to why we ought (or ought not) to perform the acts identified. Let's take each of these aims in turn.

2.1 *What You Ought to Do*

We can start with the enumerative aim. An ethical theory tries to articulate a general principle that tells us the status of the various actions we could possibly face. There are four main assessments this principle might deliver: *impermissible, permissible, optional,* and *required.* These assessments are called *deontic verdicts,* because they tell us our various duties. (*Deon* is Greek for "duty.")

Having a handle on what these four deontic verdicts mean is crucial to understanding what a theory demands. One way to do this visually is by representing each of the actions you could perform at a given time as a door you could proceed through. Say, right now, you have ten possible actions you could perform. Then we could imagine you standing in front of ten doors, each representing a course of action you could take. Now to visualize what a theory says about each of these actions, we could further imagine that some doors are marked with an X. This X indicates that proceeding through the door—performing this action—is, according to the theory, impermissible. With this picture, we can now represent the verdicts a theory might issue as follows:

- An action is *impermissible* if and only if refraining from the action is required. This is a door with an X on it, telling you not to proceed.

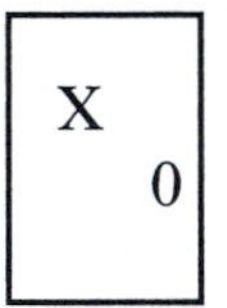

  The door represents a course of action that you could take, but ethically you shouldn't.

- An action is *permissible* if and only if it is an action that is not impermissible. This is a door without an X on it, telling you it is Okay to proceed.

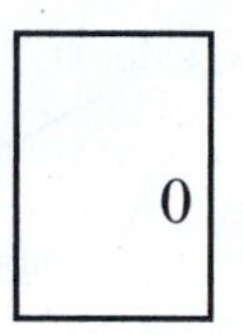

This is a course of action that you could take, and ethically it is open for you to take it.

- An action is *optional* if and only if it is permissible to perform or not perform the action. Suppose, for simplicity, that you only have three actions available to you. One of these acts is impermissible; the other two are permissible. So the choice set you face looks like this:

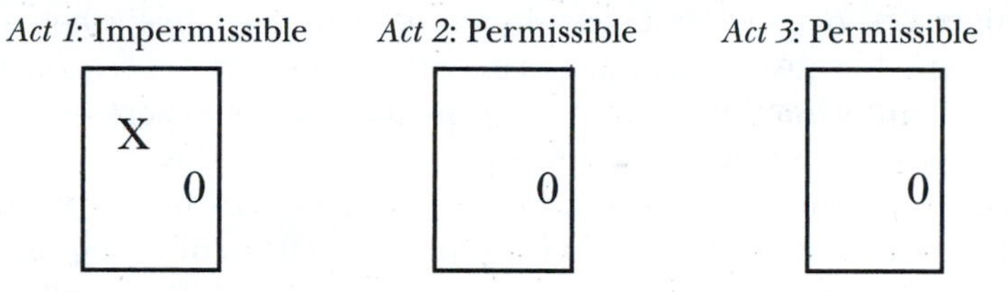

  Since you can permissibly perform *Act 2* or *Act 3*, both of these acts are *optional*. You need to make sure you refrain from performing *Act 1*, but ethically the rest is up to you.

- An action is *required* if and only if it is the uniquely permissible action available—a permissible action that is not optional. Suppose again that you only have three actions available to you. But this time two of these acts are impermissible; the remaining act is permissible. So this new choice set looks like this:

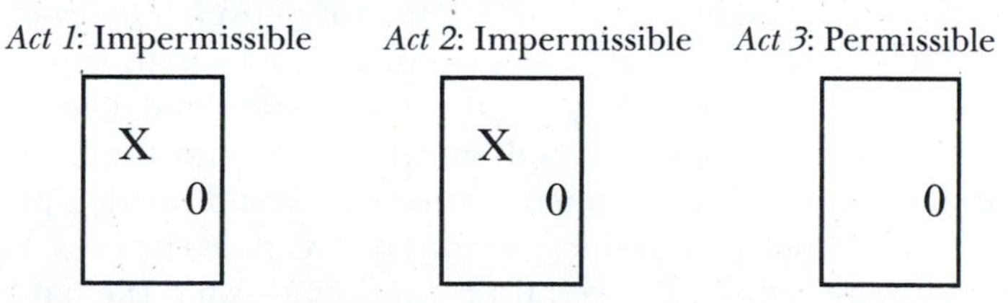

  Since you can only permissibly perform *Act 3*, this act is *required*. All of the other acts open to you are ethically blocked.

Notice how these verdicts relate to one another. For example, any action that is required will also be permissible. The below diagram illustrates these connections.

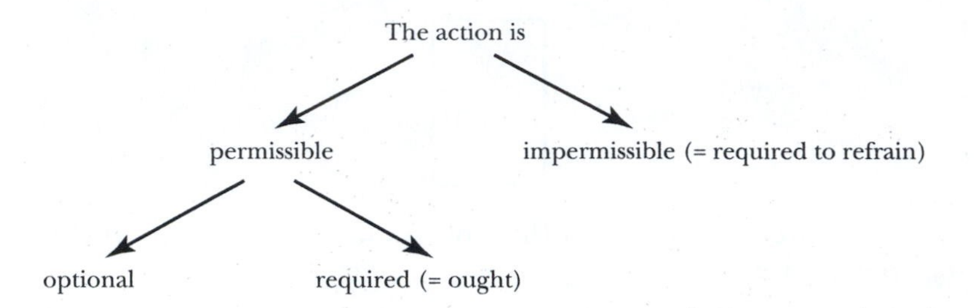

The definitions for our four deontic verdicts have been partly defined in terms of one another. That's unsatisfying. Nevertheless, we can make some headway toward more satisfying definitions if we introduce the concept of a *reason*: a consideration that counts in favor of, or justifies, our acting in certain ways. As, for instance, when we say, the fact that casting insults harms others gives you a reason not to cast them. The fact—that casting insults harms others—counts in favor of your not casting them.

By deploying the concept of a reason, we can break out of our definitional circle by analyzing "required" in the following, more informative way:

> An action is *required* if and only if there is decisive reason to perform the action. The set of reasons in favor of the action outweighs the set of reasons against it.

Defining "required", and thereby our other deontic verdicts, in terms of reasons fits well with a fairly natural way of thinking about what to do. When thinking about whether we ought to perform some action, we look to all the considerations that count in favor of acting in this way and all of the considerations against it. We then treat these considerations like weights on a scale. If the pros outweigh the cons, then we are required to perform the action. Think back to your regrettable action. There were the pros: that you wouldn't be embarrassed, that you could help out a friend, and the like. And there were the cons: that it would harm someone, that you would break a promise, and the like. Since regrettable, the cons outweighed the pros. You did what you were required to refrain from doing—what the balance of reasons failed to support.

Defining our deontic verdicts in terms of reasons sits well with what ethical theories are in the business of doing: namely, locating the considerations that count in favor of our actions. Ethics is, at base, justificatory. By citing reasons, we are not trying to explain how the world is; rather, we're trying to justify how it should be.

2.2 *Why You Ought to Do it*

In citing the reasons that deliver our deontic verdicts, however, we've made a subtle shift. We've moved to giving a specific justification—e.g., the fact that the action will harm others—for *why* an act has the deontic status it does. This brings us to the second, explanatory aim of an ethical theory. Why do acts have the deontic statuses that they do? The answer to this question tells us which facts are genuinely reason-providing. If, for example, you think you ought not have performed the regrettable action *because* it caused harm, then you take harm facts to be one of the factors that determine the deontic statuses of actions. It is, at least in part, because of the harm it would cause that you are required to refrain from acting in this regrettable way.

To get a better handle on this explanatory aim, it will be helpful to start with a broad taxonomy of the types of accounts on offer. And the best way to categorize the various approaches is to think about how you would construct a theory yourself. In constructing an ethical theory, what you would likely do is think very carefully about your life, noting the various features that seem ethically relevant. Next you would try to identify some central idea by which all of these features could be explained.

Here is how we might start such a list:

Deontic Claims	Evaluative Claims	Character Claims
Costlessly saving lives is required.	Pain is bad.	Courage is a virtue.
Favoring your children is permissible.	Injustice is bad.	Modesty is a virtue.
Murdering is impermissible.	Pleasure is good.	Beneficence is a virtue.
Torturing is impermissible.	Equality is good.	Malice is a vice.
Stealing is impermissible.	Beauty is good.	Vanity is a vice.
Lying is impermissible.	Getting one's due is good.	Envy is a vice.

Obviously, this list needs to be greatly expanded. But this gives us a start. The items on this list are symptomatic of the ethical life. We now need a diagnosis that explains all of these symptoms (or explains them away).

As this analogy suggests, constructing an ethical theory is very similar to how a doctor comes up with a diagnosis. If we were doctors, we would first look carefully at our patient, noting the numerous symptoms. We would then offer an account that we believed best explains why our patient displays these symptoms. Diagnostic medicine is, of course, a descriptive enterprise. Nevertheless, insofar as the process of inquiry is concerned—trying to offer a unified account of the data—the analogy to theory construction in ethics is apt. A diagnosis explains why a patient's body displays the symptoms it does. An ethical theory explains why a life displays the normative features it does.

By recognizing how theory construction begins, we can classify the various theories by asking: What central idea explains the various features of our ethical lives? Three different answers to this question are prevalent among ethicists. There are those that take the central idea to concern the world we create—*consequentialists.* There are those that take the central idea to concern the actions we perform—*deontologists.* And there are those that take the central idea to be the people we are—*virtue ethicists.* In terms of our list of ethically relevant features, we could classify these theories by saying that consequentialists try to explain the items on the right and left columns on our list of symptoms in terms of the items found in the middle column. Deontologists try to explain the items on the middle and right columns in terms of the items found on the left. And virtue ethicists try to explain the items on the left and middle columns in terms of the items found on the right. The question, of course, is which of these diagnoses is correct.

§3. *Consequentialism*

The normative importance of the connection between acts and outcomes is obvious. Let us thus begin with consequentialism. On this approach, we start by noting that, through our acts, we shape the world we occupy. When you are thinking about whether to do something—say, skip class—the first thought you probably have concerns what will happen if you skip and what will happen if you don't. Those that take the consequentialist approach never move past this thought. They believe that, in figuring out what to do, all that ethically matters concerns what will be brought about. This is not to suggest that consequentialists are narrowly concerned with what causally follows from the act. Rather, the outcome that an act brings about includes everything in the complete world history were the act to be performed. Concern for outcomes, in this broad sense, exhausts the ethical domain, according to consequentialists.

But how precisely do we get from outcomes to deontic verdicts? The answer involves three steps. First, we need to look at the alternatives you have available to you at the time of action. Second, we evaluate the world that would come about were you to take a given action. We associate an outcome with each action and then ask: How does this outcome compare to the other possible outcomes? Is it better or worse? Evaluating the outcomes of each action gives us a ranking. Third, we use this ranking to assign deontic verdicts to each action. And the natural thought to have concerning ranking is: Why do less than the best? The action with the best outcome is the one you ought to take. Yet, given that there could be ties for best, it is perhaps better to say that you are permitted to do (of the available actions) only what will bring about the best outcome. Doing less than the best is impermissible. Consequentialism, in a word, treats deontic verdicts as a function of the outcomes—in particular the goodness of the outcomes—our actions produce.

We can make these three steps concrete by looking at an example. Suppose you face a life-threatening illness. Your doctor gives you three options: (A) You can have a surgery with anesthetics, which will painlessly cure you. (B) You can have surgery without anesthetics, which will agonizingly cure you. Or (C) you can do nothing, in which case you will die an agonizing death. What ought you to do? If you are thinking like a consequentialist, you are thinking, "It ought to be that I am painlessly cured." And why is that? Because (A) is better than (B), and (B) is better than (C).

Option		Outcome	Deontic Verdict
A	⟶	Best (cured, no agony)	*Required*
B	⟶	2nd Best (cured, agony)	*Impermissible*
C	⟶	Worst (not cured, agony)	*Impermissible*

This example illustrates the structure of a consequentialist theory. We ought to make the world as good as we can. Facts about the goodness of outcomes are the sole reason-providing facts. They are the only facts that matter for determining the deontic status of an action. But this example also illustrates what is compelling about the view. Without a moment's reflection, it should be obvious that (A) is the option you ought to choose. Why endure unnecessary badness? The consequentialist globalizes this thought for the rest of the normative domain: It is only permissible to bring about the best outcome.

So far so good. However, in order to get from this consequentialist framework to a specific consequentialist theory, we need to nail down, with precision, what it takes for one outcome to be better than another. How should we evaluate the possible actions available to us?

In the above example, I took it for granted that your agony and death were bad. And these seem like pretty obvious candidates for bad outcomes. How well your life is going (or if it is going at all) appears to be one of the things that makes an outcome better or worse. Let's thus begin with the natural suggestion that facts about well-being are what determines the goodness of an outcome. (A discussion of the major theories of well-being can be found in the *Appendix*.)

3.1 *Egoism*

Suppose we focus exclusively on *your* well-being, holding that it alone is good. That is to say, one outcome is better than another if and only if your life is going better in that outcome. Nobody else matters. Just you. Then, combined with a consequentialist approach, this view would hold that you ought to make the world as good as you can, and the only way to do this is to make your life as good-for-you as possible. This view is known as

> *Universal Egoism.* You are required to perform an action if and only if (and because), of the acts now available to you, this act will uniquely bring about the most good-for-you. That is, you ought to perform the action whose outcome is uniquely best-for-you.

The theory thus tells each of us to do whatever will best promote our own good. This principle serves as the criterion for assessing the deontic statuses of actions. An action is *required* if and only if so acting would uniquely maximize your overall well-being. An action is *impermissible* if and only if so acting would not maximize your overall well-being. And an action is *optional* if and only if so acting would maximize your overall well-being, but there is some other available action that ties in the amount of overall well-being it would bring you.

After hearing these deontic verdicts, universal egoism might not look very promising. Is the impermissibility of an action really located in the narcissistic fact that it wouldn't be best for *you*? Can't the good of others bear noninstrumentally on what you are required to do? The thought driving these questions seems to be this: Universal egoism makes ethics overly and implausibly focused on a specific person—you. Perhaps, however, egoism can be made more plausible by thinking about what nonegoistic theories demand. An altruistic theory maintains that ethics demands, at least sometimes, that you sacrifice your well-being for the well-being of others. Egoism denies this. Thus, if we can show that you are not required to be altruistic, then we are well on our way to universal egoism.

Let's begin by assuming that an altruistic act is required. What you have most reason to do is sacrifice your well-being for the well-being of others. Suppose, for example, that you are outside of a burning building with a group of strangers stuck inside. It is too late for the fire department to help. The only hope for these strangers is you. However, to save these strangers you will be severely burned. These burns will force you to live out the remainder of your existence in agony. Any benefit that you get from saving these strangers will, we can assume, be swamped by this future agony. Now, if the number of these strangers was large enough, most ethical theories will demand that you make this sacrifice. They demand altruism. But I suspect, confronted with this situation, you would pause to ask: Why ought *I* to do what altruism claims I ought to do?

If, as we are assuming, this altruistic act is required, this question would answer itself. It would be like asking: Do I really have most reason to do what I have most reason to do? Your original question, however, does not seem to be trivial in this way. You seem to be really asking for something. What's going on? One interpretation turns to the authority of the deontic verdict altruism delivers. When you try to assume the truth of altruism and then confront a situation where it demands something at odds with what is good-for-you, the deontic verdict seems to lose its authority—it fails to bind you in the right sort of way. To use a political analogy, altruism's demands are like the laws of a country of which you are not a citizen. When a country tries to command a noncitizen it makes sense to say: Why ought *I* to do what this state claims I ought to do? This state has exceeded its jurisdiction. And so too, on this line of argument, have altruistic ethical theories. You cannot have reasons to perform actions that do not ultimately promote your well-being. Such purported reasons do not speak to you; they lack authority.

If this line of argument is correct, then for a reason to have force it must serve your well-being. And by plugging this conclusion into the consequentialist framework—that you always have most reason to bring about the best outcome—we get universal egoism. Of course, the soundness of this argument turns on the claim that only your well-being can grip you. The fact that well-being extends across your whole life should thus give the egoist pause. For this means that egoist must cash out the metaphor of "being gripped" or "spoken to" in such a way that the *present* well-being of others is excluded from consideration but your *future* well-being is included. Yet why think that your future well-being would be any more gripping? That is, why think that reasons are agent-relative (it's all about you) but time-neutral (your present well-being matters as much as your future well-being)? This asymmetry—placing special importance on *who*, while being indifferent to *when*—is hard to maintain. After all, the prevalence of procrastination, for instance, is best explained by the fact that the good-for-your-future-self does not always resonate with you now. But even if we assume the egoist can justify this asymmetry, problems remain.

Chief among these problems is that, if followed collectively, universal egoism is self-defeating. If we all act as universal egoism prescribes, each of us will bring about an outcome that is worse-for-each than had we not obeyed the theory's prescriptions. To see this, suppose that you and I each have a terrible migraine. I possess a capsule of aspirin, which, given my constitution, will make my migraine slightly less painful. But, given your constitution, the aspirin will make your migraine significantly less painful. You possess a capsule of codeine, which, given your constitution, will make your migraine slightly less painful. But, given my constitution, the codeine will make my migraine significantly less painful. A combination of both aspirin and codeine would completely eliminate the migraine for me and, likewise, for you. What does egoism say about this case? It says that no matter what I do, you are better off by giving yourself the codeine.

<table>
<tr><td colspan="2" rowspan="2"></td><td colspan="2">You</td></tr>
<tr><td>give me codeine</td><td>give yourself codeine</td></tr>
<tr><td rowspan="2">I</td><td>give you aspirin</td><td>• 2nd best-for-me (pain significantly reduced)
• 2nd best-for-you (pain significantly reduced)</td><td>• Worse-for-me (full pain)
• Best-for-you (eliminates pain)</td></tr>
<tr><td>give myself aspirin</td><td>• Best-for-me (eliminates pain)
• Worse-for-you (full pain)</td><td>• 3rd best-for-me (pain slightly reduced)
• 3rd best-for-you (pain slightly reduced)</td></tr>
</table>

Here's why: If I give you the aspirin, then you can completely eliminate your migraine by taking the codeine. But if I don't give you the aspirin, then the best you can do is make your migraine slightly less painful by taking the codeine. Either way, then, egoism prescribes that you take the codeine. Notice, however, that no matter what you do, I am better off giving myself the aspirin. So, if we both follow what egoism prescribes, we end up getting the next to worse outcome for each of us. But to do what seems like the obvious thing to do in this situation—i.e., swap painkillers—we would both need to disobey universal egoism.

3.2 *Contractarianism*

When confronted with this painkillers case, your initial reaction is probably that this coordination problem has an easy solution. What egoism should demand is that we first make an agreement to do what is mutually beneficial, and then turn to addressing the distribution of the pills. This is precisely what one approach, known as *contractarianism*, holds. This theory aims to retain the driving idea behind egoism—that all of your reasons are reasons to promote your well-being—but avoid the problem posed by the painkillers case by filtering egoism through a contractual agreement. Given the prevalence of coordination problems, egoism demands that we conform to the details of this contract. Very roughly, then, we can characterize contractarianism as endorsing the following:

> You are required to perform an action if and only if refraining from so acting is disallowed by principles that everyone would egoistically agree to (under suitable conditions).

This formulation is rough because we would need to know the conditions needed for the contract to qualify as suitable. For instance, we might want to add that the bargainers are idealized in certain ways—e.g., they are informed, rational, and so forth. Without such idealizations, we would in effect guarantee that no consensus could be reach. Misinformed and irrational people are hard to bargain with.

Still, even if we landed on suitable idealizing conditions, we would need to identify just what principles would be agreed to. To identify these principles, it will help to recall what each party wants out of the contract. We all want the benefits afforded by cooperation. We all want this contract to succeed. Yet each of us wants to secure the greatest benefit while taking on the fewest costs. What principles we end up with will largely depend on how we think this tension should be adjudicated. However, let's not pursue this issue further.

Whatever the chosen principles turn out to be, a lingering worry concerns compliance.

Remember that egoism serves as the foundation for contractarianism. So what happens when adhering to the terms of the contract is not good-for-you? Return to our painkillers case. Suppose, for example, that we both agree to the principle: If it's mutually advantageous to swap pills, we ought to swap. Next consider a twist on the original case. Suppose that you have a fake codeine pill, which initially works just like codeine but kills one week after ingestion. Moreover, this fake pill kills in a way such that the cause of death looks natural. If you give me this pill, I will give you aspirin. And, because you retained your codeine pill, you can completely eliminate your migraine. What ought you to do? Assuming this is a one-off case—you don't want to get a well-being-diminishing reputation—egoism councils you to secretly defect from our agreement. You ought to give me the fake pill. For recall, the driving idea behind egoism is that you cannot have reasons to perform actions that do not ultimately promote your well-being. And giving me codeine, when you have a substitute that can secure my aspirin without this cost, does not ultimately promote your well-being. The problem for contractarianism should now be obvious. If you can, by force or fraud, secure the benefits of the contract without incurring the cost, then egoism prescribes that you break the contract. You ought to free ride whenever it is best-for-you. Contractarianism's egoistic foundation demands this defection. Why? Because egoism claims that only well-being enhancing reasons can grip you. And, hence, in this case, since adhering to the chosen principles does not enhance your well-being, you have no reason to follow them. The contract loses its grip; it fails to bind.

This brings us back to our original worry with egoism: It heightens your own importance to the point of absurdity. If you think that you ought not kill me in the revised painkillers case or fail to live up to your side of the bargain, then you both reject egoism and think that contractarianism faces a serious problem.

3.3 *Utilitarianism*

The lesson from our discussion of egoism is that ethics should be more impersonal. Egoism tells you that your well-being, and only your well-being, matters. But what is the ethically relevant difference between the good-for-you and the good-for-me? Is there some magic in the use of the possessive—*my* well-being? It seems not. As Sidgwick famously put it, "[T]he good of any one individual is of no more importance, from the point of view . . . of the Universe, than the good of any other; unless, that is, there are special grounds for believing that more good is likely to be realized in the one case than in the other." Following Sidgwick, perhaps we should think that our well-being, taken together, is what matters. Your well-being is a goodness-making feature of an outcome, and so is mine. By extending this line of reasoning to everyone, we arrive at our next consequentialist theory—*utilitarianism*. This theory holds that one outcome is better than another if and only if the total amount of well-being is greater. According to this consequentialist approach, you ought to make the world as good as you can, and the only way to do this is to impartially maximize well-being. The following principle thus serves as the criterion for assessing the deontic statuses of actions, according to

> *Utilitarianism.* You are required to perform an action if and only if (and because) of the acts now available to you, this act will uniquely bring about the greatest sum-total of well-being. That is, you ought to perform the action whose outcome maximizes total well-being.

To see what this principle amounts to, we will need to understand precisely what promoting the *sum-total* of well-being means.

It means that the theory is aggregative. In determining the sum-total of well-being attached to the outcome of a given action, we need answers to the following questions:

> *The Increase Question.* For each entity whose well-being would be affected by the performance of the action, how much would the act increase their well-being?

> *The Decrease Question.* For each entity whose well-being would be affected by the performance of the action, how much would the act decrease their well-being?

Once we have an answer to the Increase Question, we take all of the units of well-being that will accrue to each entity and add them up. Then we do the same for the Decrease Question. Finally, we subtract the increases from decreases, giving us the net sum-total.

What utilitarianism demands is that we bring about the outcome with the highest sum-total of well-being. More precisely, an action is *required* if and only if so acting would uniquely bring about the greatest sum-total of well-being. An action is *impermissible* if and only if so acting would not bring about the greatest sum-total of well-being. And an action is *optional* if and only if so acting would bring about the greatest sum-total of well-being, but there is some other act that brings about an equal sum-total of well-being.

Unlike universal egoism, the deontic verdicts supplied by utilitarianism seem initially quite plausible. One area where this is particularly evident concerns our treatment of animals. Just as it appears that there is nothing special about *my* well-being that makes it more important than your well-being, there appears to be nothing special about *human* well-being that makes it more important than animal well-being. (This is why I used "entity" rather than "person" in the Increase and Decrease Questions above.) By utilitarianism's lights, it is just as bad for me to needlessly break your arm as it is for me to needlessly break the leg of a dog, assuming the decrease in well-being is the same. Intuitively, needlessly causing pain to a dog seems like a bad thing, something we have reason to avoid. Utilitarianism nicely explains this reason. And it locates the explanation in exactly the right place—the fact that the dog would suffer. Contrast this with egoism or contractarianism. Egoism says that if breaking the dog's leg would best promote my well-being, then I am required to do it. Contractarianism, at best, locates the reason not to break the dog's leg in an agreement with others. But this agreement has nothing directly to do with the dog. Thus, even if contractarianism can tell me not to harm the dog, it comes from the wrong place—a contract, not the dog's leg.

Despite its initial appeal, utilitarianism faces serious problems both in terms of its sum-totaling and its exclusive focus on well-being.

In focusing exclusively on the sum-total of well-being, the theory is indifferent to how well-being is distributed. A counterintuitive implication of this exclusive focus is immediately obvious once we remember that there are two ways of increasing the total sum of well-being: We can either increase the well-being of existing entities, or we can bring into existence new well-being–having entities. This latter option is where the trouble lies. Suppose, for instance, that you are in charge of the world's population. Given the earth's resources, you have two possible policy options:

> *Making People Well-Off.* Keep population levels static. Earth's available resources will then permit each member of the limited set of existing people to have exceedingly good lives. In short, have a low population with each person given a very high level of well-being.
>
> *Making Well-Off People.* Greatly increase the population. Earth's available resources will then permit each member of the enormous set of existing people to have lives barely worth living. In short, have a high population with each person given a very low level of well-being.

Now for the crucial stipulation: The sum total of well-being produced by each policy is the same. Confronted with these options, what does utilitarianism tell you to do? It tells you that since, in terms of well-being, each option is equally good, you are permitted to choose either. Yet could Making People Well-Off really be ethically on a par with Making Well-Off People? If you think that treating these two options equally is a mistake, then utilitarianism's sum-totaling must be abandoned. Of course, there are other ways of aggregating well-being. We could aim for the highest average, for example. But let's leave aside these possible revisions, and turn directly to a distribution problem that calls into question utilitarianism's exclusive focus on well-being.

Most of us hold that people getting their due is good. Intuitively, outcomes are better when people get what they deserve. Suppose, for example, your lifelong enemy wants to harm you. With malice in his heart, he tries to push you off of a cliff. However, worked up by the prospect of your destruction, his push carries him over the precipice with you. You both survive the fall, but are gravely injured. As the rescuers arrive, it is clear that, given the severity of the injuries, there is only enough time to save one of you. And now for the crucial stipulation: Whether you or your enemy is saved, the outcome, in terms of the sum-total of well-being, will be the same. What does utilitarianism tell these rescuers to do? Like the population case above, it tells them that since, in terms of well-being, the options are equally good, they are permitted to choose either option. Between saving you and saving your enemy, they could flip a coin. But that seems off. If you think, due to his culpability, the outcome would be worse if they saved your enemy—he caused this mess, after all—then you think that well-being is not the only factor that determines the level of goodness that an outcome can have. Desert also matters. The outcome is better when your enemy receives the level of well-being he deserves.[1]

3.4 *Act-Consequentialism*

Utilitarianism, in telling us that the maximization of well-being is all and only what matters ethically, thus faces serious problems. Yet these problems can be alleviated with a simple revision. We can simply drop the idea that well-being is all that matters. As we have seen, people getting their due might also influence the goodness of an outcome. And, if desert can influence the goodness of outcomes, then other goods might as well. Equality and beauty, for instance, are also plausible candidates. Each, it might be thought, is good in itself. Notice we have here moved away from the idea that for something to be good is for it to be good-for-us. Rather desert, equality, and beauty are good-*simpliciter.* These goods are impartially good, regardless of whether they are good-for-anyone. On this broad consequentialist approach, then, you ought to make the world as good as you can, and the only way to do this is to maximize the total amount of good-*simpliciter.* This broad consequentialist theory is known simply as

> *Act-Consequentialism.* You are required to perform an action if and only if (and because), of the acts now available to you, this act will uniquely bring about the most good-*simpliciter.* That is, you ought to perform the action whose outcome uniquely maximizes the good, period.

Act-consequentialism tells each agent to do whatever will best promote the good overall, impartially assessed.

To be clear, utilitarianism is a species of act-consequentialism, restricting the only thing that is good-*simpliciter* to well-being. Act-consequentialism, as the broader genus, is simply more liberal in the potential goods that may increase the goodness of an outcome. Of course, if we took this broader approach, we would need an account of these other goods, and how they interact, in order to determine the ranking of our available actions. But, once we had this account, we would be well positioned to avoid the above problems associated with the above narrower theories, while retaining consequentialism's compelling structure. Rather than trying to articulate what things are good-*simpliciter,* however, let's conclude with two serious problems for act-consequentialism generally.

Act-consequentialism says that you are permitted to act in a certain way if and only if this act would bring about the best outcome. By breaking apart the necessary and sufficient conditions of this principle,[2] we can bring out two implications of act-consequentialism that are particularly troubling: namely, its lack of (i) a wide range of permissible actions open to you, some of which will not maximize the good (*options*); and (ii) a set of impermissible actions that you simply ought not to perform even if they maximize the good (*constraints*).

Take first the

> *Necessary Condition.* Only if an action brings about the best outcome, is it permissible to perform the action.

This condition leaves little room for people to live their own lives. For you to act permissibly, you must bring about the most good. Put differently, it is always impermissible to fail to maximize the good. For example, right now you are reading this introduction. Maybe it will do some good. It will help you better understand ethics. But that, act-consequentialism says, is not enough. Your reading this introduction is not permissible unless, of the alternatives, this is the action that produces the *most* good. That is a daunting demand. Recall the deontic verdict concerning what it would take for an action to be optional—it would have to produce the most good and also be tied with some other available action that produced an equal amount of good. Accordingly, act-consequentialism doesn't hand out a lot of optional deontic verdicts. This dearth of options appears to be a serious problem. Shouldn't you have, at least once in your life, the option to favor or sacrifice yourself, even if it comes at the expense of the overall good? If you think we have such options, then you think that act-consequentialism requires too much.

Unfortunately for act-consequentialism, the problems do not end here. Turning now to the

> *Sufficient Condition.* If an action brings about the best outcome, it is permissible to perform the action.

This condition seems to permit too much. Act-consequentialism tells you that committing *any* act is permissible if it produces the most good. Put differently, it is never impermissible to maximize the good. Indeed, if an action uniquely produced the most good, it would be required. To see why this appears particularly troubling, pick an act that is as abhorrent as you can imagine—e.g., murdering, torturing, stealing, or lying. Next, rig two outcomes such that one outcome, the one where *you* are performing the abhorrent action, is infinitesimally better overall than the outcome where you do not perform the action. Act-consequentialism always comes back with the same verdict. It's not just permissible for you to perform the abhorrent action, it's required. There are no constraints placed on what consequentialism could demand from you. And that, I suspect, is a claim from which you will likely recoil.

We have, however, only scratched the surface in our investigation of consequentialism. Consequentialists have creative ways of responding to the problems raised in this section. But we've covered the basic tenets of the approach, so let's now take stock. The theories that take evaluative claims as primary sit on two extremes. Egoism, with its complete partiality toward self, appears to demand too little of us. Act-consequentialism, with its complete impartiality toward all, seems to demand too much. The seemingly troubling implications of universal egoism and act-consequentialism thus provide a helpful way to orient our discussion. The remaining ethical theories can be seen as attempts to forge a middle path. They try to resist the pull of act-consequentialism's impartiality without being driven all the way to egoism. How might this be accomplished?

§4. *Deontology*

Let's pause to remember what seems to be the force driving egoism and act-consequentialism to their extremes. Surprisingly, the source of these problems seems to be what was so compelling about consequentialist theories in the first place: that it is always permissible, indeed required, to maximize the good. Once pointed in a certain direction, with nothing holding them back, the deontic verdicts of consequentialist theories have no bounds. What we are looking for, then, is a way of directly securing certain verdicts. We want certain parts of your life to go untouched by ethics, leaving you a wealth of options. And we want certain acts to be off-limits, keeping you from getting your hands dirty. With these acts—e.g., murdering, torturing, stealing, or lying—looking to the consequences seems out of place. We don't have to see what these acts will bring about in order for us to know that you ought not to do them. The acts themselves, not their consequences, seem ethically problematic. Deontological theories try to capture this idea. They directly claim that certain actions are optional and certain acts are required. By taking a deontological approach, we could thus hold that ethics includes both options and constraints.[3]

But what would the structure of a deontological theory look like? The twin goals of securing both options and constraints supply an answer. First, a deontological theory will attempt to enumerate and explain why certain acts are impermissible for you to perform. This, in turn, will tell you what you are required to do. You are required to refrain from such actions. Second, the theory will claim that all actions that fall outside of the set of required acts are optional. If this is right, then ethics plays a limited role in governing over the actions of which your life consists. So long as you have refrained from the impermissible actions, the rest is up to you. By contrast, as we saw, consequentialism takes the jurisdiction of ethics to be all encompassing. Consequentialists have something to say about every act you could perform.

Constraints, as should be clear from this sketch, play a dominant role in deontological theories. Thus, to get a grip on the deontological approach, we need to have a better grip on the nature of constraints. As their name suggests, they are a kind of normative barrier.

They tell you that *you* are required to refrain from performing certain *types* of acts—e.g., murder, torture, stealing, and lying—even if so refraining comes at the cost of the overall good. Constraints thus have two features worth stressing. They concern certain types of acts, and they speak specifically to you. Let's take each of these features in turn.

Think back on our discussion of consequentialism. There we always spoke of specific actions. The explanation for this should be obvious. If consequentialists treat deontic verdicts as a function of evaluative claims, then we need to assess each available action for the amount of good it will bring about to identify which ought to be performed. But part of the worry we had about act-consequentialism stems from the thought that some acts, themselves, are simply abhorrent. And here we've arrived at an important distinction, the distinction between act-types and act-tokens. To help see this distinction, consider the question: How many letters are in the word 'fool'? This question is instructively imprecise. We might plausibly answer: four—counting each specific letter. Or, we might plausibly answer: three—counting each type of letter, and so counting 'o' only once. If we answer four, we took the question to be a question concerning letter-tokens. If we answer three, we took the question to be about letter-types. The same distinction applies to acts. If we take consequences as primary, we are only concerned with *act-tokens*. But, once we move to a deontological theory, we think in terms of *act-types*. Constraints are formulated as barriers, blocking the performance of certain act-types—for example, murder is impermissible. If you then perform the act-token—you commit murder—you've violated the constraint, and thereby done something impermissible.

Even once we've noticed this important point concerning the nature of constraints—that they are typically formulated in terms of act-types—a consequentialist thought might persist. If constraints give us the goal of not performing certain act-types, why not think that we should promote the outcome with the fewest performances of such acts? Consider a schematic case. Suppose that you are in the following position: Unless you commit murder, I will commit two murders. The consequentialist thought here is that if violations of constraints are to be avoided, then we should have the goal of minimizing such violations. If constraints are so important, then shouldn't you commit murder to prevent two additional murders? The answer, which is what drove us to deontology to begin with, is that *you* want to avoid having to be the one performing the abhorrent act. To avoid consequentialism's pull, we thus need to make a slight retreat toward egoism. We need to formulate constraints in a way that makes essential reference to *you*—the person to whom the constraint applies.

This leads us to the next feature of constraints. The reasons attached to the constraint must be *agent-relative,* not *agent-neutral.* To help see this distinction, suppose you are on a road trip with your family. Your parents tell you and your two siblings to make sure there is as little fighting as possible. Not long after, your two siblings get in a fight. Suppose you know that unless you physically intervene, the fight will continue for the rest of the trip. Your parents' command thus provides you with a reason to fight, because your intervention would bring about less fighting. The reason provided by your parents' constraint against fighting is thus agent-neutral. It gives all the children the same aim: minimize fighting. Now imagine the same scenario, but this time your parents tell you and your siblings, each individually: no fighting! Again not long after, your two siblings get in a fight, which unless you physically intervene will last the rest of the trip. Yet this time you cannot fight to reduce the fighting, for if you did, you would disobey your parents' command. In this second case, the reason provided by your parents' constraint against fighting is agent-relative; it makes essential reference to you, telling *you* not to fight. To capture the idea that it is ethically important for you to keep *your* hands clean (even if it comes at the expense of the overall good), deontology mimics your parents in this latter case. You must be given a weighty (perhaps decisive) reason to avoid violation of the constraint, even if your violation would prevent additional violations of that very constraint. If the constraint doesn't make this essential reference to you, if the reason attached to the constraint is, in other words, agent-neutral, then others' constraint violations would, in determining what *you* ought to do, be equally reason-providing as your own. The constraint would, if agent-neutral, give everyone the same aim: minimize constraint violations. Hence, in the case where unless you commit murder I will commit two murders, you would have stronger reason to murder. A deontological theory thus needs to be articulated in agent-relative terms, meaning that such a theory could potentially give different persons different aims.

Once we recognize these two features of constraints—that they focus on act-types and are backed by agent-relative reasons—we are now in a position to feel the full force of the explanatory burden that the deontologist faces. Not only do constraints wall you off from the good, they wall you off from other deontic verdicts. What you are required to do is held fixed in the face of what others do (and perhaps what your future self might do). The viability of the deontological approach thus hinges on locating a plausible source of agent-relative reasons not to perform certain act-types. In what follows, we will look at a number of different sources that may supply the grounds for such reasons. We will look at two outside sources of constraints: God and culture. And we will look at one inside source: our own rationality.[4]

4.1 *Divine Command Theory*

Most religious views take God to supply a number of agent-relative constraints. The ethical theory that draws on this theological tradition is known as the

> *Divine Command Theory.* You are required to perform an action if and only if (and because) your performance of such acts is commanded by God.

On its face, the principle divine command theory uses as the criterion for assessing deontic verdicts has some plausibility, and it seems to provide a powerful explanation of the source of our agent-relative constraints. Yet a serious difficulty lurks.

The divine command theory faces an old problem, a dilemma that directly calls into question its ability to explain why actions have the deontic verdicts that they do. Here's the dilemma: Either what is ethically required is required because God commands it, or it isn't. If performing an action is required because God commands it, then the demands of ethics are arbitrary. God could have commanded that we do the most abhorrent acts; and in so commanding, these acts would be required. But if we go for the other horn of the dilemma, maintaining that God commands certain acts because they are required, then God cannot be the source of our agent-relative constraints. God is superfluous to the ethical story. At best, God identifies the constraints we already have. God's commands, therefore, are either ethically arbitrary or unnecessary.

Nevertheless perhaps the divine command theorist is willing to accept the arbitrariness horn of this dilemma. If God commands murder, then murder is what is required. Embracing this counterintuitive implication, however, does little to help. For the underlying problem, hinted at above, comes from deriving the source of *all* ethical requirements from the commands of God. Why is this a problem? Because it seems perfectly sensible to ask: Why am I required to do what God commands? This question is not trivial. It seems to demand an answer. But what answer can the divine command theorist give? To be consistent, the answer must be that God has commanded that you ought to do what God commands.

This response, however, will not do. Either we already ought to do what God commands, in which case we are back to the superfluous horn of the dilemma. Or it is not already the case that we ought to do what God commands, in which case the command lacks ethical force, thereby leaving the original question unanswered. In other words, we need a reason, not itself provided by God's commands, to obey his commands. Yet if such a reason exists, then God is not the source of all ethical requirements. And, if no such reason exists, then God's commands lack normative authority, in which case God is not the source of all ethical requirements. Either way, then, God is not the ultimate source of ethical requirements.

4.2 *Cultural Relativism*

There's nonetheless something attractive about looking for the source of the constraints in God. That there is something outside of us handing down the constraints seems to imbue them with the special authority they seem to have. So even if God does not undergird agent-relative constraints, perhaps something outside of us still can. For example, we often hear people say that there are certain things we just don't do around here. The thought seems to be this: Certain constraints apply to people simply in virtue of being a member of a social group with certain norms and customs. Being part of a particular culture, then, provides another possible source of agent-relative reasons to refrain from performing certain act-types. This theory is known as

> *Cultural Relativism.* You are required to perform an action if and only if (and because) your performance of such acts is called for by the norms of your culture.

This theory holds that deontic verdicts are indexed to cultural norms. The idea is that ethical sentences function like sentences that use 'here' or 'now.' For example, when we say, "It's raining here," the truth of the utterance is relativized to a particular location—the location of the speaker. Similarly, according to cultural relativism, the truth of an ethical utterance is relativized to the norms of the culture from which the verdict is issued. Cultural relativism thus asserts a bold thesis. It does not merely make the uncontroversial claim that deontic verdicts are sensitive to the circumstances; rather it denies the existence of ethical truths that cut across all cultures. Cultural relativism, for instance, tells you that torture is *impermissible* because the norms of our culture include a constraint against engaging in torture. But what would make torture permissible?

Interestingly, cultural relativism gives us two answers. Torture would have been *permissible* had our culture not had norms that include a constraint against engaging in torture. Or, even if the norms of our culture contain a constraint against torture, your engaging in torture would be *permissible* from the perspective of other cultures whose norms lack such a constraint.

Having these two ways of arriving at permissibility is a puzzling feature. Could the norms of a culture really determine the correct deontic verdict concerning torture? If that seems mistaken, then we're led to accept an important desideratum on normative theories: Their deontic verdicts must be *universalizable*, applying to all persons in relevantly similar circumstances. More precisely, if a theory's verdicts are universalizable then the following is true of the theory: For all persons, each person—e.g., you—were you in so-and-so circumstances, you would have a reason to perform such-and-such action. And, accordingly, were I in these circumstances, I too would have this reason. The problem with cultural relativism is not just that it delivers implausible deontic verdicts. The deeper problem is that it violates universalizability. It tells us that the identical circumstances—where all the same facts obtain—can give rise to different deontic verdicts. That's puzzling, to say the least.

Having noted the problems with Divine Command Theory and Cultural Relativism, we now have an even better handle on what a deontological theory is after: locating an authoritative source of agent-relative reasons not to perform certain act-types while retaining universality. So, given this aim, perhaps the source of constraints can be derived from something about all of us. After all, we are the entities to whom the constraints apply. We are *agents*—beings capable of recognizing and responding to reasons.

4.3 *Kantianism*

That we are agents is a thought worth exploring. Right now you are reading this essay. If I asked you why you are doing this, you might say, "In order to learn about ethics." Here you supply me with a reason, justifying your action. Contrast yourself in this regard with a nonrational entity, say, a rose. If I asked you why does this rose bloom, you might say, "In order to attract pollinating insects for reproduction." Though this answer sounds similar to your previous one, it is not. With the rose, your cited reason is not justificatory. The rose, unlike you, does not have a rational nature. You, not the rose, are sensitive to reasons. External forces, like the sun, do not drive you. You are free in a way that the rose is not. And it is only in virtue of this freedom that ethical questions become salient. Insofar as you are responsive to reasons, you can act. The rose cannot act. It's blooming is akin to your having an involuntary spasm. The rose does not ask: Ought I to bloom? Only persons, beings with rational natures, confront normative questions.

That you have a rational nature, of course, does not mean that you always act rationally. Depressingly, most of us act irrationally all too often. But now we've arrived at an intriguing idea. Perhaps agent-relative constraints fall directly out of our own rational nature, such that violating the constraint can only be done on pain of our own rationality. That would be a neat result. Unlike the divine command theory or cultural relativism, this would locate the source of ethical requirements in you—in the mere fact that you are rational. Surely your own rationality binds you. So how could we establish this tight connection between rationality and agent-relative constraints?

To answer this question, return to universalizability—the thought that our deontic verdicts need to apply to all persons in relevantly similar circumstances. Previously, we concluded that universalizability seemed like a plausible desideratum on ethical theories. Given our discussion of rationality, we can now defend this desideratum. The connection between rationality and universalizability is easiest to see when it comes to forming beliefs. Insofar as we are rational, we cite reasons. You do not simply believe, for example, that the gas in your car is low. Rather, if you are to rationally form a belief concerning how much fuel your car has, you look for reasons. For instance, you see that your car's reliable gas light is on, and this justifies your belief that the gas is low. Notice an interesting feature concerning the evidence that your gas light provides: It is not person specific. If it's rational for you to believe that the gas is low because of the gas light, then, based on this same reason, were I in your situation, it would also be rational for me to believe the gas is low. You don't have a monopoly on gas-light reasons. Universalizability thus appears to be constitutive of rational belief formation. If some fact serves as a genuine reason for you to believe, it must serve as a genuine reason for me, assuming we are in the same circumstances. And this idea is not restricted to the formation of beliefs. Presumably, universalizability is also constitutive of rational action. To act rationally is to act on reasons I can coherently see others, in relevantly similar circumstances, acting on as well. In short, since rationality demands consistency, we are driven to universalizability.

This link between universalizability and rationality leads us to a *universalizability test.* If a purported reason for acting can't apply to all rational beings in relevantly similar circumstances, then it is not a reason. With this test in place, we are in a position to see how constraints arise from our own rationality. We apply the universalizability test broadly, identifying acts whose features are such that any purported reason in their favor fails the test. If permission-granting reasons for certain acts systematically fail, we can conclude that you have an agent-relative constraint against performing them.

To see how this test works, imagine that you are in dire need of money. Imagine further that you are over at a wealthy friend's house, where cash is carelessly left around. Suppose you are contemplating taking some of this money. It would mean little to your friend, who will not even realize it is gone. But taking some would greatly increase your well-being. Here you might be thinking

> *Steal.* The fact that taking what's not mine will increase my well-being gives me decisive reason to take it.

Now, in order to act rationally, everyone must be able to act on this reason. Our universalizability test thus begins by trying to imagine a world where everyone acts on the reason you claim to have in *Steal.* That is, we imagine a

> *Full Compliance World.* In this world, everyone complies with *Steal.* Whenever taking what's not one's own increases one's well-being, one takes it.

We next ask: Is this Full Compliance World possible? Here we are asking could all rational agents adhere to *Steal* as if a law of nature (like gravity). The answer, it seems, is No. If everyone followed *Steal,* it would destroy the very institution (property) that serves as a means to achieving the end in question (your owning the well-being-enhancing goods). In such a world where everyone complied with *Steal,* the very institution of ownership would cease. It would be pointless to steal, since no one would own anything. Accordingly, *Steal* fails the universalizability test. If not everyone could rationally act on the reason captured by *Steal,* no one could rationally act on it. Failing universalizability is the hallmark of irrationality. And since you don't have a monopoly on well-being-based reasons to take what's not yours, you are irrational if you *Steal*. But perhaps we can say more. Perhaps no reasons in favor of stealing can pass the universalizability test. If so, there would be an agent-relative constraint against stealing—stealing, the act-type, would be impermissible. That would be a substantial result; it would show the possibility of generating constraints through rationality alone.

The deontological theory we've been exploring brings us close to the theory espoused by Immanuel Kant. Kant's theory is complex, but one of his central ideas is that the reasons that serve as the determining grounds of our deontic verdicts need to be sharable by all rational beings. In his words, "Act only in accordance with that maxim [i.e., the statement describing what you are going to do, and the reason you are going to do it] through which you at the same time can will that it become a universal law." We can state this principle as follows:

> You are required to refrain from acting in a certain way if and only if (and because) you couldn't rationally will as a universal law the maxim associated with this action.

This is an elegant way of generating constraints. Rationality is what makes normativity possible; we must have agents to have reasons. But rationality, fully appreciated, is also the source of our agent-relative constraints. What's more, there is an intuitive thought—how would you feel if everyone did that?—that Kantianism nicely captures. (Think of how this thought can be deployed, with great effect, to deal with our painkillers cases from the discussion of Egoism [§3.1] and Contractarianism [§3.2]. Purported reasons to defect on a mutually advantageous agreement for personal gain are not universalizable.)

Yet there are problems for Kantianism too. The universalizability test appears to tell us that we are required to refrain from certain acts when intuitively performing them is permissible. Suppose that, because you need cash on hand, tomorrow you will pull your remaining funds out of the bank. Could all rational agents adhere to this maxim as if a law of nature? It seems not. The universalizability test thus tells us that you acted impermissibly. That looks like the wrong verdict. This action is obviously permissible. And these examples are easy to multiply: Taking the last chair in an auditorium, donating the most to charity, watching live TV shows (the content of which is not others watching live TV), and so on.

And the problems for Kantianism do not end here. The universalizability test seems to tell us that we are required to perform certain acts when intuitively refraining from them is permissible. Suppose that, out of romantic honor, were you to fight in a duel, you would aim to miss. Is a world where everyone adhered to this maxim possible? It seems not. For then, like the institution of property in *Steal*, the institution of dueling would break down. According to the universalizability test, then, it would be impermissible for you to aim to miss. Again, that seems like the wrong verdict. The universalizability test thus either needs to be refined or abandoned.

Fortunately Kantians have another, highly influential, derivation of agent-relative constraints from rational agency. Recall that rationality demands consistency. And, to state the obvious, much of our ethical lives consist of interactions with other people—i.e., other rational agents. When interacting with a person could you, without inconsistency, use your rational agency to undercut theirs?

To answer this question, return to what using your rational agency involves. Recall that rational agency is the capacity to recognize and respond to reasons. Think about how you use this capacity on a daily basis. Take any action. You see, for example, the beautiful rose, and think that having this beautiful rose would be nice. The rose then becomes your end, and you set off for some scissors. Though done a hundred times a day, this ability to set ends is a striking phenomenon. By setting ends, you seem to be able to generate reasons for yourself. But how could you have this reason-generating ability? One way—perhaps the only way—is if you yourself were an end. Yet does your being an end depend on anything else? Presumably not. You—as a rational agent—are an end in itself. Notice, however, that this same progression of thought applies to anyone with this capacity for rational agency. Accordingly, we arrive at the idea that all rational beings are ends in themselves simply by reflection on what it takes to act as a rational agent.

We now have an answer to the question whether you could, without inconsistency, use your rational agency to undercut the rational agency of another. When you act in this way, you are using a rational agent as a mere means to one of your ends. Yet, as we just saw, to act at all you are committed to treating rational agents as ends in themselves. If you undercut the rational agency of another, you are not treating a rational agent as an end in itself. So your action is inconsistent. Thus, to act in this way is to act irrationally, and hence unethically.

This line of reasoning led Kant to put forward another principle, which states: "Act in such a way that you always treat humanity [rational nature], whether in your own person or in the person of any other, never as a mere means but always as an end." We can state this principle as follows:

> You are required to refrain from acting in a certain way if and only if (and because) this act uses another rational agent merely as a means and not as an end.

When you use people as a *mere means* you use them in ways to which they could not rationally consent, thereby blocking them from sharing in your end. That is to say, you use them in a way that they cannot share your reason; you undermine their rational agency.

Given the two abilities that come with rational agency—the ability to recognize reasons and the ability to respond to them—the two most obvious ways of using someone as a mere means are deception and coercion. In cases of deception, one's ability to recognize the actual reasons in play is distorted by another. In cases of coercion, one's ability to respond to the reasons is thwarted by another.

In order to see how this principle works, consider in detail a case of deception. Suppose again that you are in dire need of money. And again, you are over at your wealthy friend's house. As it nears suppertime, you tell your friend that, if he pays, you will pick up takeout. He agrees. Your statement, however, is a lie. You plan to take the money, never to see your friend again. This deception uses your friend as a mere means. You do not allow him to share your goal; the possibility of rational consent is ruled out by the lie. You treat your friend like a tool to achieve your ends. You show your friend the same respect you might show to an ATM, not the respect due to a rational being. In short, your lie is inconsistent with seeing humanity as an end in itself. And seeing humanity as an end in itself is something, simply in virtue of acting at all, you implicitly accept. Your lie is therefore irrational. As before, if all reasons to lie were inconsistent with treating people as ends in themselves, there would be an agent-relative constraint against lying.

Still, problems remain. We can best see these problems if, as we did with act-consequentialism, we break apart the necessary and sufficient conditions of Kant's principle. Let's begin with the

> *Necessary Condition*: Only if an action uses another rational agent merely as a means and not as an end are you required to refrain from performing the action.

This condition appears to condemn too little. Although much of our ethical lives consist of interactions with other rational beings, this does not exhaust the possibilities. As we saw earlier—in the case involving the dog's leg—animals can have their well-being reduced, and such reductions seem ethically relevant. But what could a Kantian say if we substituted a dog's leg for the rose in the example above. You see the dog's leg, and think that having this leg would be nice. The leg then becomes your end, and you set off for some scissors. (Let's just assume that dogs are not rational agents. If you think dogs are rational, then we can change the example to a lower animal that can still feel pain.) Clearly, you ought to refrain from cutting off the dog's leg. But this act does not use other rational agents merely as a means. It uses a nonrational dog. And hence, the action is one you are not required to refrain from. That is hard to believe.

We can next turn to the

> *Sufficient Condition*: If an action uses another rational agent merely as a means and not as an end, you are required to refrain from performing the action.

This condition appears to condemn too much. Intuitively, it is permissible to use a person as a mere means, if the end to which they are being put is sufficiently important. Return to our schematic case where unless you murder I will commit two murders. Now let's make two revisions. First, the act in question for you is using someone as a means. You can achieve the performance of this act in a number of different ways—e.g., deception or coercion. The second revision is that the number of murders I will commit is high enough that the permissibility of you using someone as a mere means is ethically irresistible. For example, suppose that unless you use someone as a means I will commit one thousand murders. Even if we raise the number to a million, the sufficient condition of Kant's principle will always come back with the same verdict: You are required to refrain. Again, that is hard to believe.

We can now take stock. We have investigated three attempts—God, culture, and rational nature—to explain the existence of agent-relative constraints. Each faces problems. Of course, deontologists have forwarded ways of responding to the problems raised in this section. Instead of digging deeper, however, let's end by returning to options.

Our investigation into deontology was motivated by the quest to make room for options and constraints. We have been focusing on constraints because we assumed that, if constraints could be defended, the deontologist could claim that so long as you live within these barriers, the rest of your actions are optional. This claim, however, is suspect.

To see this, return to utilitarianism's plausible idea that, between two outcomes, if one outcome has a higher level of well-being than another, you have a reason to favor that outcome. Now let's suppose that among your available actions you face two outcomes, both of which involve no constraint violations but one produces a higher level of well-being. Are both of these actions optional? If well-being is reason providing, then, assuming neither action violates a constraint, the set of reasons in favor of the outcome with the higher level of well-being does not match the reasons in favor of the outcome with the lower level of well-being. You have more reason to bring about the outcome with more well-being. And you are required to perform the act that the balance of reasons favors. Thus the deontologist cannot simply say that actions that lie within the barriers set by the theory's constraints are optional. So, even if agent-relative constraints can be secured, work for the deontologist remains, if they hope to also secure options.

At this point, we might be suspicious that supplying an explanation of agent-relative constraints and options is possible. Deontological theories leave too many normative mysteries. Act-consequentialism might, at this point, appear rather alluring. However, before we succumb to consequentialism's pull, we should explore a final approach.

§5. *Virtue Ethics*

Perhaps our focus on acts and actions—on conduct—pointed us in the wrong direction. Think about eulogies or obituaries. Most do not list the actions the deceased performed. Instead, they talk about the kind of person the deceased was. In other words, they talk about the deceased's character. And this talk is not limited to funeral homes. Often, in everyday discourse, character is primary to conduct. When I was a kid, a ubiquitous Gatorade commercial demanded that young basketball players "Be like Mike." Perhaps we should follow this linguistic evidence, and treat character as primary to conduct. On this approach, it is only by first figuring out who we ought to be that we can figure out how we are required to act. We treat our deontic verdicts as a function of our character traits. We first ask what attributes you ought to possess, and then use those traits to figure out what to do.

To understand this approach, we first need to understand what it is to have a certain character. Consider Gatorade's claim that young basketball players should be like Michael Jordan. The idea seems to be that Jordan has traits or dispositions to respond in certain ways that make him a good basketball player. So, the thought continues, if you want to be a good basketball player too, then you should also try to cultivate Jordan-like dispositions. Of course, dispositions can also be bad. My dispositions, when it comes to basketball, are dispositions young basketball players should not cultivate. We might distinguish the good from the bad dispositions by calling the good dispositions *virtues*, and the bad ones *vices*. This is why those who take character claims as primary are known as virtue ethicists.

Here it is important to notice a subtle difference between evaluative claims like "pain is bad" and "Michael Jordan is a good basketball player." To differentiate this type of evaluative claim from good-for and good-*simpliciter*, we call this a claim of *attributive goodness*. Attributive uses of good pick out those things that are good-of-a-kind. For example, an eye that can see accurately at a range of 40 meters is better than an eye that can only see accurately at 20 meters. Accordingly, we call an eye that has certain traits that make it better than other eyes, within a certain comparison class, a good eye. This thought is easy to apply to Michael Jordan. He is better than most, if not all, basketball players.

Once we understand this appeal to attributive goodness, it is not hard to predict how the rest of the story unfolds. We generalize the point we've been making about Michael Jordan to human beings. The answer to the question—who should we be?—is then determined by identifying those dispositions that good humans have. But what makes for a good, distinctively human, life? One attempt to answer this question, made famous by Aristotle, leans heavily on the idea that human beings have a certain function. On this suggestion, just as what it takes to be a good eye is determined by what it takes for an eye to perform its function well, what it takes to be a good human is determined by what it takes for a human to perform its function well.

But what precisely is the function of human beings? Unlike eyes, this question is not easily answered. We might look to the activities that are unique to human beings (as opposed to plants and animals). But, needless to say, this strategy is not terribly promising. Too many distinctively human activities are either ethically irrelevant (e.g., whistling for fun) or deeply unethical (e.g., murdering for fun). However, even if this way of identifying our function fails, perhaps, by turning to modern biology, ethology, and psychology, we could identify the characteristic function of human beings. Instead of pursuing this inquiry further, let's turn to the question of how we get from character to conduct.

How do we get from the virtues to deontic verdicts? To answer this question, consider how one cultivates certain dispositions. If one wants to be a good basketball player, one does not play like me; rather, one plays like Michael Jordan. Similarly, if one wants to be a good person, one emulates what good people do. Virtuous persons serve as exemplars. They inform us how we ought to act. Looking to them tells us what to do. If you understand this point, you understand why I said, when introducing virtue ethics, that deontic verdicts are a function of our character. And here we've arrived at the principle that stands at the heart of

> *Virtue Ethics.* You are required to perform an action if and only if (and because) this action is what a fully virtuous person (acting in character) would do in the circumstances. That is, you ought to do whatever the completely virtuous agent would characteristically do.

That you ought to act only as the fully virtuous act is an attractive idea. Nevertheless, on closer inspection, the idea raises concerns. We want a theory to be capable of advising less than perfect ethical agents, but virtue ethics appears unable to do so.

Virtue ethics supplies an analysis that uses a counterfactual—were the fully virtuous person in my situation, she would (if acting in character) do such-and-such. This creates a problem. Suppose, for example, that you are a coward. Fortunately, your university is offering a class called "Cultivating Courage 101." It seems like you ought to attend. However, you are required to do only what the completely virtuous person would do. And, obviously enough, the perfectly courageous person is not going to attend. The class would be pointless for this person. Why waste time perfecting perfection? Thus if you ought to do what the perfectly virtuous person would do, you ought not attend either. But not attending would be a mistake. You are a coward and would benefit from instruction. The problem with the criterion supplied by virtue ethics for assigning deontic verdicts should now be clear. The counterfactual used to get us from character to conduct seems to rule out the requirement to do certain actions that would make us more like the virtuous. For what the *fully* virtuous would never need to do is perform actions to make themselves *more* virtuous. And that looks like a devastating problem for a view whose main focus is character development.

My disclaimer should now be familiar: Virtue ethicists have offered responses to this problem. As before, instead of pursuing these responses, now that we have an overview of the three main approaches, let's turn to how we might assess the various theories.

§6. *Theory Assessment*

After reading this introduction, you probably have a preferred theory. All the ethical theories we have looked at thus far, however, fail to get everything we want. So chances are, in your honest moments, you take your preferred theory to be a failure; it's simply that you think rival theories fail worse. But to competently make this assessment—that the others fail worse—we need to have some handle on what makes one theory better than another.

When devising a theory, the place to begin is with some paradigmatic deontic verdicts that we think any theory needs to capture. So we might start, as we did in (§2.2), with a list of intuitive ethical judgments. When constructing our theory, we want it to fit, at least initially, these judgments. If it fits, then we say it has *intuitive appeal*: The theory does not have counterintuitive implications.

Intuitive appeal, needless to say, can only take us so far. To see why, assume that all we wanted was to have a maximum fit with our ethical judgments. We could achieve this aim by simply claiming that our list of ethical judgments just is our theory. But surely this will not do, for two reasons.

First, sometimes we just don't know what to think about certain cases. I suspect, for example, you do not have a considered judgment about how many people I would need to murder before your murdering to prevent my murdering became permissible. We thus need to have a theory that can tell us, when brute intuition isn't up for the task, what to think. If a theory can tell us what to think in all ethical cases—hard and easy alike—we say it is *complete*. Theories that can only address what we owe to other human beings, for instance, appear to be incomplete. They are mute on what we owe to animals—a topic where ethical questions arise.

The second reason a theory consisting of a list of our ethical judgments will not do is this. Sometimes one's intuitions are not consistent. Perhaps what you think about one case flatly contradicts what you think about another (without you noticing it). Or perhaps you waffle about a case depending on your mood. A theory that makes inconsistent claims, however, cannot be true. So here too intuitive appeal is not enough. We also want a theory that makes consistent claims. If a theory is consistent, we call it *coherent*.

Intuitive appeal, completeness, and coherence are criteria for assessing how well a theory achieves its enumerative aim. Yet, even if a theory achieves this aim, it may turn out to fail to achieve its explanatory aim. We saw above, for example, that contractarianism can supply reason not to hurt animals, but the explanation supplied comes from a contract (not the hurt inflicted on the animal). That explanation appears misplaced, even though this seems like the correct deontic verdict. To take another example, utilitarians say that, if it fails to bring about the greatest sum total of well-being, slavery is impermissible. That, again, seems like the correct verdict. But does it seem like the correct explanation? Wouldn't the correct explanation turn to the lack of respect shown to the slave, not just the loss in well-being? As these examples help us see, we not only want our theory to come down on the right verdict, we also want it to come back with the correct explanation of that verdict. We call such a theory that can supply this proper explanation *explanatorily efficacious.*

Putting these criteria together, we want an intuitively appealing theory that can answer any ethical question we throw at it, we want to ensure that these answers do not conflict with one another, and we want a plausible explanation for the answers supplied.

A final note. When trying to achieve completeness, coherence, and explanatory efficaciousness, our initial intuitions are likely to be heavily revised. Indeed, ensuring completeness and coherence alone will force serious revision to our initial ethical judgments. Thus we should not treat our untutored intuitions as the final word. A theory that demands serious revision of our initial list of judgments might, for all that, turn out to be the best (perhaps the only) one capable of being complete and coherent. Accordingly, my practice above of introducing cases that conflict with the necessary and sufficient conditions of a theory was all too hasty. Perhaps, for example, upon reflection we are willing to live without constraints and options if act-consequentialism turns out to be the only complete, coherent, and explanatory efficacious theory. But before reaching such a conclusion much more work would need to be done.

§7. *Applied Ethics*

Having learned about the major ethical theories, we can now start thinking carefully about how they might be applied. This volume covers a wide swath of particularly vexing, and extremely important, ethical problems. Their importance should be obvious with only a cursory glance at the table of contents—most of the topics are matters of life and death. As mentioned at the outset, this importance contributes to why these problems are so vexing. They are not problems we can safely ignore. Take abortion. It could be that each of us is a bystander to the murder of millions. Take euthanasia. It could be that each of us is a bystander to the continuation of much needless suffering. These are problems where both action and inaction are both ethically weighty. So we need to be sure to land on the correct deontic verdict. The trouble is that often we face serious uncertainty.

The uncertainty we face is twofold. First, most of us are unsure which ethical theory is correct. If we knew the correct ethical theory, then we could solve most problems in applied ethics with the following argument form:

1. [Ethical Theory] is true
2. If [Ethical Theory] is true, then actions that fit [Description of Circumstances] are [Deontic Verdict].
3. Description of Circumstances.
4. Deontic Verdict

Sadly, not only do we not know (1), but we also do not know (3). That is, second, we often do not know all of the ethically relevant descriptive facts. Is the fetus a person? What will be the implications of permitting euthanasia for the society at large? Would, for example, it increase the rates of teenage suicide?

In applied ethics, we thus confront unavoidable and momentous problems compounded by normative and descriptive uncertainty. Contained in these pages are a number of attempts to puzzle through what ethics demands in these hard cases. As you shall see, much of the argumentation is tempered by the humbling fact that we have not landed on such a theory; and, even if we had, we might not have an accurate description of the circumstances when going to apply it.

As should now be clear, applying ethics is no easy task. But you should not be put off by its arduousness. Ethics is in its infancy. Much work remains. It's our goal, as we peel through the layers of the debate, to see which view comes out on top. After reading this collection, I expect you'll be left with the sense that ethicists make progress. This makes applied ethics an exciting enterprise. For we do not know what the next stage in the development of ethics will bring.

Appendix: Well-Being

Well-Being

A theory of well-being tries to answer the question: What makes a life noninstrumentally good for the subject living it? A theory of well-being has two main aims: Identify what things are good-for-you, and explain why this is so.

To help think through the various theories of well-being, it is helpful to begin with a list of what is symptomatic of a life that is good-for-you, and what is symptomatic of a life that is bad-for-you. Here are some things that might spring to mind:

Goods	Bads
Pleasure	Pain
Health	Illness
Love	Betrayal
Friendship	Manipulation
Freedom	Unfreedom
Knowledge	Deception
Accomplishment	Failure
Beauty	Ugliness

Both of these lists could be longer, but this will give us a start. Is there some feature about all of the items on this list that might explain why a life with the goods is noninstrumentally better for you than the life filled with the bads?

In trying to locate this unifying feature, it will be helpful to keep in mind why I keep adding the "noninstrumental" qualifier. This qualification is needed because the presence of many things in your life, like ice cream, may increase your well-being. But no one has an ice cream theory of well-being, because, at best, ice cream is only instrumental—it's a means—to increasing your well-being. And, in devising a theory of well-being, we are trying to capture what noninstrumentally—i.e., what ultimately—makes your life go better. Ice cream does not by itself make your life better. We might think, for example, that ice cream causes your well-being to increase because you take pleasure in experiencing ice cream, and pleasure is noninstrumentally good-for-you. If we thought that the benefits of ice cream are ultimately traceable to pleasure, then we would hold that pleasure facts are the kind of facts that are non-instrumentally good-for-you.

In searching for a unifying feature for our lists above, the importance of the instrumental/noninstrumental distinction should now be clear. Perhaps only one item is noninstrumentally good-for-you, while the rest are simply a means to bringing about the presence of that one item. If so, then just as one disease might explain many symptoms, one of the items on our list of goods might explain all of the others. If, for instance, we could deploy the same strategy we deployed for ice cream—looking to pleasure as the ultimate explanation—to all of the items on our list of goods, then we could plausibly hold that pleasure is the only thing that noninstrumentally benefits you.

Hedonism

The idea just suggested—that pleasure is what ultimately explains the presence of the other items on our list of goods—has much appeal. Take accomplishments. We can test whether your accomplishments are noninstrumentally good-for-you by asking: What makes a life full of accomplishments better-for-you? If your accomplishments ultimately make you better off, then the answer is simply the accomplishments themselves. Does that seem correct? Imagine all of the famous artists whose accomplishments came after their deaths. Was Vincent van Gogh made better off by his posthumous success? Clearly, his great works made others better off. But our question concerns only van Gogh: Did success make *him* better off? If you think his accomplishments did nothing for him—after all, he was dead when success came—then you will need to give up on the idea that we are made better off by our accomplishments themselves. Suppose that's right. We would then need an account of why accomplishments are regularly thought to be part of a life that is good-for-you. Here we might, like the case of ice cream above, point to the fact that we take pleasure in success.

If we could repeat this strategy for each of the other items on our list of goods, and use pain for our list of bads, then we could hold that your well-being is entirely constituted by facts about pleasure and pain. In support of this idea, it is worth noting that this same strategy is not easily deployed against pleasure (or pain). Pleasure does not seem instrumental to some other good. If I asked you why you are eating ice cream, and you said because it is pleasant, and I then asked why do you want to experience pleasure, you probably would not know how to respond. Pleasure is where the explanation gives out. The theory that holds that pleasure and pain exhaust the things that can be noninstrumentally good-for-you is known as

> *Hedonism.* Your well-being consists exclusively in facts about pleasure and pain. To the extent that (and because) your life contains experiences of pleasure, you are benefited. To the extent that (and because) your life contains experiences of pain, you are harmed.

We have already looked at one attractive rationale for accepting hedonism: its ability to explain many of the things contained in a life that is good for the subject living it. But, by returning to the thought that what happens after you die cannot benefit or harm you, we can proffer an additional argument in favor of hedonism. When thinking about the case of van Gogh, we noted that it seemed odd to think that he could have been made better off by his posthumous accomplishments. But why think this odd? Because van Gogh, since dead, was not around to *experience* his success. By lacking the possibility of experience, van Gogh's accomplishments never got the chance to benefit him. They never made it into his head, so to speak. If that strikes you as plausible, then you hold the

> *Experience Requirement.* Changes in your well-being must involve your experience. In order to be benefited or harmed, your experience must be affected.

The experience requirement makes hedonism, which holds that well-being essentially involves your experiences of pleasure and pain, hard to resist.

Yet, even if we accept hedonism, questions remain. In order to figure out how well your life is going, we will need to figure out how to calculate how good a particular pleasant (or painful) experience is for you. On a flat-footed proposal, we multiply intensity times duration. This view is called *quantitative hedonism.* Suppose you face a choice between an agonizing surgery and a dull headache. Quantitative hedonism plausibly holds that, if the surgery was extremely short but the headache lasted for the rest of your life, you should go with the surgery.

So far so good. Unfortunately, this invites a worry. Suppose that your life could be made much, much longer—say, a million years. Suppose further that year after year your life contained only the most mild of pleasures, such as the pleasure you get from a good stretch. Each year you get the pleasure equal to a good stretch, but since your life is so long by the time it's over you have experienced the pleasure equal to a million good stretches. That's a lot of pleasure. Compare that life to the life you have now. And let's just assume that, given your much shorter existence, you will end up with less pleasure than that resulting from a million good stretches. Would you want to swap lives?

If you wouldn't, then you reject quantitative hedonism. Presumably, what you think is missing are higher, intellectual pleasures. You think what the life of good stretches lacks is the pleasures that come from relationships, the arts, and so on. These higher pleasures are arguably different in kind from the animal, bodily pleasures associated with licking ice cream or having a good stretch. What is missing, then, from the strict quantitative calculation is the *quality* of the pleasures. This view is known as *qualitative hedonism.*[5] To accurately capture the magnitude of the pleasure, we need to multiply the intensity and duration times a quality rating. Of course, with qualitative hedonism, we will need a list of the kinds of pleasures that qualify as of higher quality. (And perhaps a similar list for pains.) But let's leave the specification of higher pleasures aside, and instead turn to a problem that plagues hedonism generally.

Hedonism, either quantitative or qualitative, says that only *experiences* of pleasure and pain matter for your well-being. This implies that your well-being consists wholly of your subjective mental states. Given the attractiveness of the experience requirement, this seems a virtue. Nonetheless, holding that your mental life fully determines your well-being has disquieting implications. For it suggests that your mental life could detach completely from reality, while leaving your well-being unaffected. Imagine, for example, that you have struggled for years to earn your university degree. Today is graduation. As you walk across the stage to shake the provost's hand, your heart is filled with joy. Would our assessment of your well-being change if your graduation were the product of an experience machine—a machine that could, without you knowing the difference, simulate reality? It is tempting to answer Yes. All other things equal, between actual graduation, and the mere experience of it, better for you that your accomplishment is actual. Yet according to hedonism, you-in-the-world and you-in-the-machine, because both enjoy the same mental states, enjoy the same level of well-being. In deciding whether to live a real life or float in a tank with electrodes attached to your brain, assuming the two were experientially identical, you could flip a coin.

Desire-Satisfactionism

If you take the connection to reality to matter essentially to how well your life is going, then hedonism must be abandoned. Perhaps it was a mistake to require that all benefits (or harms) must be experienced. Still, we do not want to venture too far away from your psychology. After all, whatever determines your well-being must benefit *you.* Perhaps, then, we should think of well-being as a fit between your mind and the world. And we have a name for the mental state that has this world-to-mind direction of fit: a desire. If we hold that the satisfaction of your desires exhausts the things that can be noninstrumentally good-for-you, then we have arrived at a theory of well-being known as

> *Desire-Satisfactionism.* Your well-being consists in having your desires satisfied. To the extent that (and because) your desires are satisfied, you are benefited. To the extent that (and because) your desires are not satisfied, you are harmed.

We can head off a potential misunderstanding by stressing that the sense of "satisfaction" in play is not a feeling. You need not feel satisfied in order to be made better off. Rather, a desire is satisfied when the object of the desire, in fact, obtains. For instance, if you desire that your mother is healthy, this desire is satisfied if and only if your mother is actually healthy. So long as you have this desire, and the world conforms to it, you are made better off. Indeed, you are made better off regardless of whether you know about it or not.

But can desire-satisfactionism supply a unified explanation of our lists of goods and bads? Arguably, it can. Note that all of the items on the list of goods are things that people generally want to have in their lives. You probably desire health, love, friendship, and so on. And you are probably averse to illness, betrayal, manipulation, and the like. So, although we did not initially include the satisfaction of desires on our list, we could hold that the reason all of these things are usually good-for-you is because, if you are like most people, these are things that you want in your life. Desire-satisfactionism can thus explain why the list of goods contains the items that it does by holding that most people desire these things, and getting the things you desire is what ultimately makes you better off. Desire-satisfactionism is thus appealing because it too, like hedonism, offers a unified explanation of what is symptomatic of a good life.

Moreover, we can mount a powerful defense of this explanation by thinking about what it would take to harm you—i.e., what it would take to make you worse off. Suppose, for instance, that I cannot take the responsibility that comes with freedom. What I most want is someone to control my life. That is, my deepest desire is to be enslaved. Now suppose that my enemy comes along and wants to harm me. It would be a very poor strategy for my enemy to make me unfree. To be sure, if my enemy enslaved me, controlling every aspect of my life, the goal of harming me would, it seems, be thwarted. We can imagine my rejoicing every day at my enslavement. The upshot of this example is that by desiring one of the items on the list of bads, it appears to cease to be bad-for-me. Desire-satisfactionism nicely explains why this is so.

Suppose this leads us to accept desire-satisfactionism. In order to figure out how well your life is going, we still need to figure out how to calculate how much the satisfaction (or frustration) of a given desire influences your well-being. The standard answer holds that the stronger the desire the greater the increase (or decrease). Return to the idea that you want the world to fit your mind. When you have desires, it is as if you are constructing a model of your dream world—what you most want the world to be like. But, clearly, parts of this dream world are more important to you than others. You'd probably be willing to give up on the part of the dream world where you are licking ice cream in order to secure the part where your mother is healthy. You prefer the latter to the former. According to the standard proportional view, having your desire that your mother is healthy satisfied increases your well-being to a proportionally greater extent than having your ice cream desire satisfied.

But should we, as our initial formulation has it, hold that *any* satisfied desire increases your well-being? Remember, a theory of well-being hopes to specify the facts that benefit *you*. And this creates a problem. For in the unrestricted form of the theory given above, even if the object of your desire has nothing to do with you, if satisfied, you are benefited. Yet it seems implausible to hold that desires that have nothing to do with you, whose satisfaction you never find out about, make you better off. The satisfaction of such desires does not redound to your well-being. To illustrate this problem, consider this: At some point, you've likely read a news story about some disaster in a far-off part of the globe. And, while reading, you probably desired that the people facing this disaster turn out all right. Then, after reading, you probably went back to living your life never to think about the disaster or the people facing it again (until now). Suppose that, in fact, unknown to you, the people facing this disaster did turn out all right. Of course, that would be good-for-them. But would it be good-for-you?

If you think not, then we need to add a restriction to desire-satisfactionism: namely, the desires need to be about you. On this restricted form of the theory, only self-regarding desires, if satisfied, increase your well-being. This restriction removes the problem posed by the case of the disaster survivors. Yet how precisely to specify this restriction proves challenging. For example, many people got their heart's desire when Armstrong took his first steps on the moon. Surely this was a good thing for these people, even though the desire involved—that Armstrong walk on the moon—was not self-regarding. But let's assume that we can properly specify this restriction, and turn to another problem.

We've assumed thus far that satisfying your actual (self-regarding) desires increases your well-being. But surely many of your actual desires are based on false beliefs or irrationality. Think back to what your dream world was like five years ago. What did your five-years-younger self most desire? With this in mind, next imagine that, at that time, your dream world was fully realized. The people that you wanted to be friends with became your friends, the stuff you wanted to own became yours, you got the career you wanted, and so on. Thinking about it now, do you think your five-years-younger self, in getting everything, would be made maximally better off? You probably think that some of the friends, the stuff, and the career would not have been good-for-you-then. And you probably think this because you have in the last five years grown older and wiser. Older and wiser, you realize that many of your desires back then were based on false information and poor reasoning. These ill-informed and irrational desires would not, if satisfied, benefit you back then. To be sure, their satisfaction may have positively harmed your five-year-younger self. If that's right, then we will need to make another revision to desire-satisfactionism. Rather than holding that the satisfaction of your *actual* desires makes you better off, we hold that the satisfaction of your *ideal* desires—the desires you would have if you were rational and fully informed of the relevant facts—make you better off.

However, like the self-regarding restriction, properly specifying this idealization proves a challenge. One immediate concern is how to specify the relevant facts needed to qualify as informed. As a first pass, we might hold that any fact that would influence our desires counts as relevant. But this will not do. Some facts would influence our desires simply by thinking about them, not because they corrected our false beliefs. If, for example, you learned what your ice cream would look like a few hours after consuming it, you might lose your desire to eat it. This implication is unwelcome. Again let's leave the proper way of specifying the idealization aside, and turn to a more general worry for desire-satisfactionism.

We noted that what makes desire-satisfactionism attractive is that it explains why someone cannot harm you by giving you what you want. In making what can benefit or harm us depend on our wants in this way, desire-satisfactionism is a subjective theory of well-being. A theory is *subjective* insofar as it says that something is noninstrumentally good-for-you just in case you take a positive attitude toward that thing—you give that thing a mental thumbs-up. Desiring (and perhaps taking pleasure) are ways of giving this thumbs-up. But note, subjectivism makes well-being hostage to people's psychology, and that can be troubling. For people's psychology can be, and this is a gross understatement, weird. Suppose, for example, that my deepest desire, even if fully informed and rational, is to pinch as many people as possible. Suppose further that everyone indulges my desire. I get what I most want. Over the course of my existence I gleefully pinch thousands of people. Desire-satisfactionism, as a subjective theory of well-being, tells us that I lived a life that was very good-for-me. But a life spent pinching people is both mildly annoying and pointless. Could such a life really be best?

Objective List Theory

If you think that my life of pinching is not best, then you will have to abandon subjectivism, appealing directly to certain objective goods. This theory is known as the

> *Objective List Theory.* Your well-being consists in having your life contain certain objective goods and lack certain objective bads. To the extent that (and because) your life contains these goods, you are benefited. To the extent that (and because) your life contains these bads, you are harmed.

The objective list theory, as its name implies, is both pluralist and objective. It is pluralistic because, as typically conceived, the approach gives up on the hope of finding a single, unifying good that makes your life noninstrumentally better-for-you. The theory instead opts for a collection of goods—like those on our list at the start of the Appendix—each of which is capable, by itself, of increasing your well-being. However, though usually pluralistic, the objective list theory need not be. For the theory may have a very short list, consisting of only one item. We would, nevertheless, want to classify this monistic account as a version of the objective list theory. The constitutive feature of the theory is thus its objectivity. The objective list theory says that the item(s) on the list of goods increase your well-being regardless of whether you take a positive attitude toward them or not. Put differently, benefits and harms can accrue to you independently of your psychology.

The appeal of the objective list theory stems primarily from the conviction most of us have that a pointless or base life cannot be good-for-you even if you endorse it. But the view also gains plausibility from reflection on how we consider the goods and bads in our lives. When thinking about love or friendship, for example, do you think these things are good-for-you because you take a positive attitude toward them, or do you take a positive attitude toward them because they are good-for-you? In answering this question, imagine trying to explain to your beloved that the reason his love makes you better off is ultimately because you take pleasure or desire it. This, I suspect, will be met with resistance. The reason for this resistance is that most of us intuitively hold that love is *desirable*; it is fitting to desire it for its own sake because it is good (and not the other way around). And the same, it seems, goes for friendship and many other goods.

Suppose, then, that we go in for an objective list theory. In order to figure out how well your life is going, we will still need to be told what items are on the list of goods, and what items are on the list of bads. Additionally, we will need to figure out just how much the presence of each good adds to your well-being, and how much the presence of each bad diminishes it.

One promising way to address both of these issues at once appeals to what it would take to live a perfect human life. On this *perfectionist* approach, our list of goods is determined by what is essential to our natures as human. If friendship and love are demanded by the development and exercise of your essential human capacities, then friendship and love will be included on the list of objective goods. By looking to what perfects you, as a human being with a certain nature, we can locate what is good-for-you. Perfectionism also provides a way of calculating the magnitude of the benefit the presence of each good brings. The goodness of each good is set by how much closer their possession brings you to the ideal. If friendships make you approximate the perfect human life to a greater extent than health, then the presence of friends increases your well-being to a greater extent than health. Of course, the plausibility of perfectionism depends on the plausibility of what is essential to being human lining up with what is good-for-you. But why think these two are connected?

We can bring out the force of this question by remembering that the objective list theory holds that the things that are good for you float free from your attitudes toward them. This attitude-independence implies that the best life for you according to the objective list theory could be one that leaves you miserable. You may be entirely averse to everything that makes for an ideal human life. You might give everything on the list of goods a mental thumbs-down. For example, suppose you are a misanthrope. You hate people. You do not want friends or lovers. They leave you cold, disgusted. Quiet solitude brings you the greatest pleasure, and is what you most desire. If human relationships are essential to living the ideal human life, then, even though you hate them, friends and lovers would be, according to the objective list theory, good-for-you. If you think that seems mistaken, then you accept the

> *Resonance Requirement.* In order for something to be good-for-you, it must resonate with you. You cannot be benefited by something that you do not endorse or that alienates you.

Accepting this requirement demands that we reject the objective list theory. For the theory's constitutive feature is its objectivity—the independence of the goods from our attitudes. The resonance requirement thus brings us back to subjectivism. The appeal of a subjectivist theory of well-being should now be obvious: It is sensitive to *you.* To maintain an objectivist theory, this sensitivity must be sacrificed.

Where does this leave us? What theory of well-being should be accepted? The answer, in the end, depends on how you come down on the experience and resonance requirements. Rejecting either seems a cost, but accepting either invites serious worries. Perhaps there is a way to adjudicate this conflict. Perhaps a hybrid theory, which holds that what makes someone's life go better is (i) the presence of one of the objective goods, and (ii) desiring or taking pleasure in that good, could get us all that we wanted. But let's leave such exotic possibilities unexplored. Surveying the above theories should be sufficient to give you a flavor of what a theory of well-being needs to accommodate. And, more importantly, it should now be clear why all plausible ethical theories take well-being to be one of the factors that determines the deontic statuses of actions.

Notes

1. Of course, if we also hold that what makes someone deserving is failing to do what is ethically required, then circularity looms.
2. p is a *necessary condition* for some q when the falsity of p guarantees the falsity of q. That is, q cannot be true unless p is true. p is a *sufficient condition* for q when the truth of p guarantees q. That is, p's being true is enough for q's being true. Being a mother is a sufficient condition for being female. "If and only if" is a way of capturing both of these conditions. The "if" captures the sufficient condition. The "only if" captures the necessary condition.

3. A terminological point. Much contemporary deontological theorizing favors the language of *rights*—e.g., the right to life, the right not to be harmed, the right to be informed, property rights, and so on. Rights are, in this sense, entitlements—claims to be treated in a certain way. Though popular, talk of constraints and options is more illuminating than talk of rights. Talk of rights often masks whether we are talking about an option or a constraint. For instance, if I say you have a property right to this book, I might be saying that, since it's yours, you have the option to use this book as you see fit—you could read it or burn it. Yet I might also be saying that, since the book is yours, I have a constraint against taking your book or interfering with your reading or burning it. Or I might mean that, if a friend is in possession of the book, she has a constraint against keeping it and you have the option to (perhaps forcibly) take it. Most of the time context makes clear which sense of "right" we are talking about. But sometimes it doesn't. Thus, to avoid ambiguity, I will speak directly in terms of options and constraints. In any case, our discussion below could, with merely cosmetic alteration, be rephrased in terms of rights.
4. A conceptual possibility is worth noting. It may turn out that these sources—God, culture, and rational nature—end up delivering a theory whose deontic verdicts align perfectly with the deontic verdicts supplied by, say, utilitarianism. That is, the views we examine below may, in the end, not turn out to enumerate deontic verdicts that include constraints. Of course, were this surprising result to occur, although both theories would give the same answer to the enumerative question of an ethical theory, they would differ in their answers to the explanatory question. Utilitarians will explain why actions have the deontic verdicts that they do by pointing to the good; whereas theorists who subscribe to one of the theories we will discuss below will point to some other explanation—e.g., God's commands. Having flagged this possibility, we can safely set it aside. As traditionally conceived, all of the theories discussed below are thought to depart significantly in terms of the deontic verdicts they deliver from the consequentialist theories examined above.
5. Is qualitative hedonism a form of hedonism? The worry can be brought out by the following dilemma: Either the quality rating is experienced as pleasant, or it isn't. If the quality rating is experienced as pleasant, then a difference in rating must be merely a difference in terms of intensity or duration, in which case we are back to quantitative hedonism. If the quality rating is not experienced as pleasant, then qualitative hedonism is not a form of hedonism, since it claims that something other than pleasure can increase well-being.

PART 

Introductory Readings

Challenges to Ethical Theory

Moral Isolationism

Mary Midgley

Some claim that the search for universal answers to moral questions is futile because morality differs from one culture to another. This view, sometimes referred to as "cultural relativism," maintains that while we can seek understanding of a particular culture's moral system, we have no basis for judging it, for morality is only a matter of custom. Mary Midgley, who was Senior Lecturer in Philosophy at Newcastle University in England, argues against cultural relativism, maintaining that moral reasoning requires the possibility of judging the practices of other cultures.

All of us are, more or less, in trouble today about trying to understand cultures strange to us. We hear constantly of alien customs. We see changes in our lifetime which would have astonished our parents. I want to discuss here one very short way of dealing with this difficulty, a drastic way which many people now theoretically favour. It

From Mary Midgley, *Heart and Mind: The Varieties of Moral Experience* (London: Routledge, 2003).

consists in simply denying that we can ever understand any culture except our own well enough to make judgements about it. Those who recommend this hold that the world is sharply divided into separate societies, sealed units, each with its own system of thought. They feel that the respect and tolerance due from one system to another forbids us ever to take up a critical position to any other culture. Moral judgement, they suggest, is a kind of coinage valid only in its country of origin.

I shall call this position "moral isolationism." I shall suggest that it is certainly not forced upon us, and indeed that it makes no sense at all. People usually take it up because they think it is a respectful attitude to other cultures. In fact, however, it is not respectful. Nobody can respect what is entirely unintelligible to them. To respect someone, we have to know enough about him to make a *favourable* judgement, however general and tentative. And we do understand people in other cultures to this extent. Otherwise a great mass of our most valuable thinking would be paralysed.

To show this, I shall take a remote example, because we shall probably find it easier to think calmly about it than we should with a contemporary one, such as female circumcision in Africa or the Chinese Cultural Revolution. The principles involved will still be the same. My example is this. There is, it seems, a verb in classical Japanese which means "to try out one's new sword on a chance wayfarer." (The word is *tsujigiri*, literally "crossroads-cut.") A samurai sword had to be tried out because, if it was to work properly, it had to slice through someone at a single blow, from the shoulder to the opposite flank. Otherwise, the warrior bungled his stroke. This could injure his honour, offend his ancestors, and even let down his emperor. So tests were needed, and wayfarers had to be expended. Any wayfarer would do—provided, of course, that he was not another Samurai. Scientists will recognize a familiar problem about the rights of experimental subjects.

Now when we hear of a custom like this, we may well reflect that we simply do not understand it; and therefore are not qualified to criticize it at all, because we are not members of that culture. But we are not members of any other culture either, except our own. So we extend the principle to cover all extraneous cultures, and we seem therefore to be moral isolationists. But this is, as we shall see, an impossible position. Let us ask what it would involve.

We must ask first: Does the isolating barrier work both ways? Are people in other cultures equally unable to criticize *us?* This question struck me sharply when I read a remark in *The Guardian* by an anthropologist about a South American Indian who had been taken into a Brazilian town for an operation, which saved his life. When he came back to his village, he made several highly critical remarks about the white Brazilians' way of life. They may very well have been justified. But the interesting point was that the anthropologist called these remarks "a damning indictment of Western civilization." Now the Indian had been in that town about two weeks. Was he in a position to deliver a damning indictment? Would we ourselves be qualified to deliver such an indictment on the Samurai, provided we could spend two weeks in ancient Japan? What do we really think about this?

My own impression is that we believe that outsiders can, in principle, deliver perfectly good indictments—only, it usually takes more than two weeks to make them damning. Understanding has degrees. It is not a slapdash yes-or-no matter. Intelligent outsiders can progress in it, and in some ways will be at an advantage over the locals. But if this is so, it must clearly apply to ourselves as much as anybody else.

Our next question is this: Does the isolating barrier between cultures block praise as well as blame? If I want to say that the Samurai culture has many virtues, or to praise the South American Indians, am I prevented from doing *that* by my outside status? Now, we certainly do need to praise other societies in this way. But it is hardly possible that we could praise them effectively if we could not, in principle, criticize them. Our praise would be worthless if it rested on no definite grounds, if it did not flow from some understanding. Certainly we may need to praise things which we do not *fully* understand. We say "there's something very good here, but I can't quite make out what it is yet." This happens when we want to learn from strangers. And we can learn from strangers. But to do this we have to distinguish between those strangers who are worth learning from and those who are not. Can we then judge which is which?

This brings us to our third question: What is involved in judging? Now plainly there is no question here of sitting on a bench in a red robe and sentencing people. Judging simply means forming an opinion, and expressing it if it is called for. Is there anything wrong about this? Naturally, we ought to avoid forming—and expressing—*crude* opinions, like that of a simple-minded missionary, who might dismiss the whole Samurai culture as entirely bad, because non-Christian. But this is a different objection. The trouble with crude opinions is that they are crude, whoever forms them, not that they are formed by the wrong people. Anthropologists, after all, are outsiders quite as much as missionaries. Moral isolationism forbids us to form *any* opinions on these matters. Its ground for doing so is that we don't understand them. But there is much that we don't understand in our own culture too. This brings us to our last question: If we can't judge other cultures, can we really judge our own? Our efforts to do so will be much damaged if we are really deprived of our opinions about other societies, because these provide the range of comparison, the spectrum of alternatives against which we set what we want to understand. We would have to stop using the mirror which anthropology so helpfully holds up to us.

In short, moral isolationism would lay down a general ban on moral reasoning. Essentially, this is the programme of immoralism, and it carries a distressing logical difficulty. Immoralists like Nietzsche are actually just a rather specialized sect of moralists. They can no more afford to put moralizing out of business than smugglers can afford to abolish customs regulations. The power of moral judgement is, in fact, not a luxury, not a perverse indulgence of the self-righteous. It is a necessity. When we judge something to be bad or good, better or worse than something else, we are taking it as an example to aim at or avoid. Without opinions of this sort, we would have no framework of comparison for our own policy, no chance of profiting by other people's insights or mistakes. In this vacuum, we could form no judgements on our own actions.

Now it would be odd if *Homo sapiens* had really got himself into a position as bad as this—a position where his main evolutionary asset, his brain, was so little use to him. None of us is going to accept this sceptical diagnosis. We cannot do so, because our involvement in moral isolationism does not flow from apathy, but from a rather acute concern about human hypocrisy and other forms of wickedness. But we polarize that concern around a few selected moral truths. We are rightly angry with those who despise, oppress or steamroll other cultures. We think that doing these things is actually *wrong*. But this is itself a moral judgement. We could not condemn oppression and insolence if we thought that all our condemnation were just a trivial local quirk of our own culture. We could still less do it if we tried to stop judging altogether.

Real moral scepticism, in fact, could lead only to inaction, to our losing all interest in moral questions, most of all in those which concern other societies. When we discuss these things, it becomes instantly clear how far we are from doing this. Suppose, for instance, that I criticize the bisecting Samurai, that I say his behaviour is brutal. What will usually happen next is that someone will protest, will say that I have no right to make criticisms like that of another culture. But it is most unlikely that he will use this move to end the discussion of the subject. Instead, he will justify the Samurai. He will try to fill in the background, to make me understand the custom, by explaining the exalted ideals of discipline and devotion which produced it. He will probably talk of the lower value which the ancient Japanese placed on individual life generally. He may well suggest that this is a healthier attitude than our own obsession with security. He may add, too, that the wayfarers did not seriously mind being bisected, that in principle they accepted the whole arrangement.

Now an objector who talks like this is implying that it *is* possible to understand alien customs. That is just what he is trying to make me do. And he implies, too, that if I do succeed in understanding them, I shall do something better than giving up judging them. He expects me to change my present judgement to a truer one—namely, one that is favourable. And the standards I must use to do this cannot just be Samurai standards. They have to be ones current in my own culture. Ideals like discipline and devotion will not move anybody unless he himself accepts them. As it happens, neither discipline nor devotion is very popular in the West at present. Anyone who appeals to them may well have to do some more arguing to make *them* acceptable, before he can use them to explain the Samurai. But if he does succeed here, he will have persuaded us, not just that there was something to be said for them in ancient Japan, but that there would be here as well.

Isolating barriers simply cannot arise here. If we accept something as a serious moral truth about one culture, we can't refuse to apply it—in however different an outward form—to other cultures as well, wherever circumstances admit it. If we refuse to do this, we just are not taking the other culture seriously. This becomes clear if we look at the last argument used by my objector—that of justification by consent of the victim. It is suggested that sudden bisection is quite in order, *provided* that it takes place between consenting adults. I cannot now discuss how conclusive this justification is. What I am pointing out is simply that it can only work if we believe that *consent* can make such a transaction respectable—and this is a thoroughly modern and Western idea. It would probably never occur to a Samurai; if it did, it would surprise him very much. It is *our* standard. In applying it, too, we are likely to make another typically Western demand. We shall ask for good factual evidence that the wayfarers actually do have this rather surprising taste—that they are really willing to be bisected.

In applying Western standards in this way, we are not being confused or irrelevant. We are asking the questions which arise *from where we stand,* questions which we can see the sense of. We do this because asking questions which you can't see the sense of is humbug. Certainly we can extend our questioning by imaginative effort. We can come to understand other societies better. By doing so, we may make their questions our own, or we may see that they are really forms of the questions which we are asking already. This is not impossible. It is just very hard work. The obstacles which often prevent it are simply those of ordinary ignorance, laziness and prejudice.

If there were really an isolating barrier, of course, our own culture could never have been formed. It is no sealed box, but a fertile jungle of different influences—Greek, Jewish, Roman, Norse, Celtic and so forth, into which further influences are still pouring—American, Indian, Japanese, Jamaican, you name it. The moral isolationist's picture of separate unmixable cultures is quite unreal. People who talk about British history usually stress the value of this fertilizing mix, no doubt rightly. But this is not just an odd fact about Britain. Except for the very smallest and most remote, all cultures are formed out of many streams. All have the problem of digesting and assimilating things which, at the start, they do not understand. All have the choice of learning something from this challenge, or, alternatively, of refusing to learn, and fighting it mindlessly instead.

This universal predicament has been obscured by the fact that anthropologists used to concentrate largely on very small and remote cultures, which did not seem to have this problem. These tiny societies, which had often forgotten their own history, made neat, self-contained subjects for study. No doubt it was valuable to emphasize their remoteness, their extreme strangeness, their independence of our cultural tradition. This emphasis was, I think, the root of moral isolationism. But, as the tribal studies themselves showed, even there the anthropologists were able to interpret what they saw and make judgements—often favourable—about the tribesmen. And the tribesmen, too, were quite equal to making judgements about the anthropologists—and about the tourists and Coca-Cola salesmen who followed them. Both sets of judgements, no doubt, were somewhat hasty, both have been refined in the light of further experience. A similar transaction between us and the Samurai might take even longer. But that is no reason at all for deeming it impossible. Morally as well as physically, there is only one world, and we all have to live in it.

Study Questions

1. What does Midgley mean by "moral isolationism"?
2. Are those opposed to our judging other cultures equally opposed to other cultures judging ours?
3. Do those who live in a culture necessarily understand it better than those who don't live in that culture?
4. If criticisms of other cultures are always inappropriate, can praise of other cultures ever be appropriate?

Egoism and Moral Scepticism

James Rachels

Whereas ethical egoism asserts that we ought never act against our own interest, psychological egoism claims that we always act in this way. James Rachels (1941–2003), who was Professor of Philosophy at the University of Alabama in Birmingham, finds both doctrines untenable. He argues, contrary to the claim made by psychological egoists, that selfishness should not be conflated with self-interest, and that feeling good after doing an action should not be confused with doing the action because it feels good. Against ethical egoism, Rachels maintains that concern for one's own welfare is compatible with concern for the welfare of others. He agrees that ethical egoism is a coherent position but concludes that it should not be accepted because it yields intuitively implausible moral verdicts.

1. Our ordinary thinking about morality is full of assumptions that we almost never question. We assume, for example, that we have an obligation to consider the welfare of other people when we decide what actions to perform or what rules to obey; we think that we must refrain from acting in ways harmful to others, and that we must respect their rights and interests as well as our own. We also assume that people are in fact capable of being motivated by such considerations, that is, that people are not wholly selfish and that they do sometimes act in the interests of others.

Both of these assumptions have come under attack by moral sceptics, as long ago as by Glaucon in Book II of Plato's *Republic*. Glaucon recalls the legend of Gyges, a shepherd who was said to have found a magic ring in a fissure opened by an earthquake. The ring would

From Steven M. Cahn, ed., *A New Introduction to Philosophy*, 1971.

make its wearer invisible and thus would enable him to go anywhere and do anything undetected. Gyges used the power of the ring to gain entry to the Royal Palace, where he seduced the Queen, murdered the King, and subsequently seized the throne. Now Glaucon asks us to imagine that there are two such rings, one given to a man of virtue and one given to a rogue. The rogue, of course, will use his ring unscrupulously and do anything necessary to increase his own wealth and power. He will recognize no moral constraints on his conduct, and, since the cloak of invisibility will protect him from discovery, he can do anything he pleases without fear of reprisal. So, there will be no end to the mischief he will do. But how will the so-called virtuous man behave? Glaucon suggests that he will behave no better than the rogue: "No one, it is commonly believed, would have such iron strength of mind as to stand fast in doing right or keep his hands off other men's goods, when he could go to the market-place and fearlessly help himself to anything he wanted, enter houses and sleep with any woman he chose, set prisoners free and kill men at his pleasure, and in a word go about among men with the powers of a god. He would behave no better than the other; both would take the same course."[1] Moreover, why shouldn't he? Once he is freed from the fear of reprisal, why shouldn't a man simply do what he pleases, or what he thinks is best for himself? What reason is there for him to continue being "moral" when it is clearly not to his own advantage to do so?

These sceptical views suggested by Glaucon have come to be known as *psychological egoism* and *ethical egoism,* respectively. Psychological egoism is the view that all men are selfish in everything that they do, that is, that the only motive from which anyone ever acts is self-interest. On this view, even when men are acting in ways apparently calculated to benefit others, they are actually motivated by the belief that acting in this way is to their own advantage, and if they did not believe this, they would not be doing that action. Ethical egoism is, by contrast, a normative view about how men *ought* to act. It is the view that, regardless of how men do in fact behave, they have no obligation to do anything except what is in their own interests. According to ethical egoists, a person is always justified in doing whatever is in his own interests, regardless of the effect on others.

Clearly, if either of these views is correct, then "the moral institution of life" (to use Butler's well-turned phrase) is very different from what we normally think. The majority of mankind is grossly deceived about what is, or ought to be, the case, where morals are concerned.

2. Psychological egoism seems to fly in the face of the facts. We are tempted to say, "Of course people act unselfishly all the time. For example, Smith gives up a trip to the country, which he would have enjoyed very much, in order to stay behind and help a friend with his studies, which is a miserable way to pass the time. This is a perfectly clear case of unselfish behavior, and if the psychological egoist thinks that such cases do not occur, then he is just mistaken." Given such obvious instances of "unselfish behavior," what reply can the egoist make? There are two general arguments by which he might try to show that all actions, including those such as the one just outlined, are in fact motivated by self-interest. Let us examine these in turn:

a. The first argument goes as follows: If we describe one person's action as selfish, and another person's action as unselfish, we are overlooking the crucial fact that in both cases, assuming that the action is done voluntarily, *the agent is merely doing what he most wants to do*. If Smith stays behind to help his friend, that only shows that he wanted to help his friend more than he wanted to go to the country. And why should he be praised for his "unselfishness" when he is only doing what he most wants to do? So, since Smith is only doing what he wants to do, he cannot be said to be acting unselfishly.

This argument is so bad that it would not deserve to be taken seriously except for the fact that so many otherwise intelligent people have been taken in by it. First, the argument rests on the premise that people never voluntarily do anything except what they want to do. But this is patently false; there are at least two classes of actions that are exceptions to this generalization. One is the set of actions which we may not want to do, but which we do anyway as a means to an end which we want to achieve, for example, going to the dentist in order to stop a toothache, or going to work every day in order to be able to draw our pay at the end of the month. These cases may be regarded as consistent with the spirit of the egoist argument, however, since the ends mentioned are wanted by the agent. But the other set of actions are those which we do, not because we want to, nor even because there is an end which we want to achieve, but because we feel ourselves *under an obligation* to do them. For example, someone may do something because he has promised to do it, and thus feels obligated, even though he does not want to do it. It is sometimes suggested that in such cases we do the action because, after all, we want to keep our promises; so, even here, we are doing what we want. However, this dodge will not work: if I have promised to do something, and if I do not want to do it, then it is simply false to say that I want to keep my promise. In such cases we feel a conflict precisely because we do *not* want to do what we feel obligated to do. It is reasonable to think that Smith's action falls roughly into this second category: he might stay behind, not because he wants to, but because he feels that this friend needs help.

But suppose we were to concede, for the sake of the argument, that all voluntary action is motivated by the agent's wants, or at least that Smith is so motivated. Even if this were granted, it would not follow that Smith is acting selfishly or from self-interest. For if Smith wants to do something that will help his friend, even when it means forgoing his own enjoyments, that is precisely what makes him *un*selfish. What else could unselfishness be, if not wanting to help others? Another way to put the same point is to say that it is the *object* of a want that determines whether it is selfish or not. The mere fact that I am acting on *my* wants does not mean that I am acting selfishly; that depends on *what it is* that I want. If I want only my own good, and care nothing for others, then I am selfish; but if I also want other people to be well-off and happy, and if I act on *that* desire, then my action is not selfish. So much for this argument.

b. The second argument for psychological egoism is this: Since so-called unselfish actions always produce a sense of self-satisfaction in the agent,[2] and since this sense of satisfaction is a pleasant state of consciousness, it follows that the point of the action is really to achieve a pleasant state of consciousness, rather than to bring about any good for others. Therefore, the action is "unselfish" only at a superficial level of analysis. Smith will feel much better with himself for having stayed to help his friend—if he had gone to the country, he would have felt terrible about it—and that is the real point of the action. According to a well-known story, this argument was once expressed by Abraham Lincoln:

> Mr. Lincoln once remarked to a fellow-passenger on an old-time mud-coach that all men were prompted by selfishness in doing good. His fellow-passenger was antagonizing this position when they were passing over a corduroy bridge that spanned a slough. As they crossed this bridge they espied an old razor-backed sow on the bank making a terrible noise because her pigs had got into the slough and were in danger of drowning. As the old coach began to climb the hill, Mr. Lincoln called out, "Driver, can't you stop just a moment?" Then Mr. Lincoln jumped out, ran back, and lifted the little pigs out of the mud and water and placed them on the bank. When he returned, his companion remarked: "Now, Abe, where does selfishness come in on

> this little episode?" "Why, bless your soul, Ed, that was the very essence of selfishness. I should have had no peace of mind all day had I gone on and left that suffering old sow worrying over those pigs. I did it to get peace of mind, don't you see?"[3]

This argument suffers from defects similar to the previous one. Why should we think that merely because someone derives satisfaction from helping others this makes him selfish? Isn't the unselfish man precisely the one who *does* derive satisfaction from helping others, while the selfish man does not? If Lincoln "got peace of mind" from rescuing the piglets, does this show him to be selfish, or, on the contrary, doesn't it show him to be compassionate and good-hearted? (If a man were truly selfish, why should it bother his conscience that *others* suffer—much less pigs?) Similarly, it is nothing more than shabby sophistry to say, because Smith takes satisfaction in helping his friend, that he is behaving selfishly. If we say this rapidly, while thinking about something else, perhaps it will sound all right; but if we speak slowly, and pay attention to what we are saying, it sounds plain silly.

Moreover, suppose we ask *why* Smith derives satisfaction from helping his friend. The answer will be, it is because Smith cares for him and wants him to succeed. If Smith did not have these concerns, then he would take no pleasure in assisting him; and these concerns, as we have already seen, are the marks of unselfishness, not selfishness. To put the point more generally: if we have a positive attitude toward the attainment of some goal, then we may derive satisfaction from attaining that goal. But the *object* of our attitude is *the attainment of that goal*; and we must want to attain the goal *before* we can find any satisfaction in it. We do not, in other words, desire some sort of "pleasurable consciousness" and then try to figure out how to achieve it; rather, we desire all sorts of different things—money, a new fishing boat, to be a better chess player, to get a promotion in our work, etc.—and because we desire these things, we derive satisfaction from attaining them. And so, if someone desires the welfare and happiness of another person, he will derive satisfaction from that; but this does not mean that this satisfaction is the object of his desire, or that he is in any way selfish on account of it.

It is a measure of the weakness of psychological egoism that these insupportable arguments are the ones most often advanced in its favor. Why, then, should anyone ever have thought it a true view? Perhaps because of a desire for theoretical simplicity: In thinking about human conduct, it would be nice if there were some simple formula that would unite the diverse phenomena of human behavior under a single explanatory principle, just as simple formulae in physics bring together a great many apparently different phenomena. And since it is obvious that self-regard is an overwhelmingly important factor in motivation, it is only natural to wonder whether all motivation might not be explained in these terms. But the answer is clearly No; while a great many human actions are motivated entirely or in part by self-interest, only by a deliberate distortion of the facts can we say that all conduct is so motivated. This will be clear, I think, if we correct three confusions which are commonplace. The exposure of these confusions will remove the last traces of plausibility from the psychological egoist thesis.

The first is the confusion of selfishness with self-interest. The two are clearly not the same. If I see a physician when I am feeling poorly, I am acting in my own interest but no one would think of calling me "selfish" on account of it. Similarly, brushing my teeth, working hard at my job, and obeying the law are all in my self-interest but none of these are examples of selfish conduct. This is because selfish behavior is behavior that ignores the interests of others, in circumstances in which their interests ought not to be ignored. This concept has a definite evaluative flavor; to call someone "selfish" is not just to describe his action but to condemn it. Thus, you would not call me selfish for eating a normal meal in normal circumstances (although it may surely be in my self-interest); but you would call me selfish for hoarding food while others about are starving.

The second confusion is the assumption that every action is done *either* from self-interest or from other-regarding motives. Thus, the egoist concludes that if there is no such thing as genuine altruism then all actions must be done from self-interest. But this is certainly a false dichotomy. The man who continues to smoke cigarettes, even after learning about the connection between smoking and cancer, is surely not acting from self-interest, not even by his own standards—self-interest would dictate that he quit smoking at once—and he is not acting altruistically either. He *is*, no doubt, smoking for the pleasure of it, but all that this shows is that undisciplined pleasure-seeking and acting from self-interest are very different. This is what led Butler to remark that "the thing to be lamented is, not that men have so great regard to their own good or interest in the present world, for they have not enough."[4]

The last two paragraphs show (*a*) that it is false that all actions are selfish, and (*b*) that it is false that all actions are done out of self-interest. And it should be noted that these two points can be made, and were, without any appeal to putative examples of altruism.

The third confusion is the common but false assumption that a concern for one's own welfare is incompatible with any genuine concern for the welfare of others. Thus, since it is obvious that everyone (or very nearly everyone) does desire his own well-being it might be thought that no one can really be concerned with others. But again, this is false. There is no inconsistency in desiring that everyone, including oneself *and* others, be well-off and happy. To be sure, it may happen on occasion that our own interests conflict with the interests of others, and in these cases we will have to make hard choices. But even in these cases we might sometimes opt for the interests of others, especially when the others involved are our family or friends. But more importantly, not all cases are like this: sometimes we are able to promote the welfare of others when our own interests are not involved at all. In these cases not even the strongest self-regard need prevent us from acting considerately toward others.

Once these confusions are cleared away, it seems to me obvious enough that there is no reason whatever to accept psychological egoism. On the contrary, if we simply observe people's behavior with an open mind, we may find that a great deal of it is motivated by self-regard, but by no means all of it; and that there is no reason to deny that "the moral institution of life" can include a place for the virtue of beneficence.[5]

3. The ethical egoist would say at this point, "Of course it is possible for people to act altruistically, and perhaps many people do act that way—but there is no reason why they *should* do so. A person is under no obligation to do anything except what is in his own interests."[6] This is really quite a radical doctrine. Suppose I have an urge to set fire to some public building (say, a department store) just for the fascination of watching the spectacular blaze: according to this view, the fact that several people might be burned to death provides no reason whatever why I should not do it. After all, this only concerns *their* welfare, not my own, and according to the ethical egoist the only person I need think of is myself.

Some might deny that ethical egoism has any such monstrous consequences. They would point out that it is really to my own advantage not to set the fire—for, if I do that I may be caught and put into prison (unlike Gyges, I have no magic ring for protection). Moreover, even if I could avoid being caught it is still to my advantage to respect the rights and interests of others, for it is to my advantage to live in a society in which people's rights and interests are respected. Only in such a society can I live a happy and secure life; so, in acting kindly toward others, I would merely be doing my part to create and maintain the sort of society which it is to my advantage to have.[7] Therefore, it is said, the egoist would not be such a bad man; he would be as kindly and considerate as anyone else, because he would see that it is to his own advantage to be kindly and considerate.

This is a seductive line of thought, but it seems to me mistaken. Certainly it is to everyone's advantage (including the egoist's) to preserve a stable society where people's interests are generally protected. But there is no reason for the egoist to think that merely because *he* will not honor the rules of the social game, decent society will collapse. For the vast majority of people are not egoists, and there is no reason to think that they will be converted by his example—especially if he is discreet and does not unduly flaunt his style of life. What this line of reasoning shows is not that the egoist himself must act benevolently, but that he must encourage *others* to do so. He must take care to conceal from public view his own self-centered method of decision making, and urge others to act on precepts very different from those on which he is willing to act.

The rational egoist, then, cannot advocate that egoism be universally adopted by everyone. For he wants a world in which his own interests are maximized; and if other people adopted the egoistic policy of pursuing their own interests to the exclusion of his interests, as he pursues his interests to the exclusion of theirs, then such a world would be impossible. So he himself will be an egoist, but he will want others to be altruists.

This brings us to what is perhaps the most popular "refutation" of ethical egoism current among philosophical writers—the argument that ethical egoism is at bottom inconsistent because it cannot be universalized.[8] The argument goes like this:

To say that any action or policy of action is *right* (or that it *ought* to be adopted) entails that it is right for *anyone* in the same sort of circumstances. I cannot, for example, say that it is right for me to lie to you, and yet object when you lie to me (provided, of course, that the circumstances are the same). I cannot hold that it is all right for me to drink your beer and then complain when you drink mine. This is just the requirement that we be consistent in our evaluations; it is a requirement of logic. Now it is said that ethical egoism cannot meet this requirement because, as we have already seen, the egoist would not want others to act in the same way that he acts. Moreover, suppose he *did* advocate the universal adoption of egoistic policies: he would be saying to Peter, "You ought to pursue your own interests even if it means destroying Paul"; and he would be saying to Paul, "You ought to pursue your own interests even if it means destroying Peter." The attitudes expressed in these two recommendations seem clearly inconsistent—he is urging the advancement of Peter's interest at one moment, and countenancing their defeat at the next. Therefore, the argument goes, there is no way to maintain the doctrine of ethical egoism as a consistent view about how we ought to act. We will fall into inconsistency whenever we try.

What are we to make of this argument? Are we to conclude that ethical egoism has been refuted? Such a conclusion, I think, would be unwarranted; for I think that we can show, contrary to this argument, how ethical egoism can be maintained consistently. We need only to interpret the egoist's position in a sympathetic way: we should say that he has in mind a certain kind of world which he would prefer over all others; it would be a world in which his own interests were maximized, regardless of the effects on the other people. The egoist's primary policy of action, then, would be to act in such a way as to bring about, as nearly as possible, this sort of world. Regardless of however morally reprehensible we might find it, there is nothing *inconsistent* in someone's adopting this as his ideal and acting in a way calculated to bring it about. And if someone did adopt this as his ideal, then he would not advocate universal egoism; as we have already seen, he would want other people to be altruists. So, if he advocates any principles of conduct for the general public, they will be altruistic principles. This could not be inconsistent; on the contrary, it would be perfectly consistent with his goal of creating a world in which his own interests are maximized. To be sure, he would have to be deceitful; in order to secure the good will of others, and a favorable hearing for his exhortations to altruism, he would have to pretend that he was himself prepared to accept altruistic principles. But again, that would be all right; from the egoist's point of view, this would merely be a matter of adopting the necessary means to the achievement of his goal—and while we might not approve of this, there is nothing inconsistent about it. Again, it might be said, "He advocates one thing, but does another. Surely *that's* inconsistent." But it is not; for what he advocates and what he does are both calculated as means to an end (the *same* end, we might note); and as such, he is doing what is rationally required in each case. Therefore, contrary to the previous argument, there is nothing inconsistent in the ethical egoist's view. He cannot be refuted by the claim that he contradicts himself.

Is there, then, no way to refute the ethical egoist? If by "refute" we mean show that he has made some *logical* error, the answer is that there is not. However, there is something more that can be said. The egoist challenge to our ordinary moral convictions amounts to a demand for an explanation of why we should adopt certain policies of action, namely, policies in which the good of others is given importance. We can give an answer to this demand, albeit an indirect one. The reason one ought not to do actions that would hurt other people is other people would be hurt. The reason one ought to do actions that would benefit other people is other people would be benefited. This may at first seem like a piece of philosophical sleight-of-hand, but it is not. The point is that the welfare of human beings is something that most of us value *for its own sake*, and not merely for the sake of something else. Therefore, when *further* reasons are demanded for valuing the welfare of human beings, we cannot point to anything further to satisfy this demand. It is not that we have no reason for pursuing these policies, but that our reason *is* that these policies are for the good of human beings.

So if we are asked, "Why shouldn't I set fire to this department store?" one answer would be, "Because if you do, people may be burned to death." This is a complete, sufficient reason which does not require qualification or supplementation of any sort. If someone seriously wants to know why this action shouldn't be done, that's the reason. If we are pressed further and asked the sceptical question, "But why shouldn't I do actions that will harm others?" we may not know what to say—but this is because the questioner has included in his question the very answer we would like to give: "Why shouldn't you do actions that will harm others? Because, doing those actions would harm others."

The egoist, no doubt, will not be happy with this. He will protest that *we* may accept this as a reason, but *he* does not. And here the argument stops: there are limits to what can be accomplished by argument, and if the egoist really doesn't care about other people—if he honestly doesn't care whether they are helped or hurt by his actions—then we have reached those limits. If we want to persuade him to act decently toward his fellow humans, we will have to make our appeal to such other attitudes as he does possess, by threats, bribes, or other cajolery. That is all that we can do.

Though some may find this situation distressing (we would like to be able to show that the egoist is just *wrong*), it holds no embarrassment for common morality. What we have come up against is simply a fundamental requirement of rational action, namely, that the existence of reasons for action always depends on the prior existence of certain attitudes in the agent. For example, the fact that a certain course of action would make the agent a lot of money is a reason for doing it only if the agent wants to make money; the fact that practicing at chess makes one a better player is a reason for practicing only if one wants to be a better player; and so on. Similarly, the fact that a certain action would help the agent is a reason for doing the action only if the agent cares about his own welfare, and the fact that an action would help others is a reason for doing it only if the agent cares about others. In this respect ethical egoism and what we might call ethical altruism are in exactly the same fix: both require that the agent *care* about himself, or about other people, before they can get started.

So a nonegoist will accept "It would harm another person" as a reason not to do an action simply because he cares about what happens to that other person. When the egoist says that he does *not* accept that as a reason, he is saying something quite extraordinary. He is saying that he has no affection for friends or family, that he never feels pity or compassion, that he is the sort of person who can look on scenes of human misery with complete indifference, so long as he is not the one suffering. Genuine egoists, people who really don't care at all about anyone other than themselves, are rare. It is important to keep this in mind when thinking about ethical egoism; it is easy to forget just how fundamental to human psychological makeup the feeling of sympathy is. Indeed, a man without any sympathy at all would scarcely be recognizable as a man; and that is what makes ethical egoism such a disturbing doctrine in the first place.

4. There are, of course, many different ways in which the sceptic might challenge the assumptions underlying our moral practice. In this essay I have discussed only two of them, the two put forward by Glaucon in the passage that I cited from Plato's *Republic*. It is important that the assumptions underlying our moral practice should not be confused with particular judgments made within that practice. To defend one is not to defend the other. We may assume—quite properly, if my analysis has been correct—that the virtue of beneficence does, and indeed should, occupy an important place in "the moral institution of life"; and yet we may make constant and miserable errors when it comes to judging when and in what ways this virtue is to be exercised. Even worse, we may often be able to make accurate moral judgments, and know what we ought to do, but not do it. For these ills, philosophy alone is not the cure.

Notes

1. *The Republic of Plato,* translated by F. M. Cornford (Oxford, 1941), p. 45.
2. Or, as it is sometimes said, "It gives him a clear conscience," or "He couldn't sleep at night if he had done otherwise," or "He would have been ashamed of himself for not doing it," and so on.
3. Frank C. Sharp, *Ethics* (New York, 1928), pp. 74–75. Quoted from the Springfield (IL) *Monitor* in the *Outlook,* vol. 56, p. 1059.
4. *The Works of Joseph Butler,* edited by W. E. Gladstone (Oxford, 1896), vol. II, p. 26. It should be noted that most of the points I am making against psychological egoism were first made by Joseph Butler. Butler made all the important points; all that is left for us is to remember them.
5. The capacity for altruistic behavior is not unique to human beings. Some interesting experiments with rhesus monkeys have shown that these animals will refrain from operating a device for securing food if this cause other animals to suffer pain. See Jules H. Masserman, Stanley Wechkin, and William Terris, "'Altruistic' Behavior in Rhesus Monkeys," *American Journal of Psychiatry,* vol. 121 (1964), pp. 584–85.
6. I take this to be the view of Ayn Rand, insofar as I understand her confused doctrine.
7. Cf. Thomas Hobbes, *Leviathan* (London, 1651), chap. 17.
8. See, for example, Brian Medlin, "Ultimate Principles and Ethical Egoism," *Australasian Journal of Philosophy,* vol. 35 (1957), pp. 111–18; and D. H. Monro, *Empiricism and Ethics* (Cambridge, 1967), chap. 16.

Study Questions

1. What is the distinction between psychological egoism and ethical egoism?
2. If you do what you want to do, are you being selfish?
3. Is a concern for yourself incompatible with a concern for others?
4. Is it self-defeating for the ethical egoist to urge everyone to act egotistically?

God and Morality

Steven M. Cahn

According to divine command theory, an act is right if and only if God wills that it is right. Steven M. Cahn, editor of this book, argues instead that whether God exists has no implications for morality. An act is not rendered right because God commands it; rather, if God commands it, God does so because the action is in accord with an independent moral standard. In that case, you could act in accord with the standard regardless of whether you believe in God.

According to many religions, although not all, the world was created by God, an all-powerful, all-knowing, all-good being. Although God's existence has been doubted, let us for the moment assume its truth. What implications of this supposition would be relevant to our lives?

Some people would feel more secure in the knowledge that the world had been planned by an all-good being. Others would feel insecure, realizing the extent to which their existence depended on a decision of this being. In any case, most people, out of either fear or respect, would wish to act in accord with God's will.

Belief in God by itself, however, provides no hint whatsoever which actions God wishes us to perform or what we ought to do to please or obey God. We may affirm that God is all-good, yet have no way of knowing the highest moral standards. All we may presume is that, whatever these standards, God always acts in accordance with them. We might expect God to have implanted the correct moral standards in our minds, but this supposition is doubtful in view of the conflicts among people's intuitions. Furthermore, even if consensus prevailed, it might be only a means by which God tests us to see whether we have the courage to dissent from popular opinion.

Some would argue that if God exists, then murder is immoral, because it destroys what God with infinite wisdom created. This argument, however, fails on several grounds. First, God also created germs, viruses, and disease-carrying rats. Because God created these things, ought they not be eliminated? Second, if God arranged for us to live, God also arranged for us to die. By killing, are we assisting the work of God? Third, God provided us with the mental and physical potential to commit murder. Does God wish us to fulfill this potential?

Thus God's existence alone does not imply any particular moral precepts. We may hope our actions are in accord with God's standards, but no test is available to check whether what we do is best in God's eyes. Some seemingly good people suffer great ills, whereas some seemingly evil people achieve happiness. Perhaps in a future life these outcomes will be reversed, but we have no way of ascertaining who, if anyone, is ultimately punished and who ultimately rewarded.

Over the course of history, those who believed in God's existence typically were eager to learn God's will and tended to rely on those individuals who claimed to possess such insight. Diviners, seers, and priests were given positions of great influence. Competition among them was severe, however, for no one could be sure which oracle to believe.

In any case prophets died, and their supposedly revelatory powers disappeared with them. For practical purposes what was needed was a permanent record of God's will. This requirement was met by the writing of holy books in which God's will was revealed to all.

But even though many such books were supposed to embody the will of God, they conflicted with one another. Which was to be accepted? Belief in the existence of God by itself yields no answer.

Let us suppose, however, that an individual becomes persuaded that a reliable guide to God's will is contained in the Ten Commandments. This person, therefore, believes to murder, steal, or commit adultery is wrong.

But why is it wrong? Is it wrong because God says so, or does God say so because it *is* wrong?

This crucial issue was raised more than two thousand years ago in Plato's remarkable dialogue, the *Euthyphro*. Plato's teacher, Socrates, who in most of Plato's works is given the leading role, asks the overconfident Euthyphro whether actions are right because God says they are right, or whether God says actions are right because they are right.

In other words, Socrates is inquiring whether actions are right because of God's fiat or whether God is subject to moral standards. If actions are right because of God's command, then anything God commands would be right. Had God commanded adultery, stealing, and murder, then adultery, stealing, and murder would be right—surely an unsettling and to many an unacceptable conclusion.

Granted, some may be willing to adopt this discomforting view, but then they face another difficulty. If the good is whatever God commands, to say that God's commands are good amounts to saying that God's commands are God's commands, a mere tautology or repetition of words. In that case, the possibility of meaningfully praising the goodness of God would be lost.

The lesson here is that might does not make right, even if the might is the infinite might of God. To act morally is not to act out of fear of punishment; it is not to act as one is commanded to act. Rather, it is to act as one ought to act, and how one ought to act is not dependent on anyone's power, even if the power be divine.

Thus actions are not right because God commands them; on the contrary, God commands them because they are right. What is right is independent of what God commands, for to be right, what God commands must conform to an independent standard.

We could act intentionally in accord with this standard without believing in the existence of God; therefore morality does not rest on that belief. Consequently those who do not believe in God can be highly moral (as well as immoral) people, and those who do believe in the existence of God can be highly immoral (as well as moral) people. This conclusion should come as no surprise to anyone who has contrasted the benevolent life of the inspiring teacher, the Buddha, an atheist, with the malevolent life of the monk Torquemada, who devised and enforced the boundless cruelties of the Spanish Inquisition.

In short, believing in the existence of God does not by itself imply any specific moral principles, and knowing God's will does not provide any justification for morality. Thus regardless of our religious commitments, the moral dimension of our lives remains to be explored.

Study Questions

1. If God exists, is murder immoral?
2. Is murder wrong because God prohibits it, or does God prohibit it because it is wrong?
3. Can those who do not believe in God be moral?
4. Can adherents of different religions resolve moral disagreements?

B.

Varieties of Ethical Theory

Leviathan

Thomas Hobbes

Thomas Hobbes (1588–1679) was an English philosopher who played a crucial role in the history of social thought. He develops a moral and political theory that views justice and other ethical ideals as resting on an implied agreement among individuals. Hobbes argues that reason requires that we should relinquish the right to do whatever we please in exchange for all others limiting their rights in a similar manner, thus achieving security for all. Outside the social order, each human life is, as Hobbes famously puts it, "solitary, poor, nasty, brutish, and short."

Chapter XIII

Of the Natural Condition of Mankind as Concerning Their Felicity, and Misery

Nature hath made men so equal, in the faculties of the body, and mind; as that though there be found one man sometimes manifestly stronger in body, or of quicker mind than another; yet when all is

From Thomas Hobbes, *Leviathan* (1660).

reckoned together, the difference between man, and man, is not so considerable, as that one man can thereupon claim to himself any benefit, to which another may not pretend, as well as he. For as to the strength of body, the weakest has strength enough to kill the strongest, either by secret machination, or by confederacy with others, that are in the same danger with himself.

And as to the faculties of the mind, setting aside the arts grounded upon words, and especially that skill of proceeding upon general, and infallible rules, called science; which very few have, and but in few things; as being not a native faculty, born with us; nor attained, as prudence, while we look after somewhat else, I find yet a greater equality amongst men, than that of strength. For prudence, is but experience; which equal time, equally bestows on all men, in those things they equally apply themselves unto. That which may perhaps make such equality incredible, is but a vain conceit of one's own wisdom, which almost all men think they have in a greater degree, than the vulgar; that is, than all men but themselves, and a few others, whom by fame, or for concurring with themselves, they approve. For such is the nature of men, that howsoever they may acknowledge many others to be more witty, or more eloquent, or more learned; yet they will hardly believe there be many so wise as themselves; for they see their own wit at hand, and other men's at a distance. But this proveth rather that men are in that point equal, than unequal. For there is not ordinarily a greater sign of the equal distribution of any thing, than that every man is contented with his share.

From this equality of ability, ariseth equality of hope in the attaining of our ends. And therefore if any two men desire the same thing, which nevertheless they cannot both enjoy, they become enemies; and in the way to their end, which is principally their own conservation, and sometimes their delectation only, endeavour to destroy, or subdue one another. And from hence it comes to pass, that where an invader hath no more to fear, than another man's single power; if one plant, sow, build, or possess a convenient seat, others may probably be expected to come prepared with forces united, to dispossess, and deprive him, not only of the fruit of his labour, but also of his life, or liberty. And the invader again is in the like danger of another.

And from this diffidence of one another, there is no way for any man to secure himself, so reasonable, as anticipation; that is, by force, or wiles, to master the persons of all men he can, so long, till he see no other power great enough to endanger him: and this is no more than his own conservation requireth, and is generally allowed. Also because there be some, that taking pleasure in contemplating their own power in the acts of conquest, which they pursue farther than their security requires; if others, that otherwise would be glad to be at case within modest bounds, should not by invasion increase their power, they would not be able, long time, by standing only on their defence, to subsist. And by consequence, such augmentation of dominion over men being necessary to a man's conservation, it ought to be allowed him.

Again, men have no pleasure, but on the contrary a great deal of grief, in keeping company, where there is no power able to over-awe them all. For every man looketh that his companion should value him, at the same rate he sets upon himself: and upon all signs of contempt, or undervaluing, naturally endeavours, as far as he dares, (which amongst them that have no common power to keep them in quiet, is far enough to make them destroy each other), to extort a greater value from his contemners, by damage; and from others, by the example.

So that in the nature of man, we find three principal causes of quarrel. First, competition; secondly, diffidence; thirdly, glory.

The first, maketh man invade for gain; the second, for safety; and the third, for reputation. The first use violence, to make themselves masters of other men's persons, wives, children, and cattle; the second, to defend them; the third, for trifles, as a word, a smile, a different opinion, and any other sign of undervalue, either direct in their persons, or by reflection in their kindred, their friends, their nation, their profession, or their name.

Hereby it is manifest, that during the time men live without a common power to keep them all in awe, they are in that condition which is called war; and such a WAR, as is of every man, against every man. For war, consisteth not in battle only, or the act of fighting; but in a tract of time, wherein the will to contend by battle is sufficiently known: and therefore the notion of *time*, is to be considered in the nature of war; as it is in the nature of weather. For as the nature of foul weather, lieth not in a shower or two of rain; but in an inclination thereto of many days together: so the nature of war, consisteth not in actual fighting; but in the known disposition thereto, during all the time there is no assurance to the contrary. All other time is PEACE.

Whatsoever therefore is consequent to a time of war, where every man is enemy to every man; the same is consequent to the time, wherein men live without other security, than what their own strength, and their own invention shall furnish them withal. In such condition, there is no place for industry; because the fruit thereof is uncertain: and consequently no culture of the earth; no navigation nor use of the commodities that may be imported by sea; no commodious building: no instruments of moving, and removing, such things as require much force; no knowledge of the face of the earth; no account of time; no arts; no letters; no society; and which is worst of all, continual fear, and danger of violent death; and the life of man, solitary, poor, nasty, brutish, and short.

It may seem strange to some man, that has not well weighed these things; that nature should thus dissociate, and render men apt to invade, and destroy one another: and he may therefore, not trusting to this inference, made from the passions, desire perhaps to have the same confirmed by experience. Let him therefore consider with himself, when taking a journey, he arms himself, and seeks to go well accompanied; when going to sleep, he locks his doors; when even in his house he locks his chests; and this when he knows there be laws, and public offices, armed, to revenge all injuries shall be done him; what opinion he has of his fellow-subjects, when he rides armed; of his fellow citizens, when he locks his doors; and of his children, and servants, when he locks his chests. Does he not there as much accuse mankind by his actions, as I do by my words? But neither of us accuse man's nature in it. The desires, and other passions of man, are in themselves no sin. No more are the actions, that proceed from those passions, till they know a law that forbids them: which till laws be made they cannot know: nor can any law be made, till they have agreed upon the person that shall make it.

It may peradventure be thought, there was never such a time, nor condition of war as this; and I believe it was never generally so, over all the world: but there are many places, where they live so now, For the savage people in many places of America, except the government of small families, the concord whereof dependeth on natural lust, have no government at all; and live at this day in that brutish manner, as I said before. Howsoever, it may be perceived what manner of life there would be, where there were no common power to fear, by the manner of life, which men that have formerly lived under a peaceful government, use to degenerate into, in a civil war.

But though there had never been any time, wherein particular men were in a condition of war one against another; yet in all times, kings, and persons of sovereign authority, because of their independency, are in continual jealousies, and in the state and posture of gladiators; having their weapons pointing, and their eyes fixed on one another; that is, their forts, garrisons, and guns upon the frontiers of their kingdoms; and continual spies upon their neighbours;

which is a posture of war. But because they uphold thereby, the industry of their subjects; there does not follow from it, that misery, which accompanies the liberty of particular men.

To this war of every man, against every man, this also is consequent; that nothing can be unjust. The notions of right and wrong, justice and injustice have there no place, where there is no common power, there is no law: where no law, no injustice. Force, and fraud, are in war the two cardinal virtues. Justice, and injustice are none of the faculties neither of the body, nor mind. If they were, they might be in a man that were alone in the world, as well as his senses, and passions. They are qualities, that relate to men in society, not in solitude. It is consequent also to the same condition, that there be no propriety, no dominion, no *mine* and *thine* distinct; but only that to be every man's, that he can get: and for so long, as he can keep it. And thus much for the ill condition, which man by mere nature is actually placed in; though with a possibility to come out of it, consisting partly in the passions, partly in his reason.

The passions that incline men to peace, are fear of death; desire of such things as are necessary to commodious living; and a hope by their industry to obtain them. And reason suggesteth convenient articles of peace, upon which men may be drawn to agreement. These articles, are they, which otherwise are called the Laws of Nature: whereof I shall speak more particularly, in the two following chapters.

Chapter XIV

Of the First and Second Natural Laws, and of Contracts

The RIGHT OF NATURE, which writers commonly call *jus naturale*, is the liberty each man hath, to use his own power, as he will himself, for the preservation of his own nature; that is to say, of his own life; and consequently, of doing any thing, which in his own judgment, and reason, he shall conceive to be the aptest means thereunto.

By LIBERTY, is understood, according to the proper signification of the word, the absence of external impediments: which impediments, may oft take away part of a man's power to do what he would; but cannot hinder him from using the power left him, according as his judgment, and reason shall dictate to him.

A LAW OF NATURE, *lex naturalis*, is a precept or general rule, found out by reason, by which a man is forbidden to do that, which is destructive of his life, or taketh away the means of preserving the same; and to omit that, by which he thinketh it may be best preserved. For though they that speak of this subject, use to confound *jus*, and *lex*, *right* and *law:* yet they ought to be distinguished; because right, consisteth in liberty to do, or to forbear: whereas LAW, determineth, and bindeth to one of them: so that law, and right, differ as much, as obligation, and liberty; which in one and the same matter are inconsistent.

And because the condition of man, as hath been declared in the precedent chapter, is a condition of war of every one against every one; in which case every one is governed by his own reason; and there is nothing he can make use of, that may not be a help unto him, in preserving his life against his enemies; it followeth, that in such a condition, every man has a right to every thing; even to one another's body. And therefore, as long as this natural right of every man to every thing endureth, there can be no security to any man, how strong or wise soever he be, of living out the time, which nature ordinarily alloweth men to live. And consequently it is a precept, or general rule of reason, *that every man, ought to endeavour peace, as far as he has hope of obtaining it; and when he cannot obtain it, that he may seek, and use, all helps, and advantages of war.* The first branch of which rule, containeth the first, and fundamental law of nature; which is, to *seek peace, and follow it.* The second, the sum of the right of nature; which is, *by all means we can, to defend ourselves.*

From this fundamental law of nature, by which men are commanded to endeavour peace, is derived this second law; *that a man be willing, when others are so too, as far-forth, as for peace, and defence of himself he shall think it necessary, to lay down this right to all things; and be contented with so much liberty against other men; as he would allow other men against himself.* For as long as every man holdeth this right, of doing any thing he liketh; so long are all men in the condition of war. But if other men will not lay down their right, as well as he; then there is no reason for any one, to divest himself of his; for that were to expose himself to prey, which no man is bound to, rather than to dispose himself to peace. This is that law of the Gospel; *whatsoever you require that others should do to you, that do yet to them. . . .*

To *lay down* a man's *right* to any thing, is to *divest* himself of the *liberty*, of hindering another of the benefit of his own right to the same. For he that renounceth, or passeth away his right, giveth not to any other man a right which he had not before; because there is nothing to which every man had not right by nature: but only standeth out of his way, that he may enjoy his own original right, without hindrance from him: not without hindrance from another. So that the effect which redoundeth to one man, by another man's defect of right, is but so much diminution of impediments to the use of his own right original. Right is laid aside, either by simply renouncing it; or by transferring it to another. By *simply* RENOUNCING; when he cares not to whom the benefit thereof redoundeth. By TRANSFERRING; when he intendeth the benefit thereof to some certain person, or persons. And when a man hath in either manner abandoned, or granted away his right; then he is said to be OBLIGED, or BOUND, not to hinder those, to whom such right is granted, or abandoned, from the benefit of it; and that he *ought*, and it is his DUTY, not to make void that voluntary act of his own: and that such hindrance is INJUSTICE, and INJURY, as being *sine jure;* the right being before renounced, or transferred. So that *injury*, or *injustice*, in the controversies of the world, is somewhat like to that, which in the disputations of scholars is called absurdity. For as it is there called an *absurdity*, to contradict what one maintained in the beginning: so in the world, it is called injustice, and injury, voluntarily to undo that, which from the beginning he had voluntarily done. The way by which a man either simply renounceth, or transferreth his right, is a declaration, or signification, by some voluntary and sufficient sign, or signs, that he doth so renounce, or transfer; or hath so renounced, or transferred the same, to him that accepteth it. And these signs are either words only, or actions only; or, as it happeneth most often, both words, and actions. And the same are the BONDS, by which men are bound, and obliged; bonds, that have their strength, not from their own nature, for nothing is more easily broken than a man's word, but from fear of some evil consequences upon the rupture.

Whensoever, a man transferreth his right, or renounceth it; it is either in consideration of some right reciprocally transferred to himself; or for some other good he hopeth for thereby. For it is a voluntary act: and of the voluntary acts of every man, the object is some *good to himself*. And therefore there be some rights, which no man can be understood by any words, or other signs, to have abandoned, or transferred. As first a man cannot lay down the right of resisting them, that assault him by force, to take away his life; because he cannot be understood to aim thereby, at any good to himself. The same may be said of wounds, and chains, and imprisonment; both because there is no benefit consequent to such patience; as there is to the patience of suffering another to be wounded, or imprisoned; as also because a man cannot tell, when he seeth men proceed against him by violence, whether they intend his death or not. And lastly the motive, and end for which this renouncing, and transferring of right is introduced, is nothing else but the security of a man's person, in his life, and in the means of so preserving life, as not to be weary of it. And therefore if a man by words, or other signs, seem to despoil himself of the end, for which those signs were intended; he is not to be understood as if he meant it, or that it was his will; but that he was ignorant of how such words and actions were to be interpreted.

The mutual transferring of right, is that which men call CONTRACT. . . .

Chapter XV

Of Other Laws of Nature

From that law of nature, by which we are obliged to transfer to another, such rights, as being retained, hinder the peace of mankind, there followeth a third; which is this, *that men perform their covenants made:* without which, covenants are in vain, and but empty words; and the right of all men to all things remaining, we are still in the condition of war.

And in this law of nature, consisteth the fountain and original of JUSTICE. For where no covenant hath preceded, there hath no right been transferred, and every man has right to every thing; and consequently, no action can be unjust. But when a covenant is made, then to break it is *unjust:* and the definition of INJUSTICE, is no other than *the not performance of covenant.* And whatsoever is not unjust, is *just.*

But because covenants of mutual trust, where there is a fear of not performance on either part, as hath been said in the former chapter, are invalid; though the original of justice be the making of covenants; yet injustice actually there can be none, till the cause of such fear be taken away; which while men are in the natural condition of war, cannot be done. Therefore before the names of just, and unjust can have place, there must be some coercive power, to compel men equally to the performance of their covenants, by the terror of some punishment, greater than the benefit they expect by the breach of their covenant; and to make good that propriety, which by mutual contract men acquire, in recompense of the universal right they abandon: and such power there is none before the erection of a commonwealth. And this is also to be gathered out of the ordinary definition of justice in the Schools: for they say, that *justice is the constant will of giving to every man his own.* And therefore where there is no *own*, that is no propriety, there is no injustice; and where there is no coercive power erected, that is, where there is no commonwealth, there is no propriety; all men having right to all things: therefore where there is no commonwealth, there nothing is unjust. So that the nature of justice, consisteth in keeping of valid covenants: but the validity of covenants begins not but with the constitution of a civil power, sufficient to compel men to keep them: and then it is also that propriety begins.

The fool hath said in his heart, there is no such thing as justice; and sometimes also with his tongue; seriously alleging, that every man's conservation, and contentment, being committed to his own care, there could be no reason, why every man might not do what he thought conduced thereunto: and therefore also to make, or not make; keep, or not keep covenants, was not against reason, when it conduced to one's benefit. He does not therein deny, that there be covenants; and that they are sometimes broken, sometimes kept; and that such breach of them may be called injustice, and the observance of them justice: but he questioneth, whether injustice, taking away the fear of God, (for the same fool hath said in his heart there is no God,) may not sometimes stand with that reason, which dictateth to every man his own good; and particularly then, when it conduceth to such a benefit, as shall put a man in a condition, to neglect not only the dispraise, and revilings, but also the power of other men. The kingdom of God is gotten by violence; but what if it could be gotten by unjust violence? were it against reason so to get it, when it is impossible to receive hurt by it? and if it be not against reason, it is not against justice; or else justice is not to be approved for good. From such reasoning as this, successful wickedness hath obtained the name of virtue: and some that in all other things have disallowed the violation of faith; yet have allowed it, when it is for the getting of a kingdom. . . . This specious reasoning is nevertheless false.

For the question is not of promises mutual, where there is no security of performance on either side; as when there is no civil power erected over the parties promising; for such promises are no covenants: but either where one of the parties has performed already; or where there is a power to make him perform; there is the question whether it be against reason, that is, against the benefit of the other to perform, or not. And I say it is not against reason. For the manifestation whereof, we are to consider; first, that when a man doth a thing, which notwithstanding any thing can be foreseen, and reckoned on, tendeth to his own destruction, howsoever some accident which he could not expect, arriving may turn it to his benefit; yet such events do not make it reasonably or wisely done. Secondly, that in a condition of war, wherein every man to every man, for want of a common power to keep them all in awe, is an enemy, there is no man can hope by his own strength, or wit, to defend himself from destruction, without the help of confederates; where every one expects the same defence by the confederation, that any one else does: and therefore he which declares he thinks it reason to deceive those that help him, can in reason expect no other means of safety, than what can be had from his own single power. He therefore that breaketh his covenant, and consequently declareth that he thinks he may with reason do so, cannot be received into any society, that unite themselves for peace and defence, but by the error of them that receive him; nor when he is received, be retained in it, without seeing the danger of their error; which errors a man cannot reasonably reckon upon as the means of his security: and therefore if he be left, or cast out of society, he perisheth; and if he live in society, it is by the errors of other men, which he could not foresee, nor reckon upon; and consequently against the reason of his preservation; and so, as all men that contribute not to his destruction, forbear him only out of ignorance of what is good for themselves.

Study Questions

1. Without government to enforce laws, would life be, as Hobbes says, "nasty, brutish, and short"?
2. What does Hobbes mean by "a law of nature"?
3. According to Hobbes, what does the "fool" believe?
4. Does Hobbes provide a satisfying response to the fool?

Groundwork for the Metaphysics of Morals

Immanuel Kant

Immanuel Kant (1724–1804) was a dominant figure in the history of modern philosophy, making groundbreaking contributions in virtually every area of the subject. He argues that the moral worth of an action is to be judged not by its consequences but by the nature of the maxim or principle that motivated the action. Thus, right actions are not necessarily those with favorable consequences but those performed in accord with correct maxims. But which maxims are correct? According to Kant, the only correct ones are those that can serve as universal laws because they are applicable without exception to every person at any time. In other words, you should act only on a maxim that can be universalized without contradiction. Kant refers to his supreme moral principle as the "categorical imperative," categorical because it does not depend on anyone's particular desires and imperative because it is a command of reason. Kant also claims that the categorical imperative can be reformulated as follows: Act in such a way that you treat humanity, whether in your own person or in any other person, always at the same time as an end, never merely as a means. In short, treat others as rational beings worthy of respect. Kant believes that acting otherwise is immoral and irrational.

First Section

Transition from Common Rational Moral Cognition to Philosophical Moral Cognition

There is nothing it is possible to think of anywhere in the world, or indeed anything at all outside it, that can be held to be good without

From Immanuel Kant, *Groundwork for the Metaphysics of Morals*, translated by Allen W. Wood (New Haven: Yale University Press, 2002).

limitation, excepting only a **good will**. Understanding, wit, the power of judgment, and like *talents* of the mind, whatever they might be called, or courage, resoluteness, persistence in an intention, as qualities of *temperament,* are without doubt in some respects good and to be wished for; but they can also become extremely evil and harmful, if the will that is to make use of these gifts of nature, and whose peculiar constitution is therefore called *character,* is not good. It is the same with *gifts of fortune.* Power, wealth, honor, even health and that entire well-being and contentment with one's condition, under the name of *happiness,* make for courage and thereby often also for arrogance, where there is not a good will to correct their influence on the mind, and thereby on the entire principle of action, and make them universally purposive; not to mention that a rational impartial spectator can never take satisfaction even in the sight of the uninterrupted welfare of a being, if it is adorned with no trait of a pure and good will; and so the good will appears to constitute the indispensable condition even of the worthiness to be happy.

Some qualities are even conducive to this good will itself and can make its work much easier, but still have despite this no inner unconditioned worth, yet always presuppose a good will, which limits the esteem that one otherwise rightly has for them, and does not permit them to be held absolutely good. Moderation in affects and passions, self-control, and sober reflection not only are good for many aims, but seem even to constitute a part of the *inner* worth of a person; yet they lack much in order to be declared good without limitation (however unconditionally they were praised by the ancients). For without the principles of a good will they can become extremely evil, and the cold-bloodedness of a villain makes him not only far more dangerous but also immediately more abominable in our eyes than he would have been held without it.

The good will is good not through what it effects or accomplishes, not through its efficacy for attaining any intended end, but only through its willing, i.e., good in itself, and considered for itself, without comparison, it is to be estimated far higher than anything that could be brought about by it in favor of any inclination, or indeed, if you prefer, of the sum of all inclinations. Even if through the peculiar disfavor of fate, or through the meager endowment of a stepmotherly nature, this will were entirely lacking in the resources to carry out its aim, if with its greatest effort nothing of it were accomplished, and only the good will were left over (to be sure, not a mere wish, but as the summoning up of all the means insofar as they are in our control): then it would shine like a jewel for itself, as something that has its full worth in itself. . . .

To be beneficent where one can is a duty, and besides this there are some souls so sympathetically attuned that, even without any other motive of vanity or utility to self, take an inner gratification in spreading joy around them, and can take delight in the contentment of others insofar as it is their own work. But I assert that in such a case the action, however it may conform to duty and however amiable it is, nevertheless has no true moral worth, but is on the same footing as other inclinations, e.g., the inclination to honor, which, when it fortunately encounters something that in fact serves the common good and is in conformity with duty, and is thus worthy of honor, deserves praise and encouragement, but not esteem; for the maxim lacks moral content, namely of doing such actions not from inclination but *from duty*. Thus suppose the mind of that same friend of humanity were clouded over with his own grief, extinguishing all his sympathetic participation in the fate of others; he still has the resources to be beneficent to those suffering distress, but the distress of others does not touch him because he is sufficiently busy with his own; and now, where no inclination any longer stimulates him to it, he tears himself out of this deadly insensibility and does the action without any inclination, solely from duty; only then does it for the first time have its authentic moral worth. Even more: if nature had put little sympathy at all in the heart of this or that person, if he (an honest man, to be sure) were by temperament cold and indifferent toward the sufferings of others, perhaps because he himself is provided with particular gifts of patience and strength to endure his own, and also presupposes or even demands the same of others; if nature has not really formed such a man into a friend of humanity (although he would not in truth be its worst product), nevertheless would he not find a source within himself to give himself a far higher worth than that which a good-natured temperament might have? By all means! Just here begins the worth of character, which is moral and the highest without any comparison, namely that he is beneficent not from inclination but from duty. . . .

An action from duty has its moral worth *not in the aim* that is supposed to be attained by it, but rather in the maxim in accordance with which it is resolved upon; thus that worth depends not on the actuality of the object of the action, but merely on the *principle of the volition,* in accordance with which the action is done, without regard to any object of the faculty of desire. It is clear from the preceding that the aims we may have in actions, and their effects, as ends and incentives of the will, can impart to the actions no unconditioned and moral worth. In what, then, can this worth lie, if it is not supposed to exist in the will, in the relation of the actions to the effect hoped for? It can lie nowhere else *than in the principle of the will,* without regard to the ends that can be effected through such action; for the will is at a crossroads, as it were, between its principle *a priori. Duty is the necessity of an action from respect for the law.* For the object, as an effect of my proposed action, I can of course have an *inclination,* but *never respect,* just because it is merely an effect and not the activity of a will. Just as little can I have respect for inclination in general, whether my own or another's; I can at most approve it in the first case, in the second I can sometimes even love it, i.e., regard it as favorable to my own advantage. Only that which is connected with my will merely as a ground, never as an effect, only what does not serve my inclination but outweighs it, or at least wholly excludes it from the reckoning in a choice, hence only the mere law for itself, can be an object of respect and hence a command. Now an action from duty is supposed entirely to abstract from the influence of inclination, and with it every object of the will, so nothing is left over for the will that can determine it except the *law* as what is objective and subjectively *pure respect* for this practical law, hence the maxim[1] of complying with such a law, even when it infringes all my inclinations.

The moral worth of the action thus lies not in the effect to be expected from it; thus also not in any principle of action which needs to get its motive from this expected effect. For all these effects (agreeableness of one's condition, indeed even the furthering of the happiness of others) could be brought about through other causes, and for them the will of a rational being is therefore not needed; but in it alone the highest and unconditioned good can nevertheless be encountered. Nothing other than the *representation of the law* in itself, *which obviously occurs only in the rational being* insofar as it, and not the hoped-for effect, is the determining ground of the will, therefore constitutes that so pre-eminent good which we call 'moral', which is already present in the person himself who acts in accordance with it, but must not first of all be expected from the effect.

But what kind of law can it be, whose representation, without even taking account of the effect expected from it, must determine the will, so that it can be called good absolutely and without limitation? Since I have robbed the will of every impulse that could have arisen from the obedience to any law, there is nothing left over except the universal lawfulness of the action in general which alone is to serve the will as its principle, i.e., I ought never to conduct myself except so *that I could also will that my maxim become a universal law.* Here it is mere lawfulness in general (without grounding it on any law determining certain actions) that serves the will as its principle, and also must so serve it, if duty is not to be everywhere an empty delusion and a chimerical concept; common human reason, indeed, agrees perfectly with this in its practical judgment, and has the principle just cited always before its eyes. . . .

Second Section

Transition from Popular Moral Philosophy to the Metaphysics of Morals

Every thing in nature works in accordance with laws. Only a rational being has the faculty to act *in accordance with the representation* of laws, i.e., in accordance with principles, or a *will.* Since for the derivation of actions from laws *reason* is required, the will is nothing other than practical reason. If reason determines the will without exception, then the actions of such a being, which are recognized as objectively necessary, are also subjectively necessary, i.e., the will is a faculty of choosing *only that* which reason, independently of inclination, recognizes as practically necessary, i.e., as good. But if reason for itself alone does not sufficiently determine the will, if the will is still subject to subjective conditions (to certain incentives) which do not always agree with the objective conditions, in a word, if the will is not *in itself* fully in accord with reason (as it actually is with human beings), then the actions which are objectively recognized as necessary are subjectively contingent, and the determination of such a will, in accord with objective laws, is *necessitation,* i.e., the relation of objective laws to a will which is not thoroughly good is represented as the determination of the will of a rational being through grounds of reason to which, however, this will in accordance with its nature is not necessarily obedient.

The representation of an objective principle, insofar as it is necessitating for a will, is called a 'command' (of reason), and the formula of the command is called an **imperative**.

All imperatives are expressed through an *ought* and thereby indicate the relation of an objective law of reason to a will which in its subjective constitution is not necessarily determined by that law (a necessitation). They say that it would be good to do or refrain from something, but they say it to a will that does not always do something just because it is represented to it as good to do. Practical *good*, however, is that which determines the will by means of representations of reason, hence not from subjective causes, but objectively, i.e., from grounds that are valid for every rational being as such. It is distinguished from the *agreeable*, as that which has influence on the will only by means of sensation from merely subjective causes, those which are valid only for the senses of this or that one, and not as a principle of reason, which is valid for everyone. . . .

Now all *imperatives* command either *hypothetically* or *categorically*. The former represent the practical necessity of a possible action as a means to attain something else which one wills (or which it is possible that one might will). The categorical imperative would be that one which represented an action as objectively necessary for itself, without any reference to another end.

Because every practical law represents a possible action as good, and therefore as necessary for a subject practically determinable by reason, all imperatives are formulas of the determination of action, which is necessary in accordance with the principle of a will which is good in some way. Now if the action were good merely as a means to *something else*, then the imperative is *hypothetical*; if it is represented as good *in itself*, hence necessary, as the principle of the will, in a will that in itself accords with reason, then it is *categorical*.

The imperative thus says which action possible through me would be good, and represents the practical rule in relation to a will that does not directly do an action because it is good, in part because the subject does not always know that it is good, in part because if it did know this, its maxims could still be contrary to the objective principles of a practical reason. . . .

There is *one* end, however, that one can presuppose as actual for all rational beings (insofar as imperatives apply to them, namely as dependent beings) and thus one aim that they not merely *can* have, but of which one can safely presuppose that without exception they *do have* it in accordance with a natural necessity, and that is the aim at *happiness*. The hypothetical imperative that represents the practical necessity of the action as a means to furthering happiness is **assertoric**. One may expound it as necessary not merely to an uncertain, merely possible aim, but to an aim that one can presuppose safely and *a priori* with every human being, because it belongs to his essence. Now one can call skill in the choice of means to his own greatest well-being *prudence* in the narrowest sense. Thus the imperative that refers to the choice of means to one's own happiness, i.e., the precept of prudence, is always *hypothetical;* the action is commanded not absolutely but only as a means to another aim.

Finally, there is one imperative that, without being grounded on any other aim to be achieved through a certain course of conduct as its condition, commands this conduct immediately. This imperative is **categorical**. It has to do not with the matter of the action and what is to result from it, but with the form and the principle from which it results; and what is essentially good about it consists in the disposition, whatever the result may be. This imperative may be called that **of morality**. . . .

Now the question arises: How are all these imperatives possible? This question does not demand the knowledge how to think the execution of the action that the imperative commands, but rather merely how to think the necessitation of the will that the imperative expresses in the problem. How an imperative of skill is to be possible probably needs no particular discussion. Whoever wills the end, also wills (insofar as reason has decisive influence on his actions) the means that are indispensably necessary to it that are in his control. . . .

By contrast, how the imperative of *morality* is possible is without doubt the sole question in need of a solution, since it is not at all hypothetical, and thus the necessity, represented as objective, cannot be based on any presupposition, as with the hypothetical imperatives. Yet in this connection it must not be left out of account that whether there is any such imperative anywhere cannot be settled *by any example,* hence not empirically; but the worry is rather that all those that seem categorical might be, in some hidden wise, hypothetical. E.g., if it is said: "You ought not to make a deceiving promise," and one assumes that the necessity of this omission is not mere advice for the avoidance of some ill or other, so that it might really mean: "You should not make a lying promise, so that if it were revealed then you would lose your credit"; if an action of this kind must be considered as evil for itself, then the imperative forbidding it would be categorical; then one still cannot with certainty give an example in which the will is determined merely by the law, without any other incentive, although it might appear so; for it is always possible that fear of disgrace, or perhaps also an obscure worry about other dangers, might secretly have had an influence on the will. Who can prove through experience the nonexistence of a cause, since experience teaches us nothing beyond the fact that we do not perceive one? But in such a case the so-called moral imperative, which appears as such to be categorical and unconditioned, would in fact be only a pragmatic precept, which alerts us to our own advantage and merely teaches us to pay attention to it. . . .

If I think of a *hypothetical* imperative in general, then I do not know beforehand what it will contain until the condition is given to me. But if I think of a *categorical* imperative, then I know directly what it contains. For since besides the law, the imperative contains only the necessity of the maxim,[2] that it should accord with this law, but the law contains no condition to which it is limited, there remains nothing left over with which the maxim of the action is to be in accord, and this accordance alone is what the imperative really represents necessarily.

The categorical imperative is thus only a single one, and specifically this: *Act only in accordance with that maxim through which you can at the same time will that it become a universal law.* . . .

Now we will enumerate some duties, in accordance with their usual division into duties toward ourselves and toward other human beings, and into perfect and imperfect duties:[3]

(1) One person, through a series of evils that have accumulated to the point of hopelessness, feels weary of life but is still so far in possession of his reason that he can ask himself whether it might be contrary to the duty to himself to take his own life. Now he tries out whether the maxim of his action could become a universal law of nature. But his maxim is: 'From self-love, I make it my principle to shorten my life when by longer term it threatens more ill than it promises agreeableness'. The question is whether this principle of self-love could become a universal law of nature. But then one soon sees that a nature whose law it was to destroy life through the same feeling whose vocation it is to impel the furtherance of life would contradict itself, and thus could not subsist as nature; hence that maxim could not possibly obtain as a universal law of nature, and consequently it entirely contradicts the supreme principle of all duty.

(2) Another sees himself pressured by distress into borrowing money. He knows very well that he will not be able to pay, but he also sees that nothing will be lent him if he does not firmly promise to pay at a determinate time. He wants to make such a promise; yet he has conscience enough to ask himself: "Is it not impermissible and contrary to duty to get out of distress in such a way?" Supposing he nevertheless resolved on it, his maxim would be stated as follows: 'If I believe myself to be in pecuniary distress, then I will borrow money and promise to pay it back, although I know this will never happen'.

Now this principle of self-love, or of what is expedient for oneself, might perhaps be united with my entire future welfare, yet the question now is: "Is it right?" I thus transform this claim of self-love into a universal law and set up the question thus: "How would it stand if my maxim became a universal law?" Yet I see right away that it could never be valid as a universal law of nature and still agree with itself, but rather it would necessarily contradict itself. For the universality of a law that everyone who believes himself to be in distress could promise whatever occurred to him with the intention of not keeping it would make impossible the promise and the end one might have in making it, since no one would believe that anything has been promised him, but rather would laugh about every such utterance as vain pretense.

(3) A third finds in himself a talent, which could, by means of some cultivation, make him into a human being who is useful for all sorts of aims. But he sees himself as in comfortable circumstances and sooner prefers to indulge in gratification than to trouble himself with the expansion and improvement of his fortunate natural predispositions. Yet he still asks whether, apart from the agreement of his maxim of neglecting his gifts of nature with his propensity to amusement, it also agrees with what one calls 'duty'. Then he sees that, although a nature could still subsist in accordance with such a universal law, though then the human being (like the South Sea Islanders) would think only of letting his talents rust and applying his life merely to idleness, amusement, procreation, in a word, to enjoyment; yet it is impossible for him to **will** that this should become a universal law of nature, or that it should be implanted in us as such by natural instinct. For as a rational being he necessarily wills that all the faculties in him should be developed, because they are serviceable and given to him for all kinds of possible aims.

(4) Yet a *fourth—for* whom it is going well, while he sees that others have to struggle with great hardships (with which he could well help them)—thinks: "What has it to do with me? Let each be as happy as heaven wills, or as he can make himself, I will not take anything from him or even envy him; only I do not want to contribute to his welfare or to his assistance in distress!" Now to be sure, if such a way of thinking were to become a universal law of nature, then the human race could well subsist, and without doubt still better than when everyone chatters about sympathetic participation and benevolence, and even on occasion exerts himself to practice them, but, on the contrary also deceives wherever he can, sells out, or otherwise infringes on the

right of human beings. But although it is possible that a universal law of nature could well subsist in accordance with that maxim, yet it is impossible to **will** that such a principle should be valid without exception as a natural law. For a will that resolved on this would conflict with itself, since the case could sometimes arise in which he needs the love and sympathetic participation of others, and where, through such a natural law arising from his own will, he would rob himself of all the hope of assistance that he wishes for himself.

Now these are some of the many actual duties, or at least of what we take to be duties, whose partitioning from the single principle just adduced clearly meets the eye. One must *be able to will* that a maxim of our action should become a universal law: this is the canon of the moral judgment of this action in general. Some actions are so constituted that their maxim cannot even be *thought* without contradiction as a universal law of nature, much less could one *will* that it *ought* to become one. With others, that internal impossibility is not to be encountered, but it is impossible to *will* that their maxims should be elevated to the universality of a natural law, because such a will would contradict itself. One easily sees that the first conflict with strict or narrow (unremitting) duty, the second only with wide (meritorious) duty, and thus all duties regarding the kind of obligation (not the object of their action) have been completely set forth through these examples in their dependence on the one principle.

Now if we attend to ourselves in every transgression of a duty, then we find that we do not actually will that our maxim should become a universal law, for that is impossible for us, but rather will that its opposite should remain a law generally; yet we take the liberty of making an *exception* for ourselves, or (even only for this once) for the advantage of our inclination. Consequently, if we weighed everything from one and the same point of view, namely that of reason, then we would encounter a contradiction in our own will, namely that objectively a certain principle should be necessary as a universal law and yet subjectively that it should not be universally valid, but rather that it should admit of exceptions. . . .

But suppose there were something *whose existence in itself* had an absolute worth, something that, as *end in itself,* could be a ground of determinate laws; then in it and only in it alone would lie the ground of a possible categorical imperative, i.e., of a practical law.

Now I say that the human being, and in general every rational being, *exists* as end in itself, *not merely as means* to the discretionary use of this or that will, but in all its actions, those directed toward itself as well as those directed toward other rational beings, it must always *at the same time* be considered as an *end.* All objects of inclinations have only a conditioned worth; for if the inclinations and the needs grounded on them did not exist, then their object would be without worth. The inclinations themselves, however, as sources of needs, are so little of absolute worth, to be wished for in themselves, that rather to be entirely free of them must be the universal wish of every rational being. Thus the worth of all objects *to be acquired* through our action is always conditioned. The beings whose existence rests not on our will but on nature nevertheless have, if they are beings without reason, only a relative worth as means, and are called *things;* rational beings, by contrast, are called *persons,* because their nature already marks them out as ends in themselves, i.e., as something that may not be used merely as means, hence to that extent limits all arbitrary choice (and is an object of respect). These are not merely subjective ends whose existence as effect of our action has a worth *for us;* but rather *objective ends,* i.e., things whose existence in itself is an end, and specifically an end such that no other end can be set in place of it, to which it should do service *merely* as means, because without this nothing at all of *absolute worth* would be encountered anywhere; but if all worth were conditioned, hence contingent, then for reason no supreme practical principle could anywhere be encountered.

If, then, there is supposed to be a supreme practical principle, and in regard to the human will a categorical imperative, then it must be such from the representation of that which, being necessarily an end for everyone, because it is an *end in itself,* constitutes an *objective* principle of the will, hence can serve as a universal practical law. The ground of this principle is: *Rational nature exists as end in itself.* The human being necessarily represents his own existence in this way; thus to that extent it is a *subjective* principle of human actions. But every other rational being also represents his existence in this way as consequent on the same rational ground as is valid for me; thus it is at the same time an *objective* principle, from which, as a supreme practical ground, all laws of the will must be able to be derived. The practical imperative will thus be the following: *Act so that you use humanity, as much in your own person as in the person of every other, always at the same time as end and never merely as means.* We will see whether this can be accomplished.

In order to remain with the previous examples:

First, . . . the one who has suicide in mind will ask himself whether his action could subsist together with the idea of humanity *as an end in itself.* If he destroys himself in order to flee from a burdensome condition, then he makes use of a person merely as *a means,* for the preservation of a bearable condition up to the end of life. The human being, however, is not a thing, hence not something that can be used *merely* as a means, but must in all his actions always be considered as an end in itself. Thus I cannot dispose of the human being in my own person, so as to maim, corrupt, or kill him. (The nearer determination of this principle, so as to avoid all misunderstanding, e.g., the amputation of limbs in order to preserve myself, or the risk at which I put my life in order to preserve my life, etc., I must here pass over; they belong to morals proper.)

Second, . . . the one who has it in mind to make a lying promise to another will see right away that he wills to make use of another human being *merely as means,* without the end also being contained in this other. For the one I want to use for my aims through such a promise cannot possibly be in harmony with my way of conducting myself toward him and thus contain in himself the end of this action. Even more distinctly does this conflict with the principle of other human beings meet the eye if one approaches it through examples of attacks on the freedom and property of others. For then it is clearly evident that the one who transgresses the rights of human beings is disposed to make use of the person of others merely as a means, without taking into consideration that as rational beings, these persons ought always to be esteemed at the same time as ends, i.e., only as beings who have to be able to contain in themselves the end of precisely the same action.

Third, it is not enough that the action does not conflict with humanity in our person as end in itself; it must also *harmonize with it.* Now in humanity there are predispositions to greater perfection, which belong to ends of nature in regard to the humanity in our subject; to neglect these would at most be able to subsist with the *preservation* of humanity as end in itself, but not with the *furthering* of this end.

Fourth, the natural end that all human beings have is their own happiness. Now humanity would be able to subsist if no one contributed to the happiness of others yet did not intentionally remove anything from it; only this is only a negative and not a positive agreement with *humanity as end in itself,* if everyone does not aspire, as much as he can, to further the ends of others. For regarding the subject which is an end in itself: if that representation is to have its *total* effect on me, then its ends must as far as possible also be *my* ends. . . .

Notes

1. A *maxim* is the subjective principle of the volition; the objective principle (i.e., that which would serve all rational beings also subjectively as a practical principle if reason had full control over the faculty of desire) is the practical *law.*
2. A *maxim* is the subjective principle for action, and must be distinguished from the *objective principle,* namely the practical law. The former contains the practical rule that reason determines in accord with the conditions of the subject (often its ignorance or also its inclinations), and is thus the principle in accordance with which the subject *acts;* but the law is the objective principle, valid for every rational being, and the principle in accordance with which it *ought to act,* i.e., an imperative.
3. I understand by a perfect duty that which permits no exception to the advantage of inclination, and I do have *perfect duties* that are not merely external but also internal, which runs contrary to the use of words common in the schools; but I do not mean to defend that here, because for my aim it is all the same whether or not one concedes it to me.

Study Questions

1. What is Kant's distinction between a hypothetical and a categorical imperative?
2. According to Kant, why does empirical inquiry not provide a sound basis for morality?
3. Can you imagine circumstances in which lying would be morally acceptable?
4. Does Kant's moral philosophy recognize special duties to relatives or friends?

Utilitarianism

John Stuart Mill

John Stuart Mill (1806–1873), the most prominent English philosopher of the nineteenth century, published widely in philosophy, political theory, and economics. He defends utilitarianism, the view that "actions are right in proportion as they tend to promote happiness and wrong as they tend to produce the reverse of happiness," each person to be counted equally. By "happiness," Mill means pleasure and the absence of pain. He grants, however, that some pleasures are more valuable than others, and these higher pleasures are those that would be chosen by knowledgeable judges. Mill maintains that utilitarianism cannot be strictly proven, yet some considerations can be presented in its favor. In particular, he argues that our desiring something is evidence that the thing is desirable. Thus, because happiness is the only end that people desire for its own sake, the evidence suggests that happiness is, in fact, intrinsically desirable.

What Utilitarianism Is

. . . The creed which accepts as the foundation of morals "utility" or the "greatest happiness principle" holds that actions are right in proportion as they tend to promote happiness; wrong as they tend to produce the reverse of happiness. By happiness is intended pleasure and the absence of pain; by unhappiness, pain and the privation of pleasure. To give a clear view of the moral standard set up by the theory, much more requires to be said; in particular, what things it includes in the ideas of pain and pleasure, and to what extent this is left an open question. But these supplementary explanations do not affect the theory of life on which this theory of morality is

From "Utilitarianism," John Stuart Mill (1861).

grounded—namely, that pleasure and freedom from pain are the only things desirable as ends; and that all desirable things (which are as numerous in the utilitarian as in any other scheme) are desirable either for pleasure inherent in themselves or as means to the promotion of pleasure and the prevention of pain.

Now such a theory of life excites in many minds, and among them in some of the most estimable in feeling and purpose, inveterate dislike. To suppose that life has (as they express it) no higher end than pleasure—no better and nobler object of desire and pursuit—they designate as utterly mean and groveling, as a doctrine worthy only of swine. . . .

But there is no known . . . theory of life which does not assign to the pleasures of the intellect, of the feelings and imagination, and of the moral sentiments a much higher value as pleasures than to those of mere sensation. It must be admitted, however, that utilitarian writers in general have placed the superiority of mental over bodily pleasures chiefly in the greater permanency, safety, uncostliness, etc., of the former—that is, in their circumstantial advantages rather than in their intrinsic nature. And on all these points utilitarians have fully proved their case; but they might have taken the other and, as it may be called, higher ground with entire consistency. It is quite compatible with the principle of utility to recognize the fact that some kinds of pleasure are more desirable and more valuable than others. It would be absurd that, while in estimating all other things quality is considered as well as quantity, the estimation of pleasure should be supposed to depend on quantity alone.

If I am asked what I mean by difference in quality in pleasures, or what makes one pleasure more valuable than another, merely as a pleasure, except its being greater in amount, there is but one possible answer. Of two pleasures, if there be one to which all or almost all who have experience of both give a decided preference, irrespective of any feeling of moral obligation to prefer it, that is the more desirable pleasure. If one of the two is, by those who are competently acquainted with both, placed so far above the other that they prefer it, even though knowing it to be attended with a greater amount of discontent, and would not resign it for any quantity of the other pleasure which their nature is capable of, we are justified in ascribing to the preferred enjoyment a superiority in quality so far outweighing quantity as to render it, in comparison, of small account.

Now it is an unquestionable fact that those who are equally acquainted with and equally capable of appreciating and enjoying both do give a most marked preference to the manner of existence which employs their higher faculties. Few human creatures would consent to be changed into any of the lower animals for a promise of the fullest allowance of a beast's pleasures; no intelligent human being would consent to be a fool, no instructed person would be an ignoramus, no person of feeling and conscience would be selfish and base, even though they should be persuaded that the fool, the dunce, or the rascal is better satisfied with his lot than they are with theirs. They would not resign what they possess more than he for the most complete satisfaction of all the desires which they have in common with him. If they ever fancy they would, it is only in cases of unhappiness so extreme that to escape from it they would exchange their lot for almost any other, however undesirable in their own eyes. A being of higher faculties requires more to make him happy, is capable probably of more acute suffering, and certainly accessible to it at more points, than one of an inferior type; but in spite of these liabilities, he can never really wish to sink into what he feels to be a lower grade of existence. . . .

It is better to be a human being dissatisfied than a pig satisfied; better to be Socrates dissatisfied than a fool satisfied. And if the fool, or the pig, are of a different opinion, it is because they only know their own side of the question. The other party to the comparison knows both sides.

It may be objected that many who are capable of the higher pleasures occasionally, under the influence of temptation, postpone them to the lower. But this is quite compatible with a full appreciation of the intrinsic superiority of the higher. Men often, from infirmity of character, make their election for the nearer good, though they know it to be the less valuable; and this no less when the choice is between two bodily pleasures than when it is between bodily and mental. They pursue sensual indulgences to the injury of health, though perfectly aware that health is the greater good. It may be further objected that many who begin with youthful enthusiasm for everything noble, as they advance in years, sink into indolence and selfishness. But I do not believe that those who undergo this very common change voluntarily choose the lower description of pleasures in preference to the higher. I believe that, before they devote themselves exclusively to the one, they have already become incapable of the other. Capacity for the nobler feelings is in most natures a very tender plant, easily killed, not only by hostile influences, but by mere want of sustenance; and in the majority of young persons it speedily dies away if the occupations to which their position in life has devoted them, and the society into which it has thrown them, are not favorable to keeping that higher capacity in exercise. Men lose their high aspirations as they lose their intellectual tastes, because they have not time or opportunity for indulging them; and they addict themselves to inferior pleasures, not because they deliberately prefer them, but because they are either the only ones to which they have access or the only ones which they are any longer capable of enjoying. It may be questioned whether anyone who has remained equally susceptible to both classes of pleasures ever knowingly and calmly preferred the lower, though many, in all ages, have broken down in an ineffectual attempt to combine both.

From this verdict of the only competent judges, I apprehend there can be no appeal. On a question which is the best worth having of two pleasures, or which of the two modes of existence is the most grateful to the feelings, apart from its moral attributes and from its consequences, the judgment of these who are qualified by knowledge of both, or, if they differ, that of the majority among them, must be admitted as final. And there needs to be the less hesitation to accept this judgment respecting the quality of pleasures, since there is no other tribunal to be referred to even on the question of quantity. What means are there of determining which is the acutest of two pains, or the intensest of two pleasurable sensations, except the general suffrage of those who are familiar with both? . . .

I must again repeat what the assailants of utilitarianism seldom have the justice to acknowledge, that the happiness which forms the utilitarian standard of what is right in conduct is not the agent's own happiness but that of all concerned. As between his own happiness and that of others, utilitarianism requires him to be as strictly impartial as a disinterested and benevolent spectator. In the golden rule of Jesus of Nazareth, we read the complete spirit of the ethics of utility. "To do as you would be done by," and "to love your neighbor as yourself," constitute the ideal perfection of utilitarian morality. As the means of making the nearest approach to this ideal, utility would enjoin, first, that laws and social arrangements should place the happiness or (as, speaking practically, it may be called) the interest of every individual as nearly as possible in harmony with the interest of the whole; and, secondly, that education and opinion, which have so vast a power over human character, should so use that power as to establish in the mind of every individual an indissoluble association between his own happiness and the good of the whole, especially between his own happiness and the practice of such modes of conduct, negative and positive, as regard for the universal happiness prescribes; so that not only he may be unable to conceive the possibility of happiness to himself, consistently with conduct opposed to the general good, but also that a direct impulse to promote the general good may be in every individual one of the habitual motives of action, and the sentiments connected therewith may fill a large and prominent place in every human being's sentient existence. If the impugners of the utilitarian morality represented it to their own minds in this its true character, I know not what recommendation possessed by any other morality they could possibly affirm to be wanting to it; what more beautiful or more exalted developments of human nature any other ethical system can be supposed to foster; or what springs of action, not accessible to the utilitarian, such systems rely on for giving effect to their mandates.

The objectors to utilitarianism cannot always be charged with representing it in a discreditable light. On the contrary, those among them who entertain anything like a just idea of its disinterested character sometimes find fault with its standard as being too high for humanity. They say it is exacting too much to require that people shall always act from the inducement of promoting the general interest of society. But this is to mistake the very meaning of a standard of morals and confound the rule of action with the motive of it. It is the business of ethics to tell us what are our duties, or by what test we may know them; but no system of ethics requires that the sole motive of all we do shall be a feeling of duty; on the contrary, ninety-nine hundredths of all our actions are done from other motives, and rightly so done if the rule of duty does not condemn them. It is the more unjust to utilitarianism that this particular misapprehension should be made a ground of objection to it, inasmuch as utilitarian moralists have gone beyond almost all others in affirming that the motive has nothing to do with the morality of the action, though much with the worth of the agent. He who saves a fellow creature from drowning does what is morally right, whether his motive be duty or the hope of being paid for his trouble; he who betrays the friend that trusts him is guilty of a crime, even if his object be to serve another friend to whom he is under greater obligations. But to speak only of actions done from the motive of duty, and in direct obedience to principle: it is a misapprehension of the utilitarian mode of thought to conceive it as implying that people should fix their minds upon so wide a generality as the world, or society at large. The greatest majority of good actions are intended not for the benefit of the world, but for that of individuals, of which the good of the world is made up; and the thoughts of the most virtuous man need not on these occasions travel beyond the particular persons concerned, except so far as is necessary to assure himself that in benefiting them he is not violating the rights, that is, the legitimate and authorized expectations, of anyone else. The multiplication of happiness is, according to the utilitarian ethics, the object of virtue: the occasions on which any person (except one in a thousand) has it in his power to do this on an extended scale—in other words, to be a public benefactor—are but exceptional; and on these occasions alone is he called on to consider public utility; in every other case, private utility, the interest or happiness of some few persons, is all he has to attend to. Those alone the influence of whose actions extends to society in general need concern themselves habitually about so large an object. In the case of abstinences indeed—of things which people forbear to do from moral considerations, though the consequences in the particular case might be beneficial—it would be unworthy of an intelligent agent not to be consciously aware that the action is of a class which, if practiced generally, would be generally injurious, and that this is the ground of the obligation to abstain from it. The amount of regard for the public interest implied in this recognition is no greater than is demanded by every system of morals, for they all enjoin to abstain from whatever is manifestly pernicious to society. . . .

Again, utility is often summarily stigmatized as an immoral doctrine by giving it the name of "expediency," and taking advantage of the popular use of that term to contrast it with principle. But the expedient, in the sense in which it is opposed to the right, generally means that which is expedient for the particular interest of the agent himself, as when a minister sacrifices the interests of his country to keep himself in place. When it means anything better than this, it means that which is expedient for some immediate object, some temporary purpose, but which violates a rule whose observance is expedient in a much higher degree. The expedient, in this sense, instead of being the same thing with the useful, is a branch of the hurtful. Thus it would often be expedient, for the purpose of getting over some momentary embarrassment, or attaining some object immediately useful to ourselves or others, to tell a lie. But inasmuch as the cultivation in ourselves of a sensitive feeling on the subject of veracity is one of the most useful, and the enfeeblement of that feeling one of the most hurtful, things to which our conduct can be instrumental; and inasmuch as any, even unintentional, deviation from truth does that much toward weakening the trustworthiness of human assertion, which is not only the principal support of all present social well-being, but the insufficiency of which does more than any one thing that can be named to keep back civilization, virtue, everything on which human happiness on the largest scale depends—we feel that the violation, for a present advantage, of a rule of such transcendent expediency is not expedient, and that he who, for the sake of convenience to himself or to some other individual, does what depends on him to deprive mankind of the good, and inflict upon them the evil, involved in the greater or less reliance which they can place in each other's words, acts the part of one of their worst enemies. Yet that even this rule, sacred as it is, admits of possible exceptions is acknowledged by all moralists, the chief of which is when the withholding of some fact (as of information from a malefactor, or of bad news from a person dangerously ill) would save an individual (especially an individual other than oneself) from great and unmerited evil, and when the withholding can only be effected by denial. But in order that the exception may not extend itself beyond the need, and may have the least possible effect in weakening reliance on veracity, it ought to be recognized and, if possible, its limits defined; and, if the principle of utility is good for anything, it must be good for weighing these conflicting utilities against one another and marking out the region within which one or the other preponderates.

Again, defenders of utility often find themselves called upon to reply to such objections as this—that there is not time, previous to action, for calculating and weighing the effects of any line of conduct on the general happiness. This is exactly as if anyone were to say that it is impossible to guide our conduct by Christianity because there is not time, on every occasion on which anything has to be done, to read through the Old and New Testaments. The answer to the objection is that there has been ample time, namely, the whole past duration of the human species. During all that time mankind have been learning by experience the tendencies of actions, on which experience all the prudence as well as all the morality of life are dependent. People talk as if the commencement of this course of experience had hitherto been put off, and as if, at the moment when some man feels tempted to meddle with the property or life of another, he had to begin considering for the first time whether murder and theft are injurious to human happiness. Even then I do not think that he would find the question very puzzling; but, at all events, the matter is now done to his hand. It is truly a whimsical supposition that, if mankind were agreed in considering utility to be the test of morality, they would remain without any agreement as to what *is* useful, and would take no measures for having their notions on the subject taught to the young and enforced by law and opinion. There is no difficulty in proving any ethical standard whatever to work ill if we suppose universal idiocy to be conjoined with it; but on any hypothesis short of that, mankind must by this time have acquired positive beliefs as to the effects of some actions on their happiness; and the beliefs which have thus come down are the rules of morality for the multitude, and for the philosopher until he has succeeded in finding better. That philosophers might easily do this, even now, on many subjects; that the received code of ethics is by no means of divine right; and that mankind have still much to learn as to the effects of actions on the general happiness, I admit or rather earnestly maintain. The corollaries from the principle of utility, like the precepts of every practical art, admit of indefinite improvement, and, in a progressive state of the human mind, their improvement is perpetually going on. But to consider the rules of morality as improvable is one thing; to pass over the intermediate generalization entirely and endeavor to test each individual action directly by the first principle is another. It is a strange notion that the acknowledgment of a first principle is inconsistent with the admission of secondary ones. To inform a traveler respecting the place of his ultimate destination is not to forbid the use of landmarks and direction-posts on the way. The proposition that happiness is the end and aim of morality does not mean that no road ought to be laid down to that goal, or that persons going thither should not be advised to take one direction rather than another. Men really ought to leave off talking a kind of nonsense on this subject, which they would neither talk nor listen to on other matters of practical concernment. Nobody argues that the art of navigation is not founded on astronomy because sailors cannot wait to calculate the Nautical Almanac. Being rational creatures, they go to sea with it ready calculated; and all rational creatures go out upon the sea of life with their minds made up on the common questions of right and wrong, as well as on many of the far more difficult questions of wise and foolish. And this, as long as foresight is a human quality, it is to be presumed they will continue to do. Whatever we adopt as the fundamental principle of morality, we require subordinate principles to apply it by; the impossibility of doing without them, being common to all systems, can afford no argument against any one in particular; but gravely to argue as if no such secondary principles could be had, and as if mankind had remained till now, and always must remain, without drawing any general conclusions from the experience of human life is as high a pitch, I think, as absurdity has ever reached in philosophical controversy. . . .

Of What Sort of Proof the Principle of Utility Is Susceptible

. . . Questions about ends are . . . questions about what things are desirable. The utilitarian doctrine is that happiness is desirable and the only thing desirable as an end, all other things being only desirable as means to that end. What ought to be required of the doctrine, what conditions is it requisite that the doctrine should fulfill—to make good its claim to be believed?

The only proof capable of being given that an object is visible is that people actually see it. The only proof that a sound is audible is that people hear it; and so of the other sources of our experience. In like manner, I apprehend, the sole evidence it is possible to produce that anything is desirable is that people do actually desire it. If the end which the utilitarian doctrine proposes to itself were not, in theory and in practice, acknowledged to be an end, nothing could ever convince any person that it was so. No reason can be given why the general happiness is desirable, except that each person, so far as he believes it to be attainable, desires his own happiness. This, however, being a fact, we have not only all the proof which the case admits of, but all which it is possible to require, that happiness is a good, that each person's happiness is a good to that person, and the general happiness, therefore, a good to the aggregate of all persons. Happiness has made out its title as *one* of the ends of conduct and, consequently, one of the criteria of morality.

But it has not, by this alone, proved itself to be the sole criterion. To do that it would seem, by the same rule, necessary to show not only that people desire happiness but that they never desire anything else. Now it is palpable that they do desire things which, in common language, are decidedly distinguished from happiness. They desire, for example, virtue and the absence of vice no less really than pleasure and the absence of pain. The desire of virtue is not as universal, but it is as authentic a fact as the desire of happiness. And hence the opponents of the utilitarian standard deem that they have a right to infer that there are other ends of human action besides happiness, and that happiness is not the standard of approbation and disapprobation.

But does the utilitarian doctrine deny that people desire virtue, or maintain that virtue is not a thing to be desired? The very reverse. It maintains not only that virtue is to be desired, but that it is to be desired disinterestedly, for itself. Whatever may be the opinion of utilitarian moralists as to the original conditions by which virtue is made virtue, however they may believe (as they do) that actions and dispositions are only virtuous because they promote another end than virtue, yet this being granted, and it having been decided, from considerations of this description, what *is* virtuous, they not only place virtue at the very head of the things which are good as means to the ultimate end, but they also recognize as a psychological fact the possibility of its being, to the individual, a good in itself, without looking to any end beyond it; and hold that the mind is not in a right state, not in a state conformable to utility, not in the state most conducive to the general happiness, unless it does love virtue in this manner—as a thing desirable in itself, even although, in the individual instance, it should not produce those other desirable consequences which it tends to produce, and on account of which it is held to be virtue. This opinion is not, in the smallest degree, a departure from the happiness principle. The ingredients of happiness are very various, and each of them is desirable in itself, and not merely when considered as swelling an aggregate. The principle of utility does not mean that any given pleasure, as music, for instance, or any given exemption from pain, as for example health, is to be looked upon as means to a collective something termed happiness, and to be desired on that account. They are desired and desirable in and for themselves; besides being means, they are a part of the end. Virtue, according to the utilitarian doctrine, is not naturally and originally part of the end, but it is capable of becoming so; and in those who live it disinterestedly it has become so, and is desired and cherished, not as a means to happiness, but to a part of their happiness.

To illustrate this further, we may remember that virtue is not the only thing originally a means, and which if it were not a means to anything else would be and remain indifferent, but which by association with what it is a means to comes to be desired for itself, and that too with the utmost intensity. What, for example, shall we say of the love of money? There is nothing originally more desirable about money than about any heap of glittering pebbles. Its worth is solely that of the things which it will buy; the desires for other things than itself, which it is a means of gratifying. Yet the love of money is not one of the strongest moving forces of human life, but money is, in many cases, desired in and for itself; the desire to possess it is often stronger than the desire to use it, and goes on increasing when all the desires which point to ends beyond it, to be compassed by it, are falling off. It may, then, be said truly that money is desired not for the sake of an end, but as part of the end. From being a means to happiness, it has come to be itself a principal ingredient of the individual's conception of happiness. The same may be said of the majority of the great objects of human life: power, for example, or fame, except that to each of these there is a certain amount of immediate pleasure annexed, which has at least the semblance of being naturally inherent in them—a thing which cannot be said of money. Still, however, the strongest natural attraction, both of power and of fame, is the immense aid they give to the attainment of our other wishes; and it is the strong association thus generated between them and all our objects of desire which gives to the direct desire of them the intensity it often assumes, so as in some characters to surpass in strength all other desires. In these cases the means have become a part of the end, and a more important part of it than any of the things which they are means to. What was once desired as an instrument for the attainment of happiness has come to be desired for its own sake. In being desired for its own sake it is, however, desired as *part* of happiness. The person is made, or thinks he would be made, happy by its mere possession and is made unhappy by failure to obtain it. The desire of it is not a different thing from the desire of happiness any more than the love of music or the desire of health. They are included in happiness. They are some of the elements of which the desire of happiness is made up. Happiness is not an abstract idea but a concrete whole; and these are some of its parts. And the utilitarian standard sanctions and approves their being so. Life would be a poor thing, very ill provided with sources of happiness, if there were not this provision of nature by which things originally indifferent, but conducive to, or otherwise associated with, the satisfaction of our primitive desires, become in themselves sources of pleasure more valuable than the primitive pleasures, both in permanency, in the space of human existence that they are capable of covering, and even in intensity.

Virtue, according to the utilitarian conception, is a good of this description. There was no original desire of it, or motive to it, save its conduciveness to pleasure, and especially to protection from pain. But through the association thus formed it may be felt a good in itself, and desired as such with as great intensity as any other good; and with this difference between it and the love of money, of power, or of fame—that all of these may, and often do, render the individual noxious to the other members of the society to which he belongs, whereas there is nothing which makes him so much a blessing to them as the cultivation of the disinterested love of virtue. And consequently, the utilitarian standard, while it tolerates and approves those other acquired desires, up to the point beyond which they would be more injurious to the general happiness than promotive of it, enjoins and requires the cultivation of the love of virtue up to the greatest strength possible, as being above all things important to the general happiness.

It results from the preceding considerations that there is in reality nothing desired except happiness. Whatever is desired otherwise than as a means to some end beyond itself, and ultimately to happiness, is desired as itself a part of happiness, and is not desired for itself until it has become so. Those who desire virtue for its own sake desire it either because the consciousness of it is a pleasure, or because the consciousness of being without it is a pain, or for both reasons united, as in truth the pleasure and pain seldom exist separately, but almost always together—the same person feeling pleasure in the degree of virtue attained, and pain in not having attained more. If one of these gave him no pleasure, and the other no pain, he would not love or desire virtue, or would desire it only for the other benefits which it might produce to himself or to persons whom he cared for.

We have now, then, an answer to the question, of what sort of proof the principle of utility is susceptible.

Study Questions

1. According to Mill, what is utilitarianism?
2. If people knowledgeable about both poetry and video games prefer the latter, are video games therefore more worthwhile?
3. Does Mill believe the principle of utilitarianism can be proven?
4. What evidence do we have that the general happiness is intrinsically desirable?

Virtue Ethics

Julia Driver

Julia Driver, professor of philosophy at Washington University in St. Louis, explains the ethical theory known as virtue ethics. Virtue ethics focuses on understanding moral character rather than formulating rules for right action. Moral inquiry is thus not a search for a formula that provides the right answer to every moral problem. Instead, the development of ethical understanding is akin to mastering a practical skill, such as playing music, that we acquire by emulating people who are more expert. They know how to respond appropriately to the particularities of complex situations, and we should seek to act likewise.

Sometimes, in deciding on what we ought to do, we first consider how we ought to be. For example, if faced with a situation that involves social injustice, we might pick someone whom we admired and wanted to be like—Gandhi, let's say, or Mother Teresa—and then ask "What would Gandhi do?" This doesn't give us a rigid formula or decision procedure to employ. Instead, it asks us to consider a virtuous person, to consider his or her virtues, and then ask what behavior people with these good traits and dispositions exemplify. Some writers have thought that a picture like this better reflects how people should go about making their moral decisions. They should do so on the basis of concrete virtue judgments instead of abstract principles, such as "Maximize the good" or "Never treat another person merely as a means," and so forth. . . .

. . . [V]irtue ethics has actually been around in one form or another for thousands of years. Current virtue ethicists in fact tend to take their inspiration from Aristotle. . . . Aristotle wrote the *Nicomachean*

From Julia Driver, *Ethics: The Fundamentals* (Malden, MA: Blackwell, 2007).

Ethics, which—as an aid to his son—spelled out the steps to a good life. Of course, "good" is a bit ambiguous—Is that morally good, or prudentially good, or intellectually good, or all of the above? Well, for Aristotle, the good human life had all these ingredients. A good human being was virtuous in the sense that he embodied all the excellences of human character. . . .

Aristotle famously believed in the claim that virtue is a mean state, that it lies between two opposed vices. This is referred to as the doctrine of the mean. The basic idea is that virtue will tend to lie between two extremes, each of which is a vice. So, bravery lies between cowardice and foolhardiness; temperance lies between gluttony and abstinence; and so forth. Some virtues can be hard to model on this view. Take honesty. Of course, failure to tell the truth—telling a lie—would be one extreme, but is there a vice of telling too much truth? Maybe . . . though I suspect there might be some disagreement over this. Part of the mean state concerned our emotions, however, and not just our actions. The virtuous person not only does the right thing, but he does the right thing in the right way—in the right sort of emotional or psychological state. Our emotions can be excessive or deficient as well. The person who runs into the battle to fight, but who is excessively fearful, is not fully virtuous. The truly well-functioning person is able to control and regulate his feelings and emotions, as well as act rightly.

Aristotle's picture, then, of the virtuous person is the person who functions harmoniously—his desires and emotions do not conflict with what he knows to be right. They go together. This leads him to view a person who acts rightly, but who feels badly about it, as not being virtuous. This person is merely "continent"—this person can control his actions, but needs to work on bringing his emotions in line with what reason tells him is the right and appropriate thing to do. So the excellent human being is not conflicted; he does not suffer inner turmoil and the struggle between reason and passion. . . .

Many challenges have been posed to virtue ethics. . . . One *general* criticism of the whole approach is that it fails to conform to what we know about how best to explain human behavior. . . .

For example, John Doris proposes that the globalism of traditional virtue ethics be rejected.[1] There is no one "honesty" trait, for example. Instead, we may have 50 or more "honesties"; that is, narrowly circumscribed traits or dispositions to tell the truth. So, Joe might not have honesty 1, which is the disposition to tell the truth about how well he does on exams, but he might have honesty 34, the disposition to tell the truth about how tall he is. So, Doris thinks that . . . the experimental evidence supports the view that there are no robust traits; that is, traits to tell the truth over all or even most contexts or situations. And this is a problem for a virtue ethics that understands virtue as a "stable" or "reliable" character trait.

Another challenge has been that virtue ethics doesn't provide a guide to action. "Be nice, dear"—Well, what is nice, and what are the circumstances under which I should be nice? That's what we really want to know. This shows that it is these other reasons that actually justify our behavior. This has been raised as a very standard problem for the theory, but virtue ethicists have spent a good deal of time trying to show how their theories could be applied. . . .

This challenge can be expanded by noting that virtue ethics has trouble telling us the right thing to do in conflict situations, where two virtues may conflict, and thus the corresponding rules—such as "Be honest" or "Be kind"—may conflict. But some virtue ethicists think that this is simply the way morality is—it is messy, and for any situation there may be more than one right answer. Insisting that morality is neat and tidy is simply to impose a misleading clarity on moral decision-making.

Note

1. John Doris, *Lack of Character: Personality and Moral Behavior* (Cambridge, UK: Cambridge University Press, 2002), p. 31.

Study Questions

1. When you make a moral judgment, should you ask "What should I do?" or "What sort of person should I be?"
2. Should moral decisions always be based on rules?
3. How is a person's character revealed?
4. Do exemplars play a significant role in your moral reasoning?

The Ethics of Care

Virginia Held

Virginia Held is Professor Emerita of Philosophy at Hunter College and the Graduate Center of the City University of New York. She develops what she terms "the ethics of care," which some philosophers have viewed as one form of virtue ethics. She emphasizes, however, that while the two are in some ways similar, virtue ethics focuses on the character of individuals, whereas the ethics of care is concerned especially with fostering connectedness among people.

1
The Ethics of Care as Moral Theory

The ethics of care is only a few decades old. Some theorists do not like the term 'care' to designate this approach to moral issues and have tried substituting 'the ethic of love,' or 'relational ethics,' but the discourse keeps returning to 'care' as the so far more satisfactory of the terms considered, though dissatisfactions with it remain. The concept of care has the advantage of not losing sight of the work involved in caring for people and of not lending itself to the interpretation of morality as ideal but impractical to which advocates of the ethics of care often object. . . .

Features of the Ethics of Care

. . . I think one can discern among various versions of the ethics of care a number of major features.

From Virginia Held, *The Ethics of Care: Personal, Political and Global* (Oxford: Oxford University Press, 2006).

First, the central focus of the ethics of care is on the compelling moral salience of attending to and meeting the needs of the particular others for whom we take responsibility. Caring for one's child, for instance, may well and defensibly be at the forefront of a person's moral concerns. The ethics of care recognizes that human beings are dependent for many years of their lives, that the moral claim of those dependent on us for the care they need is pressing, and that there are highly important moral aspects in developing the relations of caring that enable human beings to live and progress. All persons need care for at least their early years. Prospects for human progress and flourishing hinge fundamentally on the care that those needing it receive, and the ethics of care stresses the moral force of the responsibility to respond to the needs of the dependent. Many persons will become ill and dependent for some periods of their later lives, including in frail old age, and some who are permanently disabled will need care the whole of their lives. Moralities built on the image of the independent, autonomous, rational individual largely overlook the reality of human dependence and the morality for which it calls. The ethics of care attends to this central concern of human life and delineates the moral values involved. It refuses to relegate care to a realm "outside morality." How caring for particular others should be reconciled with the claims of, for instance, universal justice is an issue that needs to be addressed. But the ethics of care starts with the moral claims of particular others, for instance, of one's child, whose claims can be compelling regardless of universal principles.

Second, in the epistemological process of trying to understand what morality would recommend and what it would be morally best for us to do and to be, the ethics of care values emotion rather than rejects it. Not all emotion is valued, of course, but in contrast with the dominant rationalist approaches, such emotions as sympathy, empathy, sensitivity, and responsiveness are seen as the kind of moral emotions that need to be cultivated not only to help in the implementation of the dictates of reason but to better ascertain what morality recommends. Even anger may be a component of the moral indignation that should be felt when people are treated unjustly or inhumanely, and it may contribute to (rather than interfere with) an appropriate interpretation of the moral wrong. This is not to say that raw emotion can be a guide to morality; feelings need to be reflected on and educated. But from the care perspective, moral inquiries that rely entirely on reason and rationalistic deductions or calculations are seen as deficient.

The emotions that are typically considered and rejected in rationalistic moral theories are the egoistic feelings that undermine universal moral norms, the favoritism that interferes with impartiality, and the aggressive and vengeful impulses for which morality is to provide restraints. The ethics of care, in contrast, typically appreciates the emotions and relational capabilities that enable morally concerned persons in actual interpersonal contexts to understand what would be best. Since even the helpful emotions can often become misguided or worse—as when excessive empathy with others leads to a wrongful degree of self-denial or when benevolent concern crosses over into controlling domination—we need an *ethics* of care, not just care itself. The various aspects and expressions of care and caring relations need to be subjected to moral scrutiny and *evaluated,* not just observed and described.

Third, the ethics of care rejects the view of the dominant moral theories that the more abstract the reasoning about a moral problem the better because the more likely to avoid bias and arbitrariness, the more nearly to achieve impartiality. The ethics of care respects rather than removes itself from the claims of particular others with whom we share actual relationships. It calls into question the universalistic and abstract rules of the dominant theories. When the latter consider such actual relations as between a parent and child, if they say anything about them at all, they may see them as and cultivating them a preference that a person may have. Or they may recognize a universal obligation for all parents to care for their children. But they do not permit actual relations ever to take priority over the requirements of impartiality. . . .

The ethics of care may seek to limit the applicability of universal rules to certain domains where they are more appropriate, like the domain of law, and resist their extension to other domains. Such rules may simply be inappropriate in, for instance, the contexts of family and friendship, yet relations in these domains should certainly be *evaluated,* not merely described, hence morality should not be limited to abstract rules. We should be able to give moral guidance concerning actual relations that are trusting, considerate, and caring and concerning those that are not.

Dominant moral theories tend to interpret moral problems as if they were conflicts between egoistic individual interests on the one hand, and universal moral principles on the other. The extremes of "selfish individual" and "humanity" are recognized, but what lies between these is often overlooked. The ethics of care, in contrast, focuses especially on the area between these extremes. Those who conscientiously care for others are not seeking primarily to further their own *individual* interests; their interests are intertwined with the persons they care for. Neither are they acting for the sake of *all others* or *humanity in general*; they seek instead to preserve or promote an actual human relation between themselves and *particular others*. Persons in caring relations are acting for self-and-other together. Their characteristic stance is neither egoistic nor altruistic; these are the options in a conflictual situation, but the well-being of a caring relation involves the cooperative well-being of those in the relation and the well-being of the relation itself. . . .

A fourth characteristic of the ethics of care is that like much feminist thought in many areas, it reconceptualizes traditional notions about the public and the private. The traditional view, built into the dominant moral theories, is that the household is a private sphere beyond politics into which government, based on consent, should not intrude. Feminists have shown how the greater social, political, economic, and cultural power of men has structured this "private" sphere to the disadvantage of women and children, rendering them vulnerable to domestic violence without outside interference, often leaving women economically dependent on men and subject to a highly inequitable division of labor in the family. The law has not hesitated to intervene into women's private decisions concerning reproduction but has been highly reluctant to intrude on men's exercise of coercive power within the "castles" of their homes.

Dominant moral theories have seen "public" life as relevant to morality while missing the moral significance of the "private" domains of family and friendship. Thus the dominant theories have assumed that morality should be sought for unrelated, independent, and mutually indifferent individuals assumed to be equal. They have posited an abstract, fully rational "agent as such" from which to construct morality, while missing the moral issues that arise between interconnected persons in the contexts of family, friendship, and social groups. In the context of the family, it is typical for relations to be between persons with highly unequal power who did not choose the ties and obligations in which they find themselves enmeshed. For instance, no child can choose her parents yet she may well have obligations to care for them. Relations of this kind are standardly noncontractual, and conceptualizing them as contractual would often undermine or at least obscure the trust on which their worth depends. The ethics of care addresses rather than neglects moral issues arising in relations among the unequal and dependent, relations that are often laden with emotion and involuntary, and then notices how often these attributes apply not only in the household but in the wider society as well. For instance, persons do not choose which gender, racial, class, ethnic, religious, national, or cultural groups to be brought up in, yet these sorts of ties may be important aspects of who they are and how their experience can contribute to moral understanding.

A fifth characteristic of the ethics of care is the conception of persons with which it begins. This will be dealt with in the next section.

The Critique of Liberal Individualism

The ethics of care usually works with a conception of persons as relational, rather than as the self-sufficient independent individuals of the dominant moral theories. The dominant theories can be interpreted as importing into moral theory a concept of the person developed primarily for liberal political and economic theory, seeing the person as a rational, autonomous agent, or a self-interested individual. . . .

The ethics of care, in contrast, characteristically sees persons as relational and interdependent, morally and epistemologically. Every person starts out as a child dependent on those providing us care, and we remain interdependent with others in thoroughly fundamental ways throughout our lives. That we can think and act as if we were independent depends on a network of social relations making it possible for us to do so. And our relations are part of what constitute our identity. This is not to say that we cannot become autonomous; feminists have done much interesting work developing an alternative conception of autonomy in place of the liberal individualist one. Feminists have much experience rejecting or reconstituting relational ties that are oppressive. But it means that from the perspective of an ethics of care, to construct morality *as if* we were Robinson Crusoes . . . is misleading. And it obscures the innumerable ways persons and groups are interdependent in the modern world.

Not only does the liberal individualist conception of the person foster a false picture of society and the persons in it, it is, from the perspective of the ethics of care, impoverished also as an ideal. The ethics of care values the ties we have with particular other persons and the actual relationships that partly constitute our identity. Although persons often may and should reshape their relations with others—distancing themselves from some persons and groups and developing or strengthening ties with others—the autonomy sought within the ethics of care is a capacity to reshape and cultivate new relations, not to ever more closely resemble the unencumbered abstract rational self of liberal political and moral theories. Those motivated by the ethics of care would seek to become more admirable relational persons in better caring relations. . . .

Justice and Care

Some conceptions of the ethics of care see it as contrasting with an ethic of justice in ways that suggest one must choose between them. Carol Gilligan's suggestion of alternative perspectives in interpreting and organizing the elements of a moral problem lent itself to this implication. . . .

An ethic of justice focuses on questions of fairness, equality, individual rights, abstract principles, and the consistent application of them. An ethic of care focuses on attentiveness, trust, responsiveness to need, narrative nuance, and cultivating caring relations. Whereas an ethic of justice seeks a fair solution between competing individual interests and rights, an ethic of care sees the interests of carers and cared-for as importantly intertwined rather than as simply competing. Whereas justice protects equality and freedom, care fosters social bonds and cooperation.

These are very different emphases in what morality should consider. Yet both deal with what seems of great moral importance. This has led many to explore how they might be combined in a satisfactory morality. One can persuasively argue, for instance, that justice is needed in such contexts of care as the family, to protect against violence and the unfair division of labor or treatment of children. One can also persuasively argue that care is needed in such contexts of justice as the streets and the courts, where persons should be treated humanely, and in the way education and health and welfare should be dealt with as social responsibilities. . . .

Few would hold that considerations of justice have no place at all in care. One would not be caring well for two children, for instance, if one showed a persistent favoritism toward one of them that could not be justified on the basis of some such factor as greater need. The issues are rather what constellation of values have priority and which predominate in the practices of the ethics of care and the ethics of justice. It is quite possible to delineate significant differences between them. In the dominant moral theories of the ethics of justice, the values of equality, impartiality, fair distribution, and noninterference have priority; in practices of justice, individual rights are protected, impartial judgments are arrived at, punishments are deserved, and equal treatment is sought. In contrast, in the ethics of care, the values of trust, solidarity, mutual concern, and empathetic responsiveness have priority; in practices of care, relationships are cultivated, needs are responded to, and sensitivity is demonstrated. . . .

The question remains, however, whether justice should be thought to be incorporated into any ethic of care that will be adequate or whether we should keep the notions of justice and care and their associated ethics conceptually distinct. There is much to be said for recognizing how the ethics of care values interrelatedness and responsiveness to the needs of particular others, how the ethics of justice values fairness and rights, and how these are different emphases. Too much integration will lose sight of these valid differences. I am more inclined to say that an adequate, comprehensive moral theory will have to include the insights of both the ethics of care and the ethics of justice, among other insights, rather than that either of these can be incorporated into the other in the sense of supposing that it can provide the grounds for the judgments characteristically found in the other. Equitable caring is not necessarily better caring, it is fairer caring. And humane justice is not necessarily better justice, it is more caring justice. . . .

My own suggestions for integrating care and justice are to keep these concepts conceptually distinct and to delineate the domains in which they should have priority. In the realm of law, for instance, justice and the assurance of rights should have priority, although the humane considerations of care should not be absent. In the realm of the family and among friends, priority should be given to expansive care, though the basic requirements of justice surely should also be met. . . .

Care is probably the most deeply fundamental value. There can be care without justice: There has historically been little justice in the family, but care and life have gone on without it. There can be no justice without care, however, for without care no child would survive and there would be no persons to respect.

Care may thus provide the wider and deeper ethics within which justice should be sought, as when persons in caring relations may sometimes compete and in doing so should treat each other fairly, or, at the level of society, within caring relations of the thinner kind we can agree to treat each other for limited purposes as if we were the abstract individuals of liberal theory. But although care may be the more fundamental value, it may well be that the ethics of care does not itself provide adequate theoretical resources for dealing with issues of justice. Within its appropriate sphere and for its relevant questions, the ethics of justice may be best for what we seek. What should be resisted is the traditional inclination to expand the reach of justice in such a way that it is mistakenly imagined to be able to give us a comprehensive morality suitable for all moral questions. . . .

The Ethics of Care and Virtue Ethics

Insofar as the ethics of care wishes to cultivate in persons the characteristics of a caring person and the skills of activities of caring, might an ethic of care be assimilated to virtue theory? . . .

Certainly there are some similarities between the ethics of care and virtue theory. Both examine practices and the moral values they embody. Both see more hope for moral development in reforming practices than in reasoning from abstract rules. Both understand that the practices of morality must be cultivated, nurtured, shaped.

Until recently, however, virtue theory has not paid adequate attention to the practices of caring in which women have been so heavily engaged. Although this might be corrected, virtue theory has characteristically seen the virtues as incorporated in various traditions or traditional communities. In contrast, the ethics of care as a feminist ethic is wary of existing traditions and traditional communities: Virtually all are patriarchal. The ethics of care envisions caring not as practiced under male domination, but as it should be practiced in postpatriarchal society, of which we do not yet have traditions or wide experience. Individual egalitarian families are still surrounded by inegalitarian social and cultural influences.

In my view, although there are similarities between them and although to be caring is no doubt a virtue, the ethics of care is not simply a kind of virtue ethics. Virtue ethics focuses especially on the states of character of individuals, whereas the ethics of care concerns itself especially with caring *relations*. Caring relations have primary value. . . .

2
Care as Practice and Value

What *is* care? What do we mean by the term 'care'? Can we define it in anything like a precise way? There is not yet anything close to agreement among those writing on care on what exactly we should take the meaning of this term to be, but there have been many suggestions, tacit and occasionally explicit.

For over two decades, the concept of care as it figures in the ethics of care has been assumed, explored, elaborated, and employed in the development of theory. But definitions have often been imprecise, or trying to arrive at them has simply been postponed (as in my own case), in the growing discourse. Perhaps this is entirely appropriate for new explorations, but the time may have come to seek greater clarity. Some of those writing on care have attempted to be precise, with mixed results, whereas others have proceeded with the tacit understanding that of course to a considerable extent we know what we are talking about when we speak of taking care of a child or providing care for the ill. But care has many forms, and as the ethics of care evolves, so should our understanding of what care is.

Taking Care

The last words I spoke to my older brother after a brief visit and with special feeling were: "take care." He had not been taking good care of himself, and I hoped he would do better; not many days later he died, of problems quite possibly unrelated to those to which I had been referring. "Take care" was not an expression he and I grew up with. I acquired it over the years in my life in New York City. It may be illuminating to begin thinking about the meaning of 'care' with an examination of this expression.

We often say "take care" as routinely as "goodbye" or some abbreviation and with as little emotion. But even then it does convey some sense of connectedness. More often, when said with some feeling, it means something like "take care of yourself because I care about you." Sometimes we say it, especially to children or to someone embarking on a trip or an endeavor, meaning "I care what happens to you, so please don't do anything dangerous or foolish." Or, if we know the danger is inevitable and inescapable, it may be more like a wish that the elements will let the person take care so the worst can be evaded. And sometimes we mean it as a plea: Be careful not to harm yourself or others because our connection will make us feel with and for you. We may be harmed ourselves or partly responsible, or if you do something you will regret we will share that regret.

One way or another, this expression (like many others) illustrates human relatedness and the daily reaffirmations of connection. It is the relatedness of human beings, built and rebuilt, that the ethics of care is being developed to try to understand, evaluate, and guide. The expression has more to do with the feelings and awareness of the persons expressing and the persons receiving such expressions than with the actual tasks and work of "taking care" of a person who is dependent on us, or in need of care, but such attitudes and shared awareness seem at least one important component of care.

Some Distinctions

A seemingly easy distinction to make is between care as the activity of taking care of someone and the mere "caring about" of how we feel about certain issues. Actually "caring for" a small child or a person who is ill is quite different from merely "caring for" something (or not) in the sense of liking it or not, as in "I don't care for that kind of music." But these distinctions may not be as clear as they appear, since when we take care of a child, for instance, we usually also care about him or her, and although we could take care of a child we do not like, the caring will usually be better care if we care for the child in both senses. If we really do care about world hunger, we will probably be doing something about it, such as at least giving money to alleviate it or to change the conditions that bring it about, and thus establishing some connection between ourselves and the hungry we say we care about. And if we really do care about global climate change and the harm it will bring to future generations, we imagine a connection between ourselves and those future people who will judge our irresponsibility, and we change our consumption practices or political activities to decrease the likely harm. . . .

Care as Practice

. . . Care is a practice involving the work of care-giving and the standards by which the practices of care can be evaluated. Care must concern itself with the effectiveness of its efforts to meet needs, but also with the motives with which care is provided. It seeks good caring relations. In normal cases, recipients of care sustain caring relations through their responsiveness—the look of satisfaction in the child, the smile of the patient. Where such responsiveness is not possible—with a severely mentally ill person, for instance—sustaining the relation may depend entirely on the caregiver, but it is still appropriate to think in terms of caring relations: The caregiver may be trying to form a relation or must imagine a relation. Relations between persons can be criticized when they become dominating, exploitative, mistrustful, or hostile. Relations of care can be encouraged and maintained.

Consider, for instance, mothering, in the sense of caring for children. It had long been imagined in the modern era after the establishment of the public/private distinction to be "outside morality" because it was based on instinct. Feminist critique has been needed to show how profoundly mistaken such a view is. Moral issues are confronted constantly in the practice of mothering and other caring work. There is constant need for the cultivation of the virtues appropriate to these practices, and of moral evaluation of how the practices are being carried out. To get a hint of how profoundly injustice has been embedded in the practice of mothering, one can compare the meaning of "mothering" with that of "fathering," which standardly has meant no more than impregnating a woman and being the genetic father of a child. "Mothering" suggests that this activity must or should be done by women, whereas, except for lactation, there is no part of it that cannot be done by men as well. Many feminists argue that for actual practices of child care to be morally acceptable, they will have to be radically transformed to accord with principles of equality, though existing conceptions of equality should probably not be the primary moral focus of practices of care. This is only the beginning of the moral scrutiny to which they should be subject.

This holds also for other practices that can be thought of as practices of care. We need, then, not only to examine the practices and discern with new sensitivities the values already embedded or missing within them but also to construct the appropriate normative theory with which to evaluate them, reform them, and shape them anew. This, I think, involves understanding care as a value worthy of the kind of theoretical elaboration justice has received. Understanding the value of care involves understanding how it should not be limited to the household or family; care should be recognized as a political and social value also.

Care as Value

We all agree that justice is a value. There are also practices of justice: law enforcement, court proceedings, and so on. Practices incorporate values but also need to be evaluated by the normative standards values provide. A given actual practice of justice may only very inadequately incorporate within it the value of justice, and we need justice as a value to evaluate such a practice. The value of justice picks out certain aspects of the overall moral spectrum, those having to do with fairness, equality, and so on, and it would not be satisfactory to have only the most general value terms, such as 'good' and 'right,' 'bad' and 'wrong,' with which to do the evaluating of a practice of justice. Analogously, for actual practices of care we need care as a value to pick out the appropriate cluster of moral considerations, such as sensitivity, trust, and mutual concern, with which to evaluate such practices. It is not enough to think of care as simply work, describable empirically, with 'good' and 'right' providing all the normative evaluation of actual practices of care. Such practices are often morally deficient in ways specific to care as well as to justice.

If we say of someone that "he is a caring person," this includes an evaluation that he has a characteristic that, other things being equal, is morally admirable. Attributing a virtue to someone, as when we say that she is generous or trustworthy, describes a disposition but also makes a normative judgment. It is highly useful to be able to characterize people (and societies) in specific and subtle ways, recognizing the elements of our claims that are empirically descriptive and those that are normative. The subtlety needs to be available not only at the level of the descriptive but also within our moral evaluations. "Caring" thus picks out a more specific value to be found in persons' and societies' characteristics than merely finding them to be good or bad, or morally admirable or not, on the whole. But we may resist reducing care to a virtue if by that we refer only to the dispositions of individual persons, since caring is so much a matter of the relations between them. We value caring persons in caring relations. . . .

Caring Relations

My own view, then, is that care is both a practice and a value. As a practice, it shows us how to respond to needs and why we should. It builds trust and mutual concern and connectedness between persons. It is not a series of individual actions, but a practice that develops, along with its appropriate attitudes. It has attributes and standards that can be described, but more important that can be recommended and that should be continually improved as adequate care comes closer to being good care. Practices of care should express the caring relations that bring persons together, and they should do so in ways that are progressively more morally satisfactory. Caring practices should gradually transform children and others into human beings who are increasingly morally admirable. . . .

In addition to being a practice, care is also a value. Caring persons and caring attitudes should be valued, and we can organize many evaluations of how persons are interrelated around a constellation of moral considerations associated with care or its absence. For instance, we can ask of a relation whether it is trusting and mutually considerate or hostile and vindictive. We can ask if persons are attentive and responsive to each other's needs or indifferent and self-absorbed. Care is not the same as benevolence, in my view, since it is more the characterization of a social relation than the description of an individual disposition, and social relations are not reducible to individual states. Caring relations ought to be cultivated, between persons in their personal lives and between the members of caring societies. Such relations are often reciprocal over time if not at given times. The values of caring are especially exemplified in caring relations, rather than in persons as individuals.

To advocates of the ethics of care, care involves moral considerations at least as important as those of justice. And when adequately understood, the ethics of care is as appropriate for men as for women. Both men and women should acknowledge the enormous value of the caring activities on which society relies and should share these activities fairly. They should recognize the values of care, as of justice.

Caring relations form the small societies of family and friendship on which larger societies depend. Caring relations of a weaker but still evident kind between more distant persons allow them to trust one another enough to live in peace and respect each others' rights. For progress to be made, persons need to care together for the well-being of their members and their environment. . . .

The ethics of care builds relations of care and concern and mutual responsiveness to need on both the personal and wider social levels. Within social relations in which we care enough about one another to form a social entity, we may agree on various ways to deal with one another. For instance, for limited purposes we may imagine each other as liberal individuals in the marketplace, independent, autonomous, and rational, and we may adopt liberal schemes of law and governance, and policies to maximize individual benefits. But we should not lose sight of the deeper reality of human interdependency and of the need for caring relations to undergird or surround such constructions. The artificial abstraction of the model of the liberal individual is at best suitable for a restricted and limited part of human life, rather than for the whole of it. The ethics of care provides a way of thinking about and evaluating both the more immediate and the more distant human relations with which to develop morally acceptable societies.

Study Questions

1. What does Held mean by her claim that care is both a practice and a value?
2. Is the ethics of care a form of virtue ethics?
3. Does an ethics of care require caring equally for all?
4. Does an ethics of care imply particular views on any concrete moral issues?

Natural Law

John Finnis

John Finnis is Professor Emeritus of Law at the University of Oxford. He provides an overview of the core tenets of natural law theory, arguing that the theory provides a firm foundation for making correct moral decisions. Finnis maintains that acting in accord with natural law leads us to respect the basic human goods, such as knowledge, life, health, and friendship, thus leading all human beings to flourish.

I. Why Called 'Natural'? Why Called 'Law'?

In the discourse of ethics, political theory, or *philosophie de droit* (philosophy of law), the claim that there is a natural law is an offer to explain and defend the substance of certain assertions often made in different terms in pre-theoretical discourse (moral argument, politics, and/or law). Pretheoretically (so to speak), choices, actions, and/or dispositions may be said to be 'inhuman', 'unnaturally cruel', 'perverse', or 'morally unreasonable'; proposals, policies, or conduct may be described as violations of 'human rights'; actions of states, groups, or individuals may be described as 'crimes against humanity' and citizens may claim immunity from legal liability or obligations by appealing to a 'higher law'. A natural law theory offers to explain why such assertions can be rationally warranted and true. It offers to do so by locating these assertions in the context of a general theory of good and evil in human life so far as human life is shaped by deliberation and choice.

Such a theory of good and evil can also be called a general theory of right and wrong in human choices and actions. It will contain both (i) normative propositions identifying types of choice, action,

From John Finnis, *Reasons in Action: Collected Essays* (Oxford University Press, 2011).

or disposition as right or wrong, permissible, obligatory, etc., and (ii) non-normative propositions about the objectivity and epistemological warrant of the normative propositions.

Theorists who describe their account of good and evil, right and wrong, as a 'natural law theory' are not committed to asserting that the normative propositions they defend are 'derived from Nature' or 'read off' or 'inspected in' 'the nature of things'. Indeed, it is rare for a natural law theory to make such assertions, for their sense is deeply obscure; it is difficult, if not impossible, to understand what epistemic or rational processes would be involved in such 'derivation' or 'reading off' or 'inspection in'.

Still less are natural law theorists committed to claiming that the normative propositions they defend stand in some definite relationship to, or are warranted by, the 'laws of nature' in the sense of the regularities observed, and explanatory factors adduced, by the 'natural sciences' (physics, biology, 'experimental psychology', ecology, etc.). Thomas Aquinas, a leading natural law theorist, sharply differentiates the propositions of moral and political philosophy (in which the principles and norms of natural law are identified and elaborated) from (1) the propositions which constitute the natural sciences, (2) the principles and norms of logic, and what others have called the 'laws of thought', and (3) the principles and norms of any and every human technique of manipulating matter which is subject to our will.[1]

Nor is the typical natural law theory (classical, mediaeval, or contemporary) concerned with any alleged 'state of nature', in the sense of some golden age or state of affairs prior to human wrongdoing or to the formation of human societies or of states or political communities.

As for the term 'law', as understood in the phrase 'natural law', it does not connote that the relevant principles and norms have their directive force precisely as the commands, imperatives, or dictates of a superior will. Even those natural law theorists who argue (as most do) that the most ultimate explanation of those principles and norms (as of all other realities) is a transcendent, creative, divine source of existence, meaning, and value, will also argue that the principles and norms are inherently fitting and obligatory (not fitting or obligatory because commanded), or that the source of their obligation is rather divine wisdom than divine will.

Instead, the term 'law' in the phrase 'natural law' refers to standards of right choosing, standards which are normative (that is, rationally directive and 'obligatory') because they are true and choosing otherwise than in accordance with them is unreasonable.

And the term 'natural' (and related uses of 'by nature', 'in accordance with nature', and 'of nature') in this context signifies any one or more of the following: (a) that the relevant standards (principles and norms) are not 'positive', that is, are directive prior to any positing by individual decision or group choice or convention; (b) that the relevant standards are 'higher' than positive laws, conventions, and practices, that is, provide the premises for critical evaluation and endorsement or justified rejection of or disobedience to such laws, conventions, or practices; (c) that the relevant standards conform to the most demanding requirements of critical reason and are objective, in the sense that a person who fails to accept them as standards for judgment is in error; (d) that adherence to the relevant standards tends systematically to promote human flourishing, the fulfilment of human individuals and communities.

II. Critique of Scepticism and Dogmatism

Historically, natural law theories have been articulated as part or product of a philosophical critique of ethical scepticisms (whether nihilism, relativism, subjectivism, or hedonism). Since the sceptical views thus criticized and rejected by theorists of natural law (e.g. Plato) or natural right/justice (e.g. Aristotle) were themselves articulated in reaction to uncritically accepted conventions or religiously promoted norms, the philosophical critique of scepticism included a differentiation of the rationally grounded norms of natural law (or natural right) from moral dogmatism or conventionalism.

In contemporary thought, scepticism about natural law (and about other moral theories claiming to be objective or true) is very often based upon a logically illicit and rationally unwarranted inference from certain propositions about what 'is' the case to certain propositions about what is good or obligatory. . . .

Examples of the invalid reasoning commonly encountered today include the following:

— X is not universally regarded as good/obligatory; therefore X is not good/obligatory.
— In modern thought ('modernity') X is widely regarded as not good/obligatory; therefore X is not good/obligatory.
— In contemporary society X is widely regarded as good/obligatory; therefore X is good/obligatory.
— I have a sentiment of approval of X; therefore X is good (or worthwhile . . . or obligatory . . .), at least for me.

> — I have opted for or decided upon or am committed to the practical principle that X ought to be done; therefore X ought to be done, at least by me.

As this list of *non sequiturs* suggests, there is a link between ethical scepticism (at least in its popular forms) and ethical conventionalism. There are many natural law theories, on the other hand, which are not guilty of these or other fallacies, fallacies which consist in concluding to a normative judgment from premises which include no normative proposition. . . .

III. Cognitivism and Natural Law

Not every non-sceptical ethics is appropriately called a natural law theory. Natural law theories are distinguished from the broader set of cognitivist or objectivist ethical theories in four main ways.

First, they are differentiated . . . by their willingness to identify certain basic human goods, such as knowledge, life and health, and friendship, as the core of substantive first principles of practical reasoning. Taken together, these basic human goods give shape and content to a conception of human flourishing and thus, too, to a conception of human nature. For: an axiom of Aristotle's method . . . deployed more generally by Aquinas, shows that while nature is metaphysically (ontologically) fundamental, knowledge of a thing's nature is epistemically derivative: an animate thing's nature is understood by understanding its capacities, its capacities by understanding its activities, and its activities by understanding the objects of those activities. In the case of the human being the 'objects' which must be understood before one can understand and know human nature are the basic goods which are the objects of one's will, i.e. are one's basic reasons for acting and give reason for everything which one can intelligently take an interest in choosing.

Secondly, natural law theories are distinguished from any theory which asserts that moral truths are known essentially by discrete 'intuitions'. Rather, natural law theories contend that specific moral judgments concerning obligation or right are applications or specifications of higher principles. The first principles of the 'system' are known by insight. . . . But the insights whose content is the self-evident principles of practical knowledge are not intuitions—'insights' without data. Rather they are insights whose data are, in the first place, natural and sensory appetites and emotional responses. These data are subsequently enriched by theoretical knowledge or true opinion about possibilities (e.g. about what threatens and enhances health, or about what knowledge is available), and by experience of disharmony (frustrated intentions). . . . The first principles of natural law are not inclinations, but fundamental human goods understood as reasons for action.

Thirdly, natural law theories are distinguished from any fundamentally aggregative conception of the right and the just. For: viable natural law theories postulate no one end to which all human actions might be effective means, no one value in terms of which one might commensurate alternative options as simply better or worse, and no one principle which, without further specification in other principles and norms, should guide deliberation and choice. Rather they claim to identify a number of basic human goods, none of which is simply a means to or simply a part of any other such basic good; they further identify also a number of principles to guide ('morally') the choices necessitated by (i) the variety of basic goods and reasons for action and (ii) the multiple ways of instantiating these goods and acting on these reasons for action by intelligent and creative choice (or indeed by misguided choices whose primary motivation is not reasons but emotion).

Fourthly, natural law theories typically differ from other ethical theories by offering to clarify not only the normative disciplines and bodies of discourse, but also the methods of the descriptive and explanatory social theories (political theory or political science, economics, legal theory . . .). How best can human societies and their formative concepts be understood, without illusions, but in a general way . . . Could such projects be 'value-free'? Or must even descriptive-explanatory theorists, in selecting their concepts, rely upon some definite conceptions of what is important in human existence? Must they not use such conceptions as criteria for selecting topics for study and concepts for describing those topics? Must they not also employ such criteria in judging some types and instantiations of human institutions or practices to be the 'central cases' of such institutions or practices, and also in judging some uses of terms such as 'law' or 'constitution' or 'authority' to be, for critical descriptive theory, the 'focal' uses and senses of those terms? And must not such conceptions and criteria of importance be the subject, not of selection by 'demonic' personal preference . . . or silent conformism to academic fashion or political *parti pris*, but rather of an open, public, critical justification? Natural law theories of the classical type, as Aristotle and Aquinas, claim to offer such a justification.[2]

IV. Conclusion

. . . [T]heoretical reflection has yielded a more systematic and unifying 'master principle of morality'. This principle is reached by way of the consideration that, so far as it is in one's power, one should allow nothing but the principles corresponding to the basic human goods to shape one's practical thinking. Aquinas's first principle, 'Good is to be done and pursued and evil avoided', taken as it stands, is not yet moral; it requires only that one not act pointlessly, that is, without reason; it requires only that one take at least one of the principles corresponding to a basic human good and follow through to the point at which one somehow instantiates that good through action. The first *moral* principle makes the stronger demand, not merely that one be reasonable enough to avoid pointlessness, but that one be entirely reasonable in one's practical thinking, choice, and action. It can be formulated: in voluntarily acting for human goods and avoiding what is opposed to them, one ought to choose and otherwise will those and only those possibilities whose willing is compatible with a will toward integral human fulfilment (i.e. the fulfilment of all human persons and communities).

Notes

1. Aquinas, *Sententia Libri Ethicorum*, prol.
2. On this issue see John Finnis, *Natural Law and Natural Rights* (2nd edn, OUP, 2011), 3–22.

Study Questions

1. What does Finnis mean by "natural law"?
2. Can basic goods, such as knowledge and friendship, ever come into conflict?
3. If human beings were different, would morality be different?
4. Do descriptive facts alone ever imply values facts?

C.

Good Lives

The Meaning of Life

Richard Taylor

A good life may be described as one in which you live well, attain well-being, or find meaning. But what is the essence of such a life? The issue is discussed by Richard Taylor (1919–2003), who was Professor of Philosophy at the University of Rochester. He discusses the case of Sisyphus who, according to Greek myth, was condemned for his misdeeds to the eternal task of rolling a huge stone to the top of a hill, only each time to have it roll down to the bottom again. Taylor asks whether the life of Sisyphus is meaningless and argues that the answer depends on whether Sisyphus has a desire to roll stones up hills. If he does, then he is living a good life or has found meaning in life, for his activities match his wishes.

The question whether life has any meaning is difficult to interpret, and the more you concentrate your critical faculty on it the more it seems to elude you, or to evaporate as any intelligible question. You want to turn it aside, as a source of embarrassment, as something that, if it cannot be abolished, should at least be decently covered.

From Richard Taylor, *Good and Evil* (Amherst, NY: Prometheus Books, 2000).

And yet I think any reflective person recognizes that the question it raises is important, and that it ought to have a significant answer.

If the idea of meaningfulness is difficult to grasp in this context, so that we are unsure what sort of thing would amount to answering the question, the idea of meaninglessness is perhaps less so. If, then, we can bring before our minds a clear image of meaningless existence, then perhaps we can take a step toward coping with our original question by seeing to what extent our lives, as we actually find them, resemble that image, and draw such lessons as we are able to from the comparison.

Meaningless Existence

A perfect image of meaninglessness, of the kind we are seeking, is found in the ancient myth of Sisyphus. Sisyphus, it will be remembered, betrayed divine secrets to mortals, and for this he was condemned by the gods to roll a stone to the top of a hill, the stone then immediately to roll back down, again to be pushed to the top by Sisyphus, to roll down once more, and so on again and again, *forever.* Now in this we have the picture of meaningless, pointless toil, of a meaningless existence that is absolutely *never* redeemed. It is not even redeemed by a death that, if it were to accomplish nothing more, would at least bring this idiotic cycle to a close. If we were invited to imagine Sisyphus struggling for a while and accomplishing nothing, perhaps eventually falling from exhaustion, so that we might suppose him then eventually turning to something having some sort of promise, then the meaninglessness of that chapter of his life would not be so stark. It would be a dark and dreadful dream, from which he eventually awakens to sunlight and reality. But he does not awaken, for there is nothing for him to awaken to. His repetitive toil is his life and reality, and it goes on forever, and it is without any meaning whatever. Nothing ever comes of what he is doing, except simply, more of the same. Not by one step, nor by a thousand, nor by ten thousand does he even expiate by the smallest token the sin against the gods that led him into this fate. Nothing comes of it, nothing at all.

This ancient myth has always enchanted people, for countless meanings can be read into it. Some of the ancients apparently thought it symbolized the perpetual rising and setting of the sun, and others the repetitious crashing of the waves upon the shore. Probably the commonest interpretation is that it symbolizes our eternal struggle and unquenchable spirit, our determination always to try once more in the face of overwhelming discouragement. This interpretation is further supported by that version of the myth according to which Sisyphus was commanded to roll the stone *over* the hill, so that it would finally roll down the other side, but was never quite able to make it.

I am not concerned with rendering or defending any interpretation of this myth, however. I have cited it only for the one element it does unmistakably contain, namely, that of a repetitious, cyclic activity that never comes to anything. We could contrive other images of this that would serve just as well, and no myth-makers are needed to supply the materials of it. Thus, we can imagine two persons transporting a stone—or even a precious gem, it does not matter—back and forth, relay style. One carries it to a near or distant point where it is received by the other; it is returned to its starting point, there to be recovered by the first, and the process is repeated over and over. Except in this relay nothing counts as winning, and nothing brings the contest to any close; each step only leads to a repetition of itself. Or we can imagine two groups of prisoners, one of them engaged in digging a prodigious hole in the ground that is no sooner finished than it is filled in again by the other group, the latter then digging a new hole that is at once filled in by the first group, and so on and on endlessly.

Now what stands out in all such pictures as oppressive and dejecting is not that the beings who enact these roles suffer any torture or pain, for it need not be assumed that they do. Nor is it that their labors are great, for they are no greater than the labors commonly undertaken by most people most of the time. According to the original myth, the stone is so large that Sisyphus never quite gets it to the top and must groan under every step, so that his enormous labor is all for nought. But this is not what appalls. It is not that his great struggle comes to nothing, but that his existence itself is without meaning. Even if we suppose, for example, that the stone is but a pebble that can be carried effortlessly, or that the holes dug by the prisoners are but small ones, not the slightest meaning is introduced into their lives. The stone that Sisyphus moves to the top of the hill, whether we think of it as large or small, still rolls back every time, and the process is repeated forever. Nothing comes of it, and the work is simply pointless. That is the element of the myth that I wish to capture.

Again, it is not the fact that the labors of Sisyphus continue forever that deprives them of meaning. It is, rather, the implication of this: that they come to nothing. The image would not be changed by our supposing him to push a different stone up every time, each to roll down again. But if we supposed that these stones, instead of rolling back to their places as if they had never been moved, were assembled at the top of the hill and there incorporated, say, in a beautiful and enduring temple, then the aspect of meaninglessness would disappear. His labors would then have a point, something would come of them all, and although one could perhaps still say it was not worth it, one could not say that the life of Sisyphus was devoid of meaning altogether. Meaningfulness would at least have made an appearance, and we could see what it was.

That point will need remembering. But in the meantime, let us note another way in which the image of meaninglessness can be altered by making only a very slight change. Let us suppose that the gods, while condemning Sisyphus to the fate just described, at the same time, as an afterthought, waxed perversely merciful by implanting in him a strange and irrational impulse; namely, a compulsive impulse to roll stones. We may if we like, to make this more graphic, suppose they accomplish this by implanting in him some substance that has this effect on his character and drives. I call this perverse, because from our point of view there is clearly no reason why anyone should have a persistent and insatiable desire to do something so pointless as that. Nevertheless, suppose that is Sisyphus' condition. He has but one obsession, which is to roll stones, and it is an obsession that is only for the moment appeased by his rolling them—he no sooner gets a stone rolled to the top of the hill than he is restless to roll up another.

Now it can be seen why this little afterthought of the gods, which I called perverse, was also in fact merciful. For they have by this device managed to give Sisyphus precisely what he wants—by making him want precisely what they inflict on him. However it may appear to us, Sisyphus' fate now does not appear to him as a condemnation, but the very reverse. His one desire in life is to roll stones, and he is absolutely guaranteed its endless fulfillment. Where otherwise he might profoundly have wished surcease, and even welcomed the quiet of death to release him from endless boredom and meaninglessness, his life is now filled with mission and meaning, and he seems to himself to have been given an entry to heaven. Nor need he even fear death, for the gods have promised him an endless opportunity to indulge his single purpose, without concern or frustration. He will be able to roll stones *forever.*

What we need to mark most carefully at this point is that the picture with which we began has not really been changed in the least by adding this supposition. Exactly the same things happen as before. The only change is in Sisyphus' view of them. The picture before was the image of meaningless activity and existence. It was created precisely to be an image of that. It has not lost that meaninglessness, it has now gained not the least shred of meaningfulness. The stones still roll back as before, each phase of Sisyphus' life still exactly resembles all the others, the task is never completed, nothing comes of it, no temple ever begins to rise, and all this cycle of the same pointless thing over and over goes on forever in this picture as in the other. The *only* thing that has happened is this: Sisyphus has been reconciled to it, and indeed more, he has been led to embrace it. Not, however, by reason or persuasion, but by nothing more rational than the potency of a new substance in his veins.

The Meaninglessness of Life

I believe the foregoing provides a fairly clear content to the idea of meaninglessness and, through it, some hint of what meaningfulness, in this sense might be. Meaninglessness is essentially endless pointlessness, and meaningfulness is therefore the opposite. Activity, and even long, drawn out and repetitive activity, has a meaning if it has some significant culmination, some more or less lasting end that can be considered to have been the direction and purpose of the activity. But the descriptions so far also provide something else; namely, the suggestion of how an existence that is objectively meaningless, in this sense, can nevertheless acquire a meaning for him whose existence it is.

Now let us ask: Which of these pictures does life in fact resemble? And let us not begin with our own lives, for here both our prejudices and wishes are great, but with the life in general that we share with the rest of creation. We shall find, I think, that it all has a certain pattern, and that this pattern is by now easily recognized.

We can begin anywhere, only saving human existence for our last consideration. We can, for example, begin with any animal. It does not matter where we begin, because the result is going to be exactly the same.

Thus, for example, there are caves in New Zealand, deep and dark, whose floors are quiet pools and whose walls and ceilings are covered with soft light. As you gaze in wonder in the stillness of these caves it seems that the Creator has reproduced there in microcosm the heavens themselves, until you scarcely remember the enclosing presence of the walls. As you look more closely, however, the scene is explained. Each dot of light identifies an ugly worm, whose luminous tail is meant to attract insects from the surrounding darkness. As from time to time one of these insects draws near it becomes entangled in a sticky thread lowered by the worm, and is eaten. This goes on month after month, the blind worm lying there in the barren stillness waiting to entrap an occasional bit of nourishment that will only sustain it to another bit of nourishment until. . . . Until what? What great thing awaits all this long and repetitious effort and makes it worthwhile? Really nothing. The larva just transforms itself finally to a tiny winged adult that lacks even mouth parts to feed and lives only a day or two. These adults, as soon as they have mated and laid eggs, are themselves caught in the threads and are devoured by the cannibalistic worms, often without having ventured into the day, the only point to their existence having now been fulfilled. This has been going on for millions of years, and to no end other than that the same meaningless cycle may continue for another millions of years.

All living things present essentially the same spectacle. The larva of a certain cicada burrows in the darkness of the earth for seventeen years, through season after season, to emerge finally into the daylight for a brief flight, lay its eggs, and die—this all to repeat itself during the next seventeen years, and so on to eternity. We have already noted, in another connection, the struggles of fish, made only that others may do the same after them and that this cycle, having no other point than itself, may never cease. Some birds span an entire side of the globe each year and then return, only to insure that others may follow the same incredibly long path again and again. One is led to wonder what the point of it all is, with what great triumph this ceaseless effort, repeating itself through millions of years, might finally culminate, and why it should go on and on for so long, accomplishing nothing, getting nowhere. But then you realize that there is no point to it at all, that it really culminates in nothing, that each of these cycles, so filled with toil, is to be followed only by more of the same. The point of any living thing's life is, evidently, nothing but life itself.

This life of the world thus presents itself to our eyes as a vast machine, feeding on itself, running on and on forever to nothing. And we are part of that life. To be sure, we are not just the same, but the differences are not so great as we like to think; many are merely invented, and none really cancels the kind of meaninglessness that we found in Sisyphus and that we find all around, wherever anything lives. We are conscious of our activity. Our goals, whether in any significant sense we choose them or not, are things of which we are at least partly aware and can therefore in some sense appraise. More significantly, perhaps, we have a history, as other animals do not, such that each generation does not precisely resemble all those before. Still, if we can in imagination disengage our wills from our lives and disregard the deep interest we all have in our own existence, we shall find that they do not so little resemble the existence of Sisyphus. We toil after goals, most of them—indeed every single one of them—of transitory significance and, having gained one of them, we immediately set forth for the next, as if that one had never been, with this next one being essentially more of the same. Look at a busy street any day, and observe the throng going hither and thither. To what? Some office or shop, where the same things will be done today as were done yesterday, and are done now so they may be repeated tomorrow. And if we think that, unlike Sisyphus, these labors do have a point, that they culminate in something lasting and, independently of our own deep interests in them, very worthwhile, then we simply have not considered the thing closely enough. Most such effort is directed only to the establishment and perpetuation of home and family; that is, to the begetting of others who will follow in our steps to do more of the same. Everyone's life thus resembles one of Sisyphus's climbs to the summit of his hill, and each day of it one of his steps; the difference is that whereas Sisyphus himself returns to push the stone up again, we leave this to our children. We at one point imagined that the labors of Sisyphus finally culminated in the creation of a temple, but for this to make any difference it had to be a temple that would at least endure, adding beauty to the world for the remainder of time. Our achievements, even though they are often beautiful, are mostly bubbles; and those that do last, like the sand-swept pyramids, soon become mere curiosities while around them the rest of human-kind continues its perpetual toting of rocks, only to see them roll down. Nations are built upon the bones of their founders and pioneers, but only to decay and crumble before long, their rubble then becoming the foundation for others directed to exactly the same fate. The picture of Sisyphus is the picture of existence of the individual man, great or unknown, of nations, of the human race, and of the very life of the world.

On a country road one sometimes comes upon the ruined hulks of a house and once extensive buildings, all in collapse and spread over with weeds. A curious eye can in imagination reconstruct from what is left a once warm and thriving life, filled with purpose. There was the hearth, where a family once talked, sang, and made plans; there were the rooms, where people loved, and babes were born to a rejoicing mother; there are the musty remains of a sofa, infested with bugs, once bought at a dear price to enhance an ever-growing comfort, beauty, and warmth. Every small piece of junk fills the mind with what once, not long ago, was utterly real, with children's voices, plans made, and enterprises embarked upon. That is how these stones of Sisyphus were rolled up, and that is how they became incorporated into a beautiful temple, and that temple is what now lies before you. Meanwhile other buildings, institutions, nations, and civilizations spring up all around, only to share the same fate before long. And if the question "What for?" is now asked, the answer is clear: so that just this may go on forever.

The two pictures—of Sisyphus and of our own lives, if we look at them from a distance—are in outline the same and convey to the mind the same image. It is not surprising, then, that we invent ways of denying it, our religions proclaiming a heaven that does not crumble, their hymnals and prayer books declaring a significance to life of which our eyes provide no hint whatever.[1] Even our philosophies portray some permanent and lasting good at which all may aim, from the changeless forms invented by Plato to the beatific vision of St. Thomas and the ideals of permanence contrived by the moderns. When these fail to convince, then earthly ideals such as universal justice and brotherhood are conjured up to take their places and give meaning to our seemingly endless pilgrimage, some final state that will be ushered in when the last obstacle is removed and the last stone pushed to the hilltop. No one believes, of course, that any such state will be final, or even wants it to be in case it means that human existence would then cease to be a struggle; but in the meantime such ideas serve a very real need.

The Meaning of Life

We noted that Sisyphus' existence would have meaning if there were some point to his labors, if his efforts ever culminated in something that was not just an occasion for fresh labors of the same kind. But that is precisely the meaning it lacks. And human existence resembles his in that respect. We do achieve things—we scale our towers and raise our stones to the hilltops—but every such accomplishment fades, providing only an occasion for renewed labors of the same kind.

But here we need to note something else that has been mentioned, but its significance not explored, and that is the state of mind and feeling with which such labors are undertaken. We noted that if Sisyphus had a keen and unappeasable desire to be doing just what he found himself doing, then, although his life would in no way be changed, it would nevertheless have a meaning for him. It would be an irrational one, no doubt, because the desire itself would be only the product of the substance in his veins, and not any that reason could discover, but a meaning nevertheless.

And would it not, in fact, be a meaning incomparably better than the other? For let us examine again the first kind of meaning it could have. Let us suppose that, without having any interest in rolling stones, as such, and finding this, in fact, a galling toil, Sisyphus did nevertheless have a deep interest in raising a temple, one that would be beautiful and lasting. And let us suppose he succeeded in this, that after ages of dreadful toil, all directed at this final result, he did at last complete his temple, such that now he could say his work was done, and he could rest and forever enjoy the result. Now what? What picture now presents itself to our minds? It is precisely the picture of infinite boredom! Of Sisyphus doing nothing ever again, but contemplating what he has already wrought and can no longer add anything to, and contemplating it for an eternity! Now in this picture we have a meaning for Sisyphus' existence, a point for his prodigious labor, because we have put it there; yet, at the same time, that which is really worthwhile seems to have slipped away entirely. Where before we were presented with the nightmare of eternal and pointless activity, we are now confronted with the hell of its eternal absence.

Our second picture, then, wherein we imagined Sisyphus to have had inflicted on him the irrational desire to be doing just what he found himself doing, should not have been dismissed so abruptly. The meaning that picture lacked was no meaning that he or anyone could crave, and the strange meaning it had was perhaps just what we were seeking.

At this point, then, we can reintroduce what has been until now, it is hoped, resolutely pushed aside in an effort to view our lives and human existence with objectivity; namely, our own wills, our deep interest in what we find ourselves doing. If we do this we find that our lives do indeed still resemble that of Sisyphus, but that the meaningfulness they thus lack is precisely the meaningfulness of infinite boredom. At the same time, the strange meaningfulness they possess is that of the inner compulsion to be doing just what we were put here to do, and to go on doing it forever. This is the nearest we may hope to get to heaven, but the redeeming side of that fact is that we do thereby avoid a genuine hell.

If the builders of a great and flourishing ancient civilization could somehow return now to see archaeologists unearthing the trivial remnants of what they had once accomplished with such effort—see the fragments of pots and vases, a few broken statues, and such tokens of another age and greatness—they could indeed ask themselves what the point of it all was, if this is all it finally came to. Yet, it did not seem so to them then, for it was just the building, and not what was finally built, that gave their life meaning. Similarly, if the builders of the ruined home and farm that I described a short while ago could be brought back to see what is left, they would have the same feelings. What we construct in our imaginations as we look over these decayed and rusting pieces would reconstruct itself in their very memories, and certainly with unspeakable sadness. The piece of a sled at our feet would revive in them a warm Christmas. And what rich memories would there be in the broken crib? And the weed-covered remains of a fence would reproduce the scene of a great herd of livestock, so laboriously built up over so many years. What was it all worth, if this is the final result? Yet, again, it did not seem so to them through those many years of struggle and toil, and they did not imagine they were building a Gibraltar. The things to which they bent their backs day after day, realizing one by one their ephemeral plans, were precisely the things in which their wills were deeply involved, precisely the things in which their interests lay, and there was no need then to ask questions. There is no more need of them now—the day was sufficient to itself, and so was the life.

This is surely the way to look at all of life—at one's own life, and each day and moment it contains; of the life of a nation; of the species; of the life of the world; and of every thing that breathes. Even the glow worms I described, whose cycles of existence over the millions of years seem so pointless when looked at by us, will seem entirely different to us if we can somehow try to view their existence from within. Their endless activity, which gets nowhere, is just what it is their will to pursue. This is its whole justification and meaning. Nor would it be any salvation to the birds who span the globe every year, back and forth, to have a home made for them in a cage with plenty of food and protection, so that they would not have to migrate anymore. It would be their condemnation, for it is the doing that counts for them, and not what they hope to win by it. Flying these prodigious distances, never ending, is what it is in their veins to do, exactly as it was in Sisyphus's veins to roll stones, without end, after the gods had waxed merciful and implanted this in him.

You no sooner drew your first breath than you responded to the will that was in you to live. You no more ask whether it will be worthwhile, or whether anything of significance will come of it, than the worms and the birds. The point of living is simply to be living, in the manner that it is your nature to be living. You go through life building your castles, each of these beginning to fade into time as the next is begun; yet it would be no salvation to rest from all this. It would be a condemnation, and one that would in no way be redeemed were you able to gaze upon the things you have done, even if these were beautiful and absolutely permanent, as they never are. What counts is that you should be able to begin a new task, a new castle, a new bubble. It counts only because it is there to be done and you have the will to do it. The same will be the life of your children, and of theirs; and if the philosopher is apt to see in this a pattern similar to the unending cycles of the existence of Sisyphus, and to despair, then it is indeed because the meaning and point he is seeking is not there—but mercifully so. The meaning of life is from within us, it is not bestowed from without, and it far exceeds in both its beauty and permanence any heaven of which men have ever dreamed or yearned for.

Note

1. A popular Christian hymn, sung often at funerals and typical of many hymns, expresses this thought:

   Swift to its close ebbs out life's little day;
   Earth's joys grow dim, its glories pass away:
   Change and decay in all around I see:
   O thou who changest not, abide with me.

Study Questions

1. Can a life be enjoyed yet meaningless?
2. Can a life be immoral yet meaningful?
3. Can you be mistaken about finding meaning in an activity?
4. Can an activity you find boring give meaning to your life?

Meaning of Life

Susan Wolf

Susan Wolf is Professor of Philosophy at the University of North Carolina at Chapel Hill. She defends the view that not all lives are meaningful or well-lived, but only those in which a person actively engages in projects of worth. For Wolf these include intellectual accomplishments, aesthetic enterprises, and relationships with friends, but not watching sitcoms, playing computer games, or attending aerobics classes. Thus, unlike Taylor, Wolf would not find meaning in the life of Sisyphus, even if his fondest desire was to roll stones up hills.

A meaningful life is, first of all, one that has within it the basis for an affirmative answer to the needs or longings that are characteristically described as needs for meaning. I have in mind, for example, the sort of questions people ask on their deathbeds, or simply in contemplation of their eventual deaths, about whether their lives have been (or are) worth living, whether they have had any point, and the sort of questions one asks when considering suicide and wondering whether one has any reason to go on. These questions are familiar from Russian novels and existentialist philosophy, if not from personal experience. Though they arise most poignantly in times of crisis and intense emotion, they also have their place in moments of calm reflection, when considering important life choices. Moreover, paradigms of what are taken to be meaningful and meaningless lives in our culture are readily available. Lives of great moral or intellectual accomplishment—Gandhi, Mother Teresa, Albert Einstein—come to mind as unquestionably meaningful lives (if any are); lives of waste

From Susan Wolf, "Happiness and Meaning: Two Aspects of the Good Life," *Social Philosophy & Policy*, 24 (1997).

and isolation—Thoreau's "lives of quiet desperation," typically anonymous to the rest of us, and the mythical figure of Sisyphus—represent meaninglessness.

To what general characteristics of meaningfulness do these images lead us and how do they provide an answer to the longings mentioned above? Roughly, I would say that meaningful lives are lives of active engagement in projects of worth. Of course, a good deal needs to be said in elaboration of this statement. Let me begin by discussing the two key phrases, "active engagement" and "projects of worth."

A person is actively engaged by something if she is gripped, excited, involved by it. Most obviously, we are actively engaged by the things and people about which and whom we are passionate. Opposites of active engagement are boredom and alienation. To be actively engaged in something is not always pleasant in the ordinary sense of the word. Activities in which people are actively engaged frequently involve stress, danger, exertion, or sorrow (consider, for example: writing a book, climbing a mountain, training for a marathon, caring for an ailing friend). However, there is something good about the feeling of engagement: one feels (typically without thinking about it) especially alive.

That a meaningful life must involve "projects of worth" will, I expect, be more controversial, for the phrase hints of a commitment to some sort of objective value. This is not accidental, for I believe that the idea of meaningfulness, and the concern that our lives possess it, are conceptually linked to such a commitment.[1] Indeed, it is this linkage that I want to defend, for I have neither a philosophical theory of what objective value is nor a substantive theory about what has this sort of value. What is clear to me is that there can be no sense to the idea of meaningfulness without a distinction between more and less worthwhile ways to spend one's time, where the test of worth is at least partly independent of a subject's ungrounded preferences or enjoyment.

Consider first the longings or concerns about meaning that people have, their wondering whether their lives are meaningful, their vows to add more meaning to their lives. The sense of these concerns and resolves cannot fully be captured by an account in which what one does with one's life doesn't matter, as long as one enjoys or prefers it. Sometimes people have concerns about meaning despite their knowledge that their lives to date have been satisfying. Indeed, their enjoyment and "active engagement" with activities and values they now see as shallow seem only to heighten the sense of meaninglessness that comes to afflict them. Their sense that their lives so far have been meaningless cannot be a sense that their activities have not been chosen or fun. When they look for sources of meaning or ways to add meaning to their lives, they are searching for projects whose justifications lie elsewhere.

Second, we need an explanation for why certain sorts of activities and involvements come to mind as contributors to meaningfulness while others seem intuitively inappropriate. Think about what gives meaning to your own life and the lives of your friends and acquaintances. Among the things that tend to come up on such lists, I have already mentioned moral and intellectual accomplishments and the ongoing activities that lead to them. Relationships with friends and relatives are perhaps even more important for most of us. Aesthetic enterprises (both creative and appreciative), the cultivation of personal virtues, and religious practices frequently loom large. By contrast, it would be odd, if not bizarre, to think of crossword puzzles, sitcoms, or the kind of computer games to which I am fighting off addiction as providing meaning in our lives, though there is no question that they afford a sort of satisfaction and that they are the objects of choice. Some things, such as chocolate and aerobics class, I choose even at considerable cost to myself (it is irrelevant that these particular choices may be related); so I must find them worthwhile in a sense. But they are not the sorts of things that make life worth living.[2]

"Active engagement in projects of worth," I suggest, answers to the needs an account of meaningfulness in life must meet. If a person is or has been thus actively engaged, then she does have an answer to the question of whether her life is or has been worthwhile, whether it has or has had a point. When someone looks for ways to add meaning to her life, she is looking (though perhaps not under this description) for worthwhile projects about which she can get enthused. The account also explains why some activities and projects but not others come to mind as contributors to meaning in life. Some projects, or at any rate, particular acts, are worthwhile but too boring or mechanical to be sources of meaning. People do not get meaning from recycling or from writing checks to Oxfam and the ACLU. Other acts and activities, though highly pleasurable and deeply involving, like riding a roller coaster or meeting a movie star, do not seem to have the right kind of value to contribute to meaning.

Bernard Williams once distinguished categorical desires from the rest. Categorical desires give us reasons for living—they are not premised on the assumption that we will live. The sorts of things that give meaning to life tend to be objects of categorical desire. We desire them, at least so I would suggest, because we think them worthwhile. They are not worthwhile simply because we desire them or simply because they make our lives more pleasant.

Roughly, then, according to my proposal, a meaningful life must satisfy two criteria, suitably linked. First, there must be active engagement, and second, it must be engagement in (or with) projects of worth. A life is meaningless if it lacks active engagement with anything. A person who is bored or alienated from most of what she spends her life doing is one whose life can be said to lack meaning. Note that she may in fact be performing functions of worth. A housewife and mother, a doctor, or a busdriver may be competently doing a socially valuable job, but because she is not engaged by her work (or, as we are assuming, by anything else in her life), she has no categorical desires that give her a reason to live. At the same time, someone who is actively engaged may also live a meaningless life, if the objects of her involvement are utterly worthless. It is difficult to come up with examples of such lives that will be uncontroversial without being bizarre. But both bizarre and controversial examples have their place. In the bizarre category, we might consider pathological cases: someone whose sole passion in life is collecting rubber bands, or memorizing the dictionary, or making handwritten copies of *War and Peace*. Controversial cases will include the corporate lawyer who sacrifices her private life and health for success along the professional ladder, the devotee of a religious cult, or—an example offered by Wiggins[3]—the pig farmer who buys more land to grow more corn to feed more pigs to buy more land to grow more corn to feed more pigs.

We may summarize my proposal in terms of a slogan: "Meaning arises when subjective attraction meets objective attractiveness." The idea is that in a world in which some things are more worthwhile than others, meaning arises when a subject discovers or develops an affinity for one or typically several of the more worthwhile things and has and makes use of the opportunity to engage with it or them in a positive way.

Notes

1. This point is made by David Wiggins in his brilliant but difficult essay "Truth, Invention, and the Meaning of Life," *Proceedings of the British Academy*, vol. 62 (1976).

2. Woody Allen appears to have a different view. His list of the things that make life worth living at the end of *Manhattan* includes, for example "the crabs at Sam Woo's," which would seem to be on the level of chocolates. On the other hand, the crabs' appearance on the list may be taken to show that he regards the dish as an accomplishment meriting aesthetic appreciation, where such appreciation is a worthy activity in itself; in this respect, the crabs might be akin to other items on his list such as the second movement of the *Jupiter Symphony*, Louis Armstrong's recording of "Potatohead Blues," and "those apples and pears of Cézanne." Strictly speaking, the appreciation of great chocolate might also qualify as such an activity.
3. See Wiggins, "Truth, Invention, and the Meaning of Life," p. 342.

Study Questions

1. Based on the examples she provides, what does Wolf mean by "a project of worth"?
2. How would Wolf decide whether some activity was a project of worth?
3. Could the lives of a college professor, a professional golfer, and a janitor be equally meaningful?
4. Would studying certain subjects add more meaning to life than studying other subjects?

Meaningful Lives

Christine Vitrano

Christine Vitrano is Associate Professor of Philosophy at Brooklyn College of The City University of New York. She considers the views of a good or meaningful life offered by both Richard Taylor and Susan Wolf but finds neither convincing. Vitrano argues that Taylor's view is defective in not requiring that a good life display any concern for the welfare of others, whereas Wolf's view depends on an unexplained notion of objective value. Vitrano herself defends the view that a good or meaningful life is one in which a person acts morally while achieving satisfaction. Whether that satisfaction is found in intellectual accomplishments or rolling stones up hills is a matter of individual choice.

Richard Taylor and Susan Wolf offer contrasting visions of a meaningful life. I find each account partially persuasive, but neither by itself entirely satisfactory.

For Wolf, a meaningful life is one in which you are actively engaged in projects of worth. To be engaged is to be "gripped, excited, involved." If you find your life dreary, then it is not meaningful.

Enjoying activities, however, does not by itself render them meaningful; they also need to be worthwhile. As she says, "When someone looks for ways to add meaning to her life, she is looking . . . for worthwhile projects about which she can get enthused" and "whose justifications lie elsewhere," specifically in "objective value."

According to Wolf, worthwhile activities include "[r]elationships with friends and relatives . . . [a]esthetic enterprises (both creative and appreciative), the cultivation of personal virtues, and religious practices." Specific examples include "writing a book, climbing a mountain, training for a marathon." Among the activities that lack such worth are solving crossword puzzles, watching sitcoms, playing computer games, and eating chocolate, as well as "collecting rubber bands, or memorizing the dictionary, or making handwritten copies of *War and Peace*." "Controversial cases" are the paths of the "corporate lawyer who sacrifices her private life and health for success along the professional ladder, the devotee of a religious cult, or . . . the pig farmer who buys more land to grow more corn to feed more pigs to buy more land to grow more corn to feed more pigs."

An obvious problem with Wolf's position is that by her own admission she has "neither a philosophical theory of what objective value is nor a substantive theory about what has that sort of value." She relies on supposedly shared intuitions regarding the worth of various activities, but to assume such agreement is unjustified. Some people appreciate an activity Wolf disparages, yet dismiss one she values highly. For example, spending thousands of hours training for a marathon strikes many as wearisome; they may be far more engaged by computer games. On the other hand, grappling with a *New York Times Sunday Magazine* crossword puzzle is a popular intellectual challenge, holding far more appeal for most than reading an article on metaethics, a subject Wolf finds fascinating.

She might respond to these observations by claiming that the problem with crossword puzzles lies not in their essential unimportance but in their use as mere pastimes. In other words, even those who enjoy solving them don't take them seriously.

This reply, however, only deepens Wolf's difficulty, because the same activity could be judged as meaningful or meaningless depending on why a person engages in it. Consider, for instance, a physicist who does scientific research because of the enjoyment it brings but is devoted to chess problems for their intellectual challenge. For that scholar, pursuing physics would be meaningless, but composing and solving chess problems would be meaningful—hardly the conclusion Wolf is seeking.

Furthermore suppose that in order to distract myself from the monotony of caring for my two children, I read an article on metaphysics. Why should the motive affect the worthiness of the activity?

Because Wolf's position is weakened by her commitment to an objective value that she cannot explain, we might drop that aspect of her position and accept Richard Taylor's view that a meaningful life is one that affords you long-term satisfaction, regardless of the activities you choose. Thus the life of Sisyphus would be meaningful if Sisyphus relished rolling stones up hills.

Yet even if a person's life is enjoyable, if it is morally unworthy, displaying no concern for the welfare of others, then such a life does not deserve to be judged positively by anyone with moral compunctions.

I would suggest, however, that by combining insights from Taylor and Wolf, we can understand the nature of a meaningful life. It is one in which an individual acts morally while achieving happiness.

To be happy is to be satisfied with one's life, content with one's lot, not suffering excessively from anxiety, alienation, frustration, disappointment, or depression. Satisfied people may face problems but view their lives overall more positively than negatively.

The crucial point is that how satisfaction may be achieved differs from person to person. One individual may be satisfied only by earning ten million dollars. Another may be satisfied by going each day with friends to a favorite club to swim, eat lunch, and play cards. Another may be satisfied by acting in community theatre productions. Their paths to contentment are different, yet their degree of satisfaction may be the same.

Some may be poor, yet satisfied. Others may be alone, yet satisfied. Still others may find satisfaction regardless of the depth of their learning or self-knowledge and irrespective of whatever illness or disability they may face. In any case, the judgment of satisfaction is the individual's, not anyone else's.

Does satisfaction depend on achieving one's goals? Not necessarily. You may achieve your aims only to find that doing so does not provide the satisfaction for which you had hoped. For example, you might eagerly seek and gain admission to a prestigious college only to find that its rural location, which seemed an advantage when you applied, turns out to be a disadvantage when you develop interests better pursued in an urban environment.

Furthermore, some people don't have specific goals. They can happily live here or there, engage in a variety of hobbies, or even pursue various careers. They find delight in spontaneity. Perhaps that approach doesn't appeal to you, but so what? If it works for others, why not let them have their enjoyment without derogating it?

How do you achieve satisfaction, considering that it has eluded so many? The key lies within yourself, because you cannot control the events outside you. If your satisfaction depends on whether others praise you, then they control how satisfied you will be with your life. If you wish to avoid being subject to the power of others, then you have to free yourself from dependence on their judgments.

Some, such as Philippa Foot, warn against a life spent in "childish pursuits."[1] But which pursuits are childish? How about collecting dolls, telling jokes, planting vegetables, selling cookies, running races, recounting adventures, or singing songs? While children engage in all these activities, so do adults, who may thereby find satisfaction in their lives. Assuming they meet their moral obligations, why disparage them or their interests?

An obituary provides information about an individual's life, detailing accomplishments. What we don't learn therein, however, is whether that individual found satisfaction. If so, and assuming the person displayed due respect for others, then that person's life was meaningful.[2]

Notes

1. Philippa Foot, *Natural Goodness* (Oxford: Clarendon Press, 2001), p. 86.
2. This theory is developed at length in Steven M. Cahn and Christine Vitrano, *Happiness and Goodness: Philosophical Reflections on Living Well* (New York: Columbia University Press, 2015).

Study Questions

1. What is Vitrano's objection to Wolf's account of a meaningful life?
2. What is Vitrano's objection to Taylor's account of a meaningful life?
3. Do you believe that a person who treats others with respect and finds satisfaction sunbathing, swimming, and surfing, while having the financial resources to buy luxurious clothes, cars, and homes, is living a good life?
4. On what bases, if any, can one person judge another person's life as lacking in well-being?

PART 

The Limits of Law

Free Speech

On Liberty

John Stuart Mill

Bring to your mind an opinion so outrageous that it would be repudiated by any sensible person. Now suppose that stating this opinion openly would be an affront to the vast majority of listeners. Under such circumstances, why shouldn't the representatives of the people be empowered to pass a law banning the public expression of this foolishness, thus ensuring that no one is offended by it or tempted to repeat it? If an opinion is wrongheaded and repugnant, why does it merit protection? The most celebrated and eloquent reply is provided in John Stuart Mill's classic work, *On Liberty*. What is most surprising about Mill's presentation is that he defends an individual's free speech by appealing not to the majority's kindheartedness but to its welfare. As he puts it, "He who knows only his own side of the case knows little of that." He maintains that those who have not heard and carefully considered the arguments against their position will soon hold their views as dead dogma, shorn of significance.

From *On Liberty* by John Stuart Mill (1859).

Chapter I

Introductory

The object of this essay is to assert one very simple principle, as entitled to govern absolutely the dealings of society with the individual in the way of compulsion and control, whether the means used be physical force in the form of legal penalties or the moral coercion of public opinion. That principle is that the sole end for which mankind are warranted, individually or collectively, in interfering with the liberty of action of any of their number is self-protection. That the only purpose for which power can be rightfully exercised over any member of a civilized community, against his will, is to prevent harm to others. His own good, either physical or moral, is not a sufficient warrant. He cannot rightfully be compelled to do or forbear because it will be better for him to do so, because it will make him happier, because, in the opinions of others, to do so would be wise or even right. These are good reasons for remonstrating with him, or reasoning with him, or persuading him, or entreating him, but not for compelling him or visiting him with any evil in case he do otherwise. To justify that, the conduct from which it is desired to deter him must be calculated to produce evil to someone else. The only part of the conduct of anyone for which he is amenable to society is that which concerns others. In the part which merely concerns himself, his independence is, of right, absolute. Over himself, over his own body and mind, the individual is sovereign. . . .

This, then, is the appropriate region of human liberty. It comprises, first, the inward domain of consciousness, demanding liberty of conscience in the most comprehensive sense, liberty of thought and feeling, absolute freedom of opinion and sentiment on all subjects, practical or speculative, scientific, moral, or theological. The liberty of expressing and publishing opinions may seem to fall under a different principle, since it belongs to that part of the conduct of an individual which concerns other people, but, being almost of as much importance as the liberty of thought itself and resting in great part on the same reasons, is practically inseparable from it. Secondly, the principle requires liberty of tastes and pursuits, of framing the plan of our life to suit our own character, of doing as we like, subject to such consequences as may follow, without impediment from our fellow creatures, so long as what we do does not harm them, even though they should think our conduct foolish, perverse, or wrong. Thirdly, from this liberty of each individual follows the liberty, within the same limits, of combination among individuals; freedom to unite for any purpose not involving harm to others: the persons combining being supposed to be of full age and not forced or deceived.

No society in which these liberties are not, on the whole, respected is free, whatever may be its form of government; and none is completely free in which they do not exist absolute and unqualified. The only freedom which deserves the name is that of pursuing our own good in our own way, so long as we do not attempt to deprive others of theirs or impede their efforts to obtain it. Each is the proper guardian of his own health, whether bodily *or* mental and spiritual. Mankind are greater gainers by suffering each other to live as seems good to themselves than by compelling each to live as seems good to the rest. . . .

It will be convenient for the argument if, instead of at once entering upon the general thesis, we confine ourselves in the first instance to a single branch of it on which the principle here stated is, if not fully, yet to a certain point, recognized by the current opinions. This one branch is the Liberty of Thought, from which it is impossible to separate the cognate liberty of speaking and of writing. Although these liberties, to some considerable amount, form part of the political morality of all countries which profess religious toleration and free institutions, the grounds, both philosophical and practical, on which they rest are perhaps not so familiar to the general mind, nor so thoroughly appreciated by many, even of the leaders of opinion, as might have been expected. . . .

Chapter II

Of the Liberty of Thought and Discussion

The time, it is to be hoped, is gone by when any defense would be necessary of the "liberty of the press" as one of the securities against corrupt or tyrannical government. No argument, we may suppose, can now be needed against permitting a legislature or an executive, not identified in interest with the people, to prescribe opinions to them and determine what doctrines or what arguments they shall be allowed to hear. . . . Let us suppose, therefore, that the government is entirely at one with the people, and never thinks of exerting any power of coercion unless in agreement with what it conceives to be their voice. But I deny the right of the people to exercise such coercion, either by themselves or by their government. The power itself is illegitimate. The best government has no more title to it than the worst. It is as noxious, or more noxious, when exerted in accordance with public opinion than when in opposition to it. If all mankind minus one were of one opinion, and only one person were of the contrary opinion, mankind would be no more justified in silencing that one person than he, if he had the power, would be justified in silencing mankind. Were an opinion a personal possession of no value except to the owner, if to be obstructed in the enjoyment of it were simply a private injury, it would make some difference whether the injury was inflicted only on a few persons or on many. But the peculiar evil of silencing the expression of an opinion is that it is robbing the human race, posterity as well as the existing generation—those who dissent from the opinion, still more than those who hold it. If the opinion is right, they are deprived of the opportunity of exchanging error for truth; if wrong, they lose, what is almost as great a benefit, the clearer perception and livelier impression of truth produced by its collision with error.

It is necessary to consider separately these two hypotheses, each of which has a distinct branch of the argument corresponding to it. We can never be sure that the opinion we are endeavoring to stifle is a false opinion; and if we were sure, stifling it would be an evil still.

First, the opinion which it is attempted to suppress by authority may possibly be true. Those who desire to suppress it, of course, deny its truth; but they are not infallible. They have no authority to decide the question for all mankind and exclude every other person from the means of judging. To refuse a hearing to an opinion because they are sure that it is false is to assume that *their* certainty is the same thing as *absolute* certainty. All silencing of discussion is an assumption of infallibility. Its condemnation may be allowed to rest on this common argument, not the worse for being common.

Unfortunately for the good sense of mankind, the fact of their fallibility is far from carrying the weight in their practical judgment which is always allowed to it in theory; for while everyone well knows himself to be fallible, few think it necessary to take any precautions against their own fallibility, or admit the supposition that any opinion of which they feel very certain may be one of the examples of the error to which they acknowledge themselves to be liable. Absolute princes, or others who are accustomed to unlimited deference, usually feel this complete confidence in their own opinions on nearly all subjects. People more happily situated, who sometimes hear their opinions disputed and are not wholly unused to be set right when they are wrong, place the same unbounded reliance only on such of their opinions as are shared by all who surround them, or to whom they habitually defer; for in proportion to a man's want of confidence in his own solitary judgment does he usually repose, with implicit trust, on the infallibility of "the world" in general. And the world, to each individual, means the part of it with which he comes in contact his party, his sect, his church, his class of society; the man may be called, by comparison, almost liberal and large-minded to whom it means anything so comprehensive as his own country or his own age. Nor is his faith in this collective authority at all shaken by his being aware that other ages, countries, sects, churches, classes, and parties have thought, and even now think, the exact reverse. He devolves upon his own world the responsibility of being in the right against the dissentient worlds of other people; and it never troubles him that mere accident has decided which of these numerous worlds is the object of his reliance, and that the same causes which make him a churchman in London would have made him a Buddhist or a Confucian in Peking. Yet it is as evident in itself, as any amount of argument can make it, that ages are no more infallible than individuals—every age having held many opinions which subsequent ages have deemed not only false but absurd; and it is as certain that many opinions, now general, will be rejected by future ages, as it is that many, once general, are rejected by the present.

The objection likely to be made to this argument would probably take some such form as the following. There is no greater assumption of infallibility in forbidding the propagation of error than in any other thing which is done by public authority on its own judgment and responsibility. Judgment is given to men that they may use it. Because it may be used erroneously, are men to be told that they ought not to use it at all? To prohibit what they think pernicious is not claiming exemption from error, but fulfilling the duty incumbent on them, although fallible, of acting on their conscientious conviction. If we were never to act on our opinions, because those opinions may be wrong, we should leave all our interests uncared for, and all our duties unperformed. An objection which applies to all conduct can be no valid objection to any conduct in particular. It is the duty of governments, and of individuals, to form the truest opinions they can; to form them carefully, and never impose them upon others unless they are quite sure of being right. But when they are sure (such reasoners may say), it is not conscientiousness but cowardice to shrink from acting on their opinions and allow doctrines which they honestly think dangerous to the welfare of mankind, either in this life or in another, to be scattered abroad without restraint, because other people, in less enlightened times, have persecuted opinions now believed to be true. Let us take care, it may be said, not to make the same mistake; but governments and nations have made mistakes in other things which are not denied to be fit subjects for the exercise of authority: they have laid on bad taxes, made unjust wars. Ought we therefore to lay on no taxes and, under whatever provocation, make no wars? Men and governments must act to the best of their ability. There is no such thing as absolute certainty, but there is assurance sufficient for the purposes of human life. We may, and must, assume our opinion to be true for the guidance of our own conduct; and it is assuming no more when we forbid bad men to pervert society by the propagation of opinions which we regard as false and pernicious.

I answer, that it is assuming very much more. There is the greatest difference between presuming an opinion to be true because, with every opportunity for contesting it, it has not been refuted, and assuming its truth for the purpose of not permitting its refutation. Complete liberty of contradicting and disproving our opinion is the very condition which justifies us in assuming its truth for purposes of action; and on no other terms can a being with human faculties have any rational assurance of being right.

When we consider either the history of opinion or the ordinary conduct of human life, to what is it to be ascribed that the one and the other are no worse than they are? Not certainly to the inherent force of the human understanding, for on any matter not self-evident there are ninety-nine persons totally incapable of judging of it for one who is capable; and the capacity of the hundredth person is only comparative, for the majority of the eminent men of every past generation held many opinions now known to be erroneous, and did or approved numerous things which no one will now justify. Why is it, then, that there is on the whole a preponderance among mankind of rational opinions and rational conduct? If there really is this preponderance—which there must be unless human affairs are, and have always been, in an almost desperate state—it is owing to a quality of the human mind, the source of everything respectable in man either as an intellectual or as a moral being, namely, that his errors are corrigible. He is capable of rectifying his mistakes by discussion and experience. Not by experience alone. There must be discussion to show how experience is to be interpreted. Wrong opinions and practices gradually yield to fact and argument; but facts and arguments, to produce any effect on the mind, must be brought before it. Very few facts are able to tell their own story, without comments to bring out their meaning. The whole strength and value, then, of human judgment depending on the one property, that it can be set right when it is wrong, reliance can be placed on it only when the means of setting it right are kept constantly at hand. In the case of any person whose judgment is really deserving of confidence, how has it become so? Because he has kept his mind open to criticism of his opinions and conduct. Because it has been his practice to listen to all that could be said against him; to profit by as much of it as was just, and to expound to himself, and upon occasion to others, the fallacy of what was fallacious. Because he has felt that the only way in which a human being can make some approach to knowing the whole of a subject is by hearing what can be said about it by persons of every variety of opinion, and studying all modes in which it can be looked at by every character of mind. No wise man ever acquired his wisdom in any mode but this; nor is it in the nature of human intellect to become wise in any other manner. The steady habit of correcting and completing his own opinion by collating it with those of others, so far from causing doubt and hesitation in carrying it into practice, is the only stable foundation for a just reliance on it; for, being cognizant of all that can, at least obviously, be said against him, and having taken up his position against all gainsayers—knowing that he has sought for objections and difficulties instead of avoiding them, and has shut out no light which can be thrown upon the subject from any quarter—he has a right to think his judgment better than that of any person, or any multitude, who have not gone through a similar process. . . .

In order more fully to illustrate the mischief of denying a hearing to opinions because we, in our own judgment, have condemned them, it will be desirable to fix down the discussion to a concrete case; and I choose, by preference, the cases which are least favorable to me—in which the argument against freedom of opinion, both on the score of truth and on that of utility, is considered the strongest. Let the opinions impugned be the belief in a God and in a future state, or any of the commonly received doctrines of morality. To fight the battle on such ground gives a great advantage to an unfair antagonist, since he will be sure to say (and many who have no desire to be unfair will say it internally), Are these the doctrines which you do not deem sufficiently certain to be taken under the protection of law? Is the belief in a God one of the opinions to feel sure of which you hold to be assuming infallibility? But I must be permitted to observe that it is not the feeling sure of a doctrine (be it what it may) which I call an assumption of infallibility. It is the undertaking to decide that question *for others,* without allowing them to hear what can be said on the contrary side. And I denounce and reprobate this pretension not the less if put forth on the side of my most solemn convictions. However positive anyone's persuasion may be, not only of the falsity but of the pernicious consequences—not only of the pernicious consequences, but (to adopt expressions which I altogether condemn) the immorality and impiety of an opinion—yet if, in pursuance of that private judgment, though backed by the public judgment of his country or his contemporaries, he prevents the opinion from being heard in its defense, he assumes infallibility. And so far from the assumption being less objectionable or less dangerous because the opinion is called immoral or impious, this is the case of all others in which it is most fatal. These are exactly the occasions on which the men of one generation commit those dreadful mistakes which excite the astonishment and horror of posterity. It is among such that we find the instances memorable in history, when the arm of the law has been employed to root out the best men and the noblest doctrines; with deplorable success as to the men, though some of the doctrines have survived to be (as if in mockery) invoked in defense of similar conduct toward those who dissent from *them,* or from their received interpretation.

Mankind can hardly be too often reminded that there was once a man called Socrates, between whom and the legal authorities and public opinion of his time there took place a memorable collision. Born in an age and country abounding in individual greatness, this man has been handed down to us by those who best knew both him and the age as the most virtuous man in it. . . . This acknowledged master of all the eminent thinkers who have since lived—whose fame, still growing after more than two thousand years, all but outweighs the whole remainder of the names which make his native city illustrious—was put to death by his countrymen, after a judicial conviction, for impiety and immorality. Impiety, in denying the gods recognized by the State; indeed, his accuser asserted (see the *Apologia*) that he believed in no gods at all. Immorality, in being, by his doctrines and instructions, a "corruptor of youth." Of these charges the tribunal, there is every ground for believing, honestly found him guilty, and condemned the man who probably of all then born had deserved best of mankind to be put to death as a criminal.

To pass from this to the only other instance of judicial iniquity, the mention of which, after the condemnation of Socrates, would not be an anticlimax: the event which took place on Calvary rather more than eighteen hundred years ago. The man who left on the memory of those who witnessed his life and conversation such an impression of his moral grandeur that eighteen subsequent centuries have done homage to him as the Almighty in person, was ignominiously put to death, as what? As a blasphemer. Men did not merely mistake their benefactor, they mistook him for the exact contrary of what he was and treated him as that prodigy of impiety which they themselves are now held to be for their treatment of him. The feelings with which mankind now regard these lamentable transactions, especially the later of the two, render them extremely unjust in their judgment of the unhappy actors. . . . Orthodox Christians who are tempted to think that those who stoned to death the first martyrs must have been worse men than they themselves are ought to remember that one of those persecutors was Saint Paul. . . .

Let us now pass to the second division of the argument, and dismissing the supposition that any of the received opinions may be false, let us assume them to be true and examine into the worth of the manner in which they are likely to be held when their truth is not freely and openly canvassed. However unwillingly a person who has a strong opinion may admit the possibility that his opinion may be false, he ought to be moved by the consideration that, however true it may be, if it is not fully, frequently, and fearlessly discussed, it will be held as a dead dogma, not a living truth.

There is a class of persons (happily not quite so numerous as formerly) who think it enough if a person assents undoubtingly to what they think true, though he has no knowledge whatever of the grounds of the opinion and could not make a tenable defense of it against the most superficial objections. Such persons, if they can once get their creed taught from authority, naturally think that no good, and some harm, comes of its being allowed to be questioned. Where their influence prevails, they make it nearly impossible for the received opinion to be rejected wisely and considerately, though it may still be rejected rashly and ignorantly; for to shut out discussion entirely is seldom possible, and when it once gets in, beliefs not grounded on conviction are apt to give way before the slightest semblance of an argument. Waiving, however, this possibility—assuming that the true opinion abides in the mind, but abides as a prejudice, a belief independent of, and proof against, argument—this is not the way in which truth ought to be held by a rational being. This is not knowing the truth. Truth, thus held, is but one superstition the more, accidentally clinging to the words which enunciate a truth.

If the intellect and judgment of mankind ought to be cultivated, a thing which Protestants at least do not deny, on what can these faculties be more appropriately exercised by anyone than on the things which concern him so much that it is considered necessary for him to hold opinions on them? If the cultivation of the understanding consists in one thing more than in another, it is surely in learning the grounds of one's own opinions. Whatever people believe, on subjects on which it is of the first importance to believe rightly, they ought to be able to defend against at least the common objections. But, someone may say, "Let them be *taught* the grounds of their opinions. It does not follow that opinions must be merely parroted because they are never heard controverted. Persons who learn geometry do not simply commit the theorems to memory, but understand and learn likewise the demonstrations; and it would be absurd to say that they remain ignorant of the grounds of geometrical truths because they never hear anyone deny and attempt to disprove them." Undoubtedly: and such teaching suffices on a subject like mathematics, where there is nothing at all to be said on the wrong side of the question. The peculiarity of the evidence of mathematical truths is that all the argument is on one side. There are no objections, and no answers to objections. But on every subject on which difference of opinion is possible, the truth depends on a balance to be struck between two sets of conflicting reasons. Even in natural philosophy, there is always some other explanation possible of the same facts; some geocentric theory instead of heliocentric, some phlogiston instead of oxygen; and it has to be shown why that other theory cannot be the true one; and until this is shown, and until we know how it is shown, we do not understand the grounds of our opinion. But when we turn to subjects infinitely more complicated, to morals, religion, politics, social relations, and the business of life, three-fourths of the arguments for every disputed opinion consist in dispelling the appearances which favor some opinion different from it. The greatest orator, save one, of antiquity, has left it on record that he always studied his adversary's case with as great, if not still greater, intensity than even his own. What Cicero practiced as the means of forensic success requires to be imitated by all who study any subject in order to arrive at the truth. He who knows only his own side of the case knows little of that. His reasons may be good, and no one may have been able to refute them. But if he is equally unable to refute the reasons on the opposite side, if he does not so much as know what they are, he has no ground for preferring either opinion. The rational position for him would be suspension of judgment, and unless he contents himself with that, he is either led by authority or adopts, like the generality of the world, the side to which he feels most inclination. Nor is it enough that he should hear the arguments of adversaries from his own teachers, presented as they state them, and accompanied by what they offer as refutations. That is not the way to do justice to the arguments or bring them into real contact with his own mind. He must be able to hear them from persons who actually believe them, who defend them in earnest and do their very utmost for them. He must know them in their most plausible and persuasive form; he must feel the whole force of the difficulty which the true view of the subject has to encounter and dispose of, else he will never really possess himself of the portion of truth which meets and removes that difficulty. Ninety-nine in a hundred of what are called educated men are in this condition, even of those who can argue fluently for their opinions. Their conclusion may be true, but it might be false for anything they know; they have never thrown themselves into the mental position of those who think differently from them, and considered what such persons may have to say; and, consequently, they do not, in any proper sense of the word, know the doctrine which they themselves profess. . . .

We have now recognized the necessity to the mental well-being of mankind (on which all their other well-being depends) of freedom of opinion, and freedom of the expression of opinion, on four distinct grounds, which we will now briefly recapitulate:

First, if any opinion is compelled to silence, that opinion may, for aught we can certainly know, be true. To deny this is to assume our own infallibility.

Secondly, though the silenced opinion be an error, it may, and very commonly does, contain a portion of truth; and since the general or prevailing opinion on any subject is rarely or never the whole truth, it is only by the collision of adverse opinions that the remainder of the truth has any chance of being supplied.

Thirdly, even if the received opinion be not only true, but the whole truth; unless it is suffered to be, and actually is, vigorously and earnestly contested, it will, by most of those who receive it, be held in the manner of a prejudice, with little comprehension or feeling of its rational grounds. And not only this, but, fourthly, the meaning of the doctrine itself will be in danger of being lost or enfeebled, and deprived of its vital effect on the character and conduct: the dogma becoming a mere formal profession, inefficacious for good, but cumbering the ground and preventing the growth of any real and heartfelt conviction from reason or personal experience.

Chapter III

Of Individuality, as one of the Elements of Well-being

Such being the reasons which make it imperative that human beings should be free to form opinions, and to express their opinions without reserve; and such the baneful consequences to the intellectual, and through that to the moral nature of man, unless this liberty is either conceded, or asserted in spite of prohibition; let us next examine whether the same reasons do not require that men should be free to act upon their opinions—to carry these out in their lives, without hindrance, either physical or moral, from their fellow-men, so long as it is at their own risk and peril. This last proviso is of course indispensable. No one pretends that actions should be as free as opinions. On the contrary, even opinions lose their immunity, when the circumstances in which they are expressed are such as to constitute their expression a positive instigation to some mischievous act. An opinion that corndealers are starvers of the poor, or that private property is robbery, ought to be unmolested when simply circulated through the press, but may justly incur punishment when delivered orally to an excited mob assembled before the house of a corn-dealer, or when handed about among the same mob in the form of a placard. Acts of whatever kind, which, without justifiable cause, do harm to others, may be, and in the more important cases absolutely require to be, controlled by the unfavorable sentiments, and, when needful, by the active interference of mankind. The liberty of the individual must be thus far limited; he must not make himself a nuisance to other people. But if he refrains from molesting others in what concerns them, and merely acts according to his own inclination and judgment in things which concern himself, the same reasons which show that opinion should be free, prove also that he should be allowed, without molestation, to carry his opinions into practice at his own cost. That mankind are not infallible; that their truths, for the most part, are only half-truths; that unity of opinion, unless resulting from the fullest and freest comparison of opposite opinions, is not desirable, and diversity not an evil, but a good, until mankind are much more capable than at present of recognizing all sides of the truth, are principles applicable to men's modes of action, not less than to their opinions. As it is useful that while mankind are imperfect there should be different opinions, so is it that there should be different experiments of living; that free scope should be given to varieties of character, short of injury to others; and that the worth of different modes of life should be proved practically, when any one thinks fit to try them. It is desirable, in short, that in things which do not primarily concern others, individuality should assert itself. Where, not the person's own character, but the traditions of customs of other people are the rule of conduct, there is wanting one of the principal ingredients of human happiness, and quite the chief ingredient of individual and social progress. . . .

Study Questions

1. How does Mill defend his claim that "He who knows only his own side of the case knows little of that"?
2. Do we learn more from listening to those with whom we disagree than from those with whom we agree?
3. How would Mill react to the suggestion that a speaker with views demeaning some members of the student body for their race should be banned from speaking at a university campus?
4. Do you believe a society is justified in banning the expression of an opinion universally regarded as false?

Limiting Free Speech

Miles Unterreiner

Due in large part to a fraudulent article that claimed a link between vaccination and autism, measles is on the rise in states where it was previously thought eradicated. Given that the information propounded by antivaccination campaigners is false and potentially harmful, should it be limited? Miles Unterreiner, Rhodes Scholar at Oxford University, defends the case for doing so. He observes that most liberal states already limit speech, such as false advertising, that may cause harm, and he argues that spreading misinformation about vaccination should similarly be restricted.

Philosophical arguments concerning freedom of speech have traditionally focused upon which types of expression the state apparatus may justly limit, and under which circumstances it may do so. The state has therefore been the locus of history's most celebrated works on the subject, perhaps most famously J. S. Mill's *On Liberty* (1859). Mill's argument in favor of the free exchange of ideas remains today the most lasting and the most relevant, and his formulation of the "harm principle"—that "the only purpose for which power can be rightfully exercised over any member of a civilized community, against his will, is to prevent harm to others"—continues to undergird significant components of law and policy in industrialized democracies today.[1]

The modern state about which Mill wrote, however, now faces a peculiarly modern challenge that it is increasingly finding itself ill-equipped to handle: an admixture of infectious disease with a series of public campaigns intended to undermine the very vaccination programs designed to combat infectious disease.

From Miles Unterreiner.

Information spreads quickly now. So do viruses. What is the state to do when the two intertwine?

This December, an outbreak of measles erupted at Disneyland theme park in Anaheim, California, United States of America. By mid-January, the virus had spread north to San Francisco, infecting (thus far) at least 70 people across the state.[2]

Measles is a highly contagious airborne disease that typically manifests itself in a red splotchy rash that covers the entire body and is often accompanied by a fever and cough. In certain cases, however, measles is much more dangerous. According to the World Health Organization, approximately 145,700 persons died from measles worldwide in 2013.[3]

According to public health officials, the best way to stop the spread of measles is to receive a vaccine shot—an inert sample of the virus that effectively trains the body's immune system to resist the real thing. Prior to the start of the United States' national measles vaccination program in 1963, that country reported between 3 and 4 million cases of measles annually. Of persons infected each year, between 400 and 500 died and approximately 48,000 were hospitalized. Thanks to intensive national vaccination efforts, however, the measles virus has been considered eradicated in the United States since the year 2000.[4]

So why is measles back?

The answer can largely be traced not to a new or mutant form of the virus, but to the spread of something much more difficult to combat: false information.

Antivaccination campaigns now pose a significant threat to public health efforts around the globe. Such campaigns are sometimes grounded in objections based on religious, philosophical, or ethical grounds. Frequently, however, they are based upon the distribution of incorrect empirical information about vaccines themselves.

In 1998, research in *The Lancet*, a British medical journal, appeared to demonstrate a link between the MMR vaccine—the vaccine most frequently given to children to prevent measles—and increased autism rates in children. The editor-in-chief of the *British Medical Journal* (*BMJ*) announced in 2011 that this research had been found to be fraudulent,[5] and the paper's lead author was found guilty of professional misconduct and barred from practicing medicine in the United Kingdom.

By then, however, it was too late. MMR vaccination rates dropped significantly in the United Kingdom after the fraudulent *Lancet* article was published, from 91 percent in 1998 to 80 percent in 2003.

The number of new measles cases rose accordingly, from 56 in 1998 to 1,370 in 2008.[6] By 2008, the disease was endemic to the UK, a country in which it had once been eradicated.[7] Professor Dennis K. Flaherty of the University of West Virginia has called the vaccine–autism scare perhaps "the most damaging medical hoax of the last 100 years."[8]

What may the state do about all this, if anything? Certainly few people doubt that the state may permissibly spread correct information as widely as possible, or fund public health vaccination programs to encourage wider uptake of vaccines. But what if these strategies prove to be insufficient? May the state justifiably limit the free speech of antivaccination campaigners, and if so, on what grounds might it do so?

Antivaccination advocates have already begun to stake out a principled free-speech argument in favor of their cause. When every venue in Australia at which she had hoped to speak canceled her invitations this month, antivaccine campaigner Sherri Tenpenny's organization replied that this tactic amounted to "bullying by vested interests who do not believe in informed consent, free speech and respect for other's rights, and who appear to support censorship of thought and science."[9]

Persons conditioned to believe in the inherent value of free speech—myself included—are often inclined to agree with Tenpenny that limiting speech in this way is not permissible. I believe the public has in mind here some form of Mill's harm principle—that actions which do not harm others should not be limited by the state—combined with some sort of belief that speech acts do not cause "harm" in a morally relevant way.

But there are clearly at least some cases in which speech acts can be considered to cause harm, and in which the speaker may be rightly held responsible for the harm thus caused. Consider the case of John, who thinks that vaccines don't work and has decided to host a public reading of a popular antivaccine pamphlet. In order to reach the maximum number of people, John purchases a loudspeaker and advertises the reading widely online. But imagine that John, his loudspeaker, and the assembled crowd all gather in a remote mountain village where the sound waves generated by loud noises are known to trigger deadly avalanches. John boldly asserts that his right to free speech outweighs the harm to others that is likely to follow, and begins to read the antivaccine pamphlet aloud into his megaphone. The avalanche that follows kills 5 people and injures 500. I think it is clear that John has harmed these people, and harmed them in the same sense that he would have harmed them had he stood on top of the mountain and drilled away at the snow with a sledgehammer.

Moral responsibility for harm caused by speech can clearly extend even to cases where the thoughts and beliefs of other persons intermediate between speech and the harm it causes. Imagine that John knows that there are two bridges across a narrow canyon, and that one of the bridges is faulty and likely to collapse. Nonetheless, when a band of unknowing travelers arrives at the canyon, John advises them to avoid the safe bridge because its construction was sponsored by a major pharmaceutical company. In the resulting collapse of the unsafe bridge, 3 people die and 47 are injured.

Speech is far from unlimited in the real world, where the law often delineates circumstances in which the state may limit free expression when it causes sufficiently proximate harm. Virtually every democracy, for instance, prohibits false advertising, in which companies make knowingly false claims in order to sell a product—one cannot make a claim that a product is safe if it has been conclusively shown to be dangerous, for example. After a long series of legal battles, cigarette companies are now required in many countries to mark their products and advertisements with labels informing consumers of the health risks—a clear limitation on unfettered free speech. Likewise, accurate nutrition labels are almost always required on food containers so that consumers know which ingredients are in the food they are eating; companies cannot advertise a donut, for example, as containing valuable vitamins when the donut in fact consists purely of butter, sugar, and chocolate flavoring.

Is waging an antivaccination campaign sufficiently like causing avalanches, or like advertising cigarettes, to warrant legal limitation? There are several arguments one could make to contend that it is not, and that antivaccination campaigns ought to qualify for free speech protection.

The first is that by leaving themselves unvaccinated, persons are harming only themselves, and that the self-harm caused by refusing to vaccinate oneself is itself something Mill would (and we should) protect under the harm principle. This is not so. Many persons harmed by antivaccination campaigns are children deliberately left unvaccinated by their parents, and Mill himself admits that one may harm another "not only by his actions but by his inaction, and in either case he is justly accountable to them for the injury."[10] Persons who leave themselves or their children unvaccinated also pose a significant threat to the health of other parents' children below the age at which vaccinations may be administered (usually 12 months); highly contagious infectious diseases, particularly airborne ones, are very easily transmissible to babies who have not yet been vaccinated.

The second objection will be that the harm caused is too indirect to warrant state interference—that there are too many steps in between advising people to avoid vaccines and children falling sick to justify limiting the original advice. But the number of steps involved does not necessarily indicate that a chain of causation is not clear. If I pull a lever which I know will give painful electric shocks to 50 people, is it any morally different if the lever will knock over a ball which will roll into a set of dominoes which will knock over their own chains of additional dominoes and eventually trigger a switch that causes 50 people to suffer electric shocks?

A third objection may be on practical grounds—that the state cannot possibly halt such speech in an age dominated by social media. Whether it would be right to stop the spread of false information and whether it is possible or effective, however, are two different things. The fact that the state cannot stop all theft, for instance, should not prevent it from prosecuting some thieves.

Limiting speech on public safety grounds need not take the form of men in black masks kicking down doors in the night to take away those with whom we disagree. It may be, depending on the nature and proximity of the harm caused, as innocuous as mandating a warning label to keep consumers fully informed of risks. (This is tricky in the vaccine case, since it is difficult to place a warning label on nothing, and nothing is precisely what antivaccine campaigners urge their fellow citizens to inject.) The precise form speech restrictions take, however, may vary; it is the basic ethical question of whether the state may impose some form of limitation that must first be answered.

I do not pretend to have answered it. But whether antivaccination campaigns qualify for free speech protection is a question that may quite literally determine whether some people live or die, and it is at the very least a question worthy of further consideration.

Notes

1. Mill, John Stuart. *On Liberty*. London: Longman, Roberts, & Co., 1869.
2. Chang Alicia, "Measles Outbreak Casts Spotlight on Anti-Vaccine Movement," *The San Francisco Chronicle*, 23 January 2015. Accessed 23 January 2015 at http://www.sfgate.com/news/medical/article/Disney-parks-linked-measles-outbreak-grows-to-70-6031882.php.

3. World Health Organization, "Measles: Fact Sheet No. 286," November 2014. Accessed 22 January 2015 at http://www.who.int/mediacentre/factsheets/fs286/en/.
4. Centers for Disease Control and Prevention, "Frequently Asked Questions About Measles in the U.S.," 21 January 2015. Accessed 22 January 2015 at http://www.cdc.gov/measles/about/faqs.html.
5. Godlee, Fiona, Jane Smith and Harvey Marcovitch, "Wakefield's Article Linking MMR Vaccine and Autism Was Fraudulent," *BMJ*, 2011; 342:c7452. Accessed 22 January 2015 at http://www.bmj.com/content/342/bmj.c7452.full.
6. Flaherty, Dennis K., "The Vaccine-Autism Connection: A Public Health Crisis Caused by Unethical Medical Practices and Fraudulent Science." *Annals of Pharmacotherapy* October 2011 Vol. 45 No. 10. Accessed 22 January 2015 at http://aop.sagepub.com/content/45/10/1302.full.
7. Batty, David, "Record Number of Measles Cases Sparks Fear of Epidemic," *The Guardian*, 9 January 2009.
8. Flaherty, Dennis K., "The Vaccine-Autism Connection: A Public Health Crisis Caused by Unethical Medical Practices and Fraudulent Science." *Annals of Pharmacotherapy*, October 2011 Vol. 45 No. 10. Accessed 22 January 2015 at http://aop.sagepub.com/content/45/10/1302.full.
9. Medew, Julia, "Anti-Vaccination Campaigner Sherri Tenpenny's Tour in Jeopardy," *The Sydney Morning Herald*, 20 January 2015.
10. Mill, John Stuart. *On Liberty*. London: Longman, Roberts, & Co., 1869.

Study Questions

1. Does failing to vaccinate your child risk harm to others?
2. Can expressing ideas cause harm?
3. Does Unterreiner's reasoning imply that the state should be entitled to limit the expression of such revolutionary ideas as anarchism or communism?
4. Does Unterreiner's reasoning imply that the state should be entitled to limit hate speech?

Regulating Racist Speech on Campus

Charles R. Lawrence III

Charles R. Lawrence III is Professor of Law at the University of Hawai'i at Manoa. He argues in favor of the Stanford Code, which regulates speech that constitutes harassment on the basis of sex, race, color, disability, religion, sexual orientation, or national and ethnic origin. Lawrence maintains that such speech, like receiving a slap on the face, chills rather than promotes discussion. The intent of such insults is not to discover truth or initiate dialogue, but to injure the victim. Thus Lawrence argues that such slurs should be banned from universities, which are committed to maintaining open inquiry.

Much recent debate over the efficacy of regulating racist speech has focused on the efforts by colleges and universities to respond to the burgeoning incidents of racial harassment on their campuses. At Stanford, where I teach, there has been considerable controversy over whether racist and other discriminatory verbal harassment should be regulated and what form any regulation should take. Proponents of regulation have been sensitive to the danger of inhibiting expression, and the current regulation (which was drafted by my colleague Tom Grey) manifests that sensitivity. It is drafted somewhat more narrowly than I would have preferred, leaving unregulated hate speech that occurs in settings where there is a captive audience, but I largely agree with this regulation's substance and approach. I include it here as one example of a regulation of racist speech that I would argue

From Charles R. Lawrence III, "If He Hollers Let Him Go," *Duke Law Journal* 3 (1990).

violates neither first amendment precedent nor principle. The regulation reads as follows:

Fundamental Standard Interpretation: Free Expression and Discriminatory Harassment

1. Stanford is committed to the principles of free inquiry and free expression. Students have the right to hold and vigorously defend and promote their opinions, thus entering them into the life of the University, there to flourish or wither according to their merits. Respect for this right requires that students tolerate even expression of opinions which they find abhorrent. Intimidation of students by other students in their exercise of this right, by violence or threat of violence, is therefore considered to be a violation of the Fundamental Standard.

2. Stanford is also committed to principles of equal opportunity and nondiscrimination. Each student has the right to equal access to a Stanford education, without discrimination on the basis of sex, race, color, handicap, religion, sexual orientation, or national and ethnic origin. Harassment of students on the basis of any of these characteristics tends to create a hostile environment that makes access to education for those subjected to it less than equal. Such discriminatory harassment is therefore considered to be a violation of the Fundamental Standard.

3. This interpretation of the Fundamental Standard is intended to clarify the point at which protected free expression ends and prohibited discriminatory harassment begins. Prohibited harassment includes discriminatory intimidation by threats of violence, and also includes personal vilification of students on the basis of their sex, race, color, handicap, religion, sexual orientation, or national and ethnic origin.

4. Speech or other expression constitutes harassment by vilification if it:

a) is intended to insult or stigmatize an individual or a small number of individuals on the basis of their sex, race, color, handicap, religion, sexual orientation, or national and ethnic origin; and
b) is addressed directly to the individual or individuals whom it insults or stigmatizes; and
c) makes use of "fighting" words or non-verbal symbols.

In the context of discriminatory harassment, "fighting" words or nonverbal symbols are words, pictures or symbols that, by virtue of their form, are commonly understood to convey direct and visceral hatred or contempt for human beings on the basis of their sex, race, color, handicap, religion, sexual orientation, and national and ethnic origin.[1]

This regulation and others like it have been characterized in the press as the work of "thought police," but the rule does nothing more than prohibit intentional face-to-face insults, a form of speech that is unprotected by the first amendment. When racist speech takes the form of face-to-face insults, catcalls, or other assaultive speech aimed at an individual or a small group of persons, then it falls within the "fighting words" exception to first amendment protection. The Supreme Court has held that words that "by their very utterance inflict injury or tend to incite an immediate breach of the peace"[2] are not constitutionally protected.

Face-to-face racial insults, like fighting words, are undeserving of first amendment protection for two reasons. The first reason is the immediacy of the injurious impact of racial insults. The experience of being called "nigger," "spic," "Jap," or "kike" is like receiving a slap in the face. The injury is instantaneous. There is neither an opportunity for intermediary reflection on the idea conveyed nor an opportunity for responsive speech. The harm to be avoided is both clear and present. The second reason that racial insults should not fall under protected speech relates to the purpose underlying the first amendment. The purpose of the first amendment is to foster the greatest amount of speech. Racial insults disserve that purpose. Assaultive racist speech functions as a preemptive strike. The racial invective is experienced as a blow, not a proffered idea, and once the blow is struck, it is unlikely that dialogue will follow. Racial insults are undeserving of first amendment protection because the perpetrator's intention is not to discover truth or initiate dialogue, but to injure the victim.

The fighting words doctrine anticipates that the verbal slap in the face of insulting words will provoke a violent response, resulting in a breach of the peace. When racial insults are hurled at minorities, the response may be silence or flight rather than a fight, but the preemptive effect on further speech is the same. Women and minorities often report that they find themselves speechless in the face of discriminatory verbal attacks. This inability to respond is not the result of oversensitivity among these groups, as some individuals who oppose protective regulation have argued. Rather it is the product of several factors, all of which evidence the nonspeech character of the initial preemptive verbal assault. The first factor is that the visceral emotional response to personal attack precludes speech. Attack produces an instinctive, defensive psychological reaction. Fear, rage, shock, and flight all interfere with any reasoned response. Words like "nigger," "kike," and "faggot" produce physical symptoms that temporarily disable the victim, and the perpetrators often use these words with the intention of producing this effect. Many victims do not find words of response until well after the assault, when the cowardly assaulter has departed.

A second factor that distinguishes racial insults from protected speech is the preemptive nature of such insults—words of response to such verbal attacks may never be forthcoming because speech is usually an inadequate response. When one is personally attacked with words that denote one's subhuman status and untouchability, there is little, if anything, that can be said to redress either the emotional or reputational injury. This is particularly true when the message and meaning of the epithet resonates with beliefs widely held in society. This preservation of widespread beliefs is what makes the face-to-face racial attack more likely to preempt speech than other fighting words do. The racist name caller is accompanied by a cultural chorus of equally demeaning speech and symbols. Segregation and other forms of racist speech injure victims because of their dehumanizing and excluding message. Each individual message gains its power because of the cumulative and reinforcing effect of countless similar messages that are conveyed in a society where racism is ubiquitous.

The subordinated victims of fighting words also are silenced by their relatively powerless position in society. Because of the significance of power and position, the categorization of racial epithets as fighting words provides an inadequate paradigm; instead one must speak of their functional equivalent. The fighting words doctrine presupposes an encounter between two persons of relatively equal power who have been acculturated to respond to face-to-face insults with violence. . . . The fighting words doctrine is a paradigm based on a white male point of view. It captures the "macho" quality of male discourse. It is accepted, justifiable, and even praiseworthy when "real men" respond to personal insult with violence. The fighting words doctrine's responsiveness to this male stance in the world and its blindness to the cultural experience of women is another example of how neutral principles of law reflect the values of those who are dominant.

Black men also are well aware of the double standard that our culture applies in responding to insult. Part of the culture of racial domination through violence—a culture of dominance manifested historically in thousands of lynchings in the South and more recently in the racial violence at Howard Beach and Bensonhurst—is the paradoxical expectation on the part of whites that Black males will accept insult from whites without protest, yet will become violent without provocation. These expectations combine two assumptions: First, that Blacks as a group—and especially Black men—are more violent; and second, that as inferior persons, Blacks have no right to feel insulted. One can imagine the response of universities if Black men started to respond to racist fighting words by beating up white students.

In most situations, minorities correctly perceive that a violent response to fighting words will result in a risk to their own life and limb. This risk forces targets to remain silent and submissive. This response is most obvious when women submit to sexually assaultive speech or when the racist name caller is in a more powerful position—the boss on the job or a member of a violent racist group. Certainly, we do not expect the Black woman crossing the Wisconsin campus to turn on her tormentors and pummel them. Less obvious, but just as significant, is the effect of pervasive racial and sexual violence and coercion on individual members of subordinated groups, who must learn the survival techniques of suppressing and disguising rage and anger at an early age.

One of my students, a white, gay male, related an experience that is quite instructive in understanding the fighting words doctrine. In response to my request that students describe how they experienced the injury of racist speech, Michael told a story of being called "faggot" by a man on a subway. His description included all of the speech-inhibiting elements I have noted previously. He found himself in a state of semishock, nauseous, dizzy, unable to muster the witty, sarcastic, articulate rejoinder he was accustomed to making. He was instantly aware of the recent spate of gay bashing in San Francisco and that many of these incidents had escalated from verbal encounters. Even hours later when the shock subsided and his facility with words returned, he realized that any response was inadequate to counter the hundreds of years of societal defamation that one word—"faggot"—carried with it. Like the word "nigger" and unlike the word "liar," it is not sufficient to deny the truth of the word's application, to say, "I am not a faggot." One must deny the truth of the word's meaning, a meaning shouted from the rooftops by the rest of the world a million times a day. The complex response "Yes, I am a member of the group you despise and the degraded meaning of the word you use is one that I reject" is not effective in a subway encounter. Although there are many of us who constantly and in myriad ways seek to counter the lie spoken in the meaning of hateful words like "nigger" and "faggot," it is a nearly impossible burden to bear when one is ambushed by a sudden, face-to-face hate speech assault.

But there was another part of my discussion with Michael that is equally instructive. I asked if he could remember a situation when he had been verbally attacked with reference to his being a white male. Had he ever been called a "honkey," a "chauvinist pig," or "mick"? (Michael is from a working-class Irish family in Boston.) He said that he had been called some version of all three and that although he found the last one more offensive than the first two, he had not experienced—even in that subordinated role—the same disorienting powerlessness he had experienced when attacked for his membership in the gay community. The question of power, of the context of the power relationships within which speech takes place, and the connection to violence must be considered as we decide how best to foster the freest and fullest dialogue within our communities. Regulation of face-to-face verbal assault in the manner contemplated by the proposed Stanford provision will make room for more speech than it chills. The provision is clearly within the spirit, if not the letter, of existing first amendment doctrine.

The proposed Stanford regulation, and indeed regulations with considerably broader reach, can be justified as necessary to protect a captive audience from offensive or injurious speech. Courts have held that offensive speech may not be regulated in public forums such as streets and parks where listeners may avoid the speech by moving on or averting their eyes, but the regulation of otherwise protected speech has been permitted when the speech invades the privacy of unwilling listeners' homes or when unwilling listeners cannot avoid the speech. Racist posters, flyers, and graffiti in dorms, classrooms, bathrooms, and other common living spaces would fall within the reasoning of these cases. Minority students should not be required to remain in their rooms to avoid racial assault. Minimally, they should find a safe haven in their dorms and other common rooms that are a part of their daily routine. I would argue that the university's responsibility for ensuring these students receive an equal educational opportunity provides a compelling justification for regulations that ensure them safe passage in all common areas. Black, Latino, Asian, or Native American students should not have to risk being the target of racially assaulting speech every time they choose to walk across campus. The regulation of vilifying speech that cannot be anticipated or avoided would not preclude announced speeches and rallies where minorities and their allies would have an opportunity to organize counterdemonstrations or avoid the speech altogether.

Notes

1. Interpretation of the Fundamental Standard defining when verbal or nonverbal abuse violates the student conduct code adopted by the Stanford University Student Conduct Legislative Council, March 14, 1990. *SCLC Offers Revised Reading of Standard, Stanford Daily,* Apr. 4, 1990, §1, col. 4.

   It is important to recognize that this regulation is not content neutral. It prohibits "discriminatory harassment" rather than just plain harassment, and it regulates only discriminatory harassment based on "sex, race, color, handicap, religion, sexual orientation, and national and ethnic origin." It is arguably viewpoint neutral with respect to these categories, although its reference to "words . . . that, by virtue of their form, are commonly understood to convey direct and visceral hatred or contempt" probably means that there will be many more epithets that refer to subordinated groups than words that refer to superordinate groups covered by the regulation.
2. *Chaplinsky v. New Hampshire,* 315 U.S. 568, 572 (1942).

Study Questions

1. Do you find any problems with the Stanford code?
2. Are racist ideas more acceptable than racist epithets?
3. Should slurs against men and majorities be treated the same as slurs against women and minorities?
4. Should a university allow lecturers on campus who use racist speech?

Campus Speech Restrictions

Martin P. Golding

Martin Golding is Professor Emeritus of Philosophy and Law at Duke University. He argues that the Stanford Code, which bars speech that constitutes harassment, is problematic, because it is often unclear what speech is racist or sexist. Consider the much-discussed case of a college student, trying to study, who referred to a noisy group under his window as "water buffalo." Was the term a racial epithet? Some thought so; others not. Golding maintains that demeaning language should be combated by counterargument, not by punitive sanctions. He is concerned that the attempt to police speech may adversely affect the free exchange of ideas that is essential to a university's mission.

The Stanford code is tightly drafted, and it represents a noble effort on Professor Grey's part to protect campus speech to the extent it is compatible with the aim of eliminating discriminatory harassment. The code is *almost*, but not quite, acceptable to me. For even a tightly drafted code can have a chilling effect on speech.

Part of the reason I do not find it entirely acceptable is expressed in the Duke University Law School's "Rules, Policies, and Procedures":

> When students have allowed standards of civility to slip seriously in ways repeatedly hurtful to others entitled to share the campus equally with themselves the response at some universities to such recurrently offensive activities has been more rules. Such requests have been made to us to make more rules, but this is not an undertaking welcomed by us [the law school's administration] or by the faculty. We want you to know why this is so.

From Martin P. Golding, *Free Speech on Campus* (Lanham, MD: Rowman & Littlefield, 2000): pp. 60–64, 69.

> Regulation of student expression, whether of particular viewpoints, or even of the circumstances or manner of their utterance, is a very tricky undertaking. Such rules often convey their own intolerance without meaning to do so. However artfully drawn, they can chill a good deal of provocative expression that is altogether desirable, especially within a lively professional school. They also convey the message that those who carry unpopular messages are being told to be quiet. The business to "judicialize" academic life and our relationships is often also a sign of mutual failure to operate within the common sense notions discussed earlier [good judgment, self-restraint, and civility].[1]

The crucial sentences occur in the second paragraph: "Such rules often convey their own intolerance without meaning to do so. However artfully drawn, they can chill a good deal of provocative expression that is altogether desirable. . . ."

It seems to me that a prohibition on some forms of racist or sexist speech may easily be seen as a general viewpoint-based restriction; certain speech is condoned and other speech is proscribed. It conveys the broader message that speech that doesn't fit in with the official, underlying viewpoint is better not spoken.

Aside from this general concern, to which I shall return, there are other difficulties. Exactly what does Stanford's phrase (4c), "commonly understood to convey direct and visceral hatred or contempt for human beings on the basis of their sex, race," etc., cover? Would a black calling a white a racist offend against the code? Or is this an instance of "victim's privilege"? . . .

Consider the infamous "water buffalo" affair at the University of Pennsylvania, which stretched out over a number of months. On the night of January 13, 1993, a group of women from a black sorority were very loudly singing, chanting, and stomping under Eden Jacobowitz's dormitory window. He was working on a paper for a course. Jacobowitz shouted out, "Please be quiet." The noise continued and he shouted out, "Shut up, you water buffalo." Jacobowitz was then charged with a violation of Penn's policy on racial harassment. While Penn's policy is not identical to Stanford's, it is close to it. Our question is whether Stanford's provision covers this case. It shouldn't, but one doesn't really know.[2]

The Stanford policy is not problem free for people unfairly *charged* with the offense of discriminatory harassment by vilification. There are numerous reports of people, students and faculty, who have been perceived to vilify or harass someone and who were, as a result, put through the wringer. Sometimes they were vindicated in the end, but often the proceedings ended inconclusively, and they ended up being stigmatized as racists, sexists, and so on. Perhaps even more than in the public realm, merely being accused of a "speech offense" on campus can be quite serious.

A good noncampus example of the problem occurred in January 1999 in Washington, D.C. David Howard, the mayoral ombudsman, who is white, said the following at a budget meeting with two coworkers, one of whom was black: "I will have to be niggardly with this fund because it's not going to be a lot of money." The black coworker became incensed; Howard apologized and submitted his resignation, which was quickly accepted by the mayor. The word "niggardly," however, has no connection to the racial slur, which entered English about 1700, from the Latin "niger," or "black." According to etymologists the word "niggardly" goes back to the fourteenth-century Scandinavian term "niggard," meaning "miser," and some speculate that it goes back earlier to a Middle English word. Howard said that he learned the word for his S.A.T. test in high school. His problem was that the word *sounded* like the slur.[3] The indignation industry seems to have been at work here, and many people thought that the mayor did right to accept Howard's resignation immediately rather than rise to his defense; Howard should have watched his language.

But what protection does the Fundamental Standard Interpretation offer someone who is accused of using a word that *sounds* like a term "commonly understood to convey direct and visceral hatred or contempt for human beings on the basis of their sex, race," etc.? It might be answered that it is, first of all, unlikely that such an accusation will be made. After all, what we do want to get at are the egregious cases of verbal harassment, and how else get at them except with a speech code? But what about a male's deliberately calling a female student a "witch" rather than a "bitch," or a white calling a black a "chigger" rather than a "nigger"? Does that get him off the hook? Or are these terms the "equivalent" of an epithet? . . .

I don't mean to be nitpicking here; no code is perfect, and all codes need to be interpreted. However, in order to determine whether some given term has been used as the equivalent of an epithet, we would have to look at the intention of the speaker. But it is precisely this kind of inquiry, once we go beyond a definite list of words, that leads to the fear that "however artfully drawn, [codes] can chill a good deal of provocative expression that is altogether desirable," and "that those who carry unpopular messages are being told to be quiet," as the Duke Rules put it.

Now, one does hope that the Stanford community is knowledgeable enough to make proper distinctions, that enforcement of the policy will be intelligent, and that problem cases, if they arise, will be handled sagaciously. But the opportunity for misunderstanding is present, unfortunately, even for a code that is as finely drawn as Stanford's, and how much more so for more loosely formulated codes! There is little protection afforded by any code against overzealous administrators.

Granted, the Interpretation does require that the speaker "*intended* to insult or stigmatize," in order to hold him or her guilty of harassment by vilification. In contrast to some other campus speech codes, strict liability is rejected. But intent is difficult to prove. More than likely, though, it is the accused who will be put in the difficult position of establishing that he had no such intent. As a number of cases show, and as cases told to me by those involved indicate, a presumption of innocence does not always hold and the disciplinary procedures are not always fair. And even if the accused is found innocent, or the charges are eventually dropped, he will have gone through a terrible ordeal. . . .

Slurs, epithets, and vulgarity—no matter to whom they may be directed, and whether or not face-to-face—should be condemned, and maintaining a positive message of civility is important. But more crucial than the outlawing of single words—which is *almost* acceptable to me—is the general effect on the expression of ideas.

What, then, about *ideas* that stigmatize a group? Ideas, too, can "convey direct and visceral hatred or contempt," for instance, the idea that blacks are intellectually inferior to others. Plainly, a statement to this effect, with or without a gutter epithet, can be as wounding as racial slurs alone. If one wants to penalize "wounding words" it makes no sense to single out gutter epithets, as the African American academic Henry Louis Gates says.

Professor Grey takes up this question. Imagine, he says, this scenario:

> [A] student's habit of loudly proclaiming his admiration for *The Bell Curve* around the dormitory becomes the target of protest by African-American students, who say it is aimed at (and certainly has the effect of) making them feel unwelcome in the university and making it more difficult to do their work. He refuses to stop, and the dispute gets into the campus newspaper, which quotes the offending student as saying that he has no intention of letting "a bunch of affirmative action morons" silence him, and that he hopes "what I'm saying

will get some of them to think about whether they are really qualified to be here. . . ."

Under the Stanford policy that was invalidated, the result would be clear: the white student could be freely criticized, but he would not be in violation of University disciplinary standards. No racial epithet or its equivalent has been addressed to a targeted individual.[4]

Grey's claim is reassuring for those who want controversial ideas to be protected, although his remarks make it plain that the Stanford policy doesn't get to the heart of forestalling "wounded identity." Why shouldn't the student's assertions, "wounding words," after all, be regarded as the equivalent of a racial epithet? True, there was no targeted individual in Grey's example, but we can imagine a case in which there is such a one. . . .

I conclude, so far, that campus speech codes, even one as good as Stanford's, have serious formulation and enforcement problems. . . . I am not happy with this result, though. In any event, demeaning assertions should be combated by counterargument, not by punitive sanctions.

There is little doubt, on the other side, that racist speech may have a distorting effect on the operation of the marketplace of ideas. . . . However, it is not only racist speech that distorts the market. And the attempt to police all speech that might adversely affect the marketplace of ideas would be infeasible and intolerable.

I further admit that the face-to-face use of fighting words and racial slurs, in particular, may have a "silencing" effect on their recipient that impedes free trade in ideas, which trade is the work of the university, because they can impede discussion. ("More speech" will not always immediately work against a targeted attack.) This is true generally of uncivil discourse. Of course, many academic exchanges are quite heated, and the line is sometimes crossed. Again, though, it is the role of teachers to educate students on what the boundaries are and to show them by example that civil debate promotes the search for truth.

Notes

1. Duke University Law School's "Rules, Policies, and Procedures," www.law.duke.edu/general/info/s11.html#policy11-5 (Dean's Statement on Freedom of Expression in the Law School).
2. See the quotation from Grey, at n. 5 ("a racial epithet or its *equivalent*"). The water buffalo incident is described in detail in A. C. Kors and

H. A. Silvergate, *The Shadow University: The Betrayal of Liberty on America's Campuses* (New York: Free Press, 1998), 9–33. The Penn code is quoted at p. 11. The charges generated a body of scholarship on whether "water buffalo" is a racial epithet.

3. See *New York Times*, January 29, 1999, A8 ("Race Mix-Up Raises Havoc for Capital").
4. Thomas C. Grey, "How to Write a Speech Code Without Really Trying: Reflections on the Stanford Experience," 29 *U.C. Davis L. Rev.* 924 (1996). Professor Grey is at this point arguing that the Stanford code is more protective of free speech than an alternative harassment code that very likely would have been upheld, but which would have had the flaw of the potentially chilling vagueness of hostile-environment discrimination. . . . Richard J. Hernstein and Charles Murray, *The Bell Curve: Intelligence and Class in American Life* (New York: Free Press, 1994) is the subject of much debate.

Study Questions

1. Does a speech code imply that some points of view are better unspoken?
2. Should a university permit the expression of ideas that stigmatize a group?
3. How do you assess the "water buffalo" affair?
4. Should a university discipline any person who calls another a "moron"?

B.

Prostitution

Value and the Gift of Sexuality

Elizabeth Anderson

Elizabeth Anderson is Professor of Philosophy and Women's Studies at the University of Michigan. She argues against the legalization of prostitution on the grounds that the commodification of sex degrades its value by making it into something impersonal and instrumental. Sex, instead, should be freely exchanged as a gift based on mutual respect. In response to the claim that people should have the right to enjoy lesser goods in exchange for economic ones, Anderson argues that selling sex in public would lead to the degradation of sex in private. In other words, legally approving the selling of sex would result in the eradication of a sphere in which women could enjoy sex in a non-debased fashion. Thus Anderson concludes that the state should ban prostitution.

. . . In legalizing prostitution, the state would accord women property rights in their bodies that they lack at present. This would enable them to legitimately utilize their sexuality for economic gain without being tied to a particular man who provides them with subsistence. This is thought to represent an advance in women's economic freedom over the

From Elizabeth Anderson, *Value in Ethics and Economics* (Cambridge, MA: Harvard University Press, 1993).

present situation, which legally permits women only to give away their sexuality, and which enables them to gain subsistence in return only by exclusively committing themselves to one husband or lover at a time.

. . . [P]rostitution is the classic example of how commodification debases a gift value and its giver. The specifically human good of sexual acts exchanged as gifts is founded upon a mutual recognition of the partners as sexually attracted to each other and as affirming an intimate relationship in their mutual offering of themselves to each other. This is a shared good. The couple rejoices in their *union*, which can be realized only when each partner reciprocates the other's gift *in kind*, offering her own sexuality in the same spirit in which she received the other's—as a genuine offering of the self. The commodification of sexual "services" destroys the kind of reciprocity required to realize human sexuality as a shared good. Each party values the other only instrumentally, not intrinsically. But the nature of the good exchanged implies a particular degradation of the prostitute. The customer's cash payment is impersonal and fully alienable. In paying the prostitute he yields no power over his person to her. The prostitute sells her own sexuality, which is necessarily embodied in her person. In appropriating her sexuality for his own use, the customer expresses a (de)valuation of women as rightfully male sexual property, as objects to be used for men's own sexual purposes, which need not respond to the woman's own personal needs.

This argument shows that commodified sex is degraded and degrading to the prostitute. It does not show that the sale of sexual services should be prohibited. Why shouldn't people have the freedom to enjoy inferior goods? . . . [A]nd why shouldn't women have the freedom to get something of economic value from their sexuality? [T]he state has a case for prohibiting or restricting commodification of a good if doing so increases freedom—significant opportunities for people to value different kinds of goods in different ways—or if it increases autonomy; that is, the power of people to value goods in ways they reflectively endorse.

It may appear that commodification promotes . . . freedom. Liberals traditionally address plural and conflicting ideals by giving their adherents private spaces to pursue them, protected from state-sponsored interference by adherents of rival ideals. Let those who value sexuality as a higher good enjoy it in non-commodified personal relations, and those who value it as a commodity exchange it on the market. Feminist theory calls into question the viability of this proposal. Although popular ideology represents present modes of non-commodified sexuality in the sphere of personal relations as independent of and sharply contrasted with its commodified forms, there are deep connections between the ways women's sexuality is valued by men in both spheres. When heterosexual masculine identity is partly defined in terms of the power to have sex with a woman, prostitution and pornography supply the unmet demand for sexual intercourse generated internally in the personal sphere; they also provide techniques and models for sexual gratification that men import back into the sphere of personal relations and make normative for their intimate female partners there. The same "private" masculine gender identity creates a demand for virgins, lovers, wives, and prostitutes alike. Women's sexuality is still valued as male property in both spheres; the only question is how many men have rights to it.

I do not claim that women are treated only as sexual property in the personal sphere. I claim that an aspect of masculine identity imposes an appropriative, unshared dimension on heterosexual intercourse there that contradicts the valuational aspirations of both intimacy and commitment. The same power to appropriate a woman's sexuality that is partly definitive of manhood, the same masculine sexual desire, is gratified in personal and commodified sexual relations. If the state took up this same perspective and recognized women's sexuality as just another kind of property, no social space would be left to affirm women's experiences of rape as a worse crime, a deeper violation of the self, than robbery. . . . If women's sexuality is legally valued as a commodity anywhere in society, it would be even more difficult than it already is to establish insulated social spheres where it can be exclusively and fully valued as a genuinely shared and personal good, where women themselves can be sexually valued in ways fully consonant with their own dignity. The full realization of significant opportunities to value heterosexual relationships as shared and personal goods may therefore require that women's sexuality not be commodified. Pluralistic freedom, as well as the dignity of women, may therefore be enhanced by barriers to commodifying sexuality.

The case against prostitution on grounds of autonomy is clearer. The prostitute, in selling her sexuality to a man, alienates a good necessarily embodied in her person to him and thereby subjects herself to his commands. Her actions under contract express not her own valuations but the will of her customer. Her actions between sales express not her own valuations but the will of her pimp. Prostitution does not enhance women's autonomy over their sexuality—it simply constitutes another mode by which men can appropriate it for their own uses. The realization of women's autonomy requires that some goods embodied in their persons, including their own sexuality, remain market-inalienable.

These arguments establish the legitimacy of a state interest in prohibiting prostitution, but not a conclusive case for prohibition. Given the paucity of economic opportunities available to many women, they may have no alternative to selling their sexual services for money. If the prohibition of prostitution is to serve women's interests in freedom and autonomy, it should not function so as to drive them to starvation. It can serve these interests only where expanded economic opportunities eliminate women's need to resort to prostitution. (These interests already support the prohibition of pimping.) My arguments also do not show that the sale of sexual services cannot have a legitimate place in a just civil society. One could imagine a worthwhile practice of professional sex therapy aimed at helping people liberate themselves from perverse, patriarchal forms of sexuality. Such a practice would not be governed by the market norms that make present forms of prostitution objectionable. Professionals do not alienate control over their actions in selling them, but govern their activity by reflectively endorsed norms internal to the nonmarket ideals of their professions. The profession envisioned might help men eliminate the ways commodified conceptions of women's sexuality inform their valuations of women in the personal sphere. This possibility illustrates . . . that what confers commodity status on a good is not that people pay for it, but that exclusively market norms govern its production, exchange, and enjoyment. . . .

Study Questions

1. Does prostitution debase sex?
2. Would selling sex in public affect the role of sex in private relationships?
3. Would selling sex in public diminish anyone's freedom?
4. Do Anderson's arguments against the practice of paying women for sex also apply to the practice of paying men for sex?

Taking Money for Bodily Services

Martha C. Nussbaum

Martha C. Nussbaum, Professor of Law and Ethics at the University of Chicago, maintains that our attitudes toward the legalization of prostitution reflect prejudice, not reason. She examines six professions—factory worker, domestic servant, singer, professor, masseuse, and the hypothetical colonoscopy artist—that take money for bodily services. Each is legal, yet in ways Nussbaum seeks to demonstrate, each has much in common with prostitution. Then she considers the most popular arguments against prostitution. In each case, if the argument succeeds, it would condemn not only prostitution but also at least one of the noncontroversial six professions. Thus Nussbaum argues that the stigma attached to prostitution is not rationally justified. She adds that if the activity were legalized, prostitutes would be better protected than they are now.

I

It will be illuminating to consider the prostitute by situating her in relation to several other women who take money for bodily services:

1. A factory worker in the Perdue chicken factory, who plucks feathers from nearly frozen chickens.
2. A domestic servant in a prosperous upper-middle-class house.
3. A nightclub singer in middle-range clubs, who sings (often) songs requested by the patrons.
4. A professor of philosophy, who gets paid for lecturing and writing.

From Martha C. Nussbaum, "'Whether from Reason or Prejudice': Taking Money for Bodily Services," *Journal of Legal Studies* 27 (1998).

5. A skilled masseuse, employed by a health club (with no sexual services on the side).
6. A person whom I'll call the "colonoscopy artist": she gets paid for having her colon examined with the latest instruments, in order to test out their range and capability.[1]

By considering similarities and differences between the prostitute and these other bodily actors, we will make progress in identifying the distinctive features of prostitution as a form of bodily service. . . .

1. *The Prostitute and the Factory Worker.* Both prostitution and factory work are usually low-paid jobs; but, in many instances, a woman faced with the choice can (at least over the short-haul) make more money in prostitution than in this sort of factory work. . . . Both face health risks, but the health risk in prostitution can be very much reduced by legalization and regulation, whereas the particular type of work the factory worker is performing carries a high risk of nerve damage in the hands, a fact about it that appears unlikely to change. The prostitute may well have better working hours and conditions than the factory worker; especially in a legalized regime, she may have much more control over her working conditions. She has a degree of choice about which clients she accepts and what activities she performs, whereas the factory worker has no choices but must perform the same motions again and again for years. The prostitute also performs a service that requires skill and responsiveness to new situations, whereas the factory worker's repetitive motion exercises relatively little human skill and contains no variety. . . .[2]

2. *The Prostitute and the Domestic Servant.* In domestic service as in prostitution, one is hired by a client and one must do what that client wants or fail at the job. In both, one has a limited degree of latitude to exercise skills as one sees fit, and both jobs require the exercise of some developed bodily skills. In both, one is at risk of enduring bad behavior from one's client, although the prostitute is more likely to encounter physical violence. Certainly both are traditionally professions that enjoy low respect, both in society generally and from the client. Domestic service on the whole is likely to have worse hours and lower pay than (at least many types of) prostitution, but it probably contains fewer health risks. It also involves no invasion of intimate bodily space, as prostitution (consensually) does.

Both prostitution and domestic service are associated with a type of social stigma. In the case of domestic service, the stigma is, first, related to class: it is socially coded as an occupation only for the lowest classes. Domestic servants are in a vast majority of cases female, so it becomes coded by sex. In the United States, domestic service is very often racially coded as well. Not only in the South but also in many parts of the urban North, the labor market has frequently produced a clustering of African American women in these low-paying occupations. In my home in suburban Philadelphia in the 1950s and 1960s, the only African Americans we saw were domestic servants, and the only domestic servants we saw were African American. The perception of the occupation as associated with racial stigma ran very deep, producing difficult tensions and resentments that made domestic service seem to be incompatible with dignity and self-respect. (It needn't be, clearly; and I shall return to this.)

3. *The Prostitute and the Nightclub Singer.* Both of these people use their bodies to provide pleasure, and the customer's pleasure is the primary goal of what they do. This does not mean that a good deal of skill and art isn't involved, and in both cases, it usually is. Both have to respond to requests from the customer, although (in varying degrees depending on the case) both may also be free to improvise or to make suggestions. Both may be paid more or less, have better or worse working conditions, and more or less control over what they do.

How do they differ? The prostitute faces health risks and risks of violence not faced by the singer. She also allows her bodily space to be invaded, as the singer does not. It may also be that prostitution is always a cheap form of an activity that has a higher, better form, whereas this need not be the case in popular vocal performance (though of course it might be). The nightclub singer, furthermore, does not appear to be participating in, or perpetuating, any type of gender hierarchy—although in former times this would not have been the case. . . . Finally, there is no (great) moral stigma attached to being a nightclub singer, although at one time there certainly was.

4. *The Prostitute and the Professor of Philosophy.* These two figures have a very interesting similarity: both provide bodily services in areas that are generally thought to be especially intimate and definitive of selfhood. Just as the prostitute takes money for sex, which is commonly thought to be an area of intimate self-expression, so the professor takes money for thinking and writing about what she thinks—about morality, emotion, the nature of knowledge, whatever—all parts of a human being's intimate search for understanding of the world and

self-understanding. . . . The fact that we do not think that the professor (even one who regularly holds out for the highest salary offered) thereby alienates her mind or turns her thoughts into commodities—even when she writes a paper for a specific conference or volume—should put us on our guard about making similar conclusions in the case of the prostitute.

Other similarities are that in both cases, the performance involves interaction with others, and the form of the interaction is not altogether controlled by the person. In both cases, there is at least an element of producing pleasure or satisfaction (note the prominent role of teaching evaluations in the employment and promotion of professors), although in philosophy there is also a countervailing tradition of thinking that the goal of the interaction is to produce dissatisfaction and unease. . . . It may appear at first that the intimate bodily space of the professor is not invaded—but we should ask about this. When someone's unanticipated argument goes into one's mind, is this not both intimate and bodily? (And far less consensual, often, than the penetration of prostitute by customer?) Both performances involve skill. It might plausibly be argued that the professor's involves a more developed skill, or at least a more expensive training—but we should be cautious here. Our culture is all too ready to think that sex involves no skill and is simply "natural," a view that is surely false and is not even seriously entertained by many cultures.

The salary of the professor, and her working conditions, are usually a great deal better than those of (all but the most elite) prostitutes. The professor has a fair amount of control over the structure of her day and her working environment, although she also has fixed mandatory duties, as the prostitute, when self-employed, does not. If the professor is in a nation that protects academic freedom, she has considerable control over what she thinks and writes, although fads, trends, and peer pressure surely constrain her to some extent. The prostitute's need to please her customer is usually more exigent and permits less choice. . . . Finally, the professor of philosophy, if a female, both enjoys reasonably high respect in the community and also might be thought to bring credit to all women in that she succeeds at an activity commonly thought to be the preserve only of males. She thus subverts traditional gender hierarchy, whereas the prostitute, while suffering stigma herself, may be thought to perpetuate gender hierarchy.

5. *The Prostitute and the Masseuse.* These two bodily actors seem very closely related. Both use a skill to produce bodily satisfaction in

the client. Unlike the nightclub singer, both do this through a type of bodily contact with the client. Both need to be responsive to what the client wants and to a large degree take direction from the client as to how to handle his or her body. The bodily contact involved is rather intimate, although the internal space of the masseuse is not invaded. The type of bodily pleasure produced by the masseuse may certainly have an erotic element, although in the type of "respectable" masseuse I'm considering, it is not directly sexual.

The difference is primarily one of respectability. Practitioners of massage have fought for, and have to a large extent won, the right to be considered as dignified professionals who exercise a skill. Their trade is legal; it is not stigmatized; and people generally do not believe that they degrade their bodies or turn their bodies into commodities by using their bodies to give pleasure to customers. They have positioned themselves alongside physical therapists and medical practitioners, dissociating themselves from the erotic dimension of their activity. As a consequence of this successful self-positioning, they enjoy better working hours, better pay, and more respect than most prostitutes. What is the difference, we might ask? One is having sex, and the other is not. But what sort of difference is this? Is it a difference we want to defend? Are our reasons for thinking it so crucial really reasons, or vestiges of moral prejudice? A number of distinct beliefs enter in at this point: the belief that women should not have sex with strangers, the belief that commercial sex is inherently degrading and makes a woman a degraded woman, the belief that women should not have to have sex with strangers if they do not want to, and in general, the belief that women should have the option to refuse sex with anyone they do not really choose. Some of these beliefs are worth defending, and some are not. (I shall argue that the issue of choice is the really important one.) We need to sort them out and to make sure that our policies are not motivated by views we are not really willing to defend.

6. *The Prostitute and the Colonoscopy Artist.* I have included this hypothetical occupation for a reason that should now be evident: it involves the consensual invasion of one's bodily space. (The example is not so hypothetical, either: medical students need models when they are learning to perform internal exams, and young actors do earn a living playing such roles.) The colonoscopy artist uses her skill at tolerating the fiber-optic probe without anaesthesia to make a living. In the process, she permits an aperture of her body to be penetrated by another person's activity—and, we might add, far more

deeply penetrated than is generally the case in sex. She runs some bodily risk, since she is being used to test untested instruments, and she will probably have to fast and empty her colon regularly enough to incur some malnutrition and some damage to her excretory function. Her wages may not be very good . . . and it may also involve some stigma, given that people are inclined to be disgusted by the thought of intestines.

And yet, on the whole, we do not think that this is a base trade or one that makes the woman who does it a fallen woman. We might want to ban or regulate it if we thought it was too dangerous, but we would not be moved to ban it for moral reasons. Why not? Some people would point to the fact that it does not either reflect or perpetuate gender hierarchy; and this is certainly true. (Even if her being a woman is crucial to her selection for the job—they need to study, for example, both male and female colons—it won't be for reasons that seem connected with the subordination of women.) But surely a far greater part of the difference is made by the fact that most people do not think anal penetration by a doctor in the context of a medical procedure is immoral, whereas lots of people do think that vaginal or anal penetration in the context of sexual relations is (except under very special circumstances) immoral and that a woman who goes in for that is therefore an immoral and base woman.

II

Prostitution, we now see, has many features that link it with other forms of bodily service. It differs from these other activities in many subtle ways: but the biggest difference consists in the fact that it is, today, more widely stigmatized. . . . Opera singers no longer get told that they are unacceptable in polite society. Even the masseuse has won respect as a skilled professional. What is different about prostitution? Two factors stand out as sources of stigma. One is that prostitution is widely held to be immoral; the other is that prostitution (frequently at least) is bound up with gender hierarchy, with ideas that women and their sexuality are in need of male domination and control, and the related idea that women should be available to men to provide an outlet for their sexual desires. The immorality view would be hard to defend today as a justification for the legal regulation of prostitution, and perhaps even for its moral denunciation. People thought prostitution was immoral because they thought nonreproductive and especially extramarital sex was immoral; the prostitute was seen, typically, as a dangerous figure whose whole career was given over to lust. But female lust was (and still often is) commonly seen as bad and dangerous, so prostitution was seen as bad and dangerous. Some people would still defend these views today, but it seems inconsistent to do so if one is not prepared to repudiate other forms of nonmarital sexual activity on an equal basis. We have to grant, I think, that the most common reason for the stigma attached to prostitution is a weak reason, at least as a public reason: a moralistic view about female sexuality that is rarely consistently applied (to premarital sex, for example) and that seems unable to justify restriction on the activities of citizens who have different views of what is good and proper. At any rate, it seems hard to use the stigma so incurred to justify perpetuating stigma through criminalization, unless one is prepared to accept a wide range of . . . laws that interfere with chosen consensual activities, something that most feminist attackers of prostitution rarely wish to do.

More promising as a source of good moral arguments might be the stigma incurred by the connection of prostitution with gender hierarchy. But what is the connection, and how exactly does gender hierarchy explain pervasive stigma? It is only a small minority of people for whom prostitution is viewed in a negative light because of its collaboration with male supremacy; for only a small minority of people at any time have been reflective feminists, concerned with the eradication of inequality. Such people will view the prostitute as they view veiled women or women in purdah: with sympathetic anger, as victims of an unjust system. This reflective feminist critique, then, does not explain why prostitutes are actually stigmatized, held in disdain—both because it is not pervasive enough and because it leads to sympathy rather than to disdain.

The way that gender hierarchy actually explains stigma is a very different way, a way that turns out in the end to be just another form of the immorality charge. People committed to gender hierarchy, and determined to ensure that the dangerous sexuality of women is controlled by men, frequently have viewed the prostitute, a sexually active woman, as a threat to male control of women. They therefore become determined either to repress the occupation itself by criminalization or, if they also think that male sexuality needs such an outlet and that this outlet ultimately defends marriage by giving male desire a safely debased outlet, to keep it within bounds by close regulation. . . .

In short, sex hierarchy causes stigma, commonly, not through feminist critique but through a far more questionable set of social meanings, meanings that anyone concerned with justice for women should call into question. For it is these same meanings that are also used to justify the seclusion of women, the veiling of women, and the genital mutilation of women. The view boils down to the view that women are essentially immoral and dangerous and will be kept in control by men only if men carefully engineer things so that they do not get out of bounds. The prostitute, being seen as the uncontrolled and sexually free woman, is in this picture seen as particularly dangerous, both necessary to society and in need of constant subjugation. As an honest woman, a woman of dignity, she will wreck society. . . .

It appears, then, that the stigma associated with prostitution has an origin that feminists have good reason to connect with unjust background conditions and to decry as both unequal and irrational, based on a hysterical fear of women's unfettered sexuality. There may be other good arguments against the legality of prostitution, but the existence of widespread stigma all by itself does not appear to be among them. So long as prostitution is stigmatized, people are injured by that stigmatization, and it is a real injury to a person not to have dignity and self-respect in her own society. But that real injury (as with the comparable real injury to the dignity and self-respect of interracial couples or of lesbians and gay men) is not best handled by continued legal strictures against the prostitute and can be better dealt with in other ways: for example, by fighting discrimination against these people and taking measures to promote their dignity. . . .

III

Pervasive stigma itself, then, does not appear to provide a good reason for the continued criminalization of prostitution, any more than it does for the illegality of interracial marriage. Nor does the stigma in question even appear to ground a sound *moral* argument against prostitution. This is not, however, the end of the issue: for there are a number of other significant arguments that have been made to support criminalization. With our six related cases in mind, let us now turn to those arguments.

1. *Prostitution Involves Health Risks and Risks of Violence.* To this we can make two replies. First, insofar as this is true, as it clearly is, the problem is made much worse by the illegality of prostitution, which

prevents adequate supervision, encourages the control of pimps, and discourages health checking. . . .

To the extent to which risks remain an inevitable part of the way of life, we must now ask what general view of the legality of risky undertakings we wish to defend. Do we ever want to rule out risky bargains simply because they harm the agent? Or do we require a showing of harm to others (as might be possible in the case of gambling, for example)? Whatever position we take on this complicated question, we will almost certainly be led to conclude that prostitution lies well within the domain of the legally acceptable: for it is probably less risky than boxing, another activity in which working-class people try to survive and flourish by subjecting their bodies to some risk of harm. There is a stronger case for paternalistic regulation of boxing than of prostitution, and externalities (the glorification of violence as example to the young) make boxing at least as morally problematic, probably more so. And yet I would not defend the criminalization of boxing, and I doubt that very many Americans would either. Sensible regulation of both prostitution and boxing, by contrast, seems reasonable and compatible with personal liberty. . . .

2. *The Prostitute Has No Autonomy; Her Activities Are Controlled by Others.* This argument does not serve to distinguish prostitution from very many types of bodily service performed by working-class women. The factory worker does worse on the scale of autonomy, and the domestic servant no better. I think this point expresses a legitimate moral concern: a person's life seems deficient in flourishing if it consists only of a form of work that is totally out of the control and direction of the person herself. . . . It certainly does not help the problem to criminalize prostitution—any more than it would be to criminalize factory work or domestic service. A woman will not exactly achieve more control and "truly human functioning" by becoming unemployed. What we should instead think about are ways to promote more control over choice of activities, more variety, and more general humanity in the types of work that are actually available to people with little education and few options. That would be a lot more helpful than removing one of the options they actually have.

3. *Prostitution Involves the Invasion of One's Intimate Bodily Space.* This argument does not seem to support the legal regulation of prostitution so long as the invasion in question is consensual—that is, that the prostitute is not kidnapped, fraudulently enticed, a child beneath the age of consent, or under duress against leaving if she

should choose to leave. In this sense, prostitution is quite unlike sexual harassment and rape and far more like the activity of the colonoscopy artist—not to everyone's taste, and involving a surrender of bodily privacy that some will find repellant, but not for that reason necessarily bad, either for self or others. The argument does not even appear to support a moral criticism of prostitution, unless one is prepared to make a moral criticism of all sexual contact that does not involve love or marriage.

4. *Prostitution Makes It Harder for People to Form Relationships of Intimacy and Commitment.* This argument is prominently made by Elizabeth Anderson in defense of the criminalization of prostitution.[3] The first question we should ask is, Is this true? People still appear to fall in love in the Netherlands and Germany and Sweden; they also fell in love in ancient Athens, where prostitution was not only legal but also, probably, publicly subsidized. One type of relationship does not, in fact, appear to remove the need for the other—any more than a Jackie Collins novel removes the desire to read Proust. Proust has a specific type of value that is by no means found in Jackie Collins, so people who want that value will continue to seek out Proust, and there is no reason to think that the presence of Jackie Collins on the bookstand will confuse Proust lovers into thinking that Proust is really like Jackie Collins. So too, one supposes, with love in the Netherlands: people who want relationships of intimacy and commitment continue to seek them out for the special value they provide, and they do not have much trouble telling the difference between one sort of relationship and another, despite the availability of both.

Second, one should ask which women Anderson has in mind. Is she saying that the criminalization of prostitution would facilitate the formation of love relationships on the part of the women who were (or would have been) prostitutes? Or is she saying that the unavailability of prostitution as an option for working-class women would make it easier for romantic middle-class women to have the relationships they desire? The former claim is implausible, since it is hard to see how reinforcing the stigma against prostitutes or preventing some poor women from taking one of the few employment options they might have would be likely to improve their human relations. The latter claim might possibly be true (though it is hardly obvious), but it seems a repugnant idea, which I am sure Anderson would not endorse, that we should make poor women poorer so that middle-class women can find love. Third, one should ask Anderson whether she is prepared to endorse the large number of arguments of this form that might plausibly be made in the realm of popular culture and, if not, whether she has any way of showing how she could reject those as involving an unacceptable infringement of liberty and yet allowing the argument about prostitution that she endorses. For it seems plausible that making rock music illegal would increase the likelihood that people would listen to Mozart and Beethoven, that making Jackie Collins illegal would make it more likely that people would turn to Joyce Carol Oates, that making commercial advertising illegal would make it more likely that we would appraise products with high-minded ideas of value in our minds, and that making television illegal would improve children's reading skills. What is certain, however, is that we would and do utterly reject those ideas (we do not even seriously entertain them) because we do not want to live in Plato's *Republic,* with our cultural options dictated by a group of wise guardians, however genuinely sound their judgments may be.

5. *The Prostitute Alienates Her Sexuality on the Market; She Turns Her Sexual Organs and Acts into Commodities.* Is this true? It seems implausible to claim that the prostitute alienates her sexuality just on the grounds that she provides sexual services to a client for a fee. Does the singer alienate her voice, or the professor her mind? The prostitute still has her sexuality; she can use it on her own, apart from the relationship with the client, just as the domestic servant may cook for her family and clean her own house. She can also cease to be a prostitute, and her sexuality will still be with her, and hers, if she does. So she has not even given anyone a monopoly on those services, far less given them over into someone else's hands. The real issue that separates her from the professor and the singer seems to be the degree of choice she exercises over the acts she performs. But is even this a special issue for the prostitute, any more than it is for the factory worker or the domestic servant or the colonoscopy artist—all of whom choose to enter trades in which they will not have a great deal of say over what they do or (within limits) how they do it? Freedom to choose how one works is a luxury, highly desirable indeed, but a feature of few jobs that nonaffluent people perform.

As for the claim that the prostitute turns her sexuality into a commodity, we must ask what that means. If it means only that she accepts a fee for sexual services, then that is obvious; but nothing further has been said that would show us why this is a bad thing. The professor, the singer, the symphony musician—all accept a fee, and it seems plausible that this is a good state of affairs, creating spheres of freedom. Professors are more free to pursue their own thoughts now, as moneymakers, than they were in the days when they were supported by monastic orders; symphony musicians playing under the contract secured by the musicians union have more free time than nonunionized musicians and more opportunities to engage in experimental and solo work that will enhance their art. In neither case should we conclude that the existence of a contract has converted the abilities into things to be exchanged and traded separately from the body of the producer; they remain human creative abilities, securely housed in their possessor. So if, on the one hand, to "commodify" means merely to accept a fee, we have been given no reason to think that this is bad.

If, on the other hand, we try to interpret the claim of "commodification" using the narrow technical definition of "commodity" used by the Uniform Commercial Code,[4] the claim is plainly false. For that definition stresses the "fungible" nature of the goods in question, and "fungible" goods are, in turn, defined as goods "of which any unit is, by nature or usage of trade, the equivalent of any other like unit." While we may not think that the soul or inner world of a prostitute is of deep concern to the customer, she is usually not regarded as simply a set of units fully interchangeable with other units.[5] Prostitutes are probably somewhat more fungible than bassoon players, but not totally so. What seems to be the real issue is that the woman is not attended to as an individual, not considered as a special unique being. But that is true of many ways people treat one another in many areas of life, and it seems implausible that we should use that kind of disregard as a basis for criminalization. It may not even be immoral: for surely we cannot deeply know all the people with whom we have dealings in life, and many of those dealings are just fine without deep knowledge. So our moral question boils down to the question, Is sex without deep personal knowledge always immoral? It seems to me officious and presuming to use one's own experience to give an affirmative answer to this question, given that people have such varied experiences of sexuality. . . .

6. *The Prostitute's Activity Is Shaped By, and In Turn Perpetuates, Male Dominance of Women.* The institution of prostitution as it has most often existed is certainly shaped by aspects of male domination of women. As I have argued, it is shaped by the perception that female sexuality is dangerous and needs careful regulation, that male sexuality

is rapacious and needs a "safe" outlet, that sex is dirty and degrading, and that only a degraded woman is an appropriate sexual object. Nor have prostitutes standardly been treated with respect or been given the dignity one might think proper to a fellow human being. They share this with working-class people of many types in many ages; but, there is no doubt that there are particular features of the disrespect that derive from male supremacy and the desire to lord it over women—as well as from a tendency to link sex to (female) defilement that is common in the history of Western European culture. . . .

Prostitution is hardly alone in being shaped by, and in reinforcing, male dominance. Systems of patrilineal property and exogamous marriage, for example, certainly do more to perpetuate not only male dominance but also female mistreatment and even death. . . .

More generally, one might argue that the institution of marriage as has most frequently been practiced both expresses and reinforces male dominance. It would be right to use law to change the most iniquitous features of that institution—protecting women from domestic violence and marital rape, giving women equal property and custody rights, and improving their exit options by intelligent shaping of the divorce law. But to rule that marriage as such should be illegal on the grounds that it reinforces male dominance would be an excessive intrusion on liberty, even if one should believe marriage irredeemably unequal. So too, I think, with prostitution: what seems right is to use law to protect the bodily safety of prostitutes from assault, to protect their rights to their incomes against the extortionate behavior of pimps, to protect poor women in developing countries from forced trafficking and fraudulent offers, and to guarantee their full civil rights in the countries where they end up—to make them, in general, equals under the law, both civil and criminal. But the criminalization of prostitution seems to pose a major obstacle to that equality. . . .

7. *Prostitution Is a Trade That People Do Not Enter by Choice; Therefore the Bargains People Make within It Should Not Be Regarded as Real Bargains.* Here we must distinguish three cases. First is the case where the woman's entry into prostitution is caused by some type of conduct that would otherwise be criminal: kidnapping, assault, drugging, rape, statutory rape, blackmail, a fraudulent offer. Here we may certainly judge that the woman's choice is not a real choice and that the law should take a hand in punishing her coercer. This is a terrible problem currently in developing countries; international human rights organizations are right to make it a major focus. . . .

Different is the case of an adult woman who enters prostitution because of bad economic options: because it seems a better alternative than the chicken factory, because there is no other employment available to her, and so forth. This too, we should insist, is a case where autonomy has been infringed, but in a different way. . . .

This seems to me the truly important issue raised by prostitution. Like work in the chicken factory, it is not an option many women choose with alacrity when many other options are on their plate. This might not be so in some hypothetical culture in which prostitutes have legal protection, dignity, and respect and the status of skilled practitioner, rather like the masseuse. But it is true now in most societies, given the reality of the (albeit irrational) stigma attaching to prostitution. But the important thing to realize is that this is not an issue that permits us to focus on prostitution in isolation from the economic situation of women in a society generally. Certainly it will not be ameliorated by the criminalization of prostitution, which reduces poor women's options still further. We may grant that poor women do not have enough options and that society has been unjust to them in not extending more options, while nonetheless respecting and honoring the choices they actually make in reduced circumstances. . . .

IV

The stigma traditionally attached to prostitution is based on a collage of beliefs, most of which are not rationally defensible and which should be especially vehemently rejected by feminists: beliefs about the evil character of female sexuality, the rapacious character of male sexuality, the essentially marital and reproductive character of "good" women and "good" sex. Worries about subordination more recently raised by feminists are much more serious concerns, but they apply to many types of work poor women do. Concerns about force and fraud should be extremely urgent concerns of the international women's movement. Where these conditions do not obtain, feminists should view prostitutes as (usually) poor working women with few options, not as threats to the intimacy and commitment that many women and men (including, no doubt, many prostitutes) seek. This does not mean that we should not be concerned about ways in which prostitution as currently practiced, even in the absence of force and fraud, undermines the dignity of women, just as domestic service in the past undermined the dignity of members of a given race or class.

But the correct response to this problem seems to be to work to enhance the economic autonomy and the personal dignity of members of that class, not to rule off-limits an option that may be the only livelihood for many poor women and to further stigmatize women who already make their living this way.

In grappling further with these issues, we should begin from the realization that there is nothing per se wrong with taking money for the use of one's body. That is the way most of us live, and formal recognition of that fact through contract is usually a good thing for people, protecting their security and their employment conditions. What seems wrong is that relatively few people in the world have the option to use their body, in their work, in what Marx would call a "truly human" manner of functioning, by which he meant (among other things) having some choices about the work to be performed, some reasonable measure of control over its conditions and outcome, and also the chance to use thought and skill rather than just to function as a cog in a machine. Women in many parts of the world are especially likely to be stuck at a low level of mechanical functioning, whether as agricultural laborers, factory workers, or prostitutes. The real question to be faced is how to expand the options and opportunities such workers face, how to increase the humanity inherent in their work, and how to guarantee that workers of all sorts are treated with dignity. In the further pursuit of these questions, we need, on balance, more studies of women's credit unions and fewer studies of prostitution.

Notes

1. Although this profession, as described, is hypothetical, medical students do employ "models" to teach students how to perform pelvic and other internal exams.
2. It is probably, however, a developed skill to come to work regularly and to work regular hours each day.
3. See Anderson, *Value in Ethics and Economics*; Anderson pulls back from an outright call for criminalization, concluding that her arguments "establish the legitimacy of a state interest in prohibiting prostitution, but not a conclusive case for prohibition," given the paucity of opportunities for working women.
4. See Richard Epstein, *Surrogacy: The Case for Full Contractual Enforcement*, 81 Va. L. Rev. 2305–41, 2327 (1995).
5. Moreover, the Uniform Commercial Code does not cover the sale of services, and prostitution should be classified as a service rather than a good.

Study Questions

1. In what ways, if any, is a prostitute different from a masseuse?
2. How does Nussbaum respond to Anderson's claim that prostitution erodes the value of non-commodified sex?
3. Would the legalization of prostitution be beneficial to prostitutes?
4. Are Nussbaum's arguments equally applicable to men as well as women who are paid for sex?

Markets in Women's Sexual Labor

Debra Satz

Debra Satz is Professor of Philosophy at Stanford University. She argues that markets in reproduction (e.g., prostitution) are unlike other labor markets (e.g., professional sports) in ways that make a moral difference. Of particular relevance is that women form a social and economically disadvantaged group that is viewed as inferior to men. Satz argues that prostitution is morally wrong because it perpetuates this view of women as subordinate. However, the immorality of prostitution on egalitarian grounds does not entail that prostitution should be illegal. Indeed, given that legalization would help undermine the image of the prostitute as of lesser moral status, Satz concludes that, despite being immoral, prostitution may be legal.

There is a widely shared intuition that markets are inappropriate for some kinds of human endeavor: that some things simply should not be bought and sold. For example, virtually everyone believes that love and friendship should have no price. The sale of other human capacities is disputed, but many people believe that there is something about sexual and reproductive activities that makes their sale inappropriate. I have called the thesis supported by this intuition the asymmetry thesis.[1] Those who hold the asymmetry thesis believe that markets in reproduction and sex are asymmetric to other labor markets. They think that treating sexual and reproductive capacities as commodities, as goods to be developed and exchanged for a price, is worse than treating our other capacities as commodities. They think that there is something wrong with commercial surrogacy and prostitution that is not wrong with teaching and professional sports.

From Debra Satz, "Markets in Women's Sexual Labor," *Ethics* 106 (1995).

The intuition that there is a distinction between markets in different human capacities is a deep one, even among people who ultimately think that the distinction does not justify legally forbidding sales of reproductive capacity and sex. I accept this intuition, which I continue to probe in this article. In particular, I ask: What justifies taking an asymmetric attitude toward markets in our sexual capacities? What, if anything, is problematic about a woman selling her sexual as opposed to her secretarial labor? And, if the apparent asymmetry can be explained and justified, what implications follow for public policy? . . .

Below I survey two types of arguments which can be used to support the asymmetry thesis: (1) essentialist arguments that the sale of sexual labor is intrinsically wrong because it is alienating or contrary to human flourishing and happiness; and (2) my own egalitarian argument that the sale of sex is wrong because, given the background conditions within which it occurs, it tends to reinforce gender inequality. I . . . claim that contemporary prostitution is wrong because it promotes injustice, and not because it makes people less happy.

The Essentialist Approach

. . . [T]he essentialist thesis views the commodification of sex as an assault on personal dignity.[2] Prostitution degrades the prostitute. Elizabeth Anderson, for example, discusses the effect of commodification on the nature of sex as a shared good, based on the recognition of mutual attraction. In commercial sex, each party now values the other only instrumentally, not intrinsically. And, while both parties are thus prevented from enjoying a shared good, it is worse for the prostitute. The customer merely surrenders a certain amount of cash; the prostitute cedes her body: the prostitute is thus degraded to the status of a thing. Call this the degradation objection.

I share the intuition that the failure to treat others as persons is morally significant; it is wrong to treat people as mere things. But I am skeptical as to whether this intuition supports the conclusion that prostitution is wrong. Consider the contrast between slavery and prostitution. Slavery was, in Orlando Patterson's memorable phrase, a form of "social death": it denied to enslaved individuals the ability to press claims, to be—in their own right—sources of value and interest. But the mere sale of the use of someone's capacities does not necessarily involve a failure of this kind, on the part of either the buyer or the seller. Many forms of labor, perhaps most, cede some control of a person's body to others. Such control can range from requirements to be in a certain place at a certain time (e.g., reporting to the office), to requirements that a person (e.g., a professional athlete) eat certain foods and get certain amounts of sleep, or maintain good humor in the face of the offensive behavior of others (e.g., airline stewardesses). Some control of our capacities by others does not seem to be ipso facto destructive of our dignity. Whether the purchase of a form of human labor power will have this negative consequence will depend on background social macrolevel and microlevel institutions. Minimum wages, worker participation and control, health and safety regulations, maternity and paternity leave, restrictions on specific performance, and the right to "exit" one's job are all features which attenuate the objectionable aspects of treating people's labor as a mere economic input. The advocates of prostitution's wrongness in virtue of its connection to self-hood, flourishing, and degradation have not shown that a system of regulated prostitution would be unable to respond to their worries. In particular, they have not established that there is something wrong with prostitution irrespective of its cultural and historical context.

There is, however, another way of interpreting the degradation objection which draws a connection between the current practice of prostitution and the lesser social status of women. This connection is not a matter of the logic of prostitution per se but of the fact that contemporary prostitution degrades women by treating them as the sexual servants of men. In current prostitution, prostitutes are overwhelmingly women and their clients are almost exclusively men. Prostitution, in conceiving of a class of women as needed to satisfy male sexual desire, represents women as sexual servants to men. The degradation objection, so understood, can be seen as a way of expressing an egalitarian concern since there is no reciprocal ideology which represents men as servicing women's sexual needs. It is to this egalitarian understanding of prostitution's wrongness that I turn in the next section.

The Egalitarian Approach

While the essentialists rightly call our attention to the different relation we have with our capacities and external things, they overstate the nature of the difference between our sexual capacities and our other capacities with respect to our personhood, flourishing, and dignity. They are also insufficiently attentive to the background conditions in which commercial sex exchanges take place. [Another] account of prostitution's wrongness stresses its causal relationship to gender inequality. . . .

The answer hinges in part on how we conceive of gender inequality. On my view, there are two important dimensions of gender inequality, often conflated. The first dimension concerns inequalities in the distribution of income, wealth, and opportunity. . . . Inequalities in income and opportunity form an important part of the backdrop against which prostitution must be viewed. While there are many possible routes into prostitution, the largest number of women who participate in it are poor, young, and uneducated. Labor market inequalities will be part of any plausible explanation of why many women "choose" to enter into prostitution.

The second dimension of gender inequality does not concern income and opportunity but status. In many contemporary contexts, women are viewed and treated as inferior to men. . . .

Both forms of inequality—income inequality and status inequality—potentially bear on the question of prostitution's wrongness. Women's decisions to enter into prostitution must be viewed against the background of their unequal life chances and their unequal opportunities for income and rewarding work. The extent to which women face a highly constrained range of options will surely be relevant to whether, and to what degree, we view their choices as autonomous. Some women may actually loathe or judge as inferior the lives of prostitution they "choose." Economic inequality may thus shape prostitution.

We can also ask, Does prostitution itself shape employment inequalities between men and women? In general, whenever there are significant inequalities between groups, those on the disadvantageous side will be disproportionately allocated to subordinate positions. What they do, the positions they occupy, will serve to reinforce negative and disempowering images of themselves. In this sense, prostitution can have an effect on labor-market inequality, associating women with certain stereotypes. For example, images reinforced by prostitution may make it less likely for women to be hired in certain jobs. Admittedly the effect of prostitution on labor-market inequality, if it exists at all, will be small. Other roles which women disproportionately occupy—secretaries, housecleaners, babysitters, waitresses, and saleswomen—will be far more significant in reinforcing (as well as constituting) a gender-segregated division of labor.

I do not think it is plausible to attribute to prostitution a direct causal role in income inequality between men and women. But I believe that it is plausible to maintain that prostitution makes an important and direct contribution to women's inferior social status. Prostitution shapes and is itself shaped by custom and culture, by cultural meanings about the importance of sex, about the nature of women's sexuality and male desire.

If prostitution is wrong it is because of its effects on how men perceive women and on how women perceive themselves. In our society, prostitution represents women as the sexual servants of men. It supports and embodies the widely held belief that men have strong sex drives which must be satisfied—largely through gaining access to some woman's body. This belief underlies the mistaken idea that prostitution is the "oldest" profession, since it is seen as a necessary consequence of human (i.e., male) nature. It also underlies the traditional conception of marriage, in which a man owned not only his wife's property but her body as well. It should not fail to startle us that until recently, most states did not recognize the possibility of "real rape" in marriage.[3]

Why is the idea that women must service men's sexual needs an image of inequality and not mere difference? My argument suggests that there are two primary, contextual reasons:

First, in our culture, there is no reciprocal social practice which represents men as serving women's sexual needs. Men are gigolos and paid escorts—but their sexuality is not seen as an independent capacity whose use women can buy. It is not part of the identity of a class of men that they will service women's sexual desires. Indeed, male prostitutes overwhelmingly service other men and not women. Men are not depicted as fully capable of commercially alienating their sexuality to women; but prostitution depicts women as sexual servants of men.

Second, the idea that prostitution embodies an idea of women as inferior is strongly suggested by the high incidence of rape and violence against prostitutes, as well as the fact that few men seek out or even contemplate prostitutes as potential marriage partners. While all women in our society are potential targets of rape and violence, the mortality rates for women engaged in streetwalking prostitution are roughly forty times higher than that of nonprostitute women.

My suggestion is that prostitution depicts an image of gender inequality, by constituting one class of women as inferior. Prostitution is a "theater" of inequality—it displays for us a practice in which women are subordinated to men. This is especially the case where women are forcibly controlled by their (male) pimps. It follows from my conception of prostitution that it need not have such a negative effect when the prostitute is male.

If, through its negative image of women as sexual servants of men, prostitution reinforces women's inferior status in society, then it is wrong. Even though men can be and are prostitutes, I think that it is unlikely that we will find such negative image effects on men as a group. Individual men may be degraded in individual acts of prostitution: men as a group are not.

Granting all of the above, one objection to the equality approach to prostitution's wrongness remains. Is prostitution's negative image effect greater than that produced by other professions in which women largely service men, for example, secretarial labor? What is special about prostitution?

The negative image effect undoubtedly operates outside the domain of prostitution. But there are two significant differences between prostitution and other gender-segregated professions.

First, most people believe that prostitution, unlike secretarial work, is especially objectionable. Holding such moral views of prostitution constant, if prostitution continues to be primarily a female occupation, then the existence of prostitution will disproportionately fuel negative images of women. Second, and relatedly, the particular image of women in prostitution is more of an image of inferiority than that of a secretary. The image embodies a greater amount of objectification, of representing the prostitute as an object without a will of her own. Prostitutes are far more likely to be victims of violence than are secretaries: the mortality rate of women in prostitution is forty times that of other women. Prostitutes are also far more likely to be raped: a prostitute's "no" does not, to the male she services, mean no.

My claim is that, unless such arguments about prostitution's causal role in sustaining a form of gender inequality can be supported, I am not persuaded that something is morally wrong with markets in sex. In particular, I do not find arguments about the necessary relationship between commercial sex and diminished flourishing and degradation convincing. If prostitution is wrong, it is not because of its effects on happiness or personhood (effects which are shared with other forms of wage-labor); rather, it is because the sale of women's sexual labor may have adverse consequences for achieving a significant form of equality between men and women. My argument for the asymmetry thesis, if correct, connects prostitution to injustice. I now turn to the question of whether, even if we assume that prostitution is wrong under current conditions, it should remain illegal.

Should Prostitution be Legalized?

It is important to distinguish between prostitution's wrongness and the legal response that we are entitled to make to that wrongness. Even if prostitution is wrong, we may not be justified in prohibiting it if that prohibition makes the facts in virtue of which it is wrong worse, or if its costs are too great for other important values, such as autonomy and privacy. For example, even if someone accepts that the contemporary division of labor in the family is wrong, they may still reasonably object to government surveillance of the family's division of household chores. To determine whether such surveillance is justified, we need to know more about the fundamental interests at stake, the costs of surveillance and the availability of alternative mechanisms for promoting equality in families. While I think that there is no acceptable view which would advocate governmental surveillance of family chores, there remains a range of plausible views about the appropriate scope of state intervention and, indeed, the appropriate scope of equality considerations.

It is also important to keep in mind that in the case of prostitution, as with pornography and hate speech, narrowing the discussion of solutions to the single question of whether to ban or not to ban shows a poverty of imagination. There are many ways of challenging existing cultural values about the appropriate division of labor in the family and the nature of women's sexual and reproductive capacities—for example, education, consciousness-raising groups, changes in employee leave policies, comparable worth programs, etc. The law is not the only way to provide women with incentives to refrain from participating in prostitution. Nonetheless, we do need to decide what the best legal policy toward prostitution should be.

I begin with an assessment of the policy which we now have. The United States is one of the few developed Western countries which criminalizes prostitution. Denmark, the Netherlands, West Germany, Sweden, Switzerland, and Austria all have legalized prostitution, although in some of these countries it is restricted by local ordinances. Where prostitution is permitted, it is closely regulated.

Suppose that we accept that gender equality is a legitimate goal of social policy. The question is whether the current legal prohibition on prostitution in the United States promotes gender equality. The answer I think is that it clearly does not. The current legal policies in the United States arguably exacerbate the factors in virtue of which prostitution is wrong.

The current prohibition on prostitution renders the women who engage in the practice vulnerable. First, the participants in the practice seek assistance from pimps in lieu of the contractual and legal remedies which are denied them. Male pimps may protect women prostitutes from their customers and from the police, but the system of pimp-run prostitution has enormous negative effects on the women at the lowest rungs of prostitution. Second, prohibition of prostitution raises the dilemma of the "double bind": if we prevent prostitution without greater redistribution of income, wealth, and opportunities, we deprive poor women of one way—in some circumstances the only way—of improving their condition. Analogously, we do not solve the problem of homelessness by criminalizing it.

Furthermore, women are disproportionately punished for engaging in commercial sex acts. Many state laws make it a worse crime to sell sex than to buy it. Consequently, pimps and clients ("johns") are rarely prosecuted. In some jurisdictions, patronizing a prostitute is not illegal. The record of arrests and convictions is also highly asymmetric. . . .

There is an additional reason why banning prostitution seems an inadequate response to the problem of gender inequality and which suggests a lack of parallel with the case of commercial surrogacy. Banning prostitution would not by itself—does not—eliminate it. While there is reason to think that making commercial surrogacy arrangements illegal or unenforceable would diminish their occurrence, no such evidence exists about prostitution. No city has eliminated prostitution merely through criminalization. Instead, criminalized prostitution thrives as a black market activity in which pimps substitute for law as the mechanism for enforcing contracts. It thereby makes the lives of prostitutes worse than they might otherwise be and without clearly counteracting prostitution's largely negative image of women. . . .

Conclusion

If the arguments I have offered here are correct, then prostitution is wrong in virtue of its contributions to perpetuating a pervasive form of inequality. In different circumstances, with different assumptions about women and their role in society, I do not think that prostitution would be especially troubling—no more troubling than many other labor markets currently allowed. It follows, then, that in other circumstances, the asymmetry thesis would be denied or less strongly felt. While the idea that prostitution is intrinsically degrading is a powerful intuition . . . I believe that this intuition is itself bound up with well-entrenched views of male gender identity and women's sexual role in the context of that identity. If we are troubled by prostitution, as I think we should be, then we should direct much of our energy to putting forward alternative models of egalitarian relations between men and women.

Notes

1. Debra Satz, "Markets in Women's Reproductive Labor," *Philosophy and Public Affairs* 21 (1992): 107–31.
2. Elizabeth Anderson, *Value in Ethics and Economics* (Cambridge, Mass.: Harvard University Press, 1993), p. 45.
3. Susan Estrich, *Real Rape* (Cambridge, Mass.: Harvard University Press, 1987).

Study Questions

1. How does Satz respond to Anderson's claim that prostitution erodes the value of noncommodified sex?
2. Do you agree that women are economically and socially disadvantaged compared to men?
3. Do the reasons Satz presents against the morality of female prostitution also apply to the morality of male prostitution?
4. Should immoral activity ever be legal?

C.

Organ Sales

Organ Procurement, Altruism, and Autonomy

Sarah McGrath

Sarah McGrath, Assistant Professor of Philosophy at Princeton University, argues against the principle that the person providing an organ for transplant must do so for reasons having to do with benefit to others. In response to the objection that nobody should have to choose between going hungry and selling body parts, McGrath maintains that the problem is not having the choice of selling the body part but lacking other options. In other words, having the opportunity to sell does not itself harm anyone.

1. Introduction

According to the President's Task Force on Organ Transplantation, when a person decides to provide one of her organs for transplant while she is alive, that decision must be "informed, voluntary, and altruistic."[1] The person providing an organ for transplant must

From Sarah McGrath, "Organ Procurement, Altruism, and Autonomy," *The Journal of Value Inquiry* 40 (2006).

provide it for reasons having to do with benefit to others, not with benefit to herself.

In this paper, we will focus on the claim that organ procurement from living persons is permissible only when the provider is motivated by altruistic reasons. This claim, also accepted by the World Health Organization, is highly controversial.[2] It is not obvious that, all things being equal, a provider's motives should disqualify her from providing a life-saving organ. Given that the current altruistic system does not make enough organs available, and that people are dying for lack of organs, it might be that a person who lacks altruistic motives but is otherwise qualified to provide an organ ought to be permitted to do so. . . .

2. Autonomy

We might begin by considering whether there are any policies that are similar to the current policy on organ procurement in the following respects: they prohibit an activity when it is done for money that they permit when it is done for other reasons, and they could be justified by appeal to something other than the claim that doing the thing for money is morally wrong.

One example of such a policy is the ban on prostitution. Prostitution is illegal everywhere in the United States except some parts of Nevada. Whether bans on prostitution are justified is a controversial topic, but what is relevant to our purposes is that the most plausible defenses of the bans on prostitution do not include appeals to the claim that exchanging sex for money is always and everywhere morally wrong. . . .

The idea that certain kinds of markets, whether in sex, or organs, or women's reproductive labor, would threaten the autonomy of would-be vendors is popular among people who argue against such markets.

[T]he view . . . seems to be that there are certain spheres of choice such that enjoying autonomy in that sphere of choice involves being screened off from certain kinds of influence or incentive. This line has been developed elsewhere, in connection with ethical questions about markets, and in connection with other issues as well.[3] It might be offered in defense of the claim that babies can be put up for adoption but not sold. Reproductive autonomy might involve being screened off from consideration of certain kinds of incentives. A woman who cannot afford to feed her older children and who can make $10,000 by selling her baby may feel compelled to do so if the option is aggressively marketed and readily available. Similarly, perhaps voter-autonomy requires being free from financial incentives to vote for one candidate over another, and perhaps academic autonomy requires freedom from financial incentives to take one position on an issue, instead of another. Similarly, it might be that enjoying bodily autonomy involves being protected from considering incentives to put the parts of our bodies up for sale. If there were financial incentives to put parts of our bodies up for sale, then, just as in the baby case, someone who needed to feed her children and could not find work might feel compelled to sell her body parts.

Such scenarios do indeed seem bad, and if adhering to the view in question, that organ procurement from living persons is permissible only when the provider is motivated by altruistic reasons, is necessary for avoiding them, then this might, at least initially, look like a compelling defense. But let us note that the notion of autonomy is not doing any real work. . . . It is not clear why sexual autonomy is a good we should aim to secure.

In the absence of further claims about what sexual autonomy is, and why it is valuable, it is unclear what role an analogous notion of bodily autonomy would have to play in a defense of the claim that organ procurement from living persons is permissible only when the provider is motivated by altruistic reasons. But instead of canvassing the possibilities of how we might develop a notion of bodily autonomy such that it both matters and is threatened by markets, let us instead bypass any mention of autonomy and appeal directly to what may be called terrible choice situations. . . . We think nobody should have to choose between feeding her children and having sex, or between feeding her older children and keeping her baby, or between going hungry and selling her body parts. It seems that there are some goods or services such that no one should ever have to choose between selling them and suffering some severe hardship. Ignoring autonomy, does consideration of terrible choice situations motivate a ban in organ sales? The argument would be that if there were a market in organs, then people who are badly off would be made worse off by the fact that they would find themselves in terrible choice situations of the kind just described. Therefore, there should be no market in organs.

But the existence of terrible choice situations does not show that restricting options makes people better off. What makes such situations terrible is not that selling the good in question is an option that people have. Instead, what is terrible is that people lack other options or incentives. Let us ask whether it is possible to make someone who is bad off worse off by offering her more options. If we are facing starvation, and someone comes by in an organ trading ship offering us the opportunity to sell our kidneys as the only way to secure rescue, has that person made us worse off? Intuitively, she has not. Admittedly, there is something wrong with what she does. But it is not that she has made us worse off. Indeed, it seems she has made us slightly better off. Instead, it seems that what is bad about what she does is that she fails to give us other options. The point is that consideration of terrible choice situations does not, by itself, motivate restricting the options people have. Consideration of terrible choice situations instead motivates taking measures to ensure that people are never faced with options all of which they find abhorrent.

3. Concluding Remarks

. . . We have not canvassed all the ways in which organ sales might injure personhood. Our conclusion was only that one line of argument from autonomy was either incomplete or unsuccessful. But the burden of proof seems to be on people who think that there is a double-bind, or a collapsing good, in the case of organ sales; it seems to be on those who think that some injury is done to personhood, or some other seriously harmful long-term effects will follow, if organ sales are permitted. It would be yet a further step to show that such harms are sufficient to outweigh the benefits to individuals. . . . It has not been argued in this paper that there is no way to defend the claim that organ procurement from living persons is permissible only when the provider is motivated by altruistic reasons; in particular it has not been argued that a market would have no ill-effects. The proponent of the claim in question might be viewed as trying to limit potential harm to the population at large that might be brought about by the medical practice of benefiting individual recipients of human organs. Many of us find objectionable the idea that organs would be procured from the poorest, least powerful people and that they would go toward increasing the well-being of the already better-off, thereby perpetuating already existing inequality between the rich and the poor. But an argument for a market in organs is not being offered in this paper; there might be good reasons for banning one. . . .

Notes

1. See "Task Force on Organ Transplantation: Issues and Recommendations, U.S. Department of Health and Human Services," Washington D.C., 1986.
2. See "World Health Organization. Human Organ Transplantation: A Report on Developments Under the Auspices of the WHO," 1992.
3. See Elizabeth Anderson, *Value in Ethics and Economics* (Cambridge, Mass.: Harvard University Press, 1993). See also S. Shiffrin, "Paternalism, Unconscionability Doctrine, and Accommodation," *Philosophy and Public Affairs*, 2000.

Study Questions

1. What is an altruistic reason?
2. Should a person be permitted to provide an organ transplant for other than altruistic reasons?
3. Might any actions be prohibited if done for monetary reasons but not otherwise?
4. Are those whose options are restricted ever better off?

The Harm of a Live Donor Organ Market

Simon Rippon

Should the state legalize an organ market? An argument in favor holds that a prohibition on sales would worsen the situation of the economically disadvantaged, taking away what they might regard as their best option. Simon Rippon, Assistant Professor of Philosophy at Central European University, maintains that this argument is mistaken, because sometimes the introduction of an option can cause harm. In the case of organ sales, offering the option to sell will change the way society sees the relationship between persons and their bodies. Those unwilling to participate may face retribution by receiving higher loan rates or a loss of bankruptcy protection. According to Rippon, such potential harms are a good reason to continue the prohibition on organ sales.

Should a market in organs such as kidneys, pieces of liver and pieces of lung from living donors be legally permitted? One form of argument in favour crops up frequently. . . . Sarah McGrath writes:

> We think nobody should have to choose between . . . going hungry and selling her body parts. It seems that there are some goods or services such that no one should ever have to choose between selling them and suffering some severe hardship . . . But . . . what makes such situations terrible is not that selling the good in question is an option that people have. Instead, what is terrible is that people lack other options or incentives . . . Let us ask whether it is possible to make someone . . . worse off by offering her more options. If we are facing starvation, and someone comes by in an organ trading ship offering us the opportunity to sell our kidneys as the only way to secure rescue,

From Simon Rippon, "Imposing Options on People in Poverty: The Harms of a Live Donor Organ Market," *Journal of Medical Ethics* 40 (2014).

has that person made us worse off? Intuitively, she has not. The point is that consideration of terrible choice situations does not, by itself, motivate restricting the options people have.[1]

These points appear, at first appraisal, to provide for a powerful defence of a legal market in organs. The argument may be presented . . . as follows:

> P1. People in poverty who would choose to sell their organs if a free market existed must regard all other options open to them as worse.
> P2. If we take away what some regard as their best option, we thereby make them worse off, at least from their own perspective.
> P3. If a policy makes some worse off from their own perspective, it would be paternalistic for us to judge otherwise and to implement the policy on their behalf. We ought not to be paternalistic in this way.
> Therefore, we ought not to prohibit organ markets for the supposed good of those in poverty who would choose to sell their organs if a free market existed.

I call the above the *Laissez-Choisir Argument* or the LC Argument for short. . . . we are concerned about the plight of potential vendors, then there are decisive welfarist or antipaternalist reasons for letting them choose for themselves whether to sell by giving them the option to do so (hence *laissez-choisir*).

I will argue that the LC Argument fails because its second premise is false and, moreover, that it is in fact the case that we ought to prohibit a live donor organ market for the good of people in poverty. . . .

I will make a positive argument that a live donor organ market should be prohibited because giving people in poverty the option to sell their organs would itself impose an impermissible harm on them. However, even if my positive argument is ultimately deemed unsuccessful, establishing the mere possibility of a successful argument of this kind will show that the second premise of the LC Argument cannot be maintained. . . .

How Having an Option May Harm

My objection to the LC Argument starts from the following claim: *Sometimes you can harm people by giving them an option that they would be better off taking. . . .*

The suggestion that giving people an option could still harm them. . . seems paradoxical because of the following widespread assumption: that it is always good, or at least that it is never bad, for you to have additional options, so long as the addition of options does not impinge on your ability to choose rationally. But this assumption is mistaken. In the case of a legal market for live donor organs, I will argue that having the option to sell an organ may result, in circumstances which are predictably common among those in poverty, in individuals being held to account by others for taking and, more importantly, for failing to take the available option. I will also argue that people in poverty would be significantly harmed by being held to account in these predictable ways, with respect to the sale of their organs. We would thus harm people in poverty by giving them the option to sell their organs not because *taking* the option would be bad for them, but rather because *having* the option subjects them to predictable harms. . . .

Why an Organ Market Would Harm People in Poverty

Let us begin with the observation that the introduction of a legal market in bodily organs would allow many of us an additional option to get cash that we would not otherwise realistically have. We should then also recognise that the introduction of this option would fundamentally change the norms of the relationships of each of us to our bodily organs and to each other. As things stand currently, organs do not generally have a monetary value for their owners. But if organs can be easily exchanged for cash they will then become *commodified*, and naturally subject to the kinds of social and legal demands and responsibilities that govern our other transactions in the marketplace. For example, faced with a rent demand and inadequate cash to pay for it under the *status quo*, a couple of the choices you could make currently would be to sell some of your possessions, or to find (additional) employment and sell some of your labour. One choice that most of us do not realistically have as things stand (and therefore do not have to consider) is to sell an organ to raise the funds. This means that even if you have no possessions to sell and cannot find a job, nobody can reasonably criticise you for, say, failing to sell a kidney to pay your rent. If a free market in organs was permitted and became widespread, then it is reasonable to assume that your organs would soon enough become economic resources like any other, in the context of the market. Selling your organs would become something that is simply expected of you as and when financial need arises. Our new 'option' can thus easily be transformed into a social or legal demand, and it can drastically change the attitudes that others adopt towards you. . . .

My contention, then, is that because people in poverty often find themselves either indebted or in need of cash to meet their own basic needs and those of their families, they would predictably find themselves faced with social or legal pressure to pay the bills by selling their organs, if selling organs were permitted. So we would harm people in poverty by introducing a legal market that would subject them to such pressures.

Are the harms at stake significant enough to prohibit a market in live donor organs? . . . Once we have come to conceptualise our 'excess' organs and organ parts as pieces of unnecessary property by commodifying them, there would naturally follow genuine social and legal costs to pay for failing to sell them when economically necessary, just as there are social and legal costs to pay for failing to take employment when you are able to do so. We should ask questions such as the following: Would those in poverty be eligible for bankruptcy protection, or for public assistance, if they have an organ that they choose not to sell? Could they be legally forced to sell an organ to pay taxes, paternity bills or rent? How would society view someone who asks for charitable assistance to meet her basic needs, if she could easily sell a healthy 'excess' organ to meet them?

Such social and legal pressures do not merely impose psychic costs, and markets that introduce them can make large numbers of people considerably worse off. It is in view of the harms imposed by pressures like these that we think it necessary to enact restrictive laws for labour markets that stipulate, for example, minimum wages, minimum vacation days, parental and sick leave, and workplace safety standards, which cannot be contracted out of. These potential harms also provide us with grounds for enacting laws aimed at preventing commodification of other things, for example, laws against prostitution or against selling our children (even into the most loving homes). Wherever there is great value in not being put under social or legal pressure to sell something as a result of economic forces, we should think carefully about whether it is right to permit a market and to thereby impose the option on everyone to sell it.

The prevalence of exploitation and the enormous impact of economic, social and legal pressure in real-world organ markets are supported empirically by research conducted by Goyal *et al.*[2] They surveyed about 300 people in Chennai, India, who had sold a kidney, on average 6 years prior to the survey. They found that 96% of participants had sold their kidneys to pay off debts, and received an average of only about $1000 in return. Moreover, they found little evidence of any long-term benefit to the participants: their participants' average family incomes had declined by a third after nephrectomy, and three-fourths of them were still in debt at the time of the survey. Seventy-nine per cent of the participants would not recommend that others sell a kidney.

Anthropologist Lawrence Cohen independently drew the following conclusions based on his fieldwork on kidney selling in Chennai:

> Persons sell a kidney to get out of debt, but the conditions of indebtedness do not disappear. All of the thirty Chennai sellers . . . were back in debt again . . . The decision to sell may be set for debtors by their lenders, who advance money through an embodied calculus of collateral value . . . [T]he aggressiveness with which moneylenders call in debts may correlate with whether a debtor lives in an area that has become a kidney zone. If so, the decision to sell is a response not simply to some naturalized state of poverty but to a debt crisis that might not have happened if the option to sell were not present.[3]

Suppose that you are convinced that permitting a live donor organ market could in fact harm people in poverty significantly. You might now be inclined to argue that any such harm would, in any case, be clearly outweighed by the benefits of having an increased supply of life-saving kidneys and other organs, combined with potential economic benefits for the vendors. But we should beware of making crude consequentialist comparisons about such matters. To take an extreme example, we could adopt a general policy permitting us to abduct and cut up a healthy person in order to take his organs and save five others who are in desperate need of organ transplants. If we did so, we would be able to save five times as many lives as are lost, and increase general life expectancy. It would nevertheless be implausible to claim that such a policy is morally justified, and the best objection to it is that it would be unjust. We do not have a right to take a living person's vital organs against his or her will, even if the overall benefits of doing so would be significant. Similarly, before permitting an organ market, we must ask whether we have a right to subject people in poverty to significant harms of social and legal pressure to give up their organs, even if our doing so is the only means of achieving potentially large life-saving benefits, and even if vendors might themselves benefit economically. I submit that we have no such right.

The Nature of the Harm of an Organ Market

Why do I regard it as especially bad to be pressured to sell an organ, in comparison with many other things, such as pieces of ordinary property or some hours of labour?

The answer to this question appeals to two particular features of our relationship to our organs, and of what is involved in removing them. The first is the peculiar importance to human beings of our having fully autonomous veto control over any physical incursions on the intimate parts of our bodies by other people. It is psychologically important to us that our negative right to exclude others from interfering with our physical bodies is protected. This is part of what explains our insistence on the principle of consent for medical interventions, our finding rape a particularly appalling crime and the way in which certain forms of physical torture strike us immediately as particularly dreadful, even if we have no reason to think that they are more psychologically painful or damaging than other methods of interrogation. It is our veto control over physical intrusions upon our bodies by others that matters here, not the physical acts in question: we may have no objection to the touching by others of parts of our bodies, or even to the taking of them, so long as we freely and autonomously choose this. The nature of this concern explains why a policy of state-sanctioned redistributive organ allocation from live donors would never find wide support. In contrast, organ donation, which is voluntary, and redistributive taxation, which is coercive but targets our property rather than parts of our bodies, are both broadly supported by the public.

The second important special feature of organ selling is the small but not insignificant life-changing risks involved (eg, in the case of nephrectomy: about 1 in 3000 mortality and rather higher morbidity risk).[4] It is plausible to think that people should be permitted to take significant risks whenever their actions flow from their own fully autonomous choices (as in cases of organ donation), but that it may harm them to put them under social or legal pressure to take equivalent risks. Sometimes the imposition of such harms could be all-things-considered justified—for example, if the country is fighting a just war and conscripts to the armed forces are necessary—but this would be conditional on a fair distribution of the risks. It does not seem fair to allocate these risks by way of market forces that de facto place nearly all the pressure to take them on those in poverty.

These two features together, I think, explain the special badness of market-driven social and legal pressure to sell organs, and go some way to explaining the intuitive but inchoate moral discomfort that many people feel about the idea of organ markets. The pressure to sell would be exerted not just on those in poverty who choose to sell their organs in a market system, but also on many of those in poverty who choose not to do so. I believe it provides us with a sufficient moral reason not to permit the sale of organs by live donors, even if such sales would increase the supply of organs overall.

Notes

1. McGrath S. Organ procurement, altruism, and autonomy. *J Value Inq* 2007; 40:297–309.
2. Goyal M, Mehta RL, Schneiderman LJ, *et al.* Economic and health consequences of selling a kidney in India. *JAMA* 2002;288:1589–93.
3. Cohen L. Where it hurts: Indian material for an ethics of organ transplantation. *Daedalus* 1999;128:135–65.
4. Taylor JS. *Stakes and Kidneys: Why Markets in Human Body Parts are Morally Imperative.* Aldershot: Ashgate, 2005.

Study Questions

1. What is a live donor organ market?
2. What does Rippon mean by the *Laissez-Choisir Argument?*
3. Can you ever be harmed by having more options?
4. Might you be worse off if you had the option to sell your kidney?

A Reply to Rippon

Luke Semrau

Luke Semrau, Lecturer at Vanderbilt University, responds to Rippon's argument that the introduction of an option to sell kidneys subjects the poor to unjustified harm. Semrau maintains that if the number of available kidneys were kept small, a market in organs would not generate serious pressure to sell. Hence the harm identified by Rippon would be minimal.

According to Rippon, if kidney sales are permitted 'many of us' will consider vending. If 'organs can be easily exchanged for cash', he claims, 'it is reasonable to assume that your organs would soon enough become economic resources like any other'. Kidney sales will be so common, Rippon insists, that people struggling to make this month's rent may be pressured to vend. These grim predictions are not merely speculative. Rippon offers, as support for this view of the market, empirical research into markets in Chennai, India. He cites a well-known study that found 96% of vendors sold to relieve debt, though most remained indebted years later. He also cites the work of anthropologist Lawrence Cohen, who found that moneylenders became more aggressive in their collection tactics in areas where vending was common. The picture that emerges depicts vending not as a means to escape poverty but as a demand accompanying that condition.

Rippon holds what I will call the 'newfound capital' view of kidney commodification, according to which permitting sales would be

From Luke Semrau, "The Best Argument against Kidney Sales Fails," *Journal of Medical Ethics* 41 (2015). Revised by the author.

substantially similar to bestowing all with a surgically accessible token redeemable for $100,000. Introducing the option to vend would cause dramatic and widespread change. If sales were permitted, everyone would become one abdominal surgery away from potentially transformative sums of cash. Of course, moneylenders would adopt more aggressive tactics. Under these conditions, we should expect the economically disadvantaged to be targeted. With so many people with a kidney to spare—now potentially worth $100,000—there would be countless new opportunities to extract handsome sums from unsavvy or otherwise vulnerable actors. In addition, this perspective further supports Rippon's claim that introducing a market will 'fundamentally change the norms of the relationships of each of us to our bodily organs and to each other'. As other critics have also noted, the compensation on offer is significant and could easily distort intimate relations in unexpected ways.

In a regulated market, kidneys will not become 'economic resources like any other'. The 'newfound capital' view is mistaken. An underappreciated fact is that in a regulated market would be geopolitically bounded, that is, vendors and recipients would reside in the same region. Such a market would be 'closed' to outsiders. This constraint, combined with the natural demand for kidneys, ensures that vending in any given region will be uncommon. To see this, consider some admittedly crude calculations: As of August 2014, according to the Organ Procurement and Transplantation Network, about 35,000 people were added to the waitlist in the USA in 2012. If this is indicative of annual demand, and if we transplant only living kidneys procured on the market, then about 1 in 9000 people would become vendors annually. This natural 'cap', combined with the fixed price, makes kidneys quite unlike other economic resources. Each of the first 35,000 transplantable kidneys offered annually would fetch $100,000, and each after that would be refused. This feature of the proposal renders Rippon's appeal to evidence from India inapt. The market studied there is 'open'; most vendors reside in the slums of Chennai, while most recipients come from elsewhere. As a result, vending is far more common and its societal influence greater.

From this empirically informed view of the market, the sad picture Rippon paints looks unrealistic. Whatever norms govern the relationship between people and their body parts, we have no reason to believe that permitting 1 in 9000 to vend annually will 'fundamentally change' them. Nor should we accept Rippon's claim that vending will be 'simply expected' of those in financial need. The facts of the matter suggest that the practice will never be sufficiently common to influence societal expectations in the ways imagined.

It also becomes clear that introducing the option to vend is unlikely to give rise to pressure to vend. This is because, in short, pressuring others to vend will not reliably result in their vending. Three considerations support this claim. First, as I have argued, because the market is geopolitically bounded, and the demand for kidneys is fixed and low, rates of vending within the general population will necessarily be low. Vending will be rare. Second, because the compensation on offer is appreciable even by middle-class standards, many people, from a range of demographics, are likely to pursue the option. And even if only 1 in 1000 find sales appealing, for every one successful vendor, there would be eight who tried and failed. Vending will be competitive. Finally, the market may be designed to include certain safety features. For example, we may provide potential vendors with the chance to discreetly disqualify themselves at the screening stage or impose a waiting period between when one qualifies to vend and when one is permitted to. The upshot is this: because pressure to vend will not reliably lead to vending, few will bother to exert it.

In closing, I want to emphasise the need for further empirical research. Though I think Rippon's resistance to kidney sales is unfounded, I readily grant that we are in a position of uncertainty. The paucity of relevant evidence means that much of the discussion on kidney sales is largely speculative. There is, unfortunately, nothing speculative about the many thousands of deaths caused by the organ shortage each year or the physical and emotional suffering this brings. For decades, many countries, including the USA, have experimented with donation-only models of organ acquisition. And for decades the shortage of transplantable kidneys has grown more acute. Rather than continue to replicate these sad results, we should take the market proposals on offer seriously. We need to try a different experiment.

Study Questions

1. What does Semrau mean by a market that is "geopolitically bounded"?
2. Why does the operation of a geopolitically bounded market imply that selling will be uncommon?
3. According to Semrau, why is introducing the option to vend unlikely to give rise to pressure to vend?
4. According to Semrau, would selling kidneys lead to their becoming akin to all other economic resources?

D.

Pornography

Pornography, Oppression, and Freedom

Helen E. Longino

Helen Longino is Professor of Philosophy at Stanford University. She argues that the production and distribution of pornography is harmful to women and therefore immoral. She defines "pornography" as material endorsing sexual behavior that is degrading or abusing. She then argues that pornography is implicated in the commission of violent crimes against women, is a means of disseminating vicious lies about women, and supports sexist attitudes that reinforce the oppression of women. Moreover, she argues that pornography is not legally protected as a matter of privacy, because its sale is public. Nor is pornography justified as freedom of expression, because pornography impinges on the rights of others. Longino concludes that pornography threatens women, and no one has a right to manufacture or circulate it.

Introduction

. . . One of the beneficial results of the sexual revolution has been a growing acceptance of the distinction between questions of sexual mores and questions of morality. This distinction underlies the old

From Helen E. Longino, "Pornography, Oppression, and Freedom: A Closer Look," in *Take Back the Night*, ed. Laura Lederer (New York: William Morrow & Co., 1980).

slogan, "Make love, not war," and takes harm to others as the defining characteristic of immorality. What is immoral is behavior which causes injury to or violation of another person or people. Such injury may be physical or it may be psychological. To cause pain to another, to lie to another, to hinder another in the exercise of her or his rights, to exploit another, to degrade another, to misrepresent and slander another are instances of immoral behavior. Masturbation or engaging voluntarily in sexual intercourse with another consenting adult of the same or the other sex, as long as neither injury nor violation of either individual or another is involved, is not immoral. Some sexual behavior is morally objectionable, but not because of its sexual character. Thus, adultery is immoral not because it involves sexual intercourse with someone to whom one is not legally married, but because it involves breaking a promise (of sexual and emotional fidelity to one's spouse). Sadistic, abusive, or forced sex is immoral because it injures and violates another.

The detachment of sexual chastity from moral virtue implies that we cannot condemn forms of sexual behavior merely because they strike us as distasteful or subversive of the Protestant work ethic, or because they depart from standards of behavior we have individually adopted. It has thus seemed to imply that no matter how offensive we might find pornography, we must tolerate it in the name of freedom from illegitimate repression. I wish to argue that this is not so, that pornography is immoral because it is harmful to people.

What Is Pornography?

I define pornography as *verbal or pictorial explicit representations of sexual behavior that,* in the words of the Commission on Obscenity and Pornography, *have as a distinguishing characteristic "the degrading and demeaning portrayal of the role and status of the human female . . . as a mere sexual object to be exploited and manipulated sexually."* In pornographic books, magazines, and films, women are represented as passive and as slavishly dependent upon men. The role of female characters is limited to the provision of sexual services to men. To the extent that women's sexual pleasure is represented at all, it is subordinated to that of men and is never an end in itself as is the sexual pleasure of men. What pleases women is the use of their bodies to satisfy male desires. While the sexual objectification of women is common to pornography, women are the recipients of even worse treatment in violent pornography, in which women characters are killed, tortured, gang-raped, mutilated, bound, and otherwise abused, as a means of providing sexual stimulation or pleasure to the male characters. It is this development which has attracted the attention of feminists and been the stimulus to an analysis of pornography in general.

Not all sexually explicit material is pornography, nor is all material which contains representations of sexual abuse and degradation pornography.

A representation of a sexual encounter between adult persons which is characterized by mutual respect is, once we have disentangled sexuality and morality, not morally objectionable. Such a representation would be one in which the desires and experiences of each participant were regarded by the other participants as having a validity and a subjective importance equal to those of the individual's own desire and experiences. In such an encounter, each participant acknowledges the other participant's basic human dignity and personhood. Similarly, a representation of a nude human body (in whole or in part) in such a manner that the person shown maintains self-respect—e.g., is not portrayed in a degrading position—would not be morally objectionable. The educational films of the National Sex Forum, as well as a certain amount of erotic literature and art, fall into this category. While some erotic materials are beyond the standards of modesty held by some individuals, they are not for this reason immoral.

A representation of a sexual encounter which is not characterized by mutual respect, in which at least one of the parties is treated in a manner beneath her or his dignity as a human being, is no longer simple erotica. That a representation is of degrading behavior does not in itself, however, make it pornographic. Whether or not it is pornographic is a function of contextual features. Books and films may contain descriptions or representations of a rape in order to explore the consequences of such an assault upon its victim. What is being shown is abusive or degrading behavior which attempts to deny the humanity and dignity of the person assaulted, yet the context surrounding the representation, through its exploration of the consequences of the act, acknowledges and reaffirms her dignity. Such books and films, far from being pornographic, are (or can be) highly moral, and fall into the category of moral realism.

What makes a work a work of pornography, then, is not simply its representation of degrading and abusive sexual encounters, but its implicit, if not explicit, approval and recommendation of sexual behavior that is immoral, i.e., that physically or psychologically violates the personhood of one of the participants. Pornography, then, is verbal or pictorial material which represents or describes sexual behavior that is degrading or abusive to one or more of the participants in *such a way as to endorse the degradation.* The participants so treated in virtually all heterosexual pornography are women or children, so heterosexual pornography is, as a matter of fact, material which endorses sexual behavior that is degrading and/or abusive to women and children. As I use the term "sexual behavior," this includes sexual encounters between persons, behavior which produces sexual stimulation or pleasure for one of the participants, and behavior which is preparatory to or invites sexual activity. Behavior that is degrading or abusive includes physical harm or abuse, and physical or psychological coercion. In addition, behavior which ignores or devalues the real interests, desires, and experiences of one or more participants in any way is degrading. Finally, that a person has chosen or consented to be harmed, abused, or subjected to coercion does not alter the degrading character of such behavior.

Pornography communicates its endorsement of the behavior it represents by various features of the pornographic context: the degradation of the female characters is represented as providing pleasure to the participant males and, even worse, to the participant females, and there is no suggestion that this sort of treatment of others is inappropriate to their status as human beings. These two features are together sufficient to constitute endorsement of the represented behavior. The contextual features which make material pornographic are intrinsic to the material. In addition to these, extrinsic features, such as the purpose for which the material is presented—i.e., the sexual arousal/pleasure/satisfaction of its (mostly) male consumers—or an accompanying text, may reinforce or make explicit the endorsement. Representations which in and of themselves do not show or endorse degrading behavior may be put into a pornographic context by juxtaposition with others that are degrading, or by a text which invites or recommends degrading behavior toward the subject represented. In such a case the whole complex—the series of representations or representations with text—is pornographic. . . .

To summarize: Pornography is not just the explicit representation or description of sexual behavior, nor even the explicit representation or description of sexual behavior which is degrading and/or abusive to women. Rather, it is material that explicitly represents or describes degrading and abusive sexual behavior so as to endorse and/or recommend the behavior as described. The contextual features, moreover, which communicate such endorsement are intrinsic to the material; that is, they are features whose removal or alteration would change the representation or description. . . .

Pornography: Lies and Violence Against Women

What is wrong with pornography, then, is its degrading and dehumanizing portrayal of women (and *not* its sexual content). Pornography, by its very nature, requires that women be subordinate to men and mere instruments for the fulfillment of male fantasies. To accomplish this, pornography must lie. Pornography lies when it says that our sexual life is or ought to be subordinate to the service of men, that our pleasure consists in pleasing men and not ourselves, that we are depraved, that we are fit subjects for rape, bondage, torture, and murder. Pornography lies explicitly about women's sexuality, and through such lies fosters more lies about our humanity, our dignity, and our personhood.

Moreover, since nothing is alleged to justify the treatment of the female characters of pornography save their womanhood, pornography depicts all women as fit objects of violence by virtue of their sex alone. Because it is simply being female that, in the pornographic vision, justifies being violated, the lies of pornography are lies about all women. Each work of pornography is on its own libelous and defamatory, yet gains power through being reinforced by every other pornographic work. The sheer number of pornographic productions expands the moral issue to include not only assessing the morality or immorality of individual works, but also the meaning and force of the mass production of pornography.

The pornographic view of women is thoroughly entrenched in a booming portion of the publishing, film, and recording industries, reaching and affecting not only all who look to such sources for sexual stimulation, but also those of us who are forced into an awareness of it as we peruse magazines at newsstands and record albums in record stores, as we check the entertainment sections of city newspapers, or even as we approach a counter to pay for groceries. It is not necessary to spend a great deal of time reading or viewing pornographic material to absorb its male-centered definition of women. No longer confined within plain brown wrappers, it jumps out from billboards that proclaim "Live X-rated Girls!" or "Angels in Pain" or "Hot and Wild," and from magazine covers displaying a woman's genital area being spread open to the viewer by her own fingers. Thus, even men who do not frequent pornographic shops and movie houses are supported in the sexist objectification of women by their environment. Women, too, are crippled by internalizing as self-images those that are presented to us by pornographers. Isolated from one another and with no source of support for an alternative view of female sexuality, we may not always find the strength to resist a message that dominates the common cultural media.

The entrenchment of pornography in our culture also gives it a significance quite beyond its explicit sexual messages. To suggest, as pornography does, that the primary purpose of women is to provide sexual pleasure to men is to deny that women are independently human or have a status equal to that of men. It is, moreover, to deny our equality at one of the most intimate levels of human experience. This denial is especially powerful in a hierarchical, class society such as ours, in which individuals feel good about themselves by feeling superior to others. Men in our society have a vested interest in maintaining their belief in the inferiority of the female sex, so that no matter how oppressed and exploited by the society in which they live and work, they can feel that they are at least superior to someone or some category of individuals—a woman or women. Pornography, by presenting women as wanton, depraved, and made for the sexual use of men, caters directly to that interest. The very intimate nature of sexuality which makes pornography so corrosive also protects it from explicit public discussion. The consequent lack of any explicit social disavowal of the pornographic image of women enables this image to continue fostering sexist attitudes even as the society publicly proclaims its (as yet timid) commitment to sexual equality.

In addition to finding a connection between the pornographic view of women and the denial to us of our full human rights, women are beginning to connect the consumption of pornography with committing rape and other acts of sexual violence against women. Contrary to the findings of the Commission on Obscenity and Pornography a growing body of research is documenting (1) a correlation between exposure to representations of violence and the committing of violent acts generally, and (2) a correlation between exposure to pornographic materials and the committing of sexually abusive or violent acts against women. While more study is needed to establish precisely what the causal relations are, clearly so-called hard-core pornography is not innocent.

From "snuff" films and miserable magazines in pornographic stores to *Hustler*, to phonograph album covers and advertisements, to *Vogue*, pornography has come to occupy its own niche in the communications and entertainment media and to acquire a quasi-institutional character (signaled by the use of diminutives such as "porn" or "porno" to refer to pornographic material, as though such familiar naming could take the hurt out). Its acceptance by the mass media, whatever the motivation, means a cultural endorsement of its message. As much as the materials themselves, the social tolerance of these degrading and distorted images of women in such quantities is harmful to us, since it indicates a general willingness to see women in ways incompatible with our fundamental human dignity and thus to justify treating us in those ways. The tolerance of pornographic representations of the rape, bondage, and torture of women helps to create and maintain a climate more tolerant of the actual physical abuse of women. The tendency on the part of the legal system to view the victim of a rape as responsible for the crime against her is but one manifestation of this.

In sum, pornography is injurious to women in at least three distinct ways:

1. Pornography, especially violent pornography, is implicated in the committing of crimes of violence against women.
2. Pornography is the vehicle for the dissemination of a deep and vicious lie about women. It is defamatory and libelous.
3. The diffusion of such a distorted view of women's nature in our society as it exists today supports sexist (i.e., male-centered) attitudes, and thus reinforces the oppression and exploitation of women.

Society's tolerance of pornography, especially pornography on the contemporary massive scale, reinforces each of these modes of injury: By not disavowing the lie, it supports the male-centered myth that women are inferior and subordinate creatures. Thus, it contributes to the maintenance of a climate tolerant of both psychological and physical violence against women.

Pornography and the Law

> Congress shall make no law respecting the establishment of religion, or prohibiting the free exercise thereof; or abridging the freedom of speech, or of the press; or the right of the people peaceably to assemble, and to petition the Government for a redress of grievances.
>
> —*First Amendment*, Bill of Rights
> of the United States Constitution

Pornography is clearly a threat to women. Each of the modes of injury cited above offers sufficient reason at least to consider proposals for the social and legal control of pornography. The almost universal response from progressives to such proposals is that constitutional guarantees of freedom of speech and privacy preclude recourse to law. . . . I find objections to such a campaign that are based on appeals to the First Amendment or to a right to privacy ultimately unconvincing.

Much of the defense of the pornographer's right to publish seems to assume that, while pornography may be tasteless and vulgar, it is basically an entertainment that harms no one but its consumers, who may at worst suffer from the debasement of their taste; and that therefore those who argue for its control are demanding an unjustifiable abridgment of the rights to freedom of speech of those who make and distribute pornographic materials and of the rights to privacy of their customers. The account of pornography given above shows that the assumptions of this position are false. Nevertheless, even some who acknowledge its harmful character feel that it is granted immunity from social control by the First Amendment, or that the harm that would ensue from its control outweighs the harm prevented by its control.

There are three ways of arguing that control of pornography is incompatible with adherence to constitutional rights. The first argument claims that regulating pornography involves an unjustifiable interference in the private lives of individuals. The second argument takes the First Amendment as a basic principle constitutive of our form of government, and claims that the production and distribution of pornographic material, as a form of speech, is an activity protected by that amendment. The third argument claims not that the pornographer's rights are violated, but that others' rights will be if controls against pornography are instituted.

The privacy argument is the easiest to dispose of. Since the open commerce in pornographic materials is an activity carried out in the public sphere, the publication and distribution of such materials, unlike their use by individuals, is not protected by rights to privacy. The distinction between the private consumption of pornographic material and the production and distribution of, or open commerce in it, is sometimes blurred by defenders of pornography. But I may entertain, in the privacy of my mind, defamatory opinions about another person, even though I may not broadcast them. So one might create without restraint—as long as no one were harmed in the course of preparing them—pornographic materials for one's personal use, but be restrained from reproducing and distributing them. In both cases what one is doing—in the privacy of one's mind or basement—may indeed be deplorable, but immune from legal proscription. Once the activity becomes public, however—i.e., once it involves others—it is no longer protected by the same rights that protect activities in the private sphere.

In considering the second argument (that control of pornography, private or public, is wrong in principle), it seems important to determine whether we consider the right to freedom of speech to be absolute and unqualified. If it is, then obviously all speech, including pornography, is entitled to protection. But the right is, in the first place, not an unqualified right: There are several kinds of speech not protected by the First Amendment, including the incitement to violence in volatile circumstances, the solicitation of crimes, perjury and misrepresentation, slander, libel, and false advertising. That there are forms of proscribed speech shows that we accept limitations on the right to freedom of speech if such speech, as do the forms listed, impinges on other rights. The manufacture and distribution of material which defames and threatens all members of a class by its recommendation of abusive and degrading behavior toward some members of that class simply in virtue of their membership in it seems a clear candidate for inclusion on the list. The right is therefore not an unqualified one.

Nor is it an absolute or fundamental right, underived from any other right: If it were there would not be exceptions or limitations. The first ten amendments were added to the Constitution as a way of guaranteeing the "blessings of liberty" mentioned in its preamble, to protect citizens against the unreasonable usurpation of power by the state. The specific rights mentioned in the First Amendment those of religion, speech, assembly, press, petition—reflect the recent experiences of the makers of the Constitution under colonial government as well as a sense of what was and is required generally to secure liberty. . . .

The right to freedom of speech is not a fundamental, absolute right, but one derivative from, possessed in virtue of, the more basic right to independence. Taking this view of liberty requires providing arguments showing that the more specific rights we claim are necessary to guarantee our status as persons "independent and equal rather than subservient." In the context of government, we understand independence to be the freedom of each individual to participate as an equal among equals in the determination of how she or he is to be governed. Freedom of speech in this context means that an individual may not only entertain beliefs concerning government privately, but may express them publicly. We express our opinions about taxes, disarmament, wars, social-welfare programs, the function of the police, civil rights, and so on. Our right to freedom of speech includes the right to criticize the government and to protest against various forms of injustice and the abuse of power. What we wish to protect is the free expression of ideas even when they are unpopular. What we do not always remember is that speech has functions other than the expression of ideas.

Regarding the relationship between a right to freedom of speech and the publication and distribution of pornographic materials, there are two points to be made. In the first place, the latter activity is hardly an exercise of the right to the free expression of ideas as understood above. In the second place, to the degree that the tolerance of material degrading to women supports and reinforces the attitude that women are not fit to participate as equals among equals in the political life of their communities, and that the prevalence of such an attitude effectively prevents women from so participating, the absolute and fundamental right of women to liberty (political independence) is violated.

This second argument against the suppression of pornographic material, then, rests on a premise that must be rejected, namely, that the right to freedom of speech is a right to utter anything one wants. It thus fails to show that the production and distribution of such material is an activity protected by the First Amendment. Furthermore, an examination of the issues involved leads to the conclusion that tolerance of this activity violates the rights of women to political independence.

The third argument (which expresses concern that curbs on pornography are the first step toward political censorship) . . . [has] an underlying assumption that the maximization of freedom is a worthy social goal. Control of pornography diminishes freedom—directly the freedom of pornographers, indirectly that of all of us. But . . . what is meant by "freedom"? It cannot be that what is to be maximized is license—as the goal of a social group whose members probably have at least some incompatible interests, such a goal would be internally inconsistent. If, on the other hand, the maximization of political independence is the goal, then that is in no way enhanced by, and may be endangered by, the tolerance of pornography. To argue that the control of pornography would create a precedent for suppressing political speech is thus to confuse license with political independence.

In addition, it ignores a crucial basis for the control of pornography, i.e., its character as libelous speech. The prohibition of such speech is justified by the need for protection from the injury (psychological as well as physical or economic) that results from libel. A very different kind of argument would be required to justify curtailing the right to speak our minds about the institutions which govern us. As long as such distinctions are insisted upon, there is little danger of the government's using the control of pornography as precedent for curtailing political speech.

In summary, neither as a matter of principle nor in the interests of maximizing liberty can it be supposed that there is an intrinsic right to manufacture and distribute pornographic material.

The only other conceivable source of protection for pornography would be a general right to do what we please as long as the rights of others are respected. Since the production and distribution of pornography violates the rights of women—to respect and to freedom from defamation, among others—this protection is not available.

Conclusion

I have defined pornography in such a way as to distinguish it from erotica and from moral realism, and have argued that it is defamatory and libelous toward women, that it condones crimes against women, and that it invites tolerance of the social, economic, and cultural oppression of women. The production and distribution of pornographic material is thus a social and moral wrong. Contrasting both the current volume of pornographic production and its growing infiltration of the communications media with the status of women in this culture makes clear the necessity for its control. Since the goal of controlling pornography does not conflict with constitutional rights, a common obstacle to action is removed.

Study Questions

1. According to Longino, what is pornography?
2. Why does Longino believe that pornography is immoral?
3. Should all immoral activity be illegal?
4. Does Longino's case against heterosexual pornography apply equally to homosexual pornography?

The Case against Pornography: An Assessment

Joel Feinberg

Joel Feinberg (1926–2004) was Professor of Philosophy at the University of Arizona. He considers a number of arguments for the legal control of pornography and finds each wanting. First, the claim that pornography harms women by defaming them lacks support, for pornography makes no explicit assertions. Whatever inferences consumers of pornography draw is influenced by their preexisting attitudes. If pornography were to meet the threshold for defamation, then so too would many other representations of women in popular culture. Second, the claim that pornography harms women by inciting violence against them lacks supporting empirical evidence. Feinberg argues that violence against women is a complex social phenomenon explained by cultural ideals of manhood. Eliminating these macho values is not the task of the criminal law but of enhanced moral education.

May the law legitimately be used to restrict the liberty of pornographers to produce and distribute, and their customers to purchase and use, erotic materials that are violently abusive of women? (I am assuming that no strong case can be made for the proscription of materials that are merely degrading in one of the relatively subtle and nonviolent ways.) Many . . . answer, often with reluctance, in the affirmative. Their arguments can be divided into two general classes. Some simply invoke the harm principle. Violent pornography wrongs and harms women, according to these arguments, either by defaming them as a group, or (more importantly) by inciting males to violent crimes against them or creating a cultural climate in which

From Joel Feinberg, *Offense to Others* (Oxford: Oxford University Press, 1985).

such crimes are likely to become more frequent. The two traditional legal categories involved in these harm-principle arguments, then, are *defamation* and *incitement*. The other class of arguments invoke the offense principle, not in order to prevent mere "nuisances," but to prevent profound offense analogous to that of the Jews in Skokie or the blacks in a town where the K.K.K. rallies.

I shall not spend much time on the claim that violent and other extremely degrading pornography should be banned on the ground that it *defames* women. In a skeptical spirit, I can begin by pointing out that there are immense difficulties in applying the civil law of libel and slander as it is presently constituted in such a way as not to violate freedom of expression. Problems with *criminal* libel and slander would be even more unmanageable, and *group* defamation, whether civil or criminal, would multiply the problems still further. The argument on the other side is that pornography is essentially propaganda—propaganda against women. It does not slander women in the technical legal sense by asserting damaging falsehoods about them, because it *asserts* nothing at all. But it spreads an image of women as mindless playthings or "objects," inferior beings fit only to be used and abused for the pleasure of men, whether they like it or not, but often to their own secret pleasure. This picture lowers the esteem men have for women, and for that reason (if defamation is the basis of the argument) is sufficient ground for proscription even in the absence of any evidence of tangible harm to women caused by the behavior of misled and deluded men.

If degrading pornography defames (libels or slanders) women, it must be in virtue of some beliefs about women—false beliefs—that it conveys, so that in virtue of those newly acquired or reenforced false beliefs, consumers lower their esteem for women in general. If a work of pornography, for example, shows a woman (or group of women) in exclusively subservient or domestic roles, that may lead the consumer to *believe* that women, in virtue of some inherent female characteristics, are only fit for such roles. There is no doubt that much pornography does portray women in subservient positions, but if that is defamatory to women in anything like the legal sense, then so are soap commercials on TV. So are many novels, even some good ones. (A good novel may yet be about some degraded characters.) That some groups are portrayed in unflattering roles has not hitherto been a ground for the censorship of fiction or advertising. Besides, it is not clearly the *group* that is portrayed at all in such works, but only one individual (or small set of individuals) and fictitious ones at that. Are fat men defamed by Shakespeare's picture of Falstaff? Are Jews defamed by the characterization of Shylock? Could any writer today even hope to write a novel partly about a fawning corrupted black, under group defamation laws, without risking censorship or worse? The chilling effect on the practice of fiction-writing would amount to a near freeze.

Moreover, . . . the degrading images and defamatory beliefs pornographic works are alleged to cause are not produced in the consumer by explicit statements asserted with the intent to convince the reader or auditor of their truth. Rather they are caused by the stimulus of the work, in the context, on the expectations, attitudes, and beliefs the viewer brings with him to the work. That is quite other than believing an assertion on the authority or argument of the party making the assertion, or understanding the assertion in the first place in virtue of fixed conventions of language use and meaning. Without those fixed conventions of language, the work has to be interpreted in order for any message to be extracted from it, and the process of interpretation. . . . What looks like sexual subservience to some looks like liberation from sexual repression to others. It is hard to imagine how a court could provide a workable, much less fair, test of whether a given work has sufficiently damaged male esteem toward women for it to be judged criminally defamatory, when so much of the viewer's reaction he brings on himself, and viewer reactions are so widely variable. . . .

The major argument for repression of violent pornography under the harm principle is that it promotes rape and physical violence. In the United States there is a plenitude both of sexual violence against women and of violent pornography. . . . This has suggested to some writers that there must be a direct causal link between violent pornography and sexual violence against women; but causal relationships between pornography and rape, if they exist, must be more complicated than that. The suspicion of direct connection is dissipated, as Aryeh Neier points out,

> . . . when one looks at the situation in other countries. For example, violence against women is common in . . . Ireland and South Africa, but pornography is unavailable in those countries. By contrast violence against women is relatively uncommon in Denmark, Sweden, and the Netherlands, even though pornography seems to be even more plentifully available than in the United States. To be sure, this proves little or nothing except that more evidence is needed to establish a causal connection between pornography and violence against women beyond the fact that both may exist at the same time. But this evidence . . . simply does not exist.[1]

On the other hand, there is evidence that novel ways of committing crimes are often suggested (usually inadvertently) by bizarre tales in films or TV, . . . and even factual newspaper reports of crimes can trigger the well-known "copy-cat crime" phenomenon. But if the possibility of copy-cat cases, by itself, justified censorship or punishment, we would have grounds for supressing films of *The Brothers Karamozov* and the TV series *Roots* (both of which have been cited as influences on imitative crimes). "There would be few books left on our library shelves and few films that could be shown if every one that had at some time 'provoked' bizarre behavior were censored."[2] A violent episode in a pornographic work may indeed be a causally necessary condition for the commission of some specific crime by a specific perpetrator on a specific victim at some specific time and place. But for his reading or viewing that episode, the perpetrator may not have done precisely what he did in just the time, place, and manner that he did it. But so large a part of the full causal explanation of his act concerns his own psychological character and predispositions, that it is likely that some similar crime would have suggested itself to him in due time. It is not likely that non-rapists are converted into rapists *simply* by reading and viewing pornography. If pornography has a serious causal bearing on the occurence of rape (as opposed to the trivial copy-cat effect) it must be in virtue of its role (still to be established) in implanting the appropriate cruel dispositions in the first place.

Rape is such a complex social phenomenon that there is probably no one simple generalization to account for it. Some rapes are no doubt ineliminable, no matter how we design our institutions. Many of these are the product of deep individual psychological problems, transferred rages, and the like. But for others, perhaps the preponderant number, the major part of the explanation is sociological, not psychological. In these cases the rapist is a psychologically normal person well adjusted to his particular subculture, acting calmly and deliberately rather than in a rage, and doing what he thinks is expected of him by his peers, what he must do to acquire or preserve standing in his group. His otherwise inexplicable violence is best explained as a consequence of the peculiar form of his socialization among his peers, his pursuit of a prevailing ideal of manliness, what the Mexicans have long called *machismo,* but which exists to some degree or other among men in most countries, certainly in our own.

The macho male wins the esteem of his associates by being tough, fearless, reckless, wild, unsentimental, hard-boiled, hard drinking, disrespectful, profane, willing to fight whenever his honor is impugned, and fight without fear of consequences no matter how extreme. He is a sexual athlete who must be utterly dominant over "his" females, who are expected to be slavishly devoted to him even though he lacks gentleness with them and shows his regard only by displaying them like trophies. . . .

Would it significantly reduce sexual violence if violent pornography were effectively banned? No one can know for sure, but if the cult of macho is the main source of such violence, as I suspect, then repression of violent pornography, whose function is to pander to the macho values already deeply rooted in society, may have little effect. Pornography does not cause normal decent chaps, through a single exposure, to metamorphoze into rapists. Pornography-reading machos commit rape, but that is because they already have macho values, not because they read the violent pornography that panders to them. Perhaps then *constant* exposure to violent porn might turn a decent person into a violence-prone macho. But that does not seem likely either, since the repugnant violence of the materials could not have any appeal in the first place to one who did not already have some strong macho predispositions, so "constant exposure" could not begin to become established. Clearly, other causes, and more foundational ones, must be at work, if violent porn is to have any initial purchase. Violent pornography is more a symptom of *machismo* than a cause of it, and treating symptoms merely is not a way to offer protection to potential victims of rapists. At most, I think there may be a small spill-over effect of violent porn on actual violence. . . .

How then can we hope to weaken and then extirpate the cultish values at the root of our problem? The criminal law is a singularly ill-adapted tool for that kind of job. We might just as well legislate against entrepreneurship on the grounds that capitalism engenders "acquisitive personalities," or against the military on the grounds that it produces "authoritarian personalities," or against certain religious sects on the grounds that they foster puritanism, as criminalize practices and institutions on the grounds that they contribute to *machismo*. But macho values are culturally, not instinctively, transmitted, and the behavior that expresses them is learned, not inherited, behavior. What is learned can be unlearned. Schools should play a role. Surely, learning to see through machismo and avoid its traps should be as important a part of a child's preparation for citizenship as the acquisition of patriotism and piety. To be effective, such teaching should be frank and direct, not totally reliant on general moral platitudes. It should talk about the genesis of children's attitudes toward the other sex, and invite discussion of male insecurity, resentment of women, cruelty, and even specific odious examples. Advertising firms and film companies should be asked (at first), then pressured (if necessary) to cooperate, as they did in the successful campaign to deglamorize cigarette smoking. Fewer exploitation films should be made. . . . Materials (especially films) should be made available to clergymen as well as teachers, youth counselors, and parole officers. A strong part of the emphasis of these materials should be on the harm that bondage to the cult of macho does to men too, and how treacherous a trap *machismo* can be. The new moral education must be careful, of course, not to preach dull prudence as a preferred style for youthful living. A zest for excitement, adventure, even danger, cannot be artificially removed from adolescent nature. Moreover, teamwork, camaraderie, and toughness of character need not be denigrated. But the cult of macho corrupts and distorts these values in ways that can be made clear to youths. The mistreatment of women, when its motivation is clearly revealed and understood, should be a sure way of eliciting the contempt of the group, not a means to greater prestige within it.

Notes

1. Aryeh Neier, "Expurgating the First Amendment," *The Nation*, June 21, 1980, p. 754.
2. Loc. cit.

Study Questions

1. How does Feinberg differentiate the "harm principle" and the "offense principle"?
2. What difficulties does Feinberg find in applying to pornography the civil law of libel and slander?
3. Can a good novel be pornographic?
4. Do you agree with Feinberg that the law is ill adapted to weaken macho values?

E.

Drug Legalization

Three Points about Drug Decriminalization

Douglas Husak

Douglas Husak is Professor of Philosophy at Rutgers University. He argues that the use of drugs should not be a criminal offense. He starts with the plausible idea that to put people in jail or fine them for engaging in a certain activity requires good reasons. Finding none in this case, he concludes that drugs should be decriminalized.

. . . Approximately 80 to 90 million people have used illicit drugs at some point in their lives. There are well over 400,000 drug offenders in jail, about 130,000 for possession alone. Unlike the case of capital murderers, it is plausible to suppose that drug users should not be punished at all, and this is what I want to argue here. . . .

I. The Meaning of Decriminalization

First, there is absolutely no consensus among those of us who work in criminal theory about the meaning of such terms as *legalization* or *decriminalization*. So I resort to stipulation. What I mean by the use of

From Douglas Husak, "Four Points about Drug Decriminalization," *Criminal Justice Ethics* 22 (2003).

the term "decriminalization" in this context is that the *use* of a given drug would not be a criminal offense. I take it to be a conceptual truth for which I will not argue here that criminal offenses render persons liable to state punishment. Thus anyone who thinks that the use of a given drug should be decriminalized believes that persons should not be punished merely for using that drug. . . .

For a number of reasons, this definition of decriminalization is deceptively simple. First, there really is little punishment for use today. In most but not all jurisdictions, what is punished is possession rather than use. Technically, then, drug use is generally not criminalized. But I take the fact that statutes punish possession rather than use to be relatively unimportant. Possession is punished rather than use because it is easier to prove. In what follows, I ignore this complication and continue to suppose that decriminalization pertains to drug use. Except perhaps in fantastic cases, no one can use a drug without possessing it.

Second, there is no clear understanding of what kinds of state responses amount to punishments. Many reformers argue that drug users should be fined rather than imprisoned, and they call this idea decriminalization. Others argue that drug users should be made to undergo treatment, and they also call this idea decriminalization. Whether these proposals are compatible with what I mean by decriminalization depends on whether fines or coerced treatment are modes *of* punishment rather than alternatives *to* punishment. I think both fines and coerced treatment are modes of punishment. Even though they are probably preferable to what we now do to drug users, these responses are ruled out by decriminalization as I construe it. But that is a quibble I hope not to worry about. Simply put, whatever you take punishment to be, that is what decriminalization forbids the state from doing to people who merely use drugs.

Third, decriminalization as I propose to define it has no implications for what should be done to persons who *produce* or *sell* drugs. Therefore, it is not really a comprehensive drug policy that can rival the status quo. The considerations that I think work in favor of decriminalizing use are somewhat different from those that apply to the decriminalization of production and sale, so I propose to put production and sale aside in this essay. . . .

Finally, I admit that there is something odd about my understanding of decriminalization. What I call decriminalization in the context of drugs is comparable to what was called prohibition in the context of alcohol from 1920 to 1933. During those memorable years, production and sale were banned, but not the use or mere possession of alcohol. If we replicated that approach in our drug policy, I would call it decriminalization. That is admittedly odd, but it underscores the fact that our response to illicit drug users today is far more punitive than anything we ever did to drinkers.

II. The Best Reason to Decriminalize Drug Use

With these preliminaries out of the way, let me proceed to the basic question to be addressed. In my judgment, the fundamental issue is not whether to *de*criminalize the use of any or all drugs, but whether to *criminalize* the use of any or all drugs. The status quo must be defended. If this is the right question to ask, I would now like to offer what I believe to be the most plausible answer to it: The best reason *not* to criminalize drug use is that no argument in favor of criminalizing drug use is any good—no argument is good enough to justify criminalization. I want to make three points about this general strategy for decriminalization.

First, I recognize that this approach is not very exciting. My reason to oppose criminalization does not invoke any deep principle worth fighting about like freedom of speech or religion. I am not sure that there is any deep principle that *all* drug prohibitions violate. . . .

Then again, *some* drug prohibitions seem to violate deep principles that philosophers should care about. This becomes more apparent when you pause to consider exactly what it is that drug proscriptions are designed to prevent. Most drugs have a legitimate use, so drug consumption per se is rarely prohibited. Instead, the use of most drugs is prohibited only for a given purpose. To get directly to the heart of the matter, the proscribed purpose is usually to produce a state of intoxication or a drug "high." In case there is any doubt, let me cite the California criminal statute regulating nitrous oxide. This statute makes it a crime for "any person [to possess] nitrous oxide . . . with the intent to breathe [or] inhale for purposes of causing a condition of intoxication, elation, euphoria, dizziness, stupefaction, or dulling of the senses or for the purpose of, in any manner, changing mental processes."[1] The ultimate objective of this statute is to prevent persons from breathing something in order to change their mental processes. It is hard to see why this objective is legitimate in a state committed to freedom of thought and expression. I am not sure that *all* drug prohibitions so transparently jeopardize our right to freedom of thought. In any event, I do not believe we need to appeal to any deep principle to resist drug prohibitions generally.

Second, my case is necessarily inconclusive. I am in the unenviable position of trying to prove a negative. How can I hope to show that no argument in favor of criminalizing drug use is good enough? All I can ever aspire to do is to respond to the best arguments that have been given. I am reminded of a remark made by Hume. "'Tis impossible to refute a system, which has never been explain'd. In such a manner of fighting in the dark, a man loses his blows in the air, and often places them where the enemy is not present."[2] This is the predicament someone faces in trying to defend drug decriminalization. I am usually asked to go first on panels convened to debate drug decriminalization, but I think I should go last so that I can respond to what others think are good reasons for criminalization.

Third, my case for decriminalization has the advantage of making minimal assumptions about justice. I assume that no one should be punished unless there are excellent reasons for doing so. Punishment, after all, is the worst thing our state can do to us. The imposition of punishment must satisfy a very demanding standard of justification. It is hard to imagine that anyone would reject this assumption.

Thus my case against criminalization depends on the claim that no case for criminalization has been adequately defended. It is utterly astounding, I think, that no very good argument for drug prohibitions has ever been given. When I am asked to recommend the best book or article that makes a philosophically plausible case for punishing drug users, I am embarrassed to say that I have little to suggest.

Let me then cut directly to my own conclusions. No single argument for decriminalization responds to all arguments for criminalization. We must respond argument-by-argument, and, I think, drug-by-drug. We may have good reasons to criminalize some drugs, but not others. For example, I do not know anyone who wants to punish persons who use caffeine. Surely this is because of empirical facts about caffeine—how it affects those who use it and society in general. I can certainly *imagine* a drug that people should be punished for using. Such drugs are easy to describe; they are vividly portrayed in great works of fiction. Consider the substance that transformed Dr. Jekyll into Mr. Hyde. If a drug literally turned users into homicidal monsters, we would have excellent reasons to prohibit its consumption. Fortunately, no such drug actually exists. In fact, I have never seen a persuasive argument for punishing persons who use any drug that I am aware is widely used for recreational purposes.

III. Criminalization

Any good reason to criminalize a kind of behavior invokes a theory of criminalization. We cannot decide whether we have a good reason to punish persons who use drugs in particular unless we know what would count as a good reason to punish anyone for anything. We do not really have a theory of criminalization in the real world, unless "more is always better" qualifies for a theory. I want to pause briefly to describe what passes for a theory of criminalization in our constitutional law today. Most laws limit or restrict liberties. When the constitutionality of these laws is challenged, courts respond by dividing liberties into two kinds: *fundamental* and *non-fundamental*. The constitutionality of legislation that restricts a fundamental liberty is subjected to "strict scrutiny" and is evaluated by applying the onerous "compelling state interest" test. Virtually all criminal laws, however, limit non-fundamental liberties, and they are assessed by applying the much less demanding "rational basis" test. Under this test, the challenged law will be upheld if it is substantially related to a legitimate government purpose. The legitimate government purpose need not be the actual objective of the legislation—only its conceivable objective. Since only those laws that lack a conceivable legitimate purpose will fail this test, courts almost never find a law to be unconstitutional when non-fundamental liberties are restricted. As a result, the state needs only some conceivable legitimate purpose to enact the great majority of criminal laws on the books today— most notably, drug prohibitions, which are always evaluated by applying the rational basis test. So persons who break these laws can be punished simply because the state has a rational basis to do so.

What is remarkable about this approach is its complete indifference to the distinction between criminal and non-criminal legislation. It is one thing to enact non-criminal laws that pass the rational basis test. But it is quite another when criminal legislation is assessed by that same standard. Criminal law is different—it is importantly dissimilar from other kinds of law. Many of the arguments I have heard for drug prohibitions do a perfectly good job explaining why rational persons might well decide not to use illicit drugs, or why the state may have good reasons to discourage people from using drugs, but I fear they do not provide a justification for *punishing* drug users.

If our theory of criminalization in the real world is so bad, one would have thought that the most distinguished criminal theorists of our day would have had lots to say to rectify the situation. But they have said surprisingly little. They mostly continue to argue about the *harm principle.* But debates about whether to accept the harm principle in our theory of criminalization do not get us very far when trying to decide whether to punish drug users. We have excellent reasons to punish people who commit theft or rape. These offenses harm others by violating their rights. But this rationale cannot explain why drug users should be punished. I do not think there is any sense of harm or any theory of rights that can be invoked to show that I harm someone or violate his rights when I inject heroin or smoke crack. At most, I risk harm to myself or to others when I use a drug. I conceptualize offenses that create only a *risk* of harm that may or may not materialize as *inchoate* offenses—similar to attempt, solicitation, or conspiracy. If I am correct, the criteria we should apply to assess the justifiability of drug proscriptions are those we should apply to assess the justifiability of inchoate offenses. Unfortunately, we have no such criteria. Almost no theorist has tried very hard to extend a theory of criminalization to conduct that creates a risk of harm rather than harm itself.

Notice, however, the enormous burden an argument for criminalization would have to bear. . . . [There] are about 80 or 90 million Americans who have used an illicit drug at some point in their lives. That is approximately 42 percent of our population aged 12 and over. About 15 million Americans used an illicit drug last year, on literally billions of occasions. Very few of these occasions produced any harm. Longitudinal studies do not indicate that the population of persons who ever have used illicit drugs is very different from the population of lifetime abstainers in any ways that seem relevant to criminalization. So any argument for punishment would have to justify punishing the many, whose behavior is innocuous, for the sake of some objective that results in a very tiny percentage of cases. Many attempted murders result in successful murders, which are harms, but very few instances of drug use bring about any result we should describe as significantly harmful.

When you cannot possibly punish *all* of the people who commit a crime, you can only punish *some.* Inevitably, those who get arrested, prosecuted, and sentenced are the least powerful. Drug prohibition would have vanished long ago had whites been sent to prison for drug offenses at the same rate as blacks. Although minorities are no more likely to use illicit drugs, they are far more likely to be arrested, prosecuted, and punished when they do. This is one of the features of drug prohibitions that should outrage us all. Some people try to package drug prohibitions as a benefit to minorities, but there is plenty of evidence that they devastate minority communities and will continue to do so as long as enforcement is so selective. And yet enforcement will always be selective, since every offender cannot possibly be punished. . . .

Notes

1. *Cal. State Penal Code*, §381(b) (2002).
2. David Hume, *A Treatise of Human Nature*, (Selby-Bigge ed, 1968), Book III Section 1 p. 464.

Study Questions

1. What does Husak mean by "decriminalization"?
2. What is the difference between criminal and noncriminal legislation?
3. Should the law treat the use of heroin differently from the use of marijuana?
4. Should the law treat the use of drugs differently from the use of alcohol?

On the Decriminalization of Drugs

George Sher

George Sher, Professor of Philosophy at Rice University, responds to Husak's contention that good arguments for criminalizing drugs don't exist by offering three. The first, the paternalistic argument, holds that the reason for criminalization rests with the harm that drug users pose to themselves. The second, the protective argument, holds that the grounds for criminalization lie with the risk of harm drug users present to others. The third, the perfectionist argument, holds that because drugs tend to make people lead less worthwhile lives, the state is justified in criminalizing their use. Together these three arguments suggest that the risks associated with the use of drugs is too great to warrant their decriminalization.

I. Three Arguments for Criminalization

I begin with two ritual disclaimers. When I say that there is a good case for continuing to attach criminal penalties to the use of narcotics, I do not mean that that case extends to any particular schedule of penalties or to any special list of drugs. I am sure that many drug sentences, both past and present, are far too harsh. I am also willing to concede that the harms and bads associated with some drugs—marijuana is the obvious example—may not be significant enough to justify attaching even minor penalties to their use. I do think, however, that the harms and bads associated with many other drugs are sufficiently weighty to justify their continued criminalization. The drugs of which I take this to be true include heroin, cocaine, methamphetamine, LSD, and ecstasy, among others.

From George Sher, "On the Decriminalization of Drugs," *Criminal Justice Ethics* 22 (2003).

What, then, are the main arguments for criminalizing these drugs? They are, I think, just the familiar ones: drug users harm themselves, they harm others, and they do not live good lives. At the risk of sounding like an eighth-grade teacher, or a drug czar, I will briefly sketch each argument.

(1) The Paternalistic Argument

The nature of the harms that drug users risk is of course a function of the drugs they use. . . . [H]eroin harms the user by sapping his motivation and initiative. Also, because heroin is addictive, using it now forecloses the option of comfortably not using it later. By contrast, cocaine and methamphetamine do not have only these effects (though "crack" is by all accounts highly addictive), but their regular use also significantly increases the risk of heart attack and stroke. Furthermore, by drastically enhancing self-confidence, aggression, and libido, these drugs elicit behavior that predictably culminates in high-speed collisions, shootouts in parking lots, and destroyed immune systems. Other drugs have still other destructive effects: LSD can trigger lasting psychosis; ecstasy harms the brain, impairs the memory, and, taken with alcohol, damages the liver; and so on. Thus, one obvious reason to continue to criminalize these drugs is simply that many persons deterred by the law from using them will thereby be spared serious injury.

(2) The Protective Argument

Just as drug use can harm the user, so, too, can it harm others. Drug use harms strangers by involving them in the collisions, shoot-outs, and other catastrophes to which the impaired and overly aggressive are prone. It harms family members by depriving them of the steady companionship and income of their addicted partners. It harms fetuses by exposing them to a toxic and permanently damaging prenatal environment. It harms children by subjecting them to the neglect and abuse of their drug-addled parents. Thus, a second obvious reason to continue criminalizing drugs is that many persons deterred by the law from using drugs will thereby be prevented from harming others.

(3) The Perfectionist Argument

Just as there is broad agreement about what constitutes harm, so, too, is there broad agreement about many factors determining both good and bad lives. Most would agree that it is bad when people stumble through life with a blurred and distorted view of reality; bad when they cannot hold a thought from one moment to the next or follow a simple chain of reasoning; bad when they drift passively with no interest in pursuing worthwhile goals; and bad when they care more about the continued repetition of pleasant sensations than about the needs and interests of those who love and depend on them. Many would agree, too, that it is doubly bad when the reason people live this way is simply because they have squandered the chance to live better. Thus, a third main argument for retaining the drug laws is that many persons whom they deter are thereby prevented from wasting their lives.

II. Criminalization and the Risk of Harm

There may be other arguments for continuing to criminalize drugs, but the three just mentioned are surely among the most influential. However, although Husak concedes that some such arguments may indeed explain "why rational persons might well decide not to use illicit drugs, or why the state may have good reasons to discourage people from using drugs," he denies that any of them "provide a justification for *punishing* drug users."[1] Why, exactly, does he deny this?

As Husak agreeably acknowledges, his opposition to criminalization is not a matter of deep principle. He . . . allows that he can easily imagine drugs so harmful that they should be criminalized: "[i]f a drug literally turned users into homicidal monsters, we would have excellent reasons to prohibit its consumption."[2] However, according to Husak, no actual drug satisfies this description because no drug causes harm in more than a small proportion of cases. As Husak points out, "[a]bout 15 million Americans used an illicit drug last year, on literally billions of occasions," but "[v]ery few of these occasions produced any harm."[3] Because the antecedent likelihood of harm is small on any given occasion, Husak maintains that there is no "sense of harm . . . that can be invoked to show that I harm someone . . . when I inject heroin or smoke crack. At most, I risk harm to myself or to others when I use a drug."[4] This is said to undermine the case for criminalization because "[a]lmost no theorist has tried very hard to extend a theory of criminalization to conduct that creates a risk of harm rather than harm itself."[5]

Although Husak's official aim in these passages is only to cast doubt on those defenses of the drug laws that appeal to the harm principle, his reasoning can also be extended to the paternalistic and perfectionist arguments. To extend it, we need note only that just as no single occasion of drug use is likely to harm anyone other than the user, so, too, is no single occasion likely either to harm the user himself or to reduce significantly the goodness of his life. Because the (un)likelihood of each effect is roughly equal, the threats that Husak's reasoning poses to our three arguments seem roughly equal as well. This, of course, makes it all the more urgent to ask whether the reasoning can in fact be sustained.

Whatever else we say, we surely must insist that all reasonable theories of criminalization *do* allow governments to criminalize behavior simply on the grounds that it is too risky. We must insist on this not only for the boring reason that all reasonable theories permit governments to attach criminal penalties to drunk driving, discharging firearms in public places, and innumerable other forms of endangerment, but also for the more interesting reason that any decision to criminalize a form of behavior must be made *before* any occurrence of that behavior for which anyone can be punished. Such a decision must be based on an *ex ante* judgment about how risky the behavior is. Husak can hardly be unaware of this, and so his point can hardly be that we are *never* justified in criminalizing behavior merely on the grounds that it is risky. Instead, I take him to be making only the more modest (but still relevant) point that we are not justified in criminalizing behavior merely on the grounds that it imposes a risk of harm *that is as small as the risk imposed by a single instance of drug use.*

Should we accept this version of Husak's claim? We might have reason to accept it if the relevant forms of low-risk behavior could all be assumed to be rare, for then the amounts of harm we would tolerate by tolerating them would also be small. However, drug use is of course not rare—Husak puts its frequency at billions of occurrences per year—so even if the risk on any given occasion is small, the total amount of harm must still be large. Even if, say, cocaine users harm no one but themselves in 999 out of 1000 cases, ten million uses of cocaine will still harm non-users ten thousand times. If there is any reason to take this number of harms less seriously when they result from ten million uses of cocaine than when they result from only ten thousand uses of some more reliably harmful drug, I must confess that I do not see what it is. Thus, if criminalizing the more reliably harmful drug to prevent this number of harms to non-users is legitimate—as it surely would be if each harm were on average as severe as the average harm done by cocaine—then criminalizing cocaine to prevent this number of harms must be legitimate too.

Even were prevention of harm to others the only legitimate rationale for criminalizing any form of behavior, the aggregative nature of the harms associated with drug use would pose a serious problem for Husak's claim about risk. However, if, as I believe, the state may also legitimately criminalize behavior for paternalistic and perfectionist reasons, then aggregation will pose problems for his claim in at least four more ways. First, just as the infrequent but serious harms that drug users do to others are bound to add up, so are the infrequent but serious harms they do to themselves. Second, if each use of a given drug does a small amount of harm to the user's brain or heart, then his frequent and repetitive use of that drug is likely to do his brain or heart a lot of harm. Third, even if no single instance of drug use has much impact on the goodness of a person's life, a life entirely given over to drug use may be very bad indeed. And, fourth, just as there can be aggregation within each category of harm or bad, so, too, can there be aggregation across the categories. If the cumulative harm that drug users do to themselves is one reason to criminalize drugs, and the cumulative harm they do to others is another, and the cumulative badness of their lives is still another, then the cumulative weight of the three cumulative reasons must surely be greater than the weight of any single one alone.

III. If Narcotics, Why Not Alcohol?

Given all this, I am unconvinced by Husak's suggestion that the risks associated with drugs are too small to warrant their criminalization. However, another objection to their criminalization—an objection which Husak does not make explicit but which hovers near the edge of much of what he says—bothers me more. This is the objection that every argument that speaks for the criminalization of drugs speaks with equal strength for the criminalization of alcohol. If this objection can be sustained, then those who favor criminalizing drugs but not alcohol—as I do—are simply giving their preferred intoxicant a free pass.

Although the parallels between drugs and alcohol are pretty obvious, it may be useful to make a few of them explicit. To bring these out, we need only remind ourselves that alcohol, too, is famous for causing people to do things that culminate in fiery collisions, parking-lot shoot-outs, and destroyed immune systems; that alcoholics are well known for neglecting their partners and abusing their children; that alcohol creates an environment that is toxic and permanently damaging to fetuses; that being drunk cuts a person off from reality and prevents him from thinking clearly; and that alcohol harms the brain, impairs the memory, and, taken with ecstasy, damages the liver. We may remind ourselves, as well, that although most instances of alcohol use have no such effects, its use is so common—Americans drink alcohol billions of times per year—that the overall amount of harm and degradation that it causes is very large indeed.

Given these impressive similarities, the arguments for criminalizing the two intoxicants appear to stand or fall together. Thus, having claimed that the arguments succeed for drug criminalization, I may seem also committed to the view that they succeed for alcohol. However, because I find a world without beer too grim to contemplate, I want to resist this conclusion if possible. Is there any wiggle room here?

Given the structure of the pro-criminalization arguments, I think there may be. The salient feature of each argument is that it appeals to a kind of harm or bad that is (relatively) infrequent but whose overall total exceeds some crucial threshold. Thus, all three of my arguments leave open the possibility that the reason drugs take us past the threshold is that alcohol has already gotten us part of the way there. It may be the case, in other words, that either alcohol or the use of drugs by itself would *not* produce more harms or bads than a reasonable society can tolerate, but that in combination they would produce harms and bads that surpass the threshold. If anything like this is true, then it will not be at all inconsistent to advocate the criminalization of drugs but not alcohol. The reason for treating drugs and alcohol differently will be that we can hold the relevant harms and bads below the threshold by legally permitting one or the other but not by permitting both; the reason for continuing to criminalize drugs but not alcohol will be that this is easier and less costly than switching—easier because it avoids divisive legislative battles and the uprooting of entrenched traditions, less costly because it does not require the dismantling of a multi-million-dollar industry.

Is what I have just described anything more than a bare logical possibility? Would the decriminalization of drugs, together with the continued non-criminalization of alcohol, really take us beyond some crucial threshold of harm and badness? I must admit that I do not know. I do not know how to conceptualize the relevant threshold, how to quantify the harms and bads to which it applies, or (therefore) how to decide whether drugs plus alcohol would add up to one legal intoxicant too many. But although I am sure that I do not know these things, I am also sure that those who favor drug decriminalization do not know them either. Thus, as long as there is *some* level of harmfulness and badness beyond which criminalization becomes reasonable, the question of whether we should legalize both intoxicants, or one of the two, or neither will remain unsettled. Although the status quo is not easy to defend, it is not clear that Husak's relaxed alternative is really any easier.

Notes

1. Douglas Husak, "Four Points about Drug Criminalization," Criminal Justice Ethics, 22 (2003), p. 6.
2. *Id.*
3. *Id.*, p. 7.
4. *Id.*, p. 6.
5. *Id.*

Study Questions

1. Are drug users likely to cause harm to others?
2. Are drug users likely to cause harm to themselves?
3. Are drug users likely to lead less worthwhile lives?
4. How does Sher respond to the claim that the use of drugs is no different from the use of alcohol?

F.

Gun Control

Arms as Insurance

Samuel C. Wheeler III

Samuel Wheeler is Professor of Philosophy at the University of Connecticut. He argues that the right to bear arms is *the* fundamental right, because it is necessary for the enjoyment of our other rights. Given that a government can, and often does, unjustly coerce its citizens, they need to be afforded the opportunity to defend themselves. Wheeler contends that the right to bear arms is justified to the extent that it serves this function.

I. Meta-Rights and Rights

I take it as obvious that having a right that x entails having a right to take steps to make it more likely that x. Making it more likely that x essentially means taking steps to prevent unjust coercions which would prevent x. So, if a person has a right to the use of his garden produce, he has a right to lower the probability that that produce will be stolen by animals or people, for instance. Such rights, of course, have to be weighed against other rights. If my garden-protection scheme involves powerful searchlights and high-decibel recordings of rock music, my

From Samuel C. Wheeler III, "Arms as Insurance," *Public Affairs Quarterly* 13 (1999).

right to protect my garden runs afoul of the rights of my neighbors not to have their environment polluted by excessive light and sound.

Government is legitimated, at a minimum, by its protection of rights to life and liberty. Its institutions are at least designed to coerce citizens into respecting others' rights. If government were absolutely reliable and effective in ensuring rights not to be assaulted or despoiled of one's goods, then any measures one took independently to ensure that one's rights were not violated would be redundant. A person could still lock his valuables in a safe in his house even though the risk of theft had been reduced to zero by effective police. Even a perfect government should permit citizens to dispose of their resources foolishly. It would entail, though, that no such steps could violate another's rights, even in the slightest.

Conflicts of Rights, Risks, and Their Rational Resolution

Consider the most obvious truisms about conflict of rights: Some steps that I might take to protect my garden would impose costs on others, as in the example above. Since my neighbors have a right not to have costs imposed on them, the assessment of the right to protect my garden depends on the gravity of the costs and the gravity of the loss to me if my garden is despoiled by raccoons or by vandals.

Other steps I may take to protect my garden do not impose costs on others except probabilistically. If I protect my garden by building a double fence within which fierce but silent dogs circle the garden, then my neighbors are exposed to a risk that some of these dogs will escape and dig up their flower beds or savage people and pets. The source of risk could be unreliable fencing, my human forgetfulness about closing and locking the gate, or the miscellaneous possibilities of vandalism of the fence, hurricanes felling a tree on the fence, thereby letting the dogs out, and so forth. My neighbors have much to be worried about, depending on the ferocity of my dogs, the quality of my fence, my reliability, and so forth.

Ideally, rights to engage in activities that impose risks on others are evaluated by weighing the expected losses on both sides. That is, we assess the losses on both sides, multiply by the probabilities, and decide. If the ruination of my garden is a small cost, then, even though there is very little chance of one of my dogs escaping into the neighborhood, the enormous cost of having a child savaged can outweigh my right to protect my garden by this means. A tiny probability of a terrible loss can outweigh a relatively large probability of a relatively small loss. Few of us want to live near even the most carefully monitored nuclear reactor. . . .

Insuring Against Criminal Coercions

We can be coerced by criminals, given the imperfections of government policing. Protection from this kind of coercion, of course, takes the form of various kinds of precautions, preventions, and preparations for meeting threats. . . . Among the clearest rights is the right to prevent serious harms to oneself and others[1] by disabling a would-be assailant, at whatever cost to the assailant. A practically useful right to resist criminal assaults entails a right to be prepared for reasonably expected assaults. The limitations of rights to such preparations derive from the risks such preparations impose on others.

When a criminal assault takes place, you have recognized rights, which your government happens to be unable to enforce. Whatever rights you are granted to prepare for such assaults by means that impose some risks on others are predicated on the government's occasional inability to effectively prevent assaults. If there were the technology available to instantly get police assistance when an assault was imminent, there would be no rights to prepare for possible assaults by other, more dangerous means. For instance, if there were instantaneous transport such as the crew of the Enterprise used, and police could be instantly fetched to any location by such devices upon a citizen pushing the button of a beeper-like device, then risks would be very different. There probably would be no right to prepare oneself for assaults by criminals by the more dangerous device of carrying a concealed handgun to balance threats against you by threats against the assailant. In our actual pre–Star Trek state, there are good reasons to think that, if risks are properly managed, there is a right to be prepared to use deadly force to prevent deadly harms to oneself and others. . . .

If we imagine a government with such ideal protection abilities, it might seem that no risk-producing means of self-protection would be permissible whatsoever. All assailants would be as effectively deterred by the institutions of the government as by any strategies an individual could come up with. So, one might conclude that the more perfect police protection is, the less right there is to, for instance, possess firearms. The implicit assumption of this argument that better police protection or more effective devices for reducing crime (education, elimination of poverty, pre-crime detention of those disposed to assault) would remove any right to privately equip oneself to resist coercion. This assumption overlooks a major player in unjust coercion, government itself.

Insuring Against Unjust Government Coercions

Given that one is a human being who has been subjected to unjust deadly assault since 1900, the conditional probability that the assailants were agents of one's own government is higher than the conditional probability that the assailant is a criminal by local standards of legitimacy. If we leave out cases of questionable injustice, and just include clearly unjust homicides, the totals from the Belgian, Turkish, Russian, German, Chinese, Ugandan, Indonesian, Cambodian, Rwandan, etc. government-sanctioned slaughters exceed the totals from the private sector by a substantial factor. So, relative to just the information that a person is a human, she is more likely to suffer deadly harms from her own government than from criminals. . . .

The rest of this essay will explore the possibility that it is always reasonable to worry about government injustice, that no institutions will remove the reasonableness of that worry, and that therefore, every just government institutionalizes the possibility of resistance to it.

II. The Right to Resist Government Assault

I assume that the right to resist unjust assaults by legitimate governments is obvious in some cases. It is obvious that the residents of the Warsaw Ghetto had a right to defend themselves and that each member of a Cambodian village had a right to resist "relocation" by the Khmer Rouge, even though the governments assaulting them were "legitimate" in the sense that they had been recognized by other governments. . . .

A right to bear arms, practically speaking, enables a government and its citizens to make a deal whereby the government does not explicitly limit its powers of enforcement and interpretation, but where in fact there is a real possibility of effective resistance to government coercion. A right to bear arms is a right to be prepared to resist government coercion, if need be, even though there is no right to resist government coercion as such. When a government is going bad, and a community comes to realize this, they are in a position to collectively take up arms, an option that was not available to Ugandans, German Jews, or Cambodians.

A right to bear arms, of course, gives only a probabilistic insurance against tyranny. If a government limits its injustices to a minority, for instance, the effect of that minority being armed is primarily to increase the costs of obvious injustice. It is much easier and cheaper to burn down a ghetto populated by unarmed people than by resisters. Untrained enthusiasts rather than trained soldiers can do the work, whereas it is generally quite difficult to convince amateurs to do the dangerous work that house-to-house fighting entails. A very few incompetent Ugandan soldiers can depopulate a village that has no guns, but armed villagers acting in concert would have made depopulation very expensive, if not prohibitively so. An armed population reduces the options for a government with some tendency to go bad, by raising costs, and even by raising doubts about the possibility of certain prima facie desired steps. The point about an armed population has appeared obvious enough to every genocidal government of this century, at least.

A right to bear arms is thus an insurance of other rights, but in the way that seat belts are an insurance against being injured in automobile accidents. The right to bear arms reduces the probability and the probable severity of a catastrophe, but by no means guarantees that catastrophe will not occur. Nothing short of having reliable and absolute power oneself can be a perfect protector of one's rights. So the probabilistic protection that a right to bear arms provides is to be expected.

A right to bear arms is likewise only a special, technology-dependent case of the more general right to be able to resist unjust coercion by whatever means available. If there is a right not to have one's rights violated, and governments are among the more serious threats to one's rights, as seems to be the case, then there is at least a prima facie right to whatever means are necessary to deflect threats to rights.

Some reflections on firearms as a defensive technology are in order, to make this point. A main effect of the invention of cheap, portable firearms was the democratization of effective deadly force. Governments before firearms relied on relatively expensive, highly trained, and expensively equipped elites. Using a broadsword or wielding a lance from a horse was a tremendous advantage over a peasant on foot equipped with a farm implement, as witness the failure of peasant uprisings ever to devolve into effective guerrilla wars. Since firearms require little training, and are deadly even against well-armed professionals, governments found themselves fighting wars with citizen armies rather than warrior elites; and found themselves faced with a serious threat to their control of coercion.

Firearms as a defensive technology have the serious defect that they defend primarily by killing and by threats to kill. We could imagine a technology of impenetrable force-fields or devices which transported one instantly out of harm's way when assaulted, but such technologies are not available. If they were, then given the drawbacks of firearms, there would be no right to bear arms. That is, there is no right to bear arms as such, there is only the right to resist violation of one's rights, and, given the state of technology and economic realities, that right entails a right to bear arms. . . .

III. Conclusion

A right to resist government coercion, while paradoxical as an explicit institutionalized right, is essential to reasonable consent to be governed. The right is in effect insured by rights to effectively arm oneself and the other political rights that a population able to resist direct coercion can retain. . . .

Note

1. One has a right to intervene on behalf of oneself, but also rights to intervene on behalf of other threatened innocents. A person can use "self-defense" as a ground for defending innocent family members, colleagues, and, one would hope, strangers. There is nothing special to the self, essentially, in "self-defense." "Self-defense" is just a very plausible case of the right to intervene against assaults on innocents.

Study Questions

1. Is assault by one's government a realistic threat?
2. Does gun ownership lessen the probability of assault by one's government?
3. Does gun ownership lessen the probability of one citizen assaulting another?
4. Do any citizens have the right to own a fighter jet?

Handguns, Moral Rights, and Physical Security

David DeGrazia

David DeGrazia, Professor of Philosophy at George Washington University, explains and critiques the argument that our right to physical security gives us the right to own handguns. He argues that gun ownership jeopardizes rather than enhances the physical security of gun owners and their families. Furthermore, the widespread accessibility to guns inflicts enormous welfare losses on our whole society. DeGrazia concludes that while his case against gun ownership is not airtight, his arguments justify placing severe restrictions on gun availability.

Introduction

Guns occupy a major—sometimes terrible—place in contemporary American life. In 2012 alone, the nation incurred over a dozen mass shooting incidents, including the Aurora, Colorado massacre that set an American record for the most shooting victims in a single spree and the Newtown, Connecticut tragedy whose victims included 20 schoolchildren. The latter incident finally overwhelmed the reluctance of some politicians, including President Obama, to discuss gun policy and the place of guns in American life.

Any serious discussion of gun policy must acknowledge that the U.S. has extremely high rates of gun ownership and gun violence as well as exceptionally permissive gun laws. At least 270 million firearms are privately owned by Americans and one or more firearms can be found in 47% of all homes.[1] In 2009—the most recent year

From David DeGrazia, "Handguns, Moral Rights, and Physical Security," *Journal of Moral Philosophy*, 13 (2016).

for which official data are available—31,347 people in the U.S. were killed by guns at a rate of 10.2 per 100,000 people.[2] Moreover, a disproportionate number of victims are children. A major Centers for Disease Control and Prevention (CDC) study found that the firearm death rate among American children was almost 12 times higher than the average rates of 25 other developed countries.[3]

It is easy to acquire firearms in the U.S. Private citizens may purchase not only rifles, handguns, and ordinary ammunition, but also—since 2004, when the Federal Assault Weapons Ban was allowed to expire—"assault weapons" (a somewhat inconsistently applied term) and high-capacity ammunition clips. Adults who lack any specific disqualifying criminal or psychiatric history are eligible buyers. There is also the "gun show loophole": the exemption of firearms sold privately from the federal requirement to conduct background checks.

Is the American gun status quo morally acceptable? . . .

The Appeal to Physical Security

That people have a basic moral right to physical security is not particularly controversial and will be assumed here. Although there is disagreement about what steps a society must take to help protect people's physical security, there is much agreement about certain negative aspects of the basic right. The right to physical security includes, uncontroversially, rights not to be assaulted, not to be raped, not to be tortured, and not to be killed. It also includes a right to self-defense. The derived right of self-defense is pivotal to alleged gun rights. For the sake of convenience, let us construe the term *self-defense* broadly (if not quite accurately) so that it refers to efforts to defend not only oneself but also family members and anyone else who is residing or visiting in one's home. Clearly, people have a right to self-defense in this sense.

With this beginning, we may explicitly outline what I believe to be the strongest argument in favor of a moral right to own handguns—contextualized to the American situation.[4] Here is the structure:

1. People have a basic right to physical security.
2. This right is violated by (unjustified) assaults and is threatened by burglaries.
3. People have a right to take measures reasonably deemed to be necessary to prevent their basic rights from being violated.
4. The right stated in 3 supports a right to self-defense.

5. In present-day circumstances in the United States, adequate self-defense requires that competent adults have the option of handgun ownership.
6. Thus, competent adults in the United States today have a moral right to handgun ownership.
7. This moral right is not justifiably overridden by appeal to the general welfare or by any conflicting moral right—at least in the case of competent, law-abiding adults.
8. So the moral right to ownership of handguns by competent, law-abiding adults should be protected by law in the United States.

This is a powerful argument. To evaluate whether it is ultimately sound, we need to examine the reasoning step by step.

Evaluating the Appeal to Physical Security

The premise stated in Step 1, that people have a basic right to physical security, is an assumption I have granted.

Step 2 asserts that the right to physical security is violated by (unjustified) assaults and is threatened by burglaries. This seems correct. Assault is a paradigm violation of someone's right to physical security—except when the assault is justified by an effort to prevent someone from harming someone else or violating her rights in a serious way. Self-defense often involves justified assault against one who threatens or commits an unjustified assault. As for burglary, even if the criminals' usual intention is to steal things of value, burglars so often harm people inside the house that burglary itself is reasonably thought to *threaten* violation of one's right to physical security. Of course, burglary also threatens one's right to maintain possession of one's property.

Step 3 claims that people have a right to do what is reasonably considered necessary to prevent their basic rights from being violated. This seems correct. So does step 4, which asserts that the right just mentioned supports a right to self-defense. (Remember that we are using "self-defense" broadly to include other household members and guests.) If a person cannot defend herself, she cannot take reasonable steps to prevent others from violating her basic right to physical security—and perhaps other rights such as her right to property.

Step 5, however, is open to challenge. It states that in the United States today, adequate self-defense requires that competent adults have the option of handgun ownership. Limiting the claim's scope to competent adults reflects the idea that only they can be expected to be able to use guns properly. The claim, importantly, is not that *no competent adult* can adequately defend himself without a handgun. Maybe some can. The present claim, sympathetically construed, is that many competent adults in the U.S. can defend themselves adequately only if they possess one or more guns. Is this correct?

Since we are focusing on the moral right to own guns rather than the right to carry them in public, let us ask what is generally necessary to protect one's household from burglars and other potential assailants. Many of us who do not own guns feel secure in our homes by taking such measures as locking doors and any windows that can be opened from outside, and being prepared to call the police if someone appears to be attempting a break-in. Some go further and install house alarms. Some get noisy dogs who are good at letting you know if anyone is on the premises. Perhaps these are sufficient means of self-defense.

Perhaps not. Especially aggressive burglars may pick locks, smash through windows, shoot the family dog, and the like. If moderate measures of house protection do not prevent someone from breaking and entering, what should an individual do as the best way of protecting herself and the family? Those of us who do not own guns would probably call the police and stay as quiet as possible.

Many believe that such measures are inadequate. Especially those who live in very unsafe neighborhoods may have good grounds for this belief. After all, many thousands of criminals in the U.S. are already well-armed (a fact that distinguishes the U.S. from some other developed nations). Thus, even if people living in unsafe neighborhoods secure their houses properly and call the police promptly, such measures may leave them unnecessarily vulnerable in the absence of firepower with which to threaten and possibly shoot intruders, who are likely to be armed. One has a right to use force to repel an intruder and, according to the argument, guns are the most effective means of doing so. Knives and baseball bats are much less effective for obvious reasons. This argument has a ring of plausibility.

At the same time, we know that guns are sometimes *misused* in the household—for example, in accidental shootings, shootings prompted by arguments, and impulsive suicides. Many of the injuries and deaths that result from such incidents would not have occurred had no guns been available. Obviously, owning handguns has risks along with whatever protective benefits it offers.

This brings us to an empirical question: *Does the option of owning handguns enable more adequate self-defense and physical security than would be possible if this option were unavailable?* If one simply consults an image of a homeowner using a gun to ward off an intruder, and being unable to do so without a gun, it might seem obvious that handgun ownership promotes effective self-defense. But the question is empirical, so the answer should be responsive to evidence.

The myriad data we could consider in addressing this question are subject to varying interpretations. I suggest, nevertheless, that an even-handed examination of available evidence casts considerable doubt on the thesis that handgun ownership enables more adequate self-defense and physical security in the home. In order to do so, handgun ownership would need to be effective in achieving its purpose and not self-defeating. In fact, there is much evidence that owning guns is self-defeating in the sense of making household members less safe, and the evidence is mixed as to whether owning guns helps with self-defense.

Regarding the first point, it appears that gun ownership makes household members less safe, on average, than they would be in a gun-free household. First, having a gun at home apparently increases one's likelihood of dying by suicide.[5] This is hardly surprising considering that many suicide attempts are impulsive, reflecting immediate stressors rather than long-term hopelessness, and that guns used at close range are highly likely to kill rather than merely injure. Second, the risk of death by homicide appears to be much greater in homes with guns than in homes without guns.[6] In homes with domestic violence, the chances that such violence will prove lethal are much higher if guns are present in the home.[7] The risk of accidental death also increases markedly in households with guns.[8] On the whole, having guns at home increases the risk of household members' suffering a violent death.[9] Thus, owning guns for the purpose of self-defense is apparently self-defeating in this sense: *Household members, on average, face a greater chance of suffering a violent death if the house contains one or more guns than if the house is free of firearms.*

Those who champion a right to commit suicide might reply that we should ignore the many cases in which guns kept at home are used for this purpose. After all, we do not normally think of self-defense as being necessary against oneself. Note, however, that even if this is a valid point with respect to suicides that are *genuinely autonomous acts,* it does not apply to cases involving minors or incompetent adults who commit suicide; nor does it apply to competent adults who kill themselves impulsively rather than after sustained deliberation that reflects their long-term values and preferences. These individuals *do* need protection against themselves. Moreover, and very importantly, one does not need a gun to commit suicide. And, of course, the present objection concerning suicide does not affect the data concerning homicides and accidental killings in the household. On the whole, then, available evidence strongly supports the thesis that gun ownership for self-defense is, on average, self-defeating.

At the same time, guns are sometimes used for the defensive purpose of protecting oneself or one's family from an intruder. How often? It is especially difficult to know because such defensive gun uses (DGUS), unlike fatalities, often leave no official trail. Experts disagree significantly on the matter.

A figure commonly cited by gun advocates—2.5 million DGUS (whether in the household or in public) per year—is based on a telephone survey of 5,000 American adults.[10] This figure is scarcely credible. Only 1% of respondents reported a DGU during the previous year; given the small sample size, with even a slight proportion of false positives, projections based on these responses could have yielded a grossly inflated estimate of DGUS per year.[11] . . . In marked contrast with the 2.5 million figure, a study by the Violence Policy Center, using federally collected data for the years 2007–2011, suggests an average of 67,740 DGUS annually.[12]

Even if we had a confident estimate of defensive uses of handguns in households per year, it would be difficult to estimate in how many of those cases the weapons were used appropriately in response to a genuine threat. Another study—which is only partly relevant to our discussion because it considered assaults both in and outside the home—found that assault victims who possessed a gun were far more likely to be shot than assault victims who did not possess a gun—a result that hardly suggests effective self-protection.[13] In order to show that the appeal to physical security is sound, one would need to advance a stronger case than is currently available that gun ownership is the *most effective* means of protecting household members' basic right to physical security. And once again, there is strong evidence that handgun ownership is self-defeating in making people, on average and on balance, less safe than they would be in a gun-free household.

Does the point that handgun ownership is self-defeating decisively undermine the appeal to physical security by destroying the credibility of premise 5? Although I am inclined to believe so, I recognize that I lack a "knock-down" argument. A gun advocate might emphasize that gun owners are not all alike. Some are more cautious and judicious, and less impulsive, than others. Some live in more dangerous neighborhoods than others. Even if there is a compelling case that gun ownership is self-defeating *on average across the American population,* it does not follow that it is self-defeating for everyone. There may be individuals for whom gun ownership is not self-defeating and who are in a position to know this about themselves. If so, they may be well-positioned to claim a right to own handguns as a reasonable means of realizing their right to physical security. Further, one might argue, the law should not try to discriminate finely among those who are and those who are not in such a position, so the law should recognize a right to handgun ownership among competent, law-abiding adults. So let us regard it as an open question whether the appeal to physical security establishes a moral right to handgun ownership among competent adults in the U.S. at this time, as asserted by the intermediate conclusion stated in step 6.

Assume, for argument's sake, that there is such a right. We noted earlier that rights are limited in scope and may sometimes be overridden. A right to own handguns would be limited in scope by restricting it to competent, law-abiding adults. Only competent adults can be assumed to be able to use guns properly. And only those who qualify as law-abiding can be entrusted to do so rather than committing crimes with guns. (Here we need not address such details as what is to count as law-abiding and how to assess competence in the relevant global sense that excludes those who are substantially cognitively disabled.) Within its scope, a right may "prevail" or it may be defeated—overridden—by conflicting rights or appeals to the public welfare. Step 7 maintains that the present right is not overridden by either of these considerations among competent, law-abiding adults, an assumption that leads to the conclusion in step 8 that the moral right to own handguns should be protected in law. Our question is whether the assumption in step 7 is correct. I will present both a respectable case in favor of this assumption and a (somewhat longer) respectable case against it.

> *Case in favor:* "The right to gun ownership is not overridden by competing moral considerations. This is a negative right—a right of noninterference—and negative rights are not to be swept away in the tide of appeals to social utility. Consider an analogy. People have a right to freedom from torture. Suppose the police decided that gang violence could be greatly reduced if they had more information about gang leaders, their hideouts and plans, and how they run their businesses. Then the police realize that they can get this information by capturing a few gang members and torturing them until they squeal.

If rights could be justifiably tossed aside in the name of the public good, then this proposal to torture gang members could easily be justified: however awful the torture is for a few people, the harms of gang violence that could be prevented by using information gathered through torture are much greater. But to torture the gang members would be a grotesque violation of their rights, a violation that is not justified by appeal to the public good. Rights, at least negative rights, serve as moral side constraints. They can be set aside, if at all, only in rare, truly extreme situations—such as a true ticking time-bomb scenario, which might justify torture—but the public harms associated with high rates of gun ownership do not come close to constituting such an emergency. Our right to own guns should be respected—and protected by law."

This is a powerful argument. Given the assumption (which we have granted for now) that there is a moral right to gun ownership, the case in favor of step 7 invokes a widely accepted understanding of the power of negative rights to resist appeals to utility. But there is another respectable way to view the matter.

Case against: "The right to own guns in the contemporary U.S. is overridden by consideration of the pernicious overall consequences of widespread gun ownership. First, there is the fact—as emphasized in the discussion of step 5—that having guns in the home makes family members, on average, less safe than they would be in a gun-free household. In addition, if we consider *society as a whole* and not simply individual households, guns pose terrible overall consequences—as indicated by the fact that gun ownership rates within a population correlate significantly with murder and suicide rates in that population."

"To be sure, correlation does not entail causation, so we cannot casually assume that high rates of gun ownership *cause* the high associated murder and suicide rates. As Gary Kleck notes, gun ownership rates might be a response to crime rates rather than a cause of it;[14] we might also speculate that gun ownership rates are, in part, a response to suicidality rather than a cause of suicide. But these logical possibilities are extremely improbable in view of further consideration of the evidence. . . . Consider one example. In a comparison of homicides of children from ages five to 14 among 26 wealthy nations, the U.S. rate was 17 times the average of the other countries in homicides involving guns *but only twice as high in homicides not involving guns*; and, in the same age group, the U.S. suicide rate was 10 times the average of the other countries where guns were used *but approximately the same where guns were not used.*[15] The very different overall murder and suicide rates across nations cannot be satisfactorily explained without recognizing gun availability as a significant causal factor."

"The moral right to gun ownership should be morally overridden. The overriding can be thought of in either of two ways. First, we might say that the right to own guns is overridden by the prospect of

> a massive gain in social good or utility: an enormous reduction in violent deaths and nonfatal injuries. Alternatively, we might say that the right to gun ownership is overridden by a conflicting right: *the right to a reasonably safe environment.* Importantly, it is not true that negative rights (including the right to own firearms) automatically take priority over positive rights (including the right to conditions that foster a safe environment). Negative property rights can be overridden to save a life, for example. It would be permissible for a starving wanderer to steal a few apples from an apple tree on someone's property in order to preserve his own life. Moreover, the right to a reasonably safe environment, which we have construed as a positive right, *involves efforts to protect negative rights*: the rights of household members, including children, not to be murdered, killed by avoidable accidents, or (wrongly or negligently) injured. Indeed, the distinction between positive and negative rights is blurred here, casting further doubt on the claim that a negative right to gun ownership should trump a right to a reasonably safe environment. In sum, whether the grounds for overriding are understood as an appeal to the public welfare or as a competing right to a safe environment, the right to handgun ownership should be overridden in American society today."

This clash between respectable arguments for and against step 7 leaves us with considerable uncertainty. It is an open question whether the appeal to physical security as the basis for an undefeated moral right to handgun ownership is successful. As we have seen, the possible success of this argument pivots on two crucial assumptions: that, in the U.S. today, the option of handgun ownership is necessary and effective for self-defense, and, if so, that this right is not justifiably overridden. My sense is that the argument fails, foundering on both step 5 and step 7, but once again I recognize that some reasonable participants in this debate may see the balance of arguments differently. In any case, even if the argument does succeed, it leaves wide open the issue of appropriate gun control, because significant gun control is compatible with the right to own handguns. The Supreme Court made this determination in connection with the legal right to gun ownership.[16] Here we underscore the point in connection with the alleged moral right and efforts to fashion morally responsible policy within the established constitutional regime.

Where to Go Amid Uncertainty about Gun Rights?

Our investigation suggests that people can reasonably disagree about whether, in the U.S. today, competent, law-abiding adults have an undefeated moral right to gun ownership. It may seem that lack of closure on the central moral issue we have explored leaves us empty-handed. But I believe that digging a bit deeper into the points of disagreement suggests the possibility of a principled compromise between responsible thinkers on both sides of the gun rights issue. Indeed, such digging reveals a plausible way of reinterpreting the scope of the putative undefeated right.

Earlier we found that gun ownership is self-defeating *on average across the American population*. What prevented this point from decisively refuting the argument appealing to physical security was the likelihood that, for some individuals, gun ownership is not self-defeating. Arguably, their prerogative to own guns for the purpose of self-defense should not be curtailed just because gun ownership is self-defeating for the majority.

Now, one might reasonably reject this argument. One might contend that it no more indicates a reason to allow gun ownership than the fact that some people can drink a lot of alcohol and drive safely—due, say, to exceptional physical coordination and a disposition to drive slowly while intoxicated—is a reason to allow drunk driving. I am sympathetic toward this counterargument. But some would reject the analogy, emphasizing that handguns (unlike assault weapons) are precision instruments that can be stored safely and used responsibly. In view of such persisting disagreement, I would like to explore how granting the present pro-gun argument, in a suitably qualified way, might lead in an unexpected and constructive direction.

So let us grant that it would be unfair to those individuals for whom gun ownership would likely *not* be self-defeating to prevent them from owning guns. The question arises: For whom would gun ownership most likely not be self-defeating? A reasonable answer is: those people who (1) have a special need for guns and (2) can be trusted to store and use them safely. For most of us, apparently, it would be safer not to own guns and to secure the home through such ordinary means as locking doors and installing house alarms, and being prepared to call the police if someone appears to be attempting a break-in. But some people live in especially unsafe neighborhoods where ordinary measures are less likely to suffice, or in neighborhoods in which police protection is clearly inadequate. In effect, these individuals cannot prudently delegate their right to fight off intruders to the police. Then again, these individuals might simply make their situation *even less safe* by owning guns (if they are among the majority for whom gun ownership is self-defeating), so we need a way to make reasonable judgments that distinguish those for whom gun ownership would represent a net gain in safety and those for whom gun ownership would represent a net loss in safety.

My proposal, which I can only sketch here, is to constrain quite drastically the scope of the presumed moral right to own handguns. We noted earlier that not everyone has a moral right to own these weapons because its scope was restricted to competent, law-abiding adults (where "competent" means, roughly, "free of substantial cognitive disability" rather than "competent to use guns"). Now I propose that not all competent, law-abiding adults have a moral right to handgun ownership. The moral right, as we found earlier, is contingent upon serving the purposes of self-defense and physical security. We also found that not everyone needs these weapons for self-defense and physical security, and that many people defeat themselves in relation to these purposes by owning handguns. *On this basis, I submit that those individuals in the U.S. who have an undefeated moral right to own handguns (if anyone does) are precisely those competent, law-abiding adults who apparently need handguns for self-defense and can be trusted to store and use them in a way that, on balance, promotes rather than threatens physical security in the home.* Accordingly, handguns should only be obtainable by legal purchase (not received as a gift), and purchases should be legal only if the buyer has a handgun license. Obtaining a license should be contingent upon meeting two conditions beyond such familiar ones as passing background checks (a requirement that should become universal). The two new conditions are to be applied prospectively, after a specified date, rather than applied to gun owners who acquired their guns prior to that date.

First, as in Canada and some western European countries, *we should allow individuals to own handguns only upon demonstrating a special need for them.* One might make the case, say, that one's urban neighborhood is exceptionally unsafe and police protection is insufficient there; or that, considering where one lives out in the country, it would take too long for police to arrive in the event of an attempted break-in. Alternatively, one might make the case that one's job (say, in security or espionage) presents a special need for a handgun. In order to facilitate consistency in applying standards, licenses should be granted by a federal agency rather than by state or local agencies. The standards themselves should be publicized, and the system of review should be conducted with professionalism and integrity so as to maintain public trust in the system.

The second condition applies to those who demonstrate a special need for a handgun. In order to provide reasonable assurance that owning a gun will not be self-defeating, *one should have to pass a demanding, in-depth, federally approved course in handgun safety—with no exceptions*. Here there is a partial analogy to drivers' licenses, which can be obtained only when one has demonstrated, after many hours of practice, competence in driving. In both cases, one's prerogative is limited by reasonable considerations of safety.

By requiring licenses that in turn require meeting these two conditions for handgun ownership, we can limit the scope of an undefeated moral right to gun ownership to those for whom owning firearms will most likely confer a net gain in physical security for themselves and others in the home. Everyone else either does not need a handgun for physical security or cannot be trusted to own one.

There are principled reasons on both sides of the debate to accept this proposal. Those who (unlike me) believe that the appeal to physical security establishes an undefeated moral right for all competent, law-abiding adults must admit that my proposal is consistent both with the centerpiece of the supporting argument—the importance of self-defense and physical security—and with available evidence about the risks of gun ownership. Those who believe that the appeal to physical security is unsound should appreciate an approach that is designed to keep guns out of the hands of precisely those individuals whose misuse of guns provides the strongest reason to reject this argument.

To clarify, what I am asserting is bolder than a basis for principled compromise. The compromise is for those who divide over whether the appeal to physical security—which attributes an undefeated moral right to all competent, law-abiding adults—is sound. I have argued that the scope of the right in question is much narrower than the appeal to physical security asserts. In other words, I claim that the latter argument, in its original form, fails—or, equivalently, that it succeeds (if at all) only in a qualified form where the qualification consists in the restricted scope. The principled compromise remains for any who are not persuaded by my present claim. The practical upshot, however, is the same whether one accepts my thesis or just the principled compromise. . . .

Notes

1. See Max Fisher, "What Makes America's Gun Culture Totally Unique in the World, in Four Charts," *The Washington Post* (updated December 15, 2012; www.washingtonpost.com/blogs/worldviews/wp/2012/12/15 what-makes-americas-gun-culture-totally-unique-in-the-world-as-demonstrated-in-four-charts/) and Lydia Saad, "Self-Reported Gun Ownership in U.S. is Highest Since 1993" (www.gallup.com/poll/150353/self-reported-gun-ownership-highest-1993.aspx).

2. Center for Disease Control and Prevention, "All Injuries" (www.cdc.gov/nchs/fastats/injury.htm).
3. CDC, "Rates of Homicide, Suicide, and Firearm-related Death among Children—26 Industrialized Countries," *Morbidity and Mortality Weekly Report* 46 (February 7, 1997): 101–5.
4. Something within the spirit of this reasoning may be found in Wheeler, "Self-Defense," though they would not limit the argument to the contemporary U.S.
5. See D. A. Brent et al., "The Presence and Accessibility of Firearms in the Homes of Adolescent Suicides: A Case-Controlled Study," *JAMA* 266 (1991): 2989–95; Arthur Kellermann et al., "Suicide in the Home in Relation to Gun Ownership," *New England Journal of Medicine* 327 (1992): 467–72; Antoine Chapdelaine and Pierre Maurice, "Firearms Injury Prevention and Gun Control in Canada," *Canadian Medical Association Journal* 155 (1996): 1285–89; Yeats Conwell, Kenneth Connor, and Christopher Cox, "Access to Firearms and Risk for Suicide in Middle-Aged and Older Adults," *American Journal of Geriatric Psychiatry* 10 (2002): 407–16; Matthew Miller, Deborah Azrael, and David Hemenway, "Firearm Availability and Unintentional Firearm Deaths, Suicide, and Homicide among 5–14 Year Olds," *Journal of Trauma Injury, Infection, and Critical Care* 52 (2002): 267–75; and Matthew Miller and David Hemenway, "Guns and Suicide in the United States," *New England Journal of Medicine* 359 (2008): 989–91.
6. See A. L. Kellermann et al., "Gun Ownership as a Risk Factor for Homicide in the Home," *New England Journal of Medicine* 329 (1993): 1084–91 and D. J. Wiebe, "Homicide and Suicide Risks Associated with Firearms in the Home: A National Case-Control Study," *Annals of Emergency Medicine* 41 (2003): 771–82.
7. See L. E. Saltzman et al., "Weapon Involvement and Injury Outcomes in Family and Intimate Assaults," *JAMA* 267 (1992): 3043–47 and J. C. Campbell et al., "Risk Factors for Femicide in Abusive Relationships: Results from a Multisite Case Control Study," *American Journal of Public Health* 93 (2003): 1089–97.
8. See Matthew Miller and David Hemenway, "Firearm Availability and Unintentional Firearm Deaths," *Accident Analysis & Prevention* 33 (2001): 477–84 and D. J. Wiebe, "Firearms in U.S. Homes as a Risk Factor for Unintentional Gunshot Fatality," *Accident Analysis and Prevention* 35 (2003): 711–16.
9. Garen Wintemute, "Guns, Fear, the Constitution, and the Public's Health," *New England Journal of Medicine* 358 (2008): 1421–24, at 1422.
10. Gary Kleck and M. Gertz, "Armed Resistance to Crime: The Prevalence and Nature of Self-Defense with a Gun," *Journal of Criminal Law and Criminology* 86 (Fall 1995): 150–187.
11. See David Hemenway, "Survey Research and Self-Defensive Gun Use: An Explanation of Extreme Overestimates," *Journal of Criminal Law and Criminology* 87 (1997): 1430–45.

12. Violence Policy Center, "Firearm Justifiable Homicides and Non-Fatal Self-Defense Gun Use: An Analysis of Federal Bureau of Investigation and National Crime Victimization Survey Data" (www.vpc.org/studies/justifiable.pdf; April 2013).
13. Charles Branas et al., "Investigating the Link Between Gun Possession and Gun Assault," *American Journal of Public Health* 99 (November 2009): 2034–40.
14. *Point Blank*, p. 191.
15. Hemenway and Miller, "Firearm Availability and Homicide Rates Across 26 High-Income Countries."
16. United States Supreme Court, Syllabus of *District of Columbia v. Heller*, sect. 2.

Study Questions

1. In what ways does owning a gun enhance your security?
2. In what ways does owning a gun reduce your security?
3. Might the case for gun control be more persuasive in one locale rather than another?
4. When cowboys all carried guns, were their towns thereby made safer?

PART 

Ultimate Harms

Terrorism

Terrorism

Michael Walzer

Michael Walzer is Professor of Social Science at the Institute for Advanced Study in Princeton, New Jersey. He defines "terrorism" as the *random* murder of innocent people with the intention of spreading fear. Victims of terrorism who are neither involved in military activities nor the administration or enforcement of laws are targeted merely because they share in a particular collective identity. The goal is to undermine the solidarity of this collective by lowering morale. According to Walzer, targeting soldiers during a war can be justified, assuming the war itself is just. Terrorism, however, is always immoral, because the indiscriminate killing of innocents can never be justified.

The word "terrorism" is used most often to describe revolutionary violence. That is a small victory for the champions of order, among whom the uses of terror are by no means unknown. The systematic terrorizing of whole populations is a strategy of both conventional

From Michael Walzer, *Just and Unjust Wars: A Moral Argument with Historical Illustrations* (New York: Basic Books, 1977).

and guerrilla war, and of established governments as well as radical movements. Its purpose is to destroy the morale of a nation or a class, to undercut its solidarity; its method is the random murder of innocent people. Randomness is the crucial feature of terrorist activity. If one wishes fear to spread and intensify over time, it is not desirable to kill specific people identified in some particular way with a regime, a party, or a policy. Death must come by chance to individual Frenchmen, or Germans, to Irish Protestants, or Jews, simply because they are Frenchmen or Germans, Protestants or Jews, or until they feel themselves fatally exposed and demand that their governments negotiate for their safety.

In war, terrorism is a way of avoiding engagement with the enemy army. It represents an extreme form of the strategy of the "indirect approach."[1] It is so indirect that many soldiers have refused to call it war at all. This is a matter as much of professional pride as of moral judgment. Consider the statement of a British admiral in World War II, protesting the terror bombing of German cities: "We are a hopelessly unmilitary nation to imagine that we [can] win the war by bombing German women and children instead of defeating their army and navy."[2] The key word here is unmilitary. The admiral rightly sees terrorism as a civilian strategy. One might say that it represents the continuation of war by political means. Terrorizing ordinary men and women is first of all the work of domestic tyranny, as Aristotle wrote: "The first aim and end [of tyrants] is to break the spirit of their subjects."[3] The British described the "aim and end" of terror bombing in the same way: what they sought was the destruction of civilian morale.

Tyrants taught the method to soldiers, and soldiers to modern revolutionaries. That is a crude history; I offer it only in order to make a more precise historical point: that terrorism in the strict sense, the random murder of innocent people, emerged as a strategy of revolutionary struggle only in the period after World War II, that is, only after it had become a feature of conventional war. In both cases, in war and revolution, a kind of warrior honor stood in the way of this development, especially among professional officers and "professional revolutionaries." The increasing use of terror by far left and ultranationalist movements represents the breakdown of a political code first worked out in the second half of the nineteenth century and roughly analogous to the laws of war worked out at the same time. Adherence to this code did not prevent revolutionary militants from being called terrorists, but in fact the violence they committed bore little resemblance to contemporary terrorism. It was not random murder but assassination, and it involved the drawing of a line that we will have little difficulty recognizing as the political parallel of the line that marks off combatants from noncombatants.

The Russian Populists, the IRA, and the Stern Gang

I can best describe the revolutionary "code of honor" by giving some examples of so-called terrorists who acted or tried to act in accordance with its norms. I have chosen three historical cases. The first will be readily recognizable, for Albert Camus made it the basis of his play *The Just Assassins.*

1. In the early twentieth century, a group of Russian revolutionaries decided to kill a Tsarist official, the Grand Duke Sergei, a man personally involved in the repression of radical activity. They planned to blow him up in his carriage, and on the appointed day one of their number was in place along the Grand Duke's usual route. As the carriage drew near, the young revolutionary, a bomb hidden under his coat, noticed that his victim was not alone; on his lap he held two small children. The would-be assassin looked, hesitated, then walked quickly away. He would wait for another occasion. Camus has one of his comrades say, accepting this decision, "Even in destruction, there's a right way and a wrong way—and there are limits."[4]

2. During the years 1938–39, the Irish Republican Army waged a bombing campaign in Britain. In the course of this campaign, a republican militant was ordered to carry a pre-set time bomb to a Coventry power station. He traveled by bicycle, the bomb in his basket, took a wrong turn, and got lost in a maze of streets. As the time for the explosion drew near, he panicked, dropped his bike, and ran off. The bomb exploded, killing five passersby. No one in the IRA (as it was then) thought this a victory for the cause; the men immediately involved were horrified. The campaign had been carefully planned, according to a recent historian, so as to avoid the killing of innocent bystanders.[5]

3. In November 1944, Lord Moyne, British Minister of State in the Middle East, was assassinated in Cairo by two members of the Stern Gang, a right-wing Zionist group. The two assassins were caught, minutes later, by an Egyptian policeman. One of them described the capture at his trial: "We were being followed by the constable on his motorcycle. My comrade was behind me. I saw the

constable approach him. . . . I would have been able to kill the constable easily, but I contented myself with . . . shooting several times into the air. I saw my comrade fall off his bicycle. The constable was almost upon him. Again, I could have eliminated the constable with a single bullet, but I did not. Then I was caught."[6]

What is common to these cases is a moral distinction, drawn by the "terrorists," between people who can and people who cannot be killed. The first category is not composed of men and women bearing arms, immediately threatening by virtue of their military training and commitment. It is composed instead of officials, the political agents of regimes thought to be oppressive. Such people, of course, are protected by the war convention and by positive international law. Characteristically (and not foolishly), lawyers have frowned on assassination, and political officials have been assigned to the class of nonmilitary persons, who are never the legitimate objects of attack.[7] But this assignment only partially represents our common moral judgments. For we judge the assassin by his victim, and when the victim is Hitler-like in character, we are likely to praise the assassin's work, though we still do not call him a soldier. The second category is less problematic: ordinary citizens, not engaged in political harming—that is, in administering or enforcing laws thought to be unjust—are immune from attack whether or not they support those laws. Thus the aristocratic children, the Coventry pedestrians, even the Egyptian policeman (who had nothing to do with British imperialism in Palestine)—these people are like civilians in wartime. They are innocent politically as civilians are innocent militarily. It is precisely these people, however, that contemporary terrorists try to kill.

The war convention and the political code are structurally similar, and the distinction between officials and citizens parallels that between soldiers and civilians (though the two are not the same). What lies behind them both, I think, and lends them plausibility, is the moral difference between aiming and not aiming—or, more accurately, between aiming at particular people because of things they have done or are doing, and aiming at whole groups of people, indiscriminately, because of who they are. The first kind of aiming is appropriate to a limited struggle directed against regimes and policies. The second reaches beyond all limits; it is infinitely threatening to whole peoples, whose individual members are systematically exposed to violent death at any and every moment in the course of their (largely innocuous) lives. A bomb planted on a street corner, hidden in a bus station, thrown into a cafe or pub—this is aimless killing, except that the victims are likely to share what they cannot avoid, a collective identity. Since some of these victims must be immune from attack (unless liability follows from original sin), any code that directs and controls the fire of political militants is going to be at least minimally appealing. It is so much of an advance over the willful randomness of terrorist attacks. One might even feel easier about killing officials than about killing soldiers, since the state rarely conscripts its political, as it does its military agents; they have chosen officialdom as a career.

Soldiers and officials are, however, different in another respect. The threatening character of the soldier's activities is a matter of fact; the unjust or oppressive character of the official's activities is a matter of political judgment. For this reason, the political code has never attained the same status as the war convention. Nor can assassins claim any rights, even on the basis of the strictest adherence to its principles. In the eyes of those of us whose judgments of oppression and injustice differ from their own, political assassins are simply murderers, exactly like the killers of ordinary citizens. The case is not the same with soldiers, who are not judged politically at all and who are called murderers only when they kill noncombatants. Political killing imposes risks quite unlike those of combat, risks whose character is best revealed by the fact that there is no such thing as benevolent quarantine for the duration of the political struggle. Thus the young Russian revolutionary, who eventually killed the Grand Duke, was tried and executed for murder, as were the Stern Gang assassins of Lord Moyne. All three were treated exactly like the IRA militants, also captured, who were held responsible for the deaths of ordinary citizens. That treatment seems to me appropriate, even if we share the political judgments of the men involved and defend their resort to violence. On the other hand, even if we do not share their judgments, these men are entitled to a kind of moral respect not due to terrorists, because they set limits to their actions. . . .

In its modern manifestations, terror is the totalitarian form of war and politics. It shatters the war convention and the political code. It breaks across moral limits beyond which no further limitation seems possible, for within the categories of civilian and citizen, there isn't any smaller group for which immunity might be claimed (except children; but I don't think children can be called "immune" if their parents are attacked and killed). Terrorists anyway make no such claim;

they kill anybody. Despite this, terrorism has been defended, not only by the terrorists themselves, but also by philosophical apologists writing on their behalf. The political defenses mostly parallel those that are offered whenever soldiers attack civilians. They represent one or another version of the argument from military necessity. It is said, for example, that there is no alternative to terrorist activity if oppressed peoples are to be liberated. And it is said, further, that this has always been so: terrorism is the only means and so it is the ordinary means of destroying oppressive regimes and founding new nations. The cases I have already worked through suggest the falsity of these assertions. Those who make them, I think, have lost their grip on the historical past; they suffer from a malign forgetfulness, erasing all moral distinctions along with the men and women who painfully worked them out.

Notes

1. But Liddell Hart, the foremost strategist of the "indirect approach," has consistently opposed terrorist tactics: see, for example, *Strategy* (2nd rev. ed., New York, 1974), pp. 349–50 (on terror bombing).
2. Rear Admiral L. H. K. Hamilton, quoted in Irving, *Destruction of Convoy* PQ 17, p. 44.
3. *Politics,* trans. Ernest Barker (Oxford, 1948), p. 288 (1314a).
4. *The Just Assassins,* in *Caligula and Three Other Plays,* trans. Stuart Gilbert (New York, 1958), p. 258. The actual historical incident is described in Roland Gaucher, *The Terrorists: From Tsarist Russia to the OAS* (London, 1965), pp. 49, 50 n.
5. J. Bowyer Bell, *The Secret Army: A History of the IRA* (Cambridge, MA, 1974), pp. 161–62.
6. Gerold Frank, *The Deed* (New York, 1963), pp. 248–49.
7. James E. Bond, *The Rules of Riot: Internal Conflict and the Law of War* (Princeton, 1974), pp. 89–90.

Study Questions

1. What is terrorism?
2. In a war, should a moral distinction be drawn between people who can legitimately be killed and those who cannot?
3. Do soldiers differ from political officials as appropriate targets of attack?
4. Do you agree with Walzer that terrorism tends to rule out any sort of compromise settlement?

Is Terrorism Distinctively Wrong?

Lionel K. McPherson

Lionel K. McPherson is Associate Professor of Philosophy at Tufts University. He defines "terrorism" as the use of violence against noncombatants with the intention of causing fear. McPherson notes that terrorists are usually unable to inflict violence on the same scale as states, because the terrorists lack access to the weapons and personnel that states possess. He claims that if terroristic violence is waged for a just cause when other, less harmful means are unavailable, terrorism may be justified on the same grounds used to justify conventional war. Recognizing no morally relevant difference between terrorism and conventional warfare, McPherson concludes that we should be more critical of war in general or less absolute in our condemnation of terrorism.

Many people, including philosophers, believe that terrorism is necessarily and egregiously wrong. I will call this "the dominant view." The dominant view maintains that terrorism is akin to murder. This forecloses the possibility that terrorism, under any circumstances, could be morally permissible—murder, by definition, is wrongful killing. The unqualified wrongness of terrorism is thus part of this understanding of terrorism.

I will criticize the dominant view. . . .

I will define "terrorism" as the deliberate use of force against ordinary noncombatants, which can be expected to cause wider fear among them, for political ends. . . .

Moral evaluation of terrorism might begin with the question of what makes terrorism wrong. A better opening question, I believe, is whether [the] use of force that leads to casualties among ordinary

From Lionel K. McPherson, "Is Terrorism Distinctively Wrong?" *Ethics* 117 (2007).

noncombatants is morally objectionable. The latter question prompts [a] comparison of terrorism and conventional war. Judging by practice and common versions of just war theory, the answer is plainly no. The journalist Chris Hedges reports these facts: "Between 1900 and 1990, 43 million soldiers died in wars. During the same period, 62 million civilians were killed. . . . In the wars of the 1990s, civilian deaths constituted between 75 and 90 percent of all war deaths."[1] Such numbers may seem counterintuitive. More noncombatants than combatants have died in war, by a sizable margin, and the margin has only grown in an era of the most advanced weapons technology. We must conclude that war generally is highly dangerous for noncombatants. I will characterize this as the brute reality of war for noncombatants. This reality cannot be attributed simply to the conduct of war departing from the laws of war.

There is an ambiguity in the data I have cited: they do not clearly support the claim that most noncombatants who died in these wars were killed by military actions, for example, through the use of bombs, artillery, and land mines. Many noncombatant deaths in war have been the result of displacement and the lack of shelter, [the] inability to get food, and the spread of disease. At the same time, modern warfare is marked by a nontrivial number of noncombatant deaths that are the direct result of military actions. The ratio of war to "war-related" noncombatant casualties and the distribution of moral responsibility for these casualties will not be at issue here. I proceed on the assumption that evaluating the ethics of war involves recognizing that war, directly or indirectly, leads to a great many noncombatant casualties. Modern warfare and widespread harm to noncombatants are virtually inextricable. . . .

Immediately doubtful is the popular notion that terrorism is distinctively wrong because of the fear it usually spreads among ordinary noncombatants. Recall that my nonmoral definition of terrorism includes a fear effects clause which descriptively distinguishes terrorism from other forms of political violence. However, this does not morally distinguish terrorism and conventional war. The brute reality of war for noncombatants indicates that in general they have more to fear from conventional war than (nonstate) terrorism, particularly since (nonstate) terrorists rarely have had the capacity to employ violence on a mass scale.[2] Noncombatants in states that are military powers might have more to fear from terrorism than conventional war, since these states are relatively unlikely to be conventionally attacked. But surely this situational advantage that does not extend more broadly to noncombatants cannot ground the claim that terrorism is distinctively wrong.

The laws of war recognize a principle that prohibits disproportionate or excessive use of force, with an emphasis on noncombatants. For example, Article 51 (5) (b) of the 1977 Geneva Protocol I rules out use of force "which may be expected to cause incidental loss of civilian life, injury to civilians, damage to civilian objects, or a combination thereof, which would be excessive in relation to the concrete and direct military advantage anticipated."[3] Standard just war theory considers this the proportionality principle. Proponents of the dominant view might take the proportionality principle to illuminate an essential moral difference between conventional war and terrorism. They might claim that, unlike proper combatants, terrorists do not care about disproportionate harm to noncombatants. But the full impact of this charge is not easily sustained for two reasons.

The first reason is that terrorists could have some concern about disproportionate harm to noncombatants. This point is most salient when proportionality is understood in instrumental terms of whether violence is gratuitous, namely, in exceeding what is minimally necessary to achieve particular military or political goals, despite the availability of an alternative course of action that would be less harmful and no less efficacious. Terrorists may possess a normative if flawed sensibility that disapproves of instrumentally gratuitous violence, for the harm done would serve no strategic purpose. So the plausible charge is that terrorists reject the proportionality principle as conventionally construed (since it implicitly rules out deliberate use of force against noncombatants), not that they lack all concern for disproportionate harm to noncombatants.

The second reason is that the proportionality principle requires rather modest due care for noncombatants. Force may be used against them, provided that the incidental, or collateral, harm to them is not excessive when measured against the expected military gains. According to one legal scholar, "the interpretation by the United States and its allies of their legal obligations concerning the prevention of collateral casualties and the concept of proportionality comprehends prohibiting only two types of attacks: first, those that intentionally target civilians; and second, those that involve negligent behavior in ascertaining the nature of a target or the conduct of the attack itself."[4] Such an interpretation seems accurately to reflect the principle's leniency. Indeed, the U.S. general and military theorist James M. Dubik argues that commanders have a special moral duty "not to waste lives of their soldiers" in balancing the responsibility to ensure that due care is afforded to noncombatants.[5] A commander may give priority to limiting risk of harm to his own combatants, for their sake, at the expense of noncombatants on the other side.

We find, then, that the proportionality principle does not express a commitment to minimizing noncombatant casualties. The principle more modestly would reduce noncombatant casualties in requiring that they be worth military interests. Perhaps my reading appears too narrow. A prominent reason for thinking that terrorism is distinctively wrong is that terrorists, unlike combatants who comply with the laws of war, do not acknowledge the moral significance of bearing burdens in order to reduce noncombatant casualties for the sake of noncombatants themselves. To reply that terrorists might well be motivated to reduce noncombatant casualties on strategic grounds, for example, to avoid eroding sympathy for their political goals, would miss the point. Basic respect for the lives of noncombatants seems evidenced instead by a willingness to bear burdens in order to reduce harm to them. Terrorists, the objection goes, do not have this respect for noncombatant lives, which is a major source of the sense that terrorism is distinctively wrong as compared to conventional war.

There are difficulties with this objection. It suggests that the laws of war are imbued with a certain moral character, namely, fundamental moral concern for noncombatants. These laws, though, are part of the war convention, adopted by states and codified in international law for reasons that seem largely to reflect their shared interests, at least in the long run. We do not have to be political realists to see this. Given that noncombatants are vulnerable enough on all sides and no state generally has much to gain by harming them, states usually are prudent to accept mutually a principle that seeks to reduce noncombatant casualties. States usually are also prudent to comply with the laws of war, since this compliance is a benchmark of moral and political respectability on the world stage. Simply put, states, like terrorists, would seem contingently motivated to accept the proportionality principle on broadly strategic grounds.

Now the objection might go that, even if a realist analysis of the proportionality principle's place in the war convention is correct, this is no barrier to states' recognizing that the principle has independent, nonprudential moral standing. But the same can be true for terrorists. Familiar characterizations of them as "evil" or unconstrained by moral boundaries are an unreliable indication of moral indifference to harming noncombatants. As Virginia Held observes,

"Terrorists often believe, whether mistakenly or not, that violence is the only course of action open to them that can advance their political objectives."[6] When terrorism is seen by its agents as a means of last resort, this provides some evidence that they acknowledge the moral significance of bearing burdens out of respect for the lives of noncombatants. Such agents will not have employed terrorism earlier, despite their grievances.

A model case is the African National Congress (ANC) in its struggle against apartheid in South Africa. Nelson Mandela, during the 1964 trial that produced his sentence of life imprisonment, summed up the ANC's position as follows:

> *a.* It was a mass political organization with a political function to fulfill. Its members had joined on the express policy of nonviolence.
>
> *b.* Because of all this, it could not and would not undertake violence. This must be stressed.
>
> *c.* On the other hand, in view of this situation I have described, ANC was prepared to depart from its fifty-year-old policy of nonviolence. . . . There is sabotage, there is guerrilla warfare, there is terrorism, and there is open revolution. We chose to adopt the first method and to exhaust it before taking any other decision.[7]

Mandela was implying that violence, including terrorism, became an option "only when all else had failed, when all channels of peaceful protest had been barred to us," which led the ANC to conclude that "to continue preaching peace and nonviolence at a time when the government met our peaceful demands with force" would be "unrealistic and wrong."[8] By the 1980s, at the height of government repression, the ANC did resort to acts of terrorism before reaffirming its earlier position on controlled violence that does not target civilians.[9] The case of the ANC demonstrates that those who employ terrorism can have and sometimes have had fundamental moral concern for noncombatants. Such moral concern, however, is overriding neither for terrorists nor for proper combatants. . . .

I have argued that terrorism is not distinctively wrong as compared to conventional war in the following respects. Both types of political violence may be waged for just or unjust causes. Both types employ use of force against noncombatants, with conventional war usually causing them many more casualties. War and terrorism hence can be expected to produce fear widely among noncombatants where force is used. . . .

If we believe that war can be justifiable on grounds of just cause and the unavailability of less harmful means, despite the harm it does to noncombatants, we must take seriously whether these same grounds could ever justify terrorism. The failures of the dominant view of terrorism should lead us to adopt either a more critical attitude toward conventional war or a less condemnatory attitude toward terrorism.

Notes

1. Chris Hedges, *What Every Person Should Know about War* (New York: Free Press, 2003), p. 7.
2. I add the qualification "nonstate" since states have employed tactics (e.g., firebombing of cities) and weapons (e.g., chemical, biological, and nuclear) that could count as terrorist.
3. Adam Roberts and Richard Guelff, eds., *Documents on the Laws of War,* 3rd ed. (Oxford: Oxford University Press, 1982), p. 489. Also see, e.g., Michael Walzer, *Just and Unjust Wars* (New York: Basic Books, 1977), pp. 145–46.
4. Judith Gail Gardam, "Proportionality and Force in International Law," *American Journal of International Law* 87 (1993): pp. 391–413, 410. To be clear, Gardam is not endorsing this interpretation. For a critical assessment of standard treatments of proportionality and an alternative approach, see Lionel K. McPherson, "Excessive Force in War: A 'Golden Rule' Test," *Theoretical Inquiries in Law* 7 (2005): pp. 81–95.
5. James M. Dubik, *Philosophy & Public Affairs* 11 (1982): pp. 354–71, 368. Dubik is responding to Walzer's more demanding requirement that combatants must accept greater costs to themselves for the sake of minimizing harm to noncombatants. See Walzer, *Just and Unjust Wars,* p. 155.
6. Virginia Held, "Terrorism and War," *Journal of Ethics* 8 (2004): pp. 59–75, 69.
7. Nelson Mandela, "I Am Prepared to Die," in *Mandela, Tambo, and the African National Congress: The Struggle against Apartheid, 1948–1990: A Documentary Survey,* ed. Sheridan Johns and R. Hunt Davis Jr. (New York: Oxford University Press, 1991), pp. 115–33, 121.
8. Ibid., p. 120.
9. Sheridan Johns and R. Hunt Davis, "Conclusion: Mandela, Tambo, and the ANC in the 1990s," in their *Mandela, Tambo, and the African National Congress,* pp. 309–17, 312.

Study Questions

1. Can modern warfare be waged without harm to noncombatants?
2. Do noncombatants have more to fear from war or from terrorism?
3. Might terrorists acknowledge the moral value of the lives of noncombatants?
4. Can terrorism be used on behalf of a just cause?

B.

Torture

Torture

Henry Shue

Is torture ever justifiable? This question is here considered by Henry Shue, Professor of Politics and International Relations at the University of Oxford. He distinguishes between "interrogational torture," torture to obtain information, and "terroristic torture," torture to intimidate people other than the victim. Shue argues that in both cases torture is morally unacceptable, because it violates the prohibition against assault upon the defenseless. He acknowledges imaginable circumstances in which interrogational torture would be justified but maintains that these rare cases do not warrant relaxing legal prohibitions against it.

But no one dies in the right place
Or in the right hour
And everyone dies sooner than his time
And before he reaches home.

—Reza Baraheni

From Henry Shue, "Torture," *Philosophy and Public Affairs* 7 (1978).

Whatever one might have to say about torture, there appear to be moral reasons for not saying it. Obviously I am not persuaded by these reasons, but they deserve some mention. Mostly, they add up to a sort of Pandora's Box objection: if practically everyone is opposed to all torture, why bring it up, start people thinking about it, and risk weakening the inhibitions against what is clearly a terrible business?

Torture is indeed contrary to every relevant international law, including the laws of war. No other practice except slavery is so universally and unanimously condemned in law and human convention. Yet, unlike slavery, which is still most definitely practiced but affects relatively few people, torture is widespread and growing. According to Amnesty International, scores of governments are now using some torture—including governments which are widely viewed as fairly civilized—and a number of governments are heavily dependent upon torture for their very survival.[1]

So, to cut discussion of this objection short, Pandora's Box is open. . . .

Assault upon the Defenseless

The laws of war include an elaborate, and for the most part long-established, code for what might be described as the proper conduct of the killing of other people. . . .

. . . [O]ne of its moral bases . . . is that it allows for a "fair fight" by means of protecting the utterly defenseless from assault. . . .

At least part of the peculiar disgust which torture evokes may be derived from its apparent failure to satisfy even this weak constraint of being a "fair fight." The supreme reason, of course, is that torture begins only after the fight is—for the victim—finished. Only losers are tortured. A "fair fight" may even in fact already have occurred and led to the capture of the person who is to be tortured. But now that the torture victim has exhausted all means of defense and is powerless before the victors, a fresh assault begins. The surrender is followed by new attacks upon the defeated by the now unrestrained conquerors. In this respect torture is indeed not analogous to the killing in battle of a healthy and well-armed foe; it is a cruel assault upon the defenseless. In combat the other person one kills is still a threat when killed and is killed in part for the sake of one's own survival. The torturer inflicts pain and damage upon another person who, by virtue of now being within his or her power, is no longer a threat and is entirely at the torturer's mercy. . . .

Torture Within Constraints?

But is all torture indeed an assault upon the defenseless? For, it could be argued in support of some torture that in many cases there is something beyond the initial surrender which the torturer wants from the victim and that in such cases the victim could comply and provide the torturer with whatever is wanted. To refuse to comply with the further demand would then be to maintain a second line of defense. The victim would, in a sense, not have surrendered—at least not fully surrendered—but instead only retreated. The victim is not, on this view, utterly helpless in the face of unrestrainable assault as long as he or she holds in reserve an act of compliance which would satisfy the torturer and bring the torture to an end.

It might be proposed, then, that there could be at least one type of morally less unacceptable torture. Obviously the torture victim must remain defenseless in the literal sense, because it cannot be expected that his or her captors would provide means of defense against themselves. But an alternative to a capability for a literal defense is an effective capability for surrender, that is, a form of surrender which will in fact bring an end to attacks. In the case of torture the relevant form of surrender might seem to be a compliance with the wishes of the torturer that provides an escape from further torture.

Accordingly, the constraint on the torture that would, on this view, make it less objectionable would be this: the victim of torture must have available an act of compliance which, if performed, will end the torture. In other words, the purpose of the torture must be known to the victim, the purpose must be the performance of some action within the victim's power to perform, and the victim's performance of the desired action must produce the permanent cessation of the torture. I shall refer to torture that provides for such an act of compliance as torture that satisfies the constraint of possible compliance. As soon becomes clear, it makes a great difference what kind of act is presented as the act of compliance. And a person with an iron will, a great sense of honor, or an overwhelming commitment to a cause may choose not to accept voluntarily cessation of the torture on the terms offered. But the basic point would be merely that there should be some terms understood so that the victim retains one last portion of control over his or her fate. Escape is not defense, but it is a manner of protecting oneself. A practice of torture that allows for escape through compliance might seem immune to the charge of engaging in assault upon the defenseless. Such is the proposal.

One type of contemporary torture, however, is clearly incapable of satisfying the constraint of possible compliance. The extraction of information from the victim, which perhaps—whatever the deepest motivations of torturers may have been—has historically been a dominant explicit purpose of torture is now, in world practice, overshadowed by the goal of the intimidation of people other than the victim.[2] Torture is in many countries used primarily to intimidate potential opponents of the government from actively expressing their opposition in any form considered objectionable by the regime. Prohibited forms of expression range, among various regimes, from participation in terroristic guerrilla movements to the publication of accurate news accounts. The extent of the suffering inflicted upon the victims of the torture is proportioned, not according to the responses of the victim, but according to the expected impact of news of the torture upon other people over whom the torture victim normally has no control. The function of general intimidation of others, or deterrence of dissent, is radically different from the function of extracting specific information under the control of the victim of torture, in respects which are central to the assessment of such torture. This is naturally not to deny that any given instance of torture may serve, to varying degrees, both purposes—and, indeed, other purposes still.

Terroristic torture, as we may call this dominant type, cannot satisfy the constraint of possible compliance, because its purpose (intimidation of persons other than the victim of the torture) cannot be accomplished and may not even be capable of being influenced by the victim of the torture. The victim's suffering—indeed, the victim—is being used entirely as a means to an end over which the victim has no control. Terroristic torture is a pure case—the purest possible case—of the violation of the Kantian principle that no person may be used *only* as a means. The victim is simply a site at which great pain occurs so that others may know about it and be frightened by the prospect. The torturers have no particular reason not to make the suffering as great and as extended as possible. Quite possibly the more terrible the torture, the more intimidating it will be—this is certainly likely to be believed to be so. . . .

The degree of need for assaults upon the defenseless initially appears to be quite different in the case of torture for the purpose of extracting information, which we may call *interrogational torture.* This type of torture needs separate examination because, however condemnable we ought in the end to consider it overall, its purpose of gaining information appears to be consistent with the observation of some constraint on the part of any torturer genuinely pursuing that purpose alone. Interrogational torture does have a built-in endpoint: when the information has been obtained, the torture has accomplished its purpose and need not be continued. Thus, satisfaction of the constraint of possible compliance seems to be quite compatible with the explicit end of interrogational torture, which could be terminated upon the victim's compliance in providing the information sought. In a fairly obvious fashion the torturer could consider himself or herself to have completed the assigned task—or probably more hopefully, any superiors who were supervising the process at some emotional distance could consider the task to be finished and put a stop to it. A pure case of interrogational torture, then, appears able to satisfy the constraint of possible compliance, since it offers an escape, in the form of providing the information wanted by the torturers, which affords some protection against further assault.

Two kinds of difficulties arise for the suggestion that even largely interrogational torture could escape the charge that it includes assaults upon the defenseless. It is hardly necessary to point out that very few actual instances of torture are likely to fall entirely within the category of interrogational torture. Torture intended primarily to obtain information is by no means always in practice held to some minimum necessary amount. To the extent that the torturer's motivation is sadistic or otherwise brutal, he or she will be strongly inclined to exceed any rational calculations about what is sufficient for the stated purpose. In view of the strength and nature of a torturer's likely passions—of, for example, hate and self-hate, disgust and self-disgust, horror and fascination, subservience toward superiors and aggression toward victims—no constraint is to be counted upon in practice.

Still, it is of at least theoretical interest to ask whether torturers with a genuine will to do so could conduct interrogational torture in a manner which would satisfy the constraint of possible compliance. In order to tell, it is essential to grasp specifically what compliance would normally involve. Almost all torture is "political" in the sense that it is inflicted by the government in power upon people who are, seem to be, or might be opposed to the government. Some torture is also inflicted by opponents of a government upon people who are, seem to be, or might be supporting the government. Possible victims of torture fall into three broad categories: the ready collaborator, the innocent bystander, and the dedicated enemy.

First, the torturers may happen upon someone who is involved with the other side but is not dedicated to such a degree that cooperation with the torturers would, from the victim's perspective, constitute a betrayal of anything highly valued. For such a person a betrayal of cause and allies might indeed serve as a form of genuine escape.

The second possibility is the capture of someone who is passive toward both sides and essentially uninvolved. If such a bystander should happen to know the relevant information—which is very unlikely—and to be willing to provide it, no torture would be called for. But what if the victim would be perfectly willing to provide the information sought in order to escape the torture but does not have the information? Systems of torture are notoriously incompetent. The usual situation is captured with icy accuracy by the reputed informal motto of the Saigon police, "If they are not guilty, beat them until they are."[3] The victims of torture need an escape not only from beatings for what they know but also from beatings for what they do not know. In short, the victim has no convincing way of demonstrating that he or she cannot comply, even when compliance is impossible. (Compare the reputed dunking test for witches: if the woman sank, she was an ordinary mortal.)

Even a torturer who would be willing to stop after learning all that could be learned, which is nothing at all if the "wrong" person is being tortured, would have difficulty discriminating among pleas. Any keeping of the tacit bargain to stop when compliance has been as complete as possible would likely be undercut by uncertainty about when the fullest possible compliance had occurred. The difficulty of demonstrating that one had collaborated as much as one could might in fact haunt the collaborator as well as the innocent, especially if his or her collaboration had struck the torturers as being of little real value.

Finally, when the torturers succeed in torturing someone genuinely committed to the other side, compliance means, in a word, betrayal; betrayal of one's ideals and one's comrades. The possibility of betrayal cannot be counted as an escape. Undoubtedly some ideals are vicious and some friends are partners in crime—this can be true of either the government, the opposition, or both. Nevertheless, a betrayal is no escape for a dedicated member of either a government or its opposition, who cannot collaborate without denying his or her highest values.

For any genuine escape must be something better than settling for the lesser of two evils. One can always try to minimize one's losses—even in dilemmas from which there is no real escape. But if accepting the lesser of two evils always counted as an escape, there would be no situations from which there was no escape, except perhaps those in which all alternatives happened to be equally evil. On such a loose notion of escape, all conscripts would become volunteers, since they could always desert. And all assaults containing any alternatives would then be acceptable. An alternative which is legitimately to count as an escape must not only be preferable but also itself satisfy some minimum standard of moral acceptability. A denial of one's self does not count.

Therefore, on the whole, the apparent possibility of escape through compliance tends to melt away upon examination. The ready collaborator and the innocent bystander have some hope of an acceptable escape, but only provided that the torturers both (a) are persuaded that the victim has kept his or her part of the bargain by telling all there is to tell and (b) choose to keep their side of the bargain in a situation in which agreements cannot be enforced upon them and they have nothing to lose by continuing the torture if they please. If one is treated as if one is a dedicated enemy, as seems likely to be the standard procedure, the fact that one actually belongs in another category has no effect. On the other hand, the dedicated enemies of the torturers, who presumably tend to know more and consequently are the primary intended targets of the torture, are provided with nothing which can be considered an escape and can only protect themselves, as torture victims always have, by pretending to be collaborators or innocents, and thereby imperiling the members of these two categories.

Morally Permissible Torture?

Still, it must reluctantly be admitted that the avoidance of assaults upon the defenseless is not the only, or even in all cases an overriding, moral consideration. And, therefore, even if terroristic and interrogational torture, each in its own way, is bound to involve attacks upon people unable to defend themselves or to escape, it is still not utterly inconceivable that instances of one or the other type of torture might sometimes, all things considered, be justified. Consequently, we must sketch the elements of an overall assessment of these two types of torture, beginning again with the dominant contemporary form: terroristic.

Anyone who thought an overall justification could be given for an episode of terroristic torture would at the least have to provide a clear statement of necessary conditions, all of which would have to be satisfied before any actions so extraordinarily cruel as terroristic torture could be morally acceptable. If the torture were actually to be justified, the conditions would, of course, have to be met in fact. An attempt to specify the necessary conditions for a morally permissible episode of terroristic torture might include conditions such as the following. A first necessary condition would be that the purpose actually being sought through the torture would need to be not only morally good but supremely important, and examples of such purposes would have to be selected by criteria of moral importance which would themselves need to be justified. Second, terroristic torture would presumably have to be the least harmful means of accomplishing the supremely important goal. Given how very harmful terroristic torture is, this could rarely be the case. And it would be unlikely unless the period of use of the torture in the society was limited in an enforceable manner. Third, it would have to be absolutely clear for what purpose the terroristic torture was being used, what would constitute achievement of that purpose, and thus, when the torture would end. The torture could not become a standard practice of government for an indefinite duration. And so on.

But is there any supremely important end to which terroristic torture could be the least harmful means? Could terroristic torture be employed for a brief interlude and then outlawed? Consider what would be involved in answering the latter question. A government could, it might seem, terrorize until the terror had accomplished its purpose and then suspend the terror. There are few, if any, clear cases of a regime's voluntarily renouncing terror after having created, through terror, a situation in which terror was no longer needed. And there is considerable evidence of the improbability of this sequence. Terroristic torture tends to become, according to Amnesty International, "administrative practice": a routine procedure institutionalized into the method of governing. Some bureaus collect taxes, other bureaus conduct torture. First a suspect is arrested, next he or she is tortured. Torture gains the momentum of an ingrained element of a standard operating procedure.

Several factors appear to point in the direction of permanence. From the perspective of the victims, even where the population does not initially feel exploited, terror is very unsuitable to the generation of loyalty. This would add to the difficulty of any transition away from reliance on terror. Where the population does feel exploited even before the torture begins, the sense of outrage (which is certainly rationally justified toward the choice of victims, as we have seen) could often prove stronger than the fear of suffering. Tragically, any unlikelihood that the terroristic torture would "work" would almost guarantee that it would continue to be used. From the perspective of the torturers, it is rare for any entrenched bureau to choose to eliminate itself rather than to try to prove its essential value and the need for its own expansion. This is especially likely if the members of the operation are either thoroughly cynical or thoroughly sincere in their conviction that they are protecting "national security" or some other value taken to be supremely important. The greater burden of proof rests, I would think, on anyone who believes that controllable terroristic torture is possible.

Rousseau says at one point that pure democracy is a system of government suitable only for angels—ordinary mortals cannot handle it. If Rousseau's assumption is that principles for human beings cannot ignore the limits of the capacity of human beings, he is surely right. . . . As devilish as terroristic torture is, in a sense it too may be a technique only for angels: perhaps only angels could use it within the only constraints which would make it permissible and, then, lay it aside. The partial list of criteria for the acceptable use of terroristic torture sketched above, in combination with strong evidence of the uncontrollability of terroristic torture, would come as close to a reductio ad absurdum as one could hope to produce in political philosophy. Observance of merely the constraints listed would require a degree of self-control and self-restraint, individual and bureaucratic, which might turn out to be saintly. If so, terroristic torture would have been shown to be justifiable only if it could be kept within constraints within which it could almost certainly not be kept.

But if the final objection against terroristic torture turned out to be empirical evidence that it is probably uncontrollable, would not the philosophical arguments themselves turn out to have been irrelevant? Why bother to show that terroristic torture assaults the defenseless, if in the end the case against it is going to rest on an empirical hypothesis about the improbability of keeping such torture within reasonable bounds?

The thesis about assault upon the defenseless matters, even though it is not in itself conclusive, because the uncontrollability thesis could only be probable and would also not be conclusive in itself. It could not be shown to be certain that terroristic torture will become entrenched, will be used for minor purposes, will be used when actually not necessary, and so on. And we sometimes go ahead and allow practices which might get out of hand. The relevance of showing the extent of the assault upon defenseless people is to establish how much is at stake if the practice is allowed and then runs amok. If the evidence for uncontrollability were strong, that fact plus the demonstration of extreme cruelty would constitute a decisive case against terroristic torture. It would, then, never be justified.

Much of what can be said about terroristic torture can also be said about instances involving interrogational torture. This is the case primarily because in practice there are evidently few pure cases of interrogational torture. An instance of torture which is to any significant degree terroristic in purpose ought to be treated as terroristic. But if we keep in mind how far we are departing from most actual practice, we may, as before, consider instances in which the *sole* purpose of torture is to extract certain information and therefore the torturer is willing to stop as soon as he or she is sure that the victim has provided all the information which the victim has.

As argued in the preceding section, interrogational torture would in practice be difficult to make into less of an assault upon the defenseless. The supposed possibility of escape through compliance turns out to depend upon the keeping of a bargain which is entirely unenforceable within the torture situation and upon the making of discriminations among victims that would usually be difficult to make until after they no longer mattered. In fact, since any sensible willing collaborator will cooperate in a hurry, only the committed and the innocent are likely to be severely tortured. More important, in the case of someone being tortured because of profoundly held convictions, the "escape" would normally be a violation of integrity.

As with terroristic torture, any complete argument for permitting instances of interrogational torture would have to include a full specification of all necessary conditions of a permissible instance, such as its serving a supremely important purpose (with criteria of importance), its being the least harmful means to that goal, its having a clearly defined and reachable endpoint, and so on. This would not be a simple matter. Also as in the case of terroristic torture, a considerable danger exists that whatever necessary conditions were specified, any practice of torture once set in motion would gain enough momentum to burst any bonds and become a standard operating procedure. Torture is the ultimate shortcut. If it were ever permitted under any conditions, the temptation to use it increasingly would be very strong.

Nevertheless, it cannot be denied that there are imaginable cases in which the harm that could be prevented by a rare instance of pure interrogational torture would be so enormous as to outweigh the cruelty of the torture itself and, possibly, the enormous potential harm which would result if what was intended to be a rare instance was actually the breaching of the dam which would lead to a torrent of torture. There is a standard philosopher's example which someone always invokes: suppose a fanatic, perfectly willing to die rather than collaborate in the thwarting of his own scheme, has set a hidden nuclear device to explode in the heart of Paris. There is no time to evacuate the innocent people or even the movable art treasures—the only hope of preventing tragedy is to torture the perpetrator, find the device, and deactivate it.

I can see no way to deny the permissibility of torture in a case *just like this.* To allow the destruction of much of a great city and many of its people would be almost as wicked as purposely to destroy it, as the Nazis did to London and Warsaw, and the Allies did to Dresden and Tokyo, during World War II. But there is a saying in jurisprudence that hard cases make bad law, and there might well be one in philosophy that artificial cases make bad ethics. If the example is made sufficiently extraordinary, the conclusion that the torture is permissible is secure. But one cannot easily draw conclusions for ordinary cases from extraordinary ones, and as the situations described become more likely, the conclusion that the torture is permissible becomes more debatable.

Notice how unlike the circumstances of an actual choice about torture the philosopher's example is. The proposed victim of our torture is not someone we suspect of planting the device: he *is* the perpetrator. He is not some pitiful psychotic making one last play for attention: he *did* plant the device. The wiring is not backwards, the mechanism is not jammed: the device *will* destroy the city if not deactivated.

Much more important from the perspective of whether general conclusions applicable to ordinary cases can be drawn are the background conditions that tend to be assumed. The torture will not be conducted in the basement of a small-town jail in the provinces by local thugs popping pills; the prime minister and chief justice are being kept informed; and a priest and a doctor are present. The victim will not be raped or forced to eat excrement and will not collapse with a heart attack or become deranged before talking; while avoiding irreparable damage, the antiseptic pain will carefully be increased only up to the point at which the necessary information is divulged, and the doctor will then immediately administer an antibiotic and a tranquilizer. The torture is purely interrogational.[4]

Most important, such incidents do not continue to happen. There are not so many people with grievances against this government that the torture is becoming necessary more often, and in the smaller cities, and for slightly lesser threats, and with a little less care, and so on. Any judgment that torture could be sanctioned in an isolated case without seriously weakening existing inhibitions against the more general use of torture rests on empirical hypotheses about the psychology and politics of torture. There *is* considerable evidence of all torture's metastatic tendency. If there is also evidence that interrogational torture can sometimes be used with the surgical precision which imagined justifiable cases always assume, such rare uses would have to be considered.

Does the possibility that torture might be justifiable in some of the rarefied situations which can be imagined provide any reason to consider relaxing the legal prohibitions against it? Absolutely not. The distance between the situations which must be concocted in order to have a plausible case of morally permissible torture and the situations which actually occur is, if anything, further reason why the existing prohibitions against torture should remain and should be strengthened by making torture an international crime. An act of torture ought to remain illegal so that anyone who sincerely believes such an act to be the least available evil is placed in the position of needing to justify his or her act morally in order to defend himself or herself legally. The torturer should be in roughly the same position as someone who commits civil disobedience. Anyone who thinks an act of torture is justified should have no alternative but to convince a group of peers in a public trial that all necessary conditions for a morally permissible act were indeed satisfied. If it is reasonable to put someone through torture, it is reasonable to put someone else through a careful explanation of why. If the situation approximates those in the imaginary examples in which torture seems possible to justify, a judge can surely be expected to suspend the sentence. Meanwhile, there is little need to be concerned about possible injustice to justified torturers and great need to find means to restrain totally unjustified torture.

Notes

1. See Amnesty International, *Report on Torture* (New York: Farrar, Straus and Giroux, 1975), pp. 21–33.
2. See Amnesty International, 69.
3. Amnesty International, 166.
4. Amnesty International, pp. 24–25, 114–242.

Study Questions

1. How does Shue distinguish between "terroristic torture" and "interrogational torture"?
2. According to Shue, might torture ever be justifiable?
3. Might moral considerations ever require illegal actions?
4. Can the use of unrealistic examples distort our ethical reasoning?

The Ticking Time-Bomb Terrorist

Alan M. Dershowitz

Suppose a terrorist sets a bomb, is captured, and refuses to provide the information needed to save thousands of lives. Should the authorities resort to torture to try to avoid disaster? Alan Dershowitz, previously Professor of Law at Harvard University, argues that they should, because the benefits outweigh the costs. Indeed, Dershowitz maintains that torture should be included as part of our legal system.

The Case for Torturing the Ticking Bomb Terrorist

[Suppose] weeks before September 11, 2001, the Immigration and Naturalization Service detained Zacarias Moussaoui after flight instructors reported suspicious statements he had made while taking flying lessons and paying for them with large amounts of cash.[1] The government decided not to seek a warrant to search his computer. Now imagine that they had, and that they discovered he was part of a plan to destroy large occupied buildings, but without any further details. They interrogated him, gave him immunity from prosecution, and offered him large cash rewards and a new identity. He refused to talk. They then threatened him, tried to trick him, and employed every lawful technique available. He still refused. They even injected him with sodium pentothal and other truth serums, but to no avail. The attack now appeared to be imminent, but the FBI still had no idea what the target was or what means would be used to attack it.

From Alan M. Dershowitz, *Why Terrorism Works: Understanding the Threat, Responding to the Challenge* (New Haven, CT: Yale University Press, 2003).

We could not simply evacuate all buildings indefinitely. An FBI agent proposes the use of nonlethal torture—say, a sterilized needle inserted under the fingernails to produce unbearable pain without any threat to health or life. . . .

The simple cost-benefit analysis for employing such non-lethal torture seems overwhelming: it is surely better to inflict nonlethal pain on one guilty terrorist who is illegally withholding information needed to prevent an act of terrorism than to permit a large number of innocent victims to die.[2] Pain is a lesser and more remediable harm than death; and the lives of a thousand innocent people should be valued more than the bodily integrity of one guilty person. If the variation on the Moussaoui case is not sufficiently compelling to make this point, we can always raise the stakes. Several weeks after September 11, our government received reports that a ten-kiloton nuclear weapon may have been stolen from Russia and was on its way to New York City, where it would be detonated and kill hundreds of thousands of people. The reliability of the source, code named Dragonfire, was uncertain, but assume for purposes of this hypothetical extension of the actual case that the source was a captured terrorist—like the one tortured by the Philippine authorities—who knew precisely how and where the weapon was being brought into New York and was to be detonated. Again, everything short of torture is tried, but to no avail. It is not absolutely certain torture will work, but it is our last, best hope for preventing a cataclysmic nuclear devastation in a city too large to evacuate in time. Should nonlethal torture be tried?. . .

The . . . argument for torturing a ticking bomb terrorist is bolstered by an argument from analogy—an *a fortiori* argument. What moral principle could justify the death penalty for past individual murders and at the same time condemn nonlethal torture to prevent future mass murders? . . . The death penalty is, of course, reserved for convicted murderers. But again, what if torture was limited to convicted terrorists who refused to divulge information about future terrorism? Consider as well the analogy to the use of deadly force against suspects fleeing from arrest for dangerous felonies of which they have not yet been convicted. Or military retaliations that produce the predictable and inevitable collateral killing of some innocent civilians. The case against torture, if made by a Quaker who opposes the death penalty, war, self-defense, and the use of lethal force against fleeing felons, is understandable. But for anyone who justifies killing on the basis of a cost-benefit analysis, the case against the use of nonlethal torture to save multiple lives is more difficult to make. In the end, absolute opposition to torture—even nonlethal torture in the ticking bomb case—may rest more on historical and aesthetic considerations than on moral or logical ones. . . .

In deciding whether the ticking bomb terrorist should be tortured, one important question is whether there would be less torture if it were done as part of the legal system, as it was in sixteenth- and seventeenth-century England, or off the books, as it is in many countries today. The English system of torture was more visible and thus more subject to public accountability, and it is likely that torture was employed less frequently in England than in France. "During these years when it appears that torture might have become routinized in English criminal procedure, the Privy Council kept the torture power under careful control and never allowed it to fall into the hands of the regular law enforcement officers," as it had in France. In England "no law enforcement officer . . . acquired the power to use torture without special warrant." Moreover, when torture warrants were abolished, "the English experiment with torture left no traces." Because it was under centralized control, it was easier to abolish than it was in France, where it persisted for many years.[3]

It is always difficult to extrapolate from history, but it seems logical that a formal, visible, accountable, and centralized system is somewhat easier to control than an ad hoc, off-the-books, and under-the-radar-screen nonsystem. I believe, though I certainly cannot prove, that a formal requirement of a judicial warrant as a prerequisite to nonlethal torture would decrease the amount of physical violence directed against suspects. At the most obvious level, a double check is always more protective than a single check. In every instance in which a warrant is requested, a field officer has already decided that torture is justified and, in the absence of a warrant requirement, would simply proceed with the torture. Requiring that decision to be approved by a judicial officer will result in fewer instances of torture even if the judge rarely turns down a request. Moreover, I believe that most judges would require compelling evidence before they would authorize so extraordinary a departure from our constitutional norms, and law enforcement officials would be reluctant to seek a warrant unless they had compelling evidence that the suspect had information needed to prevent an imminent terrorist attack. A record would be kept of every warrant granted, and although it is certainly possible that some individual agents might torture without a warrant, they would have no excuse, since a warrant procedure would be available. They could not claim "necessity," because the decision as to whether the torture is indeed necessary has been taken out of their hands and placed in the hands of a judge. In addition, even if torture were deemed totally illegal without any exception, it would still occur, though the public would be less aware of its existence.

I also believe that the rights of the suspect would be better protected with a warrant requirement. He would be granted immunity, told that he was now compelled to testify, threatened with imprisonment if he refused to do so, and given the option of providing the requested information. Only if he refused to do what he was legally compelled to do—provide necessary information, which could not incriminate him because of the immunity—would he be threatened with torture. Knowing that such a threat was authorized by the law, he might well provide the information. If he still refused to, he would be subjected to judicially monitored physical measures designed to cause excruciating pain without leaving any lasting damage. . . .

Notes

1. David Johnston and Philip Shenon, "F.B.I. Curbed Scrutiny of Man Now a Suspect in the Attacks," *New Tork Times*, 10/6/2001.
2. It is illegal to withhold relevant information from a grand jury after receiving immunity. See *Kastigarv. U.S.* 406 U.S. 441 (1972).
3. John Langbein, *Torture and the Law of Proof* (Chicago: University of Chicago Press, 1977), pp. 136–37,139.

Study Questions

1. Would you have approved the torture of Moussaoui?
2. Would you trust the answers Moussaoui provides after having undergone torture?'
3. Might torture be legally justified but morally unjustified?
4. Might torture be morally justified but legally unjustified?

Training Torturers

Jessica Wolfendale

Jessica Wolfendale is Associate Professor of Philosophy at West Virginia University. She argues that the ticking bomb scenario fails to consider the need for torturers to extract the information. How would they be prepared for their role? To be effective, they would need to develop detachment from the pain of others, a view of those being tortured as subhuman, and a willingness to follow orders from their superiors without questioning. Wolfendale concludes that a society's need to train people to engage in torture would undermine its moral appropriateness, even in the ticking–bomb scenario.

> Suppose a fanatic, perfectly willing to die rather than collaborate in the thwarting of his own scheme, has set a hidden nuclear device to explode in the heart of Paris. There is no time to evacuate the innocent people or even the movable art treasures—the only hope of preventing tragedy is to torture the perpetrator, find the device, and deactivate it.[1]

Introduction

The war against terrorism has re-ignited the debate about the permissibility of torture. Once again we are hearing variations of the "ticking bomb" argument in support of the use of torture against terrorism suspects. Terrorism is claimed to pose such an extreme threat that the prohibition against torture cannot be maintained. We are involved in a new kind of war in which the ordinary moral constraints cannot apply. In the words of Cofer Black, former head of the U.S.

From Jessica Wolfendale, "Training Torturers—A Critique of the 'Ticking Bomb' Argument," *Social Theory and Practice* 32 (2006).

Counterterrorism Center: "There was a before 9/11, and there was an after 9/11 . . . After 9/11 the gloves come off."[2]

Variations of the ticking bomb argument have been put forward by writers such as Alan Dershowitz. . . .[3] These variations have involved detailed discussions about the exact conditions under which the torture of terrorism suspects might be justified. Most often these arguments are put forward as utilitarian justifications for overriding the prohibition against torture. . . . In every case, however, one crucial issue has been missing from the analysis of these arguments: permitting torture means permitting torturers.

In this paper I argue that the scope and kind of training necessary to produce the torturer needed in the ticking bomb scenario raises serious questions about the legitimacy of these kinds of arguments for the use of torture. . . .

1. The Ticking Bomb Torturer

In the standard ticking bomb scenario, a suspect has been caught who possesses information that must be obtained quickly in order to avert huge civilian casualties. Most ticking bomb scenarios do not explain *how* the suspect was identified or caught. . . . To have identified the key terrorist, know how and where to capture him, and to be sure that he has the relevant information requires an already well established and comprehensive intelligence network involving "informants, electronic surveillance networks, and undercover agents."[4] The proponent of the ticking bomb argument must therefore be sure that the relevant information cannot be found through these (already formidable) intelligence resources. However, for the purposes of this argument we will give the supporter of the ticking bomb argument the benefit of the doubt and assume that despite the vast array of intelligence resources, the only way to find out where the bomb is hidden is to interrogate the suspect. The suspect to be interrogated is usually a fanatical terrorist willing to die for his cause—someone unlikely to be intimidated by mere threats of violence and who may well be prepared for torture.

Under these conditions, the ticking bomb torturer must be able to extract the required information in the shortest possible time . . . without killing the suspect. The torturer must be an expert in interrogational torture—excessively sadistic torture or torture for the purposes of punishment, dehumanization, or deterring others is generally agreed to be impermissible. Given these constraints, what kind of training would the ticking bomb torturer require?

Perhaps the ticking bomb torturer would not need any particular skills or training. There are numerous examples of ordinary people who have massacred, tortured, raped, and committed other atrocities without any special training. . . .

It is true that ordinary people have the capacity to commit horrendous acts of violence without any particular training. However, the ticking bomb scenario requires far more than the infliction of extreme violence. The aim of the torture and the constraints on the kind of torture that may be used require a very particular kind of torturer. Unlike deterrent or dehumanizing torture, interrogational torture requires finesse, skill, and discipline. Given the importance of the information that is required from the suspect, the ticking bomb torturer needs to be *already* trained in effective interrogational torture. It would not do to take an ordinary soldier and make him torture a terrorist suspect at the last minute. . . .

The ticking bomb scenario is far too serious to permit torturers to "get creative" with the suspect. The good interrogational torturer needs to be entirely in control of the process of torture. He must be able to torture whoever is placed in front of him without flinching and without hesitation. However, he cannot be sadistic or overly brutal. Such a person would not have the discipline or skills to extract the information without killing the captive. The need for discipline, skill, and control is emphasized in real-life torturer training manuals. The Khmer Rouge Manual for Torture makes the need for discipline quite clear: "The purpose of torturing is to get their responses. It's not something we do for the fun of it."[5] Sadism and lack of discipline undermine the effectiveness of torture.

But torture requires more than practical skills; it requires immense strength of mind. Torturers need to be trained to manage the psychological stress associated with torturing. To gain a realistic understanding of how the ticking bomb torturer should be trained, we can usefully look at how real-life torturers are trained. After all, supporters of the ticking bomb case should consider all the relevant real-life consequences of training torturers if they are to derive a realistic understanding of the ticking bomb scenario.

2. The Training of Torturers

In the real world, most torturers are soldiers or military policemen who have been trained in elite military units.[6] For example, torturers in South America, Greece, Myanmar, South Africa, and Ireland all were part of elite military units charged with gathering intelligence and other covert operations. . . .

2.1. Basic Training in the Elite Military Units

. . . [T]he training process of these specialized units involves intense, highly stressful, and often brutal exercises. Aside from the more conventional weapons and fitness training, trainees are subjected to the techniques of psychological torture, a process which is extremely distressing and humiliating and can result in dissociation and deep anxiety. Despite the severity of this training and the suffering that it can cause to trainees, this training is very effective in desensitizing trainees to the infliction and the endurance of suffering. New trainees become desensitized to their own suffering, and when they in their turn play the "torturer" in the stress inoculation training they learn to be desensitized to the infliction of pain. This desensitization reduces soldiers' empathetic reaction to physical suffering and thereby makes the infliction of pain and humiliation on the enemy psychologically easier. Given that the ticking bomb torturer might have to inflict incredibly brutal tortures without flinching, he must be thoroughly desensitized to the infliction of pain and must not be hampered by feelings of empathy or sympathy for the suspect—in the ticking bomb scenario there would be no time for hesitation. . . .

Torturers, if they are to be effective and efficient, must "feel nothing" about what they are doing. But desensitization to the infliction of suffering is not sufficient to make torturers "feel nothing" when they torture suspects. Torturers must also develop the right attitude towards their work; they need to be able to torture with a minimum of emotional engagement. Studies on real-life torturers demonstrate that this is best achieved by adopting the discourse of professionalism.

2.2. Turning Torture into a Profession

The following quotes from real-life torturers demonstrate the view of torture as a profession:

> "I'm here," the officer, whose name was Massini, told [the] prisoner. "I'm a serious professional. After the revolution, I will be at your disposal to torture whom you like."[7]
>
> I don't use . . . violence outside the standard of my conscience as a human being. I'm a conscientious professional. I know what to do and when to do it.[8]

> We didn't operate on anger or sadism or anything like that. . . . It became a function. It became part of the job. It became standard operating procedure.[9]

Professionalism discourse is used to legitimize and normalize torture. This occurs in two ways. First, the elite military units represent the pinnacle of military training and attract soldiers by appealing to the military's professional ideals. Members of these units are encouraged to see themselves as the most professional of soldiers carrying out the unpleasant duties necessary to protect the nation from terrorism and other threats. The appeal to professionalism provides a veneer of legitimacy to the use of torture by tying justifications for the use of torture to the professional goals of the military and by appealing directly to the torturer's professional pride.

Second, the characterization of torture as a profession contributes to what the sociologist Herbert Kelman calls "routinization."[10] Torture becomes a routine job subject to role-specific professional standards and justifications. The language of professionalism aids this process by reconfiguring the act of torture from a brutal act of violence against another human being to what Kelman calls the "routine application of specialized knowledge and skills."[11]. . .

The routinization of torture, aided by the language of professionalism, encourages torturers to adopt an extreme form of professional detachment. . . .

2.3. Dehumanization

Torture victims are often humiliated, filthy, terrified, and naked and this significantly aids the torturers' perception of them as sub-human. . . . Indeed, torture techniques such as hooding, sleep deprivation, denial of toilet facilities, and personal humiliations deliberately aim to make torture victims feel and look less than human, therefore making it easier for torturers to treat them as if they *were* less than human. . . .

There are good reasons why such training would result in the most effective ticking bomb torturer. The time constraints on the ticking bomb scenario mean that the torturer cannot be concerned about the suspect's guilt or the moral justifications for the use of torture—any hesitation could have devastating consequences. If the ticking bomb torturer is trained in the ways I have described he will find it far easier to torture the suspect without suffering from moral and emotional qualms. He must be able to do his work without being overcome with distress or revulsion, and this means that he must already be accustomed to inflicting suffering and he must be immune to the victim's distress. The ticking bomb torturer, if he is to be effective, must also accept his orders without question; he must be able to rest assured that the burden of responsibility lies with the authorities and that they have sufficient reason to require his talents. Adopting the discourse of professionalism will make such obedience easier because it will allow the torturer to restrict his moral concerns to how well he carries out his professional duties rather than whether the use of his professional skills is morally justified. In the words of the Khmer Rouge manual . . . ; "it is necessary to avoid any question or hesitancy or half-heartedness of not daring to do torture."[12] There is too much at stake in the ticking bomb scenario to risk having an ill-prepared novice for a torturer. The ideal ticking bomb torturer needs to be the most consummate professional, and this is best achieved by the combination of the training found in Special Forces units and the use of the discourse of professionalism.

3. What's Wrong with Training Torturers?

Supporters of the ticking bomb argument could admit that the ticking bomb torturer might need the kind of training I have described if he is to have the best chance of success. They may also admit that the need for this training has not been fully discussed before and that this training seems, at the very least, quite harsh. But should the supporter of the ticking bomb argument be concerned about the need for torturer training or is this training just another consideration easily outweighed by the magnitude of the threat in the ticking bomb scenario? . . .

By encouraging torturers not to concern themselves with the moral justifications for the use of torture, the combination of the Special Forces training and the discourse of professionalism instill dispositions of unreflective obedience. Because torturers are trained to obey orders without thinking, they are very unlikely to question whether a particular order is justified—the question of the actual guilt of the suspect is beyond their professional jurisdiction. A consequence of this is that torturers are very unlikely to restrict their professional activities only to cases that meet the stringent criteria of the ticking bomb scenario. This problem is not merely a hypothetical possibility that might occur when professional torturers are trained; it is occurring now and has occurred many times in the past.

Amnesty International has identified over 150 countries that use torture,[13] and the United States government has been using torture in Guantanamo Bay and elsewhere. In the vast majority of these cases the use of torture would never be justified under the ticking bomb argument. Instead, the use of torture in the real world is most often what sociologists Herbert Kelman and V. Lee Hamilton call a "crime of obedience"—a crime that occurs when individuals perform acts of severe violence against others, simply because such acts were ordered by an authority.[14] This is hardly surprising given that torturers are trained in ways that make obedience to illegal and immoral orders quite likely, and given that the "profession" of torture is given a veneer of legitimization by appeals to the military's professional ideals. Torturers are taught to see torture as a professional job that requires the toughest, most professional soldiers. Torturers worldwide are obeying illegal and immoral orders to torture because that is what they are trained to do. Yet the ticking bomb scenario requires these kinds of torturers—torturers who are quite *deliberately* trained not to question the morality of torture. I turn now to what a supporter of the ticking bomb argument might say in response.

4. Objections

The supporter of the ticking bomb argument may claim that *of course* the use of torture for immoral purposes should be avoided and *of course* the use of torture by the 150 countries mentioned by Amnesty International is probably both illegal and immoral. But, they may argue, training torturers for the ticking bomb scenario would be different. Trained torturers would not be given the order to torture unless the ticking bomb scenario actually arose. The fact that torture and torturers are used for many immoral purposes in the real world does not mean that there is anything wrong with training torturers per se. It's just the way torturers are used that is problematic.

The problem with this objection is straightforward. The use of torture and torturers for illegal and immoral purposes is not accidental; it is not a result of "bad apple" torturers who sell their services to immoral causes. The illegal and immoral use of torture is directly connected to how torturers are trained. The training of torturers—training that would be needed for the ticking bomb torturer—produces dispositions closely linked to crimes of obedience because it produces individuals who are very likely to obey illegal and immoral orders. Unless the ticking bomb supporter can guarantee that such orders would never be given, then they must admit that training torturers is likely to lead (and has led to) crimes of obedience. The ticking bomb argument relies on the assumption that the order to torture would only ever be given in legitimate (highly specified) circumstances and that torturers, despite their training, would know—somehow—that such orders were justified. However, there is no evidence that the use of torture would or could be restricted to such highly unusual circumstances, and there is ample evidence that torture is very frequently used for purposes that would never fit the ticking bomb criteria. . . .

A second response that a supporter of the ticking bomb argument could make would be to take into consideration the effects of training torturers and tighten the requirements that must be met before the use of torture would be justified in the ticking bomb scenario. They might claim that it is *possible* to imagine a case of torture that managed to avoid all the consequences listed above and fulfilled the necessary criteria and problematic epistemological requirements of the ticking bomb scenario. There might be a hypothetical situation in a hypothetical world where the threat was sufficiently great, and where there was no alternative but to use torture, very little evidence that the use of torture and torturers would become widespread, no infliction of excessive pain, and little or no likelihood of long-term or widespread institutional changes. Now, if such a situation were in fact possible I would be happy to admit that the use of torture might be justified. Indeed, even those who believed torture to be wrong pro tanto might concede that torture would be morally permissible if such a situation arose. Does this mean that my argument against the supporter of the ticking bomb justification has failed?

I have two responses to this objection. First, I do not believe that such a hypothetical scenario is possible. The interrogational torture needed for the ticking bomb scenario cannot effectively be achieved without a trained torturer who is able and willing to obey his orders without question. It is therefore *im*possible for me to imagine a situation in which such an act of torture could take place without the training I described and without torture also being used worldwide in illegal and immoral cases.

Second, I am just not interested in the permissibility of torture in *any* possible world or hypothetical example. I am interested in the actual arrangements needed for even isolated instances of torture to occur. Because the ticking bomb argument is used in debates about the permissibility of torture on terrorism suspects in *this* world, supporters of the ticking bomb argument cannot rely on purely hypothetical cases to support their claims. Moral arguments about the use of torture must take into consideration what permitting torture involves in reality, not in a purely hypothetical example. That torture might be justified in a hypothetical example in a hypothetical world gives absolutely no reason to think that it can be justified (or legalized) in *this* world. Henry Shue makes the same point:

> Does the possibility that torture might be justifiable in some of the rarefied situations which can be imagined provide any reason to consider relaxing the legal prohibitions against it? Absolutely not. The distance between the situations which much be concocted in order to have a plausible case of morally permissible torture and the situations which actually occur is, if anything, further reason why the existing prohibitions against torture should remain.[15]

Given the pain and suffering caused by torture, supporters of the ticking bomb argument have a positive moral duty to consider whether permitting torture in the war against terrorism could be restricted only to cases that met the ticking bomb criteria. Whatever should be the case in an ideal world in which torture and torturers would only be used in legitimate ticking bomb scenarios, in this world torture and torturers are overwhelmingly used in ways that would never meet the criteria of the ticking bomb scenario. Therefore, in order to answer the question that prompted the debate about torture in the first place—whether we should permit the torture of terrorism suspects—supporters of the ticking bomb argument need to explain how the mere possibility of a ticking bomb case arising justifies a use of torture that requires training torturers in a way that deliberately instills dispositions linked to crimes of obedience, crimes that cause and have caused immense suffering to millions of people worldwide.

5. Conclusion

. . . As we have seen from current and past uses of torture, the training of torturers—the way they would need to be trained in the ticking bomb scenario—is connected to the illegal and immoral use of torture on a vast scale. In this world torture causes far more suffering than it has ever prevented. The mere possibility of a ticking bomb scenario arising is not sufficient to justify such massive suffering. In this world, it is impossible to contain the use of torture and the use of torturers within the limits of the ticking bomb scenario.

Notes

1. Henry Shue, "Torture," *Philosophy and Public Affairs* 7 (1978): 124–43, p. 141.
2. Quoted in Major William D. Casebeer, "Torture Interrogation of Terrorists: A Theory of Exceptions (with Notes, Cautions, and Warnings)" (paper presented at the Joint Services Conference on Professional Ethics, Washington D.C., 2003). Last accessed 15 February 2005 at http://www.usafa.af.mil/jscope/JSCOPE03/Casebeer03.html.
3. See Alan Dershowitz, "Want to Torture? Get a Warrant." Last accessed 21 March 2005 at http://www.sfgate.com/cgibin/article.cgi?file=/chronicle/archive/2002/01/22/ED5329.DTL.
4. Jean Maria Arrigo, "A Utilitarian Argument against Torture Interrogation of Terrorists," *Science and Engineering Ethics* 10 (2004): 1–30, at p. 12.
5. Ronald D. Crelinsten, "In Their Own Words: The World of the Torturer," in Ronald D. Crelinsten and Alex P. Schmid (eds.), *The Politics of Pain: Torturers and Their Masters* (Boulder, Colo.: Westview Press, 1993), pp. 35–65, at p. 37.
6. Crelinsten, "In Their Own Words," pp. 58–60.
7. Quoted in Crelinsten, "In Their Own Words," *Ordinary People: The Dynamics of Torture* (New York: Alfred A. Knopf, 2000), p. 56.
8. Martha Huggins, "Legacies of Authoritarianism: Brazilian Torturers' and Murderers' Reformulation of Memory," *Latin American Perspectives* 27 (2000): 57–78, p. 63.
9. John Conroy, *Unspeakable Acts,* p. 92.
10. Herbert C. Kelman, "The Social Context of Torture: Policy Process and Authority Structure," in Crelinsten and Schmid (eds.), *The Politics of Pain,* p. 30.
11. Ibid., p. 31.
12. Crelinsten, "In Their Own Words," p. 37.
13. *Amnesty International,* "Stop Torture." Accessed 17 August 2005 at http://www.amnestyusa.org/stoptorture/index.do.
14. Herbert C. Kelman and V. Lee Hamilton, *Crimes of Obedience: Towards a Social Psychology of Authority and Responsibility* (New Haven: Yale University Press, 1989), p. 46.
15. Shue, "Torture," p. 143.

Study Questions

1. In judging the morality of an aim, are you obliged to consider the morality of the means necessary to achieve that aim?
2. Does torture require the training of torturers?
3. How would torturers be trained?
4. Would any moral person be willing to be a torturer?

C.

Capital Punishment

The Morality of Capital Punishment

Walter Berns

Walter Berns (1919–2015), who was Professor of Government at Georgetown University, argues that the death penalty is a fitting expression of our care for victims of horrendous crimes and our anger at those who have perpetrated brutal injustice. By punishing guilty persons appropriately, we hold them responsible for their actions and respect them as human beings. Furthermore, the expressed anger of the community serves as a reminder that the moral order is more important than any one of us.

"Many sorrows shall be to the wicked: but he that trusteth in the Lord, mercy shall compass him about. Be glad in the Lord, and rejoice, ye righteous: and shout for joy, all ye that are upright in heart!"[1] What is said in Psalms about the Lord must also be said about the law, and as belief in divine reward and punishment declines, it must be said more emphatically about the law: we must trust in the law, and

From Walter Berns, *For Capital Punishment: Crime and the Morality of the Death Penalty* (New York; Basic Books, 1979).

those who do will be rewarded. The law must respond to the deeds of the wicked, and the righteous must have confidence that the law will respond, and do so in an appropriate manner. It must punish the wicked because the righteous or law-abiding citizens make this demand of it. They are angered by the sight or presence of crime, and anger is not merely a selfish passion.

Roosevelt Grier, the former New York Giants defensive lineman, and the other friends of Robert Kennedy see him shot down before their eyes. They are shocked, then grief stricken, then angry; but California law cannot permit them to discharge that anger on its cause, Kennedy's assassin; they must be restrained, and the appropriate way of restraining them is to assure them that it, the law, will respond to this crime. The law must assuage that anger by satisfying it, but not . . . simply to prevent them from taking the law into their own hands.

Consider another example. A few years ago, a seven-year-old boy was brutally murdered on the lower East Side of Manhattan. The next day, in a nearby neighborhood, a twenty-eight-year-old woman was stabbed to death in the doorway to her apartment. When the police caught the man suspected of doing it, they had a hard time protecting him from an angry crowd of local residents. A week later a thirty-one-year-old man was stabbed to death by a burglar in his apartment (one of the increasing number of felony murders), this before the eyes of his wife. The *Times* account continues as follows:

> On the lower East Side, most residents seemed to agree with the police that the next time a murder suspect is identified, Tuesday's mob scene is very likely to be repeated. There is a widespread feeling that the police, the courts, the entire criminal justice system simply acts out a sort of charade, and that it is up to the community to demand that justice is done. "When the police find him, they'll just say he's a sick man and send him to a hospital for two years," said . . . a Delancey Street shopkeeper. "Then he'll be right back on the street. The only thing to do is to kill this man right away, quickly and quietly."[2]

The law must not allow that to happen, and not merely because the criminal may indeed be sick; it must provide the forms of justice in order to fulfill its educative function.

Robert Kennedy's friends were angry; that East Side mob was angry; and it is not only right that they be angry (for murder is a terrible crime), but punishment depends on it and punishment is a way of promoting justice. . . .

[A] just society is one where everyone gets what he deserves, and the wicked deserve to be punished—they deserve "many sorrows," as the Psalmist says—and the righteous deserve to be joyous. Punishment serves both these ends: it makes the criminal unhappy and it makes the law-abiding person happy. It rewards the law-abiding by satisfying the anger he feels at the sight of crime. It rewards, and by rewarding teaches, law-abidingness. . . .

[T]o the extent that men cease to be loving and hating men, they also become indifferent to what we know as crime. . . . Anger is the passion that recognizes and cares about justice. . . .

Anger is expressed or manifested on those occasions when someone has acted in a manner that is thought to be unjust, and one of its bases is the opinion that men are responsible, and should be held responsible, for what they do. Thus, anger is accompanied not only by the pain caused by him who is the object of anger, but by the pleasure arising from the expectation of exacting revenge on someone who is thought to deserve it.[3] We can become angry with an inanimate object (the door we run into and then kick in return) only by foolishly attributing responsibility to it, and we cannot do that for long, which is why we do not think of returning later to revenge ourselves on the door. For the same reason, we cannot be more than momentarily angry with an animate creature other than man; only a fool or worse would dream of taking revenge on a dog. And, finally, we tend to pity rather than to be angry with men who—because they are insane, for example—are not responsible for their acts. Anger, then, is a very human passion not only because only a human being can be angry, but also because it acknowledges the humanity of its objects: it holds them accountable for what they do. It is an expression of that element of the soul that is connected with the view that there is responsibility in the world; and in holding particular men responsible, it pays them that respect which is due them as men. Anger recognizes that only men have the capacity to be moral beings and, in so doing, acknowledges the dignity of human beings. Anger is somehow connected with justice, and it is this that modern penology has not understood; it tends, on the whole, to regard anger as merely a selfish passion.

It can, of course, be that; and if someone does not become angry with an insult or an injury suffered unjustly, we tend to think he does not think much of himself. But it need not be selfish, not in the sense of being provoked only by an injury suffered by oneself. There were many angry men in America when President Kennedy was killed; one of them—Jack Ruby—even took it upon himself to exact the punishment that, if indeed deserved, ought to have been exacted by the law. There were perhaps even angrier men when Martin Luther King was killed, for King, more than anyone else at the time, embodied a people's quest for justice; the anger—more, the "black rage"—expressed on that occasion was simply a manifestation of the great change that had occurred among black men in America, a change wrought in large part by King and his associates in the civil rights movement: the servility and fear of the past had been replaced by pride and anger, and the treatment that had formerly been accepted as a matter of course or as if it were deserved was now seen for what it was, unjust and unacceptable. King preached love but the movement he led depended on anger as well as love, and that anger was not despicable, being neither selfish nor unjustified. On the contrary, it was a reflection of what was called solidarity and may more accurately be called a profound caring for others, black for other blacks, white for blacks, and, in the world King was trying to build, American for other Americans. If men are not saddened when someone else suffers, or angry when someone else suffers unjustly, the implication is that they do not care for anyone other than themselves or that they lack some quality that befits a man. When we criticize them for this, we acknowledge that they ought to care for others. If men are not angry when a neighbor suffers at the hands of a criminal, the implication is that their moral faculties have been corrupted, that they are not good citizens.

Criminals are properly the objects of anger, and the perpetrators of terrible crimes—for example, Lee Harvey Oswald and James Earl Ray—are properly the objects of great anger. They have done more than inflict an injury on an isolated individual; they have violated the foundations of trust and friendship, the necessary elements of a moral community, the only community worth living in. A moral community, unlike a hive of bees or a hill of ants, is one whose members are expected freely to obey the laws and, unlike a tyranny, are trusted to obey the laws. The criminal has violated that trust, and in so doing has injured not merely his immediate victim but the community as such. He has called into question the very possibility of that community by suggesting that men cannot be trusted freely to respect the property, the person, and the dignity of those with whom they are associated. If, then, men are not angry when someone else is robbed, raped, or murdered, the implication is that there is no moral community because those men do not care for anyone other than themselves. Anger is an expression of that caring, and society needs men who care for each other, who share their pleasures and their pains, and do so for the sake of the others.[4] It is the passion that can cause us to act for reasons having nothing to do with selfish or mean calculation; indeed, when educated, it can become a generous passion, the passion that protects the community or country by demanding punishment for its enemies. It is the stuff from which heroes are made. . . .

Capital punishment . . . serves to remind us of the majesty of the moral order that is embodied in our law and of the terrible consequences of its breach. The law must not be understood to be merely statute that we enact or repeal at our will and obey or disobey at our convenience, especially not the criminal law. Wherever law is regarded as merely statutory, men will soon enough disobey it, and they will learn how to do so without any inconvenience to themselves. The criminal law must possess a dignity far beyond that possessed by mere statutory enactment or utilitarian and self-interested calculations; the most powerful means we have to give it that dignity is to authorize it to impose the ultimate penalty. The criminal law must be made awful, by which I mean, awe-inspiring, or commanding "profound respect or reverential fear." It must remind us of the moral order by which alone we can live as *human* beings, and in our day the only punishment that can do this is capital punishment.

Notes

1. Ps. 32:10–11.
2. *New York Times*, 26 August 1973, sec. 4, p. 6.
3. Aristotle, *Rhetoric* 1378b1–5.
4. Ibid., 1381a4–6.

Study Questions

1. Is anger ever an appropriate emotion?
2. Is capital punishment a harsher penalty than life in prison without possibility of parole?
3. What message, if any, does inflicting capital punishment send to the community?
4. Is capital punishment sometimes required in order to achieve justice?

The Death Penalty as a Symbolic Issue

Stephen Nathanson

Stephen Nathanson, Professor of Philosophy at Northeastern University, argues against the position of Walter Berns and maintains that the death penalty is inconsistent with respect for the value of human life and, therefore, ought to be renounced. Whereas Berns believes that capital punishment acknowledges the dignity of human beings, Nathanson views the death penalty as a violation of such dignity, for by taking the life of a criminal, we convey the idea that the criminal, although human, is no longer of any worth. Nathanson thus concludes that abolishing the death penalty would show respect for the dignity of human life, and also reinforce the idea that violence is only morally legitimate in self-defense.

[T]he question whether we ought to punish by death is a question with great symbolic meaning. For people on both sides, whether we impose or refrain from imposing the death penalty seems to say something about our values, about the kind of people we are, about the nature of our society. The death penalty debate is in part a field on which we champion some of our most central social and ethical ideals. We think that retaining or abolishing the death penalty conveys an important message, and we want it to be the right message. . . .

The Morality of Anger

The symbolic importance of the death penalty is strongly emphasized by Walter Berns in his defense of the death penalty. In discussing the

From Stephen Nathanson, *An Eye for an Eye? The Immorality of Punishing by Death* (Lanham, MD: Rowman & Littlefield, 2001).

symbolism of punishing by death, Berns stresses the moral significance of anger. He writes:

> If . . . men are not angry when someone else is robbed, raped, or murdered, the implication is that there is no moral community because those men do not care for anyone other than themselves. Anger is an expression of that caring, and society needs men who care for each other. . . . [Anger] is the passion that can cause us to act for reasons having nothing to do with selfish or mean calculation; indeed, when educated, it can become a generous passion, the passion that protects the community or country by demanding punishment for its enemies.

Berns wants to vindicate anger because he regards it as an expression of concern for others, and he fears that society is being undermined by a lack of other-directed concerns. . . . Anger shows that we are not simply self-interested individuals joined together in a marriage of convenience. Instead, we are a community of people who share common concerns and recognize common values.

Berns is certainly correct that anger may reveal important virtues in people, especially if a failure to be angry arises either from callousness or indifference. Nonetheless, whatever virtues are displayed by anger, everyone would agree that the actions that flow from anger must be controlled. The expression of anger needs to be limited by moral constraints. . . .

A person whose family has been killed in an automobile accident caused by the carelessness of another driver may be angry enough to kill the driver. The anger shows the depth of the person's caring for other human beings, but it does not provide a justification for killing the driver. Virtually everyone would agree that execution for carelessness is too severe a response. While some negative response to destructive and harmful actions is appropriate, it does not follow that anything done in the name of righteous anger is morally right.

I know of no one who denies that anger and outrage are the appropriate responses to the murder of innocent human beings. Nor do I know of anyone who argues that murderers should not be punished at all. The question is whether punishing by death is morally required. That we may feel angry enough to kill someone does not imply that doing so would be morally legitimate.

So, one can sympathize and agree with much of Berns's message, but that message does nothing to support the appropriateness of using death as a punishment. To favor severe but lesser punishments is in no way to express indifference or callousness toward the deaths of murder victims. The anger and grief that we feel about these deaths do not give us a license to kill. . . .

Affirming the Moral Order

Berns . . . believes that if people regard laws as conveniences for improving life, then they will not take them seriously enough. They will feel free to disobey the law when obedience is inconvenient. Part of the appeal of the death penalty for Berns is that it suggests that the law possesses a transcendent value. "Capital punishment," he writes,

> serves to remind us of the majesty of the moral order that is embodied in our law and of the terrible consequences of its breach. The law must not be understood to be merely statute that we enact or repeal at our will and obey or disobey at our convenience, especially not the criminal law. . . . The criminal law must be made awful, by which I mean, awe-inspiring. . . . It must remind us of the moral order by which alone we can live as *human* beings, and in our day the only punishment that can do this is capital punishment.

For Berns, permitting the state to punish by death is a means of affirming the moral order and its embodiment in the law.

Berns is correct about one point here. The law must support the moral order in the sense that it must provide appropriate punishments for particular crimes. Morality is subverted when terrible crimes go unpunished or are punished very leniently, since these responses would suggest that the crimes are not really serious. . . .

Berns wants to see the moral order reaffirmed, but he equates this order with the legal system. He does not want us to view the law "merely [as] statute that we enact or repeal at our will." Yet, that is precisely what the law is. While the moral order does not shift with the votes of a legislature, the legal order does. All too frequently, the legal order itself runs quite counter to what morality would require. Berns does the cause of morality no service by offering a blanket sanctification of the law.

Surely Berns is correct in his view that the nature and content of the law is a serious matter, but it is doubtful that we need to kill people in order to convey that message. Moreover, by revering the law when it does not deserve reverence, we help to perpetuate injustice. A critical and sober view of the law may do more to affirm the moral order than an attitude of awe or exaggerated respect. The critic who sees the flaws of the legal system and wants to limit its powers may be as committed to the moral order as Berns and may indeed have a better way to make the legal system conform to the moral order. . . .

The Symbolism of Abolishing the Death Penalty

What is the symbolic message that we would convey by deciding to renounce the death penalty and to abolish its use?

I think that there are two primary messages. The first is the most frequently emphasized and is usually expressed in terms of the sanctity of human life, although I think we could better express it in terms of respect for human dignity. One way we express our respect for the dignity of human beings is by abstaining from depriving them of their lives, even if they have done terrible deeds. In defense of human well-being, we may punish people for their crimes, but we ought not to deprive them of everything, which is what the death penalty does.

If we take the life of a criminal, we convey the idea that by his deeds he has made himself worthless and totally without human value. I do not believe that we are in a position to affirm that of anyone. We may hate such a person and feel the deepest anger against him, but when he no longer poses a threat to anyone, we ought not to take his life.

But, one might ask, hasn't the murderer forfeited whatever rights he might have had to our respect? Hasn't he, by his deeds, given up any rights that he had to decent treatment? Aren't we morally free to kill him if we wish?

These questions express important doubts about the obligation to accord any respect to those who have acted so deplorably, but I do not think that they prove that any such forfeiture has occurred. Certainly, when people murder or commit other crimes, they do forfeit some of the rights that are possessed by the law-abiding. They lose a certain right to be left alone. It becomes permissible to bring them to trial and, if they are convicted, to impose an appropriate—even a dreadful—punishment on them.

Nonetheless, they do not forfeit all their rights. It does not follow from the vileness of their actions that we can do anything whatsoever to them. This is part of the moral meaning of the constitutional ban on cruel and unusual punishments. No matter how terrible a person's deeds, we may not punish him in a cruel and unusual way. We may not torture him, for example. His right not to be tortured has not been forfeited. Why do these limits hold? Because this person remains a human being, and we think that there is something in him that we must continue to respect in spite of his terrible acts.

One way of seeing why those who murder still deserve some consideration and respect is by reflecting again on the idea of what it is to *deserve* something. In most contexts, we think that what people deserve depends on what they have done, intended, or tried to do. It depends on features that are qualities of individuals. The best person for the job deserves to be hired. The person who worked especially hard deserves our gratitude. We can call the concept that applies in these cases *personal* desert.

There is another kind of desert, however, that belongs to people by virtue of their humanity itself and does not depend on their individual efforts or achievements. I will call this impersonal kind of desert *human* desert. We appeal to this concept when we think that everyone deserves a certain level of treatment no matter what their individual qualities are. When the signers of the Declaration of Independence affirmed that people had inalienable rights to "life, liberty, and the pursuit of happiness," they were appealing to such an idea. These rights do not have to be earned by people. They are possessed "naturally," and everyone is bound to respect them.

According to the view that I am defending, people do not lose all of their rights when they commit terrible crimes. They still deserve some level of decent treatment simply because they remain living, functioning human beings. This level of moral desert need not be earned, and it cannot be forfeited. This view may sound controversial, but in fact everyone who believes that cruel and unusual punishment should be forbidden implicitly agrees with it. That is, they agree that even after someone has committed a terrible crime, we do not have the right to do anything whatsoever to him.

What I am suggesting is that by renouncing the use of death as a punishment, we express and reaffirm our belief in the inalienable, unforfeitable core of human dignity.

Why is this a worthwhile message to convey? It is worth conveying because this belief is both important and precarious. Throughout history, people have found innumerable reasons to degrade the humanity of one another. They have found qualities in others that they hated or feared, and even when they were not threatened by these people, they have sought to harm them, deprive them of their liberty, or take their lives from them. They have often felt that they had good reasons to do these things, and they have invoked divine commands, racial purity, and state security to support their deeds.

These actions and attitudes are not relics of the past. They remain an awful feature of the contemporary world. By renouncing the death penalty, we show our determination to accord at least minimal respect even to those whom we believe to be personally vile or morally vicious. This is, perhaps, why we speak of the sanctity of human life rather than its value or worth. That which is sacred remains, in some sense, untouchable, and its value is not dependent on its worth or usefulness to us. Kant expressed this ideal of respect in the famous second version of the Categorical Imperative; "So act as to treat humanity, whether in thine own person or in that of any other, in every case as an end withal, never as a means only."

The Problem of Moral Monsters

One may feel attracted to this ideal and yet resist it by calling to mind people like Hitler or Stalin or their various henchmen, who were responsible for the deaths of millions of innocent people. Aren't such people beyond the pale? Haven't they forfeited *all* claims to even minimal decency so that it would be appropriate to execute them as punishment for their deeds? Doesn't the existence of such people show that the death penalty is legitimate?

These troubling questions raise important issues, and death penalty opponents might meet them in diverse ways. For myself, I am willing to say that even in these cases, so long as these people no longer pose an active threat to others, it would be best not to execute them. Moreover, though their deeds were terrible beyond words, I think it best that we not renounce our respect for their humanity. . . .

Not all opponents of the death penalty would agree with the views I have expressed about figures like Hitler and Stalin, and . . . it would be possible for an opponent of the death penalty . . . to concede that Hitler and Stalin might have gone so far that they no longer merited any consideration as human beings. One could even acknowledge that they should be executed.

All of this is consistent with opposition to the death penalty. Why? Because these cases are extraordinary and atypical. The death penalty controversy is concerned with the use of death as a punishment for murders that occur within society. It is advocated as a part of our ordinary criminal justice system. One could favor executing Hitler because of his extraordinary acts and still think that executions should play no regular role in the achievement of domestic order within a society.

From the perspective of this reply, the whole issue of moral monsters is a distraction that confuses the issue. If death penalty supporters were proposing executions only for extraordinary political criminals like Hitler and Stalin, these examples would be to the point. Since they are proposing executions for people whose deeds do not begin to approach the evil of these famous persons, death penalty supporters must make a different sort of case for their view. The specter of Hitler and Stalin does not help their case at all.

The Morality of Restraint

I have argued that the first symbolic meaning conveyed by a renunciation of the death penalty is that human dignity must be respected in every person. To execute a person for murder is to treat that person as if he were nothing but a murderer and to deprive him of everything that he has. Therefore, if we want to convey the appropriate message about human dignity, we will renounce the death penalty. . . .

[T]he second important message conveyed by the renunciation of punishing by death . . . [is that when] we restrain ourselves and do not take the lives of those who kill, we communicate the importance of minimizing killing and other acts of violence. We reinforce the idea that violence is morally legitimate only as a defensive measure and should be curbed whenever possible.

We can see the point of this message by contrasting it with Walter Berns's emphasis on the morality of anger. Without discounting all that Berns says, it seems to me that the death penalty supports the morality of anger in an unacceptable way. It suggests that if someone's acts have provoked you to be very angry, then you may legitimately act violently against that person. The morality of restraint, on the other hand, requires that one control one's anger and allows one to attack another person only defensively. Anger by itself provides no justification for violence.

When the state has a murderer in its power and could execute him but does not, this conveys the idea that even though this person has done wrong and even though we may be angry, outraged, and indignant with him, we will nonetheless control ourselves in a way that he did not. We will not kill him, even though we could do so and even though we are angry and indignant. We will exercise restraint, sanctioning killing only when it serves a protective function.

Why should we do this? Partly out of a respect for human dignity. But also because we want the state to set an example of proper behavior. We do not want to encourage people to resort to violence to settle conflicts when there are other ways available. We want to avoid the cycle of violence that can come from retaliation and counter-retaliation. Violence is a contagion that arouses hatred and anger, and if unchecked, it simply leads to still more violence. The state can convey the message that the contagion must be stopped, and the most effective principle for stopping it is the idea that only defensive violence is justifiable. Since the death penalty is not an instance of defensive violence, it ought to be renounced.

We show our respect for life best by restraining ourselves and allowing murderers to live, rather than by following a policy of a life for a life. Respect for life and restraint of violence are aspects of the same ideal. The renunciation of the death penalty would symbolize our support of that ideal.

Study Questions

1. What does Nathanson hope to show with the example of the person whose family has been killed in an automobile accident by a careless driver?
2. Do moral monsters deserve the death penalty?
3. Do we have compelling reasons to treat moral monsters differently from others who commit murder?
4. Do we show respect for life by not taking the lives of those who commit murder?

PART V

Justice

A.

Distributive Justice

A Theory of Justice

John Rawls

John Rawls (1921–2002) was Professor of Philosophy at Harvard University. He proposes that a just social arrangement is one that would be chosen by the members of society if they did not know either their individual places in that society or their own personal characteristics, such as race, gender, or class. Rawls claims that in "the original position" in which all are behind "a veil of ignorance," the parties would choose two fundamental principles: first, equality of rights and liberties for all; and second, the arrangement of social and economic inequalities so that both are (a) to the greatest benefit of the least advantaged, "the difference principle," and (b) attached to positions and offices open to all.

The Main Idea of the Theory of Justice

. . . [T]he principles of justice . . . are the principles that free and rational persons concerned to further their own interests would accept in an initial position of equality. . . .

From John Rawls, *A Theory of Justice* (Cambridge, MA: The Belknap Press of Harvard University Press, 1971, 1999).

[T]he original position of equality corresponds to the state of nature in the traditional theory of the social contract. This original position is not, of course, thought of as an actual historical state of affairs, much less as a primitive condition of culture. It is understood as a purely hypothetical situation. . . . Among the essential features of this situation is that no one knows his place in society, his class position or social status, nor does any one know his fortune in the distribution of natural assets and abilities, his intelligence, strength, and the like. I shall even assume that the parties do not know their conceptions of the good or their special psychological propensities. The principles of justice are chosen behind a veil of ignorance. This ensures that no one is advantaged or disadvantaged in the choice of principles by the outcome of natural chance or the contingency of social circumstances. Since all are similarly situated and no one is able to design principles to favor his particular condition, the principles of justice are the result of a fair agreement or bargain. For given the circumstances of the original position, the symmetry of everyone's relations to each other, this initial situation is fair between individuals as moral persons, that is, as rational beings with their own ends and capable, I shall assume, of a sense of justice. The original position is, one might say, the appropriate initial status quo, and thus the fundamental agreements reached in it are fair. This explains the propriety of the name "justice as fairness": it conveys the idea that the principles of justice are agreed to in an initial situation that is fair. . . .

I shall maintain . . . that the persons in the initial situation would choose two . . . principles: the first requires equality in the assignment of basic rights and duties, while the second holds that social and economic inequalities, for example inequalities of wealth and authority, are just only if they result in compensating benefits for everyone, and in particular for the least advantaged members of society. These principles rule out justifying institutions on the grounds that the hardships of some are offset by a greater good in the aggregate. It may be expedient but it is not just that some should have less in order that others may prosper. But there is no injustice in the greater benefits earned by a few provided that the situation of persons not so fortunate is thereby improved. The intuitive idea is that since everyone's well-being depends upon a scheme of cooperation without which no one could have a satisfactory life, the division of advantages should be such as to draw forth the willing cooperation of everyone taking part in it, including those less well situated. The two principles mentioned seem to be a fair basis on which those better endowed, or more fortunate in their social position, neither of which we can be said to deserve, could expect the willing cooperation of others when some workable scheme is a necessary condition of the welfare of all. Once we decide to look for a conception of justice that prevents the use of the accidents of natural endowment and the contingencies of social circumstance as counters in a quest of political and economic advantage, we are led to these principles. They express the result of leaving aside those aspects of the social world that seem arbitrary from a moral point of view. . . .

The Original Position and Justification

. . . One should not be misled . . . by the somewhat unusual conditions which characterize the original position. The idea here is simply to make vivid to ourselves the restrictions that it seems reasonable to impose on arguments for principles of justice, and therefore on these principles themselves. Thus it seems reasonable and generally acceptable that no one should be advantaged or disadvantaged by natural fortune or social circumstances in the choice of principles. It also seems widely agreed that it should be impossible to tailor principles to the circumstances of one's own case. We should insure further that particular inclinations and aspirations, and persons' conceptions of their good, do not affect the principles adopted. The aim is to rule out those principles that it would be rational to propose for acceptance, however little the chance of success, only if one knew certain things that are irrelevant from the standpoint of justice. For example, if a man knew that he was wealthy, he might find it rational to advance the principle that various taxes for welfare measures be counted unjust; if he knew that he was poor, he would most likely propose the contrary principle. To represent the desired restrictions one imagines a situation in which everyone is deprived of this sort of information. One excludes the knowledge of those contingencies which sets men at odds and allows them to be guided by their prejudices. In this manner the veil of ignorance is arrived at in a natural way. This concept should cause no difficulty if we keep in mind the constraints on arguments that it is meant to express. At any time we can enter the original position, so to speak, simply by following a certain procedure, namely, by arguing for principles of justice in accordance with these restrictions.

It seems reasonable to suppose that the parties in the original position are equal. That is, all have the same rights in the procedure for choosing principles; each can make proposals, submit reasons for their acceptance, and so on. Obviously the purpose of these conditions is to represent equality between human beings as moral persons, as creatures having a conception of their good and capable of a sense of justice. The basis of equality is taken to be similarity in these two respects. Systems of ends are not ranked in value; and each man is presumed to have the requisite ability to understand and to act upon whatever principles are adopted. Together with the veil of ignorance, these conditions define the principles of justice as those which rational persons concerned to advance their interests would consent to as equals when none are known to be advantaged or disadvantaged by social and natural contingencies. . . .

Two Principles of Justice

I shall now state in a provisional form the two principles of justice that I believe would be chosen in the original position. . . .

The first statement of the two principles reads as follows.

First: each person is to have an equal right to the most extensive scheme of equal basic liberties compatible with a similar scheme of liberties for others.

Second: social and economic inequalities are to be arranged so that they are both (a) reasonably expected to be to everyone's advantage, and (b) attached to positions and offices open to all. . . .

These principles primarily apply . . . to the basic structure of society and govern the assignment of rights and duties and regulate the distribution of social and economic advantages. . . . [I]t is essential to observe that the basic liberties are given by a list of such liberties. Important among these are political liberty (the right to vote and to hold public office) and freedom of speech and assembly; liberty of conscience and freedom of thought; freedom of the person, which includes freedom from psychological oppression and physical assault and dismemberment (integrity of the person); the right to hold personal property and freedom from arbitrary arrest and seizure as defined by the concept of the rule of law. These liberties are to be equal by the first principle.

The second principle applies . . . to the distribution of income and wealth and to the design of organizations that make use of differences in authority and responsibility. While the distributions of wealth and income need not be equal, it must be to everyone's advantage, and at the same time, positions of authority and responsibility must be accessible to all. One applies the second principle by holding positions open, and then, subject to this constraint, arranges social and economic inequalities so that everyone benefits.

These principles are to be arranged in a serial order with the first principle prior to the second. This ordering means that infringements of the basic equal liberties protected by the first principle cannot be justified, or compensated for, by greater social and economic advantages. . . .

[I]n regard to the second principle, the distribution of wealth and income, and positions of authority and responsibility, are to be consistent with both the basic liberties and equality of opportunity. . . .

[T]hese principles are a special case of a more general conception of justice that can be expressed as follows.

> All social values—liberty and opportunity, income and wealth, and the social bases of self-respect—are to be distributed equally unless an unequal distribution of any, or all, of these values is to everyone's advantage.

Injustice, then, is simply inequalities that are not to the benefit of all. Of course, this conception is extremely vague and requires interpretation.

As a first step, suppose that the basic structure of society distributes certain primary goods, that is, things that every rational man is presumed to want. These goods normally have a use whatever a person's rational plan of life. For simplicity, assume that the chief primary goods at the disposition of society are rights and liberties, powers and opportunities, income and wealth. . . . These are the social primary goods. Other primary goods such as health and vigor, intelligence and imagination, are natural goods; although their possession is influenced by the basic structure, they are not so directly under its control. Imagine, then, a hypothetical initial arrangement in which all the social primary goods are equally distributed; everyone has similar rights and duties, and income and wealth are evenly shared. This state of affairs provides a benchmark for judging improvements. If certain inequalities of wealth and organizational powers would make everyone better off than in this hypothetical starting situation, then they accord with the general conception.

Now it is possible, at least theoretically, that by giving up some of their fundamental liberties men are sufficiently compensated by the resulting social and economic gains. The general conception of justice imposes no restrictions on what sort of inequalities are permissible; it only requires that everyone's position be improved. We need not suppose anything so drastic as consenting to a condition of slavery. Imagine instead that men forego certain political rights when the economic returns are significant and their capacity to influence the course of policy by the exercise of these rights would be marginal in any case. It is this kind of exchange which the two principles as stated rule out; being arranged in serial order they do not permit exchanges between basic liberties and economic and social gains. The serial ordering of principles expresses an underlying preference among primary social goods. When this preference is rational so likewise is the choice of these principles in this order. . . .

The Veil of Ignorance

. . . The notion of the veil of ignorance raises several difficulties. Some may object that the exclusion of nearly all particular information makes it difficult to grasp what is meant by the original position. Thus it may be helpful to observe that one or more persons can at any time enter this position, or perhaps better, simulate the deliberations of this hypothetical situation, simply by reasoning in accordance with the appropriate restrictions. . . .

It may be protested that the condition of the veil of ignorance is irrational. Surely, some may object, principles should be chosen in light of all the knowledge available. There are various replies to this contention. . . . To begin with, it is clear that since the differences among the parties are unknown to them, and everyone is equally rational and similarly situated, each is convinced by the same arguments. Therefore, we can view the agreement in the original position from the standpoint of one person selected at random. If anyone after due reflection prefers a conception of justice to another, then they all do, and a unanimous agreement can be reached. We can, to make the circumstances more vivid, imagine that the parties are required to communicate with each other through a referee as intermediary, and that he is to announce which alternatives have been suggested and the reasons offered in their support. He forbids the attempt to form coalitions, and he informs the parties when they have come to an understanding. But such a referee is actually superfluous, assuming that the deliberations of the parties must be similar.

Thus there follows the very important consequence that the parties have no basis for bargaining in the usual sense. No one knows his situation in society nor his natural assets, and therefore no one is in a position to tailor principles to his advantage. We might imagine that one of the contractees threatens to hold out unless the others agree to principles favorable to him. But how does he know which principles are especially in his interests? The same holds for the formation of coalitions: if a group were to decide to band together to the disadvantage of the others, they would not know how to favor themselves in the choice of principles. Even if they could get everyone to agree to their proposal, they would have no assurance that it was to their advantage, since they cannot identify themselves either by name or description. . . .

The restrictions on particular information in the original position are, then, of fundamental importance. Without them we would not be able to work out any definite theory of justice at all. We would have to be content with a vague formula stating that justice is what would be agreed to without being able to say much, if anything, about the substance of the agreement itself. . . . The veil of ignorance makes possible a unanimous choice of a particular conception of justice. Without these limitations on knowledge the bargaining problem of the original position would be hopelessly complicated.

Study Questions

1. What does Rawls mean by "the original position"?
2. According to Rawls, what two principles would be chosen in the original position?
3. Are Rawls's two principles shown to be just by being chosen in the original position, or are they chosen in the original position because they are just?
4. If you were in the original position, what principles would you choose?

The Entitlement Theory

Robert Nozick

Robert Nozick (1938–2002) was Professor of Philosophy at Harvard University. He argues that if we treat all goods as though they were unowned and distribute them in accord with some preferred scheme, we ignore the source of these goods, disregarding the labor and ingenuity of the people who created them. According to Nozick, past history plays a crucial role in determining entitlements. If you hold property justly, either by justly acquiring it when it was unowned or transferring it justly from someone entitled to it, then you have a right to your holding. In short, whatever arises from a just situation by just steps is itself just. Nozick concludes that any further redistribution is an infringement on liberty.

The minimal state is the most extensive state that can be justified. Any state more extensive violates people's rights. Yet many persons have put forth reasons purporting to justify a more extensive state. . . . I shall focus upon those generally acknowledged to be most weighty and influential, to see precisely wherein they fail. . . .

The term "distributive justice" is not a neutral one. Hearing the term "distribution," most people presume that some thing or mechanism uses some principle or criterion to give out a supply of things. Into this process of distributing shares some error may have crept. So it is an open question, at least, whether *re*distribution should take place; whether we should do again what has already been done once, though poorly. However, we are not in the position of children who have been given portions of pie by someone who now makes last minute adjustments to rectify careless cutting. There is no *central* distribution, no person or group entitled to control all the resources,

From Robert Nozick, *Anarchy, State, and Utopia* (New York: Basic Books, 1977).

jointly deciding how they are to be doled out. What each person gets, he gets from others who give to him in exchange for something, or as a gift. In a free society, diverse persons control different resources, and new holdings arise out of the voluntary exchanges and actions of persons. There is no more a distributing or distribution of shares than there is a distributing of mates in a society in which persons choose whom they shall marry. The total result is the product of many individual decisions which the different individuals involved are entitled to make. . . . We shall speak of people's holdings; a principle of justice in holdings describes (part of) what justice tells us (requires) about holdings. . . .

The Entitlement Theory

The subject of justice in holdings consists of three major topics. The first is the *original acquisition of holdings,* the appropriation of unheld things. This includes the issues of how unheld things may come to be held, the process, or processes, by which unheld things may come to be held, the things that may come to be held by these processes, the extent of what comes to be held by a particular process, and so on. We shall refer to the complicated truth about this topic, which we shall not formulate here, as the principle of justice in acquisition. The second topic concerns the *transfer of holdings* from one person to another. By what processes may a person transfer holdings to another? How may a person acquire a holding from another who holds it? Under this topic come general descriptions of voluntary exchange, and gift and (on the other hand) fraud, as well as reference to particular conventional details fixed upon in a given society. The complicated truth about this subject (with placeholders for conventional details) we shall call the principle of justice in transfer. (And we shall suppose it also includes principles governing how a person may divest himself of a holding, passing it into an unheld state.)

If the world were wholly just, the following inductive definition would exhaustively cover the subject of justice in holdings.

1. A person who acquires a holding in accordance with the principle of justice in acquisition is entitled to that holding.
2. A person who acquires a holding in accordance with the principle of justice in transfer, from someone else entitled to the holding, is entitled to the holding.
3. No one is entitled to a holding except by (repeated) applications of 1 and 2.

The complete principle of distributive justice would say simply that a distribution is just if everyone is entitled to the holdings they possess under the distribution.

A distribution is just if it arises from another just distribution by legitimate means. The legitimate means of moving from one distribution to another are specified by the principle of justice in transfer. The legitimate first "moves" are specified by the principle of justice in acquisition.[1] Whatever arises from a just situation by just steps is itself just. The means of change specified by the principle of justice in transfer preserve justice. As correct rules of inference are truth-preserving, and any conclusion deduced via repeated application of such rules from only true premisses is itself true, so the means of transition from one situation to another specified by the principle of justice in transfer are justice-preserving, and any situation actually arising from repeated transitions in accordance with the principle from a just situation is itself just. The parallel between justice-preserving transformations and truth-preserving transformations illuminates where it fails as well as where it holds. That a conclusion could have been deduced by truth-preserving means from premisses that are true suffices to show its truth. That from a just situation a situation *could* have arisen via justice-preserving means does *not* suffice to show its justice. The fact that a thief's victims voluntarily *could* have presented him with gifts does not entitle the thief to his ill-gotten gains. Justice in holdings is historical; it depends upon what actually has happened. . . .

Not all actual situations are generated in accordance with the two principles of justice in holdings: the principle of justice in acquisition and the principle of justice in transfer. Some people steal from others, or defraud them, or enslave them, seizing their product and preventing them from living as they choose, or forcibly exclude others from competing in exchanges. None of these are permissible modes of transition from one situation to another. And some persons acquire holdings by means not sanctioned by the principle of justice in acquisition. The existence of past injustice (previous violations of the first two principles of justice in holdings) raises the third major topic under justice in holdings: the rectification of injustice in holdings. If past injustice has shaped present holdings in various ways, some identifiable and some not, what now, if anything, ought to be done to rectify these injustices? What obligations do the performers of injustice have toward those whose position is worse than it would have been had the injustice not been done? Or, than it would have been had compensation been paid promptly? How, if at all, do things change if the beneficiaries and those made worse off are not the direct parties in the act of injustice, but, for example, their descendants? Is an injustice done to someone whose holding was itself based upon an unrectified injustice? How far back must one go in wiping clean the historical slate of injustices? What may victims of injustice permissibly do in order to rectify the injustices being done to them, including the many injustices done by persons acting through their government? I do not know of a thorough or theoretically sophisticated treatment of such issues. Idealizing greatly, let us suppose theoretical investigation will produce a principle of rectification. This principle uses historical information about previous situations and injustices done in them (as defined by the first two principles of justice and rights against interference), and information about the actual course of events that flowed from these injustices, until the present, and it yields a description (or descriptions) of holdings in the society. The principle of rectification presumably will make use of its best estimate of subjunctive information about what would have occurred . . . if the injustice had not taken place. If the actual description of holdings turns out not to be one of the descriptions yielded by the principle, then one of the descriptions yielded must be realized.[2]

The general outlines of the theory of justice in holdings are that the holdings of a person are just if he is entitled to them by the principles of justice in acquisition and transfer, or by the principle of rectification of injustice (as specified by the first two principles). If each person's holdings are just, then the total set (distribution) of holdings is just. To turn these general outlines into a specific theory we would have to specify the details of each of the three principles of justice in holdings: the principle of acquisition of holdings, the principle of transfer of holdings, and the principle of rectification of violations of the first two principles. I shall not attempt that task here. . . .

Historical Principles and End-Result Principles

The general outlines of the entitlement theory illuminate the nature and defects of other conceptions of distributive justice. The entitlement theory of justice in distribution is *historical;* whether a distribution is just depends upon how it came about. In contrast, *current time-slice principles* of justice hold that the justice of a distribution is determined by how things are distributed (who has what) as judged by some *structural* principle(s) of just distribution. A utilitarian who judges between any two distributions by seeing which has the greater sum of utility and, if the sums tie, applies some fixed equality criterion to choose the more equal distribution, would hold a current time-slice principle of justice. . . . According to a current time-slice principle, all that needs to be looked at, in judging the justice of a distribution, is who ends up with what; in comparing any two distributions one need look only at the matrix presenting the distributions. No further information need be fed into a principle of justice. It is a consequence of such principles of justice that any two structurally identical distributions are equally just. . . .

Most persons do not accept current time-slice principles as constituting the whole story about distributive shares. They think it relevant in assessing the justice of a situation to consider not only the distribution it embodies, but also how that distribution came about. If some persons are in prison for murder or war crimes, we do not say that to assess the justice of the distribution in the society we must look only at what this person has, and that person has, and that person has, . . . at the current time. We think it relevant to ask whether someone did something so that he *deserved* to be punished, deserved to have a lower share. Most will agree to the relevance of further information with regard to punishments and penalties. . . .

In contrast to end-result principles of justice, *historical principles* of justice hold that past circumstances or actions of people can create differential entitlements or differential deserts to things. An injustice can be worked by moving from one distribution to another structurally identical one, for the second, in profile the same, may violate people's entitlements or deserts; it may not fit the actual history.

Patterning

The entitlement principles of justice in holdings that we have sketched are historical principles of justice. To better understand their precise character, we shall distinguish them from another subclass of the historical principles. Consider, as an example, the principle of distribution according to moral merit. This principle requires that total distributive shares vary directly with moral merit; no person should have a greater share than anyone whose moral merit is greater. . . . Let us call a principle of distribution *patterned* if it specifies that a distribution is to vary along with some natural dimension, weighted sum of natural dimensions, or lexicographic ordering of natural dimensions. And let us say a distribution is patterned if it accords with some patterned principle. . . . The principle of distribution in accordance with moral merit is a patterned historical principle, which specifies a patterned distribution. "Distribute according to I.Q." is a patterned principle that looks to information not contained in distributional matrices. It is not historical, however, in that it does not look to any past actions creating differential entitlements to evaluate a distribution; it requires only distributional matrices whose columns are labeled by I.Q. scores. The distribution in a society, however, may be composed of such simple patterned distributions, without itself being simply patterned. Different sectors may operate different patterns, or some combination of patterns may operate in different proportions across a society. A distribution composed in this manner, from a small number of patterned distributions, we also shall term "patterned." And we extend the use of "pattern" to include the overall designs put forth by combinations of end-state principles.

Almost every suggested principle of distributive justice is patterned: to each according to his moral merit, or needs, or marginal product, or how hard he tries, or the weighted sum of the foregoing, and so on. The principle of entitlement we have sketched is *not* patterned. There is no one natural dimension or weighted sum or combination of a small number of natural dimensions that yields the distributions generated in accordance with the principle of entitlement. The set of holdings that results when some persons receive their marginal products, others win at gambling, others receive a share of their mate's income, others receive gifts from foundations, others receive interest on loans, others receive gifts from admirers, others receive returns on investment, others make for themselves much of what they have, others find things, and so on, will not be patterned. Heavy strands of patterns will run through it; significant portions of the variance in holdings will be accounted for by pattern-variables. If most people most of the time choose to transfer some of their entitlements to others only in exchange for something from them, then a large part of what many people hold will vary with what they held that others wanted. . . .

How Liberty Upsets Patterns

. . . [S]uppose a distribution favored by one of these nonentitlement conceptions is realized. Let us suppose it is your favorite one and let us call this distribution D1; perhaps everyone has an equal share, perhaps shares vary in accordance with some dimension you treasure. Now suppose that Wilt Chamberlain is greatly in demand by basketball teams, being a great gate attraction. (Also suppose contracts run only for a year, with players being free agents.) He signs the following sort of contract with a team: In each home game, twenty-five cents from the price of each ticket of admission goes to him. (We ignore the question of whether he is "gouging" the owners, letting them look out for themselves.) The season starts, and people cheerfully attend his team's games; they buy their tickets, each time dropping a separate twenty-five cents of their admission price into a special box with Chamberlain's name on it. They are excited about seeing him play; it is worth the total admission price to them. Let us suppose that in one season one million persons attend his home games, and Wilt Chamberlain winds up with $250,000, a much larger sum than the average income and larger even than anyone else has. Is he entitled to this income? Is this new distribution D_2, unjust? If so, why? There is *no* question about whether each of the people was entitled to the control over the resources they held in D_1; because that was the distribution (your favorite) that (for the purposes of argument) we assumed was acceptable. Each of these persons *chose* to give twenty-five cents of their money to Chamberlain. They could have spent it on going to the movies, or on candy bars. . . . But they all, at least one million of them, converged on giving it to Wilt Chamberlain in exchange for watching him play basketball. If D_1 was a just distribution, and people voluntarily moved from it to D_2, transferring parts of their shares they were given under D_1 (what was it for if not to do something with?), isn't D_2 also just? If the people were entitled to dispose of the resources to which they were entitled (under D_1), didn't this include their being entitled to give it to, or exchange it with, Wilt Chamberlain? Can anyone else complain on grounds of justice? Each other person already has his legitimate share under D_1. Under D_1, there is nothing that anyone has that anyone else has a claim of justice against. After someone transfers something to Wilt Chamberlain, third parties *still* have their legitimate shares; *their* shares are not changed. By what process could such a transfer among two persons give rise to a legitimate claim of distributive justice on a portion of what was transferred, by a third party who had no claim of justice on any holding of the others *before* the transfer? To cut off objections irrelevant here, we might imagine the exchanges occurring in a socialist society, after hours. After playing whatever basketball he does in his daily work, or doing whatever other daily work he does, Wilt Chamberlain decides to put in *overtime* to earn additional money. (First his work quota is set; he works time over that.) Or imagine it is a skilled juggler people like to see, who puts on shows after hours.

Why might someone work overtime in a society in which it is assumed their needs are satisfied? Perhaps because they care about things other than needs. I like to write in books that I read, and to have easy access to books for browsing at odd hours. It would be very pleasant and convenient to have the resources of Widener Library in my back yard. No society, I assume, will provide such resources close to each person who would like them as part of his regular allotment (under D_1). Thus, persons either must do without some extra things that they want, or be allowed to do something extra to get some of these things. On what basis could the inequalities that would eventuate be forbidden? Notice also that small factories would spring up in a socialist society, unless forbidden. I melt down some of my personal possessions (under D_1) and build a machine out of the material. I offer you, and others, a philosophy lecture once a week in exchange for your cranking the handle on my machine, whose products I exchange for yet other things, and so on. . . . Each person might participate to gain things over and above their allotment under D_1. Some persons even might want to leave their job in socialist industry and work full time in this private sector. . . . Here I wish merely to note how private property even in means of production would occur in a socialist society that did not forbid people to use as they wished some of the resources they are given under the socialist distribution D_1. The socialist society would have to forbid capitalist acts between consenting adults.

The general point illustrated by the Wilt Chamberlain example and the example of the entrepreneur in a socialist society is that no end-state principle or distributional patterned principle of justice can be continuously realized without continuous interference with people's lives. Any favored pattern would be transformed into one unfavored by the principle, by people choosing to act in various ways; for example, by people exchanging goods and services with other people, or giving things to other people, things the transferrers are entitled to under the favored distributional pattern. To maintain a pattern one must either continually interfere to stop people from transferring resources as they wish to, or continually (or periodically) interfere to take from some persons resources that others for some reason chose to transfer to them. . . .

Redistribution and Property Rights

Apparently, patterned principles allow people to choose to expend upon themselves, but not upon others, those resources they are entitled to (or rather, receive) under some favored distributional pattern

D_1. For if each of several persons chooses to expend some of his D_1 resources upon one other person, then that other person will receive more than his D_1 share, disturbing the favored distributional pattern. Maintaining a distributional pattern is individualism with a vengeance! Patterned distributional principles do not give people what entitlement principles do, only better distributed. For they do not give the right to choose what to do with what one has; they do not give the right to choose to pursue an end involving (intrinsically, or as a means) the enhancement of another's position. To such views, families are disturbing; for within a family occur transfers that upset the favored distributional pattern. Either families themselves become units to which distribution takes place, the column occupiers (on what rationale?), or loving behavior is forbidden. . . .

Proponents of patterned principles of distributive justice focus upon criteria for determining who is to receive holdings; they consider the reasons for which someone should have something, and also the total picture of holdings. Whether or not it is better to give than to receive, proponents of patterned principles ignore giving altogether. In considering the distribution of goods, income, and so forth, their theories are theories of recipient justice; they completely ignore any right a person might have to give something to someone. Even in exchanges where each party is simultaneously giver and recipient, patterned principles of justice focus only upon the recipient role and its supposed rights. Thus discussions tend to focus on whether people (should) have a right to inherit, rather than on whether people (should) have a right to bequeath or on whether persons who have a right to hold also have a right to choose that others hold in their place. I lack a good explanation of why the usual theories of distributive justice are so recipient oriented; ignoring givers and transferrers and their rights is of a piece with ignoring producers and their entitlements. But why is it *all* ignored?

Patterned principles of distributive justice necessitate *re*distributive activities. The likelihood is small that any actual freely-arrived-at set of holdings fits a given pattern; and the likelihood is nil that it will continue to fit the pattern as people exchange and give. From the point of view of an entitlement theory, redistribution is a serious matter indeed, involving, as it does, the violation of people's rights. (An exception is those takings that fall under the principle of the rectification of injustices.) From other points of view, also, it is serious.

Taxation of earnings from labor is on a par with forced labor. Some persons find this claim obviously true: taking the earnings of *n* hours labor is like taking *n* hours from the person; it is like forcing the person to work *n* hours for another's purpose. Others find the claim absurd. But even these, *if* they object to forced labor, would oppose forcing unemployed hippies to work for the benefit of the needy. And they would also object to forcing each person to work five extra hours each week for the benefit of the needy. But a system that takes five hours' wages in taxes does not seem to them like one that forces someone to work five hours, since it offers the person forced a wider range of choice in activities than does taxation in kind with the particular labor specified. (But we can imagine a gradation of systems of forced labor, from one that specifies a particular activity, to one that gives a choice among two activities, to . . . ; and so on up.) Furthermore, people envisage a system with something like a proportional tax on everything above the amount necessary for basic needs. Some think this does not force someone to work extra hours, since there is no fixed number of extra hours he is forced to work, and since he can avoid the tax entirely by earning only enough to cover his basic needs. This is a very uncharacteristic view of forcing for those who *also* think people are forced to do something *whenever* the alternatives they face are considerably worse. However, *neither* view is correct. The fact that others intentionally intervene, in violation of a side constraint against aggression, to threaten force to limit the alternatives, in this case to paying taxes or (presumably the worse alternative) bare subsistence, makes the taxation system one of forced labor and distinguishes it from other cases of limited choices which are not forcings.

Notes

1. Applications of the principle of justice in acquisition may also occur as part of the move from one distribution to another. You may find an unheld thing now and appropriate it. Acquisitions also are to be understood as included when, to simplify, I speak only of transitions by transfers.
2. If the principle of rectification of violations of the first two principles yields more than one description of holdings, then some choice must be made as to which of these is to be realized. Perhaps the sort of considerations about distributive justice and equality that I argue against play a legitimate role in *this* subsidiary choice. Similarly, there may be room for such considerations in deciding which otherwise arbitrary features a statute will embody, when such features are unavoidable because other considerations do not specify a precise line; yet a line must be drawn.

Study Questions

1. According to Nozick, how does a person acquire something justly?
2. According to Nozick's principles, does anyone at present have a right to their holdings?
3. What is the difference between distribution according to an *end-state principle* and distribution according to a *patterned principle?*
4. What is the general point illustrated by the Wilt Chamberlain example?

B.

Immigration

Immigration: The Case for Limits

David Miller

David Miller is Professor of Political Theory at Nuffield College, Oxford. He considers three arguments in favor of an unrestricted right to immigration, contending that none is compelling. The first holds that the right to freedom of movement includes the right to move between states. Miller argues, however, that even in the most liberal societies the right to freedom of movement is severely restricted. For example, we do not have the right to trespass on privately owned lands. The second argument stems from a person's right to leave a state. In order to be exercised, the right to exit seems to demand that the borders of other states be open. But Miller argues that having a right to exit, properly understood, is akin to a right to be married. Exercising either right is contingent on finding a party willing to cooperate. The third argument Miller considers is the claim that distributive justice demands open borders. He maintains that although cases in which individuals fall below the basic minimum of subsistence would provide a right to immigrate, such instances are sharply limited. Miller goes on to suggest that safeguarding a state's distinctive culture and controlling its population provide reasons to keep borders closed. Thus in his view states are justified in limiting immigration.

From David Miller, "Immigration: The Case for Limits," in *Contemporary Debates in Applied Ethics*, eds. Andrew I. Cohen and Christopher Heath Wellman (Malden, MA: Blackwell, 2005): pp. 193–206.

. . . In this chapter, I shall explain why nation-states may be justified in imposing restrictive immigration policies if they so choose. The argument is laid out in three stages. First, I canvass three arguments that purport to justify an unlimited right of migration between states and show why each of them fails. Second, I give two reasons, one having to do with culture, the other with population, that can justify states in limiting immigration. Third, I consider whether states nonetheless have a duty to admit a special class of potential immigrants—namely refugees—and also how far they are allowed to pick and choose among the immigrants they do admit. The third section, in other words, lays down some conditions that an ethical immigration policy must meet. But I begin by showing why there is no general right to choose one's country of residence or citizenship.

Can There Be an Unlimited Right of Migration Between States?

Liberal political philosophers who write about migration usually begin from the premise that people should be allowed to choose where in the world to locate themselves unless it can be shown that allowing an unlimited right of migration would have harmful consequences that outweigh the value of freedom of choice. . . . In other words, the central value appealed to is simply freedom itself. Just as I should be free to decide who to marry, what job to take, what religion (if any) to profess, so I should be free to decide whether to live in Nigeria, or France, or the USA. Now these philosophers usually concede that in practice some limits may have to be placed on this freedom—for instance, if high rates of migration would result in social chaos or the breakdown of liberal states that could not accommodate so many migrants without losing their liberal character. In these instances, the exercise of free choice would become self-defeating. But the presumption is that people should be free to choose where to live unless there are strong reasons for restricting their choice.

I want to challenge this presumption. Of course there is always *some* value in people having more options to choose between, in this case options as to where to live, but we usually draw a line between *basic* freedoms that people should have as a matter of right and what we might call *bare* freedoms that do not warrant that kind of protection. It would be good from my point of view if I were free to purchase an Aston Martin tomorrow, but that is not going to count as a morally significant freedom—my desire is not one that imposes any kind of obligation on others to meet it. In order to argue against immigration restrictions, therefore, liberal philosophers must do more than show that there is some value to people in being able to migrate, or that they often *want* to migrate (as indeed they do, in increasing numbers). It needs to be demonstrated that this freedom has the kind of weight or significance that could turn it into a right, and that should therefore prohibit states from pursuing immigration policies that limit freedom of movement.

I shall examine three arguments that have been offered to defend a right to migrate. The first starts with the general right to freedom of movement, and claims that this must include the freedom to move into, and take up residence in, states other than one's own. The second begins with a person's right to *exit* from her current state—a right that is widely recognized in international law—and claims that a right of exit is pointless unless it is matched by a right of entry into other states. The third appeals to international distributive justice. Given the huge inequalities in living standards that currently exist between rich and poor states, it is said, people who live in poor states have a claim of justice that can only be met by allowing them to migrate and take advantage of the opportunities that rich states provide.

The idea of a right to freedom of movement is not in itself objectionable. We are talking here about what are usually called basic rights or human rights, and I shall assume (since there is no space to defend the point) that such rights are justified by pointing to the vital interests that they protect. . . . They correspond to conditions in whose absence human beings cannot live decent lives, no matter what particular values and plans of life they choose to pursue. Being able to move freely in physical space is just such a condition, as we can see by thinking about people whose legs are shackled or who are confined in small spaces. A wider freedom of movement can also be justified by thinking about the interests that it serves instrumentally: if I cannot move about over a fairly wide area, it may be impossible for me to find a job, to practice my religion, or to find a suitable marriage partner. Since these all qualify as vital interests, it is fairly clear that freedom of movement qualifies as a basic human right.

What is less clear, however, is the physical extent of that right, in the sense of how much of the earth's surface I must be able to move to in order to say that I enjoy it. Even in liberal societies that make no attempt to confine people within particular geographical areas, freedom of movement is severely restricted in a number of ways. I cannot, in general, move to places that other people's bodies now occupy (I cannot just push them aside). I cannot move on to private property without the consent of its owner, except perhaps in emergencies or where a special right of access exists—and since most land is privately owned, this means that a large proportion of physical space does not fall within the ambit of a *right* to free movement. Even access to public space is heavily regulated: there are traffic laws that tell me where and at what speed I may drive my car, parks have opening and closing hours, the police can control my movements up and down the streets, and so forth. . . . Yet few would argue that because of these limitations, people in these societies are deprived of one of their human rights. . . .

The point here is that liberal societies in general offer their members *sufficient* freedom of movement to protect the interests that the human right to free movement is intended to protect, even though the extent of free movement is very far from absolute. So how could one attempt to show that the right in question must include the right to move to some other country and settle there? What vital interest requires the right to be interpreted in such an extensive way? Contingently, of course, it may be true that moving to another country is the only way for an individual to escape persecution, to find work, to obtain necessary medical care, and so forth. In these circumstances the person concerned may have the right to move, not to any state that she chooses, but to *some* state where these interests can be protected. But here the right to move serves only as a remedial right: its existence depends on the fact that the person's vital interests cannot be secured in the country where she currently resides. In a world of decent states—states that were able to secure their citizens' basic rights to security, food, work, medical care, and so forth—the right to move across borders could not be justified in this way.

Our present world is not, of course, a world of decent states, and this gives rise to the issue of refugees, which I shall discuss in the final section of this chapter. But if we leave aside for the moment cases where the right to move freely across borders depends upon the right to avoid persecution, starvation, or other threats to basic interests, how might we try to give it a more general rationale? One reason a person may want to migrate is in order to participate in a culture that does not exist in his native land—for instance he wants to work at an occupation for which there is no demand at home, or to join a religious community which, again, is not represented in the country from which he comes. These might be central components in his plan of life, so he will find it very frustrating if he is not able to move. But does this ground a right to free movement across borders? It seems to me that it does not. What a person can legitimately demand access to is an *adequate* range of options to choose between—a reasonable choice of occupation, religion, cultural activities, marriage partners, and so forth. Adequacy here is defined in terms of generic human interests rather than in terms of the interests of any one person in particular—so, for example, a would-be opera singer living in a society which provides for various forms of musical expression, but not for opera, can have an adequate range of options in this area even though the option she most prefers is not available. So long as they adhere to the standards of decency sketched above, all contemporary states are able to provide such an adequate range internally. So although people certainly have an *interest* in being able to migrate internationally, they do not have a basic interest of the kind that would be required to ground a human right. It is more like my interest in having an Aston Martin than my interest in having access to *some* means of physical mobility.

I turn next to the argument that because people have a right to leave the society they currently belong to, they must also have a right to enter other societies, since the first right is practically meaningless unless the second exists—there is no unoccupied space in the world to exit *to*, so unless the right to leave society A is accompanied by the right to enter societies B, C, D, etc., it has no real force. . . .

The right of exit is certainly an important human right, but once again it is worth examining why it has the significance that it does. Its importance is partly instrumental: knowing that their subjects have the right to leave inhibits states from mistreating them in various ways, so it helps to preserve the conditions of what I earlier called "decency." However, even in the case of decent states the right of exit remains important, and that is because by being deprived of exit rights individuals are forced to remain in association with others whom they may find deeply uncongenial—think of the militant atheist in a society where almost everyone devoutly practices the same religion, or the religious puritan in a society where most people behave like libertines. On the other hand, the right of exit from state A does not appear to entail an unrestricted right to enter any society of the immigrant's choice—indeed, it seems that it can be exercised provided that at least one other society, society B say, is willing to take him in. . . .

It is also important to stress that there are many rights whose exercise is contingent on finding partners who are willing to cooperate in the exercise, and it may be that the right of exit falls into this category. Take the right to marry as an example. This is a right held against the state to allow people to marry the partners of their choice (and perhaps to provide the legal framework within which marriages can be contracted). It is obviously not a right to have a marriage partner provided—whether any given person can exercise the right depends entirely on whether he is able to find someone willing to marry him, and many people are not so lucky. The right of exit is a right held against a person's current state of residence not to prevent her from leaving the state (and perhaps aiding her in that endeavor by, say, providing a passport). But it does not entail an obligation on any other state to let that person in. Obviously, if no state were ever to grant entry rights to people who were not already its citizens, the right of exit would have no value. But suppose states are generally willing to consider entry applications from people who want to migrate, and that most people would get offers from at least one such state: then the position as far as the right of exit goes is pretty much the same as with the right to marry, where by no means everyone is able to wed the partner they would ideally like to have, but most have the opportunity to marry *someone.*

So once the right of exit is properly understood, it does not entail an unlimited right to migrate to the society of one's choice. But now, finally, in this part of the chapter, I want to consider an argument for migration rights that appeals to distributive justice. It begins from the assumption of the fundamental moral equality of human beings. It then points out that, in the world in which we live, a person's life prospects depend heavily on the society into which she happens to be born, so that the only way to achieve equal opportunities is to allow people to move to the places where they can develop and exercise their talents, through employment and in other ways. In other words, there is something fundamentally unfair about a world in which people are condemned to relative poverty through no fault of their own when others have much greater opportunities, whereas if people were free to live and work wherever they wished, then each person could choose whether to stay in the community that had raised him or to look for a better life elsewhere.

The question we must ask here is whether justice demands equality of opportunity at the global level, as the argument I have just sketched assumes, or whether this principle only applies *inside* societies, among those who are already citizens of the same political community. . . . Note to begin with that embracing the moral equality of all human beings—accepting that every human being is equally an object of moral concern—does not yet tell us what we are required to do for them as a result of that equality. One answer *might* be that we should attempt to provide everyone with equal opportunities to pursue their goals in life. But another, equally plausible, answer is that we should play our part in ensuring that their basic rights are respected, where these are understood as rights to a certain minimum level of security, freedom, resources, and so forth—a level adequate to protect their basic interests, as suggested earlier in this chapter. . . .

But what if somebody does fall below this threshold? Does this not give him the right to migrate to a place where the minimum level is guaranteed? Perhaps, but it depends on whether the minimum *could* be provided in the political community he belongs to now, or whether that community is so oppressive, or so dysfunctional, that escape is the only option. So here we encounter again the issue of refugees, to be discussed in my final section. Meanwhile, the lesson for other states, confronted with people whose lives are less than decent, is that they have a choice: they must either ensure that the basic rights of such people are protected in the places where they live—by aid, by intervention, or by some other means—or they must help them to move to other communities where their lives will be better. Simply shutting one's borders and doing nothing else is not a morally defensible option here. People everywhere have a right to a decent life. But before jumping to the conclusion that the way to respond to global injustice is to encourage people whose lives are less than decent to migrate elsewhere, we should consider the fact that this policy will do little to help the very poor, who are unlikely to have the resources to move to a richer country. Indeed, a policy of open migration may make such people worse off still, if it allows doctors, engineers, and other professionals to move from economically undeveloped to economically developed societies in search of higher incomes, thereby depriving their countries of origin of vital skills. Equalizing opportunity for the few may diminish opportunities for the many. Persisting global injustice does impose on rich states the obligation to make a serious contribution to the relief of global poverty, but in most instances they should contribute to improving conditions of life on the ground, as it were, rather than bypassing the problem by allowing (inevitably selective) inward migration.

Justifications for Limiting Immigration

. . . In this section, I shall outline two good reasons that states may have for restricting immigration. One has to do with preserving culture, the other with controlling population. I don't claim that these reasons will apply to every state, but they do apply to many liberal democracies that are currently having to decide how to respond to potentially very large flows of immigrants from less economically developed societies (other states may face larger flows still, but the political issues will be different).

The first reason assumes that the states in question require a common public culture that in part constitutes the political identity of their members, and that serves valuable functions in supporting democracy and other social goals. . . . What I want to do here is to consider how the need to protect the public culture bears upon the issue of immigration. In general terms we can say (a) that immigrants will enter with cultural values, including *political* values, that are more or less different from the public culture of the community they enter; (b) that as a result of living in that community, they will absorb some part of the existing public culture, modifying their own values in the process; and (c) that their presence will also change the public culture in various ways—for instance, a society in which an established religion had formed an important part of national identity will typically exhibit greater religious diversity after accepting immigrants, and as a consequence religion will play a less significant part in defining that identity.

Immigration, in other words, is likely to change a society's public culture rather than destroy it. And since public cultures always change over time, as a result of social factors that are quite independent of immigration (participation in the established religion might have been declining in any case), it doesn't on the face of it seem that states have any good reason to restrict immigration on that basis. They might have reason to limit the *flow* of immigrants, on the grounds that the process of acculturation outlined above may break down if too many come in too quickly. But so long as a viable public culture is maintained, it should not matter that its character changes as a result of taking in people with different cultural values. . . .

What this overlooks, however, is that the public culture of their country is something that people have an interest in controlling: they want to be able to shape the way that their nation develops, including the values that are contained in the public culture. They may not of course succeed: valued cultural features can be eroded by economic and other forces that evade political control. But they may certainly have good reason to try, and in particular to try to maintain cultural continuity over time, so that they can see themselves as the bearers of an identifiable cultural tradition that stretches backward historically. Cultural continuity, it should be stressed, is not the same as cultural rigidity: the most valuable cultures are those that can develop and adapt to new circumstances, including the presence of new subcultures associated with immigrants.

Consider the example of language. In many states today the national language is under pressure from the spread of international languages, especially English. People have an incentive to learn and use one of the international languages for economic and other purposes, and so there is a danger that the national language will wither away over the course of two or three generations. If this were to happen, one of the community's most important distinguishing characteristics would have disappeared, its literature would become inaccessible except in translation, and so forth. So the states in question adopt policies to insure, for instance, that the national language is used in schools and in the media, and that exposure to foreign languages through imports is restricted. What effect would a significant influx of immigrants who did not already speak the national language have in these circumstances? It is likely that their choice of second language would be English, or one of the other international languages. So their presence would increase the incentive among natives to defect from use of the national language in everyday transactions, and make the project of language-preservation harder to carry through. The state has good reason to limit immigration, or at least to differentiate sharply among prospective immigrants between those who speak the national language and those who don't, as the government of Quebec has done in recent years. . . .

How restrictive an immigration policy this dictates depends on the empirical question of how easy or difficult it is to create a symbiosis between the existing public culture and the new cultural values of the immigrants, and this will vary hugely from case to case (in particular the experience of immigration itself is quite central to the public cultures of some states, but not to others). Most liberal democracies are now multicultural, and this is widely regarded as a source of cultural richness. But the more culturally diverse a society becomes, the greater need it has for a unifying public culture to bind its members together, and this culture has to connect to the history and physical shape of the society in question—it can't be invented from scratch. . . . So a political judgment needs to be made about the scale and type of immigration that will enrich rather than dislocate the existing public culture.

The second reason for states to limit immigration that I want to consider concerns population size. This is a huge, and hugely controversial, topic, and all I can do here is to sketch an argument that links together the issues of immigration and population control. The latter issue really arises at two different levels: global and national. At the global level, there is a concern that the carrying capacity of the earth may be stretched to [the] breaking point if the total number of human beings continues to rise as it has over the last half century or so. At [the] national level, there is a concern about the effect of population growth on quality of life and the natural environment. Let me look at each level in turn.

Although there is disagreement about just how many people the earth can sustain before resource depletion—the availability of water, for example—becomes acute, it would be hard to maintain that there is *no* upper limit. Although projections of population growth over the century ahead indicate a leveling off in the rate of increase, we must also expect—indeed should welcome—increases in the standard of living in the developing world that will mean that resource consumption per capita will also rise significantly. In such a world it is in all our interests that states whose populations are growing rapidly should adopt birth control measures and other policies to restrict the rate of growth, as both China and India have done in past decades. But such states have little or no incentive to adopt such policies if they can "export" their surplus population through international migration, and since the policies in question are usually unpopular, they have a positive incentive not to pursue them. A viable population policy at global level requires each state to be responsible for stabilizing, or even possibly reducing, its population over time, and this is going to be impossible to achieve if there are no restrictions on the movement of people between states.

At [the] national level, the effects of population growth may be less catastrophic, but can still be detrimental to important cultural values. What we think about this issue may be conditioned to some extent by the population density of the state in which we live. Those of us who live in relatively small and crowded states experience daily the way in which the sheer number of our fellow citizens, with their needs for housing, mobility, recreation, and so forth, impacts on the physical environment, so that it becomes harder to enjoy access to open space, to move from place to place without encountering congestion, to preserve important wildlife habitats, and so on. It's true, of course, that the problems arise not simply from population size, but also from a population that wants to live in a certain way—to move around a lot, to have high levels of consumption, and so on—so we could deal with them by collectively changing the way that we live, rather than by restricting or reducing population size. . . . Perhaps we should. But this, it seems to me, is a matter for political decision: members of a territorial community have the right to decide whether to restrict their numbers, or to live in a more ecologically and humanly sound way, or to do neither and bear the costs of a high-consumption, high-mobility lifestyle in a crowded territory. If restricting numbers is part of the solution, then controlling immigration is a natural corollary.

What I have tried to do in this section is to suggest why states may have good reason to limit immigration. I concede that would-be immigrants may have a strong interest in being admitted—a strong economic interest, for example—but in general they have no obligation-conferring *right* to be admitted, for reasons given in the previous section. On the other side, nation-states have a strong and legitimate interest in determining who comes in and who does not. . . . It remains now to see what conditions an admissions policy must meet if it is to be ethically justified.

Conditions for an Ethical Immigration Policy

I shall consider two issues. The first is the issue of refugees, usually defined as people who have fled their home country as a result of a well-founded fear of persecution or violence. What obligations do states have to admit persons in that category? The second is the issue of discrimination in admissions policy. If a state decides to admit some immigrants (who are not refugees) but refuses entry to others, what criteria can it legitimately use in making its selection?

As I indicated in the first section of this chapter, people whose basic rights are being threatened or violated in their current place of residence clearly do have the right to move to somewhere that offers them greater security. Prima facie, then, states have an obligation to admit refugees, indeed "refugees" defined more broadly than is often the case to include people who are being deprived of rights to subsistence, basic healthcare, etc. . . . But this need not involve treating them as long-term immigrants. They may be offered temporary sanctuary in states that are able to protect them, and then be asked to return to their original country of citizenship when the threat has passed. . . . Moreover, rather than encouraging long-distance migration, it may be preferable to establish safety zones for refugees close to their homes and then deal with the cause of the rights-violations directly—whether this means sending in food and medical aid or intervening to remove a genocidal regime from power. There is obviously a danger that the temporary solution becomes semi-permanent, and this is unacceptable because refugees are owed more than the immediate protection of their basic rights—they are owed something like the chance to make a proper life for themselves. But liberals who rightly give a high moral priority to protecting the human rights of vulnerable people are regrettably often unwilling to countenance intervention in states that are plainly violating these rights.

If protection on the ground is not possible, the question then arises *which* state should take in the refugees. It is natural to see the obligation as shared among all those states that are able to provide refuge, and in an ideal world one might envisage some formal mechanism for distributing refugees among them. However, the difficulties in devising such a scheme are formidable. . . . To obtain agreement from different states about what each state's refugee quota should be, one would presumably need to start with simple and relatively uncontroversial criteria such as population or per capita GNP. But this leaves out of the picture many other factors, such as population density, the overall rate of immigration into each state, cultural factors that make absorption of particular groups of refugees particularly easy or difficult, and so forth—all factors that would differentially affect the willingness of political communities to accept refugees and make agreement on a scheme very unlikely. Furthermore, the proposed quota system pays no attention to the choices of the refugees themselves as to where to apply for sanctuary, unless it is accompanied by a compensatory scheme that allows states that take in more refugees than their quota prescribes to receive financial transfers from states that take in less.

Realistically, therefore, states have to be given considerable autonomy to decide on how to respond to particular asylum applications: besides the refugee's own choice, they are entitled to consider the overall number of applications they face, the demands that temporary or longer-term accommodation of refugees will place on existing citizens, and whether there exists any special link between the refugee and the host community—for instance, similarities of language or culture, or a sense of historical responsibility on the part of the receiving state (which might see itself as somehow implicated among the causes of the crisis that has produced the refugees). If states are given this autonomy, there can be no guarantee that every bona fide refugee will find a state willing to take him or her in. Here we simply face a clash between two moral intuitions: on the one hand, every refugee is a person with basic human rights that deserve protection; on the other, the responsibility for insuring this is diffused among states in such a way that we cannot say that any particular state S has an obligation to admit refugee R. Each state is at some point entitled to say that it has done enough to cope with the refugee crisis. So the best we can hope for is that informal mechanisms will continue to evolve which make all refugees the *special* responsibility of one state or another. . . .

The second issue is discrimination among migrants who are not refugees. Currently, states do discriminate on a variety of different grounds, effectively selecting the migrants they want to take in. Can this be justified? Well, given that states are entitled to put a ceiling on the numbers of people they take in, for reasons canvassed in the previous section, they need to select somehow, if only by lottery (as the USA began to do in 1995 for certain categories of immigrant). So what grounds can they legitimately use? It seems to me that receiving states are entitled to consider the benefit they would receive from admitting a would-be migrant as well as the strength of the migrant's own claim to move. So it is acceptable to give precedence to people whose cultural values are closer to those of the existing population—for instance, to those who already speak the native language. This is a direct corollary of the argument in the previous section about cultural self-determination. Next in order of priority come those who possess skills and talents that are needed by the receiving community. Their claim is weakened, as suggested earlier, by the likelihood that in taking them in, the receiving state is also depriving their country of origin of a valuable resource (medical expertise, for example). In such cases, the greater the interest the potential host country has in admitting the would-be migrant, the more likely it is that admitting her will make life worse for those she leaves behind. So although it is reasonable for the receiving state to make decisions based on how much the immigrant can be expected to contribute economically if admitted, this criterion should be used with caution. What cannot be defended in any circumstances is discrimination on grounds of race, sex, or, in most instances, religion—religion could be a relevant criterion only where it continues to form an essential part of the public culture, as in the case of the state of Israel.

If nation-states are allowed to decide how many immigrants to admit in the first place, why can't they pick and choose among potential immigrants on whatever grounds they like—admitting only red-haired women if that is what their current membership prefers? I have tried to hold a balance between the interest that migrants have in entering the country they want to live in, and the interest that political communities having in determining their own character. Although the first of these interests is not strong enough to justify a right of migration, it is still substantial, and so the immigrants who are refused entry are owed an explanation. To be told that they belong to the wrong race, or sex (or have hair of the wrong color) is insulting, given that these features do not connect to anything of real significance to the society they want to join. Even tennis clubs are not entitled to discriminate among applicants on grounds such as these.

Let me conclude by underlining the importance of admitting all long-term immigrants to full and equal citizenship in the receiving society (this does not apply to refugees who are admitted temporarily until it is safe to return to their country of origin, but it does apply to refugees as soon as it becomes clear that return is not a realistic option for them). Controls on immigration must be coupled with active policies to insure that immigrants are brought into the political life of the community, and acquire the linguistic and other skills that they require to function as active citizens. . . . In several states immigrants are now encouraged to take citizenship classes leading up to a formal admissions ceremony, and this is a welcome development insofar as it recognizes that becoming a citizen isn't something that just happens spontaneously. Precisely because they aim to be "communities of character," with distinct public cultures to which new immigrants can contribute, democratic states must bring immigrants into political dialogue with natives. What is unacceptable is the emergence of a permanent class of non-citizens, whether these are guest workers, illegal immigrants, or asylum seekers waiting to have their applications adjudicated. The underlying political philosophy which informs this chapter sees democratic states as political communities formed on the basis of equality among their members, and just as this gives such states the right to exclude, it also imposes the obligation to protect the equal status of all those who live within their borders.

Study Questions

1. What is the difference between *basic* freedoms and *bare* freedoms?
2. Is the right to exit similar to the right to be married?
3. According to Miller, why does preserving culture provide a reason to limit immigration?
4. According to Miller, when should refugees be granted asylum?

Is There a Right to Immigrate?

Michael Huemer

Michael Huemer is Professor of Philosophy at the University of Colorado at Boulder. He argues that closing borders violates the rights of would-be immigrants. Everyone has the right to immigrate because everyone has the right to freedom from the use or threat of physical force, and immigration restrictions involve the use of coercion. Huemer considers three reasons often cited in favor of overriding the right to immigrate: the effects on the labor market, the financial burden of aiding immigrants, and the preservation of a state's culture. He concludes that none of these reasons overrides the right to immigrate, and thus restrictions on immigration amount to morally wrongful violations of rights.

1. The Immigration Question

Every year, close to one million individuals from foreign nations migrate to the United States legally. But many more are turned away. Individuals seeking to enter without the permission of the U.S. government are regularly barred at the border, and those discovered in the territory without authorization are forcibly removed. The government expels over one million people from the country each year.[1] Hundreds of thousands continue to try to smuggle themselves in, occasionally dying in the attempt. On the face of it, this raises ethical questions. Is it right to forcibly prevent would-be immigrants from living in the United States? Those excluded seem, on the face of it, to suffer a serious harm. Why are we justified in imposing this harm?

Some reason that, just as a private club may exercise its discretion as to whom to admit or exclude, so a nation-state has the right to choose whom to admit or exclude. Some believe that we must exclude most

From Michael Huemer, "Is There a Right to Immigrate?" *Social Theory and Practice* 36 (2010).

would-be immigrants in order to maintain the integrity of our national culture. Others argue that immigrants cause economic hardship for existing citizens—that they take jobs from American workers, depress wages, and place an undue burden on social services provided by the state. Some go so far as to warn that unchecked immigration would bring on environmental, economic, and social catastrophes that would reduce the United States to the status of a Third World country.

Few would question the state's right to exclude at least some potential migrants. For example, the state may deny entry to international terrorists or fugitives from the law. The interesting question concerns the vast majority of other potential immigrants—ordinary people who are simply seeking a new home and a better life. Does the state have the right to exclude these ordinary people?

In the following, I argue that the answer to this question is no. I shall assume that we are considering ordinary, noncriminal migrants who wish to leave their country of origin for morally innocent reasons, whether to escape persecution or economic hardship, or simply to join a society they would prefer to live in. Though I shall conduct the discussion in terms of the situation of the United States, most of my arguments apply equally well to other countries.

My strategy is to argue, first, that immigration restriction is at least a prima facie violation of the rights of potential immigrants. This imposes a burden on advocates of restriction to cite some special conditions that either neutralize or outweigh the relevant prima facie right. I then examine the most popular justifications offered for restricting immigration, finding that none of them offers a credible rationale for claiming either that such restriction does not violate rights or that the rights violation is justified. This leaves immigration restrictions ultimately unjustified. . . .

2. Immigration Restriction as a Prima Facie Rights Violation

In this section, I aim to show that immigration restriction is a prima facie rights violation. A prima facie rights violation is an action of a sort that *normally*—that is, barring any special circumstances—violates someone's rights. For example, killing a human being is a prima facie rights violation: in normal circumstances, to kill someone is to violate his rights. But there are special circumstances that may alter this verdict: euthanasia and self-defense killings do not violate rights, for instance. Furthermore, even when an action violates rights, it may sometimes be justified nevertheless, because the victim's rights may be *outweighed* by competing moral considerations. Thus, killing one innocent person may be justified, though a violation of the victim's right to life, if it is necessary to prevent the deaths of one million others. Or so it seems to me.

The claim that an action is a prima facie rights violation, then, is not a very strong claim. It does not entail that the action is wrong all things considered, for there may be special circumstances that prevent the action from being an actual rights violation, or that render it justified despite its violation of rights. But nor is the claim entirely without force: to accept that an action is a prima facie rights violation has the effect of shifting a normative presumption. It becomes the burden of those who advocate the act in question to identify the special exculpatory or justificatory circumstances that make what tends to be a wrongful rights violation either not a rights violation in this case, or a justified rights violation. Those who oppose the act in question need only rebut such efforts.

Now before we turn to the case of immigration, consider the following scenario. Marvin is in desperate need of food. Perhaps someone has stolen his food, or perhaps a natural disaster destroyed his crops; whatever the reason, Marvin is in danger of starvation. Fortunately, he has a plan to remedy the problem: he will walk to the local marketplace, where he will buy bread. Assume that in the absence of outside interference, this plan would succeed: the marketplace is open, and there are people there who are willing to trade food to Marvin in exchange for something he has. Another individual, Sam, is aware of all this and is watching Marvin. For some reason, Sam decides to detain Marvin on his way to the marketplace, forcibly preventing him from reaching it. As a result, Marvin returns home empty-handed, where he dies of starvation.

What is the proper assessment of Sam's action? Did Sam harm Marvin? Did he violate Marvin's rights? Was Sam's action wrong?

It seems to me that there are clear answers to these questions. Sam's behavior in this scenario was both extremely harmful to Marvin and a severe violation of Marvin's rights. Indeed, if Marvin's death was reasonably foreseeable, then Sam's act was an act of murder. Unless there obtained some unusual circumstances not mentioned in the preceding description, Sam's behavior was extremely wrong.

Intuitively, Sam's behavior would still be wrong if the harm suffered by Marvin were less severe. Suppose that, rather than dying soon after returning home, Marvin foreseeably suffers from serious malnutrition. Again, assume that this misfortune would have been avoided had Marvin been able to trade in the marketplace, but Sam forcibly prevented him from doing so. In this case, again, it seems that Sam violates Marvin's rights and wrongfully harms Marvin.

What do these examples show? I think they show, to begin with, that individuals have a prima facie, negative right not to be subjected to seriously harmful coercion. Sam's behavior in the scenario was, by stipulation, coercive—it involved a use or threat of physical force against Marvin, significantly restricting his freedom of action. It was also extremely harmful, resulting in Marvin's starvation. These facts seem to explain why Sam's action was a violation of Marvin's rights, and why it was wrong.

How do we know that Sam harmed Marvin? A "harm" is commonly understood as a setback to someone's interests. Marvin's death by starvation certainly sets back his interests. Moreover, in my view, no philosophical *theory* of harm is required in this case. Perhaps there are borderline cases in which one would need to appeal to a theory to determine whether an event counted as a harm or not. But the story of starving Marvin presents no such difficult case. Marvin's death is a paradigm case of a harm. . . .

I am not claiming here that all acts of coercion are harmful. Paternalistic coercion, for instance, need not be harmful. Nor are all harmful actions coercive. One might harm a person, for instance, by spreading false rumors about her, without any exercise of physical force. I am only claiming that *this* action, Sam's forcible interference with Marvin's effort to reach the marketplace, was both harmful and coercive. Similarly, I am not claiming that all coercion violates rights, nor that all harmful acts violate rights. I claim only that, when an action is seriously harmful *and* coercive, it tends for that reason to be a rights violation, other things being equal—that is, it is a prima facie rights violation. Sam's behavior in the scenario described violates Marvin's rights, because it is an act of extremely harmful coercion, and there are no relevant extenuating circumstances. Sam's behavior could be justified if, for example, it was necessary to prevent the deaths of a million innocent persons; or, perhaps, if Marvin had for some reason contracted Sam to forcibly prevent Marvin from going to the marketplace. But assume that nothing like that is the case. The case is just as originally described, with no special circumstances. Few would doubt, then, that Sam's behavior is unacceptable.

How does all this relate to U.S. immigration policy? The role of Marvin is played by those potential immigrants who seek escape from oppression or economic hardship. The marketplace is the United States: were they allowed in, most immigrants would succeed in meeting their needs (to a greater extent, at least, than they will if they are not allowed in). The role of Sam is played by the government of the United States, which has adopted severe restrictions on entry. These restrictions are imposed by coercion: armed guards are hired to patrol the borders, physically barring unauthorized entry, and armed officers of the state forcibly detain and expel immigrants who are found residing in the country illegally. As in the case of Sam's detention of Marvin, the U.S. government's exclusion of undocumented immigrants is also very harmful to most of those excluded: many suffer from oppression or poverty that could and would be remedied if only they were able to enter the country of their choice. In view of this, the actions of the U.S. government, prima facie, constitute serious violations of the rights of potential immigrants—specifically, the government violates their prima facie right not to be harmfully coerced. . . .

Sam's action might be justified if there were special circumstances not previously specified, circumstances that either cancelled the right that Marvin normally has not to be harmfully coerced, or that morally outweighed Marvin's rights. Likewise, what we have said so far does not establish that the U.S. government's restrictions on immigration are wrong *tout court*, but only that those defending the policy incur a burden of providing a justification for these restrictions. In light of the seriousness of the harms involved in this case, the justification for immigration restrictions must be correspondingly clear and powerful.

3. Reasons for Restriction

Harmful coercion is sometimes justified. It may be justified when necessary to defend an innocent party against harmful coercion. It may be justified when necessary to prevent much worse consequences. It may be justified because of a prior agreement made by the coercee. And there may be other circumstances that justify harmful coercion as well. Some believe, for instance, that harmful coercion may be justified because of a need to rectify severe economic inequality. The latter claim is controversial, as would be many other alleged justifications for harmful coercion. This illustrates one reason why a general theory of the conditions for justified harmful coercion would be difficult to devise and still more difficult to defend.

Fortunately, it may turn out that we do not need any such general theory. Some sorts of reasons . . . are generally accepted as legitimate justifications for harmful coercion. Equally, there are some sorts of reasons that we can see intuitively, even without a general theory, *not* to be legitimate justifications for harmful coercion. For instance, one is not justified in harmfully coercing a person simply because one wants the victim's shoes, or because one hates the race to which the victim belongs, or because one disagrees with the victim's philosophical beliefs. Whatever is the correct theory of justifications for harmful coercion, *those* reasons surely will not qualify. The task at hand is to determine whether there are any circumstances that justify the harmful coercion involved in immigration restrictions. Given that immigration restriction is a prima facie rights violation, the burden of proof falls on advocates of restriction. Thus, we may proceed by considering the reasons they have offered for restricting immigration. If it turns out that all of these reasons fall into the category of things that clearly do not count as valid justifications for harmful coercion, then it is fair to draw the conclusion that immigration restrictions are unjustified.

3.1. Immigration and Employment

In popular discourse, the most common sort of argument for limiting or eliminating immigration is economic. It is said that immigrants take jobs away from American workers, and that they cause a lowering of wage rates due to their willingness to work for lower wages than American workers. At the same time, economists are nearly unanimous in agreeing that the overall economic effects of immigration on existing Americans are positive. These claims are mutually consistent: there are certain industries in which immigrants are disproportionately likely to work. Preexisting workers in those industries are made worse off due to competition with immigrant workers. According to one estimate, immigration during the 1980s may have reduced the wages of native-born workers in the most strongly affected industries by about 1–2% (5% for high school dropouts).[2] At the same time, employers in those industries and customers of their businesses are made better off due to lower production costs, and the economic gains to these latter groups outweigh the economic losses to the workers. Some economists have accused immigration opponents of overlooking the economic benefits of immigration due to a bias against foreigners or members of other races.

Let us leave aside the question of the overall effects of immigration on the economy, and focus instead on the following question. Granted that immigration makes some American workers economically worse off, does this show that immigration restriction does not violate the rights of would-be immigrants, or that if it does, the rights violation is nevertheless justified? More generally, does the following constitute a valid justification for harmful coercion: that the coercive action is necessary to prevent someone else from suffering slight to moderate economic disadvantage through marketplace competition?

It seems to me that it does not. Consider two related examples. In the first example, I am being considered for a particular job, for which I know that Bob is the only other candidate. I also know that Bob is willing to work for a lower salary than the salary that I could obtain if I were the only candidate. On the day Bob is scheduled to have his job interview, I accost him and physically restrain him from going to the interview. When confronted about my seemingly unacceptable conduct, I explain that my action was necessary to protect myself against Bob's taking the job that I would otherwise have, or my being forced to accept a lower salary in order to get the job. Does this provide an adequate justification for my behavior? Does it show that, contrary to initial appearances, my harmful coercion does not really violate Bob's rights? Alternatively, does it show that my action, though a rights violation, was an ethically justified rights violation?

Certainly not. The mere fact that Bob is competing with me for a job that I desire, or that Bob is willing to accept a lower salary than I could obtain if I did not have to compete with him, does not invalidate or suspend Bob's right not to be subjected to harmful coercion. Nor does my interest in having less economic competition *outweigh* Bob's right not to be coercively harmed. If my need for the job in question were very much greater than Bob's need, then some might argue that I would be justified in overriding Bob's rights. We need not decide exactly when a right may be overridden, nor whether a greater economic need could constitute an adequate basis for overriding a competitor's right to be free from harmful coercion; we need not decide these things here, because we can simply stipulate that Bob has at least as much need for the job for which we are competing as I do. In such a case, no one would say that Bob's right to be free from coercive harms is suspended or outweighed.

My second example is a modified version of the story of Sam and Marvin. As before, Marvin plans to walk to the local marketplace to obtain life-sustaining food. Due to his economic circumstances,

Marvin will have to buy the cheapest bread available at the market. Sam's daughter, however, also plans to go to the market, slightly later in the day, to buy some of this same bread. This bread is often in short supply, so that the vendor may run out after Marvin's purchase. Sam's daughter could buy more expensive bread, but she would prefer not to. Knowing all this, Sam fears that if Marvin is allowed to go to the market, his daughter will be forced to pay a slightly higher price for bread than she would like. To prevent this from happening, he accosts Marvin on the road and physically restrains him from traveling to the market. Is Sam's action permissible?

Suppose Sam claims that his harmful coercion does not violate Marvin's rights, because it is necessary to protect his daughter from economic disadvantage. Certainly this defense falls flat. A person's right to be free from harmful coercion is not so easily swept aside. Likewise for the suggestion that Sam's action, though a rights violation, is justified because his daughter's interest in saving money outweighs Marvin's rights. No one would accept such feeble justifications.

Yet this seems analogous to the common economic argument for immigration restriction. The claim seems to be that we are justified in forcibly preventing individuals—many of whom are seeking escape from dire economic distress—from entering the American labor market, because American workers would suffer economic disadvantage through price competition. No one claims that American workers would be disadvantaged to anything like the degree that potential immigrants are disadvantaged by being forcibly excluded from the market. Nevertheless, the prospect of a modest lowering of American wages and narrowing of employment opportunities is taken to either suspend or outweigh the rights of needy foreigners. The ethical principle would have to be that a person's right to be free from extremely harmful coercion is sometimes held in abeyance simply by virtue of the fact that such coercion is necessary to protect third parties from modest economic disadvantage resulting from marketplace competition. The implausibility of this principle is shown by the examples of Bob and Marvin above.

3.2. The State's Duty to Its Citizens

Perhaps immigration restriction can be justified by reflection on the special obligations governments owe to their own citizens, as distinct from foreign nationals. Few doubt that there are such duties. States must provide their citizens protection from criminals and hostile foreign governments. A state does not have the same obligation to protect foreign citizens from criminals or other governments. . . .

Perhaps this leads to a rationale for immigration restriction. Perhaps the state has a general duty to serve the interests of its own citizens, including their economic interests, and no such duty, or no duty nearly as strong, to further the interests of foreign nationals. As a result, when the interests of American citizens come into conflict with those of foreigners, the American government must side with its own citizens, even when this results in a lowering of global social utility. Limitations on migration into the United States run contrary to the interests of would-be immigrants, but since those would-be immigrants are not presently U.S. citizens, the U.S. government has either no duty or a much weaker duty to consider their interests, as compared to the interests of its own citizens. Perhaps this gives some traction to the argument that American workers are disadvantaged because of competition with immigrants. Alternatively, one might argue that immigrants impose a financial burden on government providers of social services, such as health care, education, and law enforcement. Since these social programs are financed through revenues collected from existing U.S. citizens, the government's consideration for the interests of its current citizens dictates that it limit the amount of immigration into the country.

Begin with the observation that immigration disadvantages American workers through labor market competition. There are two obstacles to regarding this as a justification for immigration restriction, even if we accept that the state has a much stronger obligation to protect the interests of its own citizens than it has to protect the interests of others. First, only some current citizens would be disadvantaged by increased immigration—those citizens who work in industries that immigrants are disproportionately likely to join. This is a relatively small portion of the population. All other current citizens would either fail to be significantly affected or actually be benefited by increased immigration. As mentioned earlier, most economists believe that the overall economic impact of immigration on current citizens is positive. Thus, if we consider only the interests of current citizens, it is at best unclear that immigration restrictions are beneficial. If we also give *some* weight to the interests of the immigrants themselves, it seems that the case for free immigration is clear.

Second, there are some obligations that any moral agent owes to other persons, merely in virtue of their status as persons. The special obligations that governments owe to their citizens, whatever these obligations may consist of, do not eliminate the obligation to respect the human rights of noncitizens. In particular, the government's duty to give special consideration to its own citizens' interests cannot be taken to imply that the government is entitled to coercively impose grave harms on noncitizens for the sake of securing small economic benefits for citizens.

Consider again the case of starving Marvin. In the last version of the story, Sam coercively prevented Marvin from reaching the local marketplace, on the grounds that doing so was necessary to prevent his daughter from having to pay a higher than normal price for her bread. This action seems unjustified. Would Sam succeed in defending his behavior if he pointed out that, as a father, he has special obligations to his daughter, and that these imply that he must give greater weight to her interests than to the interests of non-family members? Certainly the premise is true—if anything, parents have even stronger and clearer duties to protect the interests of their offspring than a government has to protect its citizens' interests. But this does not negate the rights of non-family members not to be subjected to harmful coercion. One's special duties to one's offspring imply that if one must choose between giving food to one's own child and giving food to a non-family member, one should generally give the food to one's own child. But they do not imply that one may use force to stop non-family members from obtaining food, in order to procure modest economic advantages for one's own children.

Next, consider the charge that immigrants create a fiscal burden due to their consumption of social services. On the whole, immigrants pay slightly less in taxes than the cost of the social services they consume.[3] This is mainly because immigrants tend to have lower-than-average incomes, and thus pay relatively low taxes.[4] Some economists believe, however, that in the long run (over a period of decades), increased immigration would have a net positive fiscal impact.

Assume that immigrants impose a net fiscal burden on government. Would this fact justify forcibly preventing a large number of potential immigrants from entering the country? To answer this, first we must ask whether the state presently has an obligation to provide social services to potential immigrants, even at a net cost to the state. On some theories of distributive justice, it could be argued that the state has such an obligation, even though these potential immigrants are not presently citizens. If so, then the state obviously may not exclude potential immigrants for the purpose of shirking this duty.

Suppose, on the other hand, that the state has no such obligation to provide social services to potential immigrants, at least not without collecting from them sufficient revenues to cover the expenditure. If this is true, the state would perhaps be justified in denying social services to immigrants, raising taxes on immigrants, or charging special fees to immigrants for the use of social services. But it remains implausible that the state would be justified in excluding potential immigrants from the territory entirely. It is not typically a satisfactory defense for a harmful act of coercion to say that because of a policy one has voluntarily adopted, if one did not coerce one's victim in this way, one would instead confer a benefit on the person that one does not wish to confer.

Suppose, for example, that Sam runs a charity organization. He has made a policy of offering free food to all poor people who enter the local marketplace. Unfortunately, the organization is running short on cash, so Sam is looking for ways to cut costs. When he learns that Marvin is heading to the market to buy some food, he decides to save money by forcibly preventing Marvin from reaching the market. Marvin would be better off being allowed into the marketplace, even without free food, since he could still buy some inexpensive food with his limited funds. But Sam has already made a policy of offering free food to all poor people in the marketplace, so he would in fact offer free food to Marvin, were Marvin to make it there. Is it permissible for Sam to coercively inflict a serious harm on Marvin, in order to avoid having to either break his policy or give free food to Marvin?

Surely not. Perhaps Sam would be justified in altering his policy and refusing to give free food to Marvin when he arrives at the marketplace—this would be permissible, provided that Sam has no humanitarian obligation to assist Marvin. But whether or not Sam has any such humanitarian duties, he surely has no right to actively prevent Marvin from getting his own food. If Marvin had been coming to the market to *steal* Sam's food, perhaps then again Sam would be justified in excluding him. Even this claim would be controversial; if Marvin's condition of need were sufficiently urgent, some would say that Sam must let him take the food. But whatever one thinks about that question, surely Sam cannot justify barring Marvin from the opportunity to *buy* food from others, merely on the grounds that if Sam permits him to do so, then Sam will also voluntarily give him some food.

I have considered the possibilities both that the state owes potential immigrants a duty to help them satisfy their needs, and that the state owes them no such duty. But perhaps the situation is more complex. Perhaps the state presently owes no duty to aid potential immigrants, but if and when they become residents in its territory, the state will *then* owe them a duty to provide the same level of services as it provides to native-born citizens. If so, the state could not, ethically, protect its financial interests by opening the borders and simply providing lower levels of social services to the mass of incoming immigrants.

In assessing this view, we must take account of the distinction between residents and citizens. It is much more plausible that states are obligated to help citizens satisfy their needs, than that states are obligated to help all *residents* do so. So it is not clear that the suggestion of the preceding paragraph could justify preventing foreigners from residing in the United States, as opposed to justifying a refusal to grant citizenship. Nevertheless, let us assume that the state has a duty to offer equal levels of social services to all residents, once they are here. Even if mere residency somehow entitles one to equal levels of social services with native-born citizens, it is not plausible that this entitlement is *inalienable*, that is, that it cannot be voluntarily waived. The state therefore has at least one available strategy, apart from immigration restriction, for protecting its financial interests. This is to make a grant of legal residency or citizenship to potential immigrants contingent on the immigrants' agreement to waive their right to receive certain social services. Alternatively, the state could require new immigrants to agree to pay a higher tax rate, sufficient to cover the government's expected costs. The availability of these alternatives undercuts any justification the state could plausibly be claimed to have, in virtue of its fiscal interests, for excluding most potential immigrants from the country.

It could be questioned whether the policy suggested in the preceding paragraph is permissible. If foreigners have a *right* to immigrate, one could argue, then the state must allow them to exercise that right, whether or not they agree to waive other rights (including rights that they may come to have in the future). This may be correct. But whether or not it is correct, my argument of the preceding paragraph stands. For my claim was not that the state in fact ought to require potential immigrants to waive their (future) right to receive social services. I claim only that the state ought *not* to prohibit potential immigrants from entering the country, given that there is an alternative method of achieving the same goal, and that this alternative is less coercive and less harmful. It may of course be that *neither* alternative is permissible. But in any event, the unnecessarily coercive alternative is not permissible. In general, whether one may coercively harm innocent others to protect one's economic interests is open to debate. Perhaps there are circumstances in which one may do so. But even if one may do so, surely one may not employ *more* harmful coercion than is necessary to achieve one's goal. . . .

3.4. Cultural Preservation

In the views of some thinkers, states are justified in restricting the flow of immigration into their territories for the purposes of preserving the distinctive cultures of those nations. . . . David Miller argues that existing citizens have an interest in seeking to *control* how their culture does or does not develop, and this requires the ability to limit external influence; thus, again, we have a right to restrict immigration.[5]

To see this as a persuasive reason for restricting American immigration, we must accept two premises, one empirical and the other ethical. The empirical premise is that American culture is in danger of extinction or at least severe alteration if immigration is not restricted. The ethical premise is that the need to preserve one's culture constitutes a legitimate justification for harmful coercion of the sort involved in immigration restrictions.

Both premises are open to question. Empirically, it is doubtful whether apprehensions about the demise of American culture are warranted. Around the world, American culture, and Western culture more generally, have shown a robustness that prompts more concern about the ability of other cultures to survive influence from the West than vice versa. For example, Coca-Cola now sells its products in over 200 countries around the world, with the average human being on Earth drinking 4.8 gallons of Coke per year. McDonald's operates more than 32,000 restaurants in over 100 countries. The three highest grossing movies of all time, worldwide, were *Avatar, Titanic,* and *The Lord of the Rings: The Return of the King.* All three were made by American companies, but 70% of the box office receipts came from outside the United States. The television show *Who Wants to Be a Millionaire?* has been franchised in over 100 countries worldwide, including such diverse places as Japan, Nigeria, Venezuela, and Afghanistan. Whether one sees the phenomenon as desirable, undesirable, or neutral, Western culture has shown a remarkable ability to establish roots in a variety of societies around the world, including societies populated almost entirely by non-Western people. This robustness suggests that American culture is in no danger of being eradicated from America, even if America should drastically increase its rate of immigration. Other societies may have cause to fear the loss of their cultures due to foreign influence, but America does not.

Turning to the ethical premise of the argument for restriction, is the desire to preserve American culture a valid justification for immigration restriction? More generally, can one be justified in harmfully coercing others, solely because doing so is necessary to prevent those others from altering the culture of one's society? Miller is on plausible ground in maintaining that people have a strong interest in controlling their culture. But not everything in which one has an *interest* is something that one may, ethically, secure through harmful coercion of others, even if such coercion is required to protect one's interest. For instance, I have an interest in having my lawn mowed, but I may not force anyone to mow it, even if this is the only method I have available to secure the desired result. Even when one has a *right* to something, it is not always permissible to protect one's enjoyment of the right through coercion. Suppose that I am in need of a liver transplant, but there are no willing donors available. To preserve my life, I must take a liver by force from an unwilling donor. Even though I have both a strong interest in living and a right to life, this does not imply that I may coerce an unwilling donor.

Why, then, should we assume that our admittedly strong interest in preserving our culture entitles us to harmfully coerce others in the name of cultural preservation? Proponents of the cultural preservation argument have neglected this question. Two hypothetical examples, however, may help us to address it.

First, suppose that a number of your neighbors have been converting to Buddhism or selling their homes to Buddhists. Because of this, your neighborhood is in danger of being changed from a Christian to a Buddhist community. The Buddhists do not coercively interfere with your practice of your own religion, nor do they do anything else to violate your rights; still, you object to the transformation, because you would prefer to live among Christians. If you catch on to what is happening in the early stages, are you ethically entitled to use force to stop your neighborhood from becoming Buddhist? Consider a few ways in which you might go about this. You might forcibly interfere with your neighbors' practice of their religion. You could go to their houses, destroy their Buddha statues, and replace them with crucifixes. You could force your neighbors to attend Christian churches. You could forcibly expel all Buddhists from the neighborhood. Or you could forcibly prevent any Buddhists from moving in. All of these actions seem unacceptable. Hardly anyone would accept the suggestion that your interest in preserving a Christian neighborhood either negates or outweighs your neighbors' rights not to be harmfully coerced by you.

A society's dominant religion is an important part of its culture, though not the only important part. But similar intuitions can be elicited with respect to other aspects of culture. You may not forcibly prevent your neighbors from speaking different languages, wearing unusual clothes, listening to unfamiliar music, and so on. This suggests that the protection of one's interest in cultural preservation is not a sufficient justification for harmful coercion against others.

Second, consider another variant of the story of Marvin. Again, imagine that Sam has coercively prevented Marvin from reaching the local marketplace, where he would have bought food needed to sustain his life. His earlier justifications for his behavior having fallen flat, Sam mentions that he had yet another reason. Marvin practices very different traditions from most of the other people in the marketplace. For instance, he wears unusual clothing, belongs to a minority religion, speaks a different language from most others (though he is able to get along well enough to purchase food), and admires very different kinds of art. Sam became concerned that, if Marvin went to the marketplace and interacted with the people gathered there, he might influence the thinking and behavior of others in the marketplace. He might convert others to his religion, for example, or induce more people to speak his language. Because Sam did not want these things to happen, he decided to forcibly prevent Marvin from reaching the marketplace.

Sam had a real interest in preventing the sort of changes that Marvin might have induced. The question is whether this interest is of such a kind that it justifies the use of harmful coercion against innocent others to protect that interest. Intuitively, the answer is no. Sam's desire to be surrounded by people who think and behave in ways similar to himself does not overrule Marvin's right to be free from harmful coercion.

Is this case a fair analogy to the case of immigration restriction? One difference is that Marvin is only one person, and it seems unlikely that he could single-handedly bring about a drastic change in the culture of Sam's society. In contrast, if the United States were to open its borders, *millions* of people would come across, making drastic cultural change a much more realistic possibility.

This difference between the two cases would invalidate my argument, if the reason why Sam's action was impermissible were that Marvin would not in fact have had the effects that Sam feared. But this is not the case. In both of my examples, it should be stipulated that the agent's fears are realistic: in the first example, you have well-founded fears that your neighborhood is becoming Buddhist; in the second example, Sam had well-founded fears that Marvin would have a large impact on the other people in the marketplace. (Perhaps the marketplace is small enough that a single person can significantly influence it.) My contention, with regard to these examples, is not that the cultural change would not happen, but that the avoidance of cultural change does not seem an adequate justification for harmful coercion against innocent others. . . .

5. Conclusion

. . . Literally *millions* of lives are affected in a serious and long-term manner by immigration restrictions. Were these restrictions lifted, millions of people would see greatly expanded opportunities and would take the chance to drastically alter their lives for the better. This makes immigration law a strong candidate for the most harmful body of law in America today. In view of this, it is particularly troubling that these restrictions appear to have so little justification.

Notes

1. U.S. Department of Homeland Security, *Yearbook of Immigration Statistics: 2007,* http://www.dhs.gov/ximgtn/statistics/publications/yearbook.shtm (Washington, D.C.: U.S. Department of Homeland Security, Office of Immigration Statistics, 2008; accessed April 9, 2009), pp. 5, 95.
2. National Research Council, Panel on the Demographic and Economic Impacts of Immigration, *The New Americans: Economic, Demographic, and Fiscal Effects of Immigration,* ed. James P. Smith and Barry Edmonston (Washington, D.C.: National Academies Press, 1997), pp. 6–7.
3. The National Research Council (*The New Americans,* p. 10) estimated that a 10% increase in immigration would impose an increased annual fiscal burden of $15 to $20 per household on existing Americans. As the Congressional Budget Office reports, the most costly government services used by immigrants are public school education, health care, and law enforcement ("The Impact of Unauthorized Immigrants on the Budgets of State and Local Governments," http://www.cbo.gov/doc.cfm?index=8711 (Washington, D.C.: Congressional Budget Office, 2007; accessed April 9, 2009)).
4. National Research Council, *The New Americans,* p. 11.
5. David Miller, "Immigration: The Case for Limits," in Cohen and Wellman (eds.), *Contemporary Debates in Applied Ethics,* pp. 193–206, at pp. 200-201.

Study Questions

1. What is a prima facie rights violation?
2. According to Huemer, why is immigration restriction a prima facie rights violation?
3. According to Huemer, are all acts of coercion harmful?
4. Does Huemer agree that a state is justified in restricting the flow of immigration in order to preserve that state's distinctive culture?

C.

Injustice

Racisms

Kwame Anthony Appiah

Kwame Anthony Appiah, Professor of Philosophy at Princeton University, distinguishes three doctrines that might be called "racism." The first, which he terms *racialism*, is the view that we can group people according to certain inheritable characteristics, such as skin color. According to Appiah, racialism is morally neutral because it is merely a way to classify people. Nevertheless, racialism can be used to support two pernicious forms of racism, which Appiah terms *extrinsic racism* and *intrinsic racism*. Extrinsic racism holds that different races exhibit different moral traits, such as honesty or dishonesty, whereas intrinsic racism maintains that some races are by nature more valuable than others. Appiah concludes that racialism is false, and that both extrinsic and intrinsic racism are morally objectionable.

Racist Propositions

There are at least three distinct doctrines that might be held to express the theoretical content of what we call "racism." One is the view—which I shall call *racialism*—that there are heritable

From Kwame Anthony Appiah, "Racisms," in *Anatomy of Racism*, ed. David Goldberg (Minneapolis, MN: University of Minnesota Press, 1990).

characteristics, possessed by members of our species, that allow us to divide them into a small set of races, in such a way that all the members of these races share certain traits and tendencies with each other that they do not share with members of any other race. These traits and tendencies characteristic of a race constitute, on the racialist view, a sort of racial essence; and it is part of the content of racialism that the essential heritable characteristics of what the nineteenth century called the "Races of Man" account for more than the visible . . . characteristics—skin color, hair type, facial features—on the basis of which we make our informal classifications. Racialism is at the heart of nineteenth-century Western attempts to develop a science of racial difference. . . .

Racialism is not, in itself, a doctrine that must be dangerous, even if the racial essence is thought to entail moral and intellectual dispositions. Provided positive moral qualities are distributed across the races, each can be respected, can have its "separate but equal" place. Unlike most Western-educated people, I believe . . . that racialism is false; but by itself, it seems to be a cognitive rather than a moral problem. The issue is how the world is, not how we would want it to be.

Racialism is, however, a presupposition of other doctrines that have been called "racism," and these other doctrines have been, in the last few centuries, the basis of a great deal of human suffering and the source of a great deal of moral error.

One such doctrine we might call "extrinsic racism": extrinsic racists make moral distinctions between members of different races because they believe that the racial essence entails certain morally relevant qualities. The basis for the extrinsic racists' discrimination between people is their belief that members of different races differ in respects that *warrant* the differential treatment, respects—such as honesty or courage or intelligence—that are uncontroversially held (at least in most contemporary cultures) to be acceptable as a basis for treating people differently. Evidence that there are no such differences in morally relevant characteristics . . . should thus lead people out of their racism if it is purely extrinsic. As we know, such evidence often fails to change an extrinsic racist's attitudes substantially. . . . But at this point . . . what we have is no longer a false doctrine but a cognitive incapacity, one whose significance I shall discuss later in this essay.

I say that the *sincere* extrinsic racist may suffer from a cognitive incapacity. But some who espouse extrinsic racist doctrines are simply insincere intrinsic racists. For *intrinsic racists*, on my definition, are people who differentiate morally between members of different races because they believe that each race has a different moral status, quite independent of the moral characteristics entailed by its racial essence. Just as, for example, many people assume that the fact that they are biologically related to another person—a brother, an aunt, a cousin—gives them a moral interest in that person, so an intrinsic racist holds that the bare fact of being of the same race is a reason for preferring one person to another. (I shall return to this parallel later as well.)

For an intrinsic racist, no amount of evidence that a member of another race is capable of great moral, intellectual, or cultural achievements, or has characteristics that, in members of one's own race, would make them admirable or attractive, offers any ground for treating that person as he or she would treat similarly endowed members of his or her own race. Just so, some sexists are "intrinsic sexists," holding that the bare fact that someone is a woman (or man) is a reason for treating her (or him) in certain ways. . . .

Racist Dispositions

Most people will want to object already that this discussion of the propositional content of racist moral and factual beliefs misses something absolutely crucial to the character of the psychological and sociological reality of racism, something I touched on when I mentioned that extrinsic racist utterances are often made by people who suffer from what I called a "cognitive incapacity." Part of the standard force of accusations of racism is that their objects are in some way *irrational*. . . .

This cognitive incapacity is not, of course, a rare one. Many of us are unable to give up beliefs that play a part in justifying the special advantages we gain (or hope to gain) from our positions in the social order—in particular, beliefs about the positive characters of the class of people who share that position. Many people who express extrinsic racist beliefs . . . are beneficiaries of social orders that deliver advantages to them by virtue of their "race," so that their disinclination to accept evidence that would deprive them of a justification for those advantages is just an instance of this general phenomenon. . . .

The most interesting cases of this sort of ideological resistance to the truth are not, perhaps, the ones I have just mentioned. On the whole, it is less surprising, once we accept the admittedly problematic notion of self-deception, that people who think that certain attitudes or beliefs advantage them or those they care about should be able, as we say, to "persuade" themselves to ignore evidence that undermines those beliefs or attitudes. What is more interesting is the existence of people who resist the truth of a proposition while thinking that its wider acceptance would in no way disadvantage them or those individuals about whom they care . . . who resist the truth when they recognize that its acceptance would actually advantage them—this might be the case with some black people who have internalized negative racist stereotypes; or who fail, by virtue of their ideological attachments, to recognize what is in their own best interests at all.

My business here is not with the psychological or social processes by which these forms of ideological resistance operate, but it is important, I think, to see the refusal on the part of some extrinsic racists to accept evidence against the beliefs as an instance of a widespread phenomenon in human affairs. It is a plain fact, to which theories of ideology must address themselves, that our species is prone both morally and intellectually to such distortions of judgment, in particular to distortions of judgment that reflect partiality. An inability to change your mind in the face of appropriate evidence is a cognitive incapacity; but it is one that all of us surely suffer from in some areas of belief; especially in areas where our own interests or self-images are (or seem to be) at stake.

It is not, however, as some have held, a tendency that we are powerless to resist. No one, no doubt, can be impartial about everything—even about everything to which the notion of partiality applies; but there is no subject matter about which most sane people cannot, in the end, be persuaded to avoid partiality in judgment. And it may help to shake the convictions of those whose incapacity derives from this sort of ideological defense if we show them how their reaction fits into this general pattern. It is, indeed, because it generally *does* fit this pattern that we call such views "racism"—the suffix "-ism" indicating that what we have in mind is not simply a theory but an ideology. It would be odd to call someone brought up in a remote corner of the world with false and demeaning views about white people a "racist" if that person gave up these beliefs quite easily in the face of appropriate evidence.

Real live racists, then, exhibit a systematically distorted rationality, the kind of systematically distorted rationality that we are likely to call "ideological." And it is a distortion that is especially striking in the cognitive domain: extrinsic racists, as I said earlier, however intelligent or otherwise well informed, often fail to treat evidence against the theoretical propositions of extrinsic racism dispassionately. Like extrinsic racism, intrinsic racism can also often be seen as ideological . . . . What makes intrinsic racism similarly ideological is not so much the failure of inductive or deductive rationality that is so striking in someone . . . but rather the connection that it, like extrinsic racism, has with the interests—real or perceived—of the dominant group.

I propose to use the old-fashioned term "racial prejudice" in the rest of this essay to refer to the deformation of rationality in judgment that characterizes those whose racism is more than a theoretical attachment to certain propositions about race.

Racial Prejudice

It is hardly necessary to raise objections to what I am calling "racial prejudice"; someone who exhibits such deformations of rationality is plainly in trouble. But it is important to remember that propositional racists in a racist culture have false moral beliefs but may not suffer from racial prejudice. Once we show them how society has enforced extrinsic racist stereotypes, once we ask them whether they really believe that race in itself, independently of those extrinsic racist beliefs, justifies differential treatment, many will come to give up racist propositions, although we must remember how powerful a weight of authority our arguments have to overcome. Reasonable people may insist on substantial evidence if they are to give up beliefs that are central to their cultures.

Still in the end, many will resist such reasoning; and to the extent that their prejudices are really not subject to any kind of rational control, we may wonder whether it is right to treat such people as morally responsible for the acts their racial prejudice motivates, or morally reprehensible for holding the views to which their prejudice leads them. It is a bad thing that such people exist; they are, in a certain sense, bad people. But it is not clear to me that they are responsible for the fact that they are bad. Racial prejudice, like prejudice generally, may threaten an agent's autonomy, making it appropriate to treat or train rather than to reason with them.

But once someone has been offered evidence both (1) that their reasoning in a certain domain is distorted by prejudice, and (2) that the distortions conform to a pattern that suggests a lack of impartiality, they ought to take special care in articulating views and proposing policies in that domain. They ought to do so because, as I have already said, the phenomenon of partiality in judgment is well attested in human affairs. Even if you are not immediately persuaded that you are yourself a victim of such a distorted rationality in a certain domain, you should keep in mind always that this is the usual position of those who suffer from such prejudices. To the extent that this line of thought is not one that itself falls within the domain in question, one can be held responsible for not subjecting judgments that *are* within that domain to an especially extended scrutiny; and this is a fortiori true if the policies one is recommending are plainly of enormous consequence.

If it is clear that racial prejudice is regrettable, it is also clear in the nature of the case that providing even a superabundance of reasons and evidence will often not be a successful way of removing it. Nevertheless, the racist's prejudice will be articulated through the sorts of theoretical propositions I dubbed extrinsic and intrinsic racism. And we should certainly be able to say something reasonable about why these theoretical propositions should be rejected. . . .

Extrinsic and Intrinsic Racism

. . . Intrinsic racism is, in my view, a moral error. Even if racialism were correct, the bare fact that someone was of another race would be no reason to treat them worse—or better—than someone of my race. In our public lives, people are owed treatment independently of their biological characters: if they are to be differently treated there must be some morally relevant difference between them. In our private lives, we are morally free to have aesthetic preferences between people, but once our treatment of people raises moral issues, we may not make arbitrary distinctions. Using race in itself as a morally relevant distinction strikes most of us as obviously arbitrary. Without associated moral characteristics, why should race provide a better basis than hair color or height or timbre of voice? And if two people share all the properties morally relevant to some action we ought to do, it will be an error—a failure to apply the Kantian injunction to universalize our moral judgments—to use the bare facts of race as the basis for treating them differently. No one should deny that a common ancestry might, in particular cases, account for similarities in moral character. But then it would be the moral similarities that justified the different treatment.

It is presumably because most people . . . share the sense that intrinsic racism requires arbitrary distinctions that they are largely unwilling to express it in situations that invite moral criticism. But I do not know how I would argue with someone who was willing to announce an intrinsic racism as a basic moral idea; the best one can do, perhaps, is to provide objections to possible lines of defense of it.

Study Questions

1. According to Appiah, what is racialism?
2. How does Appiah distinguish *extrinsic* and *intrinsic* racism?
3. According to Appiah, why is extrinsic racism unjustifiable?
4. According to Appiah, why is intrinsic racism unjustifiable?

Sexism

Ann E. Cudd and Leslie E. Jones

Ann E. Cudd, Professor of Philosophy at Boston University, and Leslie E. Jones, a former doctoral student who worked with her at the University of Kansas, here explore sexism, that is, the systematic inequality between the sexes. They find sexism at three levels: in the explicit rules and implicit norms governing social institutions, so-called institutional sexism; in the interpersonal exchanges between persons that give rise to invidious sexual inequalities, so-called interpersonal sexism; and in psychological beliefs and tacit attitudes that sustain or create inequality between men and women, so-called unconscious sexism. Cudd and Jones conclude that morality demands we oppose sexism at all three levels.

. . . [W]hen we compare the life prospects of women and men, we find that a woman is far more likely to be poor, unhealthy, abused, and politically disenfranchised, even while she works longer hours and is largely responsible for the primary care of future generations.

Two general explanations could account for this remarkable disparity in life prospects: (1) women are by nature inferior to men, and so less worthy of concern or less able to benefit from equal concern, or (2) women are systematically disadvantaged by society. Under the first we include explanations based on psychology, biology, sociobiology, and so on that maintain that natural differences between men and women are sufficient to justify the comparatively sadder life prospects of women. . . .

In what follows we proceed on the assumption that the more plausible course is to take some version of the second as true. To follow

From Ann E. Cudd and Leslie E. Jones, "Sexism," in *A Companion to Applied Ethics,* eds. R. G. Frey and Christopher Heath Wellman (Malden, MA: Blackwell, 2003): 102–117.

this line in investigating the ways in which women are systematically disadvantaged is to investigate sexism. . . . We begin with a characterization of sexism. We turn then to the levels at which sexism conditions human social life, and discuss some paradigm examples of sexism. We then set out the two principal types of feminist theories of sexism. . . .

What Is Sexism?

. . . In its widest sense the term "sexism" can be used to refer to anything that creates, constitutes, promotes, sustains, or exploits an unjustifiable distinction between the sexes. . . . In this wide sense the term "sexism" (and its nominative "sexist") can be used to refer to any purported though mistaken difference between the sexes. This neutral descriptive use of the term, however, is deeply unsatisfactory. First, because the history of the term (brief as it is) shows it to have been intentionally modeled on "racism." As "racism" does not merely describe attempts to differentiate between races, but instead refers to pernicious distinctions between races, the term "sexism" is better understood as referring to pernicious distinctions between the sexes. Second, a neutral use of the term implicitly denies its conceptual role in binding together and illuminating the various faces of women's social difference, and the ways in which these differences are harmful. Again, just as racism is most accurately used to refer to various forms of oppression against non-Caucasians (at least in Western societies), in the more accurate and more specific sense with which we will be concerned here, "sexism" refers to a historically and globally pervasive form of oppression against women. It is this more specific and explicitly normative sense of sexism that is the subject of feminist inquiry. . . .

[T]here are many parallels between racism and sexism. For one thing, both are pervasive and have a high human cost. But, more importantly, the psychological mechanisms that make sexism and racism possible and desirable are similar: namely, our penchant for categorizing by social group, and making invidious distinctions between in-group and out-group members (Cudd, 1998). Furthermore, the social mechanisms that maintain sexism and racism are similar. Both sexism and racism are maintained through systematic violence and economic disadvantage. Both are difficult to pinpoint, but can be statistically documented and are much more readily perceived by the victims than by the respective dominant social groups. Both sexism and racism can have devastating psychological effects on individuals. And both inspire enormously powerful backlash when they are publicly challenged. . . .

If one holds, as we do, that sexism is pervasive, both historically and globally, then it will be no surprise that its ground will be both wide and deep. Institutions that are sexist will be both causes and effects of sexism. When regarded as a result of past sexism, such institutions will then carry on a tradition of, say, excluding women from available high-paying work. Managers and others who carry on this tradition may, of course, overtly maintain extrinsic sexism. They may sincerely, but falsely, believe women to be incapable of carrying on this work. This *intentional extrinsic sexism* should be distinguished from what might be called *individuated extrinsic sexism*, which maintains that while women (as a group) are capable of carrying on this work, no individual woman is. In either case it will be extremely difficult to persuasively establish such trenchant attitudes as sexist. In the latter case though women in general are held to be able to do this work, the technique of holding that each one now applying cannot do the job will effectively, if unintentionally, maintain the sexist tradition. Within that tradition such judgments are considered to be matters of keeping high standards, not sexism. As this practice requires an increasingly high degree of dubious judgment the longer it continues, over time it becomes correspondingly less reasonable to attribute to managers and others the sincere belief that women (as a group) are equally capable. In the case of intentional extrinsic sexism the fact that there are currently no or few women in the field contributes to the view that women cannot or do not want to do the work. The tradition of excluding women is, in this case, *intentional*. . . .

One important effect of the practice of excluding women in these ways is, of course, that women are made more dependent on others, usually men. By reducing the opportunities women have available to them, women are less able to clearly establish, both to themselves and to others, their general ability to accomplish high-paying (or high-status) tasks. Where these patterns are left unchallenged there is thus little to counter the claim that women are, by nature, more dependent. Moreover, these effects of sexist hiring practices are reinforced in a number of ways. They are reinforced by patterns of language which mark and delimit appropriate activities and attitudes on the basis of sex, and relegate the activities and attitudes of women to a lower status (i.e. sexist language). And they are reinforced by systems of education and enculturation which support, if not create and coerce, discrete proclivities for girls and boys, and relegate the proclivities of girls to a lower status. These social aspects of sexism are further mirrored in psychological dispositions, desires, and self-concepts. Accepting the activities, attitudes, and proclivities which are typically associated with men as "normal" or "standard" for human beings (i.e. the man standard) would render the activities, attitudes, and proclivities which are typically associated with women, when different, abnormal or substandard. For instance, women will appear "highly emotional" or "hysterical" when they display more emotion and concern than men, or "brooding" and "moody" when less. More pertinently, recognition of the man standard enables us to make as much sense as one can of the characterization of pregnancy as a form of illness or a temporary disability.

We stated earlier that sexism involves systematic inequality. Our discussion to this point has attempted to elucidate this notion. On our view sexism is a systematic, pervasive, but often subtle, force that maintains the oppression of women, and that is at work through institutional structures, in interpersonal interactions and the attitudes that are expressed in them, and in the cognitive, linguistic, and emotional processes of individual minds. In short, sexism structures our very experience of the world, and makes that world on the whole worse for women than for men.

Levels of Sexism

Sexism can be seen as a force responding to and molding human interactions. As a force, it can be seen, roughly, to operate at three levels: institutional sexism, which works on and through the level of social institutions; interpersonal sexism, which works on and through interactions among individuals who are not explicitly mediated by institutional structures; and unconscious sexism, which works at the personal level of the cognitive and affective processes of individuals. It is helpful to sort out these levels in order to explain why some charges of sexism are relatively uncontroversial, while others are difficult to see or evidence conclusively.

Institutional Sexism

Institutional sexism refers to invidious sexual inequalities in the explicit rules and implicit norms governing and structuring social institutions. Religious institutions provide a useful example of how explicit rules and implicit norms structure institutions. In the Catholic

Church, for instance, it is an explicit rule that all priests are men and all nuns are women. Only priests can run the church hierarchy, and priests outrank nuns in most decision-making situations. While it is clear how explicit rules can govern and structure institutions, this example can also help us to see that implicit norms also structure Catholic experience and create sexual inequality. While it is no longer widely accepted as an explicit rule that in heterosexual marriage the man is the head of the household and the woman is the helpmeet, it is implied by the relative rank of priests and nuns in the church and by its sacred writings. This implicit norm positions men above women in marriage (as in all other social institutions in which both sexes are present), clearly an invidious sexual inequality. In addition to the more explicitly rule-governed institutions of government, religion, family, health care, and education, there are crucially important informally or implicitly structured institutions prime among them being language, and the sites of cultural and artistic production. . . .

Interpersonal Sexism

Whereas institutional sexism involves the explicit rules and their implicit norms that sustain oppressive social institutions, interpersonal sexism involves interactions between persons that are not governed by explicit rules. Interpersonal sexism comprises actions and other expressions between persons that create, constitute, promote, sustain, and/or exploit invidious sexual inequalities.

The person who is acting in a sexist way or making a sexist expression need not intend sexism; there are intentional and unintentional forms of interpersonal sexism. Here are some examples from our experiences:

- As a child, the girl is not allowed the free play of her brothers; she is prevented by her parents and teachers from engaging in rough-and-tumble play, not included in activities involving building, transportation, etc., not encouraged to try or expected to succeed at sports, mathematics, or leadership activities, and required, unlike her brothers, to do domestic chores.
- In school the teachers require her to speak less and restrain her behavior more than boys. Teachers reward her with better grades for her passivity, but boys exclude her from their games and begin to take the superior attitudes of their fathers.
- In sports she sees males and manhood extolled, females and womanhood ridiculed. Coaches and team-mates insult male

athletes by calling them "woman" or "girl," and praise them with the term "man."

- When a man and a woman negotiate a car loan or a home loan, or buy an expensive machine, the salesperson speaks only to the man. Supermarket ads are aimed, meanwhile, at women as housewives.
- In conversations between colleagues men are routinely deferred to while women's remarks are ignored. When a male colleague repeats what a female has said, he is complimented for his good idea.

Sexism is a key motif that unifies this otherwise seemingly disparate set of personal experiences. . . . For society's ground of legitimacy seems to require that injustice be recognized and socially opposed. Yet the injustice of sexism is built into the very fabric of everyone's everyday experiences from infancy on.

Unconscious Sexism

"Unconscious sexism" refers to the psychological mechanisms and tacit beliefs, emotions, and attitudes that create, constitute, promote, sustain, and/or exploit invidious sexual inequalities. This category will be denied by many as vague, unprovable, or too easily invoked. But there are both conceptual and empirical arguments in favor of its existence. The conceptual argument is that the statistical evidence concerning the lesser lives that women live would be completely puzzling given the legal guarantees of equality for men and women in many countries were it not for the possibility of such unconscious sexism. Institutional and interpersonal sexism cannot alone account for all the data. That implies that there are unconscious attitudes and beliefs that allow persons in positions of power unconsciously to prefer men to women when social rewards are distributed, and yet not to see themselves or be seen as applying sexist standards.

The empirical argument is widely diffused, but accessible. It consists first of all in evidence for the existence of unconscious motivations, which is vast in the psychological literature. Second, there is evidence that when the same work is attributed to a woman it is judged of less value than when attributed to a man (Valian, 1998). Third, there is evidence that women find it more painful to think of themselves as oppressed, and men find it more painful to think of themselves as the privileged gender. Thus, there is motivation for neither women nor men to think of women as oppressed and men as dominant (Branscombe, 1998). Fourth, there is a great deal of evidence from social cognitive psychology to suggest that persons make invidious distinctions among salient social categories, that we tend to amplify them well beyond the real differences between individuals in those categories, and that sex is one of those categories (Tajfel, 1981). Now since it surely cannot be argued that men get the worse end of this deal, this fact constitutes evidence for the claim that such cognitive processes tend to create unconscious sexist attitudes and beliefs. There is, no doubt, a great deal more evidence that could be cited, but this much should be sufficient to make the point that unconscious sexism is a real, documented, psychological phenomenon.

Having demonstrated its reality, however, some discussion and examples will be helpful to see how unconscious sexism is manifested and how one might go about discovering it. The key to recognizing unconscious motivations, especially unsavory ones that persons are reluctant to acknowledge in themselves, is to look for decisions or actions that could not be justified by a reasonable assessment of the available evidence. What counts as "reasonable" and "available" are crucial issues here, of course. By "reasonable" we mean consistent with one's other explicitly held beliefs and widely shared, non-sexist, knowledge in the community. We insist on explicit beliefs here because, of course, if one has tacit sexist beliefs the action could be reasonable but sexist, and yet not counted as unconscious. By "available evidence" we are referring to reports that would be made by a member of the community who does not have sexist beliefs or attitudes, or whose sexist beliefs played no role in the reports, or to widely shared, non-sexist, knowledge in the community. Of course, there may be no non-sexist members of any community. The practices of sexism affect one's self-conception. Internal critique may not be enough to free oneself from identification with those practices. But we must begin to identify sexist practices somewhere. Granting that it is possible that we will not recognize all unconscious (or, indeed, all conscious) sexism, we can still begin by finding the more obvious cases. Consider the following examples:

- A philosophy department is looking to hire a new faculty member. One-third of the applicants are women. One-third of the interview list is made up of women. In the interviews the women are judged as doing worse than the men. The comments afterwards are that they don't seem "as polished" or "professional" as the men. The fact is that the women do not meet the interviewers' expectations of what a philosopher or a faculty member is supposed to look like, a stereotype that includes being a man. . . .

- A drug is being tested for its effectiveness in preventing heart disease. All the research subjects are men. When asked to account for this the research team leader responds that women's hormones would interfere with the study. While it is surely true that the drug could affect women differently from men as a result of female hormones, it is equally true that it could affect men differently from women as a result of male hormones. This symmetry is lost on the research team, who, like most of us, tend to think of women as the ones with the "interfering" or abnormal hormones.

Unconscious sexism often seems to be innocent, in the sense that the beliefs or feelings that make it up are never voiced, and often based on widely shared stereotypes. Whether or not it is innocent surely depends on the degree to which the individual has access to information that counters the unconscious sexist beliefs and attitudes, a condition that depends on larger social factors. Although we do believe that "sexism" names not only a mistake but a prima facie wrong, there are cases where one can commit this wrong and yet not be culpable.

These levels of sexism are, of course, interrelated. Understood as institutional discrimination, sexism concerns the interactions between men and women only as symptoms of a more pervasive problem. Social institutions guide, and on some accounts cause, our interpersonal attitudes. Our self-conceptions and our conception of others are at least partially a product of the social structures through which we interact with one another. How they are interrelated is a central question within feminism, feminist philosophy, and feminist social science. Different ways of understanding the interrelations between these levels result in different, and sometimes quite divergent, accounts. Two types of account are prominent in the feminist literature. In the next section we discuss these two types.

Two Feminist Views of Sexism

Though feminists agree that sexism structures our very experience of the world, feminist theories of sexism vary considerably. Nonetheless, they can be very roughly divided into two categories. First, what can be labeled "equality feminism" maintains that social institutions are the primary medium of sexism. Men and women do not differ markedly in their potential capacities, interests, and abilities. Given similar training, men and women would develop fairly similar talents, at least as similar as those between men or between women.

Thus if we are to transform society it will require that we resist and undermine those institutions that enforce sex differences and disproportionately deprive women of opportunities to develop highly valued social skills. Equality feminists need not accept what we have above called "the man standard." Rather, most contemporary equality feminists employ measures of social value such as utility, respect for human rights, or hypothetical agreement in order to develop gender-neutral standards by which to judge the opportunities, activities, and proclivities of men and women.

Alternatively, "difference feminists" maintain that unconscious desires are the primary medium of sexism. Accordingly, social institutions are the result, rather than the cause, of sexism. Recently a variety of feminists holding this view have attempted to both articulate the differences between men and women and re-evaluate equality feminism. Some . . . have argued that women's "different voice" involves a greater emphasis on responsiveness, caring, and the maintenance of particular, concrete relationships. This voice is undervalued in society, they argue, because of the dominance of "responsibility"—a notion which involves a strict adherence to principle and which, they argue, typifies the male point of view. Others skeptical of gender neutrality are also skeptical of the idea that caring and relationship maintenance best characterize women's difference. They thus seek to identify a different difference. . . .

Both views aim to transform institutional sexism, interpersonal sexism, and unconscious sexism. They differ, however, over just what form such a transformation would take. For equality feminists the notion that there is a significant difference between men and women, a difference that makes a difference, seems more likely to sustain the global disparity existing between men and women since this disparity has been built on the basis of sex differentiation. For difference feminists, on the other hand, the notion that there is no significant difference between men and women, seems likely to undermine women's emancipation. Since women have been defined and have defined themselves in relation to men, as subordinate to dominant, women's independence depends on discovering, or perhaps imaginatively inventing, a different identity. Importantly, both equality feminists and difference feminists have the same worry. For both, the idea that an attempted transformation of society will result in a mere modification of sexism rather than its elimination is, given its evident though under-acknowledged depth and pervasiveness, a predominant, reasonable, and clearly practical concern. . . .

In conclusion, sexism is alive and well in contemporary Western society, and to an even greater degree in much of the rest of the world. Sexism is a serious form of oppression, and, as such, it is incumbent on decent people to oppose it, though the form that opposition should take remains a serious matter for theorists and activists alike.

References

Branscombe, N. (1998) Thinking About One's Gender Group's Privileges or Disadvantages: Consequences for Well-Being in Women and Men. *British Journal of Social Psychology*, 37: 167–84.

Cudd, A. E. (1998) Psychological Explanations of Oppression. In C. Willett (ed.), *Theorizing Multiculturalism*. Malden, MA: Blackwell.

Tajfel, H. (1981) *Human Groups and Social Categories*. Cambridge: Cambridge University Press.

Valian, V. (1998) *Why So Slow? The Advancement of Women*. Cambridge, MA: MIT Press.

Study Questions

1. What do Cudd and Jones mean by *sexism?*
2. Is sexism implicit in any claim of differences between men and women?
3. Does the structure of sexism differ from the structure of racism?
4. How would we know if we were making progress in combatting sexism?

Five Faces of Oppression

Iris Marion Young

Iris Marion Young (1949–2006) was Professor of Political Science at the University of Chicago. She explores the concept of oppression and argues that various groups in American society have been subject to exploitation, marginalization, powerlessness, cultural imperialism, and violence. She claims that many groups are oppressed in several of these ways, and some have experienced them all. Young concludes that her analysis makes possible comparisons as to which groups have been more oppressed than others.

Politics is partly a struggle over the language people use to describe social and political experience. Most people in the United States would not use the term "oppression" to name injustice in this society. For a minority of Americans, on the other hand—such as socialists, radical feminists, American Indian activists, black activists, gay and lesbian activists, and others identifying with new left social movements of the 1960s and '70s—oppression is a central category of political discourse. Speaking the political language in which oppression is a central word involves adopting a whole mode of analyzing and evaluating social structures and practices that is quite incommensurate with the language of liberal individualism that dominates political discourse in the United States.

Consequently, those of us who identify with at least one of the movements I have named have a major political project: we must persuade people that the discourse of oppression makes sense of much of our social experience. We are ill prepared for this task, however, if we have no clear account of the meaning of the concept of oppression.

From Iris Marion Young, "Five Faces of Oppression," *The Philosophical Forum* 6 (1988).

While we commonly find the term used in the diverse philosophical and theoretical literature spawned by radical social movements in the United States, we find little direct discussion of the meaning of the concept of oppression as used by these movements.

In this chapter I offer some explication of the concept as I understand its use by new social movements in the United States since the 1960s. I offer you an explication of this concept, an unfolding of its meaning. I do not think the concept of oppression can be strictly defined, that is, corralled within one clear boundary. There is no attribute or set of attributes that all oppressed people have in common.

In the following account of oppression I reflect on the situation and experience of those groups said by new left social movements to be oppressed in U.S. society: at least women, blacks, Chicanos, Puerto Ricans, and most other Spanish-speaking Americans, Native Americans, Jews, lesbians, gay men, Arabs, Asians, old people, working-class people, poor people, and physically or mentally disabled people.

Obviously, these groups are not oppressed to the same degree or in the same ways. In the most general sense, all oppressed people share some inhibition of their ability to develop and exercise their capacities and express their needs, thoughts, and feelings. Nevertheless, reflection on the concrete uses of the term "oppression" in radical political discourse convinces me that the term refers to several distinct structures or situations. I label these with five disparate categories: exploitation, marginality, powerlessness, cultural imperialism, and violence. . . .

Exploitation

The central function of Marx's theory of exploitation is to explain how class structure can exist in the absence of legally and normatively sanctioned class distinctions. In precapitalist societies domination is overt and carried on through direct political means. In both slave society and feudal society the right to appropriate the product of the labor of others partly defines class privilege, and these societies legitimate class distinctions with ideologies of natural superiority and inferiority.

Capitalist society, on the other hand, removes traditional juridically enforced class distinctions and promotes a belief in the legal freedom of persons. Workers freely contract with employers, receive a wage, and no formal mechanisms of law or custom force them to work for that employer or any employer. Thus, the mystery of capitalism arises: when everyone is formally free, how can there be class domination?

Why does there continue to be class distinction between the wealthy, who own the means of production, and the mass of people, who work for them? The theory of exploitation answers this question.

Profit, the basis of capitalist power and wealth, is a mystery if we assume that in the market goods exchange at their values. Marx's use of the labor theory of value, however, dispels this mystery. Every commodity's value is a function of the labor time necessary for the production of labor power. Labor power is the one commodity that in the process of being consumed produces new value. Profit then comes from the difference between the actual labor and the value of that capacity to labor that the capitalist purchases and puts to work. The owner of capital appropriates this surplus value, which accounts for the possibility of realizing a profit. . . .

The central insight expressed with the concept of exploitation, then, is that domination occurs through a steady process of the transfer of the results of the labor of some people to benefit others. The injustice of class division does not consist only in the fact that some people have great wealth while most people have little and some are severely deprived.[1] The theory of exploitation shows that this relation of power and inequality is produced and reproduced through a systematic process in which the energies of the have-nots are continuously expended to maintain and augment the power, status, and wealth of the haves.

Many writers have cogently argued that the Marxian concept of exploitation is too narrow to encompass all forms of domination and oppression.[2] In particular, by confining itself to examining class domination and oppression, the Marxist concept of exploitation does not contribute to an understanding of such group oppressions as sexism and racism. The question, then, is whether the concept of exploitation can be broadened to include other ways that the labor and energy expenditure of one group benefits another, thus reproducing a relation of domination between them.

Feminists have had little difficulty showing that women's oppression consists partly in a systematic and unreciprocated transfer of powers from women to men. Women's oppression consists not merely in an inequality of status, power, and wealth resulting from men's excluding women from privileged activities. The freedom, power, status, and self-realization of men is possible precisely because women work for them. Gender exploitation has two aspects, transfer of the fruits of material labor to men, and the transfer of nurturing and sexual energies to men.

. . . Thus, for example, in most systems of agricultural production in the world, men take to market goods women have produced, and more often than not men receive the status and often the entire income from this labor. . . .

Most feminist theories of gender exploitation have concentrated on the institutional structure of the patriarchal family. Recently, however, feminists have begun to theorize relations of gender exploitation enacted in the contemporary workplace and through the state. Carol Brown argues that as men have removed themselves from responsibility for children, many women have become dependent on the state for subsistence as they continue to bear nearly total responsibility for child rearing.[3] This creates a new system of the exploitation of women's domestic labor mediated by those state institutions, which she calls public patriarchy.

In twentieth-century capitalist economies, the workplaces that women have been entering in increasing numbers serve as another important site of gender exploitation. David Alexander argues that most typically feminine jobs have gender tasks involving sexual labor, nurturing, caring for a person's body, or smoothing over relations through personality.[4] In these ways, women's energies are expended in workplaces that enhance the status of, please, or comfort others, usually men; and these gender-based labors of waitresses, clerical workers, nurses, and other caretakers often go unnoticed and undercompensated.

To summarize, women are exploited in the Marxian sense to the degree that they are wage workers. Some have argued that women's domestic labor is also a form of capitalist class exploitation insofar as it is labor covered by the wages a family receives. As a class, however, women undergo specific forms of gender exploitation—ways the energies and power of women are expended, often unnoticed and unacknowledged, usually to benefit men by releasing them for more important and creative work, enhancing their status or the environment around them, or providing men with sexual or emotional service.

Race is a structure of oppression at least as basic as class or gender. Are there, then, racially specific forms of exploitation? This is different from the question of whether racial groups are subjected to intense capitalist exploitation. Racial groups in the United States, especially blacks and Latinos, are oppressed through capitalist superexploitation resulting from a segmented labor market that tends to reserve skilled, high-paying, unionized jobs for whites. . . .

However one answers the question about capitalist superexploitation of racial groups, is it also possible to conceptualize a form of exploitation that is racially specific on analogy with the gender-specific forms I have discussed? The category of *menial* labor might provide an opening for such conceptualization. In its derivation "menial" means the labor of servants. Wherever there is racism, including the United States today, there is the assumption, more or less enforced, that members of the oppressed racial groups are or ought to be servants of those, or some of those, in the privileged group. In white racist societies this generally means that many white people have dark- or yellow-skinned domestic servants, and in the United States today there remains significant race structuring of private household service.

In the United States today much service labor has gone public: anybody can have servants if they go to a good hotel, a good restaurant, or hire a cleaning service. Servants often attend the daily—and nightly—activities of business executives, government officials, and other high-status professionals. In our society there remains strong cultural pressure to fill servant jobs—like bell hop, porter, chamber maid, bus boy, and so on—with black and Latin workers. These jobs entail a transfer of energies whereby the servers enhance the status of the served, to place them in an aristocracy—the rule of the best.

Menial labor today refers to more than service, however; it refers to any servile, unskilled, low-paying work lacking in autonomy, and in which a person is subject to orders from several people. Menial work tends to be auxiliary work, instrumental to another person's work, in which that other person receives primary recognition for doing the job. Laborers on a construction site, for example, are at the beck and call of welders, electricians, carpenters, and other skilled workers, who receive recognition for the job done. In the history of the United States, explicit racial discrimination reserved menial work for blacks, Chicanos, American Indians, and Chinese, and menial work still tends to be linked to black and Latino workers. I offer this category of menial labor as a form of racially specific exploitation, only as a proposal, however, that needs discussion.

Marginalization

Increasingly in the United States, racial oppression occurs more in the form of marginalization than exploitation. Marginals are people the system of labor markets cannot or will not employ. Not only in Third World capitalist countries, but also in most Western capitalist societies, there is a growing underclass of people permanently confined to lives of social marginality, the majority of whom are racially marked—blacks or Indians in Latin America, blacks, East Indians, Eastern Europeans, or North Africans in Europe.

Marginalization is by no means the fate only of racially marked groups, however. In the United States a shamefully large proportion of the population is marginal: old people, and increasingly people who are not very old but get laid off from their jobs and cannot find new work; young people, especially black or Latino, who cannot find first or second jobs; many single mothers and their children; other people involuntarily unemployed; many mentally or physically disabled people; and American Indians, especially those on reservations.

Marginalization is perhaps the most dangerous form of oppression. A whole category of people is expelled from useful participation in social life, then potentially subject to severe material deprivation and even extermination. The material deprivation marginalization often causes certainly is unjust, especially in a society in which others have plenty. Contemporary advanced capitalist societies in principle have acknowledged the injustice of material deprivation caused by marginalization, and have taken some steps to address it by providing welfare payments and services. The continuance of this welfare state is by no means assured, and in most welfare-state societies, especially the United States, benefits are not sufficient to eliminate large-scale suffering and deprivation.

Material deprivation, which can be addressed by redistributive social policies, is not, however, the extent of the harm caused by marginalization. Two categories of injustice beyond distribution are associated with marginality in advanced capitalist societies. The provision of welfare itself produces new injustice when it deprives dependent persons of rights and freedoms that others have. If justice requires that every person has the opportunity to develop and exercise his or her capacities, finally, then marginalization is unjust primarily because it blocks such opportunity to exercise capacities in socially defined and recognized ways. . . .

In our own society the exclusion of dependent persons from equal citizenship rights is only barely hidden beneath the surface. Because they are dependent on bureaucratic institutions for support or services, old people, poor people, and mentally or physically disabled people are subject to patronizing, punitive, demeaning, and arbitrary treatment by the policies and people associated with welfare bureaucracies. Being a dependent in this society implies being legitimately subject to often arbitrary and invasive authority of social service providers and other public and private bureaucrats, who enforce rules with which the marginal must comply, and otherwise exercise power over the conditions of his or her life. In meeting needs of the marginalized, with the aid of social scientific disciplines, the welfare agencies also construct the needs themselves. Medical and social service professionals know what is good for those they serve, and the marginals and dependents themselves do not have the right to claim to know what is good for them. Dependency thus implies in this society . . . a sufficient condition to suspend rights to privacy, respect, and individual choice.

Although dependency thus produces conditions of injustice in our society, dependency in itself should not and need not be oppressive. We cannot imagine a society in which some people would not need to be dependent on others at least some of the time: children, sick people, women recovering from childbirth, old people who have become frail, and depressed or otherwise emotionally needy persons have the moral right to be dependent on others for subsistence and support. . . .

Marginalization does not cease to be oppressive when one has shelter and food. Many old people, for example, have sufficient means to live comfortably but remain oppressed in their marginal status. Even if marginals were provided a comfortable material life within institutions that respected their freedom and dignity, injustices of marginality would remain in the form of uselessness, boredom, and lack of self-respect. Most of this society's productive and recognized activities take place in contexts of organized social cooperation, and social structures and processes that close persons out of participation in such social cooperation are unjust.

The fact of marginalization raises basic structural issues of justice. In particular, we must consider what is just about a connection between participation in productive activities of social cooperation, on the one hand, and acquisition of the means of consumption, on the other. As marginalization is increasing, with no sign of abatement, some social policy analysts have introduced the idea of a "social wage" as a socially provided, guaranteed income not tied to the wage system. Restructuring activities of production and service provision to ensure that everyone able and willing has socially recognized work to do, moreover, also implies organization of socially productive activity at least partly outside of a wage system.[5]

Powerlessness

As I have indicated, the Marxian idea of class is important because it helps reveal the structure of exploitation: that some people have their power and wealth because they profit from the labor of others. For this reason I reject the claim of some that a traditional class exploitation model fails to capture the structure of contemporary society. It is still the case that the labor of most people in the society augments the power of a few; whatever their differences from nonprofessional workers, most professional workers share with them not being members of the capitalist class.

An adequate conception of oppression, however, cannot ignore the experience of social division colloquially referred to as the difference between the "middle class" and the "working class," a division structured by the social division of labor between professionals and nonprofessionals. Rather than expanding or revising the Marxian concept of class to take account of this experience, as some writers do, I suggest that we . . . describe this as a difference in *status* rather than class. Being a professional entails occupying a status position that nonprofessionals lack, creating a condition of oppression that nonprofessionals suffer. I shall call this kind of oppression "powerlessness."

The absence of genuine democracy in the United States means that most people do not participate in making decisions that regularly affect the conditions of their lives and actions. In this sense most people lack significant power. Powerlessness, however, describes the lives of people who have little or no work autonomy, exercise little creativity or judgment in their work, have no technical expertise or authority, express themselves awkwardly, especially in public or bureaucratic settings, and do not command respect. . . .

The clearest way for me to think of this powerless status is negatively: the powerless lack the status and sense of self that professionals tend to have. There are three aspects of status privilege that professionals have, the lack of which produces oppression for nonprofessionals.

First, acquiring and practicing a profession has an expansive, progressive character. Being professional usually requires a college education and learning a specialized knowledge that entails working with symbols and concepts. In acquiring one's profession, a person experiences progress in learning the necessary expertise, and usually when one begins practicing one enters a career, that is, a working life of growth or progress in professional development. The life of the nonprofessional by comparison is powerless in the sense that it lacks this orientation toward the progressive development of one's capacities.

Second, while most professionals have supervisors and do not have power to affect many decisions or the action of very many people, most nevertheless have considerable day-to-day work autonomy. Professionals usually have some authority over others, moreover, either over workers they supervise or over auxiliaries or clients. Nonprofessionals, on the other hand, lack autonomy, and both in their working lives and in their consumer-client lives, they often stand under the authority of professionals.

Though having its material basis in a division of labor between mental and manual work, the group division between middle class and working class designates not a division only in working life, but also in nearly all aspects of social life. Professionals and nonprofessionals belong to different cultures in the United States. The two groups tend to live in segregated neighborhoods or even different towns, not least because of the actions and decisions of real estate people. They tend to have different tastes in food, decor, clothes, music, and vacations. Members of the two groups socialize for the most part with others in the same status group. While there is some intergroup mobility between generations, for the most part the children of professionals become professionals and the children of nonprofessionals do not.

Thus, third, the privileges of the professional extend beyond the workplace to elevate a whole way of life, which consists in being "respectable." To treat someone with respect is to be prepared to listen to what they have to say or to do what they request because they have some authority, expertise, or influence.

The norms of respectability in our society are associated specifically with professional culture. Professional dress, speech, tastes, and demeanor all connote respectability. Generally professionals expect and receive respect from others. In restaurants, banks, hotels, real estate offices, and many other such public places, professionals typically receive more respectful treatment than nonprofessionals. For this reason nonprofessionals seeking a loan or a job, or to buy a house or a car, will often try to look "professional" and "respectable" in these settings. The privilege of this professional respectability starkly appears in the dynamics of racism and sexism. In daily interchange women and men of color must prove their respectability. At first they are often not treated by strangers with respectful distance or deference. Once people discover that this woman or that Puerto Rican man is a college teacher or a business executive, however, people often behave more respectfully toward her or him. Working class white men, on the other hand, are often treated with respect until their working class status is revealed.

Cultural Imperialism

Exploitation, marginality, and powerlessness all refer to relations of power and oppression that occur by virtue of the social division of labor: who works for whom, who does not work, and how the content of work in one position is defined in relation to others. These three categories refer to the structural and institutional relations that delimit people's material lives, including but not limited to the resources they have access to, the concrete opportunity they have or do not have to develop and exercise capacities in involving, socially recognized ways that enhance rather than diminish their lives. These kinds of oppression are a matter of concrete power in relation to others, who benefits from whom, and who is dispensable.

Recent theorists of movements of group liberation, especially feminists and black liberation theorists, have also given prominence to a rather different experience of oppression, which I shall call cultural imperialism. This is the experience of existing in a society whose dominant meanings render the particular perspectives and point of view of one's own group invisible at the same time as they stereotype one's group and mark it out as "other."

Cultural imperialism consists in the universalization of one group's experience and culture and its establishment as the norm. Some groups have exclusive or primary access to . . . the means of interpretation and communication in a society. As a result, the dominant cultural products of the society, that is, those most widely disseminated, express the experience, values, goals, and achievements of the groups that produce them. The cultural products also express their perspective on and interpretation of events and elements in the society, including the other groups in the society, insofar as they are noticed at all. Often without noticing they do so, the dominant groups project their own experience as representative of humanity as such.

An encounter with groups different from the dominant group, however, challenges its claim to universality. The dominant group saves its position by bringing the other group under the measure of its dominant norms. Consequently, the difference of women from men, Native Americans or Africans from Europeans, Jews from Christians, homosexuals from heterosexuals, or workers from professionals becomes reconstructed as deviance and inferiority. The dominant groups and their cultural expressions are the normal, the universal, and thereby unremarkable. Since the dominant group's cultural expressions are the only expressions that receive wide dissemination, the dominant groups construct the differences that some groups exhibit as lack and negation in relation to the norms, and those groups become marked out as "other."

Victims of cultural imperialism experience a paradoxical oppression in that they are both marked out by stereotypes and rendered invisible. As remarkable, deviant beings, the culturally dominated are stamped with an essence. In contrast, the privileged are indefinable because they are individual; each is whatever he or she wants to be, they are what they do, and by their doings they are judged. The stereotype marks and defines the culturally dominated, confines them to a nature that is usually attached in some way to their bodies, and thus that cannot easily be denied. These stereotypes so permeate the society that they are not noticed as contestable. Just as everyone knows that the earth goes around the sun, so everyone knows that gay people are promiscuous, that Indians are alcoholics, and that women are good with children.

Those living under cultural imperialism find themselves defined from the outside, positioned, and placed by a system of dominant meanings they experience as arising from elsewhere, from those with whom they do not identify and who do not identify with them. The dominant culture's stereotyped, marked, and inferiorized images of the group must be internalized by group members at least to the degree that they are forced to react to behaviors of others that express or are influenced by those images. This creates for the culturally oppressed the experience that W. E. B. DuBois called "double consciousness." "This sense of always looking at one's self through the eyes of others, of measuring one's soul by the tape of a world that looks on in amused contempt and pity."[6] This consciousness is double because the oppressed subject refuses to coincide with these devalued, objectified, stereotyped visions of herself or himself. The subject desires recognition as human, capable of activity, full of hope and possibility, but receives from the dominant culture only the judgment that he or she is different, marked, or inferior.

People in culturally oppressed groups often maintain a sense of positive subjectivity because they can affirm and recognize one another as sharing similar experiences and perspectives on social life.

The group defined by the dominant culture as deviant, as a stereotyped other, *is* culturally different from the dominant group because the status of otherness creates specific experiences not shared by the dominant group and because culturally oppressed groups also are often socially segregated and occupy specific positions in the social division of labor. They express their specific group experiences and interpretations of the world to one another, developing and perpetuating their own culture. Double consciousness, then, occurs because one finds one's being defined by two cultures: a dominant and a subordinate culture.

Cultural imperialism involves the paradox of experiencing oneself as invisible at the same time that one is marked out and noticed as different. The perspectives of other groups dominate the culture without their noticing it as a perspective, and their cultural expressions are widely disseminated. These dominant cultural expressions often simply pay no attention to the existence and experience of those other groups, only to mention or refer to them in stereotyped or marginalized ways. This, then, is the injustice of cultural imperialism: that the oppressed group's experience and interpretation of social life finds no expression that touches the dominant culture, while that same culture imposes on the oppressed group its experience and interpretations of social life.

Violence

Finally, many groups suffer the oppression of systematic and legitimized violence. The members of some groups live with the fear of random, unprovoked attacks on their persons or property, which have no motive but to damage, humiliate, or destroy them. In U.S. society women, blacks, Asians, Arabs, gay men, and lesbians live under such threats of violence, and in at least some regions Jews, Puerto Ricans, Chicanos, and other Spanish-speaking Americans must fear such violence as well. Violation may also take the form of name-calling or petty harassment intended to degrade or humiliate, and always signals an underlying threat of physical attack.

Such violence is systematic because it is directed at any member of the group simply because he or she is a member of that group. Any woman, for example, has reason to fear rape. The violence to which these oppressed groups are subject, moreover, is usually legitimate in the sense that most people regard it as unsurprising, and so it usually goes unpunished. Police beatings or killings of black youths, for example, are rarely publicized, rarely provoke moral outrage on the part of most white people, and rarely receive punishment.

An important aspect of the kind of random but systematic violence I am referring to here is its utter irrationality. Xenophobic violence is different from the violence of state or ruling-class repression. Repressive violence has a rational, though evil, motive: rulers use it as a coercive tool to maintain their power. Many accounts of racist, sexist, or homophobic violence try to explain it as motivated by a desire to maintain group privilege or domination. I agree that fear of violence functions to help keep these oppressed groups subordinate. I think the causes of such violence must be traced to unconscious structures of identity formation that project onto some groups the fluid, bodily aspect of the subject that threatens the rigid unity of that identity.

Conclusion

The five faces of oppression that I have explicated here function as criteria of oppression, not as a full theoretical account of oppression. With them we can tell whether a group is oppressed, according to objective social structures and behaviors. Being subject to any one of these five conditions is sufficient for calling a group oppressed. Most of the groups I listed earlier as oppressed in U.S. society experience more than one of these forms, and some experience all five.

Nearly all, if not all, groups said by contemporary social movements to be oppressed in our society suffer cultural imperialism. Which other oppressions are experienced by which groups, however, is quite variable. Working class people are exploited and powerless, for example, but if employed and white do not experience marginalization and violence. Gay men, on the other hand, are not *qua* gay exploited or powerless, but they experience severe cultural imperialism and violence. Similarly, Jews and Arabs as groups are victims of cultural imperialism and violence, though many members of these groups also suffer exploitation or powerlessness. Old people are oppressed by marginalization and cultural imperialism, and this is also true of physically or mentally disabled people. As a group women are subject to gender-based exploitation, powerlessness, cultural imperialism, and violence. Racism in the United States associates blacks and Latinos with marginalization, even though many members of these groups escape that condition; members of these groups often suffer all five forms of oppression.

With these criteria I have specifically avoided defining structures and kinds of oppression according to the groups oppressed: racism, classism, sexism, hetero-sexism, ageism. The forms of group oppression these terms name are not homologous, and the five criteria can help describe how and why not. The five criteria also help show that while no group oppression is reducible to or explained by any other group oppression, the oppression of one group is not a closed system with its own attributes, but overlaps with the oppression of other groups. With these criteria, moreover, we can claim that one group is more oppressed than another, insofar as it is subject to more of these five conditions, without thereby theoretically privileging a particular form of oppression or one oppressed group.

Are there any connections among these five forms of oppression? Why are particular groups subject to various combinations of them? The answers to these questions are beyond the scope of this chapter. My project here is analytical and descriptive, not explanatory. Answering these questions is important to the theoretical project of understanding oppression. I believe they cannot be answered by an *a priori* account, however, but require a specific explanatory account of the connections among forms of oppression for each social context and for each group.

Notes

1. Alan Buchanan, *Marx and Justice* (Totowa, N.J.: Rowman & Allanheld, 1982), 44–49; Nancy Holmstrom, "Exploitation," *Canadian Journal of Philosophy*, VII, no. 2 (1977):353–69.
2. Anthony Giddens, *A Contemporary Critique of Historical Materialism* (Berkeley: University of California Press, 1981), 242; Arthur Brittan and Mary Maynard, *Sexism, Racism and Oppression* (Oxford: Basil Blackwell, 1984), 93; Raymond Murphy, "Exploitation or Exclusion?" *Sociology* 19, no. 2 (May, 1985):225–43; Herbert Gintis and Samuel Bowles, *Capitalism and Democracy* (New York: Basic Books, 1986).
3. Carol Brown, "Mothers, Fathers and Children: From Private to Public Patriarchy" in *Women and Revolution*, ed. Lydia Sargent (Boston: South End Press, 1981), 239–68.
4. David Alexander, "Gendered Job Traits and Women's Occupations" (Ph.D. Dissertation, University of Massachusetts, 1987).
5. Claus Offe, *Disorganized Capitalism: Contemporary Transformation of Work and Politics* (Cambridge: M.I.T. Press, 1986), Chapters 1–3.
6. W. E. B. DuBois, *The Souls of Black Folks* (New York: Signet, 1903, 1969).

Study Questions

1. What does Young mean by *oppression*?
2. According to Young, how does *marginalization* differ from *cultural imperialism?*
3. Are any groups in the United States oppressed but not mentioned by Young?
4. Have any of the groups Young mentions become less oppressed in recent years?

D.

Reparations

The Morality of Reparation

Bernard R. Boxill

Bernard Boxill is Professor Emeritus at the University of North Carolina at Chapel Hill. He argues that while the aim of compensation is to secure present justice, the justification for reparation is to rectify past injustice. Because the ancestors of blacks in the United States were treated unjustly, blacks living in the United States today are entitled to reparation from whites. While Boxill does not specify the amount of the reparation or the means of collecting or distributing it, he emphasizes that reparation is owed and should be paid.

. . . By a discussion of the justification and aims of reparation and compensation, I shall . . . show that, though both are parts of justice, they have different aims, and hence compensation cannot replace reparation.

Let me begin with a discussion of how compensation may be justified. Because of the scarcity of positions and resources relative to aspiring individuals, every society that refuses to resort to paternalism or a strict regimentation of aspirations must incorporate competition

From Bernard R. Boxill, "The Morality of Reparation," *Social Theory and Practice* 2 (1972).

among its members for scarce positions and resources. Given that freedom of choice necessitates at least the possibility of competition, I believe that justice requires that appropriate compensatory programs be instituted both to ensure that the competition is fair, and that the losers be protected.

If the minimum formal requirement of justice is that persons be given equal consideration, then it is clear that justice requires that compensatory programs be implemented in order to ensure that none of the participants suffer from a removable handicap. The same reasoning supports the contention that the losers in the competition be given, if necessary, sufficient compensation to enable them to reenter the competition on equal terms with the others. In other words, the losers can demand equal opportunity as well as can the beginners.

In addition to providing compensation in the above cases, the community has the duty to provide compensation to the victims of accident where no one was in the wrong, and to the victims of "acts of God" such as floods, hurricanes, and earthquakes. Here again, the justification is that such compensation is required if it is necessary to ensure equality of opportunity.

Now, it should be noted that, in all the cases I have stated as requiring compensation, no prior injustice need have occurred. This is clear, of course, in the case of accidents and "acts of God"; but it is also the case that in a competition, even if everyone abides by the rules and acts fairly and justly, some will necessarily be losers. In such a case, I maintain, if the losers are rendered so destitute as to be unable to compete equally, they can demand compensation from the community. Such a right to compensation does not render the competition nugatory; the losers cannot demand success—they can demand only the minimum necessary to reenter the competition. Neither is it the case that every failure has rights of compensation against the community. As we shall see, the right to compensation depends partly on the conviction that every individual has an equal right to pursue what he considers valuable; the wastrel or indolent man has signified what he values by what he has freely chosen to be. Thus, even if he seems a failure and considers himself a failure, he does not need or have a right of compensation. Finally, the case for compensation sketched is not necessarily paternalistic. It is not argued that society or government can decide what valuable things individuals should have and implement programs to see to it that they have them. Society must see to it that its members can pursue those things they consider valuable.

The justification of compensation rests on two premises: first, each individual is equal in dignity and worth to every other individual, and hence has a right, equal to that of any other, to arrange his life as he sees fit, and to pursue and acquire what he considers valuable; and second, the individuals involved must be members of a community. Both premises are necessary in order to show that compensation is both good and, in addition, mandatory or required by justice. One may, for example, concede that a man who is handicapped by some infirmity should receive compensation; but if the man is a member of no community, and if his infirmity is due to no injustice, then one would be hard put to find the party who could be legitimately forced to bear the cost of such compensation. Since persons can be legitimately compelled to do what justice dictates, then it would seem that in the absence of a community, and if the individual has suffered his handicap because of no injustice, that compensation cannot be part of justice. But given that the individual is a member of a community, then I maintain that he can legitimately demand compensation from that community. The members of a community are, in essential respects, members of a joint undertaking; the activities of the members of a community are interdependent and the community benefits from the efforts of its members even when such efforts do not bring the members what they individually aim at. It is legitimate to expect persons to follow the spirit and letter of rules and regulations, to work hard and honestly, to take calculated risks with their lives and fortunes, all of which helps society generally, only if such persons can demand compensation from society as a whole when necessary.

The case for rights of compensation depends, as I have argued above, on the fact that the individuals involved are members of a single community the very existence of which should imply a tacit agreement on the part of the whole to bear the costs of compensation. The case for reparation I shall try to show is more primitive in the sense that it depends only on the premise that every person has an equal right to pursue and acquire what he values. Recall that the crucial difference between compensation and reparation is that whereas the latter is due only after injustice, the former may be due when no one has acted unjustly to anyone else. It is this relative innocence of all the parties concerned which made it illegitimate, in the absence of prior commitments, to compel anyone to bear the cost of compensation.

In the case of reparation, however, this difficulty does not exist. When reparation is due, it is not the case that no one is at fault, or that everyone is innocent; in such a case, necessarily, someone has infringed unjustly on another's right to pursue what he values. This could happen in several different ways, dispossession being perhaps the most obvious. When someone possesses something, he has signified by his choice that he values it. By taking it away from him one infringes on his equal right to pursue and possess what he values. On the other hand, if I thwart, unfairly, another's legitimate attempt to do or possess something, I have also acted unjustly; finally, an injustice has occurred when someone makes it impossible for others to pursue a legitimate goal, even if these others never actually attempt to achieve that goal. These examples of injustice differ in detail, but what they all have in common is that no supposition of prior commitment is necessary in order to be able to identify the parties who must bear the cost of reparation; it is simply and clearly the party who has acted unjustly. . . .

The case for reparation thus requires for its justification less in the way of assumptions than the case for compensation. Examination of the justifications of reparation and compensation also reveals the difference in their aims.

The characteristic of compensatory programs is that they are essentially "forward looking"; by that I mean that such programs are intended to alleviate disabilities which stand in the way of some *future* good, *however* these disabilities may have come about. Thus, the history of injustices suffered by black and colonial people is quite irrelevant to their right to compensatory treatment. What is strictly relevant to this is that such compensatory treatment is necessary if some future goods such as increased happiness, equality of incomes, and so on, are to be secured. To put it another way, given the contingency of causal connections, the present condition of black and colonial people could have been produced in any one of a very large set of different causal sequences. Compensation is concerned with the remedying of the present situation however it may have been produced; and to know the present situation, and how to remedy it, it is not, strictly speaking, necessary to know just how it was brought about, or whether it was brought about by injustice.

On the other hand, the justification of reparation is essentially "backward looking"; reparation is due only when a breach of justice *has* occurred. Thus, as opposed to the case of compensation, the case for reparation to black and colonial people depends precisely on the fact that such people have been reduced to their present condition by a history of injustice. In sum, while the aim of compensation is to procure some future good, that of reparation is to rectify past injustices; and rectifying past injustices may not insure equality of opportunity.

The fact that reparation aims precisely at correcting a prior injustice suggests one further important difference between reparation and compensation. Part of what is involved in rectifying an injustice is an acknowledgment on the part of the transgressor that what he is doing is required of him because of his prior error. This concession of error seems required by the premise that every person is equal in worth and dignity. Without the acknowledgment of error, the injurer implies that the injured has been treated in a manner that befits him; hence, he cannot feel that the injured party is his equal. In such a case, even if the unjust party repairs the damage he has caused, justice does not yet obtain between himself and his victim. For, if it is true that when someone has done his duty nothing can be demanded of him, it follows that if, in my estimation, I have acted dutifully even when someone is injured as a result, then I must feel that nothing can be demanded of me and that any repairs I may make are gratuitous. If justice can be demanded, it follows that I cannot think that what I am doing is part of justice.

It will be objected, of course, that I have not shown in this situation that justice cannot obtain between injurer and victim, but only that the injurer does not *feel* that justice can hold between himself and the one he injures. The objection depends on the distinction between the objective transactions between the individuals and their subjective attitudes, and assumes that justice requires only the objective transactions. The model of justice presupposed by this objection is, no doubt, that justice requires equal treatment of equals, whereas the view I take is that justice requires equal consideration between equals; that is to say, justice requires not only that we *treat* people in a certain way, for whatever reason we please, but that we treat them as equals precisely because we believe they are our equals. In particular, justice requires that we acknowledge that our treatment of others can be required of us; thus, where an unjust injury has occurred, the injurer reaffirms his belief in the other's equality by conceding that repair can be demanded of him, and the injured rejects the allegation of his inferiority contained in the other's behavior by demanding reparation.

Consequently, when injustice has reduced a people to indigency, compensatory programs alone cannot be all that justice requires. Since the avowed aim of compensatory programs is forward looking, such programs *necessarily* cannot affirm that the help they give is required because of a prior injustice. This must be the case even if it is the unjustly injuring party who makes compensation. Thus, since the acknowledgment of error is required by justice as part of what it means to give equal consideration, compensatory programs cannot take the place of reparation.

In sum, *compensation* cannot be substituted for *reparation* where reparation is due, because they satisfy two differing requirements of justice. In addition, practically speaking, since it is by demanding and giving justice where it is due that the members of a community continually reaffirm their belief in each other's equality, a stable and equitable society is not possible without reparation being given and demanded when it is due.

Consider now the assertion that the present generation of white Americans owe the present generation of black Americans reparation for the injustices of slavery inflicted on the ancestors of the black population by the ancestors of the white population. To begin, consider the very simplest instance of a case where reparation may be said to be due: Tom has an indisputable moral right to possession of a certain item, say a bicycle, and Dick steals the bicycle from Tom. Here, clearly, Dick owes Tom, at least the bicycle and a concession or error, in reparation. Now complicate the case slightly; Dick steals the bicycle from Tom and "gives" it to Harry. Here again, even if he is innocent of complicity in the theft, and does not know that his "gift" was stolen, Harry must return the bicycle to Tom with the acknowledgment that, though innocent or blameless, he did not rightfully possess the bicycle. Consider a final complication; Dick steals the bicycle from Tom and gives it to Harry; in the meantime Tom dies, but leaves a will clearly conferring his right to ownership of the bicycle to his son, Jim. Here again we should have little hesitation in saying that Harry must return the bicycle to Jim.

Now, though it involves complications, the case for reparation under consideration is essentially the same as the one last mentioned: the slaves had an indisputable moral right to the products of their labour; these products were stolen from them by the slave masters who ultimately passed them on to their descendants; the slaves presumably have conferred their rights of ownership to the products of their labour to their descendants; thus, the descendants of slave masters are in possession of wealth to which the descendants of slaves have rights; hence, the descendants of slave masters must return this wealth to the descendants of slaves with a concession that they were not rightfully in possession of it.

It is not being claimed that the descendants of slaves must seek reparation from those among the white population who happen to be descendants of slave owners. This perhaps would be the case if slavery had produced for the slave owners merely specific hoards of gold, silver or diamonds, which could be passed on in a very concrete way from father to son. As a matter of fact, slavery produced not merely specific hoards, but wealth which has been passed down mainly to descendants of the white community to the relative exclusion of the descendants of slaves. Thus, it is the white community as a whole that prevents the descendants of slaves from exercising their rights of ownership, and the white community as a whole that must bear the cost of reparation.

The above statement contains two distinguishable arguments. In the first argument the assertion is that each white person, individually, owes reparation to the black community because membership in the white community serves to identify an individual as a recipient of benefits to which the black community has a rightful claim. In the second argument, the conclusion is that the white community as a whole, considered as a kind of corporation or company, owes reparation to the black community.

In the first of the arguments sketched above, individuals are held liable to make reparation even if they have been merely passive recipients of benefits; that is, even if they have not deliberately chosen to accept the benefits in question. This argument invites the objection that, for the most part, white people are simply not in a position to choose to receive or refuse benefits belonging to the descendants of slaves and are, therefore, not culpable or blameable and hence not liable to make reparation. But this objection misses the point. The argument under consideration simply does not depend on or imply the claim that white people are culpable or blameable; the argument is that merely by being white, an individual receives benefits to which others have at least partial rights. In such cases, whatever one's choice or moral culpability, reparation must be made. Consider an extreme case: Harry has an unexpected heart attack and is taken unconscious to the hospital. In the same hospital Dick has recently died. A heart surgeon transplants the heart from Dick's dead body to Harry without permission from Dick's family. If Harry recovers, he must make suitable reparation to Dick's family, conceding that he is not in rightful possession of Dick's heart even if he had no part in choosing to receive it.

The second of the arguments distinguished above concluded that for the purpose in question, the white community can be regarded as a corporation or company which, as a whole, owes reparation to the sons of slaves. Certainly the white community resembles a corporation or company in some striking ways; like such companies, the white community has interests distinct from, and opposed to, other groups in the same society, and joint action is often taken by the members of the white community to protect and enhance their interests. Of course, there are differences; people are generally born into the white community and do not deliberately choose their membership in it; on the other hand, deliberate choice is often the standard procedure for gaining membership in a company. But this difference is unimportant; European immigrants often deliberately choose to become part of the white community in the United States for the obvious benefits this brings, and people often inherit shares and so, without deliberate choice, become members of a company. What is important here is not how deliberately one chooses to become part of a community or a company; what is relevant is that one chooses to continue to accept the benefits which circulate exclusively within the community, sees such benefits as belonging exclusively to the members of the community, identifies one's interests with those of the community, viewing them as opposed to those of others outside the community, and finally, takes joint action with other members of the community to protect such interests. In such a case, it seems not unfair to consider the present white population as members of a company that incurred debts before they were members of the company, and thus to ask them justly to bear the cost of such debts.

It may be objected that the case for reparation depends on the validity of inheritance; for, only if the sons of slaves inherit the rights of their ancestors can it be asserted that they have rights against the present white community. If the validity of inheritance is rejected, a somewhat different, but perhaps even stronger, argument for reparation can still be formulated. For if inheritance is rejected with the stipulation that the wealth of individuals be returned to the whole society at their deaths, then it is even clearer that the white community owes reparation to the black community. For the white community has appropriated, almost exclusively, the wealth from slavery in addition to the wealth from other sources; but such wealth belongs jointly to all members of the society, white as well as black; hence, it owes them reparation. The above formulation of the argument is entirely independent of the fact of slavery and extends the rights of the black community to its just portion of the total wealth of the society.

Study Questions

1. How does Boxill distinguish between "compensation" and "reparation"?
2. What does Boxill mean by "black and colonial people"?
3. On Boxill's view, are whites who descend from slave masters as well as whites who descend from those killed fighting slave masters in the Civil War equally obligated to provide reparation?
4. Would Boxill's reasoning lead to the conclusion that Native Americans are owed reparation, and, if so, would blacks be among those obligated to provide it?

Reparations and the Problem of Agency

Chandran Kukathas

Chandran Kukathas is Professor of Government at the London School of Economics. He argues that reparations are almost always morally unjustified. They require locating those who owe the reparations as well as those to whom the reparations are due. In the case of the descendants of American slaves, for example, should we count children of mixed descent? And how should we identify those who should pay? How about Native Americans whose land was taken away but some of whom held slaves? And what of recent immigrants who have come to the United States to escape persecution? Should they pay reparations? Kukathas concludes that, given such difficulties, the prospects for justifying reparations look dim.

If a person is wronged, whether by a physical violation of his person or by having his property unjustly taken, or even by the besmirching of his reputation, he is, most people agree, entitled to some form of compensation or restitution from the person or persons responsible for the wrong. What form the reparation should take, and how great it should be, are sometimes difficult problems, but this does not change the fact that something is owed and someone must be held to account. If a restaurant goes bust because a supplier fails to fulfill his commitments and a newspaper publishes false reports of the restaurant's allegedly unethical practices, the business owner can seek compensation from those responsible for the harm he has suffered. The fact that apportioning responsibility will not be easy makes no difference: the law must try to find an answer that rectifies the injustice.

From Chandran Kukathas, "Who? Whom? Reparations and the Problem of Agency," *Journal of Social Philosophy* 37 (2006).

Similarly, it can be argued, the harm suffered by the descendants of victims of unredressed injustices of the past cries out no less urgently for attention. Many people today suffer as a consequence of wrongs committed in the past, and they too, some say, are entitled to some form of restitution. The fact that matters are complex is no reason for them to give up their claims, or for others to give up on the task [of] finding answers to the question of who owes what to whom.

It seems fair to say that the complexity of the problem of apportioning responsibility, and of settling the nature and extent of compensation owed, should not deter us from trying to do justice. We seek only as much precision as we can plausibly hope for, and make compromises to ensure that *some* justice is done, imperfect justice being better than no justice at all. Yet matters are importantly different when the problem is not so much determining the form of restitution but establishing who the relevant parties are in the case. In cases of past injustice, the problem of identifying the parties often turns out to be especially troublesome. Indeed, the more remote the original wrong, the more difficult it is to establish who has cause for complaint and who can rightly be held responsible.

In this paper, I argue that the pursuit of justice by making reparation for past wrongs, and particularly for wrongs done more than a generation ago, is not morally justifiable except in some special cases. For the paying of reparations to be defensible, it must be possible to identify two kinds of agent: the victim of injustice, to whom reparation is owed, and the perpetrator or beneficiary of injustice who can be held accountable for the wrong or liable for the cost of restitution. If both agents cannot be identified, there cannot be a case for reparation. It may be possible to justify, say, the return of some lands to people who have been dispossessed, if we can identify the dispossessed and also those who can be held accountable; but it is not possible to justify, say, compensation for the descendants of slavery generally. Some persons can be held responsible for some of the wrongs of the past, but one *generation* cannot be asked to atone for the sins of earlier ones. . . .

I

Many people and communities that are the descendants of victims of injustice in the past live disadvantaged lives. The descendants of American slaves are on average worse-off than are the rest of the population of the United States; the descendants of Australian Aborigines are generally worse-off than the non-Aboriginal population; and the Maori of New Zealand do less well than their *pakeha* counterparts on most measures of well-being, from life expectancy to rates of incarceration. There are many reasons why a political community might want to acknowledge the wrongs of the past. For one thing, it seems likely that the events of the past have had a significant bearing on who fares well and who fares poorly: the probability of one's life going well is affected substantially by the community into which one is born. For another thing, the fact that people are suffering itself gives us some reason to attend to them, and when that suffering has a long history, that very history may need to be acknowledged.

If, however, we wish to do justice to specific individuals or groups, we need to do more than take note of history's injustices. We need to identify with some precision who is a victim of injustice, and who can rightly be held responsible—or liable. But why do we need to be precise if we know that there has been injustice in the past and that there are people who are suffering in the present? One reason is that this is, at least implicitly, what those who see themselves as victims of past injustice demand. Their claim is not that their condition should be remedied because they have simply done badly out of history. It is that they should be compensated in some way because they have been treated unjustly. Their claim is different from that which might be made by the poor more generally: that the background institutions under which they have remained poor are unfair or systematically biased in favor of others or not conducive to equality. Their claim is, rather, that particular wrongs were committed and that it is the further injustices that were consequent upon them that need to be rectified. If this is indeed their contention, then their claims can only be addressed by identifying the agents who deserve restitution and those who are liable for providing it. For them, it will not do simply to lump them in with the poor more generally, for their claim is of a very specific nature.

Irrespective of the claims of the descendants of victims of past injustice, however, it is necessary to identify the agents involved in matters of historical injustice because justice in restitution generally demands that we know who is obliged to restore whom. . . . This means that the question of justice in restitution is at least a different kind of question to that of distributive justice, even if it might be held, in the end, to be an aspect of the problem of distributive justice understood more broadly[1]. . . .

When the issue of how to redress historical injustice arises, the problem is to work out who has a claim upon whom for compensation for past wrongs. This means working out which agents have claims against which other agents for actions taken in the past that have damaged some and benefited others. Claims might be made by individuals against other individuals, individuals against groups, groups against groups, and groups against individuals. The validity of any claim would depend, among other things, on the proper identification of the agents in question as persons entitled to make claims or persons liable for fulfilling them. The issue is: how readily can this be done?

II

The problem of identifying the relevant agents in trying to establish claims for restitution for past injustice is more difficult than has been recognized. Who is entitled to compensation for a wrong committed, and who is liable to pay is sometimes easy enough to ascertain when victim and perpetrator are both alive, though it can get progressively more difficult to establish the extent of entitlement and responsibility as time goes on. When generations have passed, even identifying the parties to the case is difficult.

To begin with, let us consider the problem of identifying the claimants, before turning to the problem of establishing who is liable for providing restitution to those who are harmed. . . . The question is: *who* are the individual descendants of the victims of past injustice?

This question may be read in different ways. One way of reading it is by taking it to mean "who should *count* as a descendant of a victim of past injustice?" If this is the question, the answer in any given society could be a relatively small or a worryingly large number. It would be a very large number if we considered anyone a descendant of a victim if he or she could identify *any* ancestor who had suffered injustice. If we confined our analysis to a single society, like the United States, we would get a collection of individuals that included at least the following: the descendants of African slaves, the descendants of Native Americans, the descendants of people who were the victims of war, the descendants of conscripts and neglected war veterans, the descendants of people unjustly incarcerated (including but not only the Japanese imprisoned during World War II), the descendants of anyone who was cheated, swindled, or taken unfair advantage of by governments, businesses, unions, criminal organizations, or individuals. Depending on how broadly injustice was defined, that number could easily encompass the majority of the population. If, for example, we took severe punishment for possessing and selling drugs to be unjust, then many people have been the victims of injustice; but if we took severe punishment in this instance to be warranted, many people are in fact the descendants of the victims of justice. We could also stipulate how broadly or narrowly we wish to construe injustice by determining a strong or weak minimum standard by which we deem whether an injustice has been committed. If being verbally abused by a policeman is sufficient for someone to claim victimhood, the number of victims could be impossibly large. Finally, if we took the victims of injustice to include women who had been treated unjustly in the workplace, in the home, or by laws limiting their right to work or to receive equal pay, the descendants of the victims of past injustice might include everyone.

The point here, of course, is not to suggest that no one could be distinguished as a descendant of a victim of past injustice because everyone is a descendant. It is, rather, to say that identifying the set of people to be recognized as the descendants of victims is a complex and contentious matter. It requires determining not only who to include but who to exclude from consideration.

Another way of reading the question is by taking it to mean "how do we tell if someone is a *descendant* of a victim of past injustice?" In some cases, this may be relatively straightforward: the child of a slave or former slave is clearly in this category. But what of the children, and grandchildren, of mixed descent? Does a person with one black grandparent or one black great-grandparent count as black or white? Even if we assume that the world is divided conveniently into victims and perpetrators or beneficiaries of injustice, it is not obvious how we should categorize those with ancestors on both sides of the divide—leaving to one side the issue of whether descent should be understood purely biologically or to include relationship through adoption.

A further complexity arises when we consider whether the category of descendants of victims of past injustice should be extended to include people beyond the borders of the political community. Many people around the world are the descendants of refugees who fled persecution, often leaving behind both the experience of violent treatment and their personal wealth or livelihoods. Intermarriage over the generations has created many people who are the descendants of people who have suffered great injustice. Sometimes it is difficult to identify these people. On other occasions it is not: if we take the case of Liberia for example, a country founded by the forcible repatriation of black Americans to African soil, we might say that almost everyone there is the descendant of victims of injustice, although many people there may have only one American ancestor.

The general problem in distinguishing the descendants of victims of past injustice is that it is too easy to reach the point at which a very large proportion of the population can be identified as descendants. If that happens, the moral force of the claims made by some people will be diminished to the extent that many others in the society might simply respond that they too have injustice in their histories. Is there a better way of separating out the descendants of injustice who have strong claims from those who do not?

An obvious alternative is to identify not individuals but groups that are the descendants of victims of past injustice. This might have the immediate advantage of giving us an entity that is easier to isolate and distinguish from other potential claimants because it has persisted over a greater length of time and because tracing an ancestry will not be a problem. Moreover, the most serious injustices of the past, which cry out for rectification, were committed against groups or people as members of groups. The two issues that have to be settled, however, are which groups to count, and whom to include within them. This may be difficult, and we should consider why.

To begin with the matter of which groups to count, it may seem plain that certain groups are almost self-evidently candidates. The descendants of African slaves in modern America, and the indigenous peoples dispossessed of their lands in many parts of the world come to mind. It would be impossible to deny that slaves and dispossessed people were the victims of injustice many generations ago, or that the injustice the people of these groups continued to suffer was injustice in succeeding generations. The main point of contention is not whether such groups are plausible candidates for restitution but whether excluding the descendants of other victims of past injustice is warranted. The question is not just "why these groups and not others?" but also "why not people who don't fall into notable groups, but are the descendants of victims of serious injustice all the same?" One powerful reason for picking out particular groups but not others may be that the injustice suffered by these groups has had a particularly significant impact on the life of the society as a whole—perhaps so much so that it would make a difference to the quality of life in that society if these particular grievances were addressed. While this is an important reason, and one that may well justify attempting to offer restitution to the descendants of some groups, it is not, in the end, a reason that invokes the importance of doing justice for its own sake. . . .

The issue of who is to be included within a group being recognized as descending from victims of past injustice raises different problems.

Most of these problems stem from the fact that groups are made up of individuals, and subgroups of individuals, with different histories, and often quite complex identities. Morally speaking, those histories themselves can be quite mixed. Consider, for example, the case of the Seminole Indians. The Seminoles were bands of Creek Indians who separated from the tribe and settled in northern Florida in the seventeenth century. They practiced slavery, not only of other Indians captured in battle, but also of Africans whom they purchased or were given as gifts by the British. By the nineteenth century, however, the black Seminole population had grown and established a strong, independent community, which actually joined with the Seminoles to resist the attempt of Americans to annex Florida. They fought against General Andrew Jackson in the First Seminole War (1817–18), and later in the Second Seminole War (1835–42), and gained a measure of independence. But they were then forced to face the Creek Indians, who were intent on enslaving them, and reintegrating the Seminole Indians into Creek society. Many fled to Mexico to escape Creek slave-hunters, though a good number returned after the Civil War to work as Indian Scouts. They claim that they were promised their own land in Texas in return, but in the end the War Department denied that they had land to offer, and the Bureau of Indian Affairs refused to give them land on the grounds that they were not really Indians.

How should these groups be understood if the issue is the rectification of past injustice? The Seminoles and Creeks were certainly victims of injustice, since theirs is a history of dispossession; but they were also perpetrators of some serious injustices against each other and against Africans, in collaboration with Americans. The black Seminoles appear to have a less ambiguous history, but even they returned to work as scouts in an American army intent on clearing the southwest of Comanches and Apaches to make room for white settlements. Even they were complicit in serious injustices.

The question is whether the complexity of history and identity should be assumed away in order to focus on the larger story of injustice, in this case the story of African slavery and the dispossession of indigenous peoples. If the detail is obliterated in the moral accounting, however, it is not clear that what would be guiding the decision to rectify past injustice are the injustices themselves but other ethical considerations.

More generally, there is a problem in determining whom to include in groups that might be candidates for restitution to the extent that individuals may be of mixed descent, having ancestors who were both victims and perpetrators of injustice. Others might be descended from a mix of immigrants and ancestors who suffered injustice. This problem may be compounded by the fact that some groups refuse to recognize some individuals or subgroups as members of their communities. At present, for example, the existence of black members of the Seminole Indians is a contentious issue because the sums paid to the Seminoles in compensation for dispossession would have to be further divided if Indians of African descent were included. . . .

Yet even if the identities of the descendants of victims of past injustice can be settled, there remains the problem of establishing who should be held liable for restitution. This problem is more serious because even if it is true that injustices were committed in the past and the descendants of victims have suffered as a consequence, this may not be sufficient reason to hold many—or indeed, any—people today responsible for rectifying the situation.

A number of difficulties stand in the way of establishing responsibility for past injustice. One set of difficulties stems from the problem of determining who was responsible for the original injustices that might now generate claims on the part of descendants of victims. If one takes the case of African slavery, the perpetrators of injustice certainly include slave owners, slave traders, and those who supported the institution of slavery, whether by backing governments who upheld it or serving as officials who enforced the law protecting it. But this means some responsibility for the original injustice must be borne by people from other countries who captured and sold slaves. Equally, it is difficult to hold responsible for the injustice of slavery those who had no part in it, or who disapproved of it, or who worked to eliminate it.

It might be argued that all who benefited from slavery can be held responsible to some degree, and one might conclude from this that no one in the United States was free from the taint of this particular injustice.[2] But those who benefited from slavery included not only those whites who lived in the United States but others as well. American assets, including slave enterprises, were held by people in Europe who invested their money abroad; the products of slave labor were sold all around the world; and even some Africans and American Indians took advantage of the slave trade to enrich themselves. White Americans may bear the heaviest burden of responsibility for slavery, as they might also for the dispossession of indigenous peoples, but they do not bear it alone. If that is so, the case for holding their descendants peculiarly responsible for these injustices of the past would be weakened.

The argument for holding these descendants responsible is weakened further by the fact that, with the passing of generations, many countries such as Australia and the United States have admitted immigrants who have had no part in the injustices of the past insofar as they have no ancestors who were even indirectly implicated in wrongs committed in their new country. . . .

Finally, the argument for holding the descendants of the perpetrators or beneficiaries of injustice liable for making restitution is weakened by intermarriage and the fact that people's identities are complex mixtures of different inheritances. If responsibility for rectifying past injustice is to be sheeted home to anyone, it would have to be to a different kind of agent.

One possibility here is that we might hold liable not individual persons but certain kinds of group agents. There are a number of candidates, including companies, private organizations such as churches, and governments, from the local to state and national. Such entities might be held responsible for restitution for past injustice because, at least in some cases, they might be not so much the descendants of perpetrators of injustice in the past as entities whose complicity in past injustice is real because they are the same agents as those that originated in the past. Coca-Cola today is the same entity as the Coca-Cola of fifty years ago, and the Catholic Church of today is the same entity as the church of a millennium ago. Companies and churches can be held accountable for the injustices of the past if they themselves committed them. The same might hold for governments, which do not change with each new administration but remain continuous for as long as the polity remains stable and the personnel change without affecting the regime.

This solution might have some merit, but a couple of difficulties ought to be recognized nonetheless. First, there are relatively few companies that have operated for long enough, and continue to exist, which might be found responsible and so held liable for compensating the descendants of their own injustice. There have been many companies in history that were guilty of committing serious injustices in pursuit of profit: the British and Dutch East India Companies are obvious examples. But the number of such corporations that can be identified today as having been responsible for wrongs in the past may be small, if only because corporations are often taken over, or decline and disappear.

Second, if we consider churches to be possible candidates for being held liable for past injustice, we need to ask whether and how far a charitable organization can be held responsible for wrongs committed by those under its authority, and how this should be balanced against the contributions it has made to ameliorating the condition of the poor and the destitute.

In the light of these considerations, perhaps the only entities that can properly be held responsible for rectifying past injustice are the political ones. In part, this is because there may be an argument for holding governments responsible for the wrongs committed in the societies they rule. But more generally, governments could be charged with the task of remedying precisely those wrongs for which it is difficult to identify the real culprits.

III

Governments can clearly be held responsible for rectifying past injustices when they themselves have committed them. If governments can be sued or required to compensate people for taking their property, then they can surely be required to restore people who have been harmed by injustices the government committed a long time ago.

But should governments, or more particularly, the state, be considered a kind of moral agent that can be charged with the duty of acting as a kind of rectifier of last resort of the injustices that societies have been unable to remedy? It is often difficult to establish clear lines of responsibility for many of the wrongs we see in society. . . . [I]t seems evident that some injustices of the past have an enduring legacy, and it surely will not do to let them go unaddressed because clean lines of responsibility cannot readily be drawn. Perhaps it is a part of the role of the state to address precisely these problems: to do justice by considering the relations between different groups and communities that comprise it, and that have shaped the larger political society.

Tempting though this thought may be, it should be resisted. Particularly if the state in question is a liberal democratic state, accountable to its citizens, it is, in the end, obliged to do only what it can justify to those citizens. If there is no plausible justification for holding one part of society responsible for compensating another for injustices committed in the past, there is no warrant for calling upon the state to take any particular action. Or at least, any action it takes in the name of rectifying past injustice could only be seen as having a symbolic quality. In order to repair, not the wrongs done to people in the past, but the fabric of a society that has been torn by serious injustices in its history, it might move to compensate the descendants of victims of past injustice. Its move here would, however, be primarily of symbolic importance. And it could not go too far without raising among the citizenry the question of whether its actions are what justice really demands.

Notes

1. It might be argued, for example, that a complete theory of distributive justice will encompass a theory of justice in rectification. Nozick's theory of justice, for example, seems to do just that. See Robert Nozick, *Anarchy, State and Utopia* (Oxford: Blackwell, 1974), pt. II.
2. For a defense of this view, see Bernard Boxill, "A Lockean Argument for Black Reparations," *The Journal of Ethics* 7 (2003): 63–91.

Study Questions

1. What concerns about reparations are raised by the case of the Seminoles?
2. Due to a complex historical record, might two people owe each other reparations?
3. Might reparations be owed to those discriminated against on bases other than race, such as religion, nationality, or sexual orientation?
4. Might reparations be owed by impoverished people to those who are wealthy?

E.

Affirmative Action

Two Concepts of Affirmative Action

Steven M. Cahn

Steven M. Cahn, editor of this book, distinguishes between procedural and preferential affirmative action. The former seeks to ensure that matters of race, sex, and ethnic origin play no role in judging individuals. The latter urges that we pay attention to these characteristics so as to ensure that individuals are chosen in proportion to the availability of particular groups to which they belong. While defending procedural affirmative action, Cahn argues that preferential affirmative action encourages stereotypical thinking and overlooks that each individual adds to a group's diversity in some ways but not others. After all, why is racial, sexual, and ethnic diversity to be valued more highly than diversity of religion, economic class, military experience, sexual orientation, and so on? Cahn concludes that before embracing preferential affirmative action, we should try scrupulous enforcement of procedural affirmative action.

In March 1961, less than two months after assuming office, President John F. Kennedy issued Executive Order 10925, establishing the President's Committee on Equal Employment Opportunity. Its

From Steven M. Cahn, "Two Concepts of Affirmative Action," *Academe* 83 (1997).

mission was to end discrimination in employment by the government and its contractors. The order required every federal contract to include the pledge that "The contractor will not discriminate against any employe[e] or applicant for employment because of race, creed, color, or national origin. The contractor will take affirmative action to ensure that applicants are employed, and that employe[e]s are treated during employment, without regard to their race, creed, color, or national origin."

Here, for the first time in the context of civil rights, the government called for "affirmative action." The term meant taking appropriate steps to eradicate the then widespread practices of racial, religious, and ethnic discrimination.[1] The goal, as the President stated, was "equal opportunity in employment." In other words, *procedural* affirmative action, as I shall call it, was instituted to ensure that applicants for positions would be judged without any consideration of their race, religion, or national origin. These criteria were declared irrelevant. Taking them into account was forbidden.

The Civil Rights Act of 1964 restated and broadened the application of this principle. Title VI declared that "No person in the United States shall, on the ground of race, color or national origin, be excluded from participation in, be denied the benefits of, or be subjected to discrimination under any program or activity receiving Federal financial assistance."

Before one year had passed, however, President Lyndon B. Johnson argued that fairness required more than a commitment to such procedural affirmative action. In his 1965 commencement address at Howard University, he said, "You do not take a person who for years has been hobbled by chains and liberate him, bring him up to the starting line of a race and then say, 'you're free to compete with all the others,' and still justly believe that you have been completely fair."

Several months later, President Johnson issued Executive Order 11246, stating that "It is the policy of the Government of the United States to provide equal opportunity in Federal employment for all qualified persons, to prohibit discrimination in employment because of race, creed, color or national origin, and to promote the full realization of equal employment opportunity through a positive, continuing program in each department and agency." Two years later the order was amended to prohibit discrimination on the basis of sex.

While the aim of President Johnson's order is stated in language similar to that of President Kennedy's, President Johnson abolished the Committee on Equal Employment Opportunity, transferred its responsibilities to the Secretary of Labor, and authorized the Secretary to "adopt such rules and regulations and issue such orders as he deems necessary and appropriate to achieve the purposes thereof."

Acting on this mandate, the Department of Labor in December 1971, during the administration of President Richard M. Nixon, issued Revised Order No. 4, requiring all federal contractors to develop "an acceptable affirmative action program," including "an analysis of areas within which the contractor is deficient in the utilization of minority groups and women, and further, goals and timetables to which the contractor's good faith efforts must be directed to correct the deficiencies." Contractors were instructed to take the term "minority groups" to refer to "Negroes, American Indians, Orientals, and Spanish Surnamed Americans." (No guidance was given as to whether having only one parent, grandparent, or great-grandparent from a group would suffice to establish group membership.) The concept of "underutilization," according to the Revised Order, meant "having fewer minorities or women in a particular job classification than would reasonably be expected by their availability." "Goals" were not to be "rigid and inflexible quotas," but "targets reasonably attainable by means of applying every good faith effort to make all aspects of the entire affirmative action program work."[2]

Such preferential affirmative action, as I shall call it, requires that attention be paid to the same criteria of race, sex, and ethnicity that procedural affirmative action deems irrelevant. Is such use of these criteria justifiable in employment decisions?[3]

Return to President Johnson's claim that a person hobbled by discrimination cannot in fairness be expected to be competitive. How are we to determine which specific individuals are entitled to a compensatory advantage? To decide each case on its own merits would be possible, but this approach would undermine the argument for instituting preferential affirmative action on a group basis. For if some members of a group are able to compete, why not others? Thus defenders of preferential affirmative action maintain that the group, not the individual, is to be judged. If the group has suffered discrimination, then all its members are to be treated as hobbled runners.

Note, however, that while a hobbled runner, provided with a sufficient lead in a race, may cross the finish line first, giving that person an edge prevents the individual from being considered as fast a runner as others. An equally fast runner does not need an advantage to be competitive. This entire racing analogy thus encourages stereotypical thinking. For example, recall those men who played in baseball's Negro Leagues. That these athletes were barred from competing in the Major Leagues is the greatest stain on the history of the sport. While they suffered discrimination, these players were as proficient as their counterparts in the Major Leagues. They needed only to be judged by the same criteria as all others, and ensuring such equality of consideration is the essence of procedural affirmative action.

Granted, if individuals are unprepared or ill-equipped to compete, then they ought to be helped to try to achieve their goals. But such aid is appropriate for all who need it, not merely for members of particular racial, sexual, or ethnic groups.

Victims of discrimination deserve compensation. Former players in the Negro Leagues ought to receive special consideration in the arrangement of pension plans and any other benefits formerly denied these athletes due to unfair treatment. The case for such compensation, however, does not imply that present black players vying for jobs in the Major Leagues should be evaluated in any other way than their performance on the field. To assume their inability to compete is derogatory and erroneous.

Such considerations have led recent defenders of preferential affirmative action to rely less heavily on any argument that implies the attribution of noncompetitiveness to an entire population.[4] Instead, the emphasis has been placed on recognizing the benefits society is said to derive from encouraging expression of the varied experiences, outlooks, and values of members of different groups.

This approach makes a virtue of what has come to be called "diversity."[5] As a defense of preferential affirmative action, diversity has at least two advantages. First, those previously excluded are now included not as a favor to them but as a means of enriching all. Second, no one is viewed as hobbled; each competes on a par, although with varied strengths.

Note that diversity requires preferential hiring. Those who enhance diversity are to be preferred to those who do not. Those preferred, however, are not being chosen because of their deficiency; the larger group is deficient, lacking diversity.

What does it mean to say that a group lacks diversity? Or to put the question another way, could we decide, for example, which member of a ten-person group to eliminate in order to decrease most markedly its diversity?

So stated, the question is reminiscent of a provocative puzzle in *The Tyranny of Testing*, a 1962 book by the scientist Banesh Hoffman. In this attack on the importance placed on multiple-choice tests, he quotes the following letter to the editor of the *Times* of London:

> Sir—Among the "odd one out" type of questions which my son had to answer for a school entrance examination was: "Which is the odd one out among cricket, football, billiards, and hockey?" [In England "football" refers to the game Americans call "soccer," and "hockey" here refers to "field hockey."] The letter continued: I said billiards because it is the only one played indoors. A colleague says football because it is the only one in which the ball is not struck by an implement. A neighbour says cricket because in all the other games the object is to put the ball into a net. . . . Could any of your readers put me out of my misery by stating what is the correct answer . . . ?

A day later the *Times* printed the following two letters:

> Sir.—"Billiards" is the obvious answer . . . because it is the only one of the games listed which is not a team game.
>
> Sir.—football is the odd one out because . . . it is played with an inflated ball as compared with the solid ball used in each of the other three.

Hoffman then continued his own discussion:

> When I had read these three letters it seemed to me that good cases had been made for football and billiards, and that the case for cricket was particularly clever . . . At first I thought this made hockey easily the worst of the four choices and, in effect, ruled it out. But then I realized that the very fact that hockey was the only one that could be thus ruled out gave it so striking a quality of separateness as to make it an excellent answer after all—perhaps the best. Fortunately, for my peace of mind, it soon occurred to me that hockey is the only one of the four games that is played with a curved implement.

The following day the *Times* published yet another letter, this from a philosophically sophisticated thinker.

> Sir.—[The author of the original letter] . . . has put his finger on what has long been a matter of great amusement to me. Of the four—cricket, football, billiards, hockey—each is unique in a multitude of respects. For example, billiards is the only one played with more than one ball at once, the only one played on a green cloth and not on a field. . . . It seems to me that those who have been responsible for inventing this kind of brain teaser have been ignorant of the elementary philosophical fact that every thing is at once unique and a member of a wider class.

With this sound principle in mind, return to the problem of deciding which member of a ten-person group to eliminate in order to decrease most markedly its diversity. Unless the sort of diversity is specified, the question has no rational answer.

In searches for college and university faculty members, we know what sorts of diversity are typically of present concern: race, sex, and certain ethnicities. Why should these characteristics be given special regard?

Consider, for example, other nonacademic respects in which prospective faculty appointees can differ: age, religion, nationality, regional background, economic class, social stratum, military experience, bodily appearance, physical soundness, sexual orientation, marital status, ethical standards, political commitments, and cultural values. Why should we not seek diversity of these sorts?

To some extent schools do. Many colleges and universities indicate in advertisements for faculty positions that the schools seek veterans or persons with disabilities. The City University of New York requires all searches to give preference to individuals of Italian-American descent.

The crucial point is that the appeal to diversity never favors any particular candidate. Each one adds to some sort of diversity but not another. In a department of ten, one individual might be the only Black, another the only woman, another the only bachelor, another the only veteran, another the only one over fifty, another the only Catholic, another the only Republican, another the only Scandinavian, another the only socialist, and the tenth the only Southerner.

Suppose the suggestion is made that the sorts of diversity to be sought are those of groups that have suffered discrimination. This approach leads to another problem, clearly put by John Kekes:

> It is true that American blacks, Native Americans, Hispanics, and women have suffered injustice as a group. But so have homosexuals, epileptics, the urban and the rural poor, the physically ugly, those whose careers were ruined by McCarthyism, prostitutes, the obese, and so forth . . .
>
> There have been some attempts to deny that there is an analogy between these two classes of victims. It has been said that the first were unjustly discriminated against due to racial or sexual prejudice and that this is not true of the second. This is indeed so. But why should we accept the suggestion . . . that the only form of injustice relevant to preferential treatment is that which is due to racial or sexual prejudice? Injustice occurs in many forms, and those who value justice will surely object to all of them.[6]

Kekes's reasoning is cogent. In addition, another difficulty looms for the proposal to seek diversity only of groups that have suffered discrimination. For diversity is supposed to be valued not as compensation to the disadvantaged but as a means of enriching all.

Consider a department in which most of the faculty members are women. In certain fields, for example, nursing and elementary education, such departments are common. If diversity by sex is of value, then such a department, when making its next appointment, should prefer a man. Yet men as a group have not been victims of discrimination. To achieve valued sorts of diversity, the question is not which groups have been discriminated against, but which valued groups are not represented. The question thus reappears as to which sorts of diversity are to be most highly valued. I know of no compelling answer.

Seeking to justify preferential affirmative action in terms of its contribution to diversity raises another difficulty. For preferential affirmative action is commonly defended as a temporary rather than a permanent measure.[7] Preferential affirmative action to achieve diversity, however, is not temporary.

Suppose it were. Then once an institution had appointed an appropriate number of members of a particular group, preferential affirmative action would no longer be in effect. Yet the institution may later find that it has too few members of that group. Because lack of valuable diversity is presumably no more acceptable at one time than another, preferential affirmative action would have to be reinstituted. Thereby it would in effect become a permanent policy.

Why do so many of its defenders wish it to be only transitional? They believe the policy was instituted in response to irrelevant criteria for appointment having mistakenly been treated as relevant. To adopt any policy that continues to treat essentially irrelevant criteria as relevant is to share the guilt of those who discriminated originally. Irrelevant criteria should be recognized as such and abandoned as soon as feasible.

Some defenders of preferential affirmative action argue, however, that an individual's race, sex, or ethnicity is germane to fulfilling the responsibilities of a faculty member. They believe, therefore, that preferential affirmative action should be a permanent feature of search processes, because it takes account of criteria that should be considered in every appointment.

At least three reasons have been offered to justify the claim that those of a particular race, sex, or ethnicity are well-suited to be faculty members: first, they would be especially effective teachers of any student who shares their race, sex, or ethnicity;[8] second, they would be particularly insightful researchers because of their experiencing the world from distinctive standpoints;[9] third, they would be role models, demonstrating that those of a particular race, sex, or ethnicity can be effective faculty members.[10]

Consider each of these claims in turn. As to the presumed teaching effectiveness of the individuals in question, no empirical study supports the claim.[11] But assume compelling evidence were presented. It would have no implications for individual cases. A particular person who does not share race, sex, or ethnicity with students might teach them superbly. An individual of the students' own race, sex, or ethnicity might be ineffective. Regardless of statistical correlations, what is crucial is that individuals be able to teach effectively all sorts of students, and seeking individuals who give evidence of satisfying this criterion is entirely consistent with procedural affirmative action. But knowing an individual's race, sex, or ethnicity does not reveal whether that person will be effective in the classroom.

Do members of a particular race, sex, or ethnicity share a distinctive intellectual perspective that enhances their scholarship? Celia Wolf-Devine has aptly described this claim as a form of "stereotyping" that is "demeaning." As she puts it, "A Hispanic who is a Republican is no less a Hispanic, and a woman who is not a feminist is no less a woman."[12] Furthermore, are Hispanic men and women supposed to have the same point of view in virtue of their common ethnicity, or are they supposed to have different points of view in virtue of their different genders?

If our standpoints are thought to be determined by our race, sex, and ethnicity, why not also by the numerous other significant respects in which people differ, such as age, religion, sexual orientation, and so on? Because each of us is unique, can anyone else share my point of view?

That my own experience is my own is a tautology that does not imply the keenness of my insight into my experience. The victim of a crime may as a result embrace an outlandish theory of racism. But neither who you are nor what you experience guarantees the truth of your theories.

To be an effective researcher calls for discernment, imagination, and perseverance. These attributes are not tied to one's race, sex, ethnicity, age, or religion. Black scholars, for example, may be more inclined to study Black literature than are non-Black scholars. But some non-Black literary critics are more interested in and more knowledgeable about Black literature than are some Black literary critics. Why make decisions based on fallible racial generalizations when judgments of individual merit are obtainable and more reliable?

Perhaps the answer lies in the claim that only those of a particular race, sex, or ethnicity can serve as role models, exemplifying to members of a particular group the possibility of their success. Again, no empirical study supports the claim, but it has often been taken as self-evident that, for instance, only a woman can be a role model for a woman, only a Black for a Black, and only a Catholic for a Catholic. In other words, the crucial feature of a person is supposed to be not what the person does but who the person is.

The logic of the situation, however, is not so clear. Consider, for example, a Black man who is a Catholic. Presumably he serves as a role model for Blacks, men, and Catholics. Does he serve as a role model for Black women, or can only a Black woman serve that purpose? Does he serve as a role model for all Catholics or only for those who are Black? Can I serve as a role model for anyone else, because no one else shares all my characteristics? Perhaps I can serve as a role model for everyone else, because everyone else belongs to at least one group to which I belong.

Putting aside these conundrums, the critical point is supposed to be that in a field in which discrimination has been rife, a successful individual who belongs to the discriminated group demonstrates that members of the group can succeed in that field. Obviously success is possible without a role model, for the first successful individual had none. But suppose persuasive evidence were offered that a role model, while not necessary, sometimes is helpful, not only to those who belong to the group in question but also to those prone to believe that no members of the group can perform effectively within the field. Role models would then both encourage members of a group that had suffered discrimination and discourage further discrimination against the group.

To serve these purposes, however, the person chosen would need to be viewed as having been selected by the same criteria as all others. If not, members of the group that has suffered discrimination as well as those prone to discriminate would be confirmed in their common view that members of the group never would have been chosen unless membership in the group had been taken into account. Those who suffered discrimination would conclude that it still exists, while those prone to discriminate would conclude that members of the group lack the necessary attributes to compete equally.

How can we ensure that a person chosen for a position has been selected by the same criteria as all others? Preferential affirmative action fails to serve the purpose, because by definition it differentiates among people on the basis of criteria other than performance. The approach that ensures merit selection is procedural affirmative action. It maximizes equal opportunity by demanding vigilance against every form of discrimination.

The policy of appointing others than the best qualified has not produced a harmonious society in which prejudice is transcended and all enjoy the benefits of self-esteem. Rather, the practice has bred doubts about the abilities of those chosen while generating resentment in those passed over.

Procedural affirmative action had barely begun before it was replaced by preferential affirmative action. The difficulties with the latter are now clear. Before deeming them necessary evils in the struggle to overcome pervasive prejudice, why not try scrupulous enforcement of procedural affirmative action? We might thereby most directly achieve that equitable society so ardently desired by every person of good will.

Notes

1. A comprehensive history of one well-documented case of such discrimination is Dan A. Oren, *Joining the Club: A History of Jews and Yale* (New Haven and London: Yale University Press, 1985). Prior to the end of World War II, no Jew had ever been appointed to the rank of full professor in Yale College.
2. 41 C.F.R. 60-2.12. The Order provides no suggestion as to whether a "good faith effort" implies only showing preference among equally qualified candidates (the "tiebreaking" model), preferring a strong candidate to an even stronger one (the "plus factor" model), preferring a merely qualified candidate to a strongly qualified candidate (the "trumping" model), or canceling a search unless a qualified candidate of the preferred sort is available (the "quota" model).

   A significant source of misunderstanding about affirmative action results from both the government's failure to clarify which type of preference is called for by a "good faith effort" and the failure on the part of those conducting searches to inform applicants which type of preference is in use. Regarding the latter issue, see my "Colleges Should Be Explicit About Who Will Be Considered for Jobs," *The Chronicle of Higher Education, 35* (30), 1989, reprinted in *Affirmative Action and the University: A Philosophical Inquiry*, Steven M. Cahn (ed.), (Philadelphia: Temple University Press, 1993), pp. 3–4.

3. Whether their use is appropriate in a school's admission and scholarship decisions is a different issue, involving other considerations, and I shall not explore that subject in this article.
4. See, for example, Leslie Pickering Francis, "In Defense of Affirmative Action," in Cahn, op. cit., especially pp. 24–26. She raises concerns about unfairness to those individuals forced by circumstances not of their own making to bear all the costs of compensation, as well as injustices to those who have been equally victimized but are not members of specified groups.
5. The term gained currency when Justice Lewis Powell, in his pivotal opinion in the Supreme Court's 1978 *Bakke* decision, found "the attainment of a diverse student body" to be a goal that might justify the use of race in student admissions. An incisive analysis of that decision is Carl Cohen, *Naked Racial Preference* (Lanham, MD: Madison Books, 1995), pp. 55–80.
6. Cahn, op. cit., p. 151.
7. Consider Michael Rosenfeld, *Affirmative Action and Justice: A Philosophical and Constitutional Inquiry* (New Haven and London: Yale University Press, 1991), p. 336: "Ironically, the sooner affirmative action is allowed to complete its mission, the sooner the need for it will altogether disappear."
8. See, for example, Francis, op. cit., p. 31.
9. See, for example, Richard Wasserstrom, "The University and the Case for Preferential Treatment," *American Philosophical Quarterly*, 13(4), 1976, pp. 165–70.
10. See, for example, Joel J. Kupperman, "Affirmative Action: Relevant Knowledge and Relevant Ignorance," in Cahn, op. cit., pp. 181–88.
11. Consider Judith Jarvis Thomson, "Preferential Hiring," *Philosophy and Public Affairs*, 2(4), 1973, p. 368: "I do not think that as a student I learned any better, or any more, from the women who taught me than from the men, and I do not think that my own women students now learn any better or any more from me than they do from my male colleagues."
12. Cahn, op. cit., p. 230.

Study Questions

1. Explain the distinction Cahn draws between procedural and preferential affirmative action.
2. Does preferential affirmative action imply that on occasion a highly qualified candidate should be passed over in favor of one who is not as highly qualified?
3. According to Cahn, why does the appeal to diversity never favor any particular candidate?
4. Are one's sex, race, or ethnicity germane to fulfilling the responsibilities of a faculty member?

Facing Facts and Responsibilities

Karen Hanson

Karen Hanson, Professor of Philosophy at the University of Minnesota, defends preferential treatment for women and minority group men, while admitting that such a system may contain flaws that need correction. She argues that a professoriate that is mostly white and male sends the unfortunate message that the university is an institution primarily for white men. While some argue that preferential appointments may result in a stigma being attached to women and minority men, Hanson points out that many men have been appointed without superior qualifications, and no stigma attaches to them. In short, to address the injustices of racism and sexism requires taking special account of race and sex.

. . . [O]ne of the continuing intellectual problems in the debates about affirmative action is determining where the burden of proof should lie. If women and minority group men are not employed in academia in numbers and at levels proportional to their numbers in qualified applicant pools, are we entitled to assume the likelihood of unfair hiring and promotion practices and to insist that opponents of affirmative action prove opportunities really are equal for all? Or should we suppose that all racial and gender biases must be identifiable, so that, absent any specification of a problematic practice, we are entitled to rely on the fairness of sex-blind and race-blind employment procedures? If we admit that there has been racial and sexual injustice in the past, and we want to give some special treatment to

From Karen Hanson, "Facing Facts and Responsibilities: The White Man's Burden and the Burden of Proof," in Steven M. Cahn, ed., *Affirmative Action and the University: A Philosophical Inquiry* (Philadelphia, PA: Temple University Press, 1993).

those who have been disadvantaged, is it reasonable to extend this special treatment to all members of a racial group and to all women? Or should we proceed to attend immediately to disadvantage, formulating race- and sex-neutral policies that respond more directly to the specific disadvantages that are the ground of our concern? Although I grant that no general formula can be given concerning where, in discussion of actual circumstances and proposed policies, the burden of proof must lie, it seems to me that we should be inclined to doubt equality of opportunity and inclined to think race and sex are relevant categories to attempted amelioration. This inclination may be more widely shared if we begin our discussion of affirmative action only after open reflection on a couple of very basic, very general, very simple questions: Do we think our society, as a whole, has eliminated all traces of racism and sexism? And do we take the academy—and ourselves, as members of the academy—to be isolated from, or insulated against, the practices and institutions of the larger society?

I do not think we can responsibly deny that racism and sexism are still very much a part of American life; and, once we admit that, it becomes difficult to insist that we must always begin in a race-neutral and sex-neutral fashion as we try to attend to the "disadvantages" of some members of our society. An important part of the evidence of continuing racism and sexism is economic, but we must not reduce these problems to their economic markers and associated deprivations. An African American boy whose parents can afford to send him to a fine private prep school will still be exposed, throughout his life, to vicious racial epithets. As a young man, even after he has completed college and graduate school and has begun a promising professional career, he may not be able to jog in old clothes through an affluent white neighborhood without attracting undue attention and unpleasant suspicion. A young girl's interest in science may be encouraged and supported by her family, and they may, when the time comes, pay her tuition to, say, MIT. But she will grow up in a society rife with special contests for women only—those, for example, where young women parade about in swimsuits and evening gowns, seeking appearance points from their judges, and where, perhaps in quirky response to feminist criticism, more points can be earned for the appearance of "poise." She will notice, with or without rueful hilarity, that the events themselves are now often dubbed "scholarship pageants." And however our young woman finances her years at MIT, she may still be reasonably reluctant, as her male colleagues are not, to walk alone to the library at night. . . .

Thus . . . I find untenable the suggestion that we can address the injustices of racism and sexism without taking special account of race and sex. Ethnicity and gender play important roles in the social experience of every American, and racism and sexism are special, distinctive difficulties for all women and all members of some minority groups, whether or not there is, in an individual case, economic deprivation as well. This of course does not mean that every African American male and every woman has suffered more or had to overcome more in life than any white male. It does mean, however, that it is inappropriate to insist on a common category of generic "disadvantages" in our initial consideration of and responses to the problems of racism and sexism. The distinctiveness of racism and sexism also suggests that it may simply be a red herring to note, in these discussions, that many white men have had to suffer and overcome economic and other disadvantages. There are indeed other structural injustices in our society—as well as plain individual misfortunes—and perhaps there should be, from the academy, an institutional response to these problems. But if the topic on the table is racism and sexism, and the question being pursued is whether the academy should use any form of affirmative action to attack *these* injustices, we do not show that it should not by noting that the world may already contain other injustices as well.

The adversion to other injustices would not be irrelevant if it could be shown that all forms of affirmative action must exacerbate these other standing problems. It is, however, exceedingly unlikely that such a demonstration could ever be made. What unbreakable link could there possibly be between attempting to improve the lot of women and minority group men and positively worsening the condition of, say, economically exploited white males? That these groups may sometimes be pitted against one another is one thing. It would be quite a different matter to show that in all social and economic arrangements these groups' fortunes must be inversely related. In fact, the usual worry about other injustices is rather different. The concern is that affirmative action may generate new injustices. White males, especially young white males, may suddenly be deprived of equal opportunity and fair treatment; and women and minority group males may be freshly stigmatized by being treated once again in terms of group identity and as if they were in need of special allowances, help, or protection. Raising these possibilities of injustice opens wider questions about the conditions for equal opportunity and about the nature of fair treatment, and we may once again be barred from progress by disagreements about the appropriate location of the burden of proof.

While I do not deny that there could be policies of preferential treatment for women and minorities that would be unjust to white men and harmful to the academy, and I do not deny there could be affirmative action procedures that would treat white men unfairly, it seems to me that we should be able, in each such case, to identify precisely the elements we judge unjust, harmful, or unfair. . . . We do not, however, need such specific worries to feel intellectually respectable anxiety about the extent to which our employment and promotion practices provide fair opportunity for women and racial minorities. To arouse that anxiety we should, I suggest, ask ourselves the second of my two very general questions: Is the academy—and are we, as members of the academy—untouched by the sexism and racism pervading the surrounding society?

What could be the ground of the requisite confidence that we—and all our colleagues on hiring and promotion committees—have escaped the pernicious social influences that maintain racism and sexism? We might want to insist that our disciplinary training and our allegiance to a meritocratic academy force judgments free of racist and sexist taints. But the fact that the academy has in the past undeniably practiced unfair discrimination and the fact that many academic disciplines have in the past undeniably supplied specious theoretical underpinnings for racism and sexism should give us pause. Are the social and economic pressures on the academy—and the psychological pressures on its inhabitants—entirely different from those at play in the larger society?

The academy's reaction to the infusion of women and minorities into its ranks has not been dissimilar to the reaction to integration elsewhere in the world of work. There has been, from some quarters, a begrudging attitude and a diffuse sense that white males are being denied fair treatment and equal opportunity. Does anything beyond an unwarranted sense of entitlement stand behind this sense? . . .

A bit of distemper should be expected. If a pie once enjoyed by our group alone now must be shared with individuals from groups formerly denied a piece, then unless we can make a bigger pie, some of us are going to get less than before or none at all. Even if we are now making an equitable distribution, if the field of distribution has been enlarged, the expectations of individuals in the group with a once exclusive claim will have to be lowered. Is this all that has happened with extant policies of affirmative action? Perhaps not, but when we have seen the morally indefensible resistance to integration in various other segments of the work world, can we simply assume that all academic uneasiness is a product of sound reasoning?

Whether or not we are willing to entertain the idea of an academic parallel to the meanly self-interested opposition to integration in other sections of society, we should attend not only to the similarities between the academy and other institutions but also to the articulation of our own institution with others. Even if we cherish some ideal of an ivory tower, we must recognize that the denizens of the tower in fact live in ordinary communities and in ordinary families; that work done in the tower affects the nation and the world; that the tower and its staff are visible to those outside it. Even if we could be certain that the hiring and promotion procedures within academia were fair and untinged by racism and sexism, if conditions outside the tower clearly tend to impede participation by women and minority group males, should we rest content that we have done our bit for equal opportunity? . . .

Our institutional self-reflection cannot be undertaken from a perspective wholly within our institution, and our reflection on society is not from a point outside our society. Facing the fact that the professoriate is mainly white and male, we may show some proper respect for individual autonomy when we explain this profile by alluding to the "different choices" made and "alternative career paths" taken by women and minority group males. But it is a shallow morality and a faulty analysis that portrays these "different choices" as made, the "alternative paths" as taken, in circumstances unrelated to the legacy and the continuing existence of racism and sexism.

Insofar as we want to end racism and sexism and insofar as we value academia and believe in the social and personal importance of our enterprise, we should want to see a fair proportion of women and minority group males participating in our profession. It is not just the content of our courses and our research results but also the structure of our institution that teaches lessons to our students and to the wider society. Until recently, one of the lessons we taught was that higher education is conducted mostly by white men, that the professionals who are equipped to train our society's professionals are mostly white men, that the keepers and extenders of a significant portion of our society's intellectual tradition and activity are mostly white men. When an argument for affirmative action adverts to the value of diversity within academia, the rationale need not be only the assumption that women and minority group men are likely to bring fresh and different perspectives to the academy's search for truth. The idea may also be that our society now has a stale perspective *on* women and minority group males and that the visible faculty diversity encouraged by policies of affirmative action could be properly edifying.

The haste with which opponents of affirmative action contend that what will be visible is a stigma on all women and minority faculty, the quick assurance that affirmative action hiring will brand as inferior the women and minority males thus hired, should provoke a further moment of institutional and personal self-reflection. If we have granted that members of these groups are, in our society, already stigmatized by sexism and racism, what, exactly, do we think will be added by our proposed procedures? Are we sure that we are, in our claims about stigmatization, doing more than expressing our resolve not to see women and minority males as full members of the academy? For most of the life of American higher education, white men have been hired to the faculty not through the fairest and most open procedures but through friendships and old school ties. Prestigious all-male colleges have had special "legacy" admissions, and family connections have meant more than individual merit. Did these practices ever stigmatize all white males? Did they even cast general doubt on the competence of the specific white males who were their specific beneficiaries?

I raise these questions not to suggest that we should, for the sake of a crude balance, replace one flawed system with another. I suggest instead that, as we take up the issue of whether there are genuine flaws in various policies of affirmative action, as we consider the need for affirmative action at all, we ask ourselves again: Are we sure that we—in our individual consciousnesses and judgments and in the academy as a whole—have left behind the unfairness of a racist, sexist past?

Study Questions

1. What does Hanson mean by the "burden of proof"?
2. Do preferential appointments help to overcome prejudice?
3. Who else besides women and minority group men suffer from what Hanson refers to as "structural injustices in our society"?
4. Would Hanson recommend passing over candidates with superior qualifications for faculty positions for others who are unanimously believed to lack such qualifications?

What Good Am I?

Laurence Thomas

Laurence Thomas is Professor of Philosophy and Political Science at Syracuse University. He rejects the role-model argument for affirmative action, because in his view it comes close to implying that, at most, minorities can teach whites how not to be racist. Thomas, however, favors affirmative action as a corrective to the unconscious prejudices of those who overtly believe in greater equality. Furthermore, he argues that the mission of education depends on bonds of trust between students and teachers, and that these are enhanced by affirmative action.

What good am I as a black professor? The raging debate over affirmative action surely invites me to ask this searching question of myself, just as it must invite those belonging to other so-called suspect categories to ask it of themselves. If knowledge is color blind, why should it matter whether the face in front of the classroom is a European white, a Hispanic, an Asian, and so on? Why should it matter whether the person is female or male?

One of the most well-known arguments for affirmative action is the role-model argument. It is also the argument that I think is the least satisfactory—not because women and minorities do not need role models—everyone does—but because as the argument is often presented, it comes dangerously close to implying that about the only thing a black, for instance, can teach a white is how not to be a racist. Well, I think better of myself than that. And I hope that all women and minorities feel the same about themselves . . .

From Laurence Thomas, "What Good Am I?" in Steven M. Cahn, ed., *Affirmative Action and the University: A Philosophical Inquiry* (Philadelphia, PA: Temple University Press, 1993).

But even if the role-model argument were acceptable in some version or the other, affirmative action would still seem unsavory, as the implicit assumption about those hired as affirmative action appointments is that they are less qualified than those who are not. For, so the argument goes, the practice would be unnecessary if, in the first place, affirmative action appointees were the most qualified for the position, since they would be hired by virtue of their merits. I call this the counterfactual argument from qualifications.

Now, while I do not want to say much about it, this argument has always struck me as extremely odd. In a morally perfect world, it is no doubt true that if women and minorities were the most qualified they would be hired by virtue of their merits. But this truth tells me nothing about how things are in this world. It does not show that biases built up over decades and centuries do not operate in the favor of, say, white males over nonwhite males. It is as if one argued against feeding the starving simply on the grounds that in a morally perfect world starvation would not exist. Perhaps it would not. But this is no argument against feeding the starving now.

It would be one thing if those who advance the counterfactual argument from qualifications addressed the issue of built-up biases that operate against women and minorities. Then I could perhaps suppose that they are arguing in good faith. But for them to ignore these built-up biases in the name of an ideal world is sheer hypocrisy. It is to confuse what the ideal should be with the steps that should be taken to get there. Sometimes the steps are very simple or, in any case, purely procedural: instead of *A*, do *B*; or perform a series of well-defined steps that guarantee the outcome. Not so with nonbiased hiring, however, since what is involved is a change in attitude and feelings—not even merely a change in belief. After all, it is possible to believe something quite sincerely and yet not have the emotional wherewithal to act in accordance with that belief. . . .

The philosophical debate over affirmative action has stalled . . . because so many who oppose it, and some who do not, are unwilling to acknowledge the fact that sincere belief in equality does not entail a corresponding change in attitude and feelings in day-to-day interactions with women and minorities. Specifically, sincere belief does not eradicate residual and, thus, unintentional sexist and racist attitudes. So, joviality among minorities may be taken by whites as the absence of intellectual depth or sincerity on the part of those minorities, since such behavior is presumed to be uncommon among high-minded intellectual whites. Similarly, it is a liability for academic women to be too fashionable in their attire, since fashionably attired women are often taken by men as aiming to be seductive.

Lest there be any misunderstanding, nothing I have said entails that unqualified women and minorities should be hired. I take it to be obvious, though, that whether someone is the best qualified is often a judgment call. On the other hand, what I have as much as said is that there are built-up biases in the hiring process that disfavor women and minorities and need to be corrected. I think of it as rather on the order of correcting for unfavorable moral headwinds. It is possible to be committed to gender and racial equality and yet live a life in which residual, and thus unintentional, sexism and racism operate to varying degrees of explicitness.

I want to return now to the question with which I began this essay: What good am I as a black professor? I want to answer this question because, insofar as our aim is a just society, I think it is extremely important to see the way in which it does matter that the person in front of the class is not always a white male, notwithstanding the truth that knowledge, itself, is color blind.

Teaching is not just about transmitting knowledge. If it were, then students could simply read books and professors could simply pass out tapes or lecture notes. Like it or not, teachers are the object of intense emotions and feelings on the part of students [who are] solicitous of faculty approval and affirmation. Thus, teaching is very much about intellectual affirmation; and there can be no such affirmation of the student by the mentor in the absence of deep trust between them, be the setting elementary or graduate school. Without this trust, a mentor's praise will ring empty; constructive criticism will seem mean spirited; and advice will be poorly received, if sought after at all. A student needs to be confident that he can make a mistake before the professor without being regarded as stupid in the professor's eyes and that the professor is interested in seeing beyond his weaknesses to his strengths. Otherwise, the student's interactions with the professor will be plagued by uncertainty; and that uncertainty will fuel the self-doubts of the student.

Now, the position that I should like to defend, however, is not that only women can trust women, only minorities can trust minorities, and only whites can trust whites. That surely is not what we want. Still, it must be acknowledged, first of all, that racism and sexism have very often been a bar to such trust between mentor and student, when the professor has been a white male and the student has been either a woman or a member of a minority group. Of course, trust between mentor and student is not easy to come by in any case. This, though, is compatible with women and minorities having even greater problems if the professor is a white male.

Sometimes a woman professor will be necessary if a woman student is to feel the trust of a mentor that makes intellectual affirmation possible; sometimes a minority professor will be necessary for a minority student; indeed, sometimes a white professor will be necessary for a white student. (Suppose the white student is from a very sexist and racist part of the United States, and it takes a white professor to undo the student's biases.)

Significantly, though, in an academy where there is gender and racial diversity among the faculty, that diversity alone gives a woman or minority student the hope that intellectual affirmation is possible. This is so even if the student's mentor should turn out to be a white male. For part of what secures our conviction that we are living in a just society is not merely that we experience justice, but that we see justice around us. A diverse faculty serves precisely this end in terms of women and minority students believing that it is possible for them to have an intellectually affirming mentor relationship with a faculty member regardless of the faculty's gender or race.

Naturally, there are some women and minority students who will achieve no matter what the environment. Harriet Jacobs and Frederick Douglass were slaves who went on to accomplish more than many of us will who have never seen the chains of slavery. Neither, though, would have thought their success a reason to leave slavery intact. Likewise, the fact that there are some women and minorities who will prevail in spite of the obstacles is no reason to leave the status quo in place.

There is another part of the argument. Where there is intellectual affirmation, there is also gratitude. When a student finds that affirmation in a faculty member, a bond is formed, anchored in the student's gratitude, that can weather almost anything. Without such ties there could be no "ole boy" network—a factor that is not about racism, but a kind of social interaction running its emotional course. When women and minority faculty play an intellectually affirming role in the lives of white male students, such faculty undermine a nonracist and nonsexist pattern of emotional feelings that has unwittingly served the sexist and racist end of passing the intellectual mantle from white male to white male. For what we want, surely, is not just blacks passing the mantle to blacks, women to women, and white males to white males, but a world in which it is possible for all to see one another as proper recipients of the intellectual mantle. Nothing serves this end better than the gratitude between mentor and student that often enough ranges over differences between gender and race or both.

Ideally, my discussion of trust, intellectual affirmation, and gratitude should have been supplemented with a discussion of nonverbal behavior. For it seems to me that what has been ignored . . . is the way in which judgments are communicated not simply by what is said but by a vast array of nonverbal behavior. Again, a verbal and sincere commitment to equality, without the relevant change in emotions and feelings, will invariably leave nonverbal behavior intact. Mere voice intonation and flow of speech can be a dead giveaway that the listener does not expect much of substance to come from the speaker. Anyone who doubts this should just remind her- or himself that it is a commonplace to remark to someone over the phone that he sounds tired or "down" or distracted, where the basis for this judgment, obviously, can only be how the individual sounds. One can get the clear sense that one called at the wrong time just by the way in which the other person responds or gets involved in the conversation. So, ironically, there is a sense in which it can be easier to convince ourselves that we are committed to gender and racial equality than it is to convince a woman or a minority person, for the latter see and experience our nonverbal behavior in a way that we ourselves do not. Specifically, it so often happens that a woman or minority can see that a person's nonverbal behavior belies their verbal support of gender and racial equality in faculty hiring—an interruption here, or an all-too-quick dismissal of a remark there. And this is to say nothing of the ways in which the oppressor often seems to know better than the victim how the victim is affected by the oppression that permeates her or his life, an arrogance that is communicated in myriad ways. . . .

Before moving on let me consider an objection to my view. No doubt some will balk at the very idea of women and minority faculty intellectually affirming white male students. But this is just so much nonsense on the part of those [who are] balking. For I have drawn attention to a most powerful force in the lives of all individuals, namely, trust and gratitude; and I have indicated that just as these feelings have unwittingly served racist and sexist ends, they can serve ends that are morally laudable. Furthermore, I have rejected the idea, often implicit in the role-model argument, that women and minority faculty are only good for their own kind. What is more, the position I have advocated is not one of subservience in the least, as I have spoken of an affirming role that underwrites an often unshakable debt of gratitude.

So, to return to the question with which I began this essay: I matter as a black professor and so do women and minority faculty generally, because collectively, if not in each individual case, we represent the hope, sometimes in a very personal way, that the university is an environment where the trust that gives rise to intellectual affirmation and the accompanying gratitude is possible for all, and between all peoples. Nothing short of the reality of diversity can permanently anchor this hope for ourselves and posterity. . . .

I do not advocate the representation of given viewpoints or the position that the ethnic and gender composition of faculty members should be proportional to their numbers in society. The former is absurd because it is a mistake to insist that points of view are either gender- or color-coded. The latter is absurd because it would actually entail getting rid of some faculty, since the percentage of Jews in the academy far exceeds their percentage in the population. If one day this should come to be true of blacks or Hispanics, they in turn would be fair game. . . .

[T]he continued absence of any diversity whatsoever draws attention to itself. My earlier remarks about nonverbal behavior taken in conjunction with my observations about trust, affirmation, and gratitude are especially apropos here. The complete absence of diversity tells departments more about themselves than no doubt they are prepared to acknowledge.

I would like to conclude with a concrete illustration of the way in which trust and gratitude can make a difference in the academy. As everyone knows, being cited affirmatively is an important indication of professional success. Now, who gets cited is not just a matter of what is true and good. On the contrary, students generally cite the works of their mentors and the work of others introduced to them by their mentors; and, on the other hand, mentors generally cite the work of those students of theirs for whom they have provided considerable intellectual affirmation. Sexism and racism have often been obstacles to faculty believing that women and minorities can be proper objects of full intellectual affirmation. It has also contributed to the absence of women and minority faculty which, in turn, has made it well-nigh impossible for white male students to feel an intellectual debt of gratitude to women and minority faculty. Their presence in the academy cannot help but bring about a change with regard to so simple a matter as patterns of citation, the professional ripple effect of which will be significant beyond many of our wildest dreams.

If social justice were just a matter of saying or writing the correct words, then equality would have long ago been a *fait accompli* in the academy. For I barely know anyone who is a faculty member who has not bemoaned the absence of minorities and women in the academy, albeit to varying degrees. So, I conclude with a very direct question: Is it really possible that so many faculty could be so concerned that women and minorities should flourish in the academy, and yet so few do? You will have to forgive me for not believing that it is. . . .

Study Questions

1. What is the role-model argument?
2. What does Thomas mean by "unintentional sexist and racist attitudes"?
3. According to Thomas, does an effective mentor need to be of the same race or sex as the student?
4. Do Thomas's arguments in favor of appointing women and minorities also imply the importance of adding members of any other specific groups to the faculty?

Proportional Representation

Celia Wolf-Devine

Celia Wolf-Devine is Professor Emerita of Philosophy at Stonehill College. She argues that numbers alone do not prove discrimination. She questions the assumption that women and members of racial and ethnic minority groups have equal interest in participating in any particular career path. After all, different cultures value different professions. Furthermore, Wolf-Devine doubts that an individual's race or sex is a reliable indicator of what that individual believes. Hence intellectual diversity is not necessarily a consequence of racial or sexual diversity.

I begin by asking a question, an affirmative answer to which seems presupposed by the current debate on affirmative action:[1] Is there necessarily something wrong if there is a low percentage of African Americans or women or Hispanics, et cetera, in the field of college teaching relative to their proportion in the population at large? Why is this a goal we should aim at? I do not mean to deny that women and racial and ethnic minorities have been victims of discrimination in academia (although this is by no means limited to blacks, Asians, Hispanics, and Native Americans—consider, for example, Polish, Lebanese, or Portuguese Americans) or that some discrimination still persists. Such discrimination is bad and should be eliminated; in fact, we ought to put more resources into enforcing antidiscrimination laws. My argument here is that there is no reason to believe that proportional representation of minorities and women among the professoriate is a requirement of justice or that a situation where such

From Celia Wolf-Devine, "Proportional Representation," in Steven M. Cahn, ed., *Affirmative Action and the University: A Philosophical Inquiry* (Philadelphia, PA: Temple University Press, 1993).

proportional representation obtained would necessarily be better than one in which it did not.

Arguments that might be advanced in favor of the claim that something is wrong if women and minorities are not proportionally represented fall into two general categories: those that take the existence of such statistical disparities to be evidence of discrimination or injustice, and those based on the value of diversity. These two types of arguments differ in that those based on the need for diversity would not prove that universities are required as a matter of justice to appoint more women and minorities, but merely that it would be educationally desirable were they to do so. But if it could be shown that the lack of proportional representation of minority groups among the professoriate either itself constituted an injustice or provided adequate evidence of the existence of ongoing injustice, then the case for involvement of the federal government to correct this becomes stronger.

Is Proportional Representation a Requirement of Justice?

Does the lack of proportional representation of women and minorities among the professoriate constitute an injustice? Or is it necessarily evidence of discrimination or injustice of any sort? It would be evidence of injustice or discrimination only if it is reasonable to believe that, in the absence of discrimination and injustice, women and all racial and ethnic minorities would be proportionately represented in college teaching (and other professions). But *is* it reasonable to believe this?

The important issue here philosophically is where we place the burden of proof. Should we assume that the statistics reflect some sort of discrimination or injustice unless we have evidence to the contrary? But why put the burden of proof here? While it is legitimate to put the burden of proof on the employer in cases where the proportion of women and minorities hired is radically lower than their proportion *in the applicant pool*, the case is totally different when we are comparing the proportion of women and minorities in the professoriate with their proportion in the population as a whole.

Looking first at racial and ethnic groups, there is no prima facie reason to suppose that members of different racial and ethnic minorities would be equally likely to want to go into the professoriate and, on the contrary, many reasons to expect that they would not.

To the extent that ethnic and racial groups form at least partially self-contained communities (and they do), members of one community will value different sorts of character traits, encourage the acquisition of different skills, and have different ideas about what sorts of jobs carry the most prestige. Most arguments in favor of affirmative action in fact suppose that racial and ethnic groups differ in these sorts of ways; if they did not, then bringing in a wider variety of such groups would not contribute to diversity.

In one culture, scientists might be particularly respected, while in another being a media personality might be viewed as the height of success. Sometimes traditional patterns in a culture predispose members toward certain professions, as the great respect for Torah scholars in Jewish culture fits very naturally with aspirations for careers as scholars or lawyers. Cultures that are highly verbal might be expected to produce more teachers than others. In addition, of course, as some members of a community go into a particular field, others aspire to go into it also since they already know something about it from their friends and relatives and have contacts in the field.

So even if equal percentages of the members of all racial and ethnic groups might desire some sort of prestigious job, there is no reason to suppose that all of them would regard the same jobs as prestigious. Or to put the point more bluntly, not everyone would regard being a professor as prestigious. And there are special reasons why college teaching might be less attractive than other professions to those (for example, blacks and Hispanics) who are trying to struggle out of poverty. Due to its low salaries relative to the amount of training required, college teaching has long tended to attract people brought up in relatively secure financial conditions, plus a few other individuals who feel a strong calling to the intellectual life. . . .

Ambitious young members of minority groups may quite reasonably prefer careers in law, politics, industry, or the media. Indeed, the problem of how to attract bright young people of *any* racial or ethnic group into college teaching is becoming increasingly severe. Even students who feel strongly drawn to the intellectual life are often deterred from pursuing academic careers by poor salaries and by what they hear about academic politics.

If I am right, then, one important reason why racial and ethnic minorities are not proportionately represented in the professiorate is because those who are in a position to acquire the credentials are going into other professions. Bright, ambitious members of such groups who have B.A.s often find careers in other areas more attractive than college teaching. This is partly a function of their cultures, which may not accord high prestige to professors relative to other professions, and partly a result of low salaries and demoralization among many (although certainly not all) professors. And in order to attract them into the professoriate, it is essential to begin by improving the situation of those already in the field in a number of ways (and not just salary, although that is important). We should then make it clear to minority members that they are genuinely welcome in academia and will receive fair consideration.

Another reason why racial and ethnic minorities are not proportionally represented in the professoriate is because large numbers of them have been deeply scarred by poverty (and often racism) and do not enter college. They are therefore not even in the running for becoming college teachers or for pursuing most careers with high status and pay. The difficulties involved in remedying this situation are massive, and the universities can play only a limited role. Universities could, for example, set up tutorial programs aimed at helping disadvantaged students (and staffed by faculty and student volunteers). Or they could offer scholarships for college and graduate school to talented disadvantaged students or have need-blind admissions if they can afford to do so. Since such programs are costly, government assistance would probably be necessary.

The big question that arises at this point is to what extent such remedial programs should be directed at racial and ethnic minorities. At this point I believe another background fact becomes relevant—one that is too often overlooked by supporters of affirmative action. During the Reagan years, American society underwent a marked polarization between rich and poor. We have, in fact, the most extreme polarization of any industrialized country (measured by the gap between the wealth of the upper fifth of society and that of the lower fifth). And it is arguable that affirmative action has contributed to this polarization (at least it has done nothing to prevent it), since those women and blacks who were in a position to take advantage of it (i.e., those who had suffered less discrimination) did so, leaving the really poor no better off and simply displacing other groups and pushing them down into poverty.[2]

The problem of the widening gap of rich and poor should be confronted directly, rather than gearing remedial programs too closely to race and ethnic group (as affirmative action does). In addition to making people more rather than less race conscious and generating resentments along racial and ethnic lines, such programs are not radical enough, because they lead people to think that by appointing middle-class blacks, Hispanics, or Asians they have thereby really helped the poor.

The poor need direct assistance, and it is not only minority members who are poor. There are enormous numbers of white poor, particularly in rural areas of the South. Many ethnic groups are impoverished and have suffered discrimination at least as severe as that against Hispanics and Asians. The children of single mothers of all races and ethnic groups have been pushed down into severe poverty, and many blue-collar workers have been impoverished (e.g., small farmers or residents of the Minnesota Iron Range). Programs targeted at the economically disadvantaged should perhaps be supplemented by special compensatory programs aimed at blacks and Native Americans (since most Hispanics and Asians are recent immigrants, compensatory arguments do not carry the same force in their case). I do not here take a position on this thorny issue, except to say that not all scholarships and special assistance programs should be earmarked for such groups, but a significant proportion should be awarded on the basis of merit and financial need alone.

The more poor people are brought up into the middle class, the more of them will obtain B.A.s and be in a position to consider college teaching as a career. We will still need to improve the situation of the professoriate if we are to be able to attract good Ph.D. candidates. But at least more people will have a chance to enter the profession, especially if graduate school scholarships are available to talented students who need them. The poor who are not upwardly mobile (e.g., the retired, the chronically ill, the mentally retarded, etc.) will still need direct financial and medical assistance.

The situation of women in academia is somewhat different from that of ethnic and racial minorities, in that they are closer to being proportionally represented, at least in the humanities, although they tend still to be absent from some scientific and technical fields and from the most prestigious positions. Does this prove they are being discriminated against? Certainly in some cases they have been and still are discriminated against (especially in promotion and pay), and these abuses should be corrected. But here also the statistics alone do not establish discrimination. Their own choices to spend more time with their children may account for their failure to advance as far or as quickly as their male colleagues and for the fact that they hold part-time positions more frequently. Certainly not all women make these sorts of choices, but enough do to affect the statistics.

(It could, of course, be argued to be unjust that women take on a larger share of child care, but we should beware of paternalistically telling people what choices they ought to make.)

In order to establish the presence of injustice or discrimination, we need to know more about the actual preferences of the women in question, and not just adopt a bureaucratic approach of trying to get the numbers to come out right. Suppose an academic couple who wish to combine career and family decide between themselves that he will work full time and she will work part time in order to spend time with the children. Then suppose that due to affirmative action he is unable to get a full-time job and she is forced to take full-time work to support the family. The statistics may look better, but both people are less happy than they would have been without affirmative action.

Proportional representation of women and of blacks, Hispanics, Native Americans, and Asians in the professoriate, then, is not a requirement of justice, and a situation where such proportional representation is present is not necessarily more just than one where it is not—for example, if it was obtained by overriding the preferences of those concerned without some reason other than a desire to get the statistics to come out right. Furthermore, a society where such proportional representation was present along with a vast and unbridgeable gap between rich and poor would be less just than one with a more equitable distribution of wealth and opportunities for advancement but which lacked proportional representation of women and minorities in some professions.

Promoting Diversity

Affirmative action is often defended as a means to greater diversity on college faculties, and a faculty that does not have proportional representation of women and minorities is regarded as not diverse enough. Diversity, unfortunately, has become something of a buzzword these days, and it is necessary to give thought to what sorts of diversity should be promoted and why. And this requires some reflection about what the purposes of the university are. Diversity of opinion is not enough, but neither is diversity of methodology. Not all methodologies deserve representation. Consider, for example, astrology, or the systematic vilification of one's opponents.

If one agrees that encouraging intelligent dialogue about important issues is one of the purposes of the university (and I do), then this has at least some implications for the sort of diversity we want.

If dialogue is of central importance, then it is desirable to have intellectual diversity. But limitless intellectual diversity is not good; the value of diversity must be weighed against the value of community. Certainly, there can be communities that are too ingrown and homogenous. If a psychology department appoints only behaviorists, then students are deprived of exposure to other quite legitimate traditions of thought within their discipline. And the same is true if an economics department appoints only followers of Milton Friedman, or a philosophy department appoints only Thomists or only phenomenologists. But on the other hand, too much diversity leads to the breakdown of communication between groups. If this occurs, faculty become unable to talk with each other and work within totally different conceptual frameworks, making no attempts to respond to positions other than their own. Students, then, tend to become hopelessly confused, give up even trying to develop coherent beliefs of their own, and retreat into just giving each professor what he or she wants. Maintaining community is, thus, just as important for education as introducing intellectual diversity.

Suppose, then, we are agreed that intellectual diversity, per se, is not simply a good to be maximized (and in real life, no one, not even the defenders of affirmative action, believes in the value of limitless diversity); we then must specify what sorts of diversity will contribute to stimulating intelligent dialogue and learning on college campuses. And I see no reason why proportional representation of groups now officially recognized as protected minorities should be expected to produce the right sort of diversity. First of all, diversity of skin color is quite consistent with total ideological conformity and therefore need not conduce to dialogue at all.

Furthermore . . . we ought not to suppose that because a person is black or Hispanic he or she will have some particular set of beliefs or espouse a particular methodology. This expectation is a form of racial stereotyping and as such is demeaning to the person. Pressures toward ideological conformity among members of minority groups are increased by this sort of dishonest attempt to smuggle in one's ideological agendas under the guise of affirmative action. A Hispanic who is a Republican is no less a Hispanic, and a woman who is not a feminist is no less a woman.

There is, then, no good reason to suppose that proportional representation of the minority groups now officially recognized will yield the right sort of intellectual diversity. And the same sorts of arguments developed above could be applied to cultural diversity as well as to intellectual diversity. People from the same cultural background share common prereflective attitudes, patterns of feeling and imagination, ways of talking, and styles of behavior. But although it is educationally valuable for students to be exposed to people from different cultures, limitless cultural diversity is not a good thing (for the same reasons that limitless intellectual diversity is not), and skin color is not a reliable guide to culture. An enormous amount of cultural diversity exists, for example, among blacks and Hispanics. Poor rural Southern blacks, for example, may be culturally more similar to poor rural Southern whites than they are to Northern middle-class urban blacks.

In short, one cannot generate the right sort of diversity (intellectual or cultural) by simply pursuing neatly measurable goals like proportional representation of women, blacks, Hispanics, Asians, and Native Americans. In addition, the sort of diversity needed at a given school will itself be a function of a number of factors, such as the character of the faculty already there, the student body, and the sorts of vocations for which students are preparing. A school preparing students for careers in international business or diplomacy might find that the sort of diversity introduced by appointing foreign nationals to their faculty is particularly valuable, for example. These sorts of judgments involve a great many complex considerations and cannot be made mechanically by trying to get statistics to meet some target percentages (comforting though it would be if things were so simple).

Notes

1. By affirmative action, I mean preferential treatment and not just things like announcing openings and encouraging women and minorities to apply. . . .
2. See Kevin Phillips, *The Politics of Rich and Poor* (New York: Random House, 1990), pp. 18, 203, 207.

Study Questions

1. If few women or members of a racial, religious, or ethnic group enter a particular profession, does that circumstance prove that the members of that profession are guilty of discrimination?
2. What does Wolf-Devine mean by "intellectual diversity"?
3. Which types of diversity are most important?
4. How would we know when diversity of a particular sort has been achieved?

PART VI

Sex

Sex and Consent

Seduction, Rape, and Coercion

Sarah Conly

Pressuring a person into having sex is morally problematic. But according to Sarah Conly, Associate Professor of Philosophy at Bowdoin College, most exploitative forms of psychological pressure are significantly different from physical coercion. For example, if one person pressures another to have sex by threatening to leave the relationship, doing so can be legitimate, because the other person is free to leave the relationship. Even seduction, while morally questionable, is not on a par with the threat of physical force.

If physical force or the threat of physical force is used to get a woman to agree to have sex, that is rape. If psychological force is used, can that also be rape?

From Sarah Conly, "Seduction, Rape, and Coercion," *Ethics* 115 (2004).

I. Verbal Coercion

What is at issue here? The question is about what is sometimes called verbal coercion, but the issue is not merely about the use of words rather than actual physical violence. Of course words alone can result in rape, if the words threaten physical violence. The issue here is distinct. Proponents of an expansion of our definition of rape argue that, just as physical force is a form of coercion which invalidates consent so that ensuing sex is rape, it is "verbal coercion" if a person agrees to have sex because of the use of words which cause or threaten to cause (only) emotional duress. . . . The question is whether such pressure, if it results in a person having sex who would not otherwise have wanted to, is indeed coercive; that is, whether it is truly sufficiently harmful and sufficiently wrongful that we may say that the person who changes her mind as a result of such pressure has been raped. What if the motivation to have sex comes not from fear of physical violence but from fear of emotional harm? What if the force used to overcome a woman's resistance is not physical force but emotional pressure? Can this be rape? The answer, I think, is that it may or may not be. Infliction of emotional harm can invalidate consent, and sex that arises as a result of this can thus be rape. Other emotional harms (even if perhaps more painful) can be consistent with valid consent. What we need to do is differentiate between the different circumstances of harm to understand when consent is and is not valid. . . . This turns our attention to the means used to bring a reluctant person to having sex.

Here, too, there is controversy about what (if any) kind of emotional pressure should count as coercive. Campus behavior codes, freed from the evidentiary requirements of a court of law (and freed from the responsibility of sending the perpetrator to prison), have recently seen more prosecutions for what once would have been considered consensual sex, precisely because some have adopted standards of assault which include overbearing of the other's will through emotional pressure. In such cases, the charge of rape seems to stem from the fact that, while the victims were not physically constrained to have sex, they were in some sense browbeaten into having intercourse they would not otherwise have chosen to have. Thus, it is argued, the sex was not truly voluntary. Even the widely accepted admonition that "No Means No" has been the subject of controversy for this reason: what follows from a woman's saying "no" to sex? To proceed immediately to penetration would clearly be wrong, but what about trying to talk her into sex, to press with blandishments or tears, to harangue; in short, to refuse to give up? Opinion is divided: some feel that "no" means simply that you should not advance physically on someone who has told you to stop, but others feel that the spirit of the rule is violated by continuing to verbally press the issue after one person has stated her desire. Especially in the conditions in which such pressure is likely to occur (when it is late and we are tired and/or to some degree inebriated) the pursuit of the sexual goal in the face of opposition has seemed to some to constitute a force which, while not violent, nullifies consent in the same way physical force does.[1]

Proponents of such changes, and corresponding changes in the law, worry about the susceptibility of one person to certain sorts of psychological force brought to bear by another. The psychological forces brought to bear may be various and may be used singly, or . . . conjointly. The aggressor may implore and wheedle until the other feels guilt; he may tease her with jealousy, berate her for her coldness and immaturity, chastise her for the harm she does him, refute her reasoning when she tries to articulate her position, and subject her to a barrage of angry words. Ultimately she may find herself in a state of psychological exhaustion, feeling unable to resist in the face of what seems an implacable will. In these cases, it is argued, the woman has been forced against her will as surely as if the aggressor had used physical violence.

To some, then, the recognition of the potency of some sorts of speech, of the psychological pressure it can convey, is a long-delayed recognition of the true dynamics of (some, many, or all, depending on whom you talk to) sexual encounters. To others this sort of interpretation of a sexual encounter represents a deviation from good sense. It may be unjust in that it castigates as rapists those who simply are persuasive at getting what they want. It may also be harmful to those who concede to such pressure, in particular to women, since they are most often thought of as the victims of such verbal coercion. If we accept that (some) women are unable to withstand the psychological force brought to bear upon them, this makes them seem like less than autonomous agents. If these women had sex when they didn't want to, why then did they have sex? Physical force or the threat of it makes sense of having sex against one's will, it is thought, but absent physical force, how are we to make sense of someone who does something she really doesn't want to do? For some, accepting that psychological pressure could be a means to rape wrongly suggests that women are weak minded, prone to collapse under "emotional pressure" and to concede to the desires of the stronger-minded male. . . .

This is a dilemma. It seems intuitively right to many (and certainly to me) that we should hold the delinquent fathers and foster fathers who threatened their children into sex responsible for being rapists and that the man who had intercourse with the eight-year-old girl was clearly forcing himself upon an innocent victim, whether or not he threatened to hit her if she wouldn't have sex. Yet, it seems implausible to say that whenever someone gives into irrational suasion to have sex, or has sex only out of fear of displeasing someone she cares for, or out of a desire to please, a rape has occurred.

Deciding to Have Sex

The differing notions of choice and rape turn in part on different accounts of the psychology involved—on how the decision about having sex is made. One central issue seems to be whether or not the woman wanted to do what she did, but this is a complex question. What is it not to want to have sex? We are seldom univocal as to reasons for doing anything. A woman may want to have sex to express love, even if she is not physically aroused. Perhaps she is tired, but her husband is leaving for a two-week trip, and she wants to have sex to feel closer to him. Perhaps she even wants to do it just because he wants to do it. He has read a lot of feminist literature, however, and is a sensitive guy and won't sulk or become angry if she doesn't have sex; he just won't feel as happy as he would if she did. She loves him, however, and wants him to feel loved. Even in the latter case, where his attitude contributes to her decision—where indeed, were it not for his desire she wouldn't want to have sex—her having sex doesn't plausibly seem to be rape, any more than my buying Girl Scout cookies only to avoid hurting the feelings of the little girl selling them means I've been robbed. Having a reason to oppose having sex as well as positive reasons to have sex doesn't mean that when she does have sex at another's behest it must be rape. Similarly, however, we cannot say that if a woman had some positive motivation to have sex that means any ensuing sex must have been consensual. Anyone might have a desire to have sex (she was physically aroused, she wants to please the man she is in love with) and have lots of reasons not to have sex—she's afraid of sexually transmitted diseases, she has contrary religious convictions, and so forth. Saying that she wanted to have sex in some ways does not determine whether the ensuing sex is consensual.

What seems to determine the question, then, is not simply whether or not the person had some desire to have or not have sex, or even whether the desire to have sex is a function of another person's antecedent desire, but whether the motivation which decides her to have sex is a result of coercive pressure. If she weighs the religious conviction against her physical arousal and decides that all things considered, she prefers to have sex, she has not been raped. If she weighs her desire not to have sex against the threat of violence by a knife-wielding rapist and decides that, given the choice of sex or death, she, all things considered, prefers to have sex, she has been raped. If her desire to have sex is a result of coercive pressure, then the fact that she did what she wanted to do is neither here nor there, because the options from which she had to choose were illegitimately narrow. The question here, then, is when is psychological pressure coercive?

II. But What Is Coercion?

We need to examine when the criteria we generally feel are required for coercion to be present are also present in cases of psychological pressure. None of these is seen as sufficient for coercion, but all are seen as necessary, and when psychological pressure doesn't meet these criteria, it is not coercive.

Intent

One requirement for coercion is that the coercer is doing what he does intentionally. Accidentally doing something which causes another to decide to have sex with you can't be considered coercive. The question of *mens rea* guilty mind has long played a role in the legal determination of rape. While our discussion is not of what constitutes legal rape but of what constitutes rape from the moral perspective, it may still be held that there can be no wrongdoing unless there is a perpetrator who has acted with a blameworthy frame of mind. In the case of legal rape, the idea is that the perpetrator either knows that the woman has given no valid consent, or should have known, in that he would have known with a reasonable amount of perspicacity or concern. Can the person who has placed psychological pressure be in a sufficiently culpable frame of mind to be held a rapist when he has sex with someone who, without threat of violence, has said that she would, given the circumstances, prefer to have sex?

It seems possible. The culpable frame of mind required for the legal designation of rape is not one where the perpetrator recognizes that he is morally or legally in the wrong. Rather, the perpetrator has simply to know that the victim did not consent or to be in a situation where he should have known. The fact that he may sincerely believe himself to be in the right (because the woman owed him sex, or whatever) does not excuse him. Similarly, while the person who places psychological pressure may believe himself to be in the right in having achieved the other's consent by threatening (mere) psychological pain, this does not suffice to excuse him from the charge of rape. If he knows that the other's consent was obtained only through the pressure he has brought to bear, he is aware of the relevant facts. The question is whether what he has done invalidates consent in the way physical force does, so that the ensuing sex is rape.

Choice

Some may argue that psychological pressure cannot be properly coercive because in typical cases of psychological pressure one has a choice of whether or not to yield, whereas in cases of physical force no such decision is possible. It is possible that, in some cases of psychological pressure, the victim of pressure is so demoralized as to literally lose the ability to choose—and this may be true in the incest cases described earlier—but we cannot assume that this is typical, at least among adults. More normally, in the case of psychological pressure, the victim is not forced to have sex, but rather chooses to have sex in order to prevent losing a relationship, to avoid an angry confrontation, or to avoid other pain. In cases of physical force, it is argued, no such choice is possible.

This looks like a distinction initially, but it does not reflect our modern beliefs about rape. While at one point in time it was true that, both culturally and legally, sex was only considered rape if the woman was literally physically overwhelmed such that she could not stop the assailant in any way, this narrow concept of rape is outmoded. A woman confronted with an armed rapist may yield to the mere threat of force, without our saying she consented to have sex. There is a sense, no doubt, in which she chooses to have sex when she chooses to have sex rather than to be beaten or killed. She was nonetheless raped because the choice is not free, and to say that the choice is not free is to say that she is placed under coercive pressure and made to choose between illegitimate options. Choice under psychological pressure might, then, be equally unfree: the mere ability to choose the better of two alternatives doesn't mean that there was insufficient force for sex to count as rape. That she can choose whether or not to have sex or suffer psychological harm does not in itself mean she has not been raped, any more than the fact that a woman might choose to have sex rather than be violently abused means she hasn't been raped.

Harm

For a choice to be coerced, however, it is necessary that the person doing the choosing has no reasonable choice between doing what the coercer wants and the bad option which the coercer has introduced. Not every threat constitutes coercion, because some threats don't introduce harms great enough to affect my decision procedure. My neighbor can't say he was coerced into supporting my bid for election because I told him I would make terribly unfriendly faces at him if he didn't do so; while I shouldn't be making faces at people who don't support me, it's not so bad that he can claim that he had no other option than to vote my way. Can psychological pain be sufficient to say that the person subjected to threats of psychological harm has no reasonable choice but to succumb to the will of the coercer?

Why not? Clearly, psychological pain can be extreme. A person might recover more quickly from a physical beating than an emotional breakup; indeed, it may be the emotional component of a beating that makes it so bad—the same amount of harm suffered from falling down the stairs would be far less traumatic. The picture the critic has here seems to be of someone who agrees to have sex to avoid some slight loss, say, so her boyfriend won't break a date with her in order to go watch football, and such critics think not having a date just doesn't seem so awful an option as to constrain a person's choice. This is true: one may agree to have sex for foolish reasons, like wanting to brag to friends that her boyfriend has never left her alone on Saturday night. To say the choice to have sex for such slight goods should not count as coerced does not, however, show that psychological pressure generally can't be coercive. The same slippery slope can occur with physical force. What if someone threatens that he will pinch the woman if she does not have sex with him? If she agrees, has she been coerced? Assuming that the woman has the normal capacity for pain, has no peculiar traumas associated with pinching, and so forth, then the threat of a slight pain would probably not count as coercive, whatever the intent of the threatener, because being pinched is a reasonable option to choose over having sex with someone you don't want to have sex with. If she concedes to his wishes, we will probably think she didn't really mind having sex to begin with, even given the uncouthness of his advance. We won't think she was raped.

The point is that, with both physical and psychological threats, there will be greater and lesser pains. Precisely what degree of pain constitutes coercive force will be difficult to say, but there is no reason to think that psychological pain cannot be awful, so awful that it makes unwanted sex the more reasonable option.

Legitimacy

For an offer to be coercive, however, it must do more than constrain the options of the chooser. It must do this illegitimately. Whether or not I coerce my son in telling him he cannot go to the Rollerworld dance unless he does his homework depends on whether I have the right to control his activities in this particular way. Sometimes a pressure may be brought to bear to make someone do something that he or she doesn't want to do and that pressure is entirely within the rights of the individual doing the pressuring. If I tell an employee I will fire him if he doesn't do a better job, I may cause him great distress and overbear his will to play computer games at work, but I haven't done anything wrong. If, on the other hand, I tell him that I will shoot him or even that I will ridicule his appearance around the office, then I have proffered a sanction which is not legitimate, even though my goal may be a reasonable one. Or, if I threaten to fire him, not because he is doing a bad job but because he refuses to enter the basketball pool, I extend my control into realms where I have no right of control. I have a right of sanction, but only in certain ways and only on certain grounds. There are ways we can bend others to our will and ways we can't, and what these are seem to be determined by the nature of the specific relationship. Is it legitimate to pressure someone to have sex? This will depend on the kind of pressure brought to bear and the legitimate parameters of the relationship in which it is brought to bear.

Clearly, in some relationships it is not legitimate to pressure someone to have sex. The cases of the parents and the daughters, above, are ones where the authority of fatherhood does not extend into the realm of sex, and using it is clearly an abuse. Demands for sex in such relationships are illegitimate. In the realm of merely social relationships, though, where there is no personal or institutional authority being extended to a use beyond its justified parameters, the issue is not so clear. Can a person legitimately threaten to break off with someone if she refuses to have sex, intending that this threat will make her have sex where normally she would choose not to? Can he legitimately do this knowing that her pain at his prospective departure will be the determining factor in her decision to have sex with him? There are two cases: he threatens to break off because that is his sincere intent if no sex is included in the relationship and he feels he should let her know this. Or, he may threaten to break off, sincerely intending to leave this unsatisfactory relationship but also hoping that his threat will motivate her to have sex, even if her other desires not to have sex remain in place. That is, in the second case he hopes to manipulate her into doing what he wants. Reflection shows that, while the second of these may be less than admirable, neither case constitutes rape.

Clearly, as the boss may fire the employee, one person may break up with another. Clearly, as the boss may threaten the employee with firing in order to improve his performance, one may threaten the other person in a relationship with a break-up if things don't improve. Can the specific area of improvement be sexual? It is not that a romantic partner has a duty, explicit or implicit, to provide sex, in the way that an employee does have a duty to do the work associated with the job. At the same time, the absence of this duty in a romantic relationship is a function of the fact that such relationships are open ended. Just as being in a relationship does not, per se, give one any duties, it is also the case that one can, without stepping out of bounds, make the relationship dependent on various conditions that suit one's own needs. Often the things which are asked are those we are so familiar with we may think of them as simply constitutive of there being a relationship, but they may in fact be conditions set by one partner for another. Person A may say she wants Person B to communicate more if they are to stay together. Person B may insist that Person A remain faithful and that, without this condition being met, person B will leave. We don't look upon these demands as being coercive, but rather as the sorts of conditions most people set on relationships, as a legitimate attempt to craft the relationship they want, even if that requires finding a different partner. This may be manipulative, in that the intent is to make someone do something she wouldn't otherwise want, but it seems manipulative in a way which we accept in dealing with others, where introducing systems of rewards and sanctions to get others to do what you want, in this less than ideal world, is sometimes necessary and often goes by the name of compromise. We may say that, if you will do the dishes, I will do the cooking; if you won't do the dishes, I won't do the cooking. It would be much nicer if we didn't pressure one another to change behaviors, as it would be nicer if we never even wanted the other to change. In the real world, though, this happens, and we recognize that this sort of trade-off is an unfortunate need when people of different desires try to stay together. Relationships are founded on odd precepts, and if one of the partners is unilaterally responsible for making the continuance of the relationship conditional on the relationship including some particular activity, that is in itself legitimate. . . .

Are such conditions always legitimate? No. As with employer-employee relationships, there are limits to what you may demand and limits to what sanctions you may threaten if even your legitimate demands are not met. Demands placed within a relationship should have reasonable bearing on the health of the relationship, and should not be inherently immoral, and sanctions offered for failure to meet even reasonable demands are limited. I am assuming, however, that engaging in sex, all things being equal, is not immoral and has reasonable bearing on the relationship, and thus that meeting its absence with discontinuing the relationship is, as argued above, a justified response.

So, it does seem within a person's rights to want sex to be a part of a romantic relationship and also within that person's rights to tell the partner that, if there is no sex, he will decamp. This does amount to a demand, indeed a threat, insofar as the fear of losing the relationship is an incentive to have sex and the one intends this fear to motivate the other to have sex, just as the wife who says she'll divorce if her husband is unfaithful again intends this fear to motivate him to change his ways. When you enter into a relationship, however, you lay yourself open to the possibility of being hurt in various ways. One is that the other person may tell you you'll be dumped if you don't change, and that may place you in a painful dilemma, that is, doing something you don't want to do or losing the relationship. This can be true if you are asked to be faithful, and it can be true if you are asked to have sex. Just as the one person has the right to ask, the other has the right to decide not to do any of the things she is asked. But no one has the right to insist that a relationship cause no pain, and no one can claim to have been coerced just because the prospect of pain changes behavior.

III. Deciding to Have Sex, Redux

Not every case of deciding to have sex is so clear, however. It would be nice if every person who decided to have sex weighed all the advantages and disadvantages of doing so, decided correctly which considerations have the most weight for her or him, and acted accordingly. In such cases we may say the person did what he or she wanted to do. What do we say, though, when we confront an agent whose actions do not accurately reflect her strongest desire? Many persons engage in sex in a way which they later regret, not just because of unforeseen consequences but because the act was, even at that time, contrary to their overall motivational structure; it was in some sense not what they truly wanted at the time. Some people have sex out of weakness of will. . . .

Not surprisingly, this happens frequently in the realm of sexuality, where on the one hand there is a strong motivation to engage in sexual activity and on the other hand there are many desires and values which mitigate against it. This in itself, however, may have nothing to do with coercion. Two people can weakly and mutually succumb to the lure of romance (or whatever) without their roles being that of victim and villain. While weakness is no doubt morally problematic in terms of each person's assessment of his or her own character, neither has anything to blame the other for, any more than the dieter can blame the whipped cream. The problem arises when one feels that one's weakness has somehow been induced by another.

A. Seduction

Weakness induced by another is what we've come to know as seduction. In seduction, a person does not simply act weakly because she finds the prospect of sex overwhelmingly tempting; she is brought to this weakness by the interference of someone else. There are two ways this can happen: the victim of seduction can be brought to do something that she in many way likes but which she is trying to resist. She can be led to succumb to temptation so that desire overcomes conviction. Or, she may be importuned to do something that she is not attracted to, and distracted by grief or fear, she may give in, without fully rational consideration. It is this which might lead one to see seduction as a species of rape, because pressure is brought to bear on the woman to act in a way that runs counter not just to what she would not want without that pressure but also to what she really wants even given that pressure. . . .

The proximity of the lure causes her to see it most vividly and to feel its attractions most poignantly, and this causes her to choose weakly, to give in to temptation. The important thing is that these appeals do not contribute to any rational decision-making process, but rather undercut it. The seducer does not allow the other time to collect herself, to think about what it really would be best to do. Thus, the circumstances may be as relevant as the content of the appeal in determining whether or not this is seduction: what in mid-afternoon over coffee in the student union might be a rational discussion about the desirability of including sex in the relationship may well be productive of an emotional maelstrom at 2:00 A.M. in the dark of his room. Were she in control of herself, she might resist, or she might, upon reflection, have a change of heart and decide that, if having sex is the only way to continue the relationship, then that is worth it. But in this circumstance reflection is not an option, and no exertion of self-control is forthcoming. She gives in, unable to resist the pressure of the moment, unable to act on the decision she would make if the circumstances of his demands did not induce weakness.

Weakness and positive temptation

If a man consciously tries to undercut a woman's decision-making process by arousing emotion and is successful in this, is the ensuing sex rape? Consider, first, an analogous case, where the seduced is already attracted to whatever it is that she is trying to resist and where the seducer increases her desires while trying to undercut her appreciation of the reasons to resist. You go into a store, where your eye is caught by the attractive but expensive item you've always wanted but know to be a luxury you can't afford. As you stand contemplating it, you are approached by the High Pressure Salesman, who is paid by commission and who is not going to be dissuaded from trying to sell you this piece by considerations of your welfare. It's him against you, and he does everything he can to overcome your defenses. Well, not everything he can—he doesn't pull a gun and threaten you with death if you don't buy the item; he doesn't tell you that your safety or the security of your children is at stake. He doesn't use violence as a threat in any sense nor induce terror. Rather, he tries to subvert your reasoning process. When you tell him, weakening, that you can't afford the a. but e. item, he tells you that in the long run the item isn't really that expensive; if, for example, you calculate how much you will be paying per hour, the amount is negligible. He argues that, in certain cases, the item may even be construed as saving you money—you'll be using the a. but e. item so much that you won't spend on all those other less attractive items and, anyway, when it's time for resale you might well get rid of the a. but e. item for more than you paid for it. . . . And most of all, whatever he says, he doesn't let you think.

He looks for a point of vulnerability, a weakness through which he can corrupt the solid reasoning process with which you came in and convince you that what he wants is really what you want. . . .

Would this work? It depends, of course, on the person. For one thing, you've got to be tempted by the a. but e. item to begin with and to have a sufficiently ingenuous character not to recognize that this is essentially an adversarial relationship. As with seduction, only some people are vulnerable to the pressure. But, as with seduction, some people are vulnerable, and they give in, only to rue an action which was expressive neither of their heartfelt desires nor their considered principles. This is bad. We look down on high pressure salesmen as being manipulative and self-interested. But while this is true, such a sales technique is not assault. The salesman does not rob you. He does not even misrepresent issues of fact. He aids you to pursue something you want by increasing your desire for it and decreasing your recognition of the reasons against it. This is like a person who wants you off your diet and wafts fresh bread under your nose while telling you that just this once won't hurt. It wouldn't work if you weren't enticed by the smell of fresh bread. It might not work if they weren't also talking to you to reduce your resistance. Combining the two things, though, sometimes does work. In the realm of sexuality, it is like someone who increases the other's already existing desire to have sex, perhaps by touch, perhaps by words, while trying to dispose of their reasons not to have sex.

Such a person is not admirable, but just as the high pressure salesman is not a robber and the bread-wafter is not guilty of assault by force-feeding, the seducer who persuades you to do something you are attracted to but might otherwise have been able to resist is not guilty of rape. If he touches you when you have told him to stop, he is guilty of assault, but if you don't try to stop him from touching you and you let him talk to you about why it is okay to have sex, changing your mind is ultimately a decision for which you are responsible.

Weakness and negative sanctions

What if you are led to act weakly, though, not because of a positive attraction but because of a threat of emotional pain? And what if the other has induced this emotional pain just in order to subvert your thinking processes and get you to do what they want? This is not so much temptation as anxiety and as such it looks much more like coercion. Again, let us take a (putative) analogy which has been defused by avoiding sexual content. Let us imagine your sleazy Cousin Beau.

Beau is a charming ne'er do well. He's always had a kind word for you, his little cousin, and when you were young, he would take you for piggy-back rides when your more sober relatives engaged in boring conversations and imitate their irritable admonitions at the dinner table. Now, though, you are a young adult, with a good job and a disposable income, and Beau approaches you with dollar signs in his eyes. His proposition is vague but urgent—that you should invest your savings in a business opportunity directed by Beau himself. You are not so blinded by affection as to think that this looks like a golden opportunity, but you don't know how to handle the situation. Beau has always been so funny and kind, and he looks so sincere, and the imagined prospect of your refusal seems to cut him, a member of your own family with whom you've enjoyed so many youthful hours, to the quick. If you had time you could think more clearly, but giving you time to think is just what he doesn't want. He stresses his own suffering, hearkens back to the many times he's helped you, and suggests that he can't possibly feel the same in the future if you won't do this little thing, which can't possibly hurt you and which could help him so much. You feel guilty, you feel sorry, you feel Beau may turn against you if you fail him, and, most of all, you feel confused. The more Beau sees this, the harder he pushes. And, suppose that he is joined in the pursuit of your money by Cousin Flo. Flo has never been a buddy. She has spent both your youths making you feel inferior for your poor sense of fashion, your inability to attract boyfriends, your ugly nose. As such things often happen, instead of rejecting Flo as unworthy of your attention, you tried all the harder to live up to her standards—after all, she was older, prettier, and obviously cooler. The one thing you want to do is avoid that sneer. When Cousin Flo castigates you for once again failing to make the grade by investing in this great opportunity, when she says she'd hoped that you would finally have caught up to her in taste and acumen and would thus take the cousins up on this proposition, you quail. You've been worn down by a youth of inferiority, and it's as hard to muster the strength to withstand her judgment now as it was then.

Cousin Beau is a sleaze. Cousin Flo has a despicable character. But for all this, I don't think we can say that they are thieves, nor even that they are extortionists. It isn't that you haven't reasonable alternatives to giving them money. It is rather that you don't, as Beau gazes at you appealingly, or as Flo curls her lip, see your way clearly as to what your choice should be. The cousins have placed pressure of a sort an honorable person wouldn't, and we evaluate their character accordingly, but they have not forced your compliance. . . .

Are these analogous to seduction? They have in common that they feature people who coax, cajole, wheedle, importune, harangue, berate, and browbeat another into doing their bidding. Certainly there are differences. Strangely, women may be more vulnerable when it comes to giving up their bodies than to giving up money. On the one hand, we recognize the body to be the locus of autonomy, not to be interfered with, but on the other hand we romanticize a man's pursuit of a hesitant woman in a way that may make a woman feel unnaturally cold, inferior, and guilty if she doesn't yield to his passion. Furthermore, the use of the body by another can be much more of a loss than the loss of money; few things hit as close to home as having one's very body taken over by another. But the fact that seduction is worse than having money wormed out of you, just as rape is worse than theft, doesn't mean the analogy is not apt. The point is that the difference between seduction and rape is the same as finagled money loss and robbery. The seducer tries to suborn the person's thought process just the way Cousin Beau does. The thief and the rapist don't try to undercut the victim's ability to decide what she should do: they don't need to, because they present her with a choice—her money or her life, sex or being beaten—that she can make quite rationally.

The question, then, is not so much whether a person is acting weakly or fully in accordance with her own judgment, or whether she is acting in a way she would not were it not for the pressures of another, rather than acting uniquely on her own desires. The question is whether these pressures placed on her, and which may make her decide against her own most considered desires, are placed on her appropriately.

But, one might ask, can it ever be proper to place pressure on adults to do what they really don't want to do, either by increasing a desire they are trying to fight or by diminishing or outweighing a desire which is really in accord with their overall motivational structure? . . .

B. Persuasion

When it comes to sex, there is no doubt that, in some cases, the lover who tries to sell sex to his reluctant partner truly thinks that she will be better off once she sees how great sex with him is. In others, the effort is surely not so disinterested, but it is again within the normal scope of relationships that we try to persuade others to do what we want and that that persuasion is not purely rational. We need perhaps a more general recognition of the fact that, when it comes to sex, the two parties involved may have a conflict of interests and that cultural stereotypes and ideologies have been invented which try to hide this fact. We cannot assume that even the most romantic of encounters is not at heart adversarial. But adversarial interests may not make an action immoral. It is often fair enough that we want different things and that we try to get the other person to do what we want.

And where such actions are immoral, where we go beyond the normal degree of dishonesty or manipulation implicit in human relationships, the resulting intercourse may not be rape. It is not rape if the person asking for sex stays within what he has a right to ask for. This is not to say that there are conditions where one has a right to have sex even if the other person does not consent: there aren't. Rather, one has a right to ask for the other's consent and to try to persuade the other to give consent as long as one does this within legitimate parameters: the other should be a competent adult, capable of making a decision; sanctions should only be those one has a right to impose, like ending the relationship, not violence; there should be no use of authority derived from extraneous positions (as father, employer, etc.). No one has a right to control our bodies or to touch us when we do not want to be touched, but it is a part of our lives as moral agents that people close to us have the right to talk to us about things we may not want to hear, even when that means they are being downright nasty. We can go away if we want and not see the person any more but, if we want to be involved in a relationship, we cannot reasonably insist that we never hear anything we don't want to hear. It is part of our life as moral agents that we need to learn to negotiate through others' desires. . . .

V. Conclusion

We need to expand our conceptual framework and our terminology so that we can capture greater differences than we typically do. There is a cultural tradition which has divided sexual intercourse into either morally unacceptable rape or morally acceptable nonrape. The truth is that there are many finer distinctions which we need to recognize and to which we need to develop a sensitivity. We do this in other areas, where we recognize actions of deceit, hurtfulness, and damage which are not the worst of transgressions and yet which are not morally neutral. We know generally that there is a difference between actions which (*a*) infringe others' rights (say, stealing), (*b*) don't infringe others' rights but are nonetheless wrong (like failing to give to someone in need), (*c*) are not wrong but which nonetheless evince bad character (giving to the needy but only to feel your own superiority), and (*d*) are none of these yet may nonetheless be regrettable for their repercussions. What we need to understand is that sex is at least as complex as other areas of human interaction and has just as many varieties of wrong as well as of good, and as we have been accustomed to differentiate within other areas of human interaction so should we here.

To subsume all areas of sexual wrong under the heading of rape does a disservice to all concerned. It hurts those whose laudable goal is just to show that sex can be dark and hurtful; they lose credibility when they are perceived as exaggerating, and their perfectly appropriate criticisms of sexual practice may be dismissed. It is bad for those who are the aggressors in any sexual situation, who may feel that, as long as they have not committed rape, their actions are morally neutral: they need to learn that actions outside of rape can be despicable and to cultivate awareness as to which are and which are not morally acceptable forms of suasion. To call all sexual wrongdoing rape also does a disservice to those who have suffered the absolute terror of violent assault and whose suffering can't, I think, be compared to that of the person who has reluctantly agreed to have sex to avoid emotional distress. This may be a case where analytical philosophy, with its conceptual distinctions and semantic precision, can indeed explain something to our sense of order and can actually be useful.

Note

1. One well-known example of a college sexual offense policy which deviates greatly from the law is the Antioch College Sexual Offense policy. While the Antioch policy does not specifically address verbal coercion, it articulates two common concerns; first, it says that rape can occur even where there is no physical force or threat of physical force; second, it introduces a far more stringent standard of what real consent is than that in use in rape law. . . .

Study Questions

1. What does Conly mean by "coercion"?
2. What is "weakness of will"?
3. Is pressuring someone to have sex ever legitimate?
4. According to Conly, why can philosophy be useful in understanding the subject of seduction?

Sex under Pressure

Scott A. Anderson

Scott Anderson, Assistant Professor of Philosophy at the University of British Columbia, argues against the views of Sarah Conly, who treats the psychological pressure to have sex as analogous to pressure from an unscrupulous salesperson. Anderson argues that social conditions make these cases disanalogous. Because we live in a male-dominated society, the psychological pressure to have sex differs importantly from the psychological pressure to buy a new item at the store.

Seduction is not always a matter of charms, flatteries, and sparks; sometimes it is less like runaway passion and more like sexual assault. But even when it is not criminal, it can be ethically suspect. Seducers often use plain and not-so-plain pressure to get the objects of their desires to acquiesce to sexual proposals. Further problems stem from the way background forces and injustices—systematic gender hierarchy, for instance—empower some seducers and weaken their targets. How are we to evaluate the ethics of such pressuring? And in particular, how useful is it to ask whether such pressure amounts to a kind of coercion, or to ask whether the person seduced consents under such pressure? . . .

A recent essay by Sarah Conly throws a useful light on this question.[1] She explores the issues in sexual pressuring by investigating the ethics of similar techniques as they are used in non-sexual contexts. Although Conly's approach manifests great good sense, . . . there are problems with some of its central insights. We cannot fully appraise the pressures seducers use without attending to the wider context

From Scott A. Anderson, "Sex under Pressure: Jerks, Boorish Behavior, and Gender Hierarchy," *Res Publica* 11 (2005).

in which they occur. This context includes our hierarchical gender system, as well as the many other sources of pressure to have (or sometimes not to have) sex that come from friends, peers, parents, and the social organization of many spheres of (especially young) adulthood.

One might suppose that as long as the pressures involved in seduction do not undermine or disregard the target's consent, then such pressures are ethically unexceptional. But a proper appreciation of the place of consent requires us to attend to certain structural aspects of human interaction, especially sexual interaction, which may affect consent's value. I will argue that Conly, like some others who have recently tackled the topic, overlooks these deeper structural matters. Male seducers, unlike women, are able to draw upon advantages conferred by male dominance within a gender hierarchy. If we fail to attend to such contextual features of gender relations, it will be difficult to see why ordinary sexual pressuring ('seduction') by men is ethically more serious than many other ways one might be a jerk; conversely, attending to this context may indicate ways to undercut these advantages, and thereby to promote women's autonomy and satisfaction in their sexual relationships with men.

Consent to Sex Under Pressure

Our laws, social norms, religious views, and personal values give us numerous, sometimes conflicting directions for what is good or bad, permissible or impermissible, in the pursuit of sexual relationships with others. Some methods are ruled out entirely, while others are at least ethically suspect. Philosophers have taken to investigating the relationship between sex and laws, norms and values in part because we want to protect the autonomy of people in making decisions about whom to have sex with, when, how, and so on. Among the suspect methods of starting or furthering a sexual relationship is the use of psychological pressure aimed to overcome the hesitation or resistance of a prospective sexual partner. The difficulty in evaluating the use of pressure techniques can be brought out by comparing them to rape or sexual assault. These latter violations are accomplished by direct physical force or by using the threat of such force, or by use of disabling drugs, or when someone is physically unable to consent. These uses of power against a person allow an aggressor to proceed to have sex with his victim regardless of what she wants, thus manifesting complete disregard for her consent, and undercutting her autonomy. We have no difficulty, we may presume, in agreeing that any such conduct is wrong and should be illegal. Using pressure techniques to achieve a seduction, however, seems trivial by comparison. Hence there is an opening and use for a dedicated philosophical account of the ethics of pressuring someone into having sex.

In Conly's essay we find . . . guidance on a variety of cases where one person uses various forms of psychological pressure or manipulation in order to get another to acquiesce to sex. . . . Conly focuses the heart of her essay on less extreme cases of seduction involving ordinary, competent adults. She analyzes common seduction as a kind of intentionally induced 'weakness of the will'. The seduced party is brought to engage in or consent to activity that she would reject if allowed a cool moment and time to reflect. The seduced party yields because the seducer has applied various forms of pressure to her that breaks down or circumvents her ability to follow her best interests, rightly viewed. The pressures of interest here are limited to those of ordinary, if not laudable, social or familial interaction—e.g., wheedling, whining, emotional manipulation, mild intimidation, petty deceits, and threats to alter or end one's relationship with someone who refuses to bend to one's will. (I will refer to the lot of these as 'pressures' or 'boorishness' where these terms will then exclude more objectionable means. Those who engage in such activities I will call 'jerks'.) Seducers intentionally use these pressure techniques precisely because they tend to induce people to acquiesce to the wishes of seducers, even though doing so is against what the seduced person (at least initially) regarded as her best interests.

There are a number of ways one might evaluate the ethics of using pressure techniques in sexual pursuits, but any such evaluation must be wary of condemning activity which, even if not ideal, is in the interests of the parties involved, and carries no serious external costs. Conly holds that the key issue in evaluating a jerk's use of pressure is whether the jerk *coerces* the target of attention into sexual activity the target does not want. . . . [T]he critical elements of the test for coercion are whether a particular threatened sanction is sufficiently harmful or painful to leave the target 'no choice' but to avoid it; and whether the threatener acts illegitimately in threatening to impose such a sanction. When a use of pressure satisfies both of these conditions, it counts as coercive; otherwise, the pressure is non-coercive, and its use to obtain sexual favors is, if not benign, at least of lesser moral concern than rape or the extreme forms of seduction from which Conly begins.

Conly argues that less egregious forms of sexual pressuring are non-coercive, and thus lack the . . . moral implications that rape or sexual assault have. She notes, 'it seems implausible to say that whenever someone gives into irrational suasion to have sex, or has sex only out of fear of displeasing someone she cares for, or out of a desire to please, a rape has occurred'. Although the boorish behavior of a seducer may be problematic, within the context of a romantic relationship, the use of emotional pressures is not, she thinks, illegitimate. . . .

Conly then turns to the question of whether playing on the weaknesses or emotions of one's desired partner makes one's use of pressure illegitimate. She stacks such cases up against ones in which salespeople or relatives use similar techniques to close a sale or to cajole someone into investing in their schemes. However unpleasant or inappropriate such measures are, they fall short of criminal: if you submit to the high-pressure salesman's pitch, or invest in a good-for-nothing relative's scheme, you have nonetheless not been robbed. Similarly, she holds, if one succumbs to the temptations, badgering, or guilt-trips of a (would-be) lover, one cannot reasonably accuse him or her of rape:

> It is not rape if the person asking for sex stays within what he has a right to ask for. . . . We can go away if we want and not see the person any more but, if we want to be involved in a relationship, we cannot reasonably insist that we never hear anything we don't want to hear. It is part of our life as moral agents that we need to learn to negotiate through others' desires (118–19).

Based on these considerations, Conly . . . reasonably opposes dichotomizing sexual intercourse into either rape or non-rape. 'The truth is that there are many finer distinctions which we need to recognize and to which we need to develop a sensitivity'. She further denies that all uses of pressure to have sex are on a par; for instance, she holds that it is illegitimate for employers to use their economic leverage to pressure employees into having sex, or for parents and teachers to use their authority to seduce. . . .

Consent to Sex in Context

It is uncontroversial that coercing someone into sex is condemnable, and thus that all permissible means of inducing another to have sex must be non-coercive. Our question is whether and how to draw ethical distinctions among the various non-coercive means, and what then to do with those distinctions. . . . My aim here is not so much to defend the rhetoric connecting seduction to rape, but to argue that there is something valuable in looking for connections here. This value is easily overlooked by an account of seduction like Conly's, which analyzes it in terms of coercion, understood pressures on the will, and consent. Her account, I will suggest, fails to make sense of the reasons that have led feminists to try to forge this connection. By narrowing our analysis of seduction to the individual's use of pressure and its effects on the seducee's will, she tends to ignore background factors that are crucial to understanding the ethics of the seducer's behavior and the problems of seduction for the seduced.

We can see reason to worry about this in the generic way Conly treats ethical judgments about sex, which is insensitive to the special context of sex and sexuality that give sexual pressuring its particular urgency. She writes, for instance, that

> [T]he fact that seduction is worse than having money wormed out of you, just as rape is worse than theft, doesn't mean the analogy is not apt. The point is that the difference between seduction and rape is the same as finagled money loss and robbery.

Regarding the criminality of the conduct involved, Conly may be correct; but insofar as she is drawing a deeper lesson about how these behaviors compare as social ills, her analysis misses the deep difference that context makes in these disparate fields of ethical concern. While robberies and finagling may both point up the evils of greed and the importance we attach to money, robbing and finagling are not connected in the way that raping and pressuring into sex are. The fact that there are robbers about, and that one must take precautions against them does not greatly affect the viability of finagling or the harm involved in it. Nor do finaglers exacerbate the damages caused by robbers. By contrast, the existence and pervasiveness of violence used as a means to obtain sex is integrally connected to the hierarchical structure of gender relations. This structure in turn greatly alters the viability of a man's pressuring a woman into sex, and the harm such pressuring causes—even if she does not relent, and especially if she does.

Conly's analysis leaves no room for these contextual matters, in that it treats seduction as strictly a matter of one individual's questionable ethical conduct impacting another individual who is potentially afflicted by weakness of the will. Both of these individuals suffer from what amount to internal defects of character, which apparently have nothing to do with each other. . . .

[I]f one limits one's evaluations of sex under pressure to a choice between *consensual* versus *coerced*, one is left with little to say about what is wrong or problematic with the behavior of men who pressure women into having sex with them. In this light, we may regard those feminists who have linked such pressuring to rape as attempting to bring into view the problematic role that gender hierarchy plays in framing the situation faced by a woman targeted by a male seducer. Despite denying this connection, Conly does apparently think there is something problematic about the pressuring conduct of jerks, and not just in the cases where it oversteps the line between boorishness and assault. The question is how to explain the nature of this problem. . . .

Evaluating Sexual Pressure in a Context of Sexual Inequality

In explaining why a woman submits to sex with a man, it will often suffice to say that he threatened her with violence if she refused. We rarely feel we need to press further and ask why she assumed that he was capable of violence, why she assumed the threat was in earnest, or why she assumed that if she denied him that he would have gone ahead, against his own interests, and executed his threat. Even if he is a relative stranger to her, we do not usually press for answers to such questions. Why? Because we know what men, or at least some men, are like. That is, we know such things as that it is not uncommon for men to harm women awfully, that men often do so even against their own best interests, and that demonstrating an inclination to do so can alter the ground-rules for their interactions with women to their advantage. In other words, our understanding of how men can coerce women into unwanted sex depends upon our understanding of the kinds of powers men possess over women, when they are likely to use them, and so forth.

To understand the ethical significance of pressuring into sex, we need to have a similar understanding of how and why such pressure works. It is not wholly obvious why pressuring someone to have sex is at all likely to succeed, or work better than thoughtfulness and charm, say, or why using pressure appears to some a reasonable strategy with respect to their ends. The idea that one person could put pressure on another to do something antecedently unwanted is straightforward enough; in some sense, just asking another to do something is a form of pressure. Yet this does not explain why anyone would yield to such pressure. It is helpful here to bear in mind that all pressurings, whether towards sex or any other end, take place in a particular context that likely provides us with various facilities and obstacles concerning our ability to resist external pressure. In some contexts (say, parent–child relations), the use of pressure works largely because children have no choice but to rely on their parents. Such pressure is also entirely expected and reasonable because of the need to sway the behaviors and values of people not yet fully formed or competent to judge independently. In other contexts (say, strangers passing on the street), the use of pressure to alter personal choices is not just unexpected and culturally inappropriate, it is also fairly easy to dismiss without loss. One can walk away, and the pressurer usually has no useful avenue by which to continue or increase his pressuring.

Thus the ability of one person to pressure another into unwanted sex needs to be explained by reference to the factors that make such pressure relevant to one's ends, predictably effective in altering behavior, and socially viable (i.e., not quickly and strongly discouraged). My suggestion is that an investigation into the workings of pressuring into sex will reveal real differences in its significance when used by men as opposed to when used by women. So, for example, when a fraternity man pressures a sorority woman into sex, we would do well to notice how institutional, social, and relational factors combine to make such pressure viable. On the (relatively) more benign side are included factors such as the interest sorority women have in fitting in with their sisters and in finding dates for social functions. More problematically, there are pressures associated with proving one's physical attractiveness, attracting a steady boyfriend as a protector/shield against unwanted aggression, and in avoiding an escalation of aggression that could lead to rape. . . .

Furthermore, men pressuring women into having sex takes place against a background in which men and women differ in their ability to use or to resist violent attack. . . . Thus, we should not divorce our analysis of pressuring techniques in intimate encounters from the wider range of techniques a party has at his or her disposal. Even if men and women were equally likely to resort to boorish behavior to achieve their sexual ends, men are known to turn sometimes to much more potent and dangerous techniques than women typically are, and men are generally able to fend off the relatively few women who might be inclined to use such techniques themselves. Hence the ability to apply pressure to have unwanted sex may differ markedly between men and women on average. Men are able to pressure women more effectively because their pressure is backed by their much greater ability to escalate that pressure into the range of the very dangerous.

Of course, when a man pressures a woman to have sex with him, he may well be unwilling to engage in such escalation; that is, he may be willing to pressure or manipulate her, but not to lay a hand without consent. But once he demonstrates that he is willing to violate norms of proper respect for his intended in the first way, it may be much harder for her to tell that he is not willing to resort to more potent means. Whether he likes it or not, his ability to apply pressure is augmented by the background common knowledge that men have the ability and a non-trivial likelihood to use force and violence against women. Unless, that is, he makes special provisions to defeat this augmentation. To do so, he would have to indicate that even though he is willing to violate certain lesser ethical norms, he would refuse to violate the more vital ones. . . . [I]t is a rather tricky matter to communicate such principles, and it would also work against one's advantage to do so. So a man might need to be subtle, unfussy and explicit—all at once—to employ boorish means to pressure a woman to have sex, while refraining from drawing upon the strength conferred by his access to more deeply unethical ones. . . .

The advantages that male jerks have compared to female jerks might also help explain the fact that the reported effects of being subjected to such techniques appear to differ significantly along gender lines. Some researchers have reported that sexual aggressiveness by women against men is more acceptable than analogous aggression by men against women would be. When women are aggressive, it is often reconceived as 'romance' or 'expressing her sexuality' or being 'seductive'[2]. Some studies have also found that men's reactions to being aggressed against by a woman differ markedly depending upon the attractiveness of the aggressor.[3] By contrast, women frequently report much more negative responses to being subjected to sexual pressure from men. . . .

[T]his understanding of how pressuring into unwanted sex works, and the context in which it occurs, suggests our question is more complex than choosing between allowing women the right to have sex with jerks versus denying the validity of their consent to such sex. In the context of gender hierarchy enforced by violence (among other forms of power), the ethical defects in a man's pressuring a woman to have sex reach beyond its boorishness, and may encompass a kind of unfair advantage-taking, among other things. As the microcosm of undergraduate Greek life in the U.S. suggests, a wide range of pressures fall on individuals making decisions about sex, and many of these pressures derive from the hierarchical (and heterosexist) nature of contemporary gender relations. When a man goes ahead and violates such norms as exist to protect women's sexual autonomy, he may at the same time be availing himself of the disparity in power between men and women more generally. Hence, whether or not we should deny the possibility of a woman's consenting to sex in such conditions, we can certainly criticize the boorishness of a male jerk's sexual conduct for reasons that may not apply to analogous conduct in non-sexual matters, or even to women's sexual boorishness, for that matter.

As for positive suggestions arising from this analysis, we can agree with Conly's reluctance to equate sexual pressuring and rape, either ethically or legally, but we need not suppose that such equations exhaust the range of our potential ethical responses. It may be an advance simply to be able to say why pressuring someone to have sex she does not want is bad: for instance, by pointing out how such pressure frequently relies on a background of violence and inequality, or how such pressure tends to ally with other pressures which additively may give women many fewer opportunities for social or other fulfillment than they might have otherwise. It may also be the case that some institutions, such as fraternities, sororities, and the like, and the campuses that house them, may be in a position to develop codes or norms of sexual conduct that give individuals defenses against unwanted sexual pressure, short of charging someone with rape or assault. Given that these places are currently the sites of norms that add to the pressures to have sex, perhaps they can instead develop norms that work to neutralize at least some pressures to have sex. Taking away at least some of the advantages that male jerks employ in pressuring women to have unwanted sex would almost certainly add to women's overall happiness and autonomy with respect to sex.

Notes

1. S. Conly, 'Seduction, Rape, and Coercion', *Ethics* 115/1 (2004), 96–121.
2. See C. Struckman-Johnson and P.B. Anderson, "'Men Do and Women Don't": Difficulties in Researching Sexually Aggressive Women,'" in Anderson and Struckman-Johnson, 1998, 9–18, pp. 14–15.
3. C. Struckman-Johnson and D. Struckman-Johnson, 'The Dynamics and Impact of Sexual Coercion of Men by Women', in Anderson and Struckman-Johnson, 121–143.

Study Questions

1. What does Anderson mean by "the hierarchical structure of gender relations"?
2. What connection does Anderson draw between sex and violence?
3. What does Anderson mean by "male jerks" and "female jerks"?
4. Are you persuaded by Anderson's critique of Conly's reasoning?

B.

Sexual Harassment

Sexual Harassment in the University

N. Ann Davis

N. Ann Davis is Professor of Human Relations and Philosophy at Pomona College. She explains why reporting sexual harassment in the university is especially difficult. Davis points to the unequal power between faculty members and students, the hierarchy in the university that is difficult to navigate, and the reluctance of many professors to become involved. She concludes that to address the damage caused by sexual harassment, we need to find ways to deal with the special problems of universities that render them environments conducive to such unethical behavior.

The notion of sexual harassment entered public consciousness in the United States with the publication of a survey on sexual harassment in the workplace conducted by *Redbook* in 1976. More than nine thousand women responded to the survey, and almost nine out of ten reported experiencing some sort of sexual harassment on the job.[1]

From N. Ann Davis, "Sexual Harassment in the University," in *Morality, Responsibility, and the University: Studies in Academic Ethics*, ed. Steven M. Cahn (Philadelphia, PA: Temple University Press, 1992).

Unsurprisingly, these revelations stimulated a lot of discussion in the news media, the popular press, and academic journals.[2] . . .

In the classic *quid pro quo* case in which an instructor puts unwelcome sexual pressure on a student and makes it clear that the student's academic evaluation or professional advancement is contingent on her yielding to that pressure, what the instructor does is obviously coercive, unjust, disrespectful, and discriminatory. It is an abuse of power and a betrayal of trust. And it is inimical to the existence of a healthy educational environment in a number of ways.

Yet surveys conducted at college campuses around the nation reveal that a sizable proportion of female college students—somewhere between 25 percent and 40 percent—report they have been subjected to some sort of sexual harassment on the part of their instructors,[3] and anecdotal evidence provided by female students, faculty members, and administrators corroborates those findings. Surveys may be difficult to interpret and compare, for they do not all employ the same definition of sexual harassment, and anecdotal evidence must always be treated with caution, but it is clear that sexual harassment and other forms of sexually inappropriate behavior are no rarity in the university. Any serious participant in higher education must be puzzled and distressed by this fact. . . .

Traditionally, the influential teaching and administrative jobs in the university have been occupied by men, and it is men who have made the policies and interpreted the rules of university governance. Though things have changed considerably in the past decade or so, most of the senior faculty and administrative positions are still occupied by men. And women remain significantly in the minority in most, if not all, academic fields. This situation is thought, in itself, to be a problem. It is women, not men, who are almost always the victims of sexual harassment and men, not women, who are almost always the harassers. And men are likely both to operate with a narrower notion of sexual harassment and to have lower estimates of the incidence of sexual harassment on campus than women do. They are also likelier to view the incidents of sexual harassment they acknowledge do occur as isolated personal incidents, rather than as the expression of an institutional (or broader) problem. Commentators thus often cite the dearth of senior women and the associated inexperience and insensitivity of academic men as among the principal factors contributing to the prevalence of sexual harassment on campus. If women were less of a minority on campus or if they occupied positions of power that enabled them to have greater influence on rules, practices, and policies, then (it is thought) the incidence of sexual harassment on campus would decrease.

The women's movement and other associated movements have led many women—and many men—to question received gender stereotypes. But it is clear, nevertheless, that those stereotypes continue to exert a powerful influence on people's views about the relations between male professors and female students. Although it is a truism that social attitudes about status, gender, and sexuality frame people's expectations about "proper" relations between the sexes, most of us are blind to many of the effects of those attitudes, and implications of those expectations often go unnoticed. Though fewer people may now regard liaisons between experienced and influential older men and inexperienced, comparatively powerless younger women as the ideal sort of relationship, such liaisons are still widely thought to be acceptable (if not simply normal). And the persistence of romanticized Pygmalionesque views of the educational process appears to legitimate such relations between male professors and female students. It is clear that gender stereotypes and associated differential social expectations contribute in a number of ways to the incidence of sexual harassment on campus. . . .

II. Ignorance

It is clear that both the frequency and the seriousness of sexual harassment in the university are widely underestimated. . . . There are a number of reasons why this is so. Personal, institutional, ideological, and societal factors all conspire to deter students from reporting incidents of sexual harassment and from taking concerted action to follow through with the reports of sexual harassment that they do make. If the data on sexual harassment are correct, it is clear that very few of the victims of sexual harassment in the workplace or in the university report it at all.[4] It is worth making clear what in the university context specifically discourages students from reporting sexual harassment.

Students and professors possess unequal power, influence, confidence, experience, and social standing. And this inequality contributes to students' fears of being ridiculed, disbelieved, punished, or thought incompetent if they come forward with reports of sexually inappropriate conduct on the part of their instructors. Fear of the humiliations that befall many of the women who report rape and other forms of sexual assault evidently makes many women wary of reporting sexual offenses, especially when—as is evidently true in cases of sexual harassment—the attacker is someone who is known to the accuser. The student who has been sexually harassed by her professor is in a particularly vulnerable position, especially if she is known to have had an ongoing personal association with him or has previously submitted to his coercion. The stereotype of the professor as brilliant, principled, and passionately dedicated to his work and to the educational growth of his students leads students to doubt that their allegations would be believed. After all, professors are widely regarded as respectable members of the community. Often enough, students lose confidence in their perceptions of their own actions: if they hadn't done something wrong, then why would this respectable citizen behave so bizarrely? "Blame the victim" sensibilities pervade our society, and so it is not too hard to understand why a confused and distressed victim of sexual harassment would shoulder the blame herself, rather than attribute it to the distinguished, respectable, and (formerly) much-admired professor who was (or appeared to be) so generous with his time and concern.

There are also other factors that erode a woman's confidence, and make her fear that the instructor's harassing behavior must somehow be her fault. Late adolescence and early adulthood are vulnerable and psychologically chaotic times. Among the many difficulties that college-age students face is the struggle to come to terms with their sexuality, and it is easy for them to be insecure in the midst of that process, unclear about their own desires and unsure about how to interpret (and deal with) the many conflicting and ambivalent desires that they have. Though both men and women undoubtedly undergo personal upheaval, their behavior does not meet with the same social interpretation or response, nor are men and women supposed to handle their ambivalences the same way. Men are expected to become more confident and hence more persistent in their pursuit of sexual relationships as they mature. The myth endures that women enjoy being the object of persistent male attentions and invitations but like to play "hard to get" and thus refuse invitations they really wish to accept: when a woman says "no," what she really means is "maybe" or "ask me again later." Since, moreover, women are taught to be polite and nonconfrontational, the woman who tries to act "decently" when confronted with an unwelcome sexual invitation/offer/threat may be seen as thereby expressing ambivalence, which, according to the foregoing myth, may be construed as an expression of interest. If the woman actually does feel ambivalent—she wants to refuse the invitation, but she feels some attraction to the man who has issued it—then she may guiltily believe that she "led him on" even when she said no. And so she may regard the instructor's sexually inappropriate behavior as her fault.

Gender roles and social expectations affect perceptions in other ways as well. Traditionally, women have been judged by their appearance, and they have thus been obliged to devote considerable energy to the attempt to look "attractive," for except among the most wealthy, it was a woman's appearance and good . . . manners that were the principal determinant of whether or not she would attract a man and marry, which was essential for her economic security. Though economics have changed, the traditional view continues to exert an influence on people's thinking, and women still feel pressure to dress attractively and act politely. Yet a woman who is attractive is seen as open to, and perhaps as actually inviting, sexual responses from men. This perception, plus the myth that men's sexual self-control is so fragile that it can be overwhelmed by the presence of an attractive woman, contributes to the view that the women who are sexually harassed are those who "asked for it" (by being physically attractive, or attractively dressed).

Surveys make it clear that there is no correlation between a woman's being attractive (or "sexily" dressed) and her being sexually harassed. Sexual harassment, like rape, is primarily an issue of power, not sex. But the myth persists that it is a female student's appearance that is the cause of her instructor's sexually inappropriate behavior toward her. This myth influences female students' perceptions of both their own and their professors' conduct. And if, as she may well suppose, she bears responsibility for the instructor's behaving as he does, she is likely not to think of his conduct as being sexual harassment.

Popular academic fiction has done a lot to perpetuate these myths, and a lot to reinforce unfortunate gender stereotypes. "Co-eds" are portrayed as lusty seducers of respectable male professors, who are often portrayed as hapless victims of those feminine wiles. One can conjecture that most college-age women have read a few of the standard academic novels and that those novels provide some of the background for their interpretation of their professors' conduct.

Believing that her experience of sexual harassment is rare, believing, perhaps, the various myths surrounding the mechanics of male and female attraction, and being influenced by the myth-supporting academic fiction she reads in English courses, the sexually harassed student may believe that the whole thing is her fault. It is not something that she should report but something she should be ashamed of. And so her energies are likely to be spent trying to cope with or "manage" the incident, not reporting it or attempting to bring the sexual harasser to justice.

The asymmetrical power and influence of students and professors not only affect the student's perception of whether or not her claims of sexual harassment would be believed, they also affect her perception of the risks involved in making such a report (even when she does not fear being disbelieved). The professor holds the power of evaluation, and often enough, the student sees him as gatekeeper to her desired career. If she displeases him, then—whether it is through the mechanism of letters of reference or the more informal workings of the "old boy network"—he may, she fears, ruin her career prospects.

The structural organization of the university also serves to deter victims from reporting sexually inappropriate behavior. The myriad of departments, programs, divisions, and colleges may be quite daunting to an undergraduate, who may not understand the relations between them or be able easily to determine who has authority with respect to what. Nor does it help that some of those people to whom a student might turn appear as confused and powerless as the student herself—or altogether uninterested. A student may summon up her courage to report an incident of sexual misconduct to a professor whom she feels she can trust, only to be told to report it to the department chair, whom she may not know at all. If the department chair has not been through this before or if the chair is overworked or less than sympathetic to her plight, then the student may be met with (what she interprets as) annoyance and indifference ("Well, what do you want me to do about it?") or referred to a dean, who may seem to the student a distant, busy, and daunting individual. The organization of the university, with its convoluted procedures and divisions of responsibility, is quotidian to experienced faculty members who understand the hierarchy and the system. But they may be intimidating to someone who does not understand them and who is already traumatized and alienated.

The attitudes of academics toward their colleagues and students and their views about their own intellectual mission and personal responsibilities may also serve to discourage students from reporting sexual harassment. What is perhaps more important, however, is that those attitudes clearly serve to deter faculty members who learn of a colleague's sexually inappropriate behavior from taking action on it. . . . [Educators] are reluctant to "break ranks," to do things that they perceive as disloyal or damaging to a colleague. In some cases this reluctance may be an expression of a long-standing liberal commitment to tolerance of difference or a manifestation of the desire to uphold academic freedom or respect the autonomy of one's colleagues. In other cases, and less (ostensibly) nobly, it may be thought to stem from academics' desire to be left alone to get on with their own work, protect their own interests, or stay out of academic politics. But whatever the precise blend of factors (what might be called) the ideology of the faculty tends to support the stance of uninvolvement.

Untenured and non-tenure-track faculty are in an especially precarious position. The accused senior colleague may wield a good deal of power in the university and in his particular academic field. If displeased or moved to seek retaliation, he may do things that place the untenured faculty member's job at risk. Female faculty members—who are statistically more likely to be untenured or not tenure-track and very much in the minority in their profession—may be particularly vulnerable. Both their professional success thus far and their professional future may well depend upon their being perceived as "good colleagues," people who happen to be female in a largely male context and profession and "don't make a fuss about it." Becoming involved with a sexual harassment case may call attention to a female instructor's gender in ways that make her uncomfortable and may place her in double jeopardy, for she may feel that she is being obliged to risk her own credibility, her good relations with her colleagues, and her own professional connections. And oddly enough, though there is no shortage of good motivations for helping a student who reports an incident of sexual misconduct—a desire to help and protect a student who is hurt and frightened and feels she has nowhere else to turn, the desire to uphold the express and tacit values of the institution, the perception of the need to show students that female faculty members can act with strength and integrity—the female instructor who is willing to assist a student who complains of sexual harassment may find her own motives impugned by resentful male colleagues. As an older woman (and therefore, as convention has it, a less-attractive woman) she may be accused of projecting her unfulfilled desires for male sexual attention onto the student, of being a harridan, or a lesbian who wants to get even with men, of being bitter about her own lack of academic success (which she wrongly and wrongfully attributes to being a woman), and so on.

It is clear that both students' reluctance to come forward with complaints of sexual harassment and faculty members' disinclination to get involved when students do come forward contribute to an underestimation of the scope of the problem of sexual harassment in academia. It is not only the frequency with which sexually inappropriate behavior occurs that is underestimated, however, but the extent of the damage it causes as well. The explanation of why this is so is both complex and multifaceted.

Part of the explanation lies in the invisibility of much of the damage in question. It is easy to see the harm in an instructor's following through on a threat to take reprisals against a student who rejects his demands or in an instructor's tendering an unduly (though perhaps not deliberately or even consciously) harsh evaluation of the student who does not respond favorably to his sexual overtures. Those students are the victims of unfair academic evaluations, and both the professor's integrity and the integrity of the institutions's grading practices are severely compromised by such behavior. But other harms—to the individual student, to other students, to the educational institution, and to the society at large—are less obvious.

Many of the students who find themselves the recipients of unwelcome sexual overtures, remarks, or questions deal with the problem by "managing" it, and the most common form of management is avoidance: the student drops the course, ceases to attend the class, withdraws the application to be a lab assistant, quits coming to office hours, changes her major, or, in the most extreme cases, drops out of school altogether. Though these avoidance tactics may effectively remove the opportunity for an instructor to engage in harassing behavior, they do so at a cost. The student who thinks she can avoid being sexually harassed by simply avoiding the professor in question may thereby be deprived of valuable academic and professional opportunities, and the pool of motivated and intelligent aspirants to the relevant profession is thus reduced. Though, on such a scenario, both the damage to the individual and the loss to society are real, they are largely undetectable. If the number of women in the profession is already low, then the temptation may be to suppose, for example, that "women just aren't interested in engineering" or that "most women just aren't able to do the sort of abstract thinking required for graduate-level physics," adding the insult of misdiagnosis to the injury of sexual harassment. Women who were in fact driven out of the profession by being robbed of the opportunity to pursue their studies in peace are deemed uninterested or incapable. And viewing these women as uninterested or incapable obviously has implications for how other female aspirants to such careers are likely to be viewed, and to view themselves.

Nor does the damage stop there. When a student is given grounds for wondering whether her instructor's academic interest and encouragement were motivated by his sexual interest in her, she may well come to doubt the legitimacy of her previous accomplishments: perhaps her success thus far has owed more to sexual attributes that instructors found attractive than to her own hard work and ability. A good, serious, hardworking student may thus lose the sort of self-confidence that anyone needs to succeed in a competitive field, and that women especially need if they are to succeed in traditionally male professions that remain statistically (if not ideologically) male dominated. If, in addition, other students and instructors attribute the harassed student's academic success to sexual involvement with, or manipulation of, her instructors, then relationships with her peers and her other instructors (and with her own students, if she is a teaching assistant) may well be harmed, and suspicion may be cast on the success of other women. More subtly, both students and instructors may be drawn into a familiar form of overgeneralization and thus may come to harbor the suspicion that women's successes in the academic and professional fields in which they are a significant minority owe more to the women's skills at sexually manipulating those in power than to their hard work and ability. Generalized resentment of women or the unspoken background belief that women do not play fair or cannot "pull their own weight" may result, and this consequence may silently lead instructors to interact differently with male and female students and to approach them with different expectations. Given the insidious working of socialization, neither the students nor the instructors may be aware of the existence of such differential treatment; yet it may well be prejudicial and, ultimately, extremely detrimental. Again, both the existence of the harm and its causation are difficult to pin down in such cases and difficult to distinguish from the apparently statistically supported view that "women just aren't good at (or interested in) physics."

It should be clear from this discussion that sexual harassment (or, more broadly, sexually inappropriate behavior) can cause significant damage to the individuals who are its direct victims, to other women, and to the society at large. But it is hard to make the estimation of that damage more precise, for attempts to arrive at a more precise measure of the damage are complicated by the many other factors that make academic and professional success more difficult for women. It is not likely, after all, that a woman's first or only experience of sex discrimination will occur in a college lecture hall or in a professor's office, and it is plausible to suppose that a woman's prior experiences will influence how much damage will be done to her by an instructor's sexual harassment or other sexually inappropriate behavior. Prior experiences may both magnify the harm that is done to her by sexual harassment and, at the same time, diminish the possibility of perceiving that behavior as the cause of the harm. If women have routinely been victims of sex discrimination or societal sexist attitudes, then how can one say that it is the experience of sexual harassment in the university that is the cause of a woman's subsequent distress or the explanation of her decision to enter a "traditionally female" job or profession?

Reflection on this problem suggests a connection between the . . . widespread ignorance about the extent of sexually inappropriate behavior in the university and the seriousness of the damage it may cause, and the difficulties involved in attempting to come up with a widely acceptable definition of sexual harassment. In a society that many people would characterize as pervaded by sexist attitudes (if not actual sex discrimination) and in one in which there is disagreement about what constitutes (objectionable) sexism and what is merely a response to differences between men and women, it may be difficult, if not impossible, to reach a consensus about what constitutes sexual harassment. Any university policy that hopes to do any good must take note of this fact. . . .

Notes

1. Claire Saffran, "What Men Do to Women on the Job," *Redbook* (November 1976), pp. 149, 217–23.
2. See, e.g., Karen Lindsay, "Sexual Harassment on the Job and How to Stop It," *Ms.* (November 1977), pp. 47–48, 50–51, 74–75, 78; Margaret Mead, "A Proposal: We Need Taboos on Sex at Work," *Redbook* (April 1978), pp. 31, 33, 38; Caryl Rivers, "Sexual Harassment: The Executive's Alternative to Rape," *Mother Jones* (June 1978), pp. 21–24, 28; Claire Saffran, "Sexual Harassment: The View from the Top," *Redbook* (March 1981), pp. 45–51.
3. See Phyllis L. Crocker, "Annotated Bibliography on Sexual Harassment in Education," *Women's Rights Law Reporter* 7 (1982), 91–106. And see *Symposium on Sexual Harassment* in *Thought & Action* 5 (1989): 17–52, especially the essay by Anne Traux, "Sexual Harassment in Higher

Education: What We've Learned," pp. 25–38, for an overview of surveys and results.

4. According to Truax, "Sexual Harassment in Higher Education," p. 26, "Of those harassed, not more than one in 10 actually report the harassment."

Study Questions

1. According to Davis, why is both the frequency and seriousness of sexual harassment widely underestimated?
2. Is sexual harassment always intentional?
3. Might a male student be the victim of sexual harassment?
4. Is a professor's dating a student akin to a judge in a case dating the defendant?

Sexual Harassment in Public Places

Margaret Crouch

Margaret Crouch is Professor of Philosophy at Eastern Michigan University. She argues that sexual harassment is morally problematic because it entrenches the subordinate place of women in society. Such harassment, however, is not limited to the workplace but is a widespread phenomenon found in many public spaces. Crouch maintains that by subjecting women to unwanted attention in public, sexual harassment leads to limitations on women's freedom of movement. Thus the goal of equal opportunity requires that sexual harassment be curbed.

I

Most current writing on sexual harassment in the United States is solely about sexual harassment in the workplace and/or in academe. This is because sexual harassment has been found illegal in these locations, and the law tends to narrow our focus. However, in spite of the fact that even definitions proffered by international organizations such as the United Nations and the European Union define sexual harassment in terms of the workplace, sexual harassment should be understood much more broadly—as something that can occur anywhere, at any time. In countries other than the United States, more attention has been paid to sexual harassment in public places—on public transportation, and in the street.

In my view, the separation of workplace/academic harassment from the broader scope of sexual harassment tends to obscure the function and effect of all harassment—to *keep women in their place.*

From Margaret Crouch, "Sexual Harassment in Public Places," *Social Philosophy Today* 25 (2009).

Sexual harassment is a means of maintaining women's status as subordinate in society; it is also a means of keeping women in certain physical spaces and out of others, or, at least, of controlling women's behavior in those spaces. In this way, sexual harassment constrains women's freedom of movement both in terms of status and place. Here, I will focus on the latter, but lack of freedom of movement in space causes lack of freedom of movement in status.

In this paper, I will argue that workplace and academic harassment must be placed in the context of this broader understanding of sexual harassment to see its true nature. Women's full participation in public and private life requires that all forms of harassment be eliminated, through law, public awareness, and moral suasion. . . .

II

. . . Both the UN and the EU categorize sexual harassment as a form of sex discrimination, which comes directly from the US legal argument that sexual harassment in the workplace is a violation of Title VII. It may be because we don't have a clear legal conception of sex discrimination outside workplaces or academe that efforts to stop sexual harassment are focused on the workplace, though the Violence Against Women Act does conceive of spousal battering, date rape, and marital rape as sex discrimination.[1] However, sexual harassment in public places has existed as long as workplace harassment, is a form of sex discrimination, and is being addressed as such by women around the world.

III

. . . Sociological studies call attention to the differences, generally, in women's and men's experiences of public space. Erving Goffman described these differences in his sociological works in the 1960s and 1970s.[2] He claimed that there is a sort of default mode called "civic inattention" that characterizes relations between strangers in public places. People tend not to stare at one another or talk to strangers in public. They are aware of their surroundings but don't intrude on one another unless there is some particular reason to do so. This "civic inattention" holds generally among men and among women, but it does not hold between men and women. In sexist societies, men treat women as so-called open persons, that is, as persons for whom there is so little regard that they may be approached and intruded upon at will.[3] According to Cynthia Grant Bowman,

> Breaches of civil inattention that include a spoken component typically occur only when one encounters a person who is either very unusual (such as an individual carrying a couch, hopping on one foot, or dressed in costume), is unusually similar to oneself in some respect (for example, someone wearing the same college sweatshirt or driving the same make of car), or is accompanied by someone or something in an "open" category, such as dogs or children. Men seem to regard women generally as such "open persons."[4]

A good deal of the intrusion on women's attention and space in public places comes in the form of sexual harassment. It includes comments on their bodies or on their presence in the public space, unwanted touching, and lewd gestures. This form of sexual harassment has some characteristics that distinguish it from the type that is typical in workplaces and academe; for instance, it is typically between strangers, and because of this, the harasser is usually anonymous.

Many think that the sort of behavior I am describing is insignificant or even flattering. However, that is not how the majority of women around the world experience it. It is experienced as aggressive, as a violation of the "civil inattention" that is the norm in public space. The woman is made to pay attention to the harasser and to see herself as he sees her. If she does not respond appropriately, in the view of the harasser, she is often the target of abuse and hostility. Frequently, a nice response leads to further harassment. A dismissal might escalate the situation. Infrequently, such encounters lead to stalking, even rape. But the amount of wariness with which a woman experiences harassment is due to the fact that she cannot predict whether this instance is likely to end badly.

Even in Paris, where so-called girl-watching is supposed to be a national pastime, women organize their lives to avoid being alone in public where they know they will be harassed. Indeed, avoidance is the most common response to harassment in public places. The avoidance is motivated by fear, for in the experience of many women, there is a direct connection between public harassment that most people would regard as innocuous and truly threatening behavior. Even though there is evidence that women are more likely to be the victims of violence from intimates than from strangers, the unpredictability of stranger violence makes every encounter threatening.

Public harassment of women by men asserts the male prerogative. . . . In so-called public spaces, men of the dominant group are in a *public* space, but many other groups are not. Men of the dominant group have the power of access to the space and do anything in the space; they also have the power to exclude others from their personal or private space while in public. Women and other non-dominant groups do not share these same powers of exclusion and access. . . .

V

What to do? If women are to be equal to men in all spheres of society, the harassment of which I have been speaking must be eliminated. But how should this be done?

Whatever is done must be accompanied by advocacy that keeps the focus on sex discrimination rather than affronts to modesty, or chivalric protection. There are some grassroots organizations that have sprung up using the internet to publicize the harms of public harassment, such as Holla Back, which started in New York but now has chapters all over the world in large urban centers. Women who are harassed take photographs of harassers and post them on the internet for all to see.[5] In India, the Blank Noise Project stages public protests to educate people about public harassment. For example, a large group went to a market where men stood around leaning on a railing looking at passersby and harassing women. The women reclaimed the space, and silently surrounded a fellow who was harassing a woman. Blank Noise uses its internet to publicize actions and to fight traditional interpretations of street harassment. For example, in order to counter the view that women bring on harassment themselves by wearing skimpy clothing, Blank Noise asked women to send in the clothes they were wearing when they were harassed. They included chadors and traditional clothing, as well as western garb.[6]

Some governments have instituted women-only transportation in order to protect women from harassment on public transportation. India has had train cars reserved for women since before independence. Tokyo began reserving train cars for women during rush hour recently, as did Rio de Janeiro. Mexico City started women-only buses in February of this year. . . .

I want to emphasize the importance of recognizing that harassment can take place anywhere and is not confined to the workplace and academe. We need to remember this larger context in order to see sexual harassment for what it really is: *a means of maintaining women's status as subordinate in society; it is also a means of keeping women in certain physical spaces and out of others, or, at least, of controlling women's behavior in those spaces.*

Notes

1. Sally F. Goldfarb, "Public Rights for 'Private' Wrongs: Sexual Harassment and the Violence against Women Act," in *Directions in Sexual Harassment Law,* ed. Catharine A. MacKinnon and Reva B. Siegel (New Haven: Yale University Press, 2004), 516–34.
2. Erving Goffman, *Behavior in Public Places* (New York: Free Press, 1963); Erving Goffman, *Interaction Rituals* (New York: Pantheon, 1967).
3. Goffman, 1963, 18.
4. Bowman, "Street Harassment," 526.
5. Holla Back, Accessed September 11, 2008. http://www.hollabacknyc.blogspot.com.
6. Blank Noise. Accessed September 11, 2008. http://blog.blanknoise.org.

Study Questions

1. What does Crouch mean by "sexual harassment"?
2. According to Crouch, what makes sexual harassment in public places morally objectionable?
3. What is "civic inattention"?
4. Is overcoming sexual harassment more a matter of enacting laws or changing individual behavior?

PART VII

The Family

Marriage

Minimal Marriage

Elizabeth Brake

Elizabeth Brake is Associate Professor of Philosophy at Arizona State University. She argues that traditional marriage, which in most states comes with many entitlements, liabilities, and powers, is illiberal. Note that the term "liberal," as philosophers use it, is not to be contrasted with "conservative," but with a view of the state, held by Aristotle and others, that considers political associations to exist by nature rather than by individual choice. Liberalism in this sense is embraced by Republicans and Democrats, for members of both parties emphasize individual rights and liberties, viewing the state as protecting individuals from interference by others, not looking to the state to institute policies that will render the citizens morally worthy. According to liberalism, state action needs to be justifiable by public reasons that all may accept, regardless of moral, religious, or philosophical outlooks. For example, passing a law that tax breaks are to be given to everyone who prays before going to bed would be illiberal, because the justification for such a law appeals to a religious doctrine that not everyone supports. Brake argues that the legal benefits currently attached to monogamous

From Elizabeth Brake, "Minimal Marriage: What Political Liberalism Implies for Marriage Law," *Ethics* 120 (2010).

marriages are akin to a law that those who pray will receive tax breaks. Thus to be consistent with liberalism, Brake advocates *minimal marriage*, which would leave to each individual the choice of whether to enter into a monogamous relationship or, instead, join any possible network of multiple, significant, nonexclusive relationships.

II. Minimal Marriage

. . . I argue that a liberal state can set no principled restrictions on the sex or number of spouses and the nature and purpose of their relationships, except that they be caring relationships (a concept I will specify below). Moreover, the state cannot require exchanges of marital rights (shorthand for various entitlements, powers, and obligations) to be reciprocal and complete, as opposed to asymmetrical and divided. Minimal marriage would also reduce the marital rights available.

To show what is at stake, I will review some of the numerous entitlements, liabilities, permissions, and powers currently exchanged reciprocally and as a complete package in marriage. In U.S. federal law alone, there are "1,138 federal statutory provisions . . . in which marital status is a factor in determining or receiving benefits, rights, and privileges."[1] Laws concerning property, inheritance, and divorce are additional, falling under state jurisdiction.

Marriage entails rights "to be on each others' health, disability, life insurance, and pension plans," "jointly [to] own real and personal property, an arrangement which protects their marital estate from each other's creditors," and to automatic inheritance if a spouse dies intestate. Spouses have rights in one another's property in marriage and on divorce. They are designated next of kin "in case of death, medical emergency, or mental incapacity" and for prison visitation and military personnel arrangements.[2] They qualify for special tax and immigration status and survivor, disability, Social Security, and veterans' benefits. Marital status is implicated throughout U.S. federal law—in "Indian" affairs, homestead rights, taxes, trade and commerce, financial disclosure and conflict of interest, federal family violence law, immigration, employment benefits, federal natural resources law, federal loans and guarantees, and payments in agriculture. Marital status also confers parental rights and responsibilities—assignment of legal paternity, joint parenting and adoption rights, and legal status with regard to step-children. . . . While this may be an efficient system, it is not, I argue, currently just. . . .

Other rights directly facilitate day-to-day maintenance of a relationship or enable spouses to play significant roles in one another's lives. Special consideration for immigration is an example: spouses cannot share daily life if they are in different countries. Civil service and military spouses may receive employment and relocation assistance and preferential hiring. Out-of-state spouses may qualify for in-state tuition. Other examples are spousal immunity from testifying, spousal care leave entitlement, hospital and prison visiting rights, entitlement to burial with one's spouse in a veterans' cemetery, and emergency decision-making powers. Through such entitlements and through status designation, marriage allows spouses to express and act on their care for one another.

Another function of note is protection of the widowed through funeral and bereavement leave, pension and health care entitlements, indemnity compensation or the right to sue for a spouse's death, automatic precedence for life insurance payouts and final paychecks, control of copyright, and automatic rights to inherit if the spouse dies intestate and to make decisions about the disposal of the body. Marriage law also provides protection for spouses on divorce.

In an ideal liberal egalitarian society, minimal marriage would consist only in rights which recognize (e.g., status designation, burial rights, bereavement leave) and support (e.g., immigration rights, caretaking leave) caring relationships. Care, broadly construed, may involve physical or emotional caretaking or simply a caring attitude (an attitude of concern for a particular other). 'Relationship', as I am using the term here, implies that parties know and are known to one another, have ongoing direct contact, and share a history. I will argue that a law performing the functions of designating, recognizing, and supporting caring relationships is justifiable, even required.

Unlike current marriage, minimal marriage does not require that individuals exchange marital rights reciprocally and in complete bundles: it allows their disaggregation to support the numerous relationships, or adult care networks, which people may have. Minimal marriage would allow a person to exchange all her marital rights reciprocally with one other person or distribute them through her adult care network. In an ideal liberal egalitarian society, law should not assume a dependency relationship between spouses, and so most marital entitlements to direct financial benefits would be eliminated (except for those, such as in-state tuition eligibility, whose primary purpose is to enable relationship maintenance). Likewise, the compatibility of specific "insurance" provisions of marriage with justice will depend on their rationale. . . .

So far, the proposal might seem extravagantly removed from real life. But consider an example of how minimal marriage rights might be distributed. Rose lives with Octavian, sharing household expenses. To facilitate this ménage, Rose and Octavian form a legal entity for certain purposes—jointly owned property, bank account access, homeowner and car insurance, and so on. The arrangement is long term but not permanent. Octavian's company will relocate him in five years, and Rose will not move—but they agree to cohabit until then. They even discuss how to divide property when the household dissolves, and they agree that if either moves out sooner, the defaulter will pay the other compensation and costs. (The arrangement for default is not punitive but merely protective.)

Rose's only living relative, Aunt Alice, lives nearby. Alice lives in genteel poverty, and Rose feels a filial responsibility toward her. Rose's employer provides excellent pension and health care benefits, for which any spouse of Rose's is eligible (at a small cost), and other spousal perks, such as reduced costs for its products. Octavian is a well-off professional and does not need these benefits—he has his own—but Alice needs access to good health care and, should Rose die, she could use the pension that would go to Rose's spouse if she had one. Assuming that such entitlements comport with justice, minimal marriage would allow Rose to transfer the eligibility for these entitlements to Alice.

While Rose enjoys Octavian's company and has affection for Alice, only Marcel truly understands her. Marcel is, like Rose, a bioethicist, and he understands her complex views on end-of-life decision making. Rose wants to transfer powers of executorship and emergency decision making to him. In addition, Marcel and Rose spend a lot of time together, discussing philosophy while enjoying recreational activities, and they would like eligibility for "family rates" at tourist attractions, health clubs, and resorts. Their local city gym, for instance, has a special rate for married couples, but they do not qualify.

There could be more people in Rose's life who occupy a role usually associated with spouses. Rose might share custody of a child with an ex. Or she might cohabit platonically with Octavian, living separately from the long-term love of her life, Stella. There is no single person with whom Rose wants or needs to exchange the whole package of marital rights and entitlements. In fact, doing so would be inconvenient, requiring her to make additional contracts to override the default terms of marriage. Even worse, marrying any one person would expose her to undesired legal liabilities, such as obligatory property division, and it could interfere with her eligibility for some loans and government programs. But Rose wants and needs to exchange some marital rights with several different people.

Rose's ménage might seem strange to some—though putting all one's eggs in one basket might seem equally strange to Rose! It is certainly not obvious that each person will find another with whom their major emotional, economic, and social needs permanently mesh. But minimal marriage does not take sides on this. It allows "traditionalists" to exchange their complete sets of marital rights reciprocally, while Rose and others like her distribute and receive marital rights as needed. Minimal marriage is a law of adult care networks, including "traditional" marriages.

III. Why More-Than-Minimal Marriage Is Incompatible with Political Liberalism

. . . I will argue, in this section, that any restrictions more extensive than those of minimal marriage cannot be justified within public reason. . . .

A. Political Liberalism, Public Reason, and Neutrality

Minimal marriage, and no more extensive or restrictive law, is consistent with political liberalism. In the first stage of my argument, I will make a case that no more extensive marriage law can be justified within public reason. The ban on arguments which depend on comprehensive conceptions of the good precludes appeal to the special value of long-term dyadic sexual relationships, and without such appeal, I will argue, restriction of marriage to such relationships cannot be justified. I also show that public reason and neutrality, where invoked in the same-sex marriage debate, have not been consistently followed, even by those defending same-sex marriage.

Liberal societies are characterized by a pluralism of reasonable comprehensive (concerning all areas of life, as opposed to narrowly political) religious, philosophical, and moral doctrines. In such societies, legislators should refrain from enacting law and policy, especially in basic matters of justice, exclusively on the basis of controversial moral or religious views which many citizens may not accept. Within public reason, legislators give reasons for law and policy which those with differing comprehensive doctrines may be reasonably expected to accept; public reason excludes reasons which depend entirely on comprehensive religious, moral, and philosophical doctrines. . . . For my argument, it is sufficient that public reason applies to law makers and government officials acting in a public capacity, that it applies to matters of basic justice, and that it requires refraining from arguments which depend on contested comprehensive doctrines. . . .

While some arguments for same-sex marriage have appealed to public reason, many have appealed to the doctrine of neutrality. For neutralists, the state should remain neutral between conceptions of the good found in comprehensive doctrines, excepting any conflicting with justice. As Rawls formulates the principle, "the state is not to do anything intended to favor or promote any particular comprehensive doctrine rather than another, or to give greater assistance to those who pursue it." More broadly, "basic institutions and public policy . . . are neutral in the sense that they can be endorsed by citizens generally as within the scope of a public political conception."[3] The relevant conception is neutrality of aim, not the outrageously demanding neutrality of effect, which would require that states ensure policies have equal effect on which conceptions are adopted. The less demanding neutrality of aim, to which justice as fairness is committed, requires that the state not justify law or policy by appeal to a conception of the good within a comprehensive doctrine.

Neutrality constrains political decision making by excluding the giving of certain reasons for institutions and policy; it excludes the conceptions of the good of comprehensive doctrines. This constraint applies to the state, in the person of legislators and public officers.[4] It prevents law makers from prohibiting actions, providing subsidies, or framing institutions for the purpose of promoting any such conceptions. . . .

B. Marriage

Public reason requires that law makers not appeal to reasons depending on comprehensive moral, religious, or philosophical doctrines in framing marriage law. More fundamentally, it requires that there be publicly justifiable grounds for there being marriage law at all. . . . In this section, I will argue that public reason applied to a legal framework designating and supporting adult caring relationships entails that no law more restrictive than minimal marriage can be justified. . . .

One reason often given for marriage is that it is "for" reproduction and child rearing; if this were the case and "traditional" marriage were essential to child rearing, this could provide a justification for restrictive marriage laws in terms of public reason. It is sometimes objected that biological procreation is not the sole purpose of marriage, for spouses adopt, rear step-children, and use gamete donors. Moreover, fertility is not a condition for marriage. Nor is child rearing (whatever the provenance of the children) its only purpose: many marriages are childless, and marriages do not end when children leave home.

But this is too fast. The design of marriage law should presumably attend to its implications for child welfare, even if child rearing is not the primary purpose of marriage. . . . The objector to minimal marriage could contend that marriage law should promote optimal environments for children. To the extent that minimal marriage would encourage diverse relationships, it is likely to decrease the number of children reared by married biological parents, and this may affect child welfare.

This objection has three weaknesses: first, the nuances of the empirical evidence regarding child welfare suggest that there is no compelling reason to think that minimal marriage would have a harmful impact on children and no reason to think it would be more harmful than current marriage law; second, a parenting framework should not recognize only optimal parenting structures; third, reasons other than child welfare guide marriage legislation, for marriage has purposes other than child rearing. . . .

The objector who presses against including same-sex, polygamous, or single-parent families on child welfare grounds should consider whether he would press such an objection in the cases of high-conflict biological parents, interracial marriages where mixed-race children were seriously disadvantaged, socioeconomically worse-off families, or parents who are junk food eaters and couch potatoes. If not, his view may incorporate an arbitrary bias. What matters greatly to child psychological development is continuity of care, which is available in polygamous, same-sex, single-parent, and extended families.

A remaining concern may be that minimal marriage will increase the number of single parents. As noted, single parenting is correlated with poverty; however, justice and efficiency suggest that such poverty should be addressed by fighting its sources, not by promoting marriage.[5] Furthermore, minimal marriage would help single parents by increasing their marital options. Finally, the detrimental effects of single parenting must be weighed with the detrimental effects of high-conflict and abusive marriages. Given widespread abuse and violence within marriage and the additional harms of high-conflict marriages, women and children may often be better off outside marriage. Indeed, if we accept the objector's claim that marital forms should be judged by their implications for child welfare, we must note that current marriage law promotes a form associated with high rates of abuse and conflict.

While I cannot pursue this argument in detail here, there is reason to separate a legal framework designating and supporting adult caring relationships from one regulating and supporting parenting. The high number—roughly one-third—of U.S. children being reared outside marriages suggests that parenting frameworks independent of marriage would be better positioned to address child welfare by benefiting children outside marriage. Financial benefits for parents and incentives to stability should attach to parenting, not marriage: focusing on marriage leaves out children of unmarried and divorced parents. . . .

Typical defenses of same-sex marriage in terms of public reason and neutrality understand marriage as providing a legislative framework for certain adult relationships. They proceed by showing that same-sex relationships exhibit the features of different-sex relationships formalized by such a framework. A characteristic list is given by Ralph Wedgwood. Marriage "typically involves sexual intimacy, economic and domestic cooperation, and a voluntary mutual commitment to sustaining this relationship."[6] Wedgwood proceeds to argue that reasons supporting recognition of different-sex marriage extend to recognition of same-sex relationships with these features (and whose partners desire such recognition). However, relationships, or adult care networks, may be important without involving sexual intimacy or economic or domestic cooperation, and members of such networks may desire recognition or other benefits of marriage. . . .

Public reason implies that a legal framework for adult relationships should not endorse an ideal of relationship depending on a comprehensive doctrine—but this is just what the monogamous ideal of marriage, gay or straight, is. . . . Once it is noticed how many varying conceptions of good relationships exist within different comprehensive doctrines, it is clear that public reason and neutrality imply that marriage should not presuppose sexual or romantic relationships, aspirations to permanence or exclusivity, or a full reciprocal exchange of marital rights.

Marriage, including same-sex marriage, currently recognizes a single central exclusive relationship of a certain priority and duration, often understood as "union." But this ignores alternative ideals of relationship; for instance, networks of multiple, significant, nonexclusive relationships which provide emotional support, caretaking, and intimacy and are not (all) romantic or sexual. Such adult care networks appear in the gay community, in African American communities, and among seniors, unmarried urbanites, and polyamorists.

This diversity reflects competing conceptions of valuable relationships. Some gay and lesbian theorists and critics of heterosexism have criticized the central, exclusive relationship ideal as a heterosexual paradigm. They point out that gays and lesbians often choose relationships which are less possessive, demanding, and insular and more flexible and open. They have challenged the desirability of same-sex marriage on the grounds that instead of affirming difference, it will assimilate lesbian and gay relationships into the heterosexual model.[7] But this concern rather implies that marriage law should be reframed to accommodate difference.

Different conceptions of good relationships are not, of course, exclusive to the gay and lesbian community. Polyamorists (gay, straight, and bisexual) promote polyamory—engaging in multiple love relationships—as involving less jealousy and more honesty than exclusive monogamy. They see marriage as promoting a psychologically unhealthy norm of possessiveness. . . .

Other groups emphasize the importance of adult care networks. Quirkyalones and urban tribalists hold ideals of sociability that reach beyond an isolated dyad. The quirkyalone movement began with one woman's public musing that her friends played the role in her life that marriage or coupledom does for many. Her short article produced a flood of responses from others who felt similarly. Quirkyalones want respect for their choice to be "single"; they argue that society treats the unmarried, or uncoupled, as incomplete and immature, however old or accomplished the individuals may be, and fails to recognize the importance of non-"traditional" relationships.[8] For different reasons, many people find the ideal of a central, exclusive relationship irrelevant. Their conceptions of good relationships involve networks, "tribes," or groups of friends, and they defend these conceptions on moral and ethical grounds and by appeal to other values. . . .

The monogamous central relationship ideal is only one contested ideal among many found within different comprehensive doctrines. Framing marriage law in a way which presupposes such a relationship fails to respect public reason and reasonable pluralism. In the absence of a publicly justifiable reason for defining marital relationships as heterosexual, monogamous, exclusive, durable, romantic or passionate, and so on, the state must recognize and support all relationships—same-sex, polygamous, polyamorous, urban tribes—if it recognizes and supports any. Because it cannot assume that spouses must relate in a certain way, it also cannot assume one set of one-size-fits-all marital rights. What it can do is make available a number of rights which designate and support relationships which individuals can use as they wish. . . .

Notes

1. At the end of 2003, reported by the General Accounting Office (GAO), Dayna K. Shaw, Associate General Counsel, in a letter of January 23, 2004, to Bill Frist. The letter accompanies the 2004 GAO report, labeled "GAO-04–353R Defense of Marriage Act." See also Enclosure I, "Categories of Laws Involving Marital Status," in a letter of January 31, 1997, by Barry R. Bedrick, Associate General Counsel, GAO, to Henry J. Hyde. The letter accompanies the 1997 GAO report, labeled "GAO/OGC-97–16 Defense of Marriage Act."
2. Craig Dean, "Gay Marriage: A Civil Right," *Journal of Homosexuality* 27 (1994): 111–15, at 112.
3. Rawls, *Political Liberalism*, 192–93.
4. Rawls, *Political Liberalism*, 252; it also applies to citizens in political contexts.
5. See Fineman, *The Autonomy Myth*, 71–94; and Young, "Mothers."
6. Wedgwood, "The Fundamental Argument," 233.
7. Paula Ettelbrick, "Since When Is Marriage a Path to Liberation?" *Out/look: National Lesbian and Gay Quarterly* 6 (1989): 14–17, reprinted in Andrew Sullivan, ed., *Same-Sex Marriage: Pro and Con* (New York: Vintage, 2004), 122–28.
8. See Sasha Cagen, *Quirkyalone* (New York: HarperCollins, 2006); Cagen writes, 18, that *Time* and *The Economist* reported in 2000 on the growing number of unmarried urbanites.

Study Questions

1. According to Brake, what is "minimal marriage"?
2. Does monogamous marriage have a value that minimal marriage lacks?
3. Do you see any problems with a society that legalizes both monogamy and polygamy?
4. Can someone live a happy and moral life without entering into any particular caring relationships?

Is Civil Marriage Illiberal?

Ralph Wedgwood

Ralph Wedgwood, Professor of Philosophy at the University of Southern California, responds to Elizabeth Brake's view that monogamous marriage is illiberal. He argues that it is similar to parenthood in that it has a generally understood social meaning and gives each party certain legal benefits and burdens. Furthermore, just like parenthood, monogamous marriage can be politically justified insofar as it serves the fundamental goals of numerous citizens and causes no harm to others. Wedgwood concludes that because marriage can be justified without resorting to any controversial moral, religious, or philosophical doctrine, marriage is consistent with liberalism.

1. Liberal Criticisms of Marriage

In the last few years, after decades of campaigning, the cause of same-sex marriage has finally scored a string of successes. By the middle of 2015, same-sex marriage was legal in the Netherlands, Belgium, Spain, Canada, South Africa, Norway, Sweden, Portugal, Iceland, Argentina, Denmark, Uruguay, Brazil, France, New Zealand, England and Wales, Scotland—and, finally, in all fifty states of the USA.

At the same time, the institution of civil marriage has recently come under intense scrutiny from political philosophers who work within a broadly liberal tradition. These philosophers agree with the advocates of same-sex marriage that it is unjust to make civil marriage available to opposite-sex couples while excluding same-sex couples.

From Ralph Wedgwood, "Is Civil Marriage Illiberal?" in *After Marriage: Rethinking Marital Relationships*, ed. Elizabeth Brake (Oxford: Oxford University Press, 2016).

But many of these philosophers give only heavily qualified support to the same-sex marriage campaigners' fundamental goal—which is to give same-sex couples access to something that closely approximates the current institution of marriage. On the contrary, according to these political philosophers, civil marriage itself, in anything approximating to its current form, is incompatible with liberal principles of justice. In their view, marriage should ideally be either completely abolished or radically reformed, virtually beyond recognition; making civil marriage in anything like its current form available to same-sex couples is supportable only if these more radical reforms are unavailable.

In this essay, I shall defend the goal of the same-sex marriage campaigners against the arguments of these liberal political philosophers. I shall principally focus on the arguments of Elizabeth Brake.[1] . . . That is, I shall argue that, while making civil marriage compatible with justice does indeed require legalizing same-sex marriage, it does not require the much more radical reforms that these political philosophers call for.

In particular, I shall focus on the central argument that Brake makes for the conclusion that unless marriage is radically reformed (by being, as she puts it, "minimized"), marriage is "incompatible with political liberalism."[2] By "political liberalism," she means the principle . . . that the state's exercise of its authority must be justifiable on grounds that are acceptable to all reasonable citizens; the state must not exercise its authority in ways that can be justified only by appeal to controversial religious or philosophical doctrines or ideals that some reasonable citizens reject.[3]

To make an argument of this kind, one would have to rely on the claim that marriage, in anything like its current form, can *only* be justified by appeal to such a controversial doctrine or ideal. As Brake puts it, existing marriage law "favors one contested conception of the good and thereby fails to respect public reason and reasonable pluralism."[4] Strictly speaking, however, political liberalism does not prohibit exercises of political authority that are somehow more *favorable* to some contested conceptions of the good than to others; it prohibits exercises of political authority that can only be *justified* by appeal to such contested conceptions. On the face of it, the claim that there is *no* adequate justification of marriage, in anything like its current form, which does not rely on some such controversial doctrine or ideal, seems debatable and in need of being defended. Defending this claim would involve "proving a negative": in principle, it would require surveying *all possible* justifications of marriage, and showing that every possible justification conflicts with liberalism (or else is inadequate in some other way). This would require surveying many more possible justifications of marriage than Brake actually considers. . . .

In general, marriage undoubtedly plays a rich and complex role in our society; but the state, in justifying its involvement in the institution of marriage, does not need to take account of all these complex details.

In this essay, I shall [offer a] justification of marriage, and I shall try to show that this justification is not vulnerable to the objections that have been raised by Brake. . . . In this way, I hope to make it plausible that marriage—even in something approximating to its current form—is quite consistent with liberal principles of justice.

2. What Is Marriage?

The political philosophers who discuss marriage all agree about one thing: marriage essentially involves the *law*. More precisely, every society that has an institution of marriage must have some system of authoritative social rules, which play the role for that society that the law plays for us, and marriage is an institution that involves those social rules. Crucially, marriage is a *legal relationship*: the question "Was Chris married to Joe at such-and-such a time?" is a question that can be settled by a court of law.

Besides being a legal relationship in this sense, what other aspects of marriage law are most fundamental to the institution of marriage? Many theorists, including Brake,[5] seem to think that the most fundamental legal components of marriage are the *entitlements* that marriage confers to *third-party benefits*—that is, to benefits that a married person receives, not from their spouse, but from third parties such as the state, or from various private organizations such as their spouse's employer. These entitlements to third-party benefits include: health insurance benefits; tax breaks; hospital visitation rights; prison visitation rights; privileged immigration treatment for foreign spouses of citizens; the right not to be compelled to testify against one's spouse (and in general to claim an evidentiary privilege for spousal communications); and so on.

However, it seems doubtful to me whether these legal entitlements to third-party benefits are fundamental elements of marriage. These entitlements vary widely between different jurisdictions and different time periods: for example, the tax regimes for married couples are completely different in different jurisdictions; and in countries (like Britain and Canada) that have a national health service, any health insurance benefits that are attached to marriage are clearly a much less important element of marriage than in countries where access to health care depends on private health insurance. In general, it seems to me that these entitlements to third-party benefits could be detached from marriage, and provided on a different basis, without radically changing the nature of marriage. . . .

[M]arriage has three fundamental elements: (i) as I have already noted, it is a *legal relationship*; (ii) it has a generally understood *social meaning*—that is, there is a body of common knowledge and general expectations about marriage that is shared among practically all members of society; and (iii) spouses have *legal powers and obligations* towards each other, where these legal powers and obligations broadly reflect this social meaning.

The way in which these mutual legal powers and obligations "reflect" the social meaning of marriage is simply that these powers and obligations empower and oblige spouses to treat each other in some of the ways in which, according to this social meaning, it is generally *expected* that spouses will typically treat each other. Thus, since it is part of the social meaning of marriage that spouses are expected typically to cooperate in coping with the material necessities of life, many of the legal powers and obligations of marriage concern *property*. For example, in so-called "community property" jurisdictions (like California), property acquired during the marriage is presumed to belong jointly to both spouses; and spouses owe each other a fiduciary duty of care, good faith, and full disclosure in the management of this community property. In virtually all jurisdictions, spouses are obliged to agree to an equitable division of property in the event of divorce; and in the absence of a will, a spouse will inherit all of the other spouse's property on their death. Similarly, since it is part of the social meaning of marriage that spouses are expected typically to know each other well and to care for each other, if you are married, you will normally have priority in being recognized as having legal authority to make decisions on behalf on your spouse if your spouse is incapacitated.

In involving these three fundamental elements, marriage is broadly similar to the legal relationship of *parenthood*, which is also (i) a *legal relationship* that has (ii) a *generally understood social meaning*, and (iii) gives the parent certain *legal obligations* towards the child, as well as a degree of *legal authority* over the child. Again, the legal rights and obligations of parents reflect this social meaning because these rights and obligations oblige and empower parents to treat their children in some of the ways in which, according to this social meaning, parents are expected to treat their children. The key difference between marriage and parenthood lies in the profoundly different social meanings of the two relationships, and in the profoundly different legal rights and obligations associated with these two relationships, which reflect these different social meanings. . . .

[I]t is generally expected that typically, most marriages have the following three features: (a) *sexual intimacy* between the spouses, at least at some point in the history of their relationship; (b) *economic and domestic cooperation*—the spouses work together in coping with the necessities of life; and (c) a *mutual commitment* to sustaining the relationship, at least at the beginning of the marriage. . . .

[I]t is clear that the most that is generally expected within our society is that *most* marriages will *typically* have these three features. Everyone knows that some marriages involve much less in the way of economic and domestic cooperation than others (some married couples live apart and do not have shared finances); everyone knows that in a great many marriages, the mutual commitment to sustaining the relationship disappears as the couple separates or gets divorced; it is presumably widely assumed that some marriages involve no sexual intimacy between the spouses at any time. So these three features are unquestionably not in any sense "criteria" that marriages have to meet to count as marriages. Nonetheless, it seems plausible to me that it is generally expected that at least typically, most marriages have these three features.

The fact that marriage has this generally understood social meaning allows married couples to use marriage as a signal with a distinctive communicative power. In effect, the couple can say "We're married," confident that their audience—whoever their audience may be—will interpret their utterance in the light of this social meaning. The couple might have all sorts of reasons for having this communicative purpose . . . but one common reason for having this communicative purpose is that the couple wishes their audience to come to expect that the couple's relationship conforms to a greater or lesser extent to what is typical of married couples. There are many reasons why a couple might wish their audience to come to have this expectation about their relationship. But perhaps one of the reasons that move many couples particularly powerfully is that it helps to deepen the couple's mutual *commitment* to their relationship if they can so easily and effectively make it known to other members of their society that they have a mutual commitment of this kind.

If marriage lacked this sort of generally understood social meaning, then the couple could not be so confident that they could achieve such communicative purposes by informing others that they were married. Suppose that I told you, "James and I are each other's *blibble*." Even if there is a subculture in which being someone's *blibble* is understood as having a certain significance, if you are not a member of that subculture, I could not be confident that you would understand the significance of what I had said; and even if there is an obscure branch of the law in which being someone's *blibble* confers certain definite obligations and benefits, if you are not a lawyer specializing in that branch of the law, I could not be confident that you would understand the legal significance of what I had said either. So the fact that marriage has a stable and generally understood social meaning allows for marriage to play an effective communicative role in this way.

This reveals that the law plays two crucial roles in the institution of marriage. First, as we have seen, marriage gives spouses a package of legal powers and obligations towards each other. Many of these powers and obligations could also be acquired by making contracts, wills, trusts, power-of-attorney authorizations, and the like. But the law does more than just to enforce these mutual obligations. . . . It specifies a certain standardized package of powers and obligations, which it attaches to a special legal relationship that has a generally understood social meaning. As I have explained, this standardized package of powers and obligations reflects the social meaning of marriage; and where necessary, they are enforced. This reinforces society's expectations that, at least typically, the relationships of most married couples will have the features that are generally expected of typical marriages. In consequence, marriage law in effect stabilizes and reinforces this social meaning. The result is that this social meaning of marriage is understood throughout the whole of society. The social meaning of marriage is not just understood by members of a particular religious community or subculture. It is understood by practically everyone, regardless of the particular religious tradition or subculture that they adhere to; indeed, in our society, even quite young children have a basic understanding of the social meaning of marriage. In this way, the law protects marriage against the risk of its ceasing to have such a generally understood social meaning. . . .

In general, marriage has a communicative function of the sort that I have been describing only because it is [a] *familiar* institution—an institution that we have all grown up hearing about. Presumably, marriage can only become familiar in this way if the culture of the society has traditions surrounding marriage. Although it is crucial to marriage that it is a legal institution, it is also crucial that it is not just a legal institution, but also a social practice rooted in the society's culture. . . .

So far, however, I have only explained what marriage is and what it does. I have not explained what *justifies* the institution of marriage. I shall turn to this question in the following section.

3. The Justification of Marriage

Why is civil marriage justified? It seems clear to me that marriage is not *required* by justice: in principle, a society could be perfectly just even if it had never had the institution of marriage. But not every way of justifying a social institution need involve showing that the institution is required by justice. In the tradition of jurisprudence that built up around the Fourteenth Amendment of the American Constitution, "justifying" a law or public policy typically involves showing only that it is "rationally related" to some "legitimate government objective." What is it for a government objective to count as "legitimate?" In some sense, it seems to me, a government objective is legitimate if it is in some uncontroversial way good for society as a whole. As Rousseau would put it, even if laws and social institutions are not necessary for justice, they can be justified by appeal to the "common good" or the "common interest." As I shall argue in this section, it seems plausible that marriage is justified because in this way it promotes the common good.

Presumably, however, nothing that is *inconsistent* with justice could be justified, even if it did promote the common good. So to argue that marriage is justified because [it] promotes the common good, I must also argue that even though marriage is not *required* by justice, it is nonetheless *consistent* with justice. . . .

For the purposes of such a political justification of marriage, it is sufficient, it seems to me, to argue for the following three points: (a) it is a central part of many people's *most fundamental goals and aspirations in life* to participate in the institution of marriage, and a legal institution of civil marriage is the best way for these people to satisfy these aspirations; (b) the existence of the institution of marriage does not in itself cause any serious harms; and (c) at least *prima facie*, marriage is consistent with justice (there is no obvious reason to think that the existence of marriage violates anyone's rights or the like). For the purposes of the political justification of marriage that I am sketching here, I shall assume that an institution that has these three properties promotes the common good of society as a whole, and can in that way be justified.

Does marriage have the first property (a)? It seems undeniable that a great many people in our society aspire to participate in the institution of marriage, and that this aspiration is a central part of their most fundamental goals and aspirations in life. Moreover, the account of the nature of marriage that I gave in the previous section clarifies the precise content of these life-aspirations. The content of these life-aspirations is to have a legal relationship with another person that involves mutual legal powers and obligations, and a generally understood social meaning, of the kind that I have described. It is reasonable for people who have this aspiration to wish for the social meaning of this legal relationship to be underpinned and stabilized by the law in the way that I have explained. Thus, the best way for the state to enable these people to satisfy these life-aspirations is by maintaining the legal institution of civil marriage. So we may assume that marriage does indeed have this first property (a).

What of the second property (b)? Does the existence of marriage cause any serious harms? We might wonder here about the widespread stigmatization of unmarried people as sad pathetic losers. . . .

To assess this objection, we need to be clear about what exactly this "stigmatization" consists in. One possibility is that this stigmatization merely involves the *belief* that some members of society have, that single people are sad pathetic losers. In this case, it is not clear that the liberal state should try to engage in propaganda to eradicate this belief. According to the principle of political liberalism, the state should not take sides on disputed questions about what makes for a good life; and according to the liberal principle of autonomy, the state should leave it up to individuals to make up their own minds about such questions autonomously, without pressurizing them to adopt any particular view. In general, within a liberal framework, the state should stay neutral on the question of whether or not married life is preferable to single life. Thus, the state should not actively *promote* marriage: it should not produce propaganda to encourage people to get married, or to persuade people that married life is preferable to unmarried life. The most that the state may permissibly do is simply to make marriage available to those who wish to participate in it. . . .

Does marriage harm other non-marital relationships between individuals? It seems plausible that on balance, marriage need not be particularly harmful to what many would regard as the most important of all human relationships—the parent-child relationship. Perhaps marriage harms non-marital caring relationships between adults? But again it is not clear that the existence of the institution of marriage itself is to blame for any harm to such adult caring relationships. Marriage could still exist even if the entitlements to third-party benefits (which we discussed at the beginning of the previous section) were detached from marriage and made available to any demonstrable caring relationship. . . .

What about the third property (c)? Does marriage violate anyone's rights? Historically, marriage has unquestionably violated people's rights. In many jurisdictions, marriage still unjustly discriminates against same-sex couples by arbitrarily excluding them from the right to marry; but as I have argued, one perfectly good way of rectifying this injustice is simply to allow same-sex couples to marry.

More seriously, marriage historically violated the rights of women: it subjected wives to the power and authority of their husbands (while encouraging the marginalization of unmarried women as low-status "spinsters" or "old maids"). It was a highly significant change in the law and social meaning of marriage when it changed from being a radically hierarchical institution, in which the wife was subordinated to her husband's authority, to being, at least in theory, a partnership of equals. This change was clearly required if marriage was ever to become compatible with justice. In general, marriage can avoid violating the rights of women only if it is combined with aggressive efforts to promote gender equality, and with an explicit repudiation of marriage's egregiously sexist past. Still, it seems possible to combine marriage with an anti-sexist regime of this kind. It is presumably for this reason that marriage itself remains strikingly popular among women—even among women who have an unquestionable commitment to combating all forms of sex discrimination and other violations of the rights of women. . . .

As I said above, it seems to me that these three properties of marriage (a), (b), and (c), taken together, are enough to give a political justification of the institution of marriage. But some theorists might raise questions about this justification of marriage. For example, Brake has objected to my justification, suggesting that the desire to marry may not be a desire that the state has any reason to help citizens to satisfy.[6] In particular, she suggests, the desire to participate in a social institution that has the core social meaning of marriage is an *objectionable* preference (and in this respect, presumably, similar to a racist desire to maintain the supremacy of a certain ethnic group or the like). Her reason for taking such a dim view of this extremely common desire is that it involves desiring that marriage should maintain its core social meaning, and so in effect involves desiring that other relationships—such as polyamorous relationships or the like—should *not* be legally recognized as marriages. In this way, she suggests, this desire reveals a kind of animus against those other relationships.

However, it is surely not true that most people who seek to marry need be motivated by any such animus towards other non-marital relationships. . . . Married couples may be entirely sympathetic towards polyamorous relationships, and keen to ensure that such polyamorous groups should be entitled to all the same third-party benefits as married couples. The mere fact that such group unions are not recognized as marriages is not enough to make it the case that the wish to marry need involve any animus or hostility towards such relationships.

Prima facie, then, the simple justification that I have given seems to be an adequate political justification of marriage. In the next section, I shall investigate whether this justification is consistent with political liberalism.

4. Is This Justification of Marriage Consistent with Political Liberalism?

As we have seen, Brake argues that the institution of civil marriage, in anything like its current form, is incompatible with political liberalism. . . .

As I shall argue in this section, once we accept that the best political justification for the institution of marriage in something like its current form is the simple justification that I sketched in the previous section, then it will become clear that this justification of marriage is quite consistent with political liberalism. In order to argue for this, I shall have to make it clearer exactly what this principle of political liberalism amounts to.

. . . Political authority inevitably involves the state's bossing people around, telling them what to do and what not to do, and threatening the use of coercive measures to ensure compliance. How can bossing people around in this way be reconciled with the respect that is due to the dignity of free and autonomous individuals? . . .

The solution that Rawls's political liberalism gives to this problem is to propose that even in a highly pluralistic society, we can make sense of a standpoint of *public reason*. This is a standpoint that can be shared by all reasonable citizens, regardless of the comprehensive religious or philosophical doctrines that they accept. . . .

According to the political justification of marriage that I sketched in the previous section, marriage is not necessary for every just society; marriage is justified simply because, in societies that had a tradition of marriage, maintaining that tradition can promote the common good. According to this justification, maintaining the institution of marriage promotes the common good simply because marriage does not clearly violate any rights or cause any serious harms, and a lot of people make it a central part of their fundamental life-aspirations to participate in the institution.

On the face of it, this political justification does not appeal to any controversial comprehensive doctrine. It is clear for example that this justification does not rely on any controversial "conjugal" ideal—such as the idea that "finding true love" with one other person is the uniquely best or happiest way of life. This justification rests only on the assumption that helping members of the community to achieve such central aspects of their fundamental life-aspirations promotes the common good.

In this way, it seems to me, marriage can be justified without appealing to any controversial view about what is good or valuable in life. Moreover, marriage also need not actively promote any such view either. The state need not seek to propagate the view that marriage is more valuable or honorable than other non-marital relationships. Indeed, as I have argued, the state should not actively promote marriage; marriage should simply be made available for those who wish to participate in it.

Could any reasonable citizen simply reject the relevance of the fact that many members of the population make it a central part of their basic life-aspirations to participate in marriage? Could a reasonable citizen insist that this fact does nothing whatever to support the claim that marriage promotes the common good? . . . [I]ntuitively, it does not sound reasonable to me for participants in political debate simply to brush aside the central components of their fellow citizens' fundamental life-aspirations, at least so long as those life-aspirations do not involve imposing any serious harms on anyone else. . . .

As I said, marriage is not a requirement of justice; a society could be perfectly just even if it had never had the institution of marriage at all. My justification of marriage implies only that, given that marriage has come to inform the central life-aspirations of many citizens, it is perfectly defensible for us to maintain the institution of marriage, so long as we also ensure that it does not cause serious harms or violate any requirements of justice.

The final objection that I wish to consider focuses on the point that a significant number of people would prefer it if there were a somewhat *different* institution, instead of an institution that has the core social meaning of marriage as we know it today. In general, a great many people are not completely happy with the social meaning of marriage as it currently exists. . . . [L]et us imagine the complaint that some polyamorists might raise against my justification of marriage. These polyamorists, let us suppose, would prefer an institution that is in some ways like marriage, but in some other crucial ways quite different—since they would prefer an institution that is open to polyamorous groups with more than two members. Not everyone can have the scheme of social institutions that they would most prefer. If I am right that allowing group marriages would profoundly change the social meaning of marriage, then we cannot have an institution that has *both* the social meaning that marriage currently has *and* the social meaning that these polyamorists would prefer. So how are we to choose?

One thing that no sensible version of liberalism can say is that every citizen can reasonably veto any law or social policy whenever he or she would prefer an alternative. It can often happen that the whole society unanimously agrees that they need to have a policy of kind *K*, but everyone has some objection to every particular policy of kind *K*. For example, there could be unanimous agreement that a road needs to be built between two towns, but for every possible route that the road might take, someone objects to the road's being built along that route. The only answer seems to be that in such cases we need to reach a collective decision by means of a generally agreed democratic procedure. Presumably, in a case where there are just two policies that we have to choose between, the democratic way to make the decision will involve some kind of majoritarian procedure. Indeed, it seems that no reasonable citizen could reject resorting to a majoritarian procedure in cases of this sort: to insist on having a veto power in such cases whenever the majority's preferences differ from one's own seems to me clearly unreasonable.

So it is at this point that it becomes relevant that marriage remains a highly popular institution, vastly more popular than any of the alternatives that marriage's radical critics have proposed. (If we had a referendum tomorrow about whether to abolish marriage, we could be confident of what the outcome would be.) Of course, this might change. If polyamory becomes much more common, people may lose interest in monogamous marriage. In that case, it might make sense to replace marriage with something else. But until then, if marriage continues to enjoy such widespread support, there seems nothing wrong in persisting with it. Since such an appeal to democratic procedures seems unavoidable in any plausible version of political liberalism, this justification of marriage seems to me to be quite consistent with political liberalism. . . .

Notes

1. See Brake, *Minimizing Marriage.*
2. See Brake, *Minimizing Marriage,* 167.
3. See Rawls, *Political Liberalism* (New York: Columbia University Press, 1993), and "The Idea of Public Reason Revisited," *University of Chicago Law Review* 64:3 (1997): 765–807.
4. See Brake, *Minimizing Marriage,* 170.
5. Ibid.
6. See Brake, *Minimizing Marriage,* 173.

Study Questions

1. What is meant by "the common good"?
2. Does the institution of marriage contribute to the common good?
3. Can marriage be justified without appealing to any controversial view about what is good or valuable in life?
4. If non-monogamous marriage were available, would it undermine traditional marriage?

Adultery

Bonnie Steinbock

Bonnie Steinbock is Professor Emerita of Philosophy at the University of Albany, State University of New York. She maintains that adultery is seriously immoral, because it involves promise-breaking and deception. Steinbock finds no immorality, however, in the case of "open marriages," in which both spouses agree that fidelity is not required. Nevertheless, she maintains that sexual fidelity is a coherent and rational ideal, worth such sacrifices as may be involved.

Trust and Deception

. . . [A]dultery unlike murder, theft, and lying, is not universally forbidden. Traditional Eskimo culture, for example, regarded sharing one's wife with a visitor as a matter of courtesy. The difference can be explained by looking at the effects of these practices on social cohesiveness. Without rules protecting the lives, persons, and property of its members, no group could long endure. Indeed, rules against killing, assault, lying, and stealing seem fundamental to having a morality at all.

Not so with adultery. For adultery is a *private* matter, essentially concerning only the relationship between husband and wife. It is not essential to morality like these other prohibitions: there are stable societies with genuine moral codes which tolerate extra-marital sex. Although adultery remains a criminal offense in some jurisdictions, it is rarely prosecuted. Surely this is because it is widely regarded as

From Bonnie Steinbock, "Adultery," *Philosophy and Public Policy Quarterly* 6 (1986).

a private matter: in the words of Billie Holiday, "Ain't nobody's business if I do."

However, even if adultery is a private matter, with which the state should not interfere, it is not a morally neutral issue. Our view of adultery is connected to our thoughts and feelings about love and marriage, sex and the family, the value of fidelity, sexual jealousy, and exclusivity. How we think about adultery will affect the quality of our relationships, the way we raise our children, the kind of society we have and want to have. So it is important to consider whether our attitudes toward adultery are justifiable.

Several practical considerations militate against adultery: pregnancy and genital herpes immediately spring to mind. However, unwanted pregnancies are a risk of all sexual intercourse, within or without marriage; venereal disease is a risk of all non-exclusive sex, not just adulterous sex. So these risks do not provide a reason for objecting specifically to adultery. In any event, they offer merely pragmatic, as opposed to moral, objections. If adultery is wrong, it does not become less so because one has been sterilized or inoculated against venereal disease.

Two main reasons support regarding adultery as seriously immoral. One is that adultery is an instance of promise-breaking, on the view that marriage involves, explicitly or implicitly, a promise of sexual fidelity: to forsake all others. That there is this attitude in our culture is clear. Mick Jagger, not noted for sexual puritanism, allegedly refused to marry Jerry Hall, the mother of his baby, because he had no intention of accepting an exclusive sexual relationship. While Jagger's willingness to become an unwed father is hardly mainstream morality, his refusal to marry, knowing that he did not wish to be faithful, respects the idea that *marriage* requires such a commitment. Moreover, the promise of sexual fidelity is regarded as a very serious and important one. To cheat on one's spouse indicates a lack of concern, a willingness to cause pain, and so a lack of love. Finally, one who breaks promises cannot be trusted. And trust is essential to the intimate partnership of marriage, which may be irreparably weakened by its betrayal.

The second reason for regarding adultery as immoral is that it involves deception, for example, lying about one's whereabouts and relations with others. Perhaps a marriage can withstand the occasional lie, but a pattern of lying will have irrevocable consequences for a marriage, if discovered, and probably even if not. Like breaking promises, lying is regarded as a fundamental kind of wrongdoing, a failure to take the one lied to seriously as a moral person entitled to respect.

Open Marriage

These two arguments suffice to make most cases of adultery wrong, given the attitudes and expectations of most people. But what if marriage did not involve any promise of sexual fidelity? What if there were no need for deception, because neither partner expected or wanted such fidelity? Objections to "open marriage" cannot focus on promise-breaking and deception, for the expectation of exclusivity is absent. If an open marriage has been freely chosen by both spouses, and not imposed by a dominant on a dependent partner, would such an arrangement be morally acceptable, even desirable?

The attractiveness of extramarital affairs, without dishonesty, disloyalty, or guilt, should not be downplayed. However satisfying sex between married people may be, it cannot have the excitement of a new relationship. ("Not *better*," a friend once said defensively to his wife, attempting to explain his infidelity, "just *different*.") Might we not be better off, our lives fuller and richer, if we allowed ourselves the thrill of new and different sexual encounters?

Perhaps the expectation of sexual exclusivity in marriage stems from emotions which are not admirable: jealousy and possessiveness. That most people experience these feelings is no reason for applauding or institutionalizing them. Independence in marriage is now generally regarded as a good thing: too much "togetherness" is boring and stifling. In a good marriage, the partners can enjoy different activities, travel apart, and have separate friends. Why draw the line at sexual activity?

The natural response to this question invokes a certain conception of love and sex: sex is an expression of affection and intimacy and so should be reserved for people who love each other. Further, it is assumed that one can and should have such feelings for only one other person at any time. To make love with someone else is to express feelings of affection and intimacy that should be reserved for one's spouse alone.

This rejection of adultery assumes the validity of a particular conception of love and sex, which can be attacked in two ways. We might divorce sex from love and regard sex as a pleasurable activity in its own right, comparable to the enjoyment of a good meal. [. . . It might be suggested] that the linkage of sex with love reflects a belief that unless it is purified by a higher emotion, such as love, sex is intrinsically bad or dirty.

But this is an overly simplistic view of the connection between sex and love. Feelings of love occur between people enjoying sexual intercourse, not out of a sense that sexual pleasure must be purified, but precisely because of the mutual pleasure they give one another. People naturally have feelings of affection for those who make them happy, and sex is a very good way of making someone extraordinarily happy. At the same time, sex is by its nature intimate, involving both physical and psychological exposure. This both requires and creates trust, which is closely allied to feelings of affection and love. This is not to say that sex necessarily requires or leads to love; but a conception of the relation between love and sex that ignores these factors is inadequate and superficial.

Alternatively, one might acknowledge the connection between sex and love, but attack the assumption of exclusivity. If parents can love all their children equally and if adults can have numerous close friends, why should it be impossible to love more than one sexual partner at a time? Perhaps we could learn to love more than one sexual partner at a time? Perhaps we could learn to love more widely and to accept that a spouse's sexual involvement with another is not a sign of rejection or lack of love.

The logistics of multiple involvement are certainly daunting. Having an affair (as opposed to a roll in the hay) requires time and concentration; it will almost inevitably mean neglecting one's spouse, one's children, one's work. More important, however, exclusivity seems to be an intrinsic part of "true love." Imagine Romeo pouring out his heart to both Juliet *and* Rosalind! In our ideal of romantic love, one chooses to forgo pleasure with other partners in order to have a unique relationship with one's beloved. Such "renunciation" is natural in the first throes of romantic love; it is precisely because this stage does *not* last that we must promise to be faithful through the notoriously unromantic realities of married life.

Fidelity as an Ideal

On the view I have been defending, genuinely open marriages are not *immoral,* although they deviate from a valued ideal of what marriage should be. While this is not the only ideal, or incumbent on all rational agents, it is a moral view in that it embodies a claim about a good way for people to live. The prohibition of adultery, then, is neither arbitrary nor irrational. However, even if we are justified in accepting the ideal of fidelity, we know that people do not always live up to the ideals they accept and we recognize that some failures to do so are worse than others. We regard a brief affair, occasioned by a prolonged separation, as morally different from installing a mistress.

Further, sexual activity is not necessary for deviation from the ideal of marriage which lies behind the demand for fidelity. . . . To abandon one's spouse, whether to a career or to another person, is also a kind of betrayal.

If a man becomes deeply involved emotionally with another woman, it may be little comfort that he is able to assure his wife that "Nothing happened." Sexual infidelity has significance as a sign of a deeper betrayal—falling in love with someone else. It may be objected that we cannot control the way we feel, only the way we behave; that we should not be blamed for falling in love, but only for acting on the feeling. While we may not have direct control over our feelings, however, we are responsible for getting ourselves into situations in which certain feelings naturally arise. "It just happened," is rarely an accurate portrayal of an extra-marital love affair.

If there can be betrayal without sex, can there be sex without betrayal? . . . People do fall in love with others and out of love with their spouses. Ought they refrain from making love while still legally tied? I cannot see much, if any, moral value in remaining physically faithful, on principle, to a spouse one no longer loves. This will displease those who regard the wrongness of adultery as a moral absolute, but my account has nothing to do with absolutes and everything to do with what it means to love someone deeply and completely. It is the value of that sort of relationship that makes sexual fidelity an ideal worth the sacrifice.

Neither a mere religiously based taboo, nor a relic of a repressive view of sexuality, the prohibition against adultery expresses a particular conception of married love. It is one we can honor in our own lives and bequeath to our children with confidence in its value as a coherent and rational ideal.

Study Questions

1. According to Steinbock, what two main reasons support regarding adultery as seriously immoral?
2. What is meant by an *open marriage?*
3. Can we imagine Romeo pouring out his heart to both Juliet and Rosalind?
4. In a traditional marriage, is every instance of adultery immoral?

B.

Parents and Children

What Do Grown Children Owe Their Parents?

Jane English

Jane English (1947–1978) was Associate Professor at the University of North Carolina at Chapel Hill. She argues that the parent–child relationship is best viewed as one between friends, not debtor and creditor. Thus children do not owe anything to their parents, but obligations emerge as duties between friends. English concludes that although parents make sacrifices for their children, the duties that grown children have to their parents result from friendship, not from sacrifices.

What do grown children owe their parents? I will contend that the answer is "nothing." Although I agree that there are many things that children *ought* to do for their parents, I will argue that it is inappropriate and misleading to describe them as things "owed." I will

From Jane English, "What Do Grown Children Owe Their Parents?" in *Having Children: Philosophical and Legal Reflections on Parenthood*, Onora O'Neill and William Ruddick, eds. (Oxford: Oxford University Press, 1979).

maintain that parents' voluntary sacrifices, rather than creating "debts" to be "repaid," tend to create love or "friendship." The duties of grown children are those of friends, and result from love between them and their parents, rather than being things owed in repayment for the parents' earlier sacrifices. Thus, I will oppose those philosophers who use the word "owe" whenever a duty or obligation exists. Although the "debt" metaphor is appropriate in some moral circumstances, my argument is that a love relationship is not such a case.

Misunderstandings about the proper relationship between parents and their grown children have resulted from reliance on the "owing" terminology. For instance, we hear parents complain, "You owe it to us to write home (keep up your piano playing, not adopt a hippie lifestyle), because of all we sacrificed for you (paying for piano lessons, sending you to college)." The child is sometimes even heard to reply, "I didn't ask to be born (to be given piano lessons, to be sent to college)." This inappropriate idiom of ordinary language tends to obscure, or even to undermine, the love that is the correct ground of filial obligation.

Favors Create Debts

There are some cases, other than literal debts, in which talk of "owing," though metaphorical, is apt. New to the neighborhood, Max barely knows his neighbor, Nina, but he asks her if she will take in his mail while he is gone for a month's vacation. She agrees. If, subsequently, Nina asks Max to do the same for her, it seems that Max has a moral obligation to agree (greater than the one he would have had if Nina had not done the same for him), unless for some reason it would be a burden far out of proportion to the one Nina bore for him. I will call this a *favor:* when A, at B's request, bears some burden for B, then B incurs an obligation to reciprocate. Here, the metaphor of Max's "owing" Nina is appropriate. It is not literally a debt, of course, nor can Nina pass this IOU on to heirs, demand payment in the form of Max's taking out her garbage, or sue Max. Nonetheless, since Max ought to perform one act of a similar nature and amount of sacrifice in return, the term is suggestive. Once he reciprocates, the debt is "discharged"—that is, their obligations revert to the condition they were in before Max's initial request.

Contrast a situation in which Max simply goes on vacation and, to his surprise, finds upon his return that his neighbor has mowed his grass twice weekly in his absence. This is a voluntary sacrifice rather than a favor, and Max has no duty to reciprocate. It would be nice for him to volunteer to do so, but this would be supererogatory on his part. Rather than a favor, Nina's action is a friendly gesture. As a result, she might expect Max to chat over the back fence, help her catch her straying dog, or something similar—she might expect the development of a friendship, but Max would be chatting (or whatever) out of friendship, rather than in repayment for mown grass. If he did not return her gesture, she might feel rebuffed or miffed, but not unjustly treated or indignant, since Max has not failed to perform a duty. Talk of "owing" would be out of place in this case.

It is sometimes difficult to distinguish between favors and nonfavors, because friends tend to do favors for each other, and those who exchange favors tend to become friends, but one test is to ask how Max is motivated. Is it "to be nice to Nina" or "because she did *x* for me"? Favors are frequently performed by total strangers without any friendship developing. Nevertheless, a temporary obligation is created, even if the chance for repayment never arises. For instance, suppose that Oscar and Matilda, total strangers, are waiting in a long checkout line at the supermarket. Oscar, having forgotten the oregano, asks Matilda to watch his cart for a second. She does. If Matilda now asks Oscar to return the favor while she picks up some tomato sauce, he is obliged to agree. Even if she had not watched his cart, it would be inconsiderate of him to refuse, claiming he was too busy reading the magazines. He may have a duty to help others, but he would not "owe" it to her. However, if she has done the same for him, he incurs an additional obligation to help, and talk of "owing" is apt. It suggests an agreement to perform equal, reciprocal, canceling sacrifices.

The Duties of Friendship

The terms "owe" and "repay" are helpful in the case of favors, because the sameness of the amount of sacrifice on the two sides is important; the monetary metaphor suggests equal quantities of sacrifice. However, friendship ought to be characterized by *mutuality* rather than reciprocity: friends offer what they can give and accept what they need, without regard for the total amounts of benefits exchanged, and friends are motivated by love rather than by the prospect of repayment. Hence, talk of "owing" is singularly out of place in friendship.

For example, suppose Alfred takes Beatrice out for an expensive dinner and a movie. Beatrice incurs no obligation to "repay" him with a goodnight kiss or a return engagement. If Alfred complains that she "owes" him something, he is operating under the assumption that she should repay a favor, but on the contrary, his was a generous gesture done in the hopes of developing a friendship. We hope that he would not want her repayment in the form of sex or attention if this was done to discharge a debt rather than from friendship. Since, if Alfred is prone to reasoning in this way, Beatrice may well decline the invitation or request to pay for her own dinner, his attitude of expecting a "return" on his "investment" could hinder the development of a friendship. Beatrice should return the gesture only if she is motivated by friendship.

Another common misuse of the "owing" idiom occurs when the Smiths have dined at the Joneses' four times, but the Joneses at the Smiths' only once. People often say, "We owe them three dinners." This line of thinking may be appropriate between business acquaintances, but not between friends. After all, the Joneses invited the Smiths not in order to feed them or to be fed in turn, but because of the friendly contact presumably enjoyed by all on such occasions. If the Smiths do not feel friendship toward the Joneses, they can decline future invitations and not invite the Joneses; they owe them nothing. Of course, between friends of equal resources and needs, roughly equal sacrifices (though not necessarily roughly equal dinners) will typically occur. If the sacrifices are highly out of proportion to the resources, the relationship is closer to servility than to friendship.[1]

Another difference between favors and friendship is that, after a friendship ends, the duties of friendship end. The party that has sacrificed less owes the other nothing. For instance, suppose Elmer donated a pint of blood that his wife Doris needed during an operation. Years after their divorce, Elmer is in an accident and needs one pint of blood. His new wife, Cora, is also of the same blood type. It seems that Doris not only does not "owe" Elmer blood, but that she should actually refrain from coming forward if Cora has volunteered to donate. To insist on donating not only interferes with the newlyweds' friendship, but it belittles Doris and Elmer's former relationship by suggesting that Elmer gave blood in hopes of favors returned instead of simply out of love for Doris. It is one of the heart-rending features of divorce that it attends to quantity in a relationship previously characterized by mutuality. If Cora could not donate, Doris's obligation would be the same as that for any former spouse in need of blood; it is not increased by the fact that Elmer similarly aided her. It is affected by the degree to which they are still friends, which, in turn, may (or may not) have been influenced by Elmer's donation.

In short, unlike the debts created by favors, the duties of friendship do not require equal quantities of sacrifice. Performing equal sacrifices does not cancel the duties of friendship, as it does the debts of favors. Unrequested sacrifices do not themselves create debts, but friends have duties regardless of whether they requested or initiated the friendship. Those who perform favors may be motivated by mutual gain, whereas friends should be motivated by affection. These characteristics of the friendship relation are distorted by talk of "owing."

Parents and Children

The relationship between children and their parents should be one of friendship characterized by mutuality rather than one of reciprocal favors. The quantity of parental sacrifice is not relevant in determining what duties the grown child has. The medical assistance grown children ought to offer their ill mothers in old age depends on the mothers' need, not on whether they endured a difficult pregnancy, for example. Nor do one's duties to one's parents cease once an equal quantity of sacrifice has been performed, as the phrase "discharging a debt" may lead us to think.

Rather, what children ought to do for their parents (and parents for children) depends on (1) their respective needs, abilities, and resources and (2) the extent to which there is an ongoing friendship between them. Thus, regardless of the quantity of childhood sacrifices, an able, wealthy child has an obligation to help his or her needy parents more than does a needy child. To illustrate, suppose sisters Cecile and Dana are equally loved by their parents, even though Cecile was an easy child to care for and was seldom ill, whereas Dana was often sick and caused some trouble as a juvenile delinquent. As adults, Dana is a struggling artist living far away, whereas Cecile is a wealthy lawyer living nearby. When the parents need visits and financial aid, Cecile has an obligation to bear a higher proportion of these burdens than her sister. This results from her abilities, rather than from the quantities of sacrifice made by the parents earlier.

Sacrifices have an important causal role in creating an ongoing friendship, which may lead us to assume incorrectly that it is the sacrifices that are the source of the obligation. That the source is the friendship instead can be seen by examining cases in which the sacrifices occurred, but the friendship, for some reason, did not develop or persist. For example, if a woman gives up her newborn child for adoption, and if no feelings of love ever develop on either side, it seems that the grown child does not have an obligation to "repay" her for her sacrifices in pregnancy. For that matter, if the adopted child has an unimpaired love relationship with the adoptive parents, he or she has the same obligations to help them as a natural child would have.

The filial obligations of grown children are a result of friendship, rather than owed for services rendered. Suppose that Vance married Lola despite his parents' strong wish that he marry within their religion, and that as a result, the parents refuse to speak to him again. As the years pass, the parents are unaware of Vance's problems, his accomplishments, and the birth of his children. The love that once existed between them, let us suppose, has been completely destroyed by this event and 30 years of desuetude. At this point, it seems, Vance is under no obligation to pay his parents' medical bills in their old age, beyond his general duty to help those in need. An additional, filial obligation would only arise from whatever love he may still feel for them. It would be irrelevant for his parents to argue, "But look how much we sacrificed for you when you were young," for that sacrifice was not a favor, but occurred as part of a friendship that existed at that time but is now, we have supposed, defunct. A more appropriate message would be, "We still love you, and we would like to renew our friendship."

I hope this helps to set the question of what children ought to do for their parents in a new light. The parental argument, "You ought to do *x* because we did *y* for you," should be replaced by, "We love you, and you will be happier if you do *x*," or "We believe you love us, and anyone who loved us would do *x*." If the parents' sacrifice had been a favor, the child's reply, "I never asked you to do *y* for me," would have been relevant; to the revised parental remarks, this reply is clearly irrelevant. The child can either do *x* or dispute one of the parents' claims: by showing that a love relationship does not exist, or that love for someone does not motivate doing *x*, or that he or she will not be happier doing *x*.

Seen in this light, parental requests for children to write home, visit, and offer them a reasonable amount of emotional and financial support in life's crises are well founded, so long as a friendship still exists. Love for others does call for caring about and caring for them. Some other parental requests, such as for more sweeping changes in the child's lifestyle or life goals, can be seen to be insupportable, once we shift the justification from debts owed to love. The terminology of favors suggests the reasoning, "Since we paid for your college education, you owe it to us to make a career of engineering, rather than becoming a rock musician." This tends to alienate affection even further, since the tuition payments are depicted as investments for a return rather than done from love, as though the child's life goals could be "bought." Basing the argument on love leads to different reasoning patterns. The suppressed premise, "If A loves B, then A follows B's wishes as to A's lifelong career" is simply false. Love does not even dictate that the child adopt the parents' values as to the desirability of alternative life goals. So the parents' strongest available argument here is, "We love you, we are deeply concerned about your happiness, and in the long run you will be happier as an engineer." This makes it clear that an empirical claim is really the subject of the debate.

The function of these examples is to draw out our considered judgments as to the proper relation between parents and their grown children, and to show how poorly they fit the model of favors. What is relevant is the ongoing friendship that exists between parents and children. Although that relationship developed partly as a result of parental sacrifices for the child, the duties that grown children have to their parents result from the friendship rather than from the sacrifices. The idiom of owing favors to one's parents can actually be destructive if it undermines the role of mutuality and leads us to think in terms of quantitative reciprocal favors.

Note

1. Cf T. E. Hill, Jr. (1973) Servility and self-respect. *Monist* 57, 87–104. Thus, during childhood, most of the sacrifices will come from the parents, since they have most of the resources, and the child has most of the needs. When children are grown, the situation is usually reversed.

Study Questions

1. If your parents have sacrificed much for you, do you owe them anything?
2. If your parents have neglected you, do you owe them anything?
3. Are you morally required to help friends from whom you have drifted apart?
4. Are you morally required to help parents from whom you have drifted apart?

Can Parents and Children Be Friends?

Joseph Kupfer

Joseph Kupfer is Professor of Philosophy at Iowa State University. Contrary to Jane English, he argues that the parent–child relationship should not be understood in terms of friendship, for friendship requires that each party needs to be roughly equal in influence and power. Yet a parent–child relationship, especially early on, is characterized by inequality. Given this history, the parent and child will always share an unequal balance of autonomy. Thus what we owe parents is not analogous to what we owe friends.

It is often said by layman and philosopher alike that ideally children should grow up to be friends with their parents. Growing up and out of the one-sided dependency characteristic of the early phases of their relationship, adult children should become companions to their parents. There ought to be a mutual caring and counsel. This emphasis on friendship reflects the fact that young children become adults able to contribute to their parents' lives in ways comparable to what their parents have done for them. It also reflects the undesirability of the apparent alternatives to friendship: estrangement, continued child-dependence, or mere civility.

Part of the difficulty is that we don't have a word or clear concept to capture the ideal parent–adult child relationship, and "friendship" does indeed come closest to what it should be. How else describe

From Joseph Kupfer, "Can Parents and Children Be Friends?" *American Philosophical Quarterly* 27 (1990).

the affection, respect, and give and take into which the relationship should evolve? In what follows I argue that parents and their adult children cannot become the "true" or "complete" friends they might be with peers. Contrary to an increasingly popular view, it is a mistake to turn to friendship as an ideal by which parents and children should orient or govern their relationships (or philosophers should theorize about them).[1] Fundamental features of the ideal parent–adult child relationship keep it from developing into full-blown friendship. While peers may fail to become ideal friends, it isn't for the same reasons that parents and their grown children can't. The obstacles between parents and children are built into the structure of the relationship. . . .

I

Parents and adult children cannot become true friends for [their] relationship lacks the equality friendship requires. . . . The inequality which prevents their friendship is inequality in autonomy. By autonomy I mean the ability to be self-determining: to choose for oneself on the basis of one's own values and beliefs. The autonomous person takes into account the opinions and advice of others, but reaches conclusions and decisions based on critical reflection of the matters at hand. Adult children are not necessarily less autonomous than their parents *per se*, or in general. Rather, they are less autonomous than their parents in the relationship. Although a grown child may generally be more autonomous than her parents, in interaction with them she cannot be. Adult children can't quite "be themselves," at least not all of the selves they've become apart from their parents. Adult children's thoughts and actions are not as free as their parents' *in the context of their relationship*. Moreover, adult children cannot affect their parents in as fundamental ways as parents influenced them when young. This claim about unequal autonomy is what I shall now try to develop and defend. First, let me briefly suggest why equal autonomy is characteristic of true friendship.

Ideal friendship requires equal autonomy in the relationship for several reasons. Without it, there will be unequal influence and power. One friend will be making more of the decisions or having more impact on the decisions at which they mutually arrive. The less autonomous friend will offer less of the resistance and counterpoise upon which the best friendships stay balanced. As a consequence, the friendship of unequal autonomy will tend toward inequality in dependency, with one friend needing or relying disproportionately on the other. The more autonomous party to the relationship will receive less from the friendship, at least in terms of advice, criticism, and alternative perspective. These are important goods inherent to friendship, and their unequal enjoyment is a detriment to complete friendship. . . .

To see why grown children can't be as autonomous as their parents within the relationship, we need to examine the unequal exercise of autonomy which characterizes the young child's upbringing. I shall then argue that this history of inequality prevents equality later on, when the child is an adult. . . . To begin with, we should make much of the obvious—the parent helps *shape* who and what the young child is. Where the parent developed into an adult independently of the child, the young child grows up under the parent's influence and care. The physical, psychological, and social dependence of the child translates into . . . inequality; the parent simply is more responsible for the being or identity of the young child than the other way around. Bringing the child into the world, raising her, taking part in her successes and failures, the parent contributes to the young child's identity in ways which she cannot reciprocate. While the parent may be changed dramatically *as a result* of rearing a child, the parent is not shaped *by* the child. The parent authors change in the young child, exerting control, both intentional and unwitting, over her development.

Who the young child is, then, results in part from the parent's exercise of autonomy. Even the young child's character and degree of autonomy itself ideally are cultivated by parental industry. Their history together is a history of parents making decisions for the young child, provisionally exercising an autonomy on her behalf that the child will (should) eventually exercise for herself. . . .

II/A

But why must this history of unequal autonomy in the relationship prevent equality later on, when the child is grown up? It is because this history endures in the identities of the parent and adult child in at least two ways: in their self-concepts, and in their habits and attitudes toward each other.

The adult child's self-concept includes different aspects of her history with the parent. The parent protecting, nurturing, encouraging, and letting go all figure in. Our degree of autonomy in general depends upon our self-concept. For example, people who see themselves as able to carry out choices effectively or who have strong body images, tend to exercise greater control over their lives than those who do not. Because it includes the history of the unequal relationship with the parent, the adult child's self-concept limits the degree to which she can function autonomously with the parent. . . .

The history of the unequal autonomy affects the adult child in another way, besides informing her self-concept. It also fosters enduring habits and attitudes towards the parents which persist into the child's adulthood. Some of these enter into her self-concept, but not all. These habits and attitudes help constitute who we are. Such attitudes as respect and loyalty, as well as habits of deference and accommodation engendered in youth persist into adulthood. . . .

II/B

What has been said about the impact of unequal autonomy on the self-concept, habits, and attitudes of grown children reciprocally holds for parents as well. The parent's sense of self is informed in a complementary way by the history of unequal autonomy. The parent sees himself as provider and protector, teacher and guardian of the young child. Most people include the role of "parent" (but not child) in their self-concept. For it is, after all, something of an occupation: an arduous, rewarding job that becomes part of our self-understanding. . . .

The parent sees himself as partly responsible for the adult child's existence, growth, and well-being. He can reasonably take credit for some of her accomplishments as well as blame for various shortcomings. . . . He is an expert on the formation of his adult child's temperament and tastes, aspirations and humiliations. The adult child, of course, knows that this particular individual (however much a "friend"), unlike all others, knew her and knew all about her before she had consciousness of herself as a person.

There is an irony in the parent's superior knowledge of the young child; too often it limits parental appreciation of the adult child—even in ideal relationships. Precisely because parents know their children so well qua children they may be kept from truly seeing and appreciating who the child is as an adult, the image of the young child coloring the parent's later perceptions. . . . People who meet us as adults, however, can more readily appreciate who and what we are since unencumbered by childhood history or their role in who we've become.

As a result of interacting with their young children, parents also develop characteristic habits and attitudes. Such habits as solicitousness and helpfulness, as well as attitudes of concern and protectiveness live on in interactions with their grown children. While children should outlive their childhoods, they remain their parents' children. Even though these original parental habits and attitudes should be *modified* as the children mature, they are practically impossible to uproot. Because such habits and attitudes bespeak an inequality in autonomy, parents remain more autonomous in relation to their grown children, and this keeps them from becoming complete or true friends. . . .

IV/B

. . . [O]ur parents' contribution is unique. Only they could make us secure and loving enough, for example, to form good friendships in the first place. We are grateful to our parents for what no one else *in principle* can do. And this makes the love informed by that gratitude of a different stripe altogether. Unlike our love of friends, the love we have for our parents is grounded in gratitude. There may be more to an adult child's love for her parents, for instance, she may love them for such virtues as patience or wit. But it is the gratitude for helping shape our identities that I am calling attention to here because that is what distinguishes love for parents most sharply from friendship love.

Our relationship with our parents is enriched not only by the gratitude-love we feel for them but by its concrete expression as well. Gratitude for who and what we are is shown differently than gratitude for this or that particular act, or even gratitude for a friendship as such. For example, we may express or exhibit this gratitude indirectly, by striving to realize our natural gifts in the knowledge that this will be especially rewarding to our parents. Since they helped define and cultivate our nature, continuing this growth is especially appropriate.

Gratitude-love can also be more directly expressed toward our parents. Because they are so responsible for who we are, it is fitting for us to take care of them. While we may also take care of friends, even out of gratitude, it is not structurally part of the relationship. It is contingently connected to the friendship in a way that taking care of our parents is not. Taking care of our parents returns us to our origins by mirroring their nurturance of us. In this return to our origins we return to our parents as only *we* can: returning their unconditional love with our gratitude-love. . . .

IV/C

The parent–adult child relationship has a solidity and stability which derives from the permanence of one's status as parent and child. We outgrow childhood, but not being someone's child. No matter how functions and needs shift, so that the parent may be taken care of by the grown child, he is still the parent. The status endures, even if many of the specific role functions do not. Friendship is different. We can acquire and lose friends; the status of friend is not permanent for the lives of the parties.

The permanence of status adds a forward-looking dimension to the relationship. Just as the parents and grown children share the history of the young child's life, and know that they do, so do they also see the relationship (whatever its perturbations) as inevitably stretching into the future. They are in it for the "long haul." Of course, when the relationship is seriously lacking, the parties feel this as a burden, something to be endured. But in the ideal relationship, it provides a backbone of durability.

The stability and strength which come from the permanence of status is buttressed by the lack of choice concerning that status. Children obviously choose neither their parents nor to be anyone's child. Although parents (ideally) choose to have children, they don't choose to have just these children (even when exercising autonomy in the strong sense of shaping the child's nature). Parents choose to create the relationship, but have only limited choice and control over who is party to it. This clearly contrasts with friendship, in which parents and adult children exercise considerable choice and control. The lack of choice over the relationship solidifies the identification between parents and adult children. The identification is ineluctable, something to be accepted as part of one's lot—unlike identification with role models or professions, over which we may exercise choice.

The permanence of status, supplemented by lack of choice, adds security for both parties. We are vouched safe against the changes that can beset even the best of friendships, changes that partly hinge on the fact that friendship is so keenly owing to choice. For that reason alone friendships are more vulnerable. For example, parents and adult children as well as friends may have to make a great effort to keep their respective relationships strong during extended periods of separation. However, the permanence or irrevocability of the parent–adult child status provides an impetus for "keeping up." It is harder to let the relationship unravel knowing that this is still your parent, this is still your child. . . .

Note

1. See, for example, Jane English's "What Do Grown Children Owe Their Parents?"

Study Questions

1. Can you be friends with someone who is not your equal in terms of power, money, or fame?
2. Can friends differ widely in age?
3. If a woman says that her mother is her best friend, is that statement necessarily false?
4. Can teachers eventually become friends with those who were initially their students?

Four Theories of Filial Duty

Simon Keller

Simon Keller is Professor of Philosophy at the Victoria University of Wellington, New Zealand. He argues that the three most prominent theories of filial duties—the debt theory, the gratitude theory, and the friendship theory—all fail. In their place he maintains that parents and children have a unique relationship. It is best understood in terms of special goods that parents can receive from no one but their children, and children can receive from no one but their parents.

Even when we have become adults, we have special duties to our parents. These are *special* duties because they are not duties that we have to people generally. You might have the duty to keep in touch with your parents, or to take them into your home when they are sick or elderly, but these are not things that you are obliged to do for just anyone.

Filial duties are, as duties go, important. It is common for people to make large sacrifices in order to provide for their parents, and to do so, in part, because they feel that it is their duty to do so. Those who neglect their filial duties can evoke deep disapproval: think of a rich son who cannot be bothered to do anything to help his parents—his lonely and impoverished but perfectly loving parents, who did all they could to give him the best possible opportunities in life—and try not to disapprove.

There is reason to want a theory of how filial duties arise and of what, in broad terms, they are. Questions about what we are required to do for our parents, and what we can legitimately expect from our children, are difficult and controversial. . . .

From Simon Keller, "Four Theories of Filial Duty," *The Philosophical Quarterly* 56 (2006).

I. The Debt Theory

Your parents have done an enormous amount for you, and you owe them something in return: this is the thought behind the debt theory. As a grown child, runs the idea, you are like someone who has taken out a loan but not yet repaid it, and filial duties identify the things that you have to do in order to discharge your debt. Throughout much of the history of philosophy, in the West and in the East, the debt theory has been regarded as unproblematic and transparently true.[1]

The trouble with the debt theory is that it leads to implausible claims about what filial duties we actually have. If you give me a loan, then my duty is to repay the loan, or to meet whatever conditions I agreed to meet in return for the loan, no more or less. The nature of my debt does not alter with your needs, my financial situation, my lifestyle choices, or the ongoing state of our relationship.

As Jane English points out, filial duties do not fit this pattern.[2] There is no measure of goods such that once you have provided it to your parents your filial duties are discharged, once and for all. And filial duties do not seem to differ in nature or weightiness depending upon the exact amount of effort and energy contributed by parents; you may have been a healthy and angelic child, undemanding and a delight to nurture, but that does not mean that you have any less of an obligation to respect and help your parents than you would have had if you had been sickly and temperamental and very difficult to raise.

Your filial duties, furthermore, differ with certain aspects of your situation. You are only required to give your parents what is reasonable, given your abilities and lifestyle choices. If you are a struggling artist, to use English's example, then you do not have the duty to contribute as much to your parents' medical care (say) as you would if you had chosen a better-paying occupation. Your duties to your parents also vary according to the state of your relationship with them. If you and your parents drift apart, or have a serious and permanent falling out (for which you cannot reasonably be blamed), then you are left with fewer filial duties, perhaps none at all. The duties of grown children to parents just do not look like the duties of debtors to creditors.

II. The Gratitude Theory

II.1. The Theory

Often, when other people do good things for us, we are obliged to respond with acts of gratitude. The gratitude theory says that to fulfil your filial duties is to perform appropriate acts of gratitude in response to the good things your parents have done for you.

Duties of gratitude differ from duties of strict indebtedness in ways that allow the gratitude theory to avoid the objections to the debt theory. This is because the contents of duties of gratitude, like those of duties to parents, can be vaguely specified and heavily dependent upon circumstances. To give one example, what we ought to do out of gratitude depends upon what we reasonably can do. If you do something for me, and I am an affluent person who lives nearby, then it may be that I ought to respond by treating you to a good dinner; but if I have little money or live far away, a sincere note of thanks might suffice. . . .

II.2. Duties of Gratitude

What are duties of gratitude? . . . [T]hey are best construed as duties to demonstrate or communicate feelings of gratitude, which is to say that they are duties to show that you feel appropriately grateful (or perhaps to act as you would if you did feel appropriately grateful) for a given benefit. In demonstrating your gratitude, you show that you recognize and appreciate your benefactors' efforts, that you regard their time and energy as valuable, that you do not take their efforts for granted. . . .

Here are three reasons to think that filial duties cannot be construed as duties of gratitude. . . .

II.3. The Point of Filial Duties

First, filial duties are direct duties to help, respect, please or benefit parents, not duties to do these things in order, or in so far as they are required, to demonstrate gratitude.

Suppose you go out of your way to make sure that you are with your mother while she goes through a difficult medical procedure. What (conceivably) makes your act obligatory is the fact that she needs or wants you there, that things will be better for her in certain respects if you are around—not the fact (if it is a fact) that your presence will be understood by your mother as showing that you are grateful for the sacrifices that she has made for you in the past. . . .

II.4. Parental Sacrifice

Secondly, the extent of duties of gratitude depends upon how much discomfort, exertion and sacrifice are involved in the provision of the relevant benefit, and this makes such duties different in a further respect from filial duties.

Suppose two people each spend a day helping you move house. The first, the 'sacrificing' mover, is an avid windsurfer and the day of your move is the only day with decent winds in months; he hates moving boxes and furniture; he has a bad back that he knows will be sore for days afterwards; he lives far away and has to drive for hours to and from home; but he cares about you and wants to make the move easier, so he helps anyway. The second, the 'effortless' mover, really quite enjoys the organization and companionship of moving house; he has no other plans for the day and is happy to have something to do; he lives nearby and is strong of back and limb; he is delighted to have the chance to help and cannot think of anything he would rather be doing.

You should be grateful to both the sacrificing mover and the effortless mover, but more should be done by way of demonstrating gratitude towards the sacrificing mover. He may not have been any more helpful on the day, but he had to make a greater effort to be there, and his participation, unlike that of the effortless mover, required non-trivial sacrifices and soreness. He merits extra thanks and appreciation, and a more significant gesture of gratitude.

The two movers can be compared with two kinds of parents. 'Sacrificing' parents love their children and are happy to give them a good upbringing, but in order to be good parents they have to make an enormous effort, sacrifice other valued parts of their lives and cope with an extra degree of physical suffering. 'Effortless' parents find that they are just made to be parents; they love bringing up children and can think of nothing else that they would want to do with the time and energy involved; they find it an exhilarating breeze. It might make sense for children of sacrificing parents to feel an extra kind of gratitude for their upbringing. But the children of effortless parents do not have lesser filial duties, speaking generally, than those of sacrificing parents. Your duty to look after your father in his old age is not mitigated by his having found parenting so much fun.

II.5. The Demands of Gratitude

Thirdly, the kinds of things that might have to be done to fulfil filial duties are very different from the kinds of things that can legitimately be expected in fulfilment of duties of gratitude. Filial duties are ongoing and open-ended, and can be very demanding. Gratitude does not require ongoing commitments or significant sacrifices. . . .

Everyday gestures of gratitude tend to be isolated acts like sending a card or flowers or taking someone to dinner; they do not involve the grateful person's doing anything that counts, given the situation, as a significant sacrifice. This is so for good reason. Duties of gratitude arise in response to benevolence, to someone's doing something to benefit you and not in order to receive something in return. The point of demonstrations of gratitude is to acknowledge acts of benevolence appropriately, not to provide repayment. All of this is undermined if those who do things for others can thereby place open-ended and demanding duties upon those whom they benefit.

It is revealing to think of this from the point of view of the benefactor. If you act benevolently towards someone, then perhaps you can expect him to acknowledge your benevolence. You can feel disappointed and perhaps affronted if he shows no appreciation for what you have done. But it is quite another matter to feel that you will only be convinced of his gratitude if he gives up something he values deeply, or is still prepared to do things for you years after the event. This is plainly unreasonable, and throws your initial alleged benevolence into doubt. Acts of benevolence do not place, and should not be expected to place, significant burdens upon their intended beneficiaries. . . .

The thought that acts of enormous benevolence generate enormous ongoing duties of gratitude is, in my view, understandable but mistaken. It can be seen as a response to two truths. The first is that there is nothing in our conventional repertoire of gestures of gratitude—not chocolates or flowers or thank-you cards or anything—that represents sufficient and sincere gratitude for something so enormous. This may mean that you feel at a loss, wanting to communicate your gratitude but without clear access to a convincing way of doing so. Perhaps your best option is to make a lesser gesture—send flowers, or whatever—while making it clear that you do not take this to represent the depth of the gratitude that you really feel; or perhaps you should just say or write something that says how grateful you are, and hope that it gets the message across. Whatever you do, you are likely to feel a little inadequate.

The second relevant truth is that if someone does something very significant for your sake, like saving your life, then he may well come to give you a special place among his values and priorities, and to hope that the two of you will have an ongoing relationship. He might want to know more about you, to know what you do with your future life, and perhaps to have you as a friend. And you, of course, may well feel the same way about him. One way in which you can show that you value your benefactor and the efforts that he has made is to show that you are open to the possibility of an ongoing friendship. You might demonstrate your gratitude by having your benefactor . . . meet your family, trying to stay in touch, or doing other things that give the two of you the opportunity to form a relationship that both of you will value—not just because it commemorates a past act of benevolence, but for its own sake.

For these reasons, it is natural and perhaps desirable to feel, as a recipient of an act of immense benevolence, as though your duty to demonstrate gratitude is very demanding, or requires of you ongoing acts of gratitude. But there are ways to explain this feeling without supposing that duties to demonstrate gratitude really are open-ended, ongoing and demanding; and there is good independent reason to think that they, unlike filial duties, are not.

III. The Friendship Theory

III.1. The Theory

The friendship theory is that the source of filial duty lies not in what parents have done in the past, but in the relationship shared by children and parents in the present. According to the friendship theory, the duties between grown children and their parents are the duties of friends.[3]

Exchanges of goods between friends are controlled by a principle of mutuality, not reciprocity. It is not important that friends contribute an equal amount, but that each gives what he reasonably can. If you and I enjoy surfing together, and you own a house near the beach, then I shall probably spend more time at your house than you will at mine; this does not mean that I am failing to do my duty as a friend. We sometimes talk of ‘owing’ our friends a dinner, or whatever, but in doing so we are expressing not the worry that we are failing to honour our debts, but the worry that we are not doing our bit to keep the friendship alive and healthy.[4]

The friendship theory has some clear advantages over the debt and gratitude theories. It can explain why filial duties do not differ depending upon exactly how much parental sacrifice was involved in raising a given child; it can explain why filial duties are not the sorts of duties that can be discharged once and for all; and (like the gratitude theory but not the debt theory) it can explain why grown children only have duties to do for their parents what they reasonably can. . . .

III.2. Discretion and Weightiness

There are important respects in which friendship is a matter of ongoing choice. Whether you begin or continue a friendship with a particular person can depend, quite properly, on whether this is someone with whom you enjoy spending time, whether he brings out the best or worst in you, and whether you (still) value the shared activities—drinking, perhaps, or snorkelling—in which the friendship is grounded. Of course, friendship is not *all* about choice; you do not sit down periodically and reassess each of your friendships from scratch, and friendships do not suddenly end when one of the friends decides to pursue opportunities elsewhere. Still, as people and circumstances change, friends, even the best of them, often drift apart, in ways that are entirely natural and unobjectionable. When friendships last for ever, that is special but exceptional, and not something on which either friend is entitled to rely.

As friendships change and end, duties to friends change too. It would really be out of order for one of my old university friends, with whom I am no longer in touch, to turn up now and expect to live in my flat for a couple of weeks, even though that is something he could quite reasonably have expected in the old days. Since we have drifted apart, my duties to him are not what they were. The existence, nature and extent of our duties to our friends depend heavily upon what choices we make, and what happens to us, as time goes by.

The same is not true of duties to parents. You should not approach your relationship with your parents, as you would a friendship, with an open mind, hoping but certainly not presuming that your evolving interests and lifestyle choices will enable the relationship to stay strong. Correspondingly, there are some perfectly legitimate explanations of why you do not have certain duties to your friends which are not respectable when applied to filial duties. You cannot explain your failure to look after your parents by saying 'Look, they're great people, and I'll always value the times we spent together, but over the years we've taken different paths. I went my way, they went theirs; it seemed that the relationship wasn't taking us where we wanted to go. . . . Things just aren't the way they were'. You are stuck with your filial duties, in a way that you are not stuck with your duties of friendship.

Filial duties also differ from duties to friends with regard to what they can demand. It is very plausible to think that if your parent is in need of medical care, and you can afford to pay for it, and there is no special reason why you should not, then it is your duty to do so. It would be very odd, however, to think that you ever have a duty to do the same for a friend. You may of course choose to pay for a friend's medical care, but if you did, then it would be beyond the call of duty. A child who makes sacrifices to pay for a parent's care is doing something that is praiseworthy, but expected in the circumstances. Someone who makes sacrifices to pay the medical bills of a friend is doing something that is truly and unusually generous.

IV. The Special Goods Theory

IV.1. The Case for the Existence of Special Goods

When brought together, our thinking about filial duty suggests that it is, in structure and content, quite unlike other familiar forms of duty. One of the reasons why the prevailing accounts of filial duty fail, in my opinion, is that they try to explain it by analogy, saying that being someone's grown child is just like being in someone's debt, or the recipient of someone's benevolence, or someone's friend. But being someone's child is not really like any of these things. The kind of relationship that you have with your parents—how you think about them and the place they have in your life—does not have much in common with relationships that you are likely to have with anyone else. It hence should not be surprising that it is difficult to illuminate the moral relationship between a parent and child by grafting it onto our understanding of some other kind of moral relationship.

In what remains of this paper, I am going to say something on behalf of an alternative approach to filial duty, which I shall call 'the special goods theory'. The approach draws upon two ideas: first, that filial duty needs to be understood on its own distinctive terms; secondly, that different forms of duty can fruitfully be understood by way of an understanding of different sorts of goods, as they arise within what ideally is a reciprocal relationship.

What kinds of benefits, by which I mean improvements to the lives of individuals, are involved in a healthy parent–child relationship?

While the children are young, they receive important goods from their parents. When the parents are old, they are likely to receive important goods from their grown children. But this is not the whole story. A healthy parent–child relationship adds value to the life of both parent and child for as long as it exists.

Many people strongly desire to have children. The desire to become a parent is not a straightforwardly altruistic desire to provide help to someone who needs it, nor is it just a desire to shore up your future interests by guaranteeing that you will have a grown child around to provide benefits in your old age, nor is it (usually) a desire to do your moral or political duty. If you desire to become a parent, your desire is much more likely to be a desire about the shape of your own life. In loving and nurturing a child you will, as well as laying the foundations of a good life for the child, make your own life better.

The goods that parenting adds to a life can be, if our ordinary attitudes are to be trusted, of enormous value. We all know of people who will commit significant measures of money, time and emotional energy in their efforts to become parents. People often feel that it is very sad when someone who wants to become a parent is unable, for whatever reason, to do so, and the sadness is for the person concerned, sadness for what he is missing.

The goods of parenting are unique in kind, meaning that there are no other sources, or not many easily accessible other sources, from which they can be gained. People who enjoy all good health, wealth and professional success may nevertheless feel that if they never have children then something important will be missing from their lives. If you desperately want to have children but never do, but you do win the lottery, you are unlikely to come out thinking 'At least I gained more than I lost'. To have that thought would be to fail to understand the uniqueness of the goods of parenting.

A similar story can be told about the goods of having a strong relationship with a parent. Even if you have everything else that you could possibly want, you may feel that you are missing something if you never knew your parents, you are estranged from them, or they are no longer alive. Grown children who have lost contact with their parents will often go to enormous efforts to find them. . . . For the child, as well as the parent, there are distinctive, special goods that can come from the parent–child relationship, and this is true of the time during which the children are children, and the time during which they are adults.

IV.2. The Special Goods

I shall now say something about what these goods are. I shall draw a loose distinction between two kinds of goods that arise in the parent–child relationship: generic goods, which could in principle be received from anyone, and special goods, which the parent can receive from no one (or almost no one) but the child, or the child can receive from no one (or almost no one) but the parent.

A grown child may help the parents by providing medical care, a ride to the shops, or a place to stay whenever they want to visit; and may make sure that their basic needs are met if they fall into financial trouble. From a parent, a grown child may receive the goods just mentioned, plus perhaps such things as baby-sitting for the grandchildren, instructions on how to cook a favourite meal, and information about shots had as a child. These are all examples of generic goods. They are generic goods because there is no reason in principle why it has to be the parent who provides them to the child, or the child who provides them to the parent. They could just as well be provided by others.

There are other goods that parents might hope to receive from their grown children, but could not receive from anyone else. You might value your child's keeping in touch, but not because you want to be in touch with someone and your child is someone. The good in question is the good of having your child, the one you raised, love and care about, make an effort to keep in touch. Similarly, there is, beyond the good of having people around for Christmas, the good of having your children around for Christmas. These are goods that your children are uniquely placed to provide.

There are also larger, profounder special goods that may accrue to the parents of grown children. Having been responsible for their children's upbringing, and especially if they are the birth parents, they may have important traits in common with their children, seeing in them a kind of younger version of themselves; they are in any case likely to identify with and have a special understanding of their children. . . .

Grown children will also gain special goods through a healthy relationship with their parents. There is a special value in having a *parent* from whom to seek advice: given your history together, and the bonds that are likely to have formed, there are respects in which your parent may bring you a distinctive, and distinctively valuable, point of view and level of concern. An ongoing healthy relationship with a parent can provide a link between your life's different stages; through your parent's perspective, you can be helped to see how the various parts of your childhood and adulthood are connected, and are all yours. And an understanding of the parents who produced you can enhance your understanding of yourself.

There is another important good that you can enjoy in virtue of your relationship with your parent or grown child, which is the good of having someone who is especially committed to ensuring that your needs and interests will be met, in the particular way in which parents and children can show each other such concern. Suppose that you come to be in need of a place to live, a loan, money for an operation, or something similar. If you are like most of us, there will be only a few people who will be prepared to make significant sacrifices in order to make sure that you get what you need. And it is very likely that those people will be your parents or grown children, perhaps along with other family members or a romantic partner; it is certainly likely that they are the ones you could approach with full confidence that they will do whatever is needed. It is good to have such people around. In having such a special concern for you, they can add a level of protection against some of the worst possibilities that life might present. . . .

In the light of this fact, there is an important sense in which having someone who is especially concerned for your needs and interests is a good which is special to the parent–child relationship, in that it very naturally arises within this relationship, is very difficult to find elsewhere, and takes on a particular sort of valuable character when shared between parents and children. Even though it does not *need* to be instantiated within a parent–child relationship in order to exist, and even though it includes the disposition to produce generic goods, the good of having someone who has a special concern for your needs and interests is a kind of special good that parents and children can provide for each other.

IV.3. From Special Goods to Special Duties

There are important goods that you can provide only to your parents, and that your parents can receive from no one but you. My suggestion is that the reason why you have special duties to your parents is that you are uniquely placed to provide them with these goods, and find yourself in a relationship in which they have provided (and perhaps continue to provide) special goods to you. And the duties themselves are duties to provide the special goods to your parents, within the context of the reciprocal relationship that you and your parents share.

The special goods theory tells a plausible unifying story about the content of special duties to parents. Doing your duty as a grown child is not like giving money to a bank or charity or hosting a dinner party for friends. When you make sure that you send presents for your parents' birthdays, make an effort to keep in touch, or do what is needed for them to get the care they need, you are almost certainly providing something for your parents that they will not get otherwise; you are providing your parents with something that no one but their child could (or is at all likely to) give them.

Thinking of filial duties in terms of special goods makes it easy to see why they are ongoing and open-ended, rather than being the sorts of duties that can be discharged once and for all. The special goods that parents can receive from their grown children are not the sorts of goods that can be secured by one long holiday together or one cash payment.

There is no direct connection between the magnitude of the sacrifices made for you by your parents and the nature of the goods to which your relationship with your parents can potentially give rise. What matters is the existence of a parent–child relationship within which the special goods can be manifested, not the exact story about its history. That is why the content and extent of filial duties are not determined in any straightforward way by what the parents did during the child's upbringing. . . .

IV.5. When Do Grown Children Have Filial Duties?

Some grown children do not have duties to their parents, and one way to assess an account of filial duty is to see what it says about which children these are.

If the special goods theory is correct, then the children . . . who do not have filial duties are the ones who are not well placed to provide the special goods to the parent. Because of their utterly incompatible personalities or world-views, their sharing a destructive or dysfunctional relationship, or their respective financial and other circumstances, a parent and grown child may have very little to offer each other. When you spend time with and try to do things for your parent, the result may be not that you each enjoy the special goods distinctive of the parent–child relationship, but just that you are each left bored or angry or hurt or depressed. In such cases, the special goods theory predicts, filial duties are not what they would otherwise be. What you should do for your parents depends upon what goods you are able to generate. . . .

V. Conclusion

When philosophers have paid attention to filial duty, they have taken it to be just a special instance of duties of indebtedness or gratitude or friendship. What I have tried to show is, minimally, that filial duty is distinctive and unusual and does not fit neatly into any easily understandable independent conception of duty. More ambitiously, I have suggested that what is special about filial duty might profitably be understood by way of the special respects in which the parent–child relationship makes lives go better.

Notes

1. On filial duties as discussed in the Western tradition, see part I of Blustein, *Parents and Children*. On filial duties as discussed in Chinese philosophy, see P. J. Ivanhoe, 'Filial Piety as a Virtue', in R. Walker and P. J. Ivanhoe (eds), *Working Virtue: Virtue Ethics and Contemporary Moral Problems* (Oxford UP, 2006).
2. J. English, 'What Do Grown Children Owe Their Parents?', in O'Neill and Ruddick (eds), *Having Children*, pp. 351–6, at pp. 354–6.
3. See English, 'What Do Grown Children Owe Their Parents?'; N. Dixon, 'The Friendship Model of Filial Obligations', *Journal of Applied Philosophy*, 12 (1995), pp. 77–87.
4. English, 'What Do Grown Children Owe Their Parents?', p. 353.

Study Questions

1. According to Keller, what is the main problem with the debt theory?
2. According to Keller, what is the main problem with the gratitude theory?
3. According to Keller, what is the main problem with the friendship theory?
4. According to Keller, what special goods are involved in the relationship between parents and children?

PART 

The Limits of Life

Abortion

A Defense of Abortion

Judith Jarvis Thomson

Consider the argument that because a fetus is an innocent human being, and killing an innocent human being is always wrong, abortion is always wrong. Some would respond by denying that the earliest embryo is a human person, but putting that issue aside, is killing an innocent human being always wrong? Judith Jarvis Thomson, Professor Emerita at the Massachusetts Institute of Technology, argues that while people have a right not to be killed unjustly, they do not have an unqualified right to life. Hence even if the human fetus is a person, abortion may be morally permissible.

Most opposition to abortion relies on the premise that the fetus is a human being, a person, from the moment of conception. The premise is argued for, but, as I think, not well. Take, for example, the most common argument. We are asked to notice that the development of a human being from conception through birth into childhood is

From Judith Jarvis Thomson, "A Defense of Abortion," *Philosophy & Public Affairs* 1 (1971).

continuous; then it is said that to draw a line, to choose a point in this development and say "before this point the thing is not a person, after this point it is a person" is to make an arbitrary choice, a choice for which in the nature of things no good reason can be given. It is concluded that the fetus is, or anyway that we had better say it is, a person from the moment of conception. But this conclusion does not follow. Similar things might be said about the development of an acorn into an oak tree, and it does not follow that acorns are oak trees, or that we had better say they are. Arguments of this form are sometimes called "slippery slope arguments"—the phrase is perhaps self-explanatory—and it is dismaying that opponents of abortion rely on them so heavily and uncritically.

I am inclined to agree, however, that the prospects for "drawing a line" in the development of the fetus look dim. I am inclined to think also that we shall probably have to agree that the fetus has already become a human person well before birth. Indeed, it comes as a surprise when one first learns how early in its life it begins to acquire human characteristics. By the tenth week, for example, it already has a face, arms and legs, fingers and toes; it has internal organs, and brain activity is detectable. On the other hand, I think that the premise is false, that the fetus is not a person from the moment of conception. A newly fertilized ovum, a newly implanted clump of cells, is no more a person than an acorn is an oak tree. But I shall not discuss any of this. For it seems to me to be of great interest to ask what happens if, for the sake of argument, we allow the premise. How, precisely, are we supposed to get from there to the conclusion that abortion is morally impermissible? Opponents of abortion commonly spend most of their time establishing that the fetus is a person, and hardly any time explaining the step from there to the impermissibility of abortion. Perhaps they think the step too simple and obvious to require much comment. Or perhaps instead they are simply being economical in argument. Many of those who defend abortion rely on the premise that the fetus is not a person, but only a bit of tissue that will become a person at birth; and why pay out more arguments than you have to? Whatever the explanation, I suggest that the step they take is neither easy nor obvious, that it calls for closer examination than it is commonly given, and that when we do give it this closer examination we shall feel inclined to reject it.

I propose, then, that we grant that the fetus is a person from the moment of conception. How does the argument go from here? Something like this, I take it. Every person has a right to life. So the fetus has a right to life. No doubt the mother has a right to decide what shall happen in and to her body; everyone would grant that. But surely a person's right to life is stronger and more stringent than the mother's right to decide what happens in and to her body, and so outweighs it. So the fetus may not be killed; an abortion may not be performed.

It sounds plausible. But now let me ask you to imagine this. You wake up in the morning and find yourself back to back in bed with an unconscious violinist. A famous unconscious violinist. He has been found to have a fatal kidney ailment, and the Society of Music Lovers has canvassed all the available medical records and found that you alone have the right blood type to help. They have therefore kidnapped you, and last night the violinist's circulatory system was plugged into yours, so that your kidneys can be used to extract poisons from his blood as well as your own. The director of the hospital now tells you, "Look, we're sorry the Society of Music Lovers did this to you—we would never have permitted it if we had known. But still, they did it, and the violinist now is plugged into you. To unplug you would be to kill him. But never mind, it's only for nine months. By then he will have recovered from his ailment, and can safely be unplugged from you." Is it morally incumbent on you to accede to this situation? No doubt it would be very nice of you if you did, a great kindness. But do you *have* to accede to it? What if it were not nine months, but nine years? Or longer still? What if the director of the hospital says, "Tough luck, I agree, but you've now got to stay in bed, with the violinist plugged into you, for the rest of your life. Because remember this. All persons have a right to life, and violinists are persons. Granted you have a right to decide what happens in and to your body, but a person's right to life outweighs your right to decide what happens in and to your body. So you cannot ever be unplugged from him." I imagine you would regard this as outrageous, which suggests that something really is wrong with that plausible-sounding argument I mentioned a moment ago.

In this case, of course, you were kidnapped; you didn't volunteer for the operation that plugged the violinist into your kidneys. Can those who oppose abortion on the ground I mentioned make an exception for a pregnancy due to rape? Certainly. They can say that persons have a right to life only if they didn't come into existence because of rape; or they can say that all persons have a right to life, but that some have less of a right to life than others, in particular, that those who came into existence because of rape have less. But these statements have a rather unpleasant sound. Surely the question of whether you have a right to life at all, or how much of it you have, shouldn't turn on the question of whether or not you are the product of a rape. And in fact the people who oppose abortion on the ground I mentioned do not make this distinction, and hence do not make an exception in case of rape.

Nor do they make an exception for a case in which the mother has to spend the nine months of her pregnancy in bed. They would agree that would be a great pity, and hard on the mother; but all the same, all persons have a right to life, the fetus is a person, and so on. I suspect, in fact, that they would not make an exception for a case in which, miraculously enough, the pregnancy went on for nine years, or even the rest of the mother's life.

Some won't even make an exception for a case in which continuation of the pregnancy is likely to shorten the mother's life; they regard abortion as impermissible even to save the mother's life. Such cases are nowadays very rare, and many opponents of abortion do not accept this extreme view. All the same, it is a good place to begin: a number of points of interest come out in respect to it.

1. Let us call the view that abortion is impermissible even to save the mother's life "the extreme view." I want to suggest first that it does not issue from the argument I mentioned earlier without the addition of some fairly powerful premises. Suppose a woman has become pregnant, and now learns that she has a cardiac condition such that she will die if she carries the baby to term. What may be done for her? The fetus, being a person, has a right to life, but as the mother is a person too, so has she a right to life. Presumably they have an equal right to life. How is it supposed to come out that an abortion may not be performed? If mother and child have an equal right to life, shouldn't we perhaps flip a coin? Or should we add to the mother's right to life her right to decide what happens in and to her body, which everybody seems to be ready to grant—the sum of her rights now outweighing the fetus' right to life?

The most familiar argument here is the following: We are told that performing the abortion would be directly killing[1] the child, whereas doing nothing would not be killing the mother, but only letting her die. Moreover, in killing the child, one would be killing an innocent person, for the child has committed no crime, and is not aiming at his mother's death. And then there are a variety of ways in which this might be continued. (1) But as directly killing an innocent person is always and absolutely impermissible, an abortion may not be performed. Or, (2) as directly killing an innocent person is murder, and murder is always and absolutely impermissible, an abortion may not be performed. Or, (3) as one's duty to refrain from directly killing an innocent person is more stringent than one's duty to keep a person from dying, an abortion may not be performed. Or, (4) if one's only options are directly killing an innocent person or letting a person die, one must prefer letting the person die, and thus an abortion may not be performed.[2]

Some people seem to have thought that these are not further premises which must be added if the conclusion is to be reached, but that they follow from the very fact that an innocent person has a right to life. But this seems to me to be a mistake, and perhaps the simplest way to show this is to bring out that while we must certainly grant that innocent persons have a right to life, the theses in (1) through (4) are all false. Take (2), for example. If directly killing an innocent person is murder, and thus is impermissible, then the mother's directly killing the innocent person inside her is murder, and thus is impermissible. But it cannot seriously be thought to be murder if the mother performs an abortion on herself to save her life. It cannot seriously be said that she *must* refrain, that she *must* sit passively by and wait for her death. Let us look again at the case of you and the violinist. There you are, in bed with the violinist, and the director of the hospital says to you, "It's all most distressing, and I deeply sympathize, but you see this is putting an additional strain on your kidneys, and you'll be dead within the month. But you *have* to stay where you are all the same. Because unplugging you would be directly killing an innocent violinist, and that's murder, and that's impermissible." If anything in the world is true, it is that you do not commit murder, you do not do what is impermissible, if you reach around to your back and unplug yourself from that violinist to save your life.

The main focus of attention in writings on abortion has been on what a third party may or may not do in answer to a request from a woman for an abortion. This is in a way understandable. Things being as they are, there isn't much a woman can safely do to abort herself. So the question asked is what a third party may do, and what the mother may do, if it is mentioned at all, is deduced, almost as an afterthought, from what it is concluded that third parties may do. But it seems to me that to treat the matter in this way is to refuse to grant to the mother that very status of person which is so firmly insisted on for the fetus. For we cannot simply read off what a person may do from what a third party may do. Suppose you find yourself trapped in a tiny house with a growing child. I mean a very tiny house, and a rapidly growing child—you are already up against the wall of the house and in a few minutes you'll be crushed to death. The child on the other hand won't be crushed to death; if nothing is done to stop him from growing he'll be hurt, but in the end he'll simply burst open the house and walk out a free man. Now I could well understand it if a bystander were to say, "There's nothing we can do for you. We cannot choose between your life and his, we cannot be the ones to decide who is to live, we cannot intervene." But it cannot be concluded that you too can do nothing, that you cannot attack it to save your life. However innocent the child may be, you do not have to wait passively while it crushes you to death. Perhaps a pregnant woman is vaguely felt to have the status of house, to which we don't allow the right of self-defense. But if the woman houses the child, it should be remembered that she is a person who houses it.

I should perhaps stop to say explicitly that I am not claiming that people have a right to do anything whatever to save their lives. I think, rather, that there are drastic limits to the right of self-defense. If someone threatens you with death unless you torture someone else to death, I think you have not the right, even to save your life, to do so. But the case under consideration here is very different. In our case there are only two people involved, one whose life is threatened, and one who threatens it. Both are innocent: the one who is threatened is not threatened because of any fault, the one who threatens does not threaten because of any fault. For this reason we may feel that we bystanders cannot intervene. But the person threatened can.

In sum, a woman surely can defend her life against the threat to it posed by the unborn child, even if doing so involves its death. And this shows not merely that the theses in (1) through (4) are false; it shows also that the extreme view of abortion is false, and so we need not canvass any other possible ways of arriving at it from the argument I mentioned at the outset.

2. The extreme view could of course be weakened to say that while abortion is permissible to save the mother's life, it may not be performed by a third party, but only by the mother herself. But this cannot be right either. For what we have to keep in mind is that the mother and the unborn child are not like two tenants in a small house which has, by an unfortunate mistake, been rented to both: the mother *owns* the house. The fact that she does adds to the offensiveness of deducing that the mother can do nothing from the supposition that third parties can do nothing. But it does more than this: it casts a bright light on the supposition that third parties can do nothing. Certainly it lets us see that a third party who says "I cannot choose between you" is fooling himself if he thinks this is impartiality. If Jones has found and fastened on a certain coat, which he needs

to keep him from freezing, but which Smith also needs to keep him from freezing, then it is not impartiality that says "I cannot choose between you" when Smith owns the coat. Women have said again and again, "This body is *my* body!" and they have reason to feel angry, reason to feel that it has been like shouting into the wind. Smith, after all, is hardly likely to bless us if we say to him, "Of course it's your coat, anybody would grant that it is. But no one may choose between you and Jones who is to have it."

We should really ask what it is that says "no one may choose" in the face of the fact that the body that houses the child is the mother's body. It may be simply a failure to appreciate this fact. But it may be something more interesting, namely, the sense that one has a right to refuse to lay hands on people, even where it would be just and fair to do so, even where justice seems to require that somebody do so. Thus justice might call for somebody to get Smith's coat back from Jones, and yet you have a right to refuse to be the one to lay hands on Jones, a right to refuse to do physical violence to him. This, I think, must be granted. But then what should be said is not "no one may choose," but only "*I* cannot choose," and indeed not even this, but "*I* will not *act*," leaving it open that somebody else can or should, and in particular that anyone in a position of authority, with the job of securing people's rights, both can and should. So this is no difficulty. I have not been arguing that any given third party must accede to the mother's request that he perform an abortion to save her life, but only that he may.

I suppose that in some views of human life the mother's body is only on loan to her, the loan not being one which gives her any prior claim to it. One who held this view might well think it impartiality to say "I cannot choose." But I shall simply ignore this possibility. My own view is that if a human being has any just, prior claim to anything at all, he has a just, prior claim to his own body. And perhaps this needn't be argued for here anyway, since, as I mentioned, the arguments against abortion we are looking at do grant that the woman has a right to decide what happens in and to her body.

But although they do grant it, I have tried to show that they do not take seriously what is done in granting it. I suggest the same thing will reappear even more clearly when we turn away from cases in which the mother's life is at stake, and attend, as I propose we now do, to the vastly more common cases in which a woman wants an abortion for some less weighty reason than preserving her own life.

3. Where the mother's life is not at stake, the argument I mentioned at the outset seems to have a much stronger pull. "Everyone has

a right to life, so the unborn person has a right to life." And isn't the child's right to life weightier than anything other than the mother's own right to life, which she might put forward as ground for an abortion?

This argument treats the right to life as if it were unproblematic. It is not, and this seems to me to be precisely the source of the mistake.

For we should now, at long last, ask what it comes to, to have a right to life. In some views having a right to life includes having a right to be given at least the bare minimum one needs for continued life. But suppose that what in fact *is* the bare minimum a man needs for continued life is something he has no right at all to be given. If I am sick unto death, and the only thing that will save my life is the touch of Henry Fonda's cool hand on my fevered brow, then all the same, I have no right to be given the touch of Henry Fonda's cool hand on my fevered brow. It would be frightfully nice of him to fly in from the West Coast to provide it. It would be less nice, though no doubt well meant, if my friends flew out to the West Coast and carried Henry Fonda back with them. But I have no right at all against anybody that he should do this for me. Or again, to return to the story I told earlier, the fact that for continued life that violinist needs the continued use of your kidneys does not establish that he has a right to be given the continued use of your kidneys. He certainly has no right against you that *you* should give him continued use of your kidneys. For nobody has any right to use our kidneys unless you give him such a right; and nobody has the right against you that you shall give him this right—if you do allow him to go on using your kidneys, this is a kindness on your part, and not something he can claim from you as his due. Nor has he any right against anybody else that they should give him continued use of your kidneys. Certainly he had no right against the Society of Music Lovers that *they* should plug him into you in the first place. And if you now start to unplug yourself, having learned that you will otherwise have to spend nine years in bed with him, there is nobody in the world who must try to prevent you, in order to see to it that he is given something he has a right to be given.

Some people are rather stricter about the right to life. In their view, it does not include the right to be given anything, but amounts to, and only to, the right not to be killed by anybody. But here a related difficulty arises. If everybody is to refrain from killing that violinist, then everybody must refrain from doing a great many different sorts of things. Everybody must refrain from slitting his throat, everybody must refrain from shooting him—and everybody must refrain from unplugging you from him. But does he have a right against everybody that they shall refrain from unplugging you from him? To refrain from doing this is to allow him to continue to use your kidneys. It could be argued that he has a right against us that *we* should allow him to continue to use your kidneys. That is, while he had no right against us that we should give him the use of your kidneys, it might be argued that he anyway has a right against us that we shall not now intervene and deprive him of the use of your kidneys. I shall come back to third-party interventions later. But certainly the violinist has no right against you that *you* shall allow him to continue to use your kidneys. As I said, if you do allow him to continue to use them, it is a kindness on your part, and not something you owe him.

The difficulty I point to here is not peculiar to the right to life. It reappears in connection with all the other natural rights; and it is something which an adequate account of rights must deal with. For present purposes it is enough just to draw attention to it. But I would stress that I am not arguing that people do not have a right to life—quite to the contrary, it seems to me that the primary control we must place on the acceptability of an account of rights is that it should turn out in that account to be a truth that all persons have a right to life. I am arguing only that having a right to life does not guarantee having either a right to be given the use of or a right to be allowed continued use of another person's body—even if one needs it for life itself. So the right to life will not serve the opponents of abortion in the very simple and clear way in which they seem to have thought it would.

4. There is another way to bring out the difficulty. In the most ordinary sort of case, to deprive someone of what he has a right to is to treat him unjustly. Suppose a boy and his small brother are jointly given a box of chocolates for Christmas. If the older boy takes the box and refuses to give his brother any of the chocolates, he is unjust to him, for the brother has been given a right to half of them. But suppose that, having learned that otherwise it means nine years in bed with that violinist, you unplug yourself from him. You surely are not being unjust to him, for you gave him no right to use your kidneys, and no one else can have given him any such right. But we have to notice that in unplugging yourself, you are killing him; and violinists, like everybody else, have a right to life, and thus in the view we were considering just now, the right not to be killed. So here you do what he supposedly has a right you shall not do, but you do not act unjustly to him in doing it.

The emendation which may be made at this point is this: the right to life consists not in the right not to be killed, but rather in the right not to be killed unjustly. This runs a risk of circularity, but never mind: it would enable us to square the fact that the violinist has a right to life with the fact that you do not act unjustly toward him in unplugging yourself, thereby killing him. For if you do not kill him unjustly, you do not violate his right to life, and so it is no wonder you do him no injustice.

But if this emendation is accepted, the gap in the argument against abortion stares us plainly in the face: it is by no means enough to show that the fetus is a person, and to remind us that all persons have a right to life—we need to be shown also that killing the fetus violates its right to life, i.e., that abortion is unjust killing. And is it?

I suppose we may take it as a datum that in a case of pregnancy due to rape the mother has not given the unborn person a right to the use of her body for food and shelter. Indeed, in what pregnancy could it be supposed that the mother has given the unborn person such a right? It is not as if there were unborn persons drifting about the world, to whom a woman who wants a child says, "I invite you in."

But it might be argued that there are other ways one can have acquired a right to the use of another person's body than by having been invited to use it by that person. Suppose a woman voluntarily indulges in intercourse, knowing of the chance it will issue in pregnancy, and then she does become pregnant; is she not in part responsible for the presence, in fact the very existence, of the unborn person inside her? No doubt she did not invite it in. But doesn't her partial responsibility for its being there itself give it a right to the use of her body? If so, then her aborting it would be more like the boy's taking away the chocolates, and less like your unplugging yourself from the violinist—doing so would be depriving it of what it does have a right to, and thus would be doing it an injustice.

And then, too, it might be asked whether or not she can kill it even to save her own life: If she voluntarily called it into existence, how can she now kill it, even in self-defense?

The first thing to be said about this is that it is something new. Opponents of abortion have been so concerned to make out the independence of the fetus, in order to establish that it has a right to life, just as its mother does, that they have tended to overlook the possible support they might gain from making out that the fetus is *dependent* on the mother, in order to establish that she has a special kind of responsibility for it, a responsibility that gives it rights against her which are not possessed by any independent person—such as an ailing violinist who is a stranger to her.

On the other hand, this argument would give the unborn person a right to its mother's body only if her pregnancy resulted from a voluntary act, undertaken in full knowledge of the chance a pregnancy might result from it. It would leave out entirely the unborn person whose existence is due to rape. Pending the availability of some further argument, then, we would be left with the conclusion that unborn persons whose existence is due to rape have no right to the use of their mothers' bodies, and thus that aborting them is not depriving them of anything they have a right to and hence is not unjust killing.

And we should also notice that it is not at all plain that this argument really does go even as far as it purports to. For there are cases and cases, and the details make a difference. If the room is stuffy, and I therefore open a window to air it, and a burglar climbs in, it would be absurd to say, "Ah, now he can stay, she's given him a right to the use of her house—for she is partially responsible for his presence there, having voluntarily done what enabled him to get in, in full knowledge that there are such things as burglars, and that burglars burgle." It would be still more absurd to say this if I had had bars installed outside my windows, precisely to prevent burglars from getting in, and a burglar got in only because of a defect in the bars. It remains equally absurd if we imagine it is not a burglar who climbs in, but an innocent person who blunders or falls in. Again, suppose it were like this: people-seeds drift about in the air like pollen, and if you open your windows, one may drift in and take root in your carpets or upholstery. You don't want children, so you fix up your windows with fine mesh screens, the very best you can buy. As can happen, however, and on very, very rare occasions does happen, one of the screens is defective; and a seed drifts in and takes root. Does the person-plant who now develops have a right to the use of your house? Surely not—despite the fact that you voluntarily opened your windows, you knowingly kept carpets and upholstered furniture, and you knew that screens were sometimes defective. Someone may argue that you are responsible for its rooting, that it does have a right to your house, because after all you *could* have lived out your life with bare floors and furniture, or with sealed windows and doors. But this won't do—for by the same token anyone can avoid a pregnancy due to rape by having a hysterectomy, or anyway by never leaving home without a (reliable!) army.

It seems to me that the argument we are looking at can establish at most that there are *some* cases in which the unborn person has a right to the use of its mother's body, and therefore *some* cases in which abortion is unjust killing. There is room for much discussion and argument as to precisely which, if any. But I think we should sidestep this issue and leave it open, for at any rate the argument certainly does not establish that all abortion is unjust killing.

5. There is room for yet another argument here, however. We surely must all grant that there may be cases in which it would be morally indecent to detach a person from your body at the cost of his life. Suppose you learn that what the violinist needs is not nine years of your life, but only one hour: all you need do to save his life is to spend one hour in that bed with him. Suppose also that letting him use your kidneys for that one hour would not affect your health in the slightest. Admittedly you were kidnapped. Admittedly you did not give anyone permission to plug him into you. Nevertheless it seems to me plain you *ought* to allow him to use your kidneys for that hour—it would be indecent to refuse.

Again, suppose pregnancy lasted only an hour, and constituted no threat to life or health. And suppose that a woman becomes pregnant as a result of rape. Admittedly she did not voluntarily do anything to bring about the existence of a child. Admittedly she did nothing at all which would give the unborn person a right to the use of her body. All the same it might well be said, as in the newly emended violinist story, that she *ought* to allow it to remain for that hour—that it would be indecent of her to refuse.

Now some people are inclined to use the term "right" in such a way that it follows from the fact that you ought to allow a person to use your body for the hour he needs, that he has a right to use your body for the hour he needs, even though he has not been given that right by any person or act. They may say that it follows also that if you refuse, you act unjustly toward him. This use of the term is perhaps so common that it cannot be called wrong; nevertheless it seems to me to be an unfortunate loosening of what we would do better to keep a tight rein on. Suppose that box of chocolates I mentioned earlier had not been given to both boys jointly, but was given only to the older boy. There he sits, stolidly eating his way through the box, his small brother watching enviously. Here we are likely to say, "You ought not to be so mean. You ought to give your brother some of those chocolates." My own view is that it just does not follow from the truth of this that the brother has any right to any of the chocolates. If the boy refuses to give his brother any, he is greedy, stingy, callous—but not unjust. I suppose that the people I have in mind will say it does follow that the brother has a right to some of the chocolates, and thus that the boy does act unjustly if he refuses to give his brother any. But the effect of saying this is to obscure what we should keep distinct, namely, the difference between the boy's refusal in this case and the boy's refusal in the earlier case, in which the box was given to both boys jointly, and in which the small brother thus had what was from any point of view clear title to half.

A further objection to so using the term "right" that from the fact that A ought to do a thing for B, it follows that B has a right against A that A do it for him, is that it is going to make the question of whether or not a man has a right to a thing turn on how easy it is to provide him with it; and this seems not merely unfortunate, but morally unacceptable. Take the case of Henry Fonda again. I said earlier that I had no right to the touch of his cool hand on my fevered brow, even though I needed it to save my life. I said it would be frightfully nice of him to fly in from the West Coast to provide me with it, but that I had no right against him that he should do so. But suppose he isn't on the West Coast. Suppose he has only to walk across the room, place a hand briefly on my brow—and lo, my life is saved. Then surely he ought to do it, it would be indecent to refuse. Is it to be said, "Ah, well, it follows that in this case she has a right to the touch of his hand on her brow, and so it would be an injustice in him to refuse"? So that I have a right to it when it is easy for him to provide it, though no right when it's hard? It's rather a shocking idea that anyone's rights should fade away and disappear as it gets harder and harder to accord them to him.

So my own view is that even though you ought to let the violinist use your kidneys for the one hour he needs, we should not conclude that he has a right to do so—we should say that if you refuse, you are, like the boy who owns all the chocolates and will give none away, self-centered and callous, indecent in fact, but not unjust. And similarly, that even supposing a case in which a woman pregnant due to rape ought to allow the unborn person to use her body for the hour he needs, we should not conclude that he has a right to do so; we should conclude that she is self-centered, callous, indecent, but not unjust, if she refuses. The complaints are no less grave; they are just different. However, there is no need to insist on this point. If anyone does wish to deduce "he has a right" from "you ought," then all the same he must surely grant that there are cases in which it is not morally required of you that you allow that violinist to use your kidneys, and in which he does not have a right to use them, and in which you do not do him an injustice if you refuse. And so also for mother and unborn child. Except in such cases as the unborn person has a right to demand it—and we were leaving open the possibility that there may be such cases—nobody is morally *required* to make large sacrifices, of health, of all other interests and concerns, of all other duties and commitments, for nine years, or even for nine months, in order to keep another person alive.

6. We have in fact to distinguish between two kinds of Samaritan: the Good Samaritan and what we might call the Minimally Decent Samaritan. The story of the Good Samaritan, you will remember, goes like this:

> A certain man went down from Jerusalem to Jericho, and fell among thieves, which stripped him of his raiment, and wounded him, and departed, leaving him half dead.
>
> And by chance there came down a certain priest that way; and when he saw him, he passed by on the other side.
>
> And likewise a Levite, when he was at the place, came and looked on him, and passed by on the other side.
>
> But a certain Samaritan, as he journeyed, came where he was; and when he saw him he had compassion on him.
>
> And went to him, and bound up his wounds, pouring in oil and wine, and set him on his own beast, and brought him to an inn, and took care of him.
>
> And on the morrow, when he departed, he took out two pence, and gave them to the host, and said unto him, "Take care of him; and whatsoever thou spendest more, when I come again, I will repay thee."
>
> —(Luke 10:30–35)

The Good Samaritan went out of his way, at some cost to himself, to help one in need of it. We are not told what the options were, that is, whether or not the priest and the Levite could have helped by doing less than the Good Samaritan did, but assuming they could have, then the fact they did nothing at all shows they were not even Minimally Decent Samaritans, not because they were not Samaritans, but because they were not even minimally decent. . . .

After telling the story of the Good Samaritan, Jesus said, "Go, and do thou likewise." Perhaps he meant that we are morally required to act as the Good Samaritan did. Perhaps he was urging people to do more than is morally required of them. At all events it seems plain that . . . it is not morally required of anyone that he give long stretches of his life—nine years or nine months—to sustaining the life of a person who has no special right (we were leaving open the possibility of this) to demand it. . . .

We have . . . to look now at third-party interventions. I have been arguing that no person is morally required to make large sacrifices to sustain the life of another who has no right to demand them, and this even where the sacrifices do not include life itself; we are not morally required to be Good Samaritans or anyway Very Good Samaritans to one another. But what if a man cannot extricate himself from such a situation? What if he appeals to us to extricate him? It seems to me plain that there are cases in which we can, cases in which a Good Samaritan would extricate him. There you are, you were kidnapped, and nine years in bed with that violinist lie ahead of you. You have your own life to lead. You are sorry, but you simply cannot see giving up so much of your life to the sustaining of his. You cannot extricate yourself, and ask us to do so. I should have thought that—in light of his having no right to the use of your body—it was obvious that we do not have to accede to your being forced to give up so much. We can do what you ask. There is no injustice to the violinist in our doing so.

7. Following the lead of the opponents of abortion, I have throughout been speaking of the fetus merely as a person, and what I have been asking is whether or not the argument we began with, which proceeds only from the fetus' being a person, really does establish its conclusion. I have argued that it does not.

But of course there are arguments and arguments, and it may be said that I have simply fastened on the wrong one. It may be said that what is important is not merely the fact that the fetus is a person, but that it is a person for whom the woman has a special kind of responsibility issuing from the fact that she is its mother. And it might be argued that all my analogies are therefore irrelevant—for you do not have that special kind of responsibility for that violinist, Henry Fonda does not have that special kind of responsibility for me. . . .

I have in effect dealt (briefly) with this argument in section 4 above; but a (still briefer) recapitulation now may be in order. Surely we do not have any such "special responsibility" for a person unless we have assumed it, explicitly or implicitly. If a set of parents do not try to prevent pregnancy, do not obtain an abortion, and then at the time of birth of the child do not put it out for adoption, but rather take it home with them, then they have assumed responsibility for it, they have given it rights, and they cannot *now* withdraw support from it at the cost of its life because they now find it difficult to go on providing for it. But if they have taken all reasonable precautions against having a child, they do not simply by virtue of their biological relationship to the child who comes into existence have a special responsibility for it. They may wish to assume responsibility for it, or they may not wish to. And I am suggesting that if assuming responsibility for it would require large sacrifices, then they may refuse. A Good Samaritan would not refuse—or anyway, a Splendid Samaritan, if the sacrifices that had to be made were enormous. But then so would a Good Samaritan assume responsibility for that violinist; so would Henry Fonda, if he is a Good Samaritan, fly in from the West Coast and assume responsibility for me.

8. My argument will be found unsatisfactory on two counts by many of those who want to regard abortion as morally permissible. First, while I do argue that abortion is not impermissible, I do not argue that it is always permissible. There may well be cases in which carrying the child to term requires only Minimally Decent Samaritanism of the mother, and this is a standard we must not fall below. I am inclined to think it a merit of my account precisely that it does *not* give a general yes or a general no. It allows for and supports our sense that, for example, a sick and desperately frightened fourteen-year-old schoolgirl, pregnant due to rape, may *of course* choose abortion, and that any law which rules this out is an insane law. And it also allows for and supports our sense that in other cases resort to abortion is even positively indecent. It would be indecent in the woman to request an abortion, and indecent in the doctor to perform it, if she is in her seventh month, and wants the abortion just to avoid the nuisance of postponing a trip abroad. The very fact that the arguments I have been drawing attention to treat all cases of abortion, or even all cases of abortion in which the mother's life is not at stake, as morally on a par ought to have made them suspect at the outset.

Secondly, while I am arguing for the permissibility of abortion in some cases, I am not arguing for the right to secure the death of the unborn child. It is easy to confuse these two things in that up to a certain point in the life of the fetus it is not able to survive outside the mother's body; hence removing it from her body guarantees its death. But they are importantly different. I have argued that you are not morally required to spend nine months in bed, sustaining the life of that violinist; but to say this is by no means to say that if, when you unplug yourself, there is a miracle and he survives, you then have a right to turn round and slit his throat. You may detach yourself even if this costs him his life; you have no right to be guaranteed his death, by some other means, if unplugging yourself does not kill him. There are some people who will feel dissatisfied by this feature of my argument. A woman may be utterly devastated by the thought of a child, a bit of herself, put out for adoption and never seen or heard of again. She may therefore want not merely that the child be detached from her, but more, that it die. Some opponents of abortion are inclined to regard this as beneath contempt—thereby showing insensitivity to what is surely a powerful source of despair. All the same, I agree that the desire for the child's death is not one which anybody may gratify, should it turn out to be possible to detach the child alive.

At this place, however, it should be remembered that we have only been pretending throughout that the fetus is a human being from the moment of conception. A very early abortion is surely not the killing of a person, and so is not dealt with by anything I have said here.

Notes

1. The term "direct" in the arguments I refer to is a technical one. Roughly, what is meant by "direct killing" is either killing as an end in itself, or killing as a means to some end, for example, the end of saving someone else's life.
2. The thesis in (4) is in an interesting way weaker than those in (1), (2), and (3): they rule out abortion even in cases in which both mother *and* child will die if the abortion is not performed. By contrast, one who held the view expressed in (4) could consistently say that one needn't prefer letting two persons die to killing one.

Study Questions

1. What are the main points Thomson seeks to make by the example of the unconscious violinist?
2. Does the morality of aborting a fetus depend on the conditions surrounding its conception?
3. In your own words, what is the distinction Thomson draws between the Good Samaritan and the Minimally Decent Samaritan?
4. If the abortion controversy is described as a debate between those who believe in a right to life and those who affirm a woman's right to choose, on which side is Thomson?

On the Moral and Legal Status of Abortion

Mary Anne Warren

Mary Anne Warren (1942–2010) was a professor of philosophy at San Francisco State University. She argues that among the characteristics central to personhood are the capacity to experience pain and pleasure, feel happy or sad, solve relatively complex problems, communicate messages on many possible topics, have a concept of oneself as a member of a social group, and regulate one's own action through moral principles. Warren maintains that a fetus, lacking these characteristics, is not a person, and hence women's rights override whatever right to life a fetus may possess.

For our purposes, abortion may be defined as the act a woman performs in deliberately terminating her pregnancy before it comes to term, or in allowing another person to terminate it. Abortion usually entails the death of a fetus. Nevertheless, I will argue that it is morally permissible, and should be neither legally prohibited nor made needlessly difficult to obtain, e.g., by obstructive legal regulations.

Some philosophers have argued that the moral status of abortion cannot be resolved by rational means. If this is so then liberty should prevail; for it is not a proper function of the law to enforce prohibitions upon personal behavior that cannot clearly be shown to be morally objectionable, and seriously so. But the advocates of prohibition believe that their position is objectively correct, and not merely a result of religious beliefs or personal prejudices. They argue that the

From Mary Anne Warren, "On the Moral and Legal Status of Abortion," *The Monist* 57 (1973).

humanity of the fetus is a matter of scientific fact, and that abortion is therefore the moral equivalent of murder, and must be prohibited in all or most cases. (Some would make an exception when the woman's life is in danger, or when the pregnancy is due to rape or incest; others would prohibit abortion even in these cases.)

In response, advocates of a right to choose abortion point to the terrible consequences of prohibiting it, especially while contraception is still unreliable, and is financially beyond the reach of much of the world's population. Worldwide, hundreds of thousands of women die each year from illegal abortions, and many more suffer from complications that may leave them injured or infertile. Women who are poor, underage, disabled, or otherwise vulnerable, suffer most from the absence of safe and legal abortion. Advocates of choice also argue that to deny a woman access to abortion is to deprive her of the right to control her own body—a right so fundamental that without it other rights are often all but meaningless.

These arguments do not convince abortion opponents. The tragic consequences of prohibition leave them unmoved, because they regard the deliberate killing of fetuses as even more tragic. Nor do appeals to the right to control one's own body impress them, since they deny that this right includes the right to destroy a fetus. We cannot hope to persuade those who equate abortion with murder that they are mistaken, unless we can refute the standard anti-abortion argument: that because fetuses are human beings, they have a right to life equal to that of any other human being. Unfortunately, confusion has prevailed with respect to the two important questions which that argument raises: (1) Is a human fetus really a human being at all stages of prenatal development? and (2) If so, what (if anything) follows about the moral and legal status of abortion? . . .

My . . . inquiry will . . . have two stages. In Section I, I consider whether abortion can be shown to be morally permissible even on the assumption that a fetus is a human being with a strong right to life. I argue that this cannot be established, except in special cases. Consequently, we cannot avoid facing the question of whether or not a fetus has the same right to life as any human being.

In Section II, I propose an answer to this question, namely, that a fetus is not a member of the moral community—the set of beings with full and equal moral rights. The reason that a fetus is not a member of the moral community is that it is not yet a person, nor is it enough like a person in the morally relevant respects to be regarded the equal of those human beings who are persons. I argue that it is personhood, and not genetic humanity, which is the fundamental basis for membership in the moral community. A fetus, especially in the early stages of its development, satisfies none of the criteria of personhood. Consequently, it makes no sense to grant it moral rights strong enough to override the woman's moral rights to liberty, bodily integrity, and sometimes life itself. Unlike an infant who has already been born, a fetus cannot be granted full and equal moral rights without severely threatening the rights and well-being of women. Nor, as we will see, is a fetus's *potential* personhood a threat to the moral permissibility of abortion, since merely potential persons do not have a moral right to become actual—or none that is strong enough to override the fundamental moral rights of actual persons.

I

Judith Thomson argues that, even if a fetus has a right to life, abortion is often morally permissible. Her argument is based upon an imaginative analogy. She asks you to picture yourself waking up one day, in bed with a famous violinist, who is a stranger to you. Imagine that you have been kidnapped, and your bloodstream connected to that of the violinist, who has an ailment that will kill him unless he is permitted to share your kidneys for nine months. No one else can save him, since you alone have the right type of blood. Consequently, the Society of Music Lovers has arranged for you to be kidnapped and hooked up. If you unhook yourself, he will die. But if you remain in bed with him, then after nine months he will be cured and able to survive without further assistance from you.

Now, Thomson asks, what are your obligations in this situation? To be consistent, the anti-abortionist must say that you are obliged to stay in bed with the violinist: for violinists are human beings, and all human beings have a right to life.[1] But this is outrageous; thus, there must be something very wrong with the same argument when it is applied to abortion. It would be extremely generous of you to agree to stay in bed with the violinist; but it is absurd to suggest that your refusal to do so would be the moral equivalent of murder. The violinist's right to life does not oblige you to do whatever is required to keep him alive; still less does it justify anyone else in forcing you to do so. A law which required you to stay in bed with the violinist would be an unjust law, since unwilling persons ought not to be required to be Extremely Good Samaritans, i.e., to make enormous personal sacrifices for the sake of other individuals toward whom they have no special prior obligation.

Thomson concludes that we can grant the anti-abortionist his claim that a fetus is a human being with a right to life, and still hold that a pregnant woman is morally entitled to refuse to be an Extremely Good Samaritan toward the fetus. For there is a great gap between the claim that a human being has a right to life, and the claim that other human beings are morally obligated to do whatever is necessary to keep him alive. One has no duty to keep another human being alive *at a great personal cost,* unless one has somehow contracted a special obligation toward that individual; and a woman who is pregnant may have done nothing that morally obliges her to make the burdensome personal sacrifices necessary to preserve the life of the fetus.

This argument is plausible, and in the case of pregnancy due to rape it is probably conclusive. Difficulties arise, however, when we attempt to specify the larger range of cases in which abortion can be justified on the basis of this argument. Thomson considers it a virtue of her argument that it does not imply that abortion is *always* morally permissible. It would, she says, be indecent for a woman in her seventh month of pregnancy to have an abortion in order to embark on a trip to Europe. On the other hand, the violinist analogy shows that, "a sick and desperately frightened fourteen-year-old schoolgirl, pregnant due to rape, may *of course* choose abortion, and that any law which rules this out is an insane law."[2] So far, so good; but what are we to say about the woman who becomes pregnant not through rape but because she and her partner did not use available forms of contraception, or because their attempts at contraception failed? What about a woman who becomes pregnant intentionally, but then reevaluates the wisdom of having a child? In such cases, the violinist analogy is considerably less useful to advocates of the right to choose abortion.

It is perhaps only when a woman's pregnancy is due to rape, or some other form of coercion, that the situation is sufficiently analogous to the violinist case for our moral intuitions to transfer convincingly from the one case to the other. One difference between a pregnancy caused by rape and most unwanted pregnancies is that only in the former case is it perfectly clear that the woman is in no way responsible for her predicament. In the other cases, she *might* have been able to avoid becoming pregnant, e.g., by taking birth control pills (more faithfully), or insisting upon the use of high-quality condoms, or even avoiding heterosexual intercourse altogether throughout her fertile years. In contrast, if you are suddenly kidnapped by strange music lovers and hooked up to a sick violinist, then you are in no way responsible for your situation, which you could not have foreseen or prevented. And responsibility does seem to matter here. If a person behaves in a way which she could have avoided, and which she knows might bring into existence a human being who will depend upon her for survival, then it is not entirely clear that if and when that happens she may rightly refuse to do what she must in order to keep that human being alive.

This argument shows that the violinist analogy provides a persuasive defense of a woman's right to choose abortion only in cases where she is in no way morally responsible for her own pregnancy. In all other cases, the assumption that a fetus has a strong right to life makes it necessary to look carefully at the particular circumstances in order to determine the extent of the woman's responsibility, and hence the extent of her obligation. This outcome is unsatisfactory to advocates of the right to choose abortion, because it suggests that the decision should not be left in the woman's own hands, but should be supervised by other persons, who will inquire into the most intimate aspects of her personal life in order to determine whether or not she is entitled to choose abortion.

A supporter of the violinist analogy might reply that it is absurd to suggest that forgetting her pill one day might be sufficient to morally oblige a woman to complete an unwanted pregnancy. And indeed it is absurd to suggest this. As we will see, a woman's moral right to choose abortion does not depend upon the extent to which she might be thought to be morally responsible for her own pregnancy. But once we allow the assumption that a fetus has a strong right to life, we cannot avoid taking this absurd suggestion seriously. On this assumption, it is a vexing question whether and when abortion is morally justifiable. The violinist analogy can at best show that aborting a pregnancy is a deeply tragic act, though one that is sometimes morally justified.

My conviction is that an abortion is not always this deeply tragic, because a fetus is not yet a person, and therefore does not yet have a strong moral right to life. Although the truth of this conviction may not be self-evident, it does, I believe, follow from some highly plausible claims about the appropriate grounds for ascribing moral rights. It is worth examining these grounds, since this has not been adequately done before.

II

The question we must answer in order to determine the moral status of abortion is, How are we to define the moral community, the set of beings with full and equal moral rights? What sort of entity has the inalienable moral rights to life, liberty, and the pursuit of happiness? . . .

On the Definition of "Human"

The term "human being" has two distinct, but not often distinguished, senses. This results in a slide of meaning, which serves to conceal the fallacy in the traditional argument that, since (1) it is wrong to kill innocent human beings, and (2) fetuses are innocent human beings, therefore (3) it is wrong to kill fetuses. For if "human being" is used in the same sense in both (1) and (2), then whichever of the two senses is meant, one of these premises is question-begging. And if it is used in different senses then the conclusion does not follow.

Thus, (1) is a generally accepted moral truth,[3] and one that does not beg the question about abortion, only if "human being" is used to mean something like "a full-fledged member of the moral community, who is also a member of the human species." I will call this the *moral* sense of "human being." It is not to be confused with what I will call the *genetic* sense, i.e., the sense in which any individual entity that belongs to the human species is a human being, regardless of whether or not it is rightly considered to be an equal member of the moral community. Premise (1) avoids begging the question only if the moral sense is intended, while premise (2) avoids it only if what is intended is the genetic sense. . . .

Defining the Moral Community

Is genetic humanity sufficient for moral humanity? There are good reasons for not defining the moral community in this way. I would suggest that the moral community consists, in the first instance, of all *persons*, rather than all genetically human entities.[4] It is persons who invent moral rights, and who are (sometimes) capable of respecting them. It does not follow from this that only persons can have moral rights. However, persons are wise not to ascribe to entities that clearly are not persons moral rights that cannot in practice be respected without severely undercutting the fundamental moral rights of those who clearly are.

What characteristics entitle an entity to be considered a person? This is not the place to attempt a complete analysis of the concept of personhood; but we do not need such an analysis to explain why a fetus is not a person. All we need is an approximate list of the most basic criteria of personhood. In searching for these criteria, it is useful to look beyond the set of people with whom we are acquainted, all of whom are human. Imagine, then, a space traveler who lands on a new planet, and encounters organisms unlike any she has ever seen or heard of. If she wants to behave morally toward these organisms, she has somehow to determine whether they are people and thus have full moral rights, or whether they are things that she need not feel guilty about treating, for instance, as a source of food.

How should she go about making this determination? If she has some anthropological background, she might look for signs of religion, art, and the manufacturing of tools, weapons, or shelters, since these cultural traits have frequently been used to distinguish our human ancestors from prehuman beings, in what seems to be closer to the moral than the genetic sense of "human being." She would be right to take the presence of such traits as evidence that the extraterrestrials were persons. It would, however, be anthropocentric of her to take the absence of these traits as proof that they were not, since they could be people who have progressed beyond, or who have never needed, these particular cultural traits.

I suggest that among the characteristics which are central to the concept of personhood are the following:

1. *sentience*—the capacity to have conscious experiences, usually including the capacity to experience pain and pleasure;
2. *emotionality*—the capacity to feel happy, sad, angry, loving, etc.;
3. *reason*—the capacity to solve new and relatively complex problems;
4. *the capacity to communicate,* by whatever means, messages of an indefinite variety of types; that is, not just with an indefinite number of possible contents, but on indefinitely many possible topics;
5. *self-awareness*—having a concept of oneself as an individual and/or as a member of a social group; and finally
6. *moral agency*—the capacity to regulate one's own actions through moral principles or ideals.

It is difficult to produce precise definitions of these traits, let alone to specify universally valid behavioral indications that these traits are present. But let us assume that our explorer knows approximately what these six characteristics mean, and that she is able to observe whether or not the extraterrestrials possess these mental and behavioral capacities. How should she use her findings to decide whether or not they are persons?

An entity need not have *all* of these attributes to be a person. And perhaps none of them is absolutely necessary. For instance, the absence of emotion would not disqualify a being that was person-like in all other ways. Think, for instance, of two of the *Star Trek* characters, Mr. Spock (who is half human and half alien), and Data (who is an android). Both are depicted as lacking the capacity to feel emotion; yet both are sentient, reasoning, communicative, self-aware moral agents, and unquestionably persons. Some people are unemotional; some cannot communicate well; some lack self-awareness; and some are not moral agents. It should not surprise us that many people do not meet all of the criteria of personhood. Criteria for the applicability of complex concepts are often like this: none may be logically necessary, but the more criteria that are satisfied, the more confident we are that the concept is applicable. Conversely, the fewer criteria are satisfied, the less plausible it is to hold that the concept applies. And if none of the relevant criteria are met, then we may be confident that it does not.

Thus, to demonstrate that a fetus is not a person, all I need to claim is that an entity that has *none* of these six characteristics is not a person. Sentience is the most basic mental capacity, and the one that may have the best claim to being a necessary (though not sufficient) condition for personhood. Sentience can establish a claim to moral considerability, since sentient beings can be harmed in ways that matter to them; for instance, they can be caused to feel pain, or deprived of the continuation of a life that is pleasant to them. It is unlikely that an entirely insentient organism could develop the other mental behavioral capacities that are characteristic of persons. Consequently, it is odd to claim that an entity that is not sentient, and that has never been sentient, is nevertheless a person. Persons who have permanently and irreparably lost all capacity for sentience, but who remain biologically alive, arguably still have strong moral rights by virtue of what they have been in the past. But small fetuses, which have not yet begun to have experiences, are not persons yet and do not have the rights that persons do.

The presumption that all persons have full and equal basic moral rights may be part of the very concept of a person. If this is so, then the concept of a person is in part a moral one; once we have admitted that X is a person, we have implicitly committed ourselves to recognizing X's right to be treated as a member of the moral community. The claim that X is a *human being* may also be voiced as an appeal to treat X decently; but this is usually either because "human being" is used in the moral sense, or because of a confusion between genetic and moral humanity.

If (1)–(6) are the primary criteria of personhood, then genetic humanity is neither necessary nor sufficient for personhood. Some genetically human entities are not persons, and there may be persons who belong to other species. A man or woman whose consciousness has been permanently obliterated but who remains biologically alive is a human entity who may no longer be a person; and some unfortunate humans, who have never had any sensory or cognitive capacities at all, may not be people either. Similarly, an early fetus is a human entity which is not yet a person. It is not even minimally sentient, let alone capable of emotion, reason, sophisticated communication, self-awareness, or moral agency.[5] Thus, while it may be greatly valued as a future child, it does not yet have the claim to moral consideration that it may come to have later.

Moral agency matters to moral status, because it is moral agents who invent moral rights, and who can be obliged to respect them. Human beings have become moral agents from social necessity. Most social animals exist well enough, with no evident notion of a moral right. But human beings need moral rights, because we are not only highly social, but also sufficiently clever and self-interested to be capable of undermining our societies through violence and duplicity. For human persons, moral rights are essential for peaceful and mutually beneficial social life. So long as some moral agents are denied basic rights, peaceful existence is difficult, since moral agents justly resent being treated as something less. If animals of some terrestrial species are found to be persons, or if alien persons come from other worlds, or if human beings someday invent machines whose mental and behavioral capacities make them persons, then we will be morally obliged to respect the moral rights of these nonhuman persons—at least to the extent that they are willing and able to respect ours in turn.

Although only those persons who are moral agents can participate directly in the shaping and enforcement of moral rights, they need not and usually do not ascribe moral rights only to themselves and other moral agents. Human beings are social creatures who naturally care for small children, and other members of the social community who are not currently capable of moral agency. Moreover, we are all vulnerable to the temporary or permanent loss of the mental capacities necessary for moral agency. Thus, we have self-interested as well as altruistic reasons for extending basic moral rights to infants and other sentient human beings who have already been born, but who currently lack some of these other mental capacities. These human beings, despite their current disabilities, are persons and members of the moral community.

But in extending moral rights to beings (human or otherwise) that have few or none of the morally significant characteristics of persons, we need to be careful not to burden human moral agents with obligations that they cannot possibly fulfill, except at unacceptably great cost to their own well-being and that of those they care about. Women often cannot complete unwanted pregnancies, except at intolerable mental, physical, and economic cost to themselves and their families. And heterosexual intercourse is too important a part of the social lives of most men and women to be reserved for times when pregnancy is an acceptable outcome. . . . If fetuses were persons, then they would have rights that must be respected, even at great social or personal cost. But given that early fetuses, at least, are unlike persons in the morally relevant respects, it is unreasonable to insist that they be accorded exactly the same moral and legal status.

Fetal Development and the Right to Life

Two questions arise regarding the application of these suggestions to the moral status of the fetus. First, if indeed fetuses are not yet persons, then might they nevertheless have strong moral rights based upon the degree to which they *resemble* persons? Secondly, to what extent, if any, does a fetus's potential to *become* a person imply that we ought to accord to it some of the same moral rights? Each of these questions requires comment.

It is reasonable to suggest that the more like a person something is—the more it appears to meet at least some of the criteria of personhood—the stronger is the case for according it a right to life, and perhaps the stronger its right to life is. That being the case, perhaps the fetus gradually gains a stronger right to life as it develops. We should take seriously the suggestion that, just as "the human individual develops biologically in a continuous fashion, the rights of a human person might develop in the same way."[6] A seven-month fetus can apparently feel pain, and can respond to such stimuli as light and sound. Thus, it may have a rudimentary form of consciousness. Nevertheless, it is probably not as conscious, or as capable of emotion, as even a very young infant is; and it has as yet little or no capacity for reason, sophisticated intentional communication, or self-awareness. In these respects, even a late-term fetus is arguably less like a person than are many nonhuman animals. Many animals (e.g., large-brained mammals such as elephants, cetaceans, or apes) are not only sentient, but clearly possessed of a degree of reason, and perhaps even of self-awareness. Thus, on the basis of its resemblance to a person, even a late-term fetus can have no more right to life than do these animals.

Animals may, indeed, plausibly be held to have some moral rights, and perhaps rather strong ones. But it is impossible in practice to accord full and equal moral rights to all animals. When an animal poses a serious threat to the life or well-being of a person, we do not, as a rule, greatly blame the person for killing it; and there are good reasons for this species-based discrimination. Animals, however intelligent in their own domains, are generally not beings with whom we can reason; we cannot persuade mice not to invade our dwellings or consume our food. That is why their rights are necessarily weaker than those of a being who can understand and respect the rights of other beings.

But the probable sentience of late-term fetuses is not the only argument in favor of treating late abortion as a morally more serious matter than early abortion. Many—perhaps most—people are repulsed by the thought of needlessly aborting a late-term fetus. The late-term fetus has features which cause it to arouse in us almost the same powerful protective instinct as does a small infant.

This response needs to be taken seriously. If it were impossible to perform abortions early in pregnancy, then we might have to tolerate the mental and physical trauma that would be occasioned by the routine resort to late abortion. But where early abortion is safe, legal, and readily available to all women, it is not unreasonable to expect most women who wish to end a pregnancy to do so prior to the third trimester. Most women strongly prefer early to late abortion, because it is far less physically painful and emotionally traumatic. Other things being equal, it is better for all concerned that pregnancies that are not to be completed should be ended as early as possible. Few women would consider ending a pregnancy in the seventh month in order to take a trip to Europe. If, however, a woman's own life or health is at stake, or if the fetus has been found to be so severely abnormal as to be unlikely to survive or to have a life worth living, then late abortion may be the morally best choice. For even a late-term fetus is not a person yet, and its rights must yield to those of the woman whenever it is impossible for both to be respected.

Potential Personhood and the Right to Life

We have seen that a presentient fetus does not yet resemble a person in ways which support the claim that it has strong moral rights. But what about its *potential*, the fact that if nurtured and allowed to develop it may eventually become a person? Doesn't that potential give it at least some right to life? The fact that something is a potential person may be a reason for not destroying it; but we need not conclude from this that potential people have a strong right to life. It may be that the feeling that it is better not to destroy a potential person is largely due to the fact that potential people are felt to be an invaluable resource, not to be lightly squandered. If every speck of dust were a potential person, we would be less apt to suppose that all potential persons have a right to become actual.

We do not need to insist that a potential person has no right to life whatever. There may be something immoral, and not just imprudent, about wantonly destroying potential people, when doing so isn't necessary. But even if a potential person does have some right to life, that right could not outweigh the right of a woman to obtain an abortion; for the basic moral rights of an actual person outweigh the rights of a merely potential person, whenever the two conflict. Since this may not be immediately obvious in the case of a human fetus, let us look at another case.

Suppose that our space explorer falls into the hands of an extraterrestrial civilization, whose scientists decide to create a few thousand new human beings by killing her and using some of her cells to create clones. We may imagine that each of these newly created women will have all of the original woman's abilities, skills, knowledge, and so on, and will also have an individual self-concept; in short, that each of them will be a bona fide (though not genetically unique) person. Imagine, further, that our explorer knows all of this, and knows that these people will be treated kindly and fairly. I maintain that in such a situation she would have the right to escape if she could, thus depriving all of the potential people of their potential lives. For her right to life outweighs all of theirs put together, even though they are not genetically human, and have a high probability of becoming people, if only she refrains from acting.

Indeed, I think that our space traveler would have a right to escape even if it were not her life which the aliens planned to take, but only a year of her freedom, or only a day. She would not be obliged to stay, even if she had been captured because of her own lack of caution—or even if she had done so deliberately, knowing the possible consequences. Regardless of why she was captured, she is not obliged to remain in captivity for *any* period of time in order to permit merely potential people to become actual people. By the same token, a woman's rights to liberty and the control of her own body outweigh whatever right a fetus may have merely by virtue of its potential personhood.

The Objection from Infanticide

One objection to my argument is that it appears to justify not only abortion, but also infanticide. A newborn infant is not much more personlike than a nine-month fetus, and thus it might appear that if late-term abortion is sometimes justified then infanticide must also sometimes be justified. Yet most people believe that infanticide is a form of murder, and virtually never justified.

This objection is less telling than it may seem. There are many reasons why infanticide is more difficult to justify than abortion, even though neither fetuses nor newborn infants are clearly persons. In this period of history, the deliberate killing of newborns is virtually never justified. This is in part because newborns are so close to being persons that to kill them requires a very strong moral justification—as does the killing of dolphins, chimpanzees, and other highly person-like creatures. It is certainly wrong to kill such beings for the sake of convenience, or financial profit, or "sport." Only the most vital human needs, such as the need to defend one's own life and physical integrity, can provide a plausible justification for killing such beings.

In the case of an infant, there is no such vital need, since in the contemporary world there are usually other people who are eager to provide a good home for an infant whose own parents are unable or unwilling to care for it. Many people wait years for the opportunity to adopt a child, and some are unable to do so, even though there is every reason to believe that they would be good parents. The needless destruction of a viable infant not only deprives a sentient human being of life, but also deprives other persons of a source of great satisfaction, perhaps severely impoverishing *their* lives.

Even if an infant is unadoptable (e.g., because of some severe physical disability), it is still wrong to kill it. For most of us value the lives of infants, and would greatly prefer to pay taxes to support foster care and state institutions for disabled children, rather than to allow them to be killed or abandoned. So long as most people feel this way, and so long as it is possible to provide care for infants who are unwanted, or who have special needs that their parents cannot meet without assistance, it is wrong to let any infant die who has a chance of living a reasonably good life.

If these arguments show that infanticide is wrong, at least in today's world, then why don't they also show that late-term abortion is always wrong? After all, third-trimester fetuses are almost as personlike as infants, and many people value them and would prefer that they be preserved. As a potential source of pleasure to some family, a fetus is just as valuable as an infant. But there is an important difference between these two cases: once the infant is born, its continued life cannot pose any serious threat to the woman's life or health, since she is free to put it up for adoption or to place it in foster care. While she might, in rare cases, prefer that the child die rather than being raised by others, such a preference would not establish a right on her part.

In contrast, a pregnant woman's right to protect her own life and health outweighs other people's desire that the fetus be preserved—just as, when a person's desire for life or health is threatened by an animal, and when the threat cannot be removed without killing the animal, that person's right to self-defense outweighs the desires of those who would prefer that the animal not be killed. Thus, while the moment of birth may mark no sharp discontinuity in the degree to which an infant resembles a person, it does mark the end of the mother's right to determine its fate. Indeed, if a late abortion can be safely performed without harming the fetus, the mother has in most cases no right to insist upon its death, for the same reason that she has no right to insist that a viable infant be killed or allowed to die.

It remains true that, on my view, neither abortion nor the killing of newborns is obviously a form of murder. Perhaps our legal system is correct in its classification of infanticide as murder, since no other legal category adequately expresses the force of our disapproval of this action. But some moral distinction remains, and it has important consequences. When a society cannot possibly care for all of the children who are born, without endangering the survival of adults and older children, allowing some infants to die may be the best of a bad set of options. Throughout history, most societies—from those that lived by gathering and hunting to the highly civilized Chinese, Japanese, Greeks, and Romans—have permitted infanticide under such unfortunate circumstances, regarding it as a necessary evil. It shows a lack of understanding to condemn these societies as morally benighted for this reason alone, since in the absence of safe and effective means of contraception and abortion, parents must sometimes have had no morally better options.

Conclusion

I have argued that fetuses are neither persons nor members of the moral community. Furthermore, neither a fetus's resemblance to a person, nor its potential for becoming a person, provides an adequate basis for the claim that it has a full and equal right to life. At the same time, there are medical as well as moral reasons for preferring early to late abortion when the pregnancy is unwanted.

Women, unlike fetuses, are undeniably persons and members of the human moral community. If unwanted or medically dangerous pregnancies never occurred, then it might be possible to respect women's basic moral rights, while at the same time extending the same basic rights to fetuses. But in the real world such pregnancies do occur—often despite the woman's best efforts to prevent them. Even if the perfect contraceptive were universally available, the continued occurrence of rape and incest would make access to abortion a vital human need. Because women are persons, and fetuses are not, women's rights to life, liberty, and physical integrity morally override whatever right to life it may be appropriate to ascribe to a fetus. Consequently, laws that deny women the right to obtain abortions, or that make safe early abortions difficult or impossible for some women to obtain, are an unjustified violation of basic moral and constitutional rights.

Notes

1. Judith Jarvis Thomson, "A Defense of Abortion," *Philosophy and Public Affairs* 1, no.1 (Fall 1971), p. 174.

2. Ibid., p. 187.
3. The principle that it is always wrong to kill innocent human beings may be in need of other modifications, e.g., that it may be permissible to kill innocent human beings in order to save a larger number of equally innocent human beings; but we may ignore these complications here.
4. From here on, I will use "human" to mean "genetically human," since the moral sense of the term seems closely connected to, and perhaps derived from, the assumption that genetic humanity is both necessary and sufficient for membership in the moral community.
5. Fetal sentience is impossible prior to the development of neurological connections between the sense organs and the brain, and between the various parts of the brain involved in the processing of conscious experience. This stage of neurological development is currently thought to occur at some point in the late second or early third trimester.
6. Thomas L. Hayes, "A Biological View," *Commonweal* 85 (March 17, 1967): pp. 677–78; cited by Daniel Callahan in *Abortion: Law, Choice, and Morality* (London: Macmillan, 1970).

Study Questions

1. What characteristics entitle an entity to be considered a person?
2. What lessons does Warren draw from Thomson's case of the unconscious violinist?
3. According to Warren, who belongs to the moral community?
4. Is infanticide more difficult to justify than late-term abortion?

An Argument that Abortion is Wrong

Don Marquis

Don Marquis, Professor of Philosophy at the University of Kansas, argues that, with rare exceptions, abortion is immoral. Marquis does not base his argument on the claim that the fetus is a person but rather on the view that an aborted fetus loses the future goods of consciousness, such as the completion of projects, the pursuit of goals, aesthetic enjoyment, friendships, intellectual pursuits, and physical pleasures of various sorts. In short, premature death deprives individuals of a future of value.

The view that abortion is, with rare exceptions, seriously immoral has received little support in the recent philosophical literature. No doubt most philosophers affiliated with secular institutions of higher education believe that the anti-abortion position is either a symptom of irrational religious dogma or a conclusion generated by seriously confused philosophical argument. The purpose of this essay is to undermine this general belief. This essay sets out an argument that purports to show, as well as any argument in ethics can show, that abortion is, except possibly in rare cases, seriously immoral, that it is in the same moral category as killing an innocent adult human being. . . .

II

[W]e can start from the following unproblematic assumption concerning our own case: it is wrong to kill *us*. Why is it wrong? Some answers can be easily eliminated. It might be said that what makes killing us

From Don Marquis, "An Argument that Abortion is Wrong," *The Journal of Philosophy* 86 (1989).

wrong is that a killing brutalizes the one who kills. But the brutalization consists of being inured to the performance of an act that is hideously immoral; hence, the brutalization does not explain the immorality. It might be said that what makes killing us wrong is the great loss others would experience due to our absence. Although such hubris is understandable, such an explanation does not account for the wrongness of killing hermits, or those whose lives are relatively independent and whose friends find it easy to make new friends.

A more obvious answer is better. What primarily makes killing wrong is neither its effect on the murderer nor its effect on the victim's friends and relatives, but its effect on the victim. The loss of one's life is one of the greatest losses one can suffer. The loss of one's life deprives one of all the experiences, activities, projects, and enjoyments that would otherwise have constituted one's future. Therefore, killing someone is wrong, primarily because the killing inflicts (one of) the greatest possible losses on the victim. To describe this as the loss of life can be misleading, however. The change in my biological state does not by itself make killing me wrong. The effect of the loss of my biological life is the loss to me of all those activities, projects, experiences, and enjoyments which would otherwise have constituted my future personal life. These activities, projects, experiences, and enjoyments are either valuable for their own sakes or are means to something else that is valuable for its own sake. Some parts of my future are not valued by me now, but will come to be valued by me as I grow older and as my values and capacities change. When I am killed, I am deprived both of what I now value which would have been part of my future personal life, but also what I would come to value. Therefore, when I die, I am deprived of all of the value of my future. Inflicting this loss on me is ultimately what makes killing me wrong. This being the case, it would seem that what makes killing *any* adult human being prima facie seriously wrong is the loss of his or her future.

How should this rudimentary theory of the wrongness of killing be evaluated? It cannot be faulted for deriving an "ought" from an "is," for it does not. The analysis assumes that killing me (or you, reader) is prima facie seriously wrong. The point of the analysis is to establish which natural property ultimately explains the wrongness of the killing, given that it is wrong. A natural property will ultimately explain the wrongness of killing, only if (1) the explanation fits with our intuitions about the matter and (2) there is no other natural property that provides the basis for a better explanation of the wrongness of killing. This analysis rests on the intuition that what makes killing a particular human or animal wrong is what it does to that particular human or animal. What makes killing wrong is some natural effect or other of the killing. . . .

The claim that what makes killing wrong is the loss of the victim's future is directly supported by two considerations. In the first place, this theory explains why we regard killing as one of the worst of crimes. Killing is especially wrong, because it deprives the victim of more than perhaps any other crime. In the second place, people with AIDS or cancer who know they are dying believe, of course, that dying is a very bad thing for them. They believe that the loss of a future to them that they would otherwise have experienced is what makes their premature death a very bad thing for them. A better theory of the wrongness of killing would require a different natural property associated with killing which better fits with the attitudes of the dying. What could it be?

The view that what makes killing wrong is the loss to the victim of the value of the victim's future gains additional support when some of its implications are examined. In the first place, it is incompatible with the view that it is wrong to kill only beings who are biologically human. It is possible that there exists a different species from another planet whose members have a future like ours. Since having a future like that is what makes killing someone wrong, this theory entails that it would be wrong to kill members of such a species. Hence, this theory is opposed to the claim that only life that is biologically human has great moral worth, a claim which many anti-abortionists have seemed to adopt. This opposition . . . seems to be a merit of the theory.

In the second place, the claim that the loss of one's future is the wrong-making feature of one's being killed entails the possibility that the futures of some actual nonhuman mammals on our own planet are sufficiently like ours that it is seriously wrong to kill them also. Whether some animals do have the same right to life as human beings depends on adding to the account of the wrongness of killing some additional account of just what it is about my future or the futures of other adult human beings which makes it wrong to kill us. No such additional account will be offered in this essay. Undoubtedly, the provision of such an account would be a very difficult matter. Undoubtedly, any such account would be quite controversial. Hence, it surely should not reflect badly on this sketch of an elementary theory of the wrongness of killing that it is indeterminate with respect to some very difficult issues regarding animal rights.

In the third place, the claim that the loss of one's future is the wrong-making feature of one's being killed does not entail, as sanctity of human life theories do, that active euthanasia is wrong. Persons who are severely and incurably ill, who face a future of pain and despair, and who wish to die will not have suffered a loss if they are killed. It is, strictly speaking, the value of a human's future which makes killing wrong in this theory. This being so, killing does not necessarily wrong some persons who are sick and dying. Of course, there may be other reasons for a prohibition of active euthanasia, but that is another matter. Sanctity-of-human-life theories seem to hold that active euthanasia is seriously wrong even in an individual case where there seems to be good reason for it independently of public policy considerations. This consequence is most implausible, and it is a plus for the claim that the loss of a future of value is what makes killing wrong that it does not share this consequence.

In the fourth place, the account of the wrongness of killing defended in this essay does straightforwardly entail that it is prima facie seriously wrong to kill children and infants, for we do presume that they have futures of value. Since we do believe that it is wrong to kill defenseless . . . babies, it is important that a theory of the wrongness of killing easily account for this. Personhood theories of the wrongness of killing, on the other hand, cannot straightforwardly account for the wrongness of killing infants and young children. Hence, such theories must add special ad hoc accounts of the wrongness of killing the young. The plausibility of such ad hoc theories seems to be a function of how desperately one wants such theories to work. The claim that the primary wrong-making feature of a killing is the loss to the victim of the value of its future accounts for the wrongness of killing young children and infants directly; it makes the wrongness of such acts as obvious as we actually think it is. This is a further merit of this theory. Accordingly, it seems that this value of a future-like-ours theory of the wrongness of killing shares strengths of both sanctity-of-life and personhood accounts while avoiding weaknesses of both. In addition, it meshes with a central institution concerning what makes killing wrong.

The claim that the primary wrong-making feature of a killing is the loss to the victim of the value of its future has obvious consequences for the ethics of abortion. The future of a standard fetus includes a set of experiences, projects, activities, and such which are identical with the futures of adult human beings and are identical with the futures of young children. Since the reason that is sufficient to explain why it is wrong to kill human beings after the time of birth is a reason that also applies to fetuses, it follows that abortion is prima facie seriously morally wrong.

This argument does not rely on the invalid inference that, since it is wrong to kill persons, it is wrong to kill potential persons also. The category that is morally central to this analysis is the category of having a valuable future like ours; it is not the category of personhood. The argument to the conclusion that abortion is prima facie seriously morally wrong proceeded independently of the notion of person or potential person or any equivalent. Someone may wish to start with this analysis in terms of the value of a human future, conclude that abortion is, except perhaps in rare circumstances, seriously morally wrong, infer that fetuses have the right to life, and then call fetuses "persons" as a result of their having the right to life. Clearly, in this case, the category of person is being used to state the *conclusion* of the analysis rather than to generate the *argument* of the analysis. . . .

Of course, this value of a future-like-ours argument, if sound, shows only that abortion is prima facie wrong, not that it is wrong in any and all circumstances. Since the loss of the future to a standard fetus, if killed, is, however, at least as great a loss as the loss of the future to a standard adult human being who is killed, abortion, like ordinary killing, could be justified only by the most compelling reasons. The loss of one's life is almost the greatest misfortune that can happen to one. Presumably abortion could be justified in some circumstances, only if the loss consequent on failing to abort would be at least as great. Accordingly, morally permissible abortions will be rare indeed unless, perhaps, they occur so early in pregnancy that a fetus is not yet definitely an individual. Hence, this argument should be taken as showing that abortion is presumptively very seriously wrong, where the presumption is very strong—as strong as the presumption that killing another adult human being is wrong. . . .

V

In this essay, it has been argued that the correct ethic of the wrongness of killing can be extended to fetal life and used to show that there is a strong presumption that any abortion is morally impermissible. If the ethic of killing adopted here entails, however, that contraception is also seriously immoral, then there would appear to be a difficulty with the analysis of this essay.

But this analysis does not entail that contraception is wrong. Of course, contraception prevents the actualization of a possible future of value. Hence, it follows from the claim that futures of value should be maximized that contraception is prima facie immoral. This obligation to maximize does not exist, however; furthermore, nothing in the ethics of killing in this paper entails that it does. The ethics of killing in this essay would entail that contraception is wrong only if something were denied a human future of value by contraception. Nothing at all is denied such a future by contraception, however.

Candidates for a subject of harm by contraception fall into four categories: (1) some sperm or other, (2) some ovum or other, (3) a sperm and an ovum separately, and (4) a sperm and an ovum together. Assigning the harm to some sperm is utterly arbitrary, for no reason can be given for making a sperm the subject of harm rather than an ovum. Assigning the harm to some ovum is utterly arbitrary, for no reason can be given for making an ovum the subject of harm rather than a sperm. One might attempt to avoid these problems by insisting that contraception deprives both the sperm and the ovum separately of a valuable future like ours. On this alternative, too many futures are lost. Contraception was supposed to be wrong, because it deprived us of one future of value, not two. One might attempt to avoid this problem by holding that contraception deprives the combination of sperm and ovum of a valuable future like ours. But here the definite article misleads. At the time of contraception, there are hundreds of millions of sperm, one (released) ovum and millions of possible combinations of all of these. There is no actual combination at all. Is the subject of the loss to be a merely possible combination? Which one? This alternative does not yield an actual subject of harm either. Accordingly, the immorality of contraception is not entailed by the loss of a future-like-ours argument simply because there is no nonarbitrarily identifiable subject of the loss in the case of contraception.

VI

The purpose of this essay has been to set out an argument for the serious presumptive wrongness of abortion subject to the assumption that the moral permissibility of abortion stands or falls on the moral status of the fetus. Since a fetus possesses a property, the possession of which in adult human beings is sufficient to make killing an adult human being wrong, abortion is wrong. This way of dealing with the problem of abortion seems superior to other approaches to the ethics of abortion, because it rests on an ethics of killing which is close to self-evident, because the crucial morally relevant property clearly applies to fetuses, and because the argument avoids the usual equivocations of "human life," "human being," or "person." . . . Its soundness is compatible with the moral permissibility of euthanasia and contraception. It deals with our intuitions concerning young children.

Finally, this analysis can be viewed as resolving a standard problem—indeed, *the* standard problem—concerning the ethics of abortion. Clearly, it is wrong to kill adult human beings. Clearly, it is not wrong to end the life of some arbitrarily chosen single human cell. Fetuses seem to be like arbitrarily chosen human cells in some respects and like adult humans in other respects. The problem of the ethics of abortion is the problem of determining the fetal property that settles this moral controversy. The thesis of this essay is that the problem of the ethics of abortion, so understood, is solvable.

Study Questions

1. Is the loss of one's future as devastating for a fetus as for a child?
2. Does Marquis's argument that abortion is immoral depend on religious considerations?
3. Does Marquis's position imply that using contraception is wrong?
4. According to Marquis, in what circumstances is abortion not wrong?

Abortion and Miscarriage

Amy Berg

Many of those who oppose abortion do so on the grounds that from the moment of conception a fetus is a person. Amy Berg, Research Assistant Professor at the University of North Carolina at Chapel Hill, argues that this position faces a dilemma. We allocate few resources to the prevention of miscarriage, but if from conception the fetus is a person, then miscarriage is more deadly than any other disease. Accordingly, those opposing abortion should either advocate substantial changes to existing medical priorities or abandon the view that from conception the fetus is a person.

Public debates about abortion often get stuck on disagreement about the moral status of fetuses: whether they are persons from the moment of conception. Many opponents of abortion claim that fetuses are persons; others insist that they are not. But those who think that fetuses are persons from the moment of conception (call them PAC, or Personhood-At-Conception, opponents of abortion) are in danger of a troubling inconsistency in their views on abortion. If current statistics are correct, miscarriage is staggeringly common, probably deadlier than any familiar disease. And yet PAC opponents of abortion do not appear to give miscarriage the weight it clearly deserves on their views. This leads to a dilemma. Either PAC opponents of abortion must radically change their political and medical priorities, or else they must accept that they do not accord fetuses the status of persons from the moment of conception.

From Amy Berg, "Abortion and Miscarriage," *Philosophical Studies* 174 (2017).

1. Miscarriage

Miscarriage, also referred to as pregnancy loss, spontaneous abortion, or stillbirth, is extremely common. Between 22 and 89% of pregnancies are believed to end in miscarriage.[1] By any measure, the vast majority of miscarriages, perhaps two out of three, occur before a woman is aware she is pregnant (Simpson 2011, p. 112).

Think for a moment about the extraordinary implications of this fact. According to the CDC, heart disease kills one in four Americans (Deaths and Mortality 2015; Heart Disease Facts 2015). Cancer kills nearly as many. Strokes kill about one in twenty. Miscarriage is almost certainly deadlier than any of these—depending on which statistics about miscarriage are correct, it may be deadlier than all of these *combined*. And keep in mind that while at least 22% of all *pregnancies* end in miscarriage, about 25% of people *who have been born* die of heart disease. If we counted miscarried fetuses in our total population, the percentages of people who die of stroke, cancer, heart disease, and so on would fall dramatically. If fetuses are persons with equal status to all others, then miscarriage is very likely to be the biggest public-health crisis of our time.

But our society, including PAC opponents of abortion, does not treat miscarriage this way. Think about the campaigns to warn people of the risks of smoking. Or the foundations that raise awareness of breast cancer. Or even the pharmaceutical funding for male impotence. What miscarriage campaigns have received this level of public awareness? We don't see public service announcements; politicians don't mention miscarriage in their stump speeches; no one holds rallies at the Capitol to prevent miscarriage. Even if women receive information from their doctors on how to prevent miscarriage, this comes too late in the majority of cases. Most of us simply do not treat miscarriage like we treat the health problems of those who have already been born.

Granted, we might think that not all miscarriages are bad in the same ways. Late miscarriage, like late abortion, seems to be bad in a different way than early miscarriage is. . . . Family and friends may grieve intensely for the child who would have been. In some ways, miscarriage may be *worse* than the death of someone who has been born—we may mourn the lost potential of the fetus and worry about whether future pregnancies will be healthy. But most of us do not treat miscarriage, particularly early miscarriage, as we would a condition that kills 22–89% of born persons. Early miscarriage is not perceived to be the equivalent of the death of someone who has been born. If it were equivalent, we would treat the prevalence of miscarriage as a public-health catastrophe. And we just don't.

2. A Dilemma

Many people think fetuses are persons from the moment of conception. One YouGov poll found that 66% of Americans believe that fetuses in the womb are people and that 52% believe that life begins at conception (Moore 2015). Although public conceptions of personhood may not be philosophically rigorous, it's clear that fetal personhood at conception is not a fringe belief. And opponents of abortion frequently make use of this claim about fetal personhood, arguing that we should give persons in the womb the same consideration as persons outside of it. But when PAC opponents of abortion couple this belief with the facts about the prevalence of miscarriage, they are faced with a dilemma.

On one hand, PAC opponents of abortion could maintain this belief. This means that they must start treating miscarriage as if it is equivalent to the death of born persons. This should lead them to agitate for a massive shift in society's medical and political priorities. Think about how our society has dealt with acute public-health crises: Ebola, SARS, even flu season. Or think about the funding for the high-profile health issues which chronically plague our society: cancer, heart disease, dementia. PAC opponents of abortion should advocate a similarly huge influx of money into medical research on the causes of and ways to prevent miscarriage. But there's only so much money for medical research to go around. This means that PAC opponents of abortion should find themselves advocating for a substantial shift in funding *away* from heart disease, cancer, and the flu toward miscarriage, since almost certainly none of these conditions kill as many people as miscarriages do. They may find it regrettable that they must advocate for this shift in priorities, but given their belief that all fetuses are persons, this is obviously the right thing to do. Think about how many persons preventing miscarriage would save.

PAC opponents of abortion should also work to shift society's political and social priorities. They should all ask elected officials what they will do about this massive public-health crisis. They should refuse to vote for candidates who don't have a miscarriage plank in their platforms; think of the analogous 21% of voters who say they will only vote for a pro-life candidate (Saad 2012). They should hold rallies to get people to donate money to miscarriage research. They should encourage sexually active women, who are at risk of miscarrying without knowing it, to monitor their bodies extremely closely to determine as soon as possible whether they are even possibly pregnant.

An increased focus on miscarriage will also shift the priorities of PAC opponents of abortion *away* from abortion. Miscarriage, it turns out, is a bigger killer than abortion. According to the Guttmacher Institute, 21% of the pregnancies that *don't* end in miscarriage end in abortion (Induced Abortion 2016). Even on a conservative estimate of the rate of miscarriage, then, miscarriage ends one and a half to two times as many pregnancies as abortion does. Opponents of abortion, it turns out, should also, perhaps primarily, be opponents of miscarriage.

This shift from abortion to miscarriage makes sense because miscarriage is relatively more politically tractable. Even if abortion were completely illegal, it would probably be impossible to prevent all abortions. And because most Americans support keeping abortion legal in at least some circumstances, it seems unlikely to become completely illegal any time soon (Abortion 2016). Working to end miscarriage, on the other hand, does not face organized political opposition. If PAC opponents of abortion truly believe that fetuses are persons from the moment of conception, they should work to end *all* fetal deaths, not just those caused by abortion. The most effective way to do this may be to focus on miscarriages.

But there might be good reasons for PAC opponents of abortion not to focus on medical research into miscarriage. They may reason that even if miscarriage is politically tractable, it is an intractable medical issue. While there are many causes of miscarriage, chromosomal abnormalities form the biggest cluster of causes. Some of these abnormalities may be so severe that a pregnancy would never be viable. Perhaps there's simply nothing that can be done. In that case, PAC opponents of abortion would be justified in focusing on preventing abortions instead.

This reply makes sense if miscarriage is not equivalent to the death of a born person. If we owe fetuses less moral concern, we may not have to try to overcome the medical obstacles to preventing miscarriage. But imagine throwing up our hands about a horrible disease that kills 22–89% of born persons. Imagine saying that we should let AIDS, or cancer, or heart disease take its course, rather than expending more effort researching how we might prevent that disease or treat people who contract it. That's not what we do. Instead, public pressure has led to increased research on these diseases, causing incredible strides in preventing, treating, and curing them.

AIDS activism provides an example here. In the late 1980s, activists formed ACT UP, the AIDS Coalition to Unleash Power, to push for more and faster research into treatments for AIDS (A Timeline 2016). ACT UP's tactics—including a "die-in" in St. Patrick's Cathedral in New York and a daylong shutdown of the Food and Drug Administration—were unorthodox, maybe even offensive. But they worked. Partly because of ACT UP's pressure, the FDA changed its approval process for AIDS drugs, and some pharmaceutical companies lowered their prices. In just a couple of decades, AIDS went from a mysterious underground disease, to a devastating and fatal epidemic, to a relatively manageable chronic condition (Scandlyn 2000, p. 132). Activist groups can only do so much to promote medical research, but the example of ACT UP shows that they can be an important catalyst. Would medical research into miscarriage see similar advances if miscarriage prevention groups shut down government buildings and conducted die-ins? We don't know, because PAC opponents of abortion (among others) have not applied this kind of pressure.

So perhaps some future medical discovery will completely change our view of the intractability of miscarriage: we simply don't know. Even if some chromosomal abnormalities cannot be treated, surely there are some causes of miscarriage (other chromosomal abnormalities, thyroid problems, uterine abnormalities) that we could eventually learn how to treat. If ending miscarriage is even a remote possibility, PAC opponents of abortion should be lobbying for more research into how we can identify, treat, and prevent causes of miscarriage.

But maybe many PAC opponents of abortion don't even get to the point of considering the medical obstacles to preventing miscarriage. Maybe they simply don't know the facts about miscarriage. They might genuinely believe that fetuses are persons from the moment of conception, but they might not know that up to 89% of persons die as a result of miscarriage. Once they learn that, they may quickly shift their political and social priorities in order to push for more research on miscarriage.

But can ignorance really be the explanation? Information about the prevalence of miscarriage is freely available online.[2] If a PAC opponent of abortion learns about the number of persons who are dying as a result of miscarriage, but doesn't do anything to alert others, she seems to be in danger of a serious moral inconsistency. I suppose it's possible that no PAC opponent of abortion is aware of the prevalence of miscarriage, but it seems unlikely. Surely there are medical researchers and OB-GYNs who believe that a fetus is a person from the moment of conception. If these people do not do everything in their power to alert others of the public-health crisis they are aware of, are they being inconsistent?

Perhaps not. Perhaps there are other explanations besides ignorance for why PAC opponents of abortion do not shift their political and medical priorities to focus on miscarriage over abortion. For one thing, many of us, including many PAC opponents of abortion, believe that it is morally worse to kill someone than to let someone die. Even knowing the facts about miscarriage, PAC opponents of abortion might continue to invest resources in opposition to abortion on the ground that they should be doing more to prevent killings than to prevent unintended deaths. But given how many deaths are caused by miscarriage, it would be strange for PAC opponents of abortion not to refocus *some* of their public efforts toward supporting research into how to stop miscarriages. We do not focus all our attention on stopping murders rather than disease on the grounds that death by disease is a case of letting die rather than killing. PAC opponents of abortion can advocate for restrictions on abortion and the overturning of *Roe v. Wade* while simultaneously working to shift medical-research money to miscarriage. If millions of persons are dying before birth, mostly because of miscarriage, then PAC opponents of abortion should be doing more to prevent unintended deaths as well as killings.

Moreover, the distinction between killing and letting die does not appear to extend to *preventing* cases of killing versus letting die. . . . It may make a moral difference whether I kill someone or allow her to die, but it does not seem to matter in the same way whether I intervene to rescue someone from being killed or from being allowed to die. If PAC opponents of abortion are only considering what we can do to prevent *other people's* abortions or miscarriages, then the moral difference between abortion, as a case of killing, and miscarriage, as a case of letting die, fades away even further. If PAC opponents of abortion aren't ignorant of the biological facts, it's not clear that they have good moral grounds for treating miscarriages differently from abortions. . . .

I have argued that taking seriously the prevalence of miscarriage, especially early miscarriage, leads to a dilemma for anyone who thinks that fetuses are persons from the moment of conception. For PAC opponents of abortion to be consistent in their moral beliefs, they must work for a substantial shift in society's political and medical priorities toward the needs of fetuses, particularly very early fetuses, and away from the needs of persons who have already been born. They should do this even though miscarriage may be difficult to prevent, since they would do so for any other complicated but lethal condition. Even if they believe that killing is worse than letting die, they should shift their resources away from opposition to abortion and toward preventing miscarriage, because so many more deaths are caused by miscarriage. Truly acting according to the belief that fetuses are persons from the moment of conception would substantially alter the priorities of PAC opponents of abortion.

3. The Other Horn of the Dilemma

But there's another horn to this dilemma. Rather than making this shift in priorities from born persons to early fetuses (many of them still clinically undetectable), we might accept that very few people, even very few PAC opponents of abortion, truly believe that an early miscarriage is equivalent to the death of a born person. While miscarriage is often devastating, especially for those immediately affected by it, the medical and political priorities of PAC opponents of abortion show that they do not think it is the *same kind of* tragedy that the death of 22–89% of born persons would be. Those who think that abortion is permissible have long given reasons for why we might think this: fetuses, especially the early fetuses who are so often miscarried, lack some or all of the features that we think make the deaths of born persons bad, such as consciousness and self-awareness. If PAC opponents of abortion do not shift their priorities, this may show that they tacitly accept this reasoning.

But not all opponents of abortion are *PAC* opponents of abortion. Some might oppose abortion not because it is the death of a person but because it is the death of a *potential* person: it is morally wrong, perhaps, to kill beings that have the potential to develop into persons.[3] The same problem reoccurs here: this argument will not show why we should be concerned about the abortion of a potential person but not at all about the miscarriage of a potential person. But the challenges for these different kinds of opposition to abortion do not by themselves show that abortion is always permissible. If our moral concern for later miscarriages is because a later fetus is more plausibly a person, then accepting that a very early miscarriage is not equivalent to the death of a born person does not require us to treat all miscarriages the same.

Knowing the facts about miscarriage means that PAC opponents of abortion must think seriously about whether they can actually accept that fetuses are persons from the moment of conception. Now that they know the prevalence of early miscarriage, are they prepared to shift resources away from born persons to fetuses whose existence is still clinically undetectable? If they continue to maintain that fetuses are persons from the moment of conception, then they must make this political and medical shift immediately. If they are unwilling to change their priorities in order to prevent what they should, on pain of inconsistency, regard as the biggest public-health crisis of our time, then they should accept that they do not actually believe in the personhood of all fetuses. Arguments that abortion is wrong because fetuses are persons from the moment of conception turn out to be arguments that even PAC opponents of abortion may not accept.

References

Abortion. *Gallup*. (2016). Gallup. 2015. http://www.gallup.com/poll/1576/abortion.aspx. Accessed 13 April 2016.

A Timeline of HIV/AIDS. (2016). *AIDS.gov*. US Department of Health and Human Services. Accessed 13 April 2016.

Berghella, M., & Achenbach, A. (2012). Early pregnancy loss. In V. Berghella (Ed.), *Obstetric evidence-based guidelines* (2nd ed., pp. 142–149). London: Informa Healthcare.

Deaths and Mortality. (2015). *Centers for disease control and prevention*. US Department of Health and Human Services, 21 August. http://www.cdc.gov/nchs/fastats/deaths.htm. Accessed 13 April 2016.

Hardy, S., & Kukla, R. (2015). Making sense of miscarriage online. *Journal of Social Philosophy, 46*(1), 106–125.

Heart Disease Facts. (2015). *Centers for disease control and prevention*. US Department of Health and Human Services, 10 August. http://www.cdc.gov/heartdisease/facts.htm. Accessed 13 April 2016.

Induced Abortion in the United States. (2016). *Guttmacher Institute*. Guttmacher Institute, March 2016. http://www.guttmacher.org/pubs/fb_induced_abortion.html. Accessed 13 April 2016.

Macklon, N. S., Geraedts, J. P. M., & Fauser, B. C. J. M. (2002). Conception to ongoing pregnancy: The 'Black Box' of early pregnancy loss. *Human Reproduction Update, 8*(4), 333–343.

Marquis, D. (1989). Why abortion is immoral. *Journal of Philosophy, 86*(4), 183–202.

Miscarriage. (2014). *Medline Plus*. US National Library of Medicine. Accessed 13 April 2016.

Moore, P. (2015). "Three quarters say Longmont attack is murder." *YouGov*. YouGov. Accessed 13 April 2016.

Nepomnaschy, P., et al. (2006). Cortisol levels and very early pregnancy loss in humans. *Proceedings of the National Academy of Sciences of the United States of America, 103*(10), 3938–3942.

Saad, L. (2012). Abortion is threshold issue for one in six U.S. voters. In *Gallup*. Gallup, 4 October 2012. Accessed 13 April 2016.

Scandlyn, J. (2000). When AIDS became a chronic disease. *Western Journal of Medicine, 172*(2), 130–133.

Simpson, J. L. (2011). Early pregnancy loss. In G. Kovacs (Ed.), *The subfertility handbook: A clinician's guide* (2nd ed., p. 2011). Cambridge: Cambridge University Press.

Warren, M. A. (1973). On the moral and legal status of abortion. *Monist, 57*(4), 43–61.

Weintraub, A., & Sheiner, E. (2011). Early pregnancy loss. In E. Sheiner (Ed.), *Bleeding during pregnancy: A comprehensive guide* (pp. 25–44). New York: Springer.

Wendler, D. (1999). Understanding the 'conservative' view on abortion. *Bioethics, 13*(1), 32–56.

Notes

1. Nepomnaschy et al. (2006) report the prevalence of miscarriage as between 31 and 89%; the 22% figure comes from Weintraub and Sheiner (2011). Others give different estimates [about 70% in Macklon et al. (2002); 40–50% in Berghella and Achenbach (2012); 30% in Simpson (2011)]. Whatever the precise number, it is clearly very large.
2. Hardy and Kukla (2015) do an especially good job of pointing out the variety of resources available online for women experiencing miscarriages.
3. Marquis (1989) holds a prominent version of this view.

Study Questions

1. In what ways might a miscarriage be worse than the death of someone who has been born?
2. If someone holds that from conception the fetus is a person, is the miscarriage of a fetus morally equivalent to the death of an adult?
3. Should someone who causes a miscarriage be treated as a murderer?
4. Could you believe that a miscarriage is not murder yet oppose abortion as morally wrong?

B. Genetic Choices

Can Having Children Be Immoral?

Laura M. Purdy

Laura M. Purdy is Professor Emerita of Philosophy at Wells College. She argues that conception can sometimes be morally wrong on grounds of genetic risk, for we have a duty to try to bring into the world only individuals who are likely to have a minimally satisfying life. If this condition is not met, then parents should seek alternative ways of satisfying any desires to reproduce. Thus the right to have children is not absolute.

Is it morally permissible for me to have children? A decision to procreate is surely one of the most significant decisions a person can make. So it would seem that it ought not to be made without some moral soul-searching.

There are many reasons why one might hesitate to bring children into this world if one is concerned about their welfare. Some are rather general, like the deteriorating environment or the prospect of poverty. Others have a narrower focus, like continuing civil war

From Laura M. Purdy, "Genetics and Reproductive Risk: Can Having Children Be Immoral," in *Bioethics: Principles, Issues, and Cases*, Lewis Vaughn ed. (Oxford: Oxford University Press, 2013).

in Ireland, or the lack of essential social support for child rearing persons in the United States. Still others may be relevant only to individuals at risk of passing harmful diseases to their offspring. . . . So the question arises: can it be wrong to have a child because of genetic risk factors? . . .

My primary concern here is to argue that conception can sometimes be morally wrong on grounds of genetic risk.

Huntington's Disease

There is always some possibility that reproduction will result in a child with a serious disease or handicap. Genetic counselors can help individuals determine whether they are at unusual risk, and, as the Human Genome Project rolls on, their knowledge will increase by quantum leaps. As this knowledge becomes available, I believe we ought to use it to determine whether possible children are at risk *before* they are conceived.

I want in this paper to defend the thesis that it is morally wrong to reproduce when we know there is a high risk of transmitting a serious disease or defect. This thesis holds that some reproductive acts are wrong, and my argument puts the burden of proof on those who disagree with it to show why its conclusions can be overridden. Hence it denies that people should be free to reproduce mindless of the consequences. However, as [a] moral argument, it should be taken as a proposal for further debate and discussion. It is not, by itself, an argument in favor of legal prohibitions of reproduction.

There is a huge range of genetic diseases. Some are quickly lethal; others kill more slowly, if at all. Some are mainly physical, some mainly mental; others impair both kinds of function. Some interfere tremendously with normal functioning, others less. Some are painful, some are not. There seems to be considerable agreement that rapidly lethal diseases, especially those, like Tay-Sachs, accompanied by painful deterioration, should be prevented even at the cost of abortion. Conversely, there seems to be substantial agreement that relatively trivial problems, especially cosmetic ones, would not be legitimate grounds for abortion. In short, there are cases ranging from low risk of mild disease or disability to high risk of serious disease or disability. Although it is difficult to decide where the duty to refrain from procreation becomes compelling, I believe that there are some clear cases. I have chosen to focus on Huntington's Disease to illustrate the kinds of concrete issues such decisions entail. However, the arguments presented here are also relevant to many other genetic diseases.

The symptoms of Huntington's Disease usually begin between the ages of thirty and fifty. It happens this way:

> Onset is insidious. Personality changes (obstinacy, moodiness, lack of initiative) frequently antedate or accompany the involuntary choreic movements. These usually appear first in the face, neck, and arms, and are jerky, irregular, and stretching in character. Contractions of the facial muscles result in grimaces; those of the respiratory muscles, lips, and tongue lead to hesitating, explosive speech. Irregular movements of the trunk are present; the gait is shuffling and dancing. Tendon reflexes are increased. . . . Some patients display a fatuous euphoria; others are spiteful, irascible, destructive, and violent. Paranoid reactions are common. Poverty of thought and impairment of attention, memory, and judgment occur. As the disease progresses, walking becomes impossible, swallowing difficult, and dementia profound. Suicide is not uncommon.[1]

The illness lasts about fifteen years, terminating in death.

Huntington's Disease is an autosomal dominant disease, meaning that it is caused by a single defective gene located on a non-sex chromosome. It is passed from one generation to the next via affected individuals. Each child of such an affected person has a fifty percent risk of inheriting the gene and thus of eventually developing the disease, even if he or she was born before the parent's disease was evident.[2]

Until recently, Huntington's Disease was especially problematic because most affected individuals did not know whether they had the gene for the disease until well into their childbearing years. So they had to decide about childbearing before knowing whether they could transmit the disease or not. If, in time, they did not develop symptoms of the disease, then their children could know they were not at risk for the disease. If unfortunately they did develop symptoms, then each of their children could know there was a fifty percent chance that they, too, had inherited the gene. In both cases, the children faced a period of prolonged anxiety as to whether they would develop the disease. Then, in the 1980s, thanks in part to an energetic campaign by Nancy Wexler, a genetic marker was found that, in certain circumstances, could tell people with a relatively high degree of probability whether or not they had the gene for the disease.[3] Finally, in March 1993, the defective gene itself was discovered.[4] Now individuals can find out whether they carry the gene for the disease, and prenatal screening can tell us whether a given fetus has inherited it. These technological developments change the moral scene substantially.

How serious are the risks involved in Huntington's Disease? Geneticists often think a ten percent risk is high.[5] But risk assessment also depends on what is at stake: the worse the possible outcome the more undesirable an otherwise small risk seems. In medicine, as elsewhere, people may regard the same result quite differently. But for devastating diseases like Huntington's this part of the judgment should be unproblematic: no one wants a loved one to suffer in this way.

There may still be considerable disagreement about the acceptability of a given risk. So it would be difficult in many circumstances to say how we should respond to a particular risk. Nevertheless, there are good grounds for a conservative approach, for it is reasonable to take special precautions to avoid very bad consequences, even if the risk is small. But the possible consequences here *are* very bad: a child who may inherit Huntington's Disease has a much greater than average chance of being subjected to severe and prolonged suffering. And it is one thing to risk one's own welfare, but quite another to do so for others and without their consent.

Is this judgment about Huntington's Disease really defensible? People appear to have quite different opinions. Optimists argue that a child born into a family afflicted with Huntington's Disease has a reasonable chance of living a satisfactory life. After all, even children born of an afflicted parent still have a fifty percent chance of escaping the disease. And even if afflicted themselves, such people will probably enjoy some thirty years of healthy life before symptoms appear. It is also possible, although not at all likely, that some might not mind the symptoms caused by the disease. Optimists can point to diseased persons who have lived fruitful lives, as well as those who seem genuinely glad to be alive. One is Rick Donohue, a sufferer from the Joseph family disease: "You know, if my mom hadn't had me, I wouldn't be here for the life I have had. So there is a good possibility I will have children."[6] Optimists therefore conclude that it would be a shame if these persons had not lived.

Pessimists concede some of these facts, but take a less sanguine view of them. They think a fifty percent risk of serious disease like Huntington's appallingly high. They suspect that many children born into afflicted families are liable to spend their youth in dreadful anticipation and fear of the disease. They expect that the disease, if it appears, will be perceived as a tragic and painful end to a blighted life. They point out that Rick Donohue is still young, and has not experienced the full horror of his sickness. It is also well-known that some young persons have such a dilated sense of time that they can hardly envision themselves at thirty or forty, so the prospect of pain at that age is unreal to them.

More empirical research on the psychology and life history of sufferers and potential sufferers is clearly needed to decide whether optimists or pessimists have a more accurate picture of the experiences of individuals at risk. But given that some will surely realize pessimists' worst fears, it seems unfair to conclude that the pleasures of these who deal best with the situation simply cancel out the suffering of those others when that suffering could be avoided altogether.

I think that these points indicate that the morality of procreation in situations like this demands further investigation. I propose to do this by looking first at the position of the possible child, then at that of the potential parent.

Possible Children and Potential Parents

The first task in treating the problem from the child's point of view is to find a way of referring to possible future offspring without seeming to confer some sort of morally significant existence upon them. I will follow the convention of calling children who might be born in the future but who are not now conceived "possible" children, offspring, individuals, or persons.

Now, what claims about children or possible children are relevant to the morality of childbearing in the circumstances being considered? Of primary importance is the judgment that we ought to try to provide every child with something like a minimally satisfying life. I am not altogether sure how best to formulate this standard but I want clearly to reject the view that it is morally permissible to conceive individuals so long as we do not expect them to be so miserable that they wish they were dead. I believe that this kind of moral minimalism is thoroughly unsatisfactory and that not many people would really want to live in a world where it was the prevailing standard. Its lure is that it puts few demands on us, but its price is the scant attention it pays to human well-being. . . .

Of course, this line of reasoning confronts us with the need to spell out what is meant by "minimally satisfying" and what a standard based on this concept would require of us. Conceptions of a minimally satisfying life vary tremendously among societies and also within them. De rigueur in some circles are private music lessons and trips to Europe, while in others providing eight years of schooling is a major accomplishment. But there is no need to consider this complication at length here since we are concerned only with health as a prerequisite for a minimally satisfying life. Thus, as we draw out what such a standard might require of us, it seems reasonable to retreat to the more limited claim that parents should try to ensure something like normal health for their children. It might be thought that even this moderate claim is unsatisfactory since in some places debilitating conditions are the norm, but one could circumvent this objection by saying that parents ought to try to provide for their children health normal for that culture, even though it may be inadequate if measured by some outside standard. This conservative position would still justify efforts to avoid the birth of children at risk for Huntington's Disease and other serious genetic diseases in virtually all societies.

This view is reinforced by the following considerations. Given that possible children do not presently exist as actual individuals, they do not have a right to be brought into existence, and hence no one is maltreated by measures to avoid the conception of a possible person. Therefore, the conservative course that avoids the conception of those who would not be expected to enjoy a minimally satisfying life is at present the only fair course of action. The alternative is a laissez-faire approach which brings into existence the lucky, but only at the expense of the unlucky. Notice that attempting to avoid the creation of the unlucky does not necessarily lead to *fewer* people being brought into being; the question boils down to taking steps to bring those with better prospects into existence, instead of those with worse ones.

I have so far argued that if people with Huntington's Disease are unlikely to live minimally satisfying lives, then those who might pass it on should not have genetically related children. This is consonant with the principle that the greater the danger of serious problems, the stronger the duty to avoid them. But this principle is in conflict with what people think of as the right to reproduce. How might one decide which should take precedence?

Expecting people to forego having genetically related children might seem to demand too great a sacrifice of them. But before reaching that conclusion we need to ask what is really at stake. One reason for wanting children is to experience family life, including love, companionship, watching kids grow, sharing their pains and triumphs, and helping to form members of the next generation. Other reasons emphasize the validation of parents as individuals within a continuous family line, children as a source of immortality, or perhaps even the gratification of producing partial replicas of oneself. Children may also be desired in an effort to prove that one is an adult, to try to cement a marriage or to benefit parents economically.

Are there alternative ways of satisfying these desires? Adoption or new reproductive technologies can fulfil many of them without passing on known genetic defects. Replacements for sperm have been available for many years via artificial insemination by donor. More recently, egg donation, sometimes in combination with contract pregnancy, has been used to provide eggs for women who prefer not to use their own. Eventually it may be possible to clone individual humans, although that now seems a long way off. All of these approaches to avoiding the use of particular genetic material are controversial and have generated much debate. I believe that tenable moral versions of each do exist.

None of these methods permits people to extend both genetic lines, or realize the desire for immortality or for children who resemble both parents; nor is it clear that such alternatives will necessarily succeed in proving that one is an adult, cementing a marriage, or providing economic benefits. Yet, many people feel these desires strongly. . . .

Fortunately, further scrutiny of the situation reveals that there are good reasons why people should attempt—with appropriate social support—to talk themselves out of the desires in question or to consider novel ways of fulfilling them. Wanting to see the genetic line continued is not particularly rational when it brings a sinister legacy of illness and death. The desire for immortality cannot really be satisfied anyway, and people need to face the fact that what really matters is how they behave in their own lifetime. And finally, the desire for children who physically resemble one is understandable, but basically narcissistic, and its fulfillment cannot be guaranteed even by normal reproduction. There are other ways of proving one is an adult, and other ways of cementing marriages—and children don't necessarily do either. Children, especially prematurely ill children, may not provide the expected economic benefits anyway. Nongenetically related children may also provide benefits similar to those that would have been provided by genetically related ones, and expected economic benefit is, in many cases, a morally questionable reason for having children.

Before the advent of reliable genetic testing, the options of people in Huntington's families were cruelly limited. On the one hand, they could have children, but at the risk of eventual crippling illness and death for them. On the other, they could refrain from childbearing, sparing their possible children from significant risk of inheriting this disease, perhaps frustrating intense desires to procreate—only to discover, in some cases that their sacrifice was unnecessary because they did not develop the disease. Or they could attempt to adopt or try new reproductive approaches.

Reliable genetic testing has opened up new possibilities. Those at risk who wish to have children can get tested. If they test positive, they know their possible children are at risk. Those who are opposed to abortion must be especially careful to avoid conception if they are to behave responsibly. Those not opposed to abortion can responsibly conceive children, but only if they are willing to test each fetus and abort those who carry the gene. If individuals at risk test negative, they are home free.

What about those who cannot face the test for themselves? They can do prenatal testing and abort fetuses who carry the defective gene. A clearly positive test also implies that the parent is affected, although negative tests do not rule out that possibility. Prenatal testing can thus bring knowledge that enables one to avoid passing the disease to others, but only, in some cases, at the cost of coming to know with certainty that one will indeed develop the disease. This situation raises with peculiar force the question of whether parental responsibility requires people to get tested.

Some people think that we should recognize a right "not to know." It seems to me that such a right could be defended only where ignorance does not put others at serious risk. So if people are prepared to forego genetically related children, they need not get tested. But if they want genetically related children then they must do whatever is necessary to ensure that affected babies are not the result. There is, after all, something inconsistent about the claim that one has a right to be shielded from the truth, even if the price is to risk inflicting on one's children the same dread disease one cannot even face in oneself.

In sum, until we can be assured that Huntington's Disease does not prevent people from living a minimally satisfying life, individuals at risk for the disease have a moral duty to try not to bring affected babies into this world. There are now enough options available so that this duty needn't frustrate their reasonable desires. Society has a corresponding duty to facilitate moral behavior on the part of individuals. Such support ranges from the narrow and concrete (like making sure that medical testing and counseling is available to all) to the more general social environment that guarantees that all pregnancies are voluntary, that pronatalism is eradicated, and that women are treated with respect regardless of the reproductive options they choose.

Notes

1. *The Merck Manual* (Rahway, NJ: Merck, 1972), pp. 1363, 1346. We now know that the age of onset and severity of the disease is related to the number of abnormal replications of the glutamine code on the abnormal gene. See Andrew Revkin, "Hunting Down Huntington's," *Discover*, December 1993, p. 108.
2. Hymie Gordon, "Genetic Counseling," *JAMA*, Vol. 217, n. 9 (August 30, 1971), p. 1346.
3. See Revkin, "Hunting Down Huntington's," pp. 99–108.
4. "Gene for Huntington's Disease Discovered," *Human Genome News*, Vol. 5, n. 1 (May 1993), p. 5.
5. Charles Smith, Susan Holloway, and Alan E. H. Emery, "Individuals at Risk in Families—Genetic Disease," *Journal of Medical Genetics*, Vol. 8 (1971), p. 453.
6. *The New York Times*, September 30, 1975, p. 1, col. 6. The Joseph family disease is similar to Huntington's Disease except that symptoms start appearing in the twenties. Rick Donohue was in his early twenties at the time he made this statement.

Study Questions

1. Can having a child ever be morally impermissible?
2. What does Purdy mean by "a minimally satisfying life"?
3. Does a minimally satisfying life have to last for at least a certain length of time?
4. Is giving birth to someone who may develop a terrible disease between the ages of thirty and fifty morally worse than giving birth to someone who is likely to die by the age of eighty?

Parents and Genetic Information

Simo Vehmas

Should parents learn about their genetic information before having children? Simo Vehmas, Professor of Disability Studies at the University of Helsinki, argues that parents have a right not to know about their hereditary properties so long as they are willing to take on parenting as an unconditional commitment, carried out without concern for whether a child has an impairment. Vehmas concludes that responsible parenthood does not always imply knowing about possible risks. The decision whether to seek such information rests with the parents.

Does Ignorance Imply (IR)Responsibility?

Most of us without a clear medical family history are in the position to decide whether to seek medical assistance to make sure if we have a certain risk to have a child with an ailment. Should such prospective parents acquire genetic information about their hereditary properties in order to act responsibly? The answer is negative if they are willing to commit themselves to parenthood unconditionally. And since parenthood should be *prima facie* an unconditional project, meaning, people should not give a qualified assent for being parents of a future child, ignoring genetic information may, in fact, be advisable. This is the case if the parents think that knowing about possible risks would not help them significantly to prepare nurturing their child and if they recognise that they would be tempted to select the most convenient child merely from their own viewpoint with the help of genetics.

From Simo Vehmas, "Just Ignore It? Parents and Genetic Information," *Theoretical Medicine* 22 (2001).

This conclusion, however, seems a bit odd in the light of the fact that ensuring and improving children's capabilities and health is seen as an absolute duty of the parents and society. Most of us accept government requirements that parents warrant their children, for example, a minimum level of education and medical care. . . .

Causing a cognitive impairment to one's child, born or unborn, is reasonably seen as immoral. This is not because impairments in themselves are undesirable threats regarding one's well-being, as it usually is assumed, but, rather, that they may endanger an individual's well-being and social status in the environment she lives in due to the way society is built. Thus, the harm related to impairments is often based on social practices, not on the assumed inherent undesirable nature of impairments. However, if parents should abstain from habits and acts that may cause impairments in their children and thus disable them in the future, why should they not aim at producing children with characters suitable for the society that they will live in? If one does not consider the distinction between acts and omissions as significant, there does not seem to be a morally relevant difference between these two lines of conduct either.

The intentions of the parents seem to be crucial here. It is indeed reasonable that parents try to ensure their child a future as good as possible. Yet, impairment such as Fragile X syndrome does not necessarily endanger a child's well-being especially if her parents are committed to taking care of her. Thus, an intentional acquisition of genetic information in order to have a child without impairment can be justified if it is based on true concern for the future child's well-being. This may be the case if the society is such that a child with a certain impairment would have substantially limited opportunities for personal well-being (it is questionable whether this is the case in Western affluent societies). If this is not the case and if parents' true intention for selecting children on the basis of their individual features is based on a qualified attitude regarding parenting a child, the acquisition of genetic information would be against the project of parenthood.

Intentionally ignoring genetic information could be seen as a morally significant omission which results in the birth of a child with impairment. It could thus be parallelled to a case where a pregnant woman causes a mental retardation in her child due to excessive drinking of alcohol. This analogy, however, is false. The reason for mental retardation in a child in the latter case is based on the woman's lack of interest regarding her future child's well-being. Her own desire for the drink is more important to her than the well-being of her child, or acknowledging her parental duties and acting according to them. This does not apply to parents who consciously ignore genetic information because of their conception of parenthood as an unconditional project. They think that it would be wrong to determine qualitative standards to their intended future child and as long as the impairment of the child would not be as serious enough to cause her undue suffering. The small risk of having a child whose life would be short and filled with pain does not undermine this approach, although it certainly is a justified reason for acquiring genetic information. If a child is born whose life can with good reason be seen as not worth living, the parents are not entitled to withdraw from their parental position but, rather, they are obliged to make decisions according to the interests and good of their child. In this kind of case it would mean making the painful decision to ensure their child a death as painless as possible. . . .

[R]esponsibility requires having all *relevant* information. In the light of the argument presented here, genetics does not necessarily offer relevant information for parents when making reproductive decisions. Parents can thus make responsible choices by ignoring genetic information if they are willing to nurture a child despite her characteristics. Also, this kind of unconditional attitude towards parenting is something that prospective parents should adopt, which means that ignoring genetic information is justified, in line with responsible parenthood, and perhaps even recommendable.

The Thin Line Between Advice and Order

The liberal tradition with its emphasis on autonomy stresses the neutral and objective nature of genetic counselling. Parents have the absolute freedom to make choices which they see as fitting themselves and their families. However, the idea of non-directive counselling is clearly an illusion. It seems likely that genetic counselling will become a similar routine as prenatal diagnostic procedures are at the moment. Prenatal tests have become a practice which offer parents a limited freedom of choice. It is assumed that if a fetal abnormality is found, terminating pregnancy should automatically take place (as it mostly does). Also, the genetic counselling has concentrated almost exclusively to medical facts without paying practically any attention to social or psychological issues; what is it like to live with a particular condition or with a child with that condition. . . . Thus, the spread of the genetic technology will probably create great pressures for people to use it even if they originally saw no benefit of certain characters which gene technology was aiming at helping them to achieve. . . .

When parents get only very limited information and sometimes prejudiced thinking regarding disability, their reproductive choices are not expanded but, rather, constricted. By providing parents with only medical information, a strict framework for the decision making is established and certain kind[s] of decisions are implicitly encouraged. The received information inevitably determines what kind of choices one makes. When medical professionals counsel or give advice to people, they affect on their decisions because of the authority they have. If . . . limited information is distributed, parents do not have all relevant information in order to make responsible decisions. This being the case, parents are facing an indirect form of force which prevents them from making autonomous and responsible decisions.

To conclude, genetics is not an enterprise beyond moral suspicion. Firstly, it may in its part be a driving force in promoting discrimination against individuals with impairments. Secondly, it may undermine the concept of parenthood and prevent parents from practising duties and virtues attached to their position. And thirdly, it is likely to practice force which weakens parents' possibilities for making autonomous and responsible reproductive choices.

Some Residual Questions

I have argued that responsible parenthood does not necessarily imply the acquisition of genetic information but, on the contrary, sometimes ignoring it if the purpose is selecting children on the grounds of their individual characteristics. I have used in this paper expressions such as "advisable", "recommendable" and "preferable" as regards parents ignoring genetic information. However, when I say that parenthood is essentially an unconditional project in which parents ought to commit themselves to nurturing any kind of child, one could argue that I am imposing a parental *duty* to genetic ignorance. If this is the case, a difficult conceptual problem occurs. This is because duties ought to have an object, a child in this case. Thus, how can prospective parents have any parental duties if there does not exist a child or even an embryo to whom they could have duties in the first place?

Duty to act in a certain manner does not, however, necessarily require the existence of the party to whom these duties are directed.

Certain intentions in themselves create positions with concomitant duties. . . . By deciding to procreate prospective parents put themselves into the parental position. . . . Why have I then avoided talking about a duty to ignore genetic information and used an expression such as advisable? This is due to the complicated reality of impairments and their effects on the well-being of individuals. Even if the arguments presented in this paper regarding the social nature of the undesirability of impairments were found plausible, it would be dishonest to deny that impairments in themselves often have negative implications (such as pain and other medical problems) on people's well-being. Partly because of this, it seems highly counter-intuitive and unacceptable to suggest that impairments are neutral conditions and that we should not try to reduce their incidence. If they were, why worry about, for example, road safety, gun control, inoculation programmes, and mine-clearance? And although it can reasonably be claimed that impairment is the inherent nature of humanity and that all humans face limitations in their lives, it is also true that the level of impairments and limitations varies from the trivial to the profound. . . .

Thus, although traditional reasons offered for the unfortunateness of impairments are not convincing and even if parenthood should be an unconditional project, imposing on parents a categorical duty to have any kind of child seems unreasonable. This appears to lead into the conclusion that the final judgement and decision should be that of the parents to make. The empirical reality in which reproductive choices are made . . . is too complex for almost any universal moral norm to capture. This does not, of course, prevent us from examining and criticising ethical arguments and choices, that is, to do what philosophers are supposed to do.

Study Questions

1. According to Vehmas, why is genetics not an enterprise beyond moral suspicion?
2. According to Vehmas, do impairments necessarily endanger a child's well-being?
3. According to Vehmas, does the duty to act in a certain manner require the existence of the party to whom these duties are directed?
4. Contrasted with Shakespeare, Bach, or Einstein, are all of us cognitively impaired?

Procreative Beneficence

Julian Savulescu

Julian Savulescu is Director of the Oxford Uehiro Centre for Practical Ethics. He argues for the principle of procreative beneficence, according to which we should select, out of all the possible children we could have, the child who is expected to have at least as good a life as all the others. Savulescu concludes that we should use prenatal testing to afford potential parents both free choice as to which child to have and non-coercive advice as to which child will be expected to have the best life.

Introduction

Imagine you are having in vitro fertilisation (IVF) and you produce four embryos. One is to be implanted. You are told that there is a genetic test for predisposition to scoring well on IQ tests (let's call this intelligence). If an embryo has gene subtypes (alleles) A, B there is a greater than 50% chance it will score more than 140 if given an ordinary education and upbringing. If it has subtypes C, D there is a much lower chance it will score over 140. Would you test the four embryos for these gene subtypes and use this information in selecting which embryo to implant? . . .

Many people believe that research into the genetic contribution to intelligence should not be performed, and that if genetic tests which predict intelligence, or a range of intelligence, are ever developed, they should not be employed in reproductive decision-making. I will argue that we have a moral obligation to test for genetic contribution to non-disease states such as intelligence and to use this information in reproductive decision-making.

From Julian Savulescu, "Procreative Beneficence: Why We Should Select the Best Children," *Bioethics* 15 (2001).

Imagine now you are invited to play the Wheel of Fortune. A giant wheel exists with marks on it from 0–$1,000,000, in $100 increments. The wheel is spun in a secret room. It stops randomly on an amount. That amount is put into Box A. The wheel is spun again. The amount which comes up is put into Box B. You can choose Box A or B. You are also told that, in addition to the sum already put in the boxes, if you choose B, a [die] will be thrown and you will lose $100 if it comes up 6.

Which box should you choose?

The rational answer is Box A. Choosing genes for non-disease states is like playing the Wheel of Fortune. You should use all the available information and choose the option most likely to bring about the best outcome.

Procreative Beneficence: The Moral Obligation to Have the Best Children

I will argue for a principle which I call Procreative Beneficence:

> couples (or single reproducers) should select the child, of the possible children they could have, who is expected to have the best life, or at least as good a life as the others, based on the relevant, available information.

I will argue that Procreative Beneficence implies couples should employ genetic tests for non-disease traits in selecting which child to bring into existence and that we should allow selection for non-disease genes in some cases even if this maintains or increases social inequality. . . .

Definitions

A disease gene is a gene which causes a genetic disorder (e.g. cystic fibrosis) or predisposes to the development of disease (e.g. the genetic contribution to cancer or dementia). A non-disease gene is a gene which causes or predisposes to some physical or psychological state of the person which is not itself a disease state, e.g. height, intelligence, character (not in the subnormal range).

Selection

It is currently possible to select from a range of possible children we could have. This is most frequently done by employing fetal selection through prenatal testing and termination of pregnancy. Selection of embryos is now possible by employing in vitro fertilization and preimplantation genetic diagnosis (PGD). There are currently no genetic tests available for non-disease states except sex. However, if such tests become available in the future, both PGD and prenatal testing could be used to select offspring on the basis of non-disease genes. Selection of sex by PGD is now undertaken in Sydney, Australia. PGD will also lower the threshold for couples to engage in selection since it has fewer psychological sequelae than prenatal testing and abortion.

In the future, it may be possible to select gametes according to their genetic characteristics. This is currently possible for sex, where methods have been developed to sort X and Y bearing sperm.[1]

Behavioural Genetics

Behavioural Genetics is a branch of genetics which seeks to understand the contribution of genes to complex behaviour. . . .

An Argument for Procreative Beneficence

Consider the *Simple Case of Selection for Disease Genes.* A couple is having IVF in an attempt to have a child. It produces two embryos. A battery of tests for common diseases is performed. Embryo A has no abnormalities on the tests performed. Embryo B has no abnormalities on the tests performed except its genetic profile reveals it has a predisposition to developing asthma. Which embryo should be implanted?

Embryo B has nothing to be said in its favour over A and something against it. Embryo A should (on pain of irrationality) be implanted. This is like choosing Box A in the Wheel of Fortune analogy.

Why shouldn't we select the embryo with a predisposition to asthma? What is relevant about asthma is that it reduces quality of life. Attacks cause severe breathlessness and in extreme cases, death. Steroids may be required to treat it. These are among the most dangerous drugs which exist if taken long term. Asthma can be lifelong and require lifelong drug treatment. Ultimately it can leave the sufferer wheelchair bound with chronic obstructive airways disease. The morally relevant property of 'asthma' is that it is a state which reduces the well-being a person experiences.

Defence of Voluntary Procreative Beneficence in the Simple Case

The following example supports Procreative Beneficence. A woman has rubella. If she conceives now, she will have a blind and deaf child. If she waits three months, she will conceive another different but healthy child. She should choose to wait until her rubella is passed.

Or consider the Nuclear Accident. A poor country does not have enough power to provide power to its citizens during an extremely cold winter. The government decides to open an old and unsafe nuclear reactor. Ample light and heating are then available. Citizens stay up later, and enjoy their lives much more. Several months later, the nuclear reactor melts down and large amounts of radiation are released into the environment. The only effect is that a large number of children are subsequently born with predispositions to early childhood malignancy.

The supply of heating and light has changed the lifestyle of this population. As a result of this change in lifestyle, people have conceived children at different times than they would have if there had been no heat or light, and their parents went to bed earlier. Thus, the children born after the nuclear accident would not have existed if the government had not switched to nuclear power. They have not been harmed by the switch to nuclear power and the subsequent accident (unless their lives are so bad they are worse than death). If we object to the Nuclear Accident (which most of us would), then we must appeal to some form of harmless wrongdoing. That is, we must claim that a wrong was done, but no one was harmed. We must appeal to something like the Principle of Procreative Beneficence.

An Objection to Procreative Beneficence in the Simple Case

The following objection to Procreative Beneficence is common.

> 'If you choose Embryo A (without a predisposition to asthma), you could be discarding someone like Mozart or an olympic swimmer. So there is no good reason to select A.'

It is true that by choosing A, you could be discarding a person like Mozart. But it is equally true that if you choose B, you could be discarding someone like Mozart without asthma. A and B are equally likely (on the information available) to be someone like Mozart (and B is more likely to have asthma).

Other Principles of Reproductive Decision-Making Applied to the Simple Case

The principle of Procreative Beneficence supports selecting the embryo without the genetic predisposition to asthma. That seems intuitively correct. How do other principles of reproductive decision-making apply to this example?

1. *Procreative Autonomy:* This principle claims that couples should be free to decide when and how to procreate, and what kind of children to have.[2] If this were the only decision-guiding principle, it would imply couples might have reason to choose the embryo with a predisposition to asthma, if for some reason they wanted that.
2. *Principle of Non-Directive Counselling:* According to this principle, doctors and genetic counsellors should only provide information about risk and options available to reduce that risk.[3] They should not give advice or other direction. Thus, if a couple wanted to transfer Embryo B, and they knew that it would have a predisposition to asthma, nothing more is to be said according to Non-Directive Counselling.
3. *The 'Best Interests of the Child' Principle:* Legislation in Australia and the United Kingdom related to reproduction gives great weight to consideration of the best interests of the child. For example, the Victorian Infertility Treatment Act 1995 states '*the welfare and interests of any person born or to be born as a result of a treatment procedure are paramount.*'[4] This principle is irrelevant to this choice. The couple could choose the embryo with the predisposition to asthma and still be doing everything possible in the interests of *that* child.

None of the alternative principles give appropriate direction in the Simple Case.

Moving from Disease Genes to Non-Disease Genes: What Is the 'Best Life'?

It is not asthma (or disease) which is important, but its impact on a life in ways that matter which is important. People often trade length of life for non–health-related well-being. Non-disease genes may prevent us from leading the best life.

By 'best life', I will understand the life with the most well-being. There are various theories of well-being: hedonistic, desire-fulfilment, objective list theories. According to hedonistic theories, what matters is the quality of our experiences, for example, that we experience pleasure. According to desire-fulfilment theories, what matters is the degree to which our desires are satisfied. According to objective list theories, certain activities are good for people, such as achieving worthwhile things with your life, having dignity, having children and raising them, gaining knowledge of the world, developing one's talents, appreciating beautiful things, and so on.

On any of these theories, some non-disease genes will affect the likelihood that we will lead the best life. Imagine there is a gene which contributes significantly to a violent, explosive, uncontrollable temper, and that state causes people significant suffering. Violent outbursts lead a person to come in conflict with the law and fall out of important social relations. The loss of independence, dignity and important social relations are bad on any of the three accounts. . . .

Consider another example. Memory (M) is the ability to remember important things when you want to. Imagine there is some genetic contribution to M: Six alleles (genes) contribute to M. IVF produces four embryos. Should we test for M profiles?

Does M relate to well-being? Having to go to the supermarket twice because you forgot the baby formula prevents you doing more worthwhile things. Failing to remember can have disastrous consequences. Indeed, forgetting the compass on a long bush walk can be fatal. There is, then, a positive obligation to test for M and select the embryo (other things being equal) with the best M profile.

Does being intelligent mean one is more likely to have a better life? At a folk intuitive level, it seems plausible that intelligence would promote well-being on any plausible account of well-being. On a hedonistic account, the capacity to imagine alternative pleasures and remember the salient features of past experiences is important in choosing the best life. On a desire-fulfilment theory, intelligence is important to choosing means which will best satisfy one's ends. On an objective list account, intelligence would be important to gaining knowledge of the world, and developing rich social relations. . . .

Choice of Means of Selecting

This argument extends in principle to selection of fetuses using prenatal testing and termination of affected pregnancy. However, selection by abortion has greater psychological harms than selection by PGD and these need to be considered. Gametic selection, if it is ever possible, will have the lowest psychological cost.

Objections to the Principle of Procreative Beneficence Applied to Non-Disease Genes

1. *Harm to the child:* One common objection to genetic selection for non-disease traits is that it results in harm to the child. There are various versions of this objection, which include the harm which arises from excessive and overbearing parental expectations, using the child as a means, and not treating it as an end, and closing off possible future options on the basis of the information provided (failing to respect the child's 'right to an open future').

There are a number of responses. Firstly, in some cases, it is possible to deny that the harms will be significant. Parents come to love the child whom they have (even a child with a serious disability). Moreover, some have argued that counselling can reduce excessive expectations.[5]

Secondly, we can accept some risk of a child experiencing some state of reduced well-being in cases of selection. One variant of the harm to child objection is: 'If you select embryo A, it might still get asthma, or worse, cancer, or have a much worse life than B, and you would be responsible.' Yet selection is immune to this objection (in a way which genetic manipulation is not).

Imagine you select Embryo A and it develops cancer (or severe asthma) in later life. You have not harmed A unless A's life is not worth living (hardly plausible) because A would not have existed if you had acted otherwise. A is not made worse off than A would otherwise have been, since without the selection, A would not have existed. Thus we can accept the possibility of a bad outcome, but not the probability of a very bad outcome. (Clearly, Procreative Beneficence demands that we not choose a child with a low predisposition to asthma but who is likely to have a high predisposition to cancer.)

This is different to genetic manipulation. Imagine you perform gene therapy to correct a predisposition to asthma and you cause a mutation which results in cancer later in life. You have harmed A: A is worse off in virtue of the genetic manipulation than A would have been if the manipulation had not been performed (assuming cancer is worse than asthma).

There is, then, an important distinction between:

- interventions which are genetic manipulations of a single gamete, embryo or fetus
- selection procedures (e.g. sex selection) which select from among a range of different gametes, embryos and fetuses.

2. *Inequality:* One objection to Procreative Beneficence is that it will maintain or increase inequality. For example, it is often argued that selection for sex, intelligence, favourable physical or psychological traits, etc. all contribute to inequality in society, and this is a reason not to attempt to select the best.

In the case of selection against disease genes, similar claims are made. For example, one version of the *Disability Discrimination Claim* maintains that prenatal testing for disabilities such as Down syndrome results in discrimination against those with those disabilities both by:

- the statement it makes about the worth of such lives
- the reduction in the numbers of people with this condition.

Even if the Disability Discrimination Claim were true, it would be a drastic step in favour of equality to inflict a higher risk of having a child with a disability on a couple (who do not want a child with a disability) to promote social equality.

Consider a hypothetical rubella epidemic. A rubella epidemic hits an isolated population. Embryos produced prior to the epidemic are not at an elevated risk of any abnormality but those produced during the epidemic are at an increased risk of deafness and blindness. Doctors should encourage women to use embryos which they have produced prior to the epidemic in preference to ones produced during the epidemic. The reason is that it is bad that blind and deaf children are born when sighted and hearing children could have been born in their place.

This does not necessarily imply that the lives of those who now live with disability are less deserving of respect and are less valuable. To attempt to prevent accidents which cause paraplegia is not to say that paraplegics are less deserving of respect. It is important to distinguish between disability and persons with disability. Selection reduces the former, but is silent on the value of the latter. There are better ways to make statements about the equality of people with disability (e.g., we could direct savings from selection against embryos/fetuses with genetic abnormalities to improving well-being of existing people with disabilities).

These arguments extend to selection for non-disease genes. It is not disease which is important but its impact on well-being. In so far as a non-disease gene such as a gene for intelligence impacts on a person's well-being, parents have a reason to select for it, even if inequality results.

This claim can have counter-intuitive implications. Imagine in a country women are severely discriminated against. They are abandoned as children, refused paid employment and serve as slaves to men. Procreative Beneficence implies that couples should test for sex, and should choose males as they are expected to have better lives in this society, even if this reinforces the discrimination against women.

There are several responses. Firstly, it is unlikely selection on a scale that contributes to inequality would promote well-being. Imagine that 50% of the population choose to select boys. This would result in three boys to every one girl. The life of a male in such a society would be intolerable.

Secondly, it is social institutional reform, not interference in reproduction, which should be promoted. What is wrong in such a society is the treatment of women, which should be addressed separately to reproductive decision-making. Reproduction should not become an instrument of social change, at least not mediated or motivated at a social level.

This also illustrates why Procreative Beneficence is different to eugenics. Eugenics is selective breeding to produce a better *population*. A *public interest* justification for interfering in reproduction is different from Procreative Beneficence which aims at producing the best child, of the possible children, a couple could have. That is an essentially private enterprise. It was the eugenics movement itself which sought to influence reproduction, through involuntary sterilisation, to promote social goods. . . .

In virtually all cases of social inequality, there are other avenues to correct inequality than encouraging or forcing people to have children with disabilities or lives of restricted genetic opportunity.

CONCLUSIONS

With respect to non-disease genes, we should provide:

- information (through PGD and prenatal testing)
- free choice of which child to have
- non-coercive advice as to which child will be expected to enter life with the best opportunity of having the best life.

Selection for non-disease genes which significantly impact on well-being is *morally required* (Procreative Beneficence). . . .

Notes

1. E. F. Fugger, S. H. Black, K. Keyvanfar, J. D. Schulman. Births of normal daughters after Microsort sperm separation and intrauterine insemination, in-vitro fertilization, or intracytoplasmic sperm injection. *Hum Reprod* 1998; 13: 2367–70.
2. R. Dworkin. 1993. *Life's Dominion: An Argument about Abortion and Euthanasia.* London. Harper Collins; J. Harris. Goodbye Dolly? The ethics of human cloning. *Journal of Medical Ethics* 1997; 23: 353–60; J. Harris. 1998. Rights and Reproductive Choice, in *The Future of Reproduction,* J. Harris and S. Holm, eds. Oxford. Clarendon Press.
3. J. A. F. Roberts. 1959. *An introduction to human genetics.* Oxford. OUP.
4. The *Human Fertilization and Embryology Act 1990* in England requires that account be taken of the welfare of any child who will be born by assisted reproduction before issuing a licence for assistance (S.13(5)).
5. J. Robertson. Preconception Sex Selection. *American Journal of Bioethics* 1:1 (Winter 2001).

Study Questions

1. According to Savulescu, what is the principle of Procreative Beneficence?
2. Does the case for adhering to the principle of Procreative Beneficence depend on a particular conception of the best life?
3. Does the choice of which child to bring into existence cause harm to anyone?
4. Does the principle of Procreative Beneficence encourage parents to infringe on another person's decision how best to live?

The Case against Perfection

Michael J. Sandel

Michael J. Sandel is Professor of Government at Harvard University. He warns against the use of genetic enhancement on the grounds that it would change our attitudes toward ourselves and our place in the world. In particular, he argues that we would no longer be able to honor our talents as gifts of nature. This shift in attitude would lead us to believe we are self-made and self-sufficient, eroding our humility and sense of solidarity with others.

Breakthroughs in genetics present us with a promise and a predicament. The promise is that we may soon be able to treat and prevent a host of debilitating diseases. The predicament is that our newfound genetic knowledge may also enable us to manipulate our own nature—to enhance our muscles, memories, and moods; to choose the sex, height, and other genetic traits of our children; to make ourselves "better than well." When science moves faster than moral understanding, as it does today, men and women struggle to articulate their unease. . . .

Consider cloning. The birth of Dolly the cloned sheep, in 1997, brought a torrent of concern about the prospect of cloned human beings. There are good medical reasons to worry. Most scientists agree that cloning is unsafe, likely to produce offspring with serious abnormalities. (Dolly recently died a premature death.) But suppose technology improved to the point where clones were at no greater risk than naturally conceived offspring. Would human cloning still be objectionable? Should our hesitation be moral as well as medical?

From Michael J. Sandel, "The Case Against Perfectionism: What's Wrong with Designer Children, Bionic Athletes, and Genetic Engineering?" *Atlantic Monthly* (2004).

What, exactly, is wrong with creating a child who is a genetic twin of one parent, or of an older sibling who has tragically died—or, for that matter, of an admired scientist, sports star, or celebrity?

Some say cloning is wrong because it violates the right to autonomy: by choosing a child's genetic makeup in advance, parents deny the child's right to an open future. A similar objection can be raised against any form of bioengineering that allows parents to select or reject genetic characteristics. According to this argument, genetic enhancements for musical talent, say, or athletic prowess, would point children toward particular choices, and so designer children would never be fully free.

At first glance the autonomy argument seems to capture what is troubling about human cloning and other forms of genetic engineering. It is not persuasive, for two reasons. First, it wrongly implies that absent a designing parent, children are free to choose their characteristics for themselves. But none of us chooses his genetic inheritance. The alternative to a cloned or genetically enhanced child is not one whose future is unbound by particular talents but one at the mercy of the genetic lottery.

Second, even if a concern for autonomy explains some of our worries about made-to-order children, it cannot explain our moral hesitation about people who seek genetic remedies or enhancements for themselves. Gene therapy on somatic (that is, nonreproductive) cells, such as muscle cells and brain cells, repairs or replaces defective genes. The moral quandary arises when people use such therapy not to cure a disease but to reach beyond health, to enhance their physical or cognitive capacities, to lift themselves above the norm.

Like cosmetic surgery, genetic enhancement employs medical means for nonmedical ends—ends unrelated to curing or preventing disease or repairing injury. But unlike cosmetic surgery, genetic enhancement is more than skin-deep. If we are ambivalent about surgery or Botox injections for sagging chins and furrowed brows, we are all the more troubled by genetic engineering for stronger bodies, sharper memories, greater intelligence, and happier moods. The question is whether we are right to be troubled, and if so, on what grounds.

In order to grapple with the ethics of enhancement, we need to confront questions largely lost from view—questions about the moral status of nature, and about the proper stance of human beings toward the given world. Since these questions verge on theology, modern philosophers and political theorists tend to shrink from them.

But our new powers of biotechnology make them unavoidable. To see why this is so, consider four examples already on the horizon: muscle enhancement, memory enhancement, growth-hormone treatment, and reproductive technologies that enable parents to choose the sex and some genetic traits of their children. In each case what began as an attempt to treat a disease or prevent a genetic disorder now beckons as an instrument of improvement and consumer choice.

Muscles

Everyone would welcome a gene therapy to alleviate muscular dystrophy and to reverse the debilitating muscle loss that comes with old age. But what if the same therapy were used to improve athletic performance? Researchers have developed a synthetic gene that, when injected into the muscle cells of mice, prevents and even reverses natural muscle deterioration. The gene not only repairs wasted or injured muscles but also strengthens healthy ones. This success bodes well for human applications. H. Lee Sweeney, of the University of Pennsylvania, who leads the research, hopes his discovery will cure the immobility that afflicts the elderly. But Sweeney's bulked-up mice have already attracted the attention of athletes seeking a competitive edge. Although the therapy is not yet approved for human use, the prospect of genetically enhanced weight lifters, home-run sluggers, linebackers, and sprinters is easy to imagine. The widespread use of steroids and other performance-improving drugs in professional sports suggests that many athletes will be eager to avail themselves of genetic enhancement.

Suppose for the sake of argument that muscle-enhancing gene therapy, unlike steroids, turned out to be safe—or at least no riskier than a rigorous weight-training regimen. Would there be a reason to ban its use in sports? There is something unsettling about the image of genetically altered athletes lifting SUVs or hitting 650-foot home runs or running a three-minute mile. But what, exactly, is troubling about it? Is it simply that we find such superhuman spectacles too bizarre to contemplate? Or does our unease point to something of ethical significance?

It might be argued that a genetically enhanced athlete, like a drug-enhanced athlete, would have an unfair advantage over his unenhanced competitors. But the fairness argument against enhancement has a fatal flaw: it has always been the case that some athletes are better endowed genetically than others, and yet we do not consider this to undermine the fairness of competitive sports. From the standpoint of fairness, enhanced genetic differences would be no worse than natural ones, assuming they were safe and made available to all. If genetic enhancement in sports is morally objectionable, it must be for reasons other than fairness.

Memory

Genetic enhancement is possible for brains as well as brawn. In the mid-1990s scientists managed to manipulate a memory-linked gene in fruit flies, creating flies with photographic memories. More recently researchers have produced smart mice by inserting extra copies of a memory-related gene into mouse embryos. The altered mice learn more quickly and remember things longer than normal mice. The extra copies were programmed to remain active even in old age, and the improvement was passed on to offspring.

Human memory is more complicated, but biotech companies, including Memory Pharmaceuticals, are in hot pursuit of memory-enhancing drugs, or "cognition enhancers," for human beings. The obvious market for such drugs consists of those who suffer from Alzheimer's and other serious memory disorders. The companies also have their sights on a bigger market: the 81 million Americans over fifty, who are beginning to encounter the memory loss that comes naturally with age. A drug that reversed age-related memory loss would be a bonanza for the pharmaceutical industry: a Viagra for the brain. Such use would straddle the line between remedy and enhancement. Unlike a treatment for Alzheimer's, it would cure no disease; but insofar as it restored capacities a person once possessed, it would have a remedial aspect. It could also have purely nonmedical uses: for example, by a lawyer cramming to memorize facts for an upcoming trial, or by a business executive eager to learn Mandarin on the eve of his departure for Shanghai.

Some who worry about the ethics of cognitive enhancement point to the danger of creating two classes of human beings: those with access to enhancement technologies, and those who must make do with their natural capacities. And if the enhancements could be passed down the generations, the two classes might eventually become subspecies—the enhanced and the merely natural. But worry about access ignores the moral status of enhancement itself. Is the scenario troubling because the unenhanced poor would be denied the benefits of bioengineering, or because the enhanced affluent would somehow be dehumanized? As with muscles, so with memory: the fundamental question is not how to ensure equal access to enhancement but whether we should aspire to it in the first place.

Height

Pediatricians already struggle with the ethics of enhancement when confronted by parents who want to make their children taller. Since the 1980s human growth hormone has been approved for children with a hormone deficiency that makes them much shorter than average. But the treatment also increases the height of healthy children. Some parents of healthy children who are unhappy with their stature (typically boys) ask why it should make a difference whether a child is short because of a hormone deficiency or because his parents happen to be short. Whatever the cause, the social consequences are the same.

In the face of this argument some doctors began prescribing hormone treatments for children whose short stature was unrelated to any medical problem. By 1996 such "off-label" use accounted for 40 percent of human-growth-hormone prescriptions. Although it is legal to prescribe drugs for purposes not approved by the Food and Drug Administration, pharmaceutical companies cannot promote such use. Seeking to expand its market, Eli Lilly & Co. recently persuaded the FDA to approve its human growth hormone for healthy children whose projected adult height is in the bottom one percentile—under five feet three inches for boys and four feet eleven inches for girls. This concession raises a large question about the ethics of enhancement: If hormone treatments need not be limited to those with hormone deficiencies, why should they be available only to very short children? Why shouldn't all shorter-than-average children be able to seek treatment? And what about a child of average height who wants to be taller so that he can make the basketball team?

Some oppose height enhancement on the grounds that it is collectively self-defeating; as some become taller, others become shorter relative to the norm. . . . As the unenhanced began to feel shorter, they, too, might seek treatment, leading to a hormonal arms race that left everyone worse off, especially those who couldn't afford to buy their way up from shortness.

But the arms-race objection is not decisive on its own. Like the fairness objection to bioengineered muscles and memory, it leaves unexamined the attitudes and dispositions that prompt the drive for enhancement.

If we were bothered only by the injustice of adding shortness to the problems of the poor, we could remedy that unfairness by publicly subsidizing height enhancements. As for the relative height deprivation suffered by innocent bystanders, we could compensate them by taxing those who buy their way to greater height. The real question is whether we want to live in a society where parents feel compelled to spend a fortune to make perfectly healthy kids a few inches taller.

Sex Selection

Perhaps the most inevitable nonmedical use of bioengineering is sex selection. For centuries parents have been trying to choose the sex of their children. Today biotech succeeds where folk remedies failed.

One technique for sex selection arose with prenatal tests using amniocentesis and ultrasound. These medical technologies were developed to detect genetic abnormalities such as spina bifida and Down syndrome. But they can also reveal the sex of the fetus—allowing for the abortion of a fetus of an undesired sex. Even among those who favor abortion rights, few advocate abortion simply because the parents do not want a girl. Nevertheless, in traditional societies with a powerful cultural preference for boys, this practice has become widespread.

Sex selection need not involve abortion, however. For couples undergoing *in vitro* fertilization (IVF), it is possible to choose the sex of the child before the fertilized egg is implanted in the womb. One method makes use of pre-implantation genetic diagnosis (PGD), a procedure developed to screen for genetic diseases. Several eggs are fertilized in a petri dish and grown to the eight-cell stage (about three days). At that point the embryos are tested to determine their sex. Those of the desired sex are implanted; the others are typically discarded. Although few couples are likely to undergo the difficulty and expense of IVF simply to choose the sex of their child, embryo screening is a highly reliable means of sex selection. And as our genetic knowledge increases, it may be possible to use PGD to cull embryos carrying undesired genes, such as those associated with obesity, height, and skin color. . . .

The Genetics & IVF Institute, a for-profit infertility clinic in Fairfax, Virginia, now offers a sperm-sorting technique that makes it possible to choose the sex of one's child before it is conceived. X-bearing sperm, which produce girls, carry more DNA than Y-bearing sperm, which produce boys; a device called a flow cytometer can separate them. The process, called MicroSort, has a high rate of success.

If sex selection by sperm sorting is objectionable, it must be for reasons that go beyond the debate about the moral status of the embryo. One such reason is that sex selection is an instrument of sex discrimination—typically against girls, as illustrated by the chilling sex ratios in India and China. Some speculate that societies with substantially more men than women will be less stable, more violent, and more prone to crime or war. These are legitimate worries—but the sperm-sorting company has a clever way of addressing them. It offers MicroSort only to couples who want to choose the sex of a child for purposes of "family balancing." Those with more sons than daughters may choose a girl, and vice versa. But customers may not use the technology to stock up on children of the same sex, or even to choose the sex of their firstborn child. (So far the majority of MicroSort clients have chosen girls.) Under restrictions of this kind, do any ethical issues remain that should give us pause?

The case of MicroSort helps us isolate the moral objections that would persist if muscle-enhancement, memory-enhancement, and height-enhancement technologies were safe and available to all.

It is commonly said that genetic enhancements undermine our humanity by threatening our capacity to act freely, to succeed by our own efforts, and to consider ourselves responsible—worthy of praise or blame—for the things we do and for the way we are. It is one thing to hit seventy home runs as the result of disciplined training and effort, and something else, something less, to hit them with the help of steroids or genetically enhanced muscles. Of course, the roles of effort and enhancement will be a matter of degree. But as the role of enhancement increases, our admiration for the achievement fades—or, rather, our admiration for the achievement shifts from the player to his pharmacist. This suggests that our moral response to enhancement is a response to the diminished agency of the person whose achievement is enhanced.

Though there is much to be said for this argument, I do not think the main problem with enhancement and genetic engineering is that they undermine effort and erode human agency. The deeper danger is that they represent a kind of hyperagency—a Promethean aspiration to remake nature, including human nature, to serve our purposes and satisfy our desires. The problem is not the drift to mechanism but the drive to mastery. And what the drive to mastery misses and may even destroy is an appreciation of the gifted character of human powers and achievements.

To acknowledge the giftedness of life is to recognize that our talents and powers are not wholly our own doing, despite the effort we expend to develop and to exercise them. It is also to recognize that not everything in the world is open to whatever use we may desire or devise. Appreciating the gifted quality of life constrains the Promethean project and conduces to a certain humility. It is in part a religious sensibility. But its resonance reaches beyond religion.

It is difficult to account for what we admire about human activity and achievement without drawing upon some version of this idea. Consider two types of athletic achievement. We appreciate players like Pete Rose, who are not blessed with great natural gifts but who manage, through striving, grit, and determination, to excel in their sport. But we also admire players like Joe DiMaggio, who display natural gifts with grace and effortlessness. Now, suppose we learned that both players took performance-enhancing drugs. Whose turn to drugs would we find more deeply disillusioning? Which aspect of the athletic ideal—effort or gift—would be more deeply offended?

Some might say effort: the problem with drugs is that they provide a shortcut, a way to win without striving. But striving is not the point of sports; excellence is. And excellence consists at least partly in the display of natural talents and gifts that are no doing of the athlete who possesses them. This is an uncomfortable fact for democratic societies. We want to believe that success, in sports and in life, is something we earn, not something we inherit. Natural gifts, and the admiration they inspire, embarrass the meritocratic faith; they cast doubt on the conviction that praise and rewards flow from effort alone. In the face of this embarrassment we inflate the moral significance of striving, and depreciate giftedness. This distortion can be seen, for example, in network-television coverage of the Olympics, which focuses less on the feats the athletes perform than on heartrending stories of the hardships they have overcome and the struggles they have waged to triumph over an injury or a difficult upbringing or political turmoil in their native land.

But effort isn't everything. No one believes that a mediocre basketball player who works and trains even harder than Michael Jordan deserves greater acclaim or a bigger contract. The real problem with genetically altered athletes is that they corrupt athletic competition as a human activity that honors the cultivation and display of natural talents. From this standpoint, enhancement can be seen as the ultimate expression of the ethic of effort and willfulness—a kind of high-tech striving. The ethic of willfulness and the biotechnological powers it now enlists are arrayed against the claims of giftedness.

The ethic of giftedness, under siege in sports, persists in the practice of parenting. But here, too, bioengineering and genetic enhancement threaten to dislodge it. To appreciate children as gifts is to accept them as they come, not as objects of our design or products of our will or instruments of our ambition. Parental love is not contingent on the talents and attributes a child happens to have. We choose our friends and spouses at least partly on the basis of qualities we find attractive. But we do not choose our children. Their qualities are unpredictable, and even the most conscientious parents cannot be held wholly responsible for the kind of children they have. . . .

[T]he deepest moral objection to enhancement lies less in the perfection it seeks than in the human disposition it expresses and promotes. The problem is not that parents usurp the autonomy of a child they design. The problem lies in the hubris of the designing parents, in their drive to master the mystery of birth. Even if this disposition did not make parents tyrants to their children, it would disfigure the relation between parent and child, and deprive the parent of the humility and enlarged human sympathies that an openness to the unbidden can cultivate.

To appreciate children as gifts or blessings is not, of course, to be passive in the face of illness or disease. Medical intervention to cure or prevent illness or restore the injured to health does not desecrate nature but honors it. Healing sickness or injury does not override a child's natural capacities but permits them to flourish. . . .

The mandate to mold our children, to cultivate and improve them, complicates the case against enhancement. We usually admire parents who seek the best for their children, who spare no effort to help them achieve happiness and success. Some parents confer advantages on their children by enrolling them in expensive schools, hiring private tutors, sending them to tennis camp, providing them with piano lessons, ballet lessons, swimming lessons, SAT-prep courses, and so on. If it is permissible and even admirable for parents to help their children in these ways, why isn't it equally admirable for parents to use whatever genetic technologies may emerge (provided they are safe) to enhance their children's intelligence, musical ability, or athletic prowess?

The defenders of enhancement are right to this extent: improving children through genetic engineering is similar in spirit to the heavily managed, high-pressure child-rearing that is now common. But this similarity does not vindicate genetic enhancement. On the contrary, it highlights a problem with the trend toward hyperparenting. One conspicuous example of this trend is sports-crazed parents bent on making champions of their children. Another is the frenzied drive of overbearing parents to mold and manage their children's academic careers. . . . This demand for performance and perfection animates the impulse to rail against the given. It is the deepest source of the moral trouble with enhancement.

Some see a clear line between genetic enhancement and other ways that people seek improvement in their children and themselves. Genetic manipulation seems somehow worse—more intrusive, more sinister—than other ways of enhancing performance and seeking success. But morally speaking, the difference is less significant than it seems. Bioengineering gives us reason to question the low-tech, high-pressure child-rearing practices we commonly accept. The hyperparenting familiar in our time represents an anxious excess of mastery and dominion that misses the sense of life as a gift. . . .

The shadow of eugenics hangs over today's debates about genetic engineering and enhancement. Critics of genetic engineering argue that human cloning, enhancement, and the quest for designer children are nothing more than "privatized" or "free-market" eugenics. Defenders of enhancement reply that genetic choices freely made are not really eugenic—at least not in the pejorative sense. To remove the coercion, they argue, is to remove the very thing that makes eugenic policies repugnant.

Sorting out the lesson of eugenics is another way of wrestling with the ethics of enhancement. The Nazis gave eugenics a bad name. But what, precisely, was wrong with it? Was the old eugenics objectionable only insofar as it was coercive? Or is there something inherently wrong with the resolve to deliberately design our progeny's traits? . . .

A number of political philosophers call for a new "liberal eugenics." They argue that a moral distinction can be drawn between the old eugenic policies and genetic enhancements that do not restrict the autonomy of the child. . . . The problem with the old eugenics was that its burdens fell disproportionately on the weak and the poor, who were unjustly sterilized and segregated. But provided that the benefits and burdens of genetic improvement are fairly distributed, these bioethicists argue, eugenic measures are unobjectionable and may even be morally required.

The libertarian philosopher Robert Nozick proposed a "genetic supermarket" that would enable parents to order children by design without imposing a single design on the society as a whole: "This supermarket system has the great virtue that it involves no centralized decision fixing the future human type(s)."

Even the leading philosopher of American liberalism, John Rawls, in his classic *A Theory of Justice* (1971), offered a brief endorsement of noncoercive eugenics. Even in a society that agrees to share the benefits and burdens of the genetic lottery, it is "in the interest of each to have greater natural assets," Rawls wrote. "This enables him to pursue a preferred plan of life." The parties to the social contract "want to insure for their descendants the best genetic endowment (assuming their own to be fixed)." Eugenic policies are therefore not only permissible but required as a matter of justice. "Thus over time a society is to take steps at least to preserve the general level of natural abilities and to prevent the diffusion of serious defects."

But removing the coercion does not vindicate eugenics. The problem with eugenics and genetic engineering is that they represent the one-sided triumph of willfulness over giftedness, of dominion over reverence, of molding over beholding. Why, we may wonder, should we worry about this triumph? Why not shake off our unease about genetic enhancement as so much superstition? What would be lost if biotechnology dissolved our sense of giftedness?

From a religious standpoint the answer is clear: To believe that our talents and powers are wholly our own doing is to misunderstand our place in creation, to confuse our role with God's. Religion is not the only source of reasons to care about giftedness, however. The moral stakes can also be described in secular terms. If bioengineering made the myth of the "self-made man" come true, it would be difficult to view our talents as gifts for which we are indebted, rather than as achievements for which we are responsible. This would transform three key features of our moral landscape: humility, responsibility, and solidarity.

In a social world that prizes mastery and control, parenthood is a school for humility. That we care deeply about our children and yet cannot choose the kind we want teaches parents to be open to the unbidden. Such openness is a disposition worth affirming, not only within families but in the wider world as well. It invites us to abide the unexpected, to live with dissonance, to rein in the impulse to control. A . . . world in which parents became accustomed to specifying the sex and genetic traits of their children would be a world inhospitable to the unbidden, a gated community writ large. The awareness that our talents and abilities are not wholly our own doing restrains our tendency toward hubris.

Though some maintain that genetic enhancement erodes human agency by overriding effort, the real problem is the explosion, not the erosion, of responsibility. As humility gives way, responsibility expands to daunting proportions. We attribute less to chance and more to choice.

Parents become responsible for choosing, or failing to choose, the right traits for their children. Athletes become responsible for acquiring, or failing to acquire, the talents that will help their teams win.

One of the blessings of seeing ourselves as creatures of nature, God, or fortune is that we are not wholly responsible for the way we are. The more we become masters of our genetic endowments, the greater the burden we bear for the talents we have and the way we perform. Today when a basketball player misses a rebound, his coach can blame him for being out of position. Tomorrow the coach may blame him for being too short. Even now the use of performance-enhancing drugs in professional sports is subtly transforming the expectations players have for one another; on some teams players who take the field free from amphetamines or other stimulants are criticized for "playing naked."

The more alive we are to the chanced nature of our lot, the more reason we have to share our fate with others. Consider insurance. Since people do not know whether or when various ills will befall them, they pool their risk by buying health insurance and life insurance. As life plays itself out, the healthy wind up subsidizing the unhealthy, and those who live to a ripe old age wind up subsidizing the families of those who die before their time. Even without a sense of mutual obligation, people pool their risks and resources and share one another's fate.

But insurance markets mimic solidarity only insofar as people do not know or control their own risk factors. Suppose genetic testing advanced to the point where it could reliably predict each person's medical future and life expectancy. Those confident of good health and long life would opt out of the pool, causing other people's premiums to skyrocket. The solidarity of insurance would disappear as those with good genes fled the actuarial company of those with bad ones.

The fear that insurance companies would use genetic data to assess risks and set premiums recently led the Senate to vote to prohibit genetic discrimination in health insurance. But the bigger danger, admittedly more speculative, is that genetic enhancement, if routinely practiced, would make it harder to foster the moral sentiments that social solidarity requires.

Why, after all, do the successful owe anything to the least-advantaged members of society? The best answer to this question leans heavily on the notion of giftedness. The natural talents that enable the successful to flourish are not their own doing but, rather, their good fortune—a result of the genetic lottery. If our genetic endowments are gifts, rather than achievements for which we can claim credit, it is a mistake and a conceit to assume that we are entitled to the full measure of the bounty they reap in a market economy. We therefore have an obligation to share this bounty with those who, through no fault of their own, lack comparable gifts.

A lively sense of the contingency of our gifts—a consciousness that none of us is wholly responsible for his or her success—saves a meritocratic society from sliding into the smug assumption that the rich are rich because they are more deserving than the poor. Without this, the successful would become even more likely than they are now to view themselves as self-made and self-sufficient, and hence wholly responsible for their success. Those at the bottom of society would be viewed not as disadvantaged, and thus worthy of a measure of compensation, but as simply unfit, and thus worthy of eugenic repair. The meritocracy, less chastened by chance, would become harder, less forgiving. As perfect genetic knowledge would end the simulacrum of solidarity in insurance markets, so perfect genetic control would erode the actual solidarity that arises when men and women reflect on the contingency of their talents and fortunes. . . .

There is something appealing, even intoxicating, about a vision of human freedom unfettered by the given. It may even be the case that the allure of that vision played a part in summoning the genomic age into being. It is often assumed that the powers of enhancement we now possess arose as an inadvertent by-product of biomedical progress—the genetic revolution came, so to speak, to cure disease, and stayed to tempt us with the prospect of enhancing our performance, designing our children, and perfecting our nature. That may have the story backwards. It is more plausible to view genetic engineering as the ultimate expression of our resolve to see ourselves astride the world, the masters of our nature. But that promise of mastery is flawed. It threatens to banish our appreciation of life as a gift, and to leave us with nothing to affirm or behold outside our own will.

Study Questions

1. Why does Sandel believe that the argument from autonomy fails to capture what is wrong with genetic enhancement?
2. What does Sandel mean by "giftedness"?
3. According to Sandel, why does genetic enhancement erode human dignity?
4. To what extent are you responsible for your successes and failures?

C.

Euthanasia

Active and Passive Euthanasia

James Rachels

The American Medical Association takes the position that while at a patient's request a physician may withhold extraordinary means of prolonging the patient's life, a physician may not take steps, even if requested by the patient, to terminate that life intentionally. James Rachels (1941–2003), who was Professor of Philosophy at the University of Alabama at Birmingham, argues that killing is not in itself any worse than letting die, and therefore no moral difference between active and passive euthanasia is defensible.

The distinction between active and passive euthanasia is thought to be crucial for medical ethics. The idea is that it is permissible, at least in some cases, to withhold treatment and allow a patient to die, but it is never permissible to take any direct action designed to kill the patient. This doctrine seems to be accepted by most doctors, and it is endorsed in a statement adopted by the House of

From James Rachels, "Active and Passive Euthanasia," *New England Journal of Medicine* 292 (1975).

Delegates of the American Medical Association on 4 December 1973:

> The intentional termination of the life of one human being by another—mercy killing—is contrary to that for which the medical profession stands and is contrary to the policy of the American Medical Association.
>
> The cessation of the employment of extraordinary means to prolong the life of the body when there is irrefutable evidence that biological death is imminent is the decision of the patient and/or his immediate family. The advice and judgement of the physician should be freely available to the patient and/or his immediate family.

However, a strong case can be made against this doctrine. In what follows I will set out some of the relevant arguments, and urge doctors to reconsider their views on this matter.

To begin with a familiar type of situation, a patient who is dying of incurable cancer of the throat is in terrible pain, which can no longer be satisfactorily alleviated. He is certain to die within a few days, even if present treatment is continued, but he does not want to go on living for those days since the pain is unbearable. So he asks the doctor for an end to it, and his family joins in the request.

Suppose the doctor agrees to withhold treatment, as the conventional doctrine says he may. The justification for his doing so is that the patient is in terrible agony, and since he is going to die anyway, it would be wrong to prolong his suffering needlessly. But now notice this. If one simply withholds treatment, it may take the patient longer to die, and so he may suffer more than he would if more direct action were taken and a lethal injection given. This fact provides strong reason for thinking that, once the initial decision not to prolong his agony has been made, active euthanasia is actually preferable to passive euthanasia, rather than the reverse. To say otherwise is to endorse the opinion that leads to more suffering rather than less, and is contrary to the humanitarian impulse that prompts the decision not to prolong his life in the first place.

Part of my point is that the process of being "allowed to die" can be relatively slow and painful, whereas being given a lethal injection is relatively quick and painless. Let me give a different sort of example. In the United States about one in 600 babies is born with Down's syndrome. Most of these babies are otherwise healthy—that is, with only the usual pediatric care, they will proceed to an otherwise normal infancy. Some, however, are born with congenital defects such as intestinal obstructions that require operations if they are to live.

Sometimes, the parents and the doctor will decide not to operate, and let the infant die. Anthony Shaw describes what happens then:

> When surgery is denied [the doctor] must try to keep the infant from suffering while natural forces sap the baby's life away. As a surgeon whose natural inclination is to use the scalpel to fight off death, standing by and watching a salvageable baby die is the most emotionally exhausting experience I know. It is easy at a conference, in a theoretical discussion to decide that such infants should be allowed to die. It is altogether different to stand by in the nursery and watch as dehydration and infection wither a tiny being over hours and days. This is a terrible ordeal for me and the hospital staff—much more so than for the parents who never set foot in the nursery.[1]

I can understand why some people are opposed to all euthanasia, and insist that such infants must be allowed to live. I think I can also understand why other people favour destroying these babies quickly and painlessly. But why should anyone favour letting "dehydration and infection wither a tiny being over hours and days"? The doctrine that says a baby may be allowed to dehydrate and wither, but may not be given an injection that would end its life without suffering, seems so patently cruel as to require no further refutation. The strong language is not intended to offend, but only to put the point in the clearest possible way.

My second argument is that the conventional doctrine leads to decisions concerning life and death made on irrelevant grounds.

Consider again the case of the infants with Down's syndrome who need operations for congenital defects unrelated to the syndrome to live. Sometimes, there is no operation, and the baby dies, but when there is no such defect, the baby lives on. Now, an operation such as that to remove an intestinal obstruction is not prohibitively difficult. The reason why such operations are not performed in these cases is, clearly, that the child has Down's syndrome and the parents and the doctor judge that because of that fact it is better for the child to die.

But notice that this situation is absurd, no matter what view one takes of the lives and potentials of such babies. If the life of such an infant is worth preserving, what does it matter if it needs a simple operation? Or, if one thinks it better that such a baby should not live on, what difference does it make that it happens to have an unobstructed intestinal tract? In either case, the matter of life and death is being decided on irrelevant grounds. It is the Down's syndrome, and not the intestines, that is the issue. The matter should be decided, if at all, on that basis, and not be allowed to depend on the essentially irrelevant question of whether the intestinal tract is blocked.

What makes this situation possible, of course, is the idea that when there is an intestinal blockage, one can "let the baby die," but when there is no such defect there is nothing that can be done, for one must not "kill" it. The fact that this idea leads to such results as deciding life or death on irrelevant grounds is another good reason why the doctrine would be rejected.

One reason why so many people think that there is an important moral difference between active and passive euthanasia is that they think killing someone is morally worse than letting someone die. But is it? Is killing, in itself, worse than letting die? To investigate this issue, two cases may be considered that are exactly alike except that one involves killing whereas the other involves letting someone die. Then, it can be asked whether this difference makes any difference to the moral assessments. It is important that the cases be exactly alike, except for this one difference, since otherwise one cannot be confident that it is this difference and not some other that accounts for any variation in the assessments of the two cases. So, let us consider this pair of cases:

In the first, Smith stands to gain a large inheritance if anything should happen to his six-year-old cousin. One evening while the child is taking his bath, Smith sneaks into the bathroom and drowns the child, and then arranges things so that it will look like an accident.

In the second, Jones also stands to gain if anything should happen to his six-year-old cousin. Like Smith, Jones sneaks in planning to drown the child in his bath. However, just as he enters the bathroom Jones sees the child slip and hit his head, and fall facedown in the water. Jones is delighted; he stands by, ready to push the child's head back under if it is necessary, but it is not necessary. With only a little thrashing about, the child drowns all by himself, "accidentally," as Jones watches and does nothing.

Now Smith killed the child, whereas Jones "merely" let the child die. That is the only difference between them. Did either man behave better, from a moral point of view? If the difference between killing and letting die were in itself a morally important matter, one should say that Jones's behaviour was less reprehensible than Smith's. But does one really want to say that? I think not. In the first place, both men acted from the same motive, personal gain, and both had exactly the same end in view when they acted. It may be inferred from Smith's conduct that he is a bad man, although that judgement may be withdrawn or modified if certain further facts are learned about him—for example, that he is mentally deranged. But would not the very same thing be inferred about Jones from his conduct? And would not the same further considerations also be relevant to any modification of this judgement? Moreover, suppose

Jones pleaded, in his own defence, "After all, I didn't do anything except just stand there and watch the child drown. I didn't kill him; I only let him die." Again, if letting die were in itself less bad than killing, this defence should have at least some weight. But it does not. Such a "defence" can only be regarded as a grotesque perversion of moral reasoning. Morally speaking, it is no defence at all.

Now, it may be pointed out, quite properly, that the cases of euthanasia with which doctors are concerned are not like this at all. They do not involve personal gain or the destruction of normal, healthy children. Doctors are concerned only with cases in which the patient's life is of no further use to him, or in which the patient's life has become or will soon become a terrible burden. However, the point is the same in these cases: the bare difference between killing and letting die does not, in itself, make a moral difference. If a doctor lets a patient die, for humane reasons, he is in the same moral position as if he had given the patient a lethal injection for humane reasons. If his decision was wrong—if, for example, the patient's illness was in fact curable—the decision would be equally regrettable no matter which method was used to carry it out. And if the doctor's decision was the right one, the method used is not in itself important.

The AMA policy statement isolates the crucial issue very well; the crucial issue is "the intentional termination of the life of one human being by another." But after identifying this issue, and forbidding "mercy killing," the statement goes on to deny that the cessation of treatment is the intentional termination of a life. This is where the mistake comes in, for what is the cessation of treatment, in these circumstances, if it is not "the intentional termination of the life of one human being by another"? Of course it is exactly that, and if it were not, there would be no point to it.

Many people will find this judgement hard to accept. One reason, I think, is that it is very easy to conflate the question of whether killing is, in itself, worse than letting die, with the very different question of whether most actual cases of killing are more reprehensible than most actual cases of letting die. Most actual cases of killing are clearly terrible (think, for example, of all the murders reported in the newspapers), and one hears of such cases every day. On the other hand, one hardly ever hears of a case of letting die, except for the actions of doctors who are motivated by humanitarian reasons. So one learns to think of killing in a much worse light than of letting die. But this does not mean that there is something about killing that makes it in itself worse than letting die, for it is not the bare difference between killing and letting die that makes the difference in these cases. Rather, the other factors—the murderer's motive of personal gain, for example, contrasted with the doctor's humanitarian motivation—account for different reactions to the different cases.

I have argued that killing is not in itself any worse than letting die; if my contention is right, it follows that active euthanasia is not any worse than passive euthanasia. What arguments can be given on the other side? The most common, I believe, is the following:

> The important difference between active and passive euthanasia is that, in passive euthanasia, the doctor does not do anything to bring about the patient's death. The doctor does nothing, and the patient dies of whatever ills already afflict him. In active euthanasia, however, the doctor does something to bring about the patient's death: he kills him. The doctor who gives the patient with cancer a lethal injection has himself caused his patient's death; whereas if he merely ceases treatment, the cancer is the cause of the death.

A number of points need to be made here. The first is that it is not exactly correct to say that in passive euthanasia the doctor does nothing, for he does do one thing that is very important: he lets the patient die. "Letting someone die" is certainly different, in some respects, from other types of action—mainly in that it is a kind of action that one may perform by way of not performing certain other actions. For example, one may let a patient die by way of not giving medication, just as one may insult someone by way of not shaking his hand. But for any purpose of moral assessment, it is a type of action nonetheless. The decision to let a patient die is subject to moral appraisal in the same way that a decision to kill him would be subject to moral appraisal: it may be assessed as wise or unwise, compassionate or sadistic, right or wrong. If a doctor deliberately let a patient die who was suffering from a routinely curable illness, the doctor would certainly be to blame for what he had done, just as he would be to blame if he had needlessly killed the patient. Charges against him would then be appropriate. If so, it would be no defence at all for him to insist that he didn't "do anything." He would have done something very serious indeed, for he let his patient die.

Fixing the cause of death may be very important from a legal point of view, for it may determine whether criminal charges are brought against the doctor. But I do not think that this notion can be used to show a moral difference between active and passive euthanasia. The reason why it is considered bad to be the cause of someone's death is that death is regarded as a great evil—and so it is. However, if it has been decided that euthanasia—even passive euthanasia—is desirable in a given case, it has also been decided that in this instance death is no greater an evil than the patient's continued existence. And if this is true, the usual reason for not wanting to be the cause of someone's death simply does not apply.

Finally, doctors may think that all of this is only of academic interest—the sort of thing that philosophers may worry about but that has no practical bearing on their own work. After all, doctors must be concerned about the legal consequences of what they do, and active euthanasia is clearly forbidden by the law. But even so, doctors should also be concerned with the fact that the law is forcing upon them a moral doctrine that may be indefensible, and has a considerable effect on their practices. Of course, most doctors are not now in the position of being coerced in this matter, for they do not regard themselves as merely going along with what the law requires. Rather, in statements such as the AMA policy statement that I have quoted, they are endorsing this doctrine as a central point of medical ethics. In that statement, active euthanasia is condemned not merely as illegal but as "contrary to that for which the medical profession stands," whereas passive euthanasia is approved. However, the preceding considerations suggest that there is really no moral difference between the two, considered in themselves (there may be important moral differences in some cases in their *consequences*, but, as I pointed out, these differences may make active euthanasia, and not passive euthanasia, the morally preferable option). So, whereas doctors may have to discriminate between active and passive euthanasia to satisfy the law, they should not do any more than that. In particular, they should not give the distinction any added authority and weight by writing it into official statements of medical ethics.

Note

1. Anthony Shaw, "Doctor, Do We Have a Choice?" *New York Times Magazine*, 30 January 1972, p. 54.

Study Questions

1. According to Rachels, in passive euthanasia does the physician do anything?
2. According to Rachels, under what circumstances is active euthanasia morally preferable to passive euthanasia?
3. Is someone who allows another person to drown morally guilty of killing the person?
4. Should the punishment be the same whether you drown someone or allow someone to drown?

Killing and Letting Die

Philippa Foot

Philippa Foot (1920–2010), was Professor of Philosophy at the University of California, Los Angeles. She defends the distinction between killing and letting die on the grounds that only the former case involves an "agent of harm," that is, an originator of a sequence that causes an unfortunate result rather than merely an observer of a sequence who doesn't interfere with it. She concludes by considering the implications of the distinction between killing and letting die for the morality of abortion.

Is there a morally relevant distinction between killing and allowing to die? Many philosophers say that there is not, and further insist that there is no other closely related difference, as for instance that which divides act from omission, whichever plays a part in determining the moral character of an action. James Rachels has argued this case in his well-known article on active and passive euthanasia.[1] . . . I believe that these people are mistaken, and this is what I shall try to show in this essay. I shall first consider the question in abstraction from any particular practical moral problem, and then I shall examine the implications my thesis may have concerning the issue of abortion.

The question with which we are concerned has been dramatically posed by asking whether we are as equally to blame for allowing people in Third World countries to starve to death as we would be for killing them by sending poisoned food? In each case it is true that if we acted differently—by sending good food or by not sending poisoned food—those who are going to die because we do not

From Philippa Foot, "Killing and Letting Die," in *Abortion and Legal Perspectives*, Jay L. Garfield and Patricia Hennessey, eds. (Amherst: University of Massachusetts Press, 1984).

send the good food or do send the poisoned food would not die after all. Our agency plays a part in what happens whichever way they die. Philosophers such as Rachels . . . consider this to be all that matters in determining our guilt or innocence. Or rather . . . that although related things are morally relevant, such as our reasons for acting as we do and the cost of acting otherwise, these are only contingently related to the distinction between doing and allowing. If we hold *them* steady and vary only the way in which our agency enters into the matter, no moral differences will be found. It is of no significance, they say, whether we kill others or let them die, or whether they die by our act or our omission. Whereas these latter differences may at first seem to affect the morality of action, we shall always find on further enquiry that some other difference—such as a difference of motive or cost—has crept in.

Now this, on the face of it, is extremely implausible. We are not inclined to think that it would be no worse to murder to get money for some comfort such as a nice winter coat than it is to keep the money back before sending a donation to Oxfam or Care. We do not think that we might just as well be called murderers for one as for the other. And there are a host of other examples which seem to make the same point. We may have to allow one person to die if saving him would mean that we could not save five others, as for instance when a drug is in short supply and he needs five times as much as each of them, but that does not mean that we could carve up one patient to get "spare parts" for five.

These moral intuitions stand clearly before us, but I do not think it would be right to conclude from the fact that these examples all seem to hang on the contrast between killing and allowing to die that this is precisely the distinction that is important from the moral point of view. For example, having someone killed is not strictly *killing* him, but seems just the same morally speaking; and on the other hand, turning off a respirator might be called killing, although it seems morally indistinguishable from allowing to die. Nor does it seem that the difference between "act" and "omission" is quite what we want, in that a respirator that had to be turned on each morning would not change the moral problems that arise with the ones we have now. Perhaps there is no locution in the language which exactly serves our purposes and we should therefore invent our own vocabulary. Let us mark the distinction we are after by saying that one person may or may not be "the agent" of harm that befalls someone else.

When is one person "the agent" in this special sense of someone else's death, or of some harm other than death that befalls him? This idea can easily be described in a general way. If there are difficulties when it comes to detail, some of these ideas may be best left unsolved, for there may be an area of indefiniteness reflecting the uncertainty that belongs to our moral judgments in some complex and perhaps infrequently encountered situations. The idea of agency, in the sense that we want, seems to be composed of two subsidiary ideas. First, we think of particular effects as the result of particular sequences, as when a certain fatal sequence leads to someone's death. This idea is implied in coroners' verdicts telling us what someone died of, and this concept is not made suspect by the fact that it is sometimes impossible to pick out a single fatal sequence—as in the lawyers' example of the man journeying into the desert who had two enemies, one of whom bored a hole in his water barrel while another filled it with brine. Suppose such complications absent. Then we can pick [out] the fatal sequence and go on to ask who initiated it. If the subject died by poisoning and it was I who put the poison into his drink, then I am the agent of his death; likewise if I shot him and he died of a bullet wound. Of course there are problems about fatal sequences which would have been harmless but for special circumstances, and those which although threatening would have run out harmlessly but for something that somebody did. But we can easily understand the idea that a death comes about through our agency if we send someone poisoned food or cut him up for spare parts, but not (ordinarily) if we fail to save him when he is threatened by accident or disease. Our examples are not problem cases from *this* point of view.

Nor is it difficult to find more examples to drive our original point home, and show that it is sometimes permissible to allow a certain harm to befall someone, although it would have been wrong to bring this harm on him by one's own agency, i.e., by originating or sustaining the sequence which brings the harm. Let us consider, for instance, a pair of cases which I shall call Rescue I and Rescue II. In the first Rescue story we are hurrying in our jeep to save some people—let there be five of them—who are imminently threatened by the ocean tide. We have not a moment to spare, so when we hear of a single person who also needs rescuing from some other disaster we say regretfully that we cannot rescue him, but must leave him to die. To most of us this seems clear, and I shall take it as clear. . . . This is Rescue I and with it I contrast Rescue II. In this second story we are again hurrying to the place where the tide is coming in in order to rescue the party of people, but this time it is relevant that the road is narrow and rocky. In this version the lone individual is trapped (do not ask me how) on the path. If we are to rescue the five we would have to drive over him. But can we do so? If we stop he will be all right eventually: he is in no danger unless from us. But of course all five of the others will be drowned. As in the first story our choice is between a course of action which will leave one man dead and five alive at the end of the day and a course of action which will have the opposite result. And yet we surely feel that in one case we can rescue the five men and in the other we cannot. We can allow someone to die of whatever disaster threatens him if the cost of saving him is failing to save five: we cannot, however, drive over *him* in order to get to *them*. We cannot originate a fatal sequence, although we can allow one to run its course. Similarly, in the pair of examples mentioned earlier, we find a contrast between on the one hand refusing to give to one man the whole supply of a scarce drug, because we can use portions of it to save five, and on the other, cutting him up for spare parts. And we notice that we may not originate a fatal sequence even if the resulting death is in no sense our object. We could not knowingly subject one person to deadly fumes in the process of manufacturing some substance that would save many, even if the poisoning were a mere side effect of the process that saved lives.

Considering these examples, it is hard to resist the conclusion that it makes all the difference whether those who are going to die if we act in a certain way will die as a result of a sequence that we originate or one that we allow to continue, it being of course something that did not *start* by our agency. So let us ask how this could be? If the distinction—which is roughly that between killing and allowing to die—*is* morally relevant, because it sometimes makes the difference between what is right and what is wrong, how does this work? After all, it cannot be a magical difference, and it does not satisfy anyone to hear that what we have is just an ultimate moral fact. Moreover, those who deny the relevance can point to cases in which it seems to make no difference to the goodness or badness of an action having a certain result, as, for example, that some innocent person dies, whether due to a sequence we originate or because of one we merely allow. And if the way the result comes about *sometimes* makes no difference, how can it ever do so? If it sometimes makes an action bad that harm came to someone else as a result of a sequence we *originated*, must this not always contribute some element of badness? How can a consideration be a reason for saying that an action is bad in one place without being at least a reason for saying the same elsewhere?

Let us address these questions. As to the route by which considerations of agency enter the process of moral judgment, it seems to be through its connection with different types of rights. For there are rights to noninterference, which form one class of rights; and there are also rights to goods or services, which are different. And corresponding to these two types of rights are, on the one hand, the duty not to interfere, called a "negative duty," and on the other the duty to provide the goods or services, called a "positive duty." These rights may in certain circumstances be overridden, and this can in principle happen to rights of either kind. So, for instance, in the matter of property rights, others have in ordinary circumstances a duty not to interfere with our property, though in exceptional circumstances the right is overridden, as in Elizabeth Anscombe's example of destroying someone's house to stop the spread of fire.[2] And a right to goods or services depending, for example, on a promise will quite often be overridden in the same kind of case. There is, however, no guarantee that the special circumstances that allow one kind of right to be overridden will always allow the overriding of the other. Typically, it takes more to justify an interference than to justify the withholding of goods or services: and it is, of course, possible to think that nothing whatsoever will justify, for example, the infliction of torture or the deliberate killing of the innocent. It is not hard to find how all this connects with the morality of killing and allowing to die—and in general with harm which an agent allows to happen and harm coming about through his agency, in my special sense having to do with originating or sustaining harmful sequences. For the violation of a right to noninterference consists in interference, which implies breaking into an existing sequence and initiating a new one. It is not usually possible, for instance, to violate that right to noninterference, which is at least part of what is meant by "the right to life" by failing to save someone from death. So if, in any circumstances, the right to noninterference is the only right that exists, or if it is the only right special circumstances have not overridden, then it may not be permissible to initiate a fatal sequence, but it *may* be permissible to withhold aid.

The question now is whether we ever find cases in which the right to noninterference exists and is not overridden, but where the right to goods or services either does not exist or *is* here overridden. The answer is, of course, that this is quite a common case. It often happens that whereas someone's rights stand in the way of our interference, we owe him no *service* in relation to that which he would lose if we interfered. We may not deprive him of his property, though we do not have to help him secure his hold on it, in spite of the fact that the balance of good and evil in the outcome (counting his loss or gain and the cost to us) will be the same regardless of how they come about. Similarly, where the issue is one of life and death, it is often impermissible to kill someone—although special circumstances having to do with the good of others make it permissible, or even required, that we do not spend the time or resources needed to save his life, as for instance, in the story of Rescue I, or in that of the scarce drug.

It seems clear, therefore, that there are circumstances in which it makes all the difference, morally speaking, whether a given balance of good and evil came about through our agency (in our sense), or whether it was rather something we had the ability to prevent but, for good reasons, did not prevent. Of course, we often have a strict duty to prevent harm to others, or to ameliorate their condition. And even where they do not, strictly speaking, have a *right* to our goods or services, we should often be failing (and sometimes grossly failing) in charity if we did not help them. But, to reiterate, it may be right to allow one person to die in order to save five, although it would not be right to kill him to bring the same good to them.

How is it, then, that anyone has ever denied this conclusion, so sympathetic to our everyday moral intuitions and apparently so well grounded in a very generally recognized distinction between different types of rights? We must now turn to an argument first *given*, by James Rachels, and more or less followed by others who think as he does. Rachels told a gruesome story of a child drowned in a bathtub in two different ways: in one case someone pushed the child's head under water, and in the other he found the child drowning and did not pull him out. Rachels says that we should judge one way of acting as bad as the other, so we have an example in which killing is as bad as allowing to die. But how, he asks, can the distinction ever be relevant if it is not relevant here?[3]

Based on what has been said earlier, the answer to Rachels should be obvious. The reason why it is, in ordinary circumstances, "no worse" to leave a child drowning in a bathtub than to push it under, is that both charity and the special duty of care that we owe to children give us a positive obligation to save them, and we have no particular reason to say that it is "less bad" to fail in this than it is to be in dereliction of the negative duty by being the agent of harm. The level of badness is, we may suppose, the same, but because a different kind of bad action has been done, there is no reason to suppose that the two ways of acting will always give the same result. In other circumstances one might be worse than the other, or only one might be bad. And this last result is exactly what we find in circumstances that allow a positive but not a negative duty to be overridden. Thus, it could be right to leave someone to die by the roadside in the story of Rescue I, though wrong to run over him in the story of Rescue II: and it could be right to act correspondingly in the cases of the scarce drug. . . .

Let me now consider an objection to the thesis I have been defending. It may be said that I shall have difficulty explaining a certain range of examples in which it seems permissible, and even obligatory, to make an intervention which jeopardizes people not already in danger in order to save others who are. The following case has been discussed. Suppose a runaway trolley is heading toward a track on which five people are standing, and that there is someone who can possibly switch the points, thereby diverting the trolley onto a track on which there is only one person. It seems that he should do this, just as a pilot whose plane is going to crash has a duty to steer, if he can, toward a less crowded street than the one he sees below. But the railway man then puts the one man newly in danger, instead of allowing the five to be killed. Why does not the one man's right to noninterference stand in his way, as one person's right to noninterference impeded the manufacture of poisonous fumes when this was necessary to save five?

The answer seems to be that this is a special case, in that we have here the *diverting* of a fatal sequence and not the starting of a new one. So we could not start a flood to stop a fire, even when the fire would kill more than the flood, but we could divert a flood to an area in which fewer people would be drowned.

A second and much more important difficulty involves cases in which it seems that the distinction between agency and allowing is inexplicably irrelevant. Why, I shall be asked, is it not morally permissible to allow someone to die deliberately in order to use his body for a medical procedure that would save many lives? It might be suggested that the distinction between agency and allowing is relevant when what is allowed to happen is itself aimed at. Yet this is not quite right, because there are cases in which it does make a difference whether one originates a sequence or only allows it to continue, although the allowing is with deliberate intent. Thus, for instance, it may not be permissible to deprive someone of a possession which only harms him, but it may be reasonable to refuse to get it back for him if it is already slipping from his grasp. And it is arguable that non-voluntary passive euthanasia is sometimes justifiable although non-voluntary active euthanasia is not. What these examples have in common is that *harm* is not in question, which suggests that the "direct," i.e., deliberate, intention of *evil* is what makes it morally objectionable to allow the beggar to die. When this element is present it is impossible to justify an action by indicating that no *origination* of evil is involved. But this special case leaves no doubt about the relevance of distinguishing between originating an evil and allowing it to occur. It was never suggested that there will *always and everywhere* be a difference of permissibility between the two.

Having defended the moral relevance of the distinction which roughly corresponds to the contrast between killing and allowing to die, I shall now ask how it affects the argument between those who oppose and those who support abortion. The answer seems to be that this entirely depends on how the argument is supposed to go. The most usual defense of abortion lies in the distinction between the destruction of a fetus and the destruction of a human person, and neither side in *this* debate will have reason to refer to the distinction between being the agent of an evil and allowing it to come about. But this is not the only defense of abortion which is current at the present time. In an influential and widely read article, Judith Jarvis Thomson has suggested an argument for allowing abortion which depends on denying what I have been at pains to maintain.[4]

Thomson suggests that abortion can be justified, at least in certain cases, without the need to deny that the fetus has the moral rights of a human person. For, she says, no person has an absolute right to the use of another's body, even to save his life, and so the fetus, whatever its status, has no right to the use of the mother's body. *Her* rights override *its* rights, and justify her in removing it if it seriously encumbers her life. To persuade us to agree with her she invents an example, which is supposed to give a parallel, in which someone dangerously ill is kept alive by being hooked up to the body of another person, without that person's consent. It is obvious, she says, that the person whose body was thus being used would have no obligation to continue in that situation, suffering immobility or other serious inconvenience, for any length of time. We should not think of him as a murderer if he detached himself, and we ought to think of a pregnant woman as having the same right to rid herself of an unwanted pregnancy.

Thomson's whole case depends on this analogy. It is, however, faulty if what I have said earlier is correct. According to my thesis, the two cases must be treated quite differently because one involves the initiation of a fatal sequence and the other the refusal to save a life. It is true that someone who extricated himself from a situation in which his body was being used in the way a respirator or a kidney machine is used could, indeed, be said to kill the other person in detaching himself. But this only shows, once more, that the use of "kill" is not important; what matters is that the fatal sequence resulting in death is not initiated but is rather allowed to take its course. And although charity or duties of care could have dictated that the help be given, it seems perfectly reasonable to treat this as a case in which such presumptions are overridden by other rights—those belonging to the person whose body would be used. The case of abortion is of course completely different. The fetus is not in jeopardy because it is in its mother's womb; it is merely dependent on her in the way children are dependent on their parents for food. An abortion, therefore, originates the sequence which ends in the death of the fetus, and the destruction comes about "through the agency" of the mother who seeks the abortion. If the fetus has the moral status of a human person then her action is, at best, likened to that of killing for spare parts or in Rescue II; conversely, the act of someone who refused to let his body be used to save the life of the sick man in Thomson's story belongs with . . . that of Rescue I.

It appears, therefore, that Thomson's argument is not valid, and that we are thrown back to the old debate about the moral status of the fetus, which stands as the crucial issue in determing whether abortion is justified.

Notes

1. James Rachels. "Active and Passive Euthanasia," *New England Journal of Medicine*, 292 (January 9, 1975). 78–80.
2. G. E. M. Anscombe. "Modern Moral Philosophy," *Philosophy*, 33 (1958): 1–19.
3. Rachels. "Active and Passive Euthanasia."
4. Judith Jarvis Thomson. "A Defense of Abortion," *Philosophy and Public Affairs*, 1 (1971), 44.

Study Questions

1. What is meant by an "agent of harm"?
2. Explain in your own words the distinction between a "negative duty" and a "positive duty."
3. Do you agree with Foot's analysis of the cases Rescue I and Rescue II?
4. What does Foot's view of the distinction between killing and letting die imply about Thomson's example of the unconscious violinist?

PART IX

Obligations to Others

World Hunger

Famine, Affluence, and Morality

Peter Singer

What obligations do we have toward those around the globe who are suffering from a lack of food, shelter, or medical care? Does morality permit us to purchase luxuries for ourselves, our families, and our friends instead of providing needed resources to other people who are suffering in unfortunate circumstances? Peter Singer, who is Ira W. Decamp Professor of Bioethics at the University Center for Human Values at Princeton University, argues that if we can prevent something bad from happening without thereby sacrificing anything of comparable moral importance, we ought to do so. In short, while some view contributing to relief funds as an act of charity, Singer considers such a donation as a moral duty.

As I write this, in November 1971, people are dying in East Bengal from lack of food, shelter, and medical care. The suffering and death that are occurring there now are not inevitable, not unavoidable in any fatalistic sense of the term. Constant poverty, a cyclone, and a

From Peter Singer, "Famine, Affluence, and Morality," *Philosophy & Public Affairs* 1 (1972).

civil war have turned at least nine million people into destitute refugees: nevertheless, it is not beyond the capacity of the richer nations to give enough assistance to reduce any further suffering to very small proportions. The decisions and actions of human beings can prevent this kind of suffering. Unfortunately, human beings have not made the necessary decisions. At the individual level, people have, with very few exceptions, not responded to the situation in any significant way. Generally speaking, people have not given large sums to relief funds; they have not written to their parliamentary representatives demanding increased government assistance; they have not demonstrated in the streets, held symbolic fasts, or done anything else directed toward providing the refugees with the means to satisfy their essential needs. At the government level, no government has given the sort of massive aid that would enable the refugees to survive for more than a few days. Britain, for instance, has given rather more than most countries. It has, to date, given £14,750,000. For comparative purposes, Britain's share of the nonrecoverable development costs of the Anglo-French Concorde project is already in excess of £275,000,000, and on present estimates will reach £440,000,000. The implication is that the British government values a supersonic transport more than thirty times as highly as it values the lives of the nine million refugees. Australia is another country which, on a per capita basis, is well up in the "aid to Bengal" table. Australia's aid, however, amounts to less than one-twelfth of the cost of Sydney's new opera house. The total amount given, from all sources, now stands at about £65,000,000. The estimated cost of keeping the refugees alive for one year is £464,000,000. Most of the refugees have now been in the camps for more than six months. The World Bank has said that India needs a minimum of £300,000,000 in assistance from other countries before the end of the year. It seems obvious that assistance on this scale will not be forthcoming. India will be forced to choose between letting the refugees starve or diverting funds from her own development program, which will mean that more of her own people will starve in the future.[1]

These are the essential facts about the present situation in Bengal. So far as it concerns us here, there is nothing unique about this situation except its magnitude. The Bengal emergency is just the latest and most acute of a series of major emergencies in various parts of the world, arising both from natural and from man-made causes. There are also many parts of the world in which people die from malnutrition and lack of food independent of any special emergency.

I take Bengal as my example only because it is the present concern, and because the size of the problem has ensured that it has been given adequate publicity. Neither individuals nor governments can claim to be unaware of what is happening there.

What are the moral implications of a situation like this? In what follows, I shall argue that the way people in relatively affluent countries react to a situation like that in Bengal cannot be justified; indeed, the whole way we look at moral issues—our moral conceptual scheme—needs to be altered, and with it, the way of life that has come to be taken for granted in our society.

In arguing for this conclusion I will not, of course, claim to be morally neutral. I shall, however, try to argue for the moral position that I take, so that anyone who accepts certain assumptions, to be made explicit, will, I hope, accept my conclusion.

I begin with the assumption that suffering and death from lack of food, shelter, and medical care are bad. I think most people will agree about this, although one may reach the same view by different routes. I shall not argue for this view. People can hold all sorts of eccentric positions, and perhaps from some of them it would not follow that death by starvation is in itself bad. It is difficult, perhaps impossible, to refute such positions, and so for brevity I will henceforth take this assumption as accepted. Those who disagree need read no further.

My next point is this: if it is in our power to prevent something bad from happening, without thereby sacrificing anything of comparable moral importance, we ought, morally, to do it. By "without sacrificing anything of comparable moral importance" I mean without causing anything else comparably bad to happen, or doing something that is wrong in itself, or failing to promote some moral good, comparable in significance to the bad thing that we can prevent. This principle seems almost as uncontroversial as the last one. It requires us only to prevent what is bad, and not to promote what is good, and it requires this of us only when we can do it without sacrificing anything that is, from the moral point of view, comparably important. I could even, as far as the application of my argument to the Bengal emergency is concerned, qualify the point so as to make it: if it is in our power to prevent something very bad from happening, without thereby sacrificing anything morally significant, we ought, morally, to do it. An application of this principle would be as follows: if I am walking past a shallow pond and see a child drowning in it, I ought to wade in and pull the child out. This will mean getting my clothes muddy, but this is insignificant, while the death of the child would presumably be a very bad thing.

The uncontroversial appearance of the principle just stated is deceptive. If it were acted upon, even in its qualified form, our lives, our society, and our world would be fundamentally changed. For the principle takes, firstly, no account of proximity or distance. It makes no moral difference whether the person I can help is a neighbor's child ten yards from me or a Bengali whose name I shall never know, ten thousand miles away. Secondly, the principle makes no distinction between cases in which I am the only person who could possibly do anything and cases in which I am just one among millions in the same position.

I do not think I need to say much in defense of the refusal to take proximity and distance into account. The fact that a person is physically near to us, so that we have personal contact with him, may make it more likely that we *shall* assist him, but this does not show that we *ought* to help him rather than another who happens to be farther away. If we accept any principle of impartiality, universalizability, equality, or whatever, we cannot discriminate against someone merely because he is far away from us (or we are far away from him). Admittedly, it is possible that we are in a better position to judge what needs to be done to help a person near to us than one far away, and perhaps also to provide the assistance we judge to be necessary. If this were the case, it would be a reason for helping those near to us first. This may once have been a justification for being more concerned with the poor in one's own town than with the famine victims in India. Unfortunately for those who like to keep moral responsibilities limited, instant communication and swift transportation have changed the situation. From the moral point of view, the development of the world into a "global village" has made an important, though still unrecognized, difference to our moral situation. Expert observers and supervisors, sent out by famine relief organizations or permanently stationed in famine-prone areas, can direct our aid to a refugee in Bengal almost as effectively as we could get it to someone in our own block. There would seem, therefore, to be no possible justification for discriminating on geographical grounds.

There may be a greater need to defend the second implication of my principle—that the fact that there are millions of other people in the same position, in respect to the Bengali refugees, as I am, does not make the situation significantly different from a situation in which I am the only person who can prevent something very bad from occurring. Again, of course, I admit that there is a psychological difference between the cases; one feels less guilty about doing nothing if one can point to others, similarly placed, who have also done nothing. Yet this can make no real difference to our moral obligations.[2] Should I consider that I am less obliged to pull the drowning child out of the pond if on looking around I see other people, no farther away than I am, who have also noticed the child but are doing nothing? One has only to ask this question to see the absurdity of the view that numbers lessen obligation. It is a view that is an ideal excuse for inactivity; unfortunately most of the major evils—poverty, overpopulation, pollution—are problems in which everyone is almost equally involved.

The view that numbers do make a difference can be made plausible if stated in this way: if everyone in circumstances like mine gave £5 to the Bengal Relief Fund, there would be enough to provide food, shelter, and medical care for the refugees; there is no reason why I should give more than anyone else in the same circumstances as I am; therefore I have no obligation to give more than £5. Each premise in this argument is true, and the argument looks sound. It may convince us, unless we notice that it is based on a hypothetical premise, although the conclusion is not stated hypothetically. The argument would be sound if the conclusion were: if everyone in circumstances like mine were to give £5, I would have no obligation to give more than £5. If the conclusion were so stated, however, it would be obvious that the argument has no bearing on a situation in which it is not the case that everyone else gives £5. This, of course, is the actual situation. It is more or less certain that not everyone in circumstances like mine will give £5. So there will not be enough to provide the needed food, shelter, and medical care. Therefore by giving more than £5 I will prevent more suffering than I would if I gave just £5.

It might be thought that this argument has an absurd consequence. Since the situation appears to be that very few people are likely to give substantial amounts, it follows that I and everyone else in similar circumstances ought to give as much as possible, that is, at least up to the point at which by giving more one would begin to cause serious suffering for oneself and one's dependents—perhaps even beyond this point to the point of marginal utility, at which by giving more one would cause oneself and one's dependents as much suffering as one would prevent in Bengal. If everyone does this, however, there will be more than can be used for the benefit of the refugees, and some of the sacrifice will have been unnecessary. Thus, if everyone does what he ought to do, the result will not be as good as it would be if everyone did a little less than he ought to do, or if only some do all that they ought to do.

The paradox here arises only if we assume that the actions in question—sending money to the relief funds—are performed more or less simultaneously, and are also unexpected. For if it is to be expected that everyone is going to contribute something, then clearly each is not obliged to give as much as he would have been obliged to had others not been giving too. And if everyone is not acting more or less simultaneously, then those giving later will know how much more is needed, and will have no obligation to give more than is necessary to reach this amount. To say this is not to deny the principle that people in the same circumstances have the same obligations, but to point out that the fact that others have given, or may be expected to give, is a relevant circumstance: those giving after it has become known that many others are giving and those giving before are not in the same circumstances. So the seemingly absurd consequence of the principle I have put forward can occur only if people are in error about the actual circumstances—that is, if they think they are giving when others are not, but in fact they are giving when others are. The result of everyone doing what he really ought to do cannot be worse than the result of everyone doing less than he ought to do, although the result of everyone doing what he reasonably believes he ought to do could be.

If my argument so far has been sound, neither our distance from a preventable evil nor the number of other people who, in respect to that evil, are in the same situation as we are, lessens our obligation to mitigate or prevent that evil. I shall therefore take as established the principle I asserted earlier. As I have already said, I need to assert it only in its qualified form: if it is in our power to prevent something very bad from happening, without thereby sacrificing anything else morally significant, we ought, morally, to do it.

The outcome of this argument is that our traditional moral categories are upset. The traditional direction between duty and charity cannot be drawn, or at least, not in the place we normally draw it. Giving money to the Bengal Relief Fund is regarded as an act of charity in our society. The bodies which collect money are known as "charities." These organizations see themselves in this way—if you send them a check, you will be thanked for your "generosity." Because giving money is regarded as an act of charity, it is not thought that there is anything wrong with not giving. The charitable man may be praised, but the man who is not charitable is not condemned. People do not feel in any way ashamed or guilty about spending money on new clothes or a new car instead of giving it to famine relief. (Indeed, the alternative does not occur to them.) This way of looking at the matter cannot be justified. When we buy new clothes not to keep ourselves warm but to look "well-dressed" we are not providing for any important need. We would not be sacrificing anything significant if we were to continue to wear our old clothes, and give the money to famine relief. By doing so, we would be preventing another person from starving. It follows from what I have said earlier that we ought to give money away, rather than spend it on clothes which we do not need to keep us warm. To do so is not charitable, or generous. Nor is it the kind of act which philosophers and theologians have called "supererogatory"—an act which it would be good to do, but not wrong not to do. On the contrary, we ought to give the money away, and it is wrong not to do so.

I am not maintaining that there are no acts which are charitable, or that there are no acts which it would be good to do but not wrong not to do. It may be possible to redraw the distinction between duty and charity in some other place. All I am arguing here is that the present way of drawing the distinction, which makes it an act of charity for a man living at the level of affluence which most people in the "developed nations" enjoy to give money to save someone else from starvation, cannot be supported. It is beyond the scope of my argument to consider whether the distinction should be redrawn or abolished altogether. There would be many other possible ways of drawing the distinction—for instance, one might decide that it is good to make other people as happy as possible, but not wrong not to do so.

Despite the limited nature of the revision in our moral conceptual scheme which I am proposing, the revision would, given the extent of both affluence and famine in the world today, have radical implications. These implications may lead to further objections, distinct from those I have already considered. I shall discuss two of these.

One objection to the position I have taken might be simply that it is too drastic a revision of our moral scheme. People do not ordinarily judge in the way I have suggested they should. Most people reserve their moral condemnation for those who violate some moral norm, such as the norm against taking another person's property. They do not condemn those who indulge in luxury instead of giving to famine relief. But given that I did not set out to present a morally neutral description of the way people make moral judgments, the way people do in fact judge has nothing to do with the validity of my conclusion. My conclusion follows from the principle which I advanced earlier, and unless that principle is rejected, or the arguments shown to be unsound, I think the conclusion must stand, however strange it appears. . . .

The second objection to my attack on the present distinction between duty and charity is one which has from time to time been made against utilitarianism. It follows from some forms of utilitarian theory that we all ought, morally, to be working full time to increase the balance of happiness over misery. The position I have taken here would not lead to this conclusion in all circumstances, for if there were no bad occurrences that we could prevent without sacrificing something of comparable moral importance, my argument would have no application. Given the present conditions in many parts of the world, however, it does follow from my argument that we ought, morally, to be working full time to relieve great suffering of the sort that occurs as a result of famine or other disasters. Of course, mitigating circumstances can be adduced—for instance, that if we wear ourselves out through overwork, we shall be less effective than we would otherwise have been. Nevertheless, when all considerations of this sort have been taken into account, the conclusion remains: we ought to be preventing as much suffering as we can without sacrificing something else of comparable moral importance. This conclusion is one which we may be reluctant to face. I cannot see, though, why it should be regarded as a criticism of the position for which I have argued, rather than a criticism of our ordinary standards of behavior. Since most people are self-interested to some degree, very few of us are likely to do everything that we ought to do. It would, however, hardly be honest to take this as evidence that it is not the case that we ought to do it. . . .

A third point raised by the conclusion reached earlier relates to the question of just how much we all ought to be giving away. One possibility, which has already been mentioned, is that we ought to give until we reach the level of marginal utility—that is, the level at which, by giving more, I would cause as much suffering to myself or my dependents as I would relieve by my gift. This would mean, of course, that one would reduce oneself to very nearly the material circumstances of a Bengali refugee. It will be recalled that earlier I put forward both a strong and a moderate version of the principle of preventing bad occurrences. The strong version, which required us to prevent bad things from happening unless in doing so we would be sacrificing something of comparable moral significance, does seem to require reducing ourselves to the level of marginal utility. I should also say that the strong version seems to me to be the correct one. I proposed the more moderate version—that we should prevent bad occurrences unless, to do so, we had to sacrifice something morally significant—only in order to show that even on this surely undeniable principle a great change in our way of life is required. On the more moderate principle, it may not follow that we ought to reduce ourselves to the level of marginal utility, for one might hold that to reduce oneself and one's family to this level is to cause something significantly bad to happen. Whether this is so I shall not discuss, since, as I have said, I can see no good reason for holding the moderate version of the principle rather than the strong version. Even if we accepted the principle only in its moderate form, however, it should be clear that we would have to give away enough to ensure that the consumer society, dependent as it is on people spending on trivia rather than giving to famine relief, would slow down and perhaps disappear entirely. There are several reasons why this would be desirable in itself. The value and necessity of economic growth are now being questioned not only by conservationists, but by economists as well.[3] There is no doubt, too, that the consumer society has had a distorting effect on the goals and purposes of its members. Yet looking at the matter purely from the point of view of overseas aid, there must be a limit to the extent to which we should deliberately slow down our economy; for it might be the case that if we gave away, say, forty percent of our Gross National Product, we would slow down the economy so much that in absolute terms we would be giving less than if we gave twenty-five percent of the much larger GNP that we would have if we limited our contribution to this smaller percentage.

I mention this only as an indication of the sort of factor that one would have to take into account in working out an ideal. Since Western societies generally consider one percent of the GNP an acceptable level of overseas aid, the matter is entirely academic. Nor does it affect the question of how much an individual should give in a society in which very few are giving substantial amounts.

It is sometimes said, though less often now than it used to be, that philosophers have no special role to play in public affairs, since most public issues depend primarily on an assessment of facts. On questions of fact, it is said, philosophers as such have no special expertise, and so it has been possible to engage in philosophy without committing oneself to any position on major public issues. No doubt there are some issues of social policy and foreign policy about which it can truly be said that a really expert assessment of the facts is required before taking sides or acting, but the issue of famine is surely not one of these. The facts about the existence of suffering are beyond dispute. Nor, I think, is it disputed that we can do something about it, either through orthodox methods of famine relief or through population control or both. This is therefore an issue on which philosophers are competent to take a position. The issue is one which faces everyone who has more money than he needs to support himself and his dependents, or who is in a position to take some sort of political action. These categories must include practically every teacher and student of philosophy in the universities of the Western world. If philosophy is to deal with matters that are relevant to both teachers and students, this is an issue that philosophers should discuss.

Discussion, though, is not enough. What is the point of relating philosophy to public (and personal) affairs if we do not take our conclusions seriously? In this instance, taking our conclusion seriously means acting upon it. The philosopher will not find it any easier than anyone else to alter his attitudes and way of life to the extent that, if I am right, is involved in doing everything that we ought to be doing. At the very least, though, one can make a start. The philosopher who does so will have to sacrifice some of the benefits of the consumer society, but he can find compensation in the satisfaction of a way of life in which theory and practice, if not yet in harmony, are at least coming together.

Notes

1. There was also a third possibility: that India would go to war to enable the refugees to return to their lands. Since I wrote this paper, India has taken this way out. The situation is no longer that described above, but this does not affect my argument, as the next paragraph indicates.
2. In view of the special sense philosophers often give to the term, I should say that I use "obligation" simply as the abstract noun derived from "ought," so that "I have an obligation to" means no more, and no less, than "I ought to." This usage is in accordance with the definition of "ought" given by the *Shorter Oxford English Dictionary:* "the general verb to express duty or obligation." I do not think any issue of substance hangs on the way the term is used; sentences in which I use "obligation" could all be rewritten, although somewhat clumsily, as sentences in which a clause containing "ought" replaces the term "obligation."

3. See, for instance, John Kenneth Galbraith, *The New Industrial State* (Boston, 1967); and E. J. Mishan, *The Costs of Economic Growth* (London, 1967).

Study Questions

1. If you can prevent something bad from happening at a comparatively small cost to yourself, are you obligated to do so?
2. Is your obligation to save a drowning child affected by how often you are called on to offer such help?
3. Are you acting immorally by paying college tuition for your own children while other children have no opportunity for any schooling at all?
4. Do we have a moral obligation to try to alleviate extreme poverty in our own country before attempting to do so in other countries?

A Reply to Singer

Travis Timmerman

Peter Singer argues that you are obligated to prevent something bad from happening if you can do so without thereby sacrificing anything of comparable moral importance. For example, you are morally obligated to save a child from drowning if you can do so without inconvenience. Travis Timmerman, assistant professor of philosophy at Seton Hall University, argues that the strength of your obligation depends on how many children need to be saved. If the number is large, then Singer's line of reasoning would obligate you to spend your life saving children. Are you not, however, entitled to pursue at least some of your own interests, even if they are not as morally weighty as saving children's lives?

Peter Singer's *Famine, Affluence, and Morality* is undoubtedly one of the most influential and widely read pieces of contemporary philosophy. Yet, the majority of philosophers (including ethicists) reject Singer's conclusion that we are morally required to donate to aid agencies whenever we can do so without sacrificing anything nearly as important as the good that our donations could bring about. Many ignore Singer's argument simply because they believe morality would just be too demanding if it required people in affluent nations to donate significant sums of money to charity. Of course, merely rejecting Singer's conclusion because it seems absurd does not constitute a refutation of Singer's argument. More importantly, this standard demandingness objection is a particularly inappropriate dialectical move because Singer provides a valid argument for his (demanding) conclusion and, crucially, the argument only consists of ethical

From Travis Timmerman, "Sometimes There Is Nothing Wrong with Letting a Child Drown," *Analysis* 75 (2015). Reprinted by permission of the publisher.

premisses that Singer takes his typical readers to already accept. Singer formulates his argument as follows.

1. Suffering and death from lack of food, shelter and medical care are bad.
2. If it is in your power to prevent something bad from happening, without sacrificing anything nearly as important, it is wrong not to do so.
3. By donating to aid agencies, you can prevent suffering and death from lack of food, shelter and medical care, without sacrificing anything nearly as important.
4. Therefore, if you do not donate to aid agencies, you are doing something wrong.

If it is not true that typical readers' existing ethical commitments entail that they accept premisses one and two, then they should be able to say which premiss(es) they reject and why. Those who believe that Singer's conclusion is too demanding will need to reject premiss two. This requires addressing Singer's infamous *Drowning Child* thought experiment, which elicits a common response that Singer believes demonstrates that his readers are already committed to the truth of premiss two. As such, Singer purports to demonstrate that the ethical commitments his typical readers already accept are demanding enough to require them to donate a substantial portion of their expendable income to aid organizations. . . .

Perhaps premiss two is true, but a proposition with such strong counterintuitive implications requires a strong defence, one that gives us reason to think that certain ordinary moral intuitions are radically misguided. Singer believes he has provided such a defence with *Drowning Child.* Aren't we morally obligated to sacrifice our new clothes to save the child *because* we are obligated to prevent something bad from happening whenever we can do so without sacrificing anything nearly as important? The short answer is 'No.' Here's why. Although Singer's description of *Drowning Child* is ahistorical, the implicit assumption is that *Drowning Child* is an anomalous event. People almost never find themselves in the situation Singer describes, so when they consider their obligations in *Drowning Child,* they implicitly assume that they have not frequently sacrificed their new clothes to save children in the past and will not need to do so frequently in the future.

Giving to aid organizations is, in this respect, unlike *Drowning Child.* Every individual in an affluent nation, so long as they have some expendable income, will always be in a position to save the lives of people living in extreme poverty by donating said income. It may be quite clear that one has a moral obligation to sacrifice $200 worth of new clothing a single time to prevent a child from drowning. It is much less clear that one is morally obligated to spend one's entire life making repeated $200 sacrifices to constantly prevent children from drowning. So, we may be obligated to save the child in *Drowning Child*, but still be disposed to believe that premiss two is false. I will expand on this asymmetry . . . by providing an altered version of Singer's thought experiment that more closely resembles the position those in affluent nations are in with respect to providing aid to those in extreme poverty. I suspect that most people's intuitions in such a case will show that they reject premiss two of Singer's argument.

People almost universally have the intuition that we are morally obligated to rescue the child in *Drowning Child*, but are not morally obligated to donate all their expendable income to aid agencies. Singer attempts to explain away this intuition as a mere psychological difference, a difference that results from our evolutionary history and socialization and not a moral difference. . . . However, there *is* a moral difference between the sacrifice required to save the child in *Drowning Child* (as it is imagined) and the sacrifice Singer believes people in affluent nations are required to make in order to donate the supposed obligatory amount to aid organizations.

This moral difference is easily overlooked because Singer's *Drowning Child* thought experiment is, in a crucial way, under-described. Once the necessary details are filled in, its inability to support premiss two will be made clear. My following *Drowning Children* case is not under-described and gives us reason to believe that there are times at which it is morally permissible to *not* prevent something bad from happening, even when one can do so at a comparably insignificant personal cost.

> ***Drowning Children***: Unlucky Lisa gets a call from her 24-hr bank telling her that hackers have accessed her account and are taking $200 out of it every 5 min until Lisa shows up in person to put a hold on her account. Due to some legal loophole, the bank is not required to reimburse Lisa for any of the money she may lose nor will they. In fact, if her account is overdrawn, the bank will seize as much of her assets as is needed to pay the debt created by the hackers.
>
> Fortunately, for Lisa, the bank is just across the street from her work and she can get there in fewer than 5 min. She was even about to walk to the bank as part of her daily routine. On her way, Lisa notices a vast space of land covered with hundreds of newly formed shallow

> ponds, each of which contains a small child who will drown unless someone pulls them to safety. Lisa knows that for each child she rescues, an extra child will live who would have otherwise died. Now, it would take Lisa approximately 5 min to pull each child to safety and, in what can only be the most horrifically surreal day of her life, Lisa has to decide how many children to rescue before entering the bank. Once she enters the bank, all the children who have not yet been rescued will drown.
>
> Things only get worse for poor Lisa. For the remainder of her life, the hackers repeat their actions on a daily basis and, every day, the ponds adjacent to Lisa's bank are filled with drowning children.

The truth of premiss two would entail that Lisa is obligated to rescue children until almost all of her money and assets are gone. It might permit her to close her account before she is unable to rent a studio apartment and eat a healthy diet. However, it would require her to give up her house, her car, her books, her art and anything else not nearly as important as a child's life. That might not seem so counterintuitive if Lisa has to make this monumental sacrifice a single time. But, and here's the rub, premiss two would also prohibit Lisa from ever rebuilding her life. For every day Lisa earns money, she is forced to choose between saving children and letting the hackers steal from her. Lisa would only be permitted to go to the bank each day in time to maintain the things nearly as important as a child's life, which I take to be the basic necessities Lisa needs to lead a healthy life.

I propose that it's a viable option that morality permits Lisa to, *at least* on 1 day over the course of her entire life, stop the hackers in time to enjoy some good that is not nearly as important as a child's life. Maybe Lisa wants to experience theatre one last time before she spends the remainder of her days pulling children from shallow ponds and stopping hackers. Given the totality of the sacrifice Lisa is making, morality intuitively permits Lisa to indulge in theatre *at least* one time in, let's say, the remaining 80 years of her life. In fact, commonsense morality should permit Lisa to indulge in these comparably morally insignificant goods a non-trivial number of times, though a single instance is all that is required to demonstrate that premiss two is false and, consequently, Singer's argument is unsound. . . .

To sum up, the intuitive pull of premiss two is more apparent than real. . . . How much are we obligated to donate to aid organizations? I am not sure exactly, but it should be the same amount we would be obligated to sacrifice were we to find ourselves in Lisa's position.

Study Questions

1. In *Drowning Child*, is Lisa obligated to continue saving children no matter how many children she has already saved?
2. Are you acting morally if you study philosophy while you could be helping others in need?
3. Are you acting morally if you buy a book for yourself while other people are starving?
4. When, if ever, are you entitled to pursue your own interests while you could, instead, be helping others in need of assistance?

B. Animals

Equality for Animals

Peter Singer

Peter Singer is Ira W. Decamp Professor of Bioethics at the University Center for Human Values at Princeton University. He argues that the fundamental principle of equality is the "principle of equal consideration of interests." According to this principle, equal interests supply reasons of equal moral weight. If the only people affected by an action are A and B, and if A's interests will be adversely affected by the action to a greater extent than B's interests will be promoted, then the act ought not be performed. If A and B are both humans, then the principle enjoys much intuitive support. Singer, however, holds that the principle also holds if A is an animal and B is a human. In other words, all interests, human or nonhuman, carry equal moral weight. Singer argues that to think otherwise is to be a speciesist, engaging in the same kind of prejudicial thinking as racists or sexists.

From Peter Singer, *Practical Ethics*, 2nd ed. (Cambridge: Cambridge University Press): pp. 55–82.

Racism and Speciesism

. . . [T]he fundamental principle of equality, on which the equality of all human beings rests, is the principle of equal consideration of interests. Only a basic moral principle of this kind can allow us to defend a form of equality that embraces all human beings, with all the differences that exist between them. I shall now contend that while this principle does provide an adequate basis for human equality, it provides a basis that cannot be limited to humans. In other words I shall suggest that, having accepted the principle of equality as a sound moral basis for relations with others of our own species, we are also committed to accepting it as a sound moral basis for relations with those outside our own species—the nonhuman animals.

This suggestion may at first seem bizarre. We are used to regarding discrimination against members of racial minorities, or against women, as among the most important moral and political issues facing the world today. These are serious matters, worthy of the time and energy of any concerned person. But animals? Isn't the welfare of animals in a different category altogether, a matter for people who are dotty about dogs and cats? How can anyone waste their time on equality for animals when so many humans are denied real equality?

This attitude reflects a popular prejudice against taking the interests of animals seriously—a prejudice no better founded than the prejudice of white slaveowners against taking the interests of their African slaves seriously. It is easy for us to criticise the prejudices of our grandfathers, from which our fathers freed themselves. It is more difficult to distance ourselves from our own views, so that we can dispassionately search for prejudices among the beliefs and values we hold. What is needed now is a willingness to follow the arguments where they lead, without a prior assumption that the issue is not worth our attention.

The argument for extending the principle of equality beyond our own species is simple, so simple that it amounts to no more than a clear understanding of the nature of the principle of equal consideration of interests. . . . [T]his principle implies that our concern for others ought not to depend on what they are like, or what abilities they possess (although precisely what this concern requires us to do may vary according to the characteristics of those affected by what we do). It is on this basis that we are able to say that the fact that some people are not members of our race does not entitle us to exploit them, and similarly the fact that some people are less intelligent than others does not mean that their interests may be disregarded. But the principle also implies that the fact that beings are not members of our species does not entitle us to exploit them, and similarly the fact that other animals are less intelligent than we are does not mean that their interests may be disregarded.

... [M]any philosophers have advocated equal consideration of interests, in some form or other, as a basic moral principle. Only a few have recognised that the principle has applications beyond our own species, one of the few being Jeremy Bentham, the founding father of modern utilitarianism. In a forward-looking passage, written at a time when African slaves in the British dominions were still being treated much as we now treat nonhuman animals, Bentham wrote:

> The day may come when the rest of the animal creation may acquire those rights which never could have been withholden from them but by the hand of tyranny. The French have already discovered that the blackness of the skin is no reason why a human being should be abandoned without redress to the caprice of a tormentor. It may one day come to be recognised that the number of the legs, the villosity of the skin, or the termination of the *os sacrum*, are reasons equally insufficient for abandoning a sensitive being to the same fate. What else is it that should trace the insuperable line? Is it the faculty of reason, or perhaps the faculty of discourse? But a fullgrown horse or dog is beyond comparison a more rational, as well as a more conversable animal, than an infant of a day, or a week, or even a month, old. But suppose they were otherwise, what would it avail? The question is not, Can they *reason*? nor Can they *talk*? but, *Can they suffer*?

In this passage Bentham points to the capacity for suffering as the vital characteristic that entitles a being to equal consideration. The capacity for suffering—or more strictly, for suffering and/or enjoyment or happiness—is not just another characteristic like the capacity for language, or for higher mathematics. Bentham is not saying that those who try to mark 'the insuperable line' that determines whether the interests of a being should be considered happen to have selected the wrong characteristic. The capacity for suffering and enjoying things is a prerequisite for having interests at all, a condition that must be satisfied before we can speak of interests in any meaningful way. It would be nonsense to say that it was not in the interests of a stone to be kicked along the road by a schoolboy. A stone does not have interests because it cannot suffer. Nothing that we can do to it could possibly make any difference to its welfare. A mouse, on the other hand, does have an interest in not being tormented, because mice will suffer if they are treated in this way.

If a being suffers, there can be no moral justification for refusing to take that suffering into consideration. No matter what the nature of the being, the principle of equality requires that the suffering be counted equally with the like suffering—in so far as rough comparisons can be made—of any other being. If a being is not capable of suffering, or of experiencing enjoyment or happiness, there is nothing to be taken into account. This is why the limit of sentience (using the term as a convenient, if not strictly accurate, shorthand for the capacity to suffer or experience enjoyment or happiness) is the only defensible boundary of concern for the interests of others. To mark this boundary by some characteristic like intelligence or rationality would be to mark it in an arbitrary way. Why not choose some other characteristic, like skin colour?

Racists violate the principle of equality by giving greater weight to the interests of members of their own race when there is a clash between their interests and the interests of those of another race. Racists of European descent typically have not accepted that pain matters as much when it is felt by Africans, for example, as when it is felt by Europeans. Similarly those I would call 'speciesists' give greater weight to the interests of members of their own species when there is a clash between their interests and the interests of those of other species. Human speciesists do not accept that pain is as bad when it is felt by pigs or mice as when it is felt by humans.

That, then, is really the whole of the argument for extending the principle of equality to nonhuman animals; but there may be some doubts about what this equality amounts to in practice. In particular, the last sentence of the previous paragraph may prompt some people to reply: 'Surely pain felt by a mouse just is not as bad as pain felt by a human. Humans have much greater awareness of what is happening to them, and this makes their suffering worse. You can't equate the suffering of, say, a person dying slowly from cancer, and a laboratory mouse undergoing the same fate.'

I fully accept that in the case described the human cancer victim normally suffers more than the nonhuman cancer victim. This in no way undermines the extension of equal consideration of interests to nonhumans. It means, rather, that we must take care when we compare the interests of different species. In some situations a member of one species will suffer more than a member of another species. In this case we should still apply the principle of equal consideration of interests but the result of so doing is, of course, to give priority to relieving the greater suffering. A simpler case may help to make this clear.

If I give a horse a hard slap across its rump with my open hand, the horse may start, but it presumably feels little pain. Its skin is thick enough to protect it against a mere slap. If I slap a baby in the same way, however, the baby will cry and presumably does feel pain, for the baby's skin is more sensitive. So it is worse to slap a baby than a horse, if both slaps are administered with equal force. But there must be some kind of blow—I don't know exactly what it would be, but perhaps a blow with a heavy stick—that would cause the horse as much pain as we cause a baby by a simple slap. That is what I mean by 'the same amount of pain' and if we consider it wrong to inflict that much pain on a baby for no good reason then we must, unless we are speciesists, consider it equally wrong to inflict the same amount of pain on a horse for no good reason.

There are other differences between humans and animals that cause other complications. Normal adult human beings have mental capacities that will, in certain circumstances, lead them to suffer more than animals would in the same circumstances. If, for instance, we decided to perform extremely painful or lethal scientific experiments on normal adult humans, kidnapped at random from public parks for this purpose, adults who entered parks would become fearful that they would be kidnapped. The resultant terror would be a form of suffering additional to the pain of the experiment. The same experiments performed on nonhuman animals would cause less suffering since the animals would not have the anticipatory dread of being kidnapped and experimented upon. This does not mean, of course, that it would be *right* to perform the experiment on animals, but only that there is a reason, and one that is not speciesist, for preferring to use animals rather than normal adult humans, if the experiment is to be done at all. Note, however, that this same argument gives us a reason for preferring to use human infants—orphans perhaps—or severely intellectually disabled humans for experiments, rather than adults, since infants and severely intellectually disabled humans would also have no idea of what was going to happen to them. As far as this argument is concerned, nonhuman animals and infants and severely intellectually disabled humans are in the same category; and if we use this argument to justify experiments on nonhuman animals we have to ask ourselves whether we are also prepared to allow experiments on human infants and severely intellectually disabled adults. If we make a distinction between animals and these humans, how can we do it, other than on the basis of a morally indefensible preference for members of our own species?

There are many areas in which the superior mental powers of normal adult humans make a difference: anticipation, more detailed memory, greater knowledge of what is happening, and so on. These differences explain why a human dying from cancer is likely to suffer more than a mouse. It is the mental anguish that makes the human's position so much harder to bear. Yet these differences do not all point to greater suffering on the part of the normal human being. Sometimes animals may suffer more because of their more limited understanding. If, for instance, we are taking prisoners in wartime we can explain to them that while they must submit to capture, search, and confinement they will not otherwise be harmed and will be set free at the conclusion of hostilities. If we capture wild animals, however, we cannot explain that we are not threatening their lives. A wild animal cannot distinguish an attempt to overpower and confine from an attempt to kill; the one causes as much terror as the other.

It may be objected that comparisons of the sufferings of different species are impossible to make, and that for this reason when the interests of animals and humans clash, the principle of equality gives no guidance. It is true that comparisons of suffering between members of different species cannot be made precisely. Nor, for that matter, can comparisons of suffering between different human beings be made precisely. Precision is not essential. As we shall see shortly, even if we were to prevent the infliction of suffering on animals only when the interests of humans will not be affected to anything like the extent that animals are affected, we would be forced to make radical changes in our treatment of animals that would involve our diet, the farming methods we use, experimental procedures in many fields of science, our approach to wildlife and to hunting, trapping and the wearing of furs, and areas of entertainment like circuses, rodeos, and zoos. As a result, the total quantity of suffering caused would be greatly reduced; so greatly that it is hard to imagine any other change of moral attitude that would cause so great a reduction in the total sum of suffering in the universe.

So far I have said a lot about the infliction of suffering on animals, but nothing about killing them. This omission has been deliberate. The application of the principle of equality to the infliction of suffering is, in theory at least, fairly straightforward. Pain and suffering are bad and should be prevented or minimised, irrespective of the race, sex, or species of the being that suffers. How bad a pain is depends on how intense it is and how long it lasts, but pains of the same intensity and duration are equally bad, whether felt by humans or animals. When we come to consider the value of life, we cannot say quite so confidently that a life is a life, and equally valuable, whether it is a human life or an animal life. It would not be speciesist to hold that the life of a self-aware being, capable of abstract thought, of planning for the future, of complex acts of communication, and so on, is more valuable than the life of a being without these capacities. (I am not saying whether this view is justifiable or not; only that it cannot simply be rejected as speciesist, because it is not on the basis of species itself that one life is held to be more valuable than another.) The value of life is a notoriously difficult ethical question, and we can only arrive at a reasoned conclusion about the comparative value of human and animal life after we have discussed the value of life in general. . . . Meanwhile there are important conclusions to be derived from the extension beyond our own species of the principle of equal consideration of interests, irrespective of our conclusions about the value of life.

Speciesism in Practice

Animals as Food

For most people in modern, urbanised societies, the principal form of contact with nonhuman animals is at meal times. The use of animals for food is probably the oldest and the most widespread form of animal use. There is also a sense in which it is the most basic form of animal use, the foundation stone on which rests the belief that animals exist for our pleasure and convenience.

If animals count in their own right, our use of animals for food becomes questionable—especially when animal flesh is a luxury rather than a necessity. Eskimos living in an environment where they must kill animals for food or starve might be justified in claiming that their interest in surviving overrides that of the animals they kill. Most of us cannot defend our diet in this way. Citizens of industrialised societies can easily obtain an adequate diet without the use of animal flesh. The overwhelming weight of medical evidence indicates that animal flesh is not necessary for good health or longevity. Nor is animal production in industrialised societies an efficient way of producing food, since most of the animals consumed have been fattened on grains and other foods that we could have eaten directly. When we feed these grains to animals, only about 10 per cent of the nutritional value remains as meat for human consumption. So, with the exception of animals raised entirely on grazing land unsuitable for crops, animals are eaten neither for health, nor to increase our food supply. Their flesh is a luxury, consumed because people like its taste.

In considering the ethics of the use of animal flesh for human food in industrialised societies, we are considering a situation in which a relatively minor human interest must be balanced against the lives and welfare of the animals involved. The principle of equal consideration of interests does not allow major interests to be sacrificed for minor interests.

The case against using animals for food is at its strongest when animals are made to lead miserable lives so that their flesh can be made available to humans at the lowest possible cost. Modern forms of intensive farming apply science and technology to the attitude that animals are objects for us to use. In order to have meat on the table at a price that people can afford, our society tolerates methods of meat production that confine sentient animals in cramped, unsuitable conditions for the entire duration of their lives. Animals are treated like machines that convert fodder into flesh, and any innovation that results in a higher 'conversion ratio' is liable to be adopted. As one authority on the subject has said, 'Cruelty is acknowledged only when profitability ceases.' To avoid speciesism we must stop these practices. Our custom is all the support that factory farmers need. The decision to cease giving them that support may be difficult, but it is less difficult than it would have been for a white Southerner to go against the traditions of his society and free his slaves; if we do not change our dietary habits, how can we censure those slaveholders who would not change their own way of living?

These arguments apply to animals who have been reared in factory farms—which means that we should not eat chicken, pork, or veal, unless we know that the meat we are eating was not produced by factory farm methods. The same is true of beef that has come from cattle kept in crowded feedlots (as most beef does in the United States). Eggs will come from hens kept in small wire cages, too small even to allow them to stretch their wings, unless the eggs are specifically sold as 'free range' (or unless one lives in a relatively enlightened country like Switzerland, which has prohibited the cage system of keeping hens).

These arguments do not take us all the way to a vegetarian diet, since some animals, for instance sheep, and in some countries cattle, still graze freely outdoors. This could change. The American pattern of fattening cattle in crowded feedlots is spreading to other countries. Meanwhile, the lives of free-ranging animals are undoubtedly better than those of animals reared in factory farms. It is still doubtful if using them for food is compatible with equal consideration of interests. One problem is, of course, that using them as food involves killing them. . . . Apart from taking their lives there are also many other things done to animals in order to bring them cheaply to our dinner table. Castration, the separation of mother and young, the breaking up of herds, branding, transporting, and finally the moments of slaughter—all of these are likely to involve suffering and do not take the animals' interests into account. Perhaps animals could be reared on a small scale without suffering in these ways, but it does not seem economical or practical to do so on the scale required for feeding our large urban populations. In any case, the important question is not whether animal flesh *could* be produced without suffering, but whether the flesh we are considering buying was produced without suffering. Unless we can be confident that it was, the principle of equal consideration of interests implies that it was wrong to sacrifice important interests of the animal in order to satisfy less important interests of our own; consequently we should boycott the end result of this process.

For those of us living in cities where it is difficult to know how the animals we might eat have lived and died, this conclusion brings us close to a vegetarian way of life. I shall consider some objections to it in the final section of this chapter.

Experimenting on Animals

Perhaps the area in which speciesism can most clearly be observed is the use of animals in experiments. Here the issue stands out starkly, because experimenters often seek to justify experimenting on animals by claiming that the experiments lead us to discoveries about humans; if this is so, the experimenter must agree that human and nonhuman animals are similar in crucial respects. For instance, if forcing a rat to choose between starving to death and crossing an electrified grid to obtain food tells us anything about the reactions of humans to stress, we must assume that the rat feels stress in this kind of situation.

People sometimes think that all animal experiments serve vital medical purposes, and can be justified on the grounds that they relieve more suffering than they cause. This comfortable belief is mistaken. Drug companies test new shampoos and cosmetics they are intending to market by dripping concentrated solutions of them into the eyes of rabbits, in a test known as the Draize test. . . . Food additives, including artificial colourings and preservatives, are tested by what is known as the LD50—a test designed to find the 'lethal dose', or level of consumption that will make 50 per cent of a sample of animals die. In the process nearly all of the animals are made very sick before some finally die and others pull through. These tests are not necessary to prevent human suffering: even if there were no alternative to the use of animals to test the safety of the products, we already have enough shampoos and food colourings. There is no need to develop new ones that might be dangerous.

In many countries, the armed forces perform atrocious experiments on animals that rarely come to light. To give just one example: at the U.S. Armed Forces Radiobiology Institute, in Bethesda, Maryland, rhesus monkeys have been trained to run inside a large wheel. If they slow down too much, the wheel slows down, too, and the monkeys get an electric shock. Once the monkeys are trained to run for long periods, they are given lethal doses of radiation. Then, while sick and vomiting, they are forced to continue to run until they drop. This is supposed to provide information on the capacities of soldiers to continue to fight after a nuclear attack. . . .

In the past, argument about animal experimentation has often missed this point because it has been put in absolutist terms: would the opponent of experimentation be prepared to let thousands die from a terrible disease that could be cured by experimenting on one animal? This is a purely hypothetical question, since experiments do not have such dramatic results, but as long as its hypothetical nature is clear, I think the question should be answered affirmatively—in other words, if one, or even a dozen animals had to suffer experiments in order to save thousands, I would think it right and in accordance with equal consideration of interests that they should do so. This, at any rate, is the answer a utilitarian must give. Those who believe in absolute rights might hold that it is always wrong to sacrifice one being, whether human or animal, for the benefit of another. In that case the experiment should not be carried out, whatever the consequences.

To the hypothetical question about saving thousands of people through a single experiment on an animal, opponents of speciesism can reply with a hypothetical question of their own: would experimenters be prepared to perform their experiments on orphaned humans with severe and irreversible brain damage if that were the only way to save thousands? (I say 'orphaned' in order to avoid the complication of the feelings of the human parents.) If experimenters are not prepared to use orphaned humans with severe and irreversible brain damage, their readiness to use nonhuman animals seems to discriminate on the basis of species alone, since apes, monkeys, dogs, cats, and even mice and rats are more intelligent, more aware of what is happening to them, more sensitive to pain, and so on, than many severely braindamaged humans barely surviving in hospital wards and other institutions. There seems to be no morally relevant characteristic that such humans have that nonhuman animals lack. Experimenters, then, show bias in favour of their own species whenever they carry out experiments on nonhuman animals for purposes that they would not think justified them in using human beings at an equal or lower level of sentience, awareness, sensitivity, and so on. If this bias were eliminated, the number of experiments performed on animals would be greatly reduced. . . .

Some Objections

In this final section of the chapter I shall attempt to answer . . . objections. I shall begin with the more straightforward ones.

How Do We Know That Animals Can Feel Pain?

We can never directly experience the pain of another being, whether that being is human or not. When I see my daughter fall and scrape her knee, I know that she feels pain because of the way she behaves—she cries, she tells me her knee hurts, she rubs the sore spot, and so on. I know that I myself behave in a somewhat similar—if more inhibited—way when I feel pain, and so I accept that my daughter feels something like what I feel when I scrape my knee.

The basis of my belief that animals can feel pain is similar to the basis of my belief that my daughter can feel pain. Animals in pain behave in much the same way as humans do, and their behaviour is sufficient justification for the belief that they feel pain. It is true that, with the exception of those apes who have been taught to communicate by sign language, they cannot actually say that they are feeling pain—but then when my daughter was very young she could not talk, either. She found other ways to make her inner states apparent, thereby demonstrating that we can be sure that a being is feeling pain even if the being cannot use language.

To back up our inference from animal behaviour, we can point to the fact that the nervous systems of all vertebrates, and especially of birds and mammals, are fundamentally similar. Those parts of the human nervous system that are concerned with feeling pain are relatively old, in evolutionary terms. Unlike the cerebral cortex, which developed fully only after our ancestors diverged from other mammals, the basic nervous system evolved in more distant ancestors common to ourselves and the other 'higher' animals. This anatomical parallel makes it likely that the capacity of animals to feel is similar to our own.

It is significant that none of the grounds we have for believing that animals feel pain hold for plants. We cannot observe behaviour suggesting pain—sensational claims to the contrary have not been substantiated—and plants do not have a centrally organised nervous system like ours.

Animals Eat Each Other, So Why Shouldn't We Eat Them?

This might be called the Benjamin Franklin Objection. Franklin recounts in his *Autobiography* that he was for a time a vegetarian but his abstinence from animal flesh came to an end when he was watching some friends prepare to fry a fish they had just caught. When the fish was cut open, it was found to have a smaller fish in its stomach. 'Well', Franklin said to himself, 'if you eat one another, I don't see why we may not eat you' and he proceeded to do so.

Franklin was at least honest. In telling this story, he confesses that he convinced himself of the validity of the objection only after the fish was already in the frying pan and smelling 'admirably well'; and he remarks that one of the advantages of being a 'reasonable creature' is that one can find a reason for whatever one wants to do. The replies that can be made to this objection are so obvious that Franklin's acceptance of it does testify more to his love of fried fish than to his powers of reason. For a start, most animals who kill for food would not be able to survive if they did not, whereas we have no need to eat animal flesh. Next, it is odd that humans, who normally think of the behaviour of animals as 'beastly' should, when it suits them, use an argument that implies that we ought to look to animals for moral guidance. The most decisive point, however, is that nonhuman animals are not capable of considering the alternatives open to them or of reflecting on the ethics of their diet. Hence it is impossible to hold the animals responsible for what they do, or to judge that because of their killing they 'deserve' to be treated in a similar way. Those who read these lines, on the other hand, must consider the justifiability of their dietary habits. You cannot evade responsibility by imitating beings who are incapable of making this choice.

Sometimes people point to the fact that animals eat each other in order to make a slightly different point. This fact suggests, they think, not that animals deserve to be eaten, but rather that there is a natural law according to which the stronger prey upon the weaker, a kind of Darwinian 'survival of the fittest' in which by eating animals we are merely playing our part.

This interpretation of the objection makes two basic mistakes, one a mistake of fact and the other an error of reasoning. The factual mistake lies in the assumption that our own consumption of animals is part of the natural evolutionary process. This might be true of a few primitive cultures that still hunt for food, but it has nothing to do with the mass production of domestic animals in factory farms.

Suppose that we did hunt for our food, though, and this was part of some natural evolutionary process. There would still be an error of reasoning in the assumption that because this process is natural it is right. It is, no doubt, 'natural' for women to produce an infant every year or two from puberty to menopause, but this does not mean that it is wrong to interfere with this process. We need to know the natural laws that affect us in order to estimate the consequences of what we do; but we do not have to assume that the natural way of doing something is incapable of improvement.

Differences between Humans and Animals

That there is a huge gulf between humans and animals was unquestioned for most of the course of Western civilisation. The basis of this assumption has been undermined by Darwin's discovery of our animal origins and the associated decline in the credibility of the story of our Divine Creation, made in the image of God with an immortal soul. Some have found it difficult to accept that the differences between us and the other animals are differences of degree rather than kind. They have searched for ways of drawing a line between humans and animals. To date these boundaries have been shortlived. For instance, it used to be said that only humans used tools. Then it was observed that the Galapagos woodpecker used a cactus thorn to dig insects out of crevices in trees. Next it was suggested that even if other animals used tools, humans are the only toolmaking animals. But Jane Goodall found that chimpanzees in the jungles of Tanzania chewed up leaves to make a sponge for sopping up water, and trimmed the leaves off branches to make tools for catching insects. The use of language was another boundary line—but now chimpanzees, gorillas, and an orangutan have learnt Ameslan, the sign language of the deaf, and there is some evidence suggesting that whales and dolphins may have a complex language of their own.

If these attempts to draw the line between humans and animals had fitted the facts of the situation, they would still not carry any moral weight. As Bentham pointed out, the fact that a being does not use language or make tools is hardly a reason for ignoring its suffering. Some philosophers have claimed that there is a more profound difference. They have claimed that animals cannot think or reason, and that accordingly they have no conception of themselves, no self-consciousness. They live from instant to instant, and do not see themselves as distinct entities with a past and a future. . . . [D]oes the fact that a being is self-conscious entitle that being to some kind of priority of consideration?

The claim that self-conscious beings are entitled to prior consideration is compatible with the principle of equal consideration of interests if it amounts to no more than the claim that something that happens to self-conscious beings can be contrary to their interests while similar events would not be contrary to the interests of beings who were not self-conscious. This might be because the self-conscious creature has greater awareness of what is happening, can fit the event into the overall framework of a longer time period, has different desires, and so on. But this is a point I granted at the start of this chapter, and provided that it is not carried to ludicrous extremes—like insisting that if I am self-conscious and a veal calf is not, depriving me of veal causes more suffering than depriving the calf of his freedom to walk, stretch and eat grass—it is not denied by the criticisms I made of animal experimentation and factory farming.

It would be a different matter if it were claimed that, even when a self-conscious being did not suffer more than a being that was merely sentient, the suffering of the self-conscious being is more important because these are more valuable types of being. . . . [H]ere we are entitled to ask *why* self-conscious beings should be considered more valuable and in particular why the alleged greater value of a self-conscious being should result in preferring the lesser interests of a self-conscious being to the greater interests of a merely sentient being, even where the self-consciousness of the former being is not itself at stake. This last point is an important one, for we are not now considering cases in which the lives of self-conscious beings are at risk but cases in which self-conscious beings will go on living, their faculties intact, whatever we decide. In these cases, if the existence of self-consciousness does not affect the nature of the interests under comparison, it is not clear why we should drag self-consciousness into the discussion at all, any more than we should drag species, race or sex into similar discussions. Interests are interests, and ought to be given equal consideration whether they are the interests of human or nonhuman animals, self-conscious or non–self-conscious animals.

There is another possible reply to the claim that self-consciousness, or autonomy, or some similar characteristic, can serve to distinguish human from nonhuman animals: recall that there are intellectually disabled humans who have less claim to be regarded as self-conscious or autonomous than many nonhuman animals. If we use these characteristics to place a gulf between humans and other animals, we place these less able humans on the other side of the gulf; and if the gulf is taken to mark a difference in moral status, then these humans would have the moral status of animals rather than humans.

This reply is forceful, because most of us find horrifying the idea of using intellectually disabled humans in painful experiments, or fattening them for gourmet dinners. But some philosophers have argued that these consequences would not really follow from the use of a characteristic like self-consciousness or autonomy to distinguish humans from other animals. I shall consider three of these attempts.

The first suggestion is that severely intellectually disabled humans who do not possess the capacities that mark the normal human off from other animals should nevertheless be treated as if they did possess these capacities, since they belong to a species, members of which normally do possess them. The suggestion is, in other words, that we treat individuals not in accordance with their actual qualities, but in accordance with the qualities normal for their species.

It is interesting that this suggestion should be made in defence of treating members of our species better than members of another species, when it would be firmly rejected if it were used to justify treating members of our race or sex better than members of another race or sex. . . . [W]hatever the difference between the *average* [IQ] scores for different groups, some members of the group with the lower average score will do better than some members of groups with the higher average score, and so we ought to treat people as individuals and not according to the average score for their ethnic group, whatever the explanation of that average might be. If we accept this we cannot consistently accept the suggestion that when dealing with severely intellectually disabled humans we should grant them the status or rights normal for their species. For what is the significance of the fact that this time the line is to be drawn around the species rather than around the race or sex? We cannot insist that beings be treated as individuals in the one case, and as members of a group in the other. Membership of a species is no more relevant in these circumstances than membership of a race or sex.

A second suggestion is that although severely intellectually disabled humans may not possess higher capacities than other animals, they are nonetheless human beings, and as such we have special relations with them that we do not have with other animals. As one reviewer of *Animal Liberation* put it: 'Partiality for our own species, and within it for much smaller groupings is, like the universe, something we had better accept . . . The danger in an attempt to eliminate partial affections is that it may remove the source of all affections.'

This argument ties morality too closely to our affections. Of course some people may have a closer relationship with the most profoundly intellectually disabled human than they do with any nonhuman animal, and it would be absurd to tell them that they should not feel this way. They simply do, and as such there is nothing good or bad about it. The question is whether our moral obligations to a being should be made to depend on our feelings in this manner. Notoriously, some human beings have a closer relationship with their cat than with their neighbours. Would those who tie morality to affections accept that these people are justified in saving their cats from a fire before they save their neighbours? And even those who are prepared to answer this question affirmatively would, I trust, not want to go along with racists who could argue that if people have more natural relationships with, and greater affection towards, others of their own race, it is all right for them to give preference to the interests of other members of their own race. Ethics does not demand that we eliminate personal relationships and partial affections, but it does demand that when we act we assess the moral claims of those affected by our actions with some degree of independence from our feelings for them.

The third suggestion invokes the widely used 'slippery slope' argument. The idea of this argument is that once we take one step in a certain direction we shall find ourselves on a slippery slope and shall slither further than we wished to go. In the present context the argument is used to suggest that we need a clear line to divide those beings we can experiment upon, or fatten for dinner, from those we cannot. Species membership makes a nice sharp dividing line, whereas levels of self-consciousness, autonomy, or sentience do not. Once we allow that an intellectually disabled human being has no higher moral status than an animal, the argument goes, we have begun our descent down a slope, the next level of which is denying rights to social misfits, and the bottom of which is a totalitarian government disposing of any groups it does not like by classifying them as subhuman.

The slippery slope argument may serve as a valuable warning in some contexts, but it cannot bear too much weight. If we believe that, as I have argued in this chapter, the special status we now give to humans allows us to ignore the interests of billions of sentient creatures, we should not be deterred from trying to rectify this situation by the mere possibility that the principles on which we base this attempt will be misused by evil rulers for their own ends. And it is no more than a possibility. The change I have suggested might make no difference to our treatment of humans, or it might even improve it.

In the end, no ethical line that is arbitrarily drawn can be secure. It is better to find a line that can be defended openly and honestly. . . .

It is also important to remember that the aim of my argument is to elevate the status of animals rather than to lower the status of any humans. I do not wish to suggest that intellectually disabled humans should be force-fed with food colourings until half of them die—although this would certainly give us a more accurate indication of whether the substance was safe for humans than testing it on rabbits or dogs does. I would like our conviction that it would be wrong to treat intellectually disabled humans in this way to be transferred to nonhuman animals at similar levels of self-consciousness and with similar capacities for suffering. It is excessively pessimistic to refrain from trying to alter our attitudes on the grounds that we might start treating intellectually disabled humans with the same lack of concern we now have for animals, rather than give animals the greater concern that we now have for intellectually disabled humans. . . .

Study Questions

1. According to Singer, what is the fundamental principle of equality?
2. Is holding human interests as more morally important than animal interests mere prejudice?
3. Does Singer identify a morally relevant difference between humans and nonhumans by claiming that, unlike animals, humans cannot evade moral responsibilities?
4. How should we consider the interests of animals who have the same cognitive capacities as some intellectually disabled persons?

Speciesism and the Idea of Equality

Bonnie Steinbock

Bonnie Steinbock is Professor Emerita of Philosophy at the University of Albany, State University of New York. She maintains that animals are different from human beings in ways that are morally relevant. In particular, unlike animals, human beings possess intelligence, which is a prerequisite for moral responsibility. Steinbock argues that because humans can be held morally responsible for their actions, the interests of human beings should be given extra weight. Granted, some human beings lack the minimal intelligence needed for moral responsibility. Steinbock, however, replies that we can look on all other members of the human species and think "that could be me." By contrast, we cannot have this thought about nonhuman animals.

Most of us believe that we are entitled to treat members of other species in ways which would be considered wrong if inflicted on members of our own species. We kill them for food, keep them confined, use them in painful experiments. The moral philosopher has to ask what relevant difference justifies this difference in treatment. A look at this question will lead us to reexamine the distinctions which we have assumed make a moral difference.

It has been suggested by Peter Singer[1] that our current attitudes are "speciesist," a word intended to make one think of "racist" or "sexist." The idea is that membership in a species is in itself not relevant to moral treatment, and that much of our behaviour and attitudes toward nonhuman animals [are] based simply on this irrelevant fact.

There is, however, an important difference between racism or sexism and "speciesism." We do not subject animals to different moral

From Bonnie Steinbock, "Speciesism and the Idea of Equality," *Philosophy* 53 (1978): pp. 247–256.

treatment simply because they have fur and feathers but because they are in fact different from human beings in ways that could be morally relevant. It is false that women are incapable of being benefited by education, and therefore that claim cannot serve to justify preventing them from attending school. But this is not false of cows and dogs, even chimpanzees. Intelligence is thought to be a morally relevant capacity because of its relation to the capacity for moral responsibility.

What is Singer's response? He agrees that nonhuman animals lack certain capacities that human animals possess and that this may justify different *treatment*. But it does not justify giving less consideration to their needs and interests. According to Singer, the moral mistake which the racist or sexist makes is not essentially the factual error of thinking that blacks or women are inferior to white men. For even if there were no factual error, even if it were true that blacks and women are less intelligent and responsible than whites and men, this would not justify giving less consideration to their needs and interests. It is important to note that the term "speciesism" is in one way like, and in another way unlike, the terms "racism" and "sexism." What the term "speciesism" has in common with these terms is the reference to focusing on a characteristic which is, in itself, irrelevant to moral treatment. And it is worth reminding us of this. But Singer's real aim is to bring us to a new understanding of the idea of equality. The question is, On what do claims to equality rest? The demand for *human* equality is a demand that the interests of all human beings be considered equally unless there is a moral justification for not doing so. But why should the interests of all human beings be considered equally? In order to answer this question, we have to give some sense to the phrase, "All men (human beings) are created equal." Human beings are manifestly *not* equal, differing greatly in intelligence, virtue, and capacities. In virtue of what can the claim to equality be made?

It is Singer's contention that claims to equality do not rest on factual equality. Not only do human beings differ in their capacities, but it might even turn out that intelligence, the capacity for virtue, etc., are not distributed evenly among the races and sexes:

> The appropriate response to those who claim to have found evidence of genetically based differences in ability between the races or sexes is not to stick to the belief that the genetic explanation must be wrong, whatever evidence to the contrary may turn up; instead we should make it quite clear that the claim to equality does not depend on intelligence, moral capacity, physical strength, or similar matters of fact. Equality is a moral ideal, not a simple assertion of fact. There is no

> logically compelling reason for assuming that a factual difference in ability between two people justifies any difference in the amount of consideration we give to satisfying their needs and interests. The principle of equality of human beings is not a description of an alleged actual equality among humans: it is a prescription of how we should treat humans.[2]

. . . Singer says, quite rightly I think, "If a being suffers, there can be no moral justification for refusing to take that suffering into consideration."[3] But he thinks that the principle of equality requires that no matter what the nature of the being, its suffering be counted equally with the like suffering of any other being. In other words, sentience does not simply provide us with reasons for acting; it is the only relevant consideration for equal consideration of interests. It is this view that I wish to challenge.

I want to challenge it partly because it has such counterintuitive results. It means, for example, that feeding starving children before feeding starving dogs is just like a Catholic charity's feeding hungry Catholics before feeding hungry non-Catholics. It is simply a matter of taking care of one's own, something which is usually morally permissible. But whereas we would admire the Catholic agency which did not discriminate, but fed all children, first come, first served, we would feel quite differently about someone who had this policy for dogs and children. Nor is this, it seems to me, simply a matter of a sentimental preference for our own species. I might feel much more love for my dog than for a strange child—and yet I might feel morally obliged to feed the child before I fed my dog. If I gave in to the feelings of love and fed my dog and let the child go hungry, I would probably feel guilty. This is not to say that we can simply rely on such feelings. Huck Finn felt guilty at helping Jim escape, which he viewed as stealing from a woman who had never done him any harm. But while the existence of such feelings does not settle the morality of an issue, it is not clear to me that they can be explained away. In any event, their existence can serve as a motivation for trying to find a rational justification for considering human interests above nonhuman ones. . . .

I think we do have to justify counting our interests more heavily than those of animals. But how? Singer is right, I think, to point out that it will not do to refer vaguely to the greater value of human life, to human worth and dignity:

> Faced with a situation in which they see a need for some basis for the moral gulf that is commonly thought to separate humans and animals,

> but can find no concrete difference that will do this without undermining the equality of humans, philosophers tend to waffle. They resort to high-sounding phrases like "the intrinsic dignity of the human individual." They talk of "the intrinsic worth of all men" as if men had some worth that other beings do not have or they say that human beings, and only human beings, are "ends in themselves," while "everything other than a person can only have value for a person." . . . Why should we not attribute "intrinsic dignity" or "intrinsic worth" to ourselves? Why should we not say that we are the only things in the universe that have intrinsic value? Our fellow human beings are unlikely to reject the accolades we so generously bestow upon them and those to whom we deny the honour are unable to object.[4]

Singer is right to be skeptical of terms like "intrinsic dignity" and "intrinsic worth." These phrases are no substitute for a moral argument. But they may point to one. In trying to understand what is meant by these phrases, we may find a difference or differences between human beings and nonhuman animals that will justify different treatment while not undermining claims for human equality. While we are not compelled to discriminate among people because of different capacities, if we can find a significant difference in capacities between human and nonhuman animals, this could serve to justify regarding human interests as primary. It is not arbitrary or smug, I think, to maintain that human beings have a different moral status from members of other species because of certain capacities which are characteristic of being human. We may not all be equal in these capacities, but all human beings possess them to some measure, and nonhuman animals do not. For example, human beings are normally held to be responsible for what they do. In recognizing that someone is responsible for his or her actions, you accord that person a respect which is reserved for those possessed of moral autonomy or capable of achieving such autonomy. Secondly, human beings can be expected to reciprocate in a way that nonhuman animals cannot. Nonhuman animals cannot be motivated by altruistic or moral reasons; they cannot treat you fairly or unfairly. This does not rule out the possibility of an animal being motivated by sympathy or pity. It does rule out altruistic motivation in the sense of motivation due to the recognition that the needs and interests of others provide one with certain reasons for acting. Human beings are capable of altruistic motivation in this sense. We are sometimes motivated simply by the recognition that someone else is in pain and that pain is a bad thing, no matter who suffers it. It is this sort of reason that I claim cannot motivate an animal or any entity not possessed of fairly abstract concepts.

(If some nonhuman animals do possess the requisite concepts—perhaps chimpanzees who have learned a language—they might well be capable of altruistic motivation.) This means that our moral dealings with animals are necessarily much more limited than our dealings with other human beings. If rats invade our houses, carrying disease and biting our children, we cannot reason with them, hoping to persuade them of the injustice they do us. We can only attempt to get rid of them. And it is this that makes it reasonable for us to accord them a separate and not equal moral status, even though their capacity to suffer provides us with some reason to kill them painlessly, if this can be done without too much sacrifice of human interests. Thirdly, as Williams points out, there is the "desire for self-respect": "a certain human desire to be identified with what one is doing, to be able to realize purposes of one's own, and not to be the instrument of another's will unless one has willingly accepted such a role."[5] Some animals may have some form of this desire, and to the extent that they do, we ought to consider their interest in freedom and self-determination. (Such considerations might affect our attitudes toward zoos and circuses.) But the desire for self-respect *per se* requires the intellectual capacities of human beings, and this desire provides us with special reasons not to treat human beings in certain ways. It is an affront to the dignity of a human being to be a slave (even if a well-treated one); this cannot be true for a horse or a cow. To point this out is of course only to say that the justification for the treatment of an entity will depend on the sort of entity in question. In our treatment of other entities, we must consider the desire for autonomy, dignity, and respect, but only where such a desire exists. Recognition of different desires and interests will often require different treatment, a point Singer himself makes.

But is the issue simply one of different desires and interests justifying and requiring different treatment? I would like to make a stronger claim, namely, that certain capacities, which seem to be unique to human beings, entitle their possessors to a privileged position in the moral community. Both rats and human beings dislike pain, and so we have a *prima facie* reason not to inflict pain on either. But if we can free human beings from crippling diseases, pain, and death through experimentation which involves making animals suffer, and if this is the only way to achieve such results, then I think that such experimentation is justified because human lives are more valuable than animal lives. And this is because of certain capacities and abilities that normal human beings have which animals apparently do not and which human beings cannot exercise if they are devastated by pain or disease.

My point is not that the lack of the sorts of capacities I have been discussing gives us a justification for treating animals just as we like, but rather that it is these differences between human beings and nonhuman animals which provide a rational basis for different moral treatment and consideration. Singer focuses on sentience alone as the basis of equality, but we can justify the belief that human beings have a moral worth that nonhuman animals do not, in virtue of specific capacities and without resorting to "high-sounding phrases."

Singer thinks that intelligence, the capacity for moral responsibility, for virtue, etc., are irrelevant to equality, because we would not accept a hierarchy based on intelligence any more than one based on race. We do not think that those with greater capacities ought to have their interests weighed more heavily than those with lesser capacities, and this, he thinks, shows that differences in such capacities are irrelevant to equality. But it does not show this at all. . . . [W]hat entitles us human beings to a privileged position in the moral community is a certain minimal level of intelligence, which is a prerequisite for morally relevant capacities. The fact that we would reject a hierarchical society based on degree of intelligence does not show that a minimal level of intelligence cannot be used as a cut-off point justifying giving greater consideration to the interests of those entities which meet this standard.

Interestingly enough, Singer concedes the rationality of valuing the lives of normal human beings over the lives of nonhuman animals.[6] We are not required to value equally the life of a normal human being and the life of an animal, he thinks, but only their suffering. But I doubt that the value of an entity's life can be separated from the value of its suffering in this way. If we value the lives of human beings more than the lives of animals, this is because we value certain capacities that human beings have and animals do not. But freedom from suffering is, in general, a minimal condition for exercising these capacities, for living a fully human life. So valuing human life more involves regarding human interests as counting for more. That is why we regard human suffering as more deplorable than comparable animal suffering.

But there is one point of Singer's which I have not yet met. Some human beings (if only a very few) are less intelligent than some nonhuman animals. Some have less capacity for moral choice and responsibility. What status in the moral community are these members of our species to occupy? Are their interests to be considered equally with ours? Is experimenting on them permissible where such experiments are painful or injurious but somehow necessary for human well-being? If it is certain of our capacities which entitle us to a privileged position, it looks as if those lacking those capacities are not entitled to a privileged position. To think it is justifiable to experiment on an adult chimpanzee but not on a severely mentally incapacitated human being seems to be focusing on membership in a species where that has no moral relevance. (It is being "speciesist" in a perfectly reasonable use of the word.) How are we to meet this challenge? . . .

I doubt that anyone will be able to come up with a concrete and morally relevant difference that would justify, say, using a chimpanzee in an experiment rather than a human being with less capacity for reasoning, moral responsibility, etc. Should we then experiment on the severely retarded? . . . [W]e feel a special obligation to care for the handicapped members of our own species, who cannot survive in this world without such care. Nonhuman animals manage very well, despite their "lower intelligence" and lesser capacities; most of them do not require special care from us. This does not, of course, justify experimenting on them. However, to subject to experimentation those people who depend on us seems even worse than subjecting members of other species to it. In addition, when we consider the severely retarded, we think, "That could be me." It makes sense to think that one might have been born retarded but not to think that one might have been born a monkey. And so, although one can imagine one's self in the monkey's place, one feels a closer identification with the severely retarded human being. Here we are getting away from such things as "morally relevant differences" and talking about something much more difficult to articulate, namely, the role of feeling and sentiment in moral thinking. We would be horrified by the use of the retarded in medical research. But what are we to make of this horror? Has it moral significance or is it "mere" sentiment, of no more importance than the sentiment of whites against blacks? It is terribly difficult to know how to evaluate such feelings.[6] I am not going to say more about this, because I think that the treatment of severely incapacitated human beings does not pose an insurmountable objection to the privileged-status principle. I am willing to admit that my horror at the thought of experiments being performed on severely mentally incapacitated human beings in cases in which I would find it justifiable and preferable to perform the same experiments on nonhuman animals (capable of similar suffering) may not be a moral emotion. But it is certainly not wrong of us to extend special care to members of our own species, motivated by feelings of sympathy, protectiveness, etc. If this is speciesism, it is stripped of its tone of moral condemnation. It is not racist to provide special care to members of your own race; it is racist to fall below your moral obligation to a person because of his or her race. I have been arguing that we are morally obliged to consider the interests of all sentient creatures but not to consider those interests equally with human interests. Nevertheless, even this recognition will mean some radical changes in our attitude toward and treatment of other species.

Notes

1. Peter Singer, *Animal Liberation* (New York: Avon Books, 1977).
2. Singer, *Animal Liberation*, p. 5.
3. Singer, *Animal Liberation*, p. 9.
4. Singer, *Animal Liberation*, pp. 266–67.
5. Williams, "The Idea of Equality," p. 157.
6. Singer, *Animal Liberation*, p. 22.

Study Questions

1. What does Steinbock believe is the morally relevant difference between humans and nonhumans?
2. Does having the capacities requisite for moral responsibility affect the badness of a being's feeling pain?
3. How does Steinbock think we should weigh the interests of those humans who lack the capacities requisite for moral responsibility?
4. Is it nonsensical, when looking at a chimpanzee in pain, to think, "That could be me"?

The Case for Animal Rights

Tom Regan

Tom Regan, Professor Emeritus of Philosophy at North Carolina State University, argues for a concept of animal rights that would demand sweeping changes in our existing practices. He calls for the abolition of animal agriculture, commercial and sport hunting, and the use of animals in scientific research. Regan argues that animals have as much a right not to be exploited as we do, because, like us, animals possess inherent value. They are "subjects of life," having wants, preferences, beliefs, feelings, memories, and expectations. Regan's view puts him at odds with the utilitarian wing of the animal rights movement, which views pleasure and the absence of pain as the only intrinsic goods. He argues that utilitarianism is open to the charge that it can accept flagrant violations of individuals' rights, so long as the effect is an increase in the overall quantity of happiness. Thus Regan urges animal advocates to adopt a rights-based theory, broadened to encompass nonrational beings.

I regard myself as an advocate of animal rights—as a part of the animal rights movement. That movement, as I conceive it, is committed to a number of goals, including,

- the total abolition of the use of animals in science;
- the total dissolution of commercial animal agriculture;
- the total elimination of commercial and sport hunting and trapping.

There are, I know, people who profess to believe in animal rights but do not avow these goals. Factory farming, they say, is wrong—it violates animals' rights—but traditional animal agriculture is all right.

From Tom Regan, "The Case for Animal Rights," in *In Defense of Animals,* ed. Peter Singer (Malden, MA: Blackwell, 1985): 13–26.

Toxicity tests of cosmetics on animals violate their rights, but important medical research—cancer research, for example—does not. The clubbing of baby seals is abhorrent, but not the harvesting of adult seals. I used to think I understood this reasoning. Not anymore. You don't change unjust institutions by tidying them up.

What's wrong—fundamentally wrong—with the way animals are treated isn't the details that vary from case to case. It's the whole system. The forlornness of the veal calf is pathetic, heart wrenching; the pulsing pain of the chimp with electrodes planted deep in her brain is repulsive; the slow, tortuous death of the racoon caught in the leg-hold trap is agonizing. But what is wrong isn't the pain, isn't the suffering, isn't the deprivation. These compound what's wrong. Sometimes—often—they make it much, much worse. But they are not the fundamental wrong.

The fundamental wrong is the system that allows us to view animals as *our resources*, here for *us*—to be eaten, or surgically manipulated, or exploited for sport or money. Once we accept this view of animals—as our resources—the rest is as predictable as it is regrettable. Why worry about their loneliness, their pain, their death? Since animals exist for us, to benefit us in one way or another, what harms them really doesn't matter—or matters only if it starts to bother us, makes us feel a trifle uneasy when we eat our veal escalope, for example. So, yes, let us get veal calves out of solitary confinement, give them more space, a little straw, a few companions. But let us keep our veal escalope.

But a little straw, more space and a few companions won't eliminate—won't even touch—the basic wrong that attaches to our viewing and treating these animals as our resources. A veal calf killed to be eaten after living in close confinement is viewed and treated in this way: but so, too, is another who is raised (as they say) "more humanely." To right the wrong of our treatment of farm animals requires more than making rearing methods "more humane"; it requires the total dissolution of commercial animal agriculture. . . .

How to proceed? We begin by asking how the moral status of animals has been understood by thinkers who deny that animals have rights. Then we test the mettle of their ideas by seeing how well they stand up under the heat of fair criticism. If we start our thinking in this way, we soon find that some people believe that we have no duties directly to animals, that we owe nothing to them, that we can do nothing that wrongs them. Rather, we can do wrong acts that involve animals, and so we have duties regarding them, though none to them. Such views may be called indirect duty views. By way of illustration: suppose your neighbour kicks your dog. Then your neighbour has done something wrong. But not to your dog. The wrong that has been done is a wrong to you. After all, it is wrong to upset people, and your neighbour's kicking your dog upsets you. So you are the one who is wronged, not your dog. Or again: by kicking your dog your neighbour damages another person's property. And since it is wrong to damage another person's property, your neighbour has done something wrong—to you, of course, not to your dog. Your neighbour no more wrongs your dog than your car would be wronged if the windshield were smashed. Your neighbour's duties involving your dog are indirect duties to you. More generally, all of our duties regarding animals are indirect duties to one another—to humanity.

How could someone try to justify such a view? Someone might say that your dog doesn't feel anything and so isn't hurt by your neighbour's kick, doesn't care about pain since none is felt, is as unaware of anything as is your windshield. Someone might say this, but no rational person will, since, among other considerations, such a view will commit anyone who holds it to the position that no human being feels pain either—that human beings also don't care about what happens to them. A second possibility is that though both humans and your dog are hurt when kicked, it is only human pain that matters. But, again, no rational person can believe this. Pain is pain wherever it occurs. If your neighbour's causing you pain is wrong because of the pain that is caused, we cannot rationally ignore or dismiss the moral relevance of the pain that your dog feels. . . .

Indirect duty views, then, including the best among them, fail to command our rational assent. Whatever ethical theory we should accept rationally, therefore, it must at least recognize that we have some duties directly to animals, just as we have some duties directly to each other. The next two theories I'll sketch attempt to meet this requirement.

The first I call the cruelty-kindness view. Simply stated, this says that we have a direct duty to be kind to animals and a direct duty not to be cruel to them. Despite the familiar, reassuring ring of these ideas, I do not believe that this view offers an adequate theory. To make this clearer, consider kindness. A kind person acts from a certain kind of motive—compassion or concern, for example. And that is a virtue. But there is no guarantee that a kind act is a right act. If I am a generous racist, for example, I will be inclined to act kindly towards members of my own race, favouring their interests above those of others. My kindness would be real and, so far as it goes, good. But I trust it is too obvious to require argument that my kind acts may not be above moral reproach—may, in fact, be positively wrong because rooted in injustice. So kindness, notwithstanding its status as a virtue to be encouraged, simply will not carry the weight of a theory of right action.

Cruelty fares no better. People or their acts are cruel if they display either a lack of sympathy for or, worse, the presence of enjoyment in another's suffering. Cruelty in all its guises is a bad thing, a tragic human failing. But just as a person's being motivated by kindness does not guarantee that he or she does what is right, so the absence of cruelty does not ensure that he or she avoids doing what is wrong. Many people who perform abortions, for example, are not cruel, sadistic people. But that fact alone does not settle the terribly difficult question of the morality of abortion. The case is no different when we examine the ethics of our treatment of animals. So, yes, let us be for kindness and against cruelty. But let us not suppose that being for the one and against the other answers questions about moral right and wrong.

Some people think that the theory we are looking for is utilitarianism. A utilitarian accepts two moral principles. The first is that of equality: everyone's interests count, and similar interests must be counted as having similar weight or importance. White or black, American or Iranian, human or animal—everyone's pain or frustration matters, and matters just as much as the equivalent pain or frustration of anyone else. The second principle a utilitarian accepts is that of utility: do the act that will bring about the best balance between satisfaction and frustration for everyone affected by the outcome.

As a utilitarian, then, here is how I am to approach the task of deciding what I morally ought to do: I must ask who will be affected if I choose to do one thing rather than another, how much each individual will be affected, and where the best results are most likely to lie—which option, in other words, is most likely to bring about the best results, the best balance between satisfaction and frustration. That option, whatever it may be, is the one I ought to choose. That is where my moral duty lies.

The great appeal of utilitarianism rests with its uncompromising *egalitarianism*: everyone's interests count and count as much as the like interests of everyone else. The kind of odious discrimination . . . based on race or sex, for example [is] disallowed in principle by utilitarianism, as is speciesism, systematic discrimination based on species membership.

The equality we find in utilitarianism, however, is not the sort an advocate of animal or human rights should have in mind. Utilitarianism has no room for the equal moral rights of different individuals because it has no room for their equal inherent value or worth. What has value for the utilitarian is the satisfaction of an individual's interests, not the individual whose interests they are. A universe in which you satisfy your desire for water, food, and warmth is, other things being equal, better than a universe in which these desires are frustrated. And the same is true in the case of an animal with similar desires. But neither you nor the animal have any value in your own right. Only your feelings do.

Here is an analogy to help make the philosophical point clearer: a cup contains different liquids, sometimes sweet, sometimes bitter, sometimes a mix of the two. What has value are the liquids: the sweeter the better, the bitterer the worse. The cup, the container, has no value. It is what goes into it, not what they go into, that has value. For the utilitarian you and I are like the cup; we have no value as individuals and thus no equal value. What has value is what goes into us, what we serve as receptacles for; our feelings of satisfaction have positive value, our feelings of frustration negative value.

Serious problems arise for utilitarianism when we remind ourselves that it enjoins us to bring about the best consequences. What does this mean? It doesn't mean the best consequences for me alone, or for my family or friends, or any other person taken individually. No, what we must do is, roughly, as follows: we must add up . . . the separate satisfactions and frustrations of everyone likely to be affected by our choice, the satisfactions in one column, the frustrations in the other. We must total each column for each of the options before us. That is what it means to say the theory is aggregative. And then we must choose that option which is most likely to bring about the best balance of totalled satisfactions over totalled frustrations. Whatever act would lead to this outcome is the one we ought morally to perform—it is where our moral duty lies. And that act quite clearly might not be the same one that would bring about the best results for me personally, or for my family or friends, or for a lab animal. The best aggregated consequences for everyone concerned are not necessarily the best for each individual.

That utilitarianism is an aggregative theory—different individuals' satisfactions or frustrations are added, or summed, or totalled—is the key objection to this theory. My Aunt Bea is old, inactive, a cranky, sour person, though not physically ill. She prefers to go on living. She is also rather rich. I could make a fortune if I could get my hands on her money, money she intends to give me in any event, after she dies, but which she refuses to give me now. In order to avoid a huge tax bite, I plan to donate a handsome sum of my profits to a local children's hospital. Many, many children will benefit from my generosity, and much joy will be brought to their parents, relatives, and friends. If I don't get the money rather soon, all these ambitions will come to naught. The once-in-a-lifetime opportunity to make a real killing will be gone. Why, then, not kill my Aunt Bea? Oh, of course I *might* get caught. But I'm no fool and, besides, her doctor can be counted on to cooperate (he has an eye for the same investment and I happen to know a good deal about his shady past). The deed can be done . . . professionally, shall we say. There is *very* little chance of getting caught. And as for my conscience being guilt-ridden, I am a resourceful sort of fellow and will take more than sufficient comfort—as I lie on the beach at Acapulco—in contemplating the joy and health I have brought to so many others.

Suppose Aunt Bea is killed and the rest of the story comes out as told. Would I have done anything wrong? Anything immoral? One would have thought that I had. Not according to utilitarianism. Since what I have done has brought about the best balance between totalled satisfaction and frustration for all those affected by the outcome, my action is not wrong. Indeed, in killing Aunt Bea the physician and I did what duty required.

This same kind of argument can be repeated in all sorts of cases, illustrating, time after time, how the utilitarian's position leads to results that impartial people find morally callous. It *is* wrong to kill my Aunt Bea in the name of bringing about the best results for others. A good end does not justify an evil means. Any adequate moral theory will have to explain why this is so. Utilitarianism fails in this respect and so cannot be the theory we seek.

What to do? Where to begin anew? The place to begin, I think, is with the utilitarian's view of the value of the individual—or, rather, lack of value. In its place, suppose we consider that you and I, for example, do have value as individuals—what we'll call *inherent value*. To say we have such value is to say that we are something more than, something different from, mere receptacles. Moreover, to ensure that we do not pave the way for such injustices as slavery or sexual discrimination, we must believe that all who have inherent value have it equally, regardless of their sex, race, religion, birthplace, and so on. Similarly to be discarded as irrelevant are one's talents or skills, intelligence and wealth, personality or pathology, whether one is loved and admired or despised and loathed. The genius and the retarded child, the prince and the pauper, the brain surgeon and the fruit vendor, Mother Teresa and the most unscrupulous used-car salesman—all have inherent value, all possess it equally, and all have an equal right to be treated with respect, to be treated in ways that do not reduce them to the status of things, as if they existed as resources for others. My value as an individual is independent of my usefulness to you. Yours is not dependent on your usefulness to me. For either of us to treat the other in ways that fail to show respect for the other's independent value is to act immorally, to violate the individual's rights.

Some of the rational virtues of this view—what I call the rights view—should be evident. Unlike . . . utilitarianism, this view *in principle* denies that we can justify good results by using evil means that violate an individual's rights—denies, for example, that it could be moral to kill my Aunt Bea to harvest beneficial consequences for others. That would be to sanction the disrespectful treatment of the individual in the name of the social good, something the rights view will not—categorically will not—ever allow.

The rights view, I believe, is rationally the most satisfactory moral theory. It surpasses all other theories in the degree to which it illuminates and explains the foundation of our duties to one another—the domain of human morality. On this score it has the best reasons, the best arguments, on its side. Of course, if it were possible to show that only human beings are included within its scope, then a person like myself, who believes in animal rights, would be obliged to look elsewhere.

But attempts to limit its scope to humans only can be shown to be rationally defective. Animals, it is true, lack many of the abilities humans possess. They can't read, do higher mathematics, build a bookcase, or make *baba ghanoush*. Neither can many human beings, however, and yet we don't (and shouldn't) say that they (these humans) therefore have less inherent value, less of a right to be treated with respect, than do others. It is the *similarities* between those human beings who most clearly, most noncontroversially have such value (the people reading this, for example), not our differences, that matter most. And the really crucial, the basic similarity is simply this: we are each of us the experiencing subject of a life, a conscious creature having an individual welfare that has importance to us whatever our usefulness to others. We want and prefer things, believe and feel things, recall and expect things. And all these dimensions of our life, including our pleasure and pain, our enjoyment and suffering, our satisfaction and frustration, our continued existence or our untimely death—all make a difference to the quality of our life as lived, as experienced, by us as individuals. As the same is true of those animals that concern us (the ones that are eaten and trapped, for example), they too must be viewed as the experiencing subjects of a life, with inherent value of their own.

Some there are who resist the idea that animals have inherent value. "Only humans have such value," they profess. How might this narrow view be defended? Shall we say that only humans have the requisite intelligence, or autonomy, or reason? But there are many, many humans who fail to meet these standards and yet are reasonably viewed as having value above and beyond their usefulness to others. Shall we claim that only humans belong to the right species, the species *Homo sapiens*? But this is blatant speciesism. Will it be said, then, that all—and only—humans have immortal souls? Then our opponents have their work cut out for them. I am myself not ill-disposed to the proposition that there are immortal souls. Personally, I profoundly hope I have one. But I would not want to rest my position on a controversial ethical issue on the even more controversial question about who or what has an immortal soul. That is to dig one's hole deeper, not to climb out. Rationally, it is better to resolve moral issues without making more controversial assumptions than are needed. The question of who has inherent value is such a question, one that is resolved more rationally without the introduction of the idea of immortal souls than by its use.

Well, perhaps some will say that animals have some inherent value, only less than we have. Once again, however, attempts to defend this view can be shown to lack rational justification. What could be the basis of our having more inherent value than animals? Their lack of reason, or autonomy, or intellect? Only if we are willing to make the same judgement in the case of humans who are similarly deficient. But it is not true that such humans—the retarded child, for example, or the mentally deranged—have less inherent value than you or I. Neither, then, can we rationally sustain the view that animals like them in being the experiencing subjects of a life have less inherent value. *All* who have inherent value have it *equally*, whether they be human animals or not.

Inherent value, then, belongs equally to those who are the experiencing subjects of a life. Whether it belongs to others—to rocks and rivers, trees and glaciers, for example—we do not know and may never know. But neither do we need to know, if we are to make the case for animal rights. We do not need to know, for example, how many people are eligible to vote in the next presidential election before we can know whether I am. Similarly, we do not need to know how many individuals have inherent value before we can know that some do. When it comes to the case for animal rights, then, what we need to know is whether the animals that, in our culture, are routinely eaten, hunted, and used in our laboratories, for example, are like us in being subjects of a life. And we do know this. We do know that many—literally, billions and billions—of these animals are the subjects of a life in the sense explained and so have inherent value if we do. And since, in order to arrive at the best theory of our duties to one another, we must recognize our equal inherent value as individuals, reason—not sentiment, not emotion—reason compels us to recognize the equal inherent value of these animals and, with this, their equal right to be treated with respect.

That, *very* roughly, is the shape and feel of the case for animal rights. . . . I must, in closing, limit myself to [two] final points.

The first is how the theory that underlies the case for animal rights shows that the animal rights movement is a part of, not antagonistic to, the human rights movement. The theory that rationally grounds the rights of animals also grounds the rights of humans. Thus those involved in the animal rights movement are partners in the struggle to secure respect for human rights—the rights of women, for example, or minorities, or workers. The animal rights movement is cut from the same moral cloth as these.

Second, having set out the broad outlines of the rights view, I can now say why its implications for farming and science, among other fields, are both clear and uncompromising. In the case of the use of animals in science, the rights view is categorically abolitionist. Lab animals are not our tasters; we are not their kings. Because these animals are treated routinely, systematically as if their value were reducible to their usefulness to others, they are routinely, systematically treated with a lack of respect, and thus are their rights routinely, systematically violated. This is just as true when they are used in trivial, duplicative, unnecessary, or unwise research as it is when they are used in studies that hold out real promise of human benefits. We can't justify harming or killing a human being (my Aunt

Bea, for example) just for these sorts of reason. Neither can we do so even in the case of so lowly a creature as a laboratory rat. It is not just refinement or reduction that is called for, not just larger, cleaner cages, not just more generous use of anaesthetic or the elimination of multiple surgery, not just tidying up the system. It is complete replacement. The best we can do when it comes to using animals in science is—not to use them. That is where our duty lies, according to the rights view.

As for commercial animal agriculture, the rights view takes a similar abolitionist position. The fundamental moral wrong here is not that animals are kept in stressful close confinement or in isolation, or that their pain and suffering, their needs and preferences are ignored or discounted. All these *are* wrong, or course, but they are not the fundamental wrong. They are symptoms and effects of the deeper systematic wrong that allows these animals to be viewed and treated as lacking independent value, as resources for us—as, indeed, a renewable resource. Giving farm animals more space, more natural environments, more companions does not right the fundamental wrong, any more than giving lab animals more anaesthesia or bigger, cleaner cages would right the fundamental wrong in their case. Nothing less than the total dissolution of commercial animal agriculture will do this, just as, for similar reasons I won't develop at length here, morality requires nothing less than the total elimination of hunting and trapping for commercial and sporting ends. The rights view's implications, then, as I have said, are clear and uncompromising. . . .

Study Questions

1. What does Regan mean by "inherent value"?
2. Why does Regan believe that limiting inherent value to human beings is a mistake?
3. Does a lion that eats a zebra violate the zebra's right to life?
4. Under what circumstances, if any, are zoos morally acceptable?

Speaking of Animal Rights

Mary Anne Warren

Mary Anne Warren (1942–2010) was a professor of philosophy at San Francisco State University. Although she agrees with Regan that animals have rights, she argues that his theory is problematic for two reasons. First, she finds his notion of "inherent value" obscure. What is inherent value, and why does having it imply having rights? The second problem is that Regan needs and does not offer a sharp line distinguishing animals that have rights from those that do not. For example, do reptiles have the same rights as monkeys? If not, why not? Warren's conclusion is that some nonhuman animals have rights, but not rights as strong as human rights.

Tom Regan has produced what is perhaps the definitive defense of the view that the basic moral rights of at least some non-human animals are in no way inferior to our own. In *The Case for Animal Rights*, he argues that all normal mammals over a year of age have the same basic moral rights.[1] Non-human mammals have essentially the same right not to be harmed or killed as we do. I shall call this "the strong animal rights position," although it is weaker than the claims made by some animal liberationists in that it ascribes rights to only some sentient animals.[2]

I will argue that Regan's case for the strong animal rights position is unpersuasive and that this position entails consequences which a reasonable person cannot accept. I do not deny that some non-human animals have moral rights; indeed, I would extend the scope of the rights claim to include all sentient animals, that is, all those capable of having experiences, including experiences of pleasure or

From Mary Anne Warren, "Difficulties with the Strong Rights Position," *Between the Species* 4 (1987).

satisfaction and pain, suffering, or frustration.[3] However, I do not think that the moral rights of most nonhuman animals are identical in strength to those of persons.[4] The rights of most non-human animals may be overridden in circumstances which would not justify overriding the rights of persons. There are, for instance, compelling realities which sometimes require that we kill animals for reasons which could not justify the killing of persons. I will call this view "the weak animal rights" position, even though it ascribes rights to a wider range of animals than does the strong animal rights position.

I will begin by summarizing Regan's case for the strong animal rights position and noting two problems with it. Next, I will explore some consequences of the strong animal rights position which I think are unacceptable. Finally, I will outline the case for the weak animal rights position.

Regan's Case

Regan's argument moves through three stages. First, he argues that normal, mature mammals are not only sentient but have other mental capacities as well. These include the capacities for emotion, memory, belief, desire, the use of general concepts, intentional action, a sense of the future, and some degree of self-awareness. Creatures with such capacities are said to be subjects-of-a-life. They are not only alive in the biological sense but have a psychological identity over time and an existence which can go better or worse for them. Thus, they can be harmed or benefited. These are plausible claims, and well defended. . . . The second and third stages of the argument are more problematic.

In the second stage, Regan argues that subjects-of-a-life have inherent value. His concept of inherent value grows out of his opposition to utilitarianism. Utilitarian moral theory, he says, treats individuals as "mere receptacles" for morally significant value, in that harm to one individual may be justified by the production of a greater net benefit to other individuals. In opposition to this, he holds that subjects-of-a-life have a value independent of both the value they may place upon their lives or experiences and the value others may place upon them.

Inherent value, Regan argues, does not come in degrees. To hold that some individuals have more inherent value than others is to adopt a "perfectionist" theory, i.e., one which assigns different moral worth to individuals according to how well they are thought to exemplify some virtue(s), such as intelligence or moral autonomy. Perfectionist theories have been used, at least since the time of Aristotle, to rationalize such injustices as slavery and male domination, as well as the unrestrained exploitation of animals. Regan argues that if we reject these injustices, then we must also reject perfectionism and conclude that all subjects-of-a-life have equal inherent value. Moral agents have no more inherent value than moral patients, i.e., subjects-of-a-life who are not morally responsible for their actions.

In the third phase of the argument, Regan uses the thesis of equal inherent value to derive strong moral rights for all subjects-of-a-life. This thesis underlies the Respect Principle, which forbids us to treat beings who have inherent value as mere receptacles, i.e., mere means to the production of the greatest overall good. This principle, in turn, underlies the Harm Principle, which says that we have a direct prima facie duty not to harm beings who have inherent value. Together, these principles give rise to moral rights. Rights are defined as valid claims, claims to certain goods and against certain beings, i.e., moral agents. Moral rights generate duties not only to refrain from inflicting harm upon beings with inherent value but also to come to their aid when they are threatened by other moral agents. Rights are not absolute but may be overridden in certain circumstances. Just what these circumstances are we will consider later. But first, let's look at some difficulties in the theory as thus far presented.

The Mystery of Inherent Value

Inherent value is a key concept in Regan's theory. It is the bridge between the plausible claim that all normal, mature mammals—human or otherwise—are subjects-of-a-life and the more debatable claim that they all have basic moral rights of the same strength. But it is a highly obscure concept, and its obscurity makes it ill-suited to play this crucial role.

Inherent value is defined almost entirely in negative terms. It is not dependent upon the value which either the inherently valuable individual or anyone else may place upon that individual's life or experiences. It is not (necessarily) a function of sentience or any other mental capacity, because, Regan says, some entities which are not sentient (e.g., trees, rivers, or rocks) may, nevertheless, have inherent value. . . . It cannot attach to anything other than an individual; species, ecosystems, and the like cannot have inherent value.

These are some of the things which inherent value is not. But what is it? Unfortunately, we are not told. Inherent value appears as a mysterious non-natural property which we must take on faith. Regan says that it is a *postulate* that subjects-of-a-life have inherent value, a postulate justified by the fact that it avoids certain absurdities which he thinks follow from a purely utilitarian theory. . . . But why is [it a] postulate that *subjects-of-a-life* have inherent value? If the inherent value of a being is completely independent of the value that it or anyone else places upon its experiences, then why does the fact that it has certain sorts of experiences constitute evidence that it has inherent value? If the reason is that subjects-of-a-life have an existence which can go better or worse for them, then why isn't the appropriate conclusion that all sentient beings have inherent value, since they would all seem to meet that condition? Sentient but mentally unsophisticated beings may have a less extensive range of possible satisfactions and frustrations, but why should it follow that they have—or may have—no inherent value at all?

In the absence of a positive account of inherent value, it is also difficult to grasp the connection between being inherently valuable and having moral rights. Intuitively, it seems that value is one thing, and rights are another. It does not seem incoherent to say that some things (e.g., mountains, rivers, redwood trees) are inherently valuable and yet are not the sorts of things which can have moral rights. Nor does it seem incoherent to ascribe inherent value to some things which are not individuals, e.g., plant or animal species, though it may well be incoherent to ascribe moral rights to such things.

In short, the concept of inherent value seems to create at least as many problems as it solves. If inherent value is based on some natural property, then why not try to identify that property and explain its moral significance, without appealing to inherent value? And if it is not based on any natural property, then why should we believe in it? That it may enable us to avoid some of the problems faced by the utilitarian is not a sufficient reason, if it creates other problems which are just as serious.

Is There a Sharp Line?

Perhaps the most serious problems are those that arise when we try to apply the strong animal rights position to animals other than normal, mature mammals. Regan's theory requires us to divide all living things into two categories: those which have the same inherent value and the same basic moral rights that we do, and those which have no inherent value and presumably no moral rights. But wherever we try to draw the line, such a sharp division is implausible.

It would surely be arbitrary to draw such a sharp line between normal, mature mammals and all other living things. Some birds (e.g., crows, magpies, parrots, mynahs) appear to be just as mentally sophisticated as most mammals and thus are equally strong candidates for inclusion under the subject-of-a-life criterion. Regan is not in fact advocating that we draw the line here. His claim is only that normal mature mammals are clear cases, while other cases are less clear. Yet, on his theory, there must be such a sharp line *somewhere,* since there are no degrees of inherent value. But why should we believe that there is a sharp line between creatures that are subjects-of-a-life and creatures that are not? Isn't it more likely that "subjecthood" comes in degrees, that some creatures have only a little self-awareness, and only a little capacity to anticipate the future, while some have a little more, and some a good deal more?

Should we, for instance, regard fish, amphibians, and reptiles as subjects-of-a-life? A simple yes-or-no answer seems inadequate. On the one hand, some of their behavior is difficult to explain without the assumption that they have sensations, beliefs, desires, emotions, and memories; on the other hand, they do not seem to exhibit very much self-awareness or very much conscious anticipation of future events. Do they have enough mental sophistication to count as subjects-of-a-life? Exactly how much is enough?

It is still more unclear what we should say about insects, spiders, octopi, and other invertebrate animals which have brains and sensory organs but whose minds (if they have minds) are even more alien to us than those of fish or reptiles. Such creatures are probably sentient. Some people doubt that they can feel pain, since they lack certain neurological structures which are crucial to the processing of pain impulses in vertebrate animals. But this argument is inconclusive, since their nervous systems might process pain in ways different from ours. When injured, they sometimes act as if they are in pain. On evolutionary grounds, it seems unlikely that highly mobile creatures with complex sensory systems would not have developed a capacity for pain (and pleasure), since such a capacity has obvious survival value. It must, however, be admitted that we do not *know* whether spiders can feel pain (or something very like it), let alone whether they have emotions, memories, beliefs, desires, self-awareness, or a sense of the future.

Even more mysterious are the mental capacities (if any) of mobile microfauna. The brisk and efficient way that paramecia move about in their incessant search for food *might* indicate some kind of sentience, in spite of their lack of eyes, ears, brains, and other organs associated with sentience in more complex organisms. It is conceivable—though not very probable—that they, too, are subjects-of-a-life.

The existence of a few unclear cases need not pose a serious problem for a moral theory, but in this case, the unclear cases constitute most of those with which an adequate theory of animal rights would need to deal. The subject-of-a-life criterion can provide us with little or no moral guidance in our interactions with the vast majority of animals. That might be acceptable if it could be supplemented with additional principles which would provide such guidance. However, the radical dualism of the theory precludes supplementing it in this way. We are forced to say that either a spider has the same right to life as you and I do, or it has no right to life whatever—and that only the gods know which of these alternatives is true.

Regan's suggestion for dealing with such unclear cases is to apply the "benefit of the doubt" principle. That is, when dealing with beings that may or may not be subjects-of-a-life, we should act as if they are.[5] But if we try to apply this principle to the entire range of doubtful cases, we will find ourselves with moral obligations which we cannot possibly fulfill. In many climates, it is virtually impossible to live without swatting mosquitoes and exterminating cockroaches, and not all of us can afford to hire someone to sweep the path before we walk, in order to make sure that we do not step on ants. Thus, we are still faced with the daunting task of drawing a sharp line somewhere on the continuum of life forms—this time, a line demarcating the limits of the benefit of the doubt principle.

The weak animal rights theory provides a more plausible way of dealing with this range of cases, in that it allows the rights of animals of different kinds to vary in strength. . . .

Why Are Animal Rights Weaker than Human Rights?

How can we justify regarding the rights of persons as generally stronger than those of sentient beings which are not persons? There are a plethora of bad justifications, based on religious premises or false or unprovable claims about the differences between human and nonhuman nature. But there is one difference which has a clear moral relevance: people are at least sometimes capable of being moved to action or inaction by the force of reasoned argument. Rationality rests upon other mental capacities, notably those which Regan cites as criteria for being a subject-of-a-life. We share these capacities with many other animals. But it is not just because we are subjects-of-a-life that we are both able and morally compelled to recognize one another as beings with equal basic moral rights. It is also because we are able to "listen to reason" in order to settle our conflicts and cooperate in shared projects. This capacity, unlike the others, may require something like a human language.

Why is rationality morally relevant? It does not make us "better" than other animals or more "perfect." It does not even automatically make us more intelligent. (Bad reasoning reduces our effective intelligence rather than increasing it.) But it is morally relevant insofar as it provides greater possibilities for cooperation and for the nonviolent resolution of problems. It also makes us more dangerous than nonrational beings can ever be. Because we are potentially more dangerous and less predictable than wolves, we need an articulated system of morality to regulate our conduct. Any human morality, to be workable in the long run, must recognize the equal moral status of all persons, whether through the postulate of equal basic moral rights or in some other way. The recognition of the moral equality of other persons is the price we must each pay for their recognition of our moral equality. Without this mutual recognition of moral equality, human society can exist only in a state of chronic and bitter conflict. The war between the sexes will persist so long as there is sexism and male domination; racial conflict will never be eliminated so long as there are racist laws and practices. But, to the extent that we achieve a mutual recognition of equality, we can hope to live together, perhaps as peacefully as wolves, achieving (in part) through explicit moral principles what they do not seem to need explicit moral principles to achieve.

Why not extend this recognition of moral equality to other creatures, even though they cannot do the same for us? The answer is that we cannot. Because we cannot reason with most non-human animals, we cannot always solve the problems which they may cause without harming them—although we are always obligated to try. We cannot negotiate a treaty with the feral cats and foxes, requiring them to stop preying on endangered native species in return for suitable concessions on our part.

> If rats invade our houses . . . we cannot reason with them, hoping to persuade them of the injustice they do us. We can only attempt to get rid of them.[6]

Aristotle was not wrong in claiming that the capacity to alter one's behavior on the basis of reasoned argument is relevant to the full moral status which he accorded to free men. Of course, he was wrong in his other premise, that women and slaves by their nature cannot reason well enough to function as autonomous moral agents. Had that premise been true, so would his conclusion that women and slaves are not quite the moral equals of free men. In the case of most non-human animals, the corresponding premise is true. If, on the other hand, there are animals with whom we can (learn to) reason, then we are obligated to do this and to regard them as our moral equals.

Thus, to distinguish between the rights of persons and those of most other animals on the grounds that only people can alter their behavior on the basis of reasoned argument does not commit us to a perfectionist theory of the sort Aristotle endorsed. There is no excuse for refusing to recognize the moral equality of some people on the grounds that we don't regard them as quite as rational as we are, since it is perfectly clear that most people can reason well enough to determine how to act so as to respect the basic rights of others (if they choose to), and that is enough for moral equality.

But what about people who are clearly not rational? It is often argued that sophisticated mental capacities such as rationality cannot be essential for the possession of equal basic moral rights, since nearly everyone agrees that human infants and mentally incompetent persons have such rights, even though they may lack those sophisticated mental capacities. But this argument is inconclusive, because there are powerful practical and emotional reasons for protecting non-rational human beings, reasons which are absent in the case of most non-human animals. Infancy and mental incompetence are human conditions which all of us either have experienced or are likely to experience at some time. We also protect babies and mentally incompetent people because we care for them. We don't normally care for animals in the same way, and when we do—e.g., in the case of much-loved pets—we may regard them as having special rights by virtue of their relationship to us. We protect them not only for their sake but also for our own, lest we be hurt by harm done to them. Regan holds that such "side-effects" are irrelevant to moral rights, and perhaps they are. But in ordinary usage, there is no sharp line between moral rights and those moral protections which are not rights. The extension of strong moral protections to infants and the mentally impaired in no way proves that non-human animals have the same basic moral rights as people.

Why Speak of "Animal Rights" at All?

If, as I have argued, reality precludes our treating all animals as our moral equals, then why should we still ascribe rights to them? Everyone agrees that animals are entitled to some protection against human abuse, but why speak of animal *rights* if we are not prepared to accept most animals as our moral equals? The weak animal rights position may seem an unstable compromise between the bold claim that animals have the same basic moral rights that we do and the more common view that animals have no rights at all. . . .

The most plausible alternative to the view that animals have moral rights is that, while they do not have *rights*, we are, nevertheless, obligated not to be cruel to them. Regan argues persuasively that the injunction to avoid being cruel to animals is inadequate to express our obligations towards animals, because it focuses on the mental states of those who cause animal suffering, rather than on the harm done to the animals themselves. . . . Cruelty is inflicting pain or suffering and either taking pleasure in that pain or suffering or being more or less indifferent to it. Thus, to express the demand for the decent treatment of animals in terms of the rejection of cruelty is to invite the too easy response that those who subject animals to suffering are not being cruel because they regret the suffering they cause but sincerely believe that what they do is justified. The injunction to avoid cruelty is also inadequate in that it does not preclude the killing of animals—for any reason, however trivial—so long as it is done relatively painlessly.

The inadequacy of the anti-cruelty view provides one practical reason for speaking of animal rights. Another practical reason is that this is an age in which nearly all significant moral claims tend to be expressed in terms of rights. Thus, the denial that animals have rights, however carefully qualified, is likely to be taken to mean that we may do whatever we like to them, provided that we do not violate any human rights. In such a context, speaking of the rights of animals may be the only way to persuade many people to take seriously protests against the abuse of animals.

Why not extend this line of argument and speak of the rights of trees, mountains, oceans, or anything else which we may wish to see protected from destruction? Some environmentalists have not hesitated to speak in this way, and, given the importance of protecting such elements of the natural world, they cannot be blamed for using this rhetorical device. But, I would argue that moral rights can meaningfully be ascribed only to entities which have some capacity for sentience. This is because moral rights are protections designed to protect rights holders from harms or to provide them with benefits which matter *to them.* Only beings capable of sentience can be harmed or benefited in ways which matter to them, for only such beings can like or dislike what happens to them or prefer some conditions to others. Thus, sentient animals, unlike mountains, rivers, or species, are at least logically possible candidates for moral rights. This fact, together with the need to end current abuses of animals—e.g., in scientific research . . . —provides a plausible case for speaking of animal rights.

Conclusion

I have argued that Regan's case for ascribing strong moral rights to all normal, mature mammals is unpersuasive because (1) it rests upon the obscure concept of inherent value, which is defined only in negative terms, and (2) it seems to preclude any plausible answer to questions about the moral status of the vast majority of sentient animals. . . .

The weak animal rights theory asserts (1) that any creature whose natural mode of life includes the pursuit of certain satisfactions has the right not to be forced to exist without the opportunity to pursue those satisfactions; (2) that any creature which is capable of pain, suffering, or frustration has the right that such experiences not be deliberately inflicted upon it without some compelling reason; and (3) that no sentient being should be killed without good reason. However, moral rights are not an all-or-nothing affair. The strength of the reasons required to override the rights of a non-human organism varies, depending upon—among other things—the probability that it is sentient and (if it is clearly sentient) its probable degree of mental sophistication.

Notes

1. Tom Regan, *The Case for Animal Rights* (Berkeley: University of California Press, 1983). All page references are to this edition.
2. For instance, Peter Singer, although he does not like to speak of rights, includes all sentient beings under the protection of his basic utilitarian principle of equal respect for like interests. (*Animal Liberation* [New York: Avon Books, 1975], p. 3.)

3. The capacity for sentience, like all of the mental capacities mentioned in what follows, is a disposition. Dispositions do not disappear whenever they are not currently manifested. Thus, sleeping or temporarily unconscious persons or non-human animals are still sentient in the relevant sense (i.e., still capable of sentience), so long as they still have the neurological mechanisms necessary for the occurrence of experiences.
4. It is possible, perhaps probable that some non-human animals—such as cetaceans and anthropoid apes—should be regarded as persons. If so, then the weak animal rights position holds that these animals have the same basic moral rights as human persons.
5. See, for instance, p. 319, where Regan appeals to the benefit of the doubt principle when dealing with infanticide and late-term abortion.
6. Bonnie Steinbock, "Speciesism and the Idea of Equality," *Philosophy* 53 (1978): 253.

Study Questions

1. How does Warren distinguish the strong animal rights position and the weak one?
2. Do all human beings deserve the same rights?
3. Do all nonhuman animals deserve the same rights?
4. According to Warren, why do mountains lack rights?

C.

The Environment

Philosophical Problems for Environmentalism

Elliott Sober

Should species and ecosystems be preserved for reasons beyond their value as resources for human use? Environmentalists believe so, but what compelling argument can they offer in support of their view? Elliott Sober, Professor of Philosophy at the University of Wisconsin–Madison, maintains that environmental values are analogous to aesthetic ones. Treating environmental values as aesthetic values, he maintains, helps demarcate which objects matter for their own sakes and which do not. Species and ecosystems, like works of art, are prized for their rarity and fittingness in a context. Indeed, Sober asserts that if a striking rock formulation were found next to the ruins of a Greek temple, he would see no relevant difference in their value.

I. Introduction

A number of philosophers have recognized that the environmental movement, whatever its practical political effectiveness, faces considerable theoretical difficulties in justification.[1] It has been recognized

From Elliott Sober, "Philosophical Problems for Environmentalism," in *The Preservation of Species*, ed. Bryan G. Norton (Princeton, NJ: Princeton University Press, 1986): pp. 173–194.

that traditional moral theories do not provide natural underpinnings for policy objectives and this has led some to skepticism about the claims of environmentalists, and others to the view that a revolutionary reassessment of ethical norms is needed. In this chapter, I will try to summarize the difficulties that confront a philosophical defense of environmentalism. I also will suggest a way of making sense of some environmental concerns that does not require the wholesale jettisoning of certain familiar moral judgments. . . .

The problem for environmentalism stems from the idea that species and ecosystems ought to be preserved for reasons additional to their known value as resources for human use. The feeling is that even when we cannot say what nutritional, medicinal, or recreational benefit the preservation provides, there still is a value in preservation. It is the search for a rationale for this feeling that constitutes the main conceptual problem for environmentalism.

The problem is especially difficult in view of the holistic (as opposed to individualistic) character of the things being assigned value. Put simply, what is special about environmentalism is that it values the preservation of species, communities, or ecosystems, rather than the individual organisms of which they are composed. "Animal liberationists" have urged that we should take the suffering of sentient animals into account in ethical deliberation.[2] Such beasts are not mere things to be used as cruelly as we like no matter how trivial the benefit we derive. But in "widening the ethical circle," we are simply including in the community more individual organisms whose costs and benefits we compare. Animal liberationists are extending an old and familiar ethical doctrine—namely, utilitarianism—to take account of the welfare of other individuals. Although the practical consequences of this point of view may be revolutionary, the theoretical perspective is not at all novel. If suffering is bad, then it is bad for any individual who suffers. Animal liberationists merely remind us of the consequences of familiar principles.

But trees, mountains, and salt marshes do not suffer. They do not experience pleasure and pain, because, evidently, they do not have experiences at all. The same is true of species. Granted, individual organisms may have mental states; but the species—taken to be a population of organisms connected by certain sorts of interactions (preeminently, that of exchanging genetic material in reproduction)— does not. Or put more carefully, we might say that the only sense in which species have experiences is that their member organisms do: the attribution at the population level, if true, is true simply in virtue of its being true at the individual level. Here is a case where reductionism is correct.

So perhaps it is true in this reductive sense that some species experience pain. But the values that environmentalists attach to preserving species do not reduce to any value of preserving organisms. It is in this sense that environmentalists espouse a holistic value system. Environmentalists care about entities that by no stretch of the imagination have experiences (e.g., mountains). What is more, their position does not force them to care if individual organisms suffer pain, so long as the species is preserved. Steel traps may outrage an animal liberationist because of the suffering they inflict, but an environmentalist aiming just at the preservation of a balanced ecosystem might see here no cause for complaint. Similarly, environmentalists think that the distinction between wild and domesticated organisms is important, in that it is the preservation of "natural" (i.e., not created by the "artificial interference" of human beings) objects that matters, whereas animal liberationists see the main problem in terms of the suffering of any organism—domesticated or not. And finally, environmentalists and animal liberationists diverge on what might be called the *n + m question*. If two species—say blue and sperm whales—have roughly comparable capacities for experiencing pain, an animal liberationist might tend to think of the preservation of a sperm whale as wholly on an ethical par with the preservation of a blue whale. The fact that one organism is part of an endangered species while the other is not does not make the rare individual more intrinsically important. But for an environmentalist, this holistic property—membership in an endangered species—makes all the difference in the world: a world with n sperm and m blue whales is far better than a world with $n + m$ sperm and 0 blue whales. Here we have a stark contrast between an ethic in which it is the life situation of individuals that matters, and an ethic in which the stability and diversity of populations of individuals are what matter.[3]

Both animal liberationists and environmentalists wish to broaden our ethical horizons—to make us realize that it is not just human welfare that counts. But they do this in very different, often conflicting, ways. It is no accident that at the level of practical politics the two points of view increasingly find themselves at loggerheads. This practical conflict is the expression of a deep theoretical divide.

II. The Ignorance Argument

"Although we might not now know what use a particular endangered species might be to us, allowing it to go extinct forever closes off the possibility of discovering and exploiting a future use." According to this point of view, our ignorance of value is turned into a reason for action. The scenario envisaged in this environmentalist argument is not without precedent; who could have guessed that penicillin would be good for something other than turning out cheese? But there is a fatal defect in such arguments, which we might summarize with the phrase *out of nothing, nothing comes:* rational decisions require assumptions about what is true and what is valuable. . . . If you are completely ignorant of values, then you are incapable of making a rational decision, either for or against preserving some species. The fact that you do not know the value of a species, by itself, cannot count as a reason for wanting one thing rather than another to happen to it.

And there are so many species. How many geese that lay golden eggs are there apt to be in that number? It is hard to assign probabilities and utilities precisely here, but an analogy will perhaps reveal the problem confronting this environmentalist argument. Most of us willingly fly on airplanes, when safer (but less convenient) alternative forms of transportation are available. Is this rational? Suppose it were argued that there is a small probability that the next flight you take will crash. This would be very bad for you. Is it not crazy for you to risk this, given that the only gain to you is that you can reduce your travel time by a few hours (by not going by train, say)? Those of us who not only fly, but congratulate ourselves for being rational in doing so, reject this argument. We are prepared to accept a small chance of a great disaster in return for the high probability of a rather modest benefit. If this is rational, no wonder that we might consistently be willing to allow a species to go extinct in order to build a hydroelectric plant.

That the argument from ignorance is no argument at all can be seen from another angle. If we literally do not know what consequences the extinction of this or that species may bring, then we should take seriously the possibility that the extinction may be beneficial as well as the possibility that it may be deleterious. It may sound deep to insist that we preserve endangered species precisely because we do not know why they are valuable. But ignorance on a scale like this cannot provide the basis for any rational action.

Rather than invoke some unspecified future benefit, an environmentalist may argue that the species in question plays a crucial role in stabilizing the ecosystem of which it is a part. This will undoubtedly be true for carefully chosen species and ecosystems, but one should not generalize this argument into a global claim to the effect that *every* species is crucial to a balanced ecosystem. Although ecologists used to agree that the complexity of an ecosystem stabilizes it, this hypothesis has been subject to a number of criticisms and qualifications, both from a theoretical and an empirical perspective.[4] And for certain kinds of species (those which occupy a rather small area and whose normal population is small) we can argue that extinction would probably not disrupt the community. However fragile the biosphere may be, the extreme view that everything is crucial is almost certainly not true.

But, of course, environmentalists are often concerned by the fact that extinctions are occurring now at a rate much higher than in earlier times. It is mass extinction that threatens the biosphere, they say, and this claim avoids the spurious assertion that communities are so fragile that even one extinction will cause a crash. However, if the point is to avoid a mass extinction of species, how does this provide a rationale for preserving a species of the kind just described, of which we rationally believe that its passing will not destabilize the ecosystem? And, more generally, if mass extinction is known to be a danger to us, how does this translate into a value for preserving any particular species? Notice that we have now passed beyond the confines of the argument from ignorance; we are taking as a premise the idea that mass extinction would be a catastrophe (since it would destroy the ecosystem on which we depend). But how should that premise affect our valuing the California condor, the blue whale, or the snail darter?

III. The Slippery Slope Argument

Environmentalists sometimes find themselves asked to explain why each species matters so much to them, when there are, after all, so many. We may know of special reasons for valuing particular species, but how can we justify thinking that each and every species is important? "Each extinction impoverishes the biosphere" is often the answer given, but it really fails to resolve the issue. Granted, each extinction impoverishes, but it only impoverishes a little bit. So if it is the *wholesale* impoverishment of the biosphere that matters, one would apparently have to concede that each extinction matters a little, but only a little. But environmentalists may be loathe to concede this, for if they concede that each species matters only a little, they seem to be inviting the wholesale impoverishment that would be an unambiguous disaster. So they dig in their heels and insist that each species matters a lot. But to take this line, one must find some other rationale than the idea that mass extinction would be a great harm. Some of these alternative rationales we will examine later. For now, let us take a closer look at the train of thought involved here.

Slippery slopes are curious things: if you take even one step onto them, you inevitably slide all the way to the bottom. So if you want to avoid finding yourself at the bottom, you must avoid stepping onto them at all. To mix metaphors, stepping onto a slippery slope is to invite being nickeled and dimed to death. . . .

Starting with 10 million extant species, and valuing overall diversity, the environmentalist does not want to grant that each species matters only a little. For having granted this, commercial expansion and other causes will reduce the tally to 9,999,999. And then the argument is repeated, with each species valued only a little, and diversity declines another notch. And so we are well on our way to a considerably impoverished biosphere, a little at a time. Better to reject the starting premise—namely, that each species matters only a little—so that the slippery slope can be avoided.

Slippery slopes should hold no terror for environmentalists, because it is often a mistake to demand that a line be drawn. Let me illustrate by an example. What is the difference between being bald and not? Presumably, the difference concerns the number of hairs you have on your head. But what is the precise number of hairs marking the boundary between baldness and not being bald? There is no such number. Yet, it would be a fallacy to conclude that there is no difference between baldness and hairiness. The fact that you cannot draw a line does not force you to say that the two alleged categories collapse into one. . . . [M]y point is just that differences in degree do not demolish the possibility of there being real moral differences.

In the environmental case, if one places a value on diversity, then each species becomes more valuable as the overall diversity declines. If we begin with 10 million species, each may matter little, but as extinctions continue, the remaining ones matter more and more. According to this outlook, a better and better reason would be demanded for allowing yet another species to go extinct. Perhaps certain sorts of economic development would justify the extinction of a species at one time. But granting this does not oblige one to conclude that the same sort of decision would have to be made further down the road. This means that one can value diversity without being obliged to take the somewhat exaggerated position that each species, no matter how many there are, is terribly precious in virtue of its contribution to that diversity.

Yet, one can understand that environmentalists might be reluctant to concede this point. They may fear that if one now allows that most species contribute only a little to overall diversity, one will set in motion a political process that cannot correct itself later. The worry is that even when the overall diversity has been drastically reduced, our ecological sensitivities will have been so coarsened that we will no longer be in a position to realize (or to implement policies fostering) the preciousness of what is left. This fear may be quite justified, but it is important to realize that it does not conflict with what was argued above. The political utility of making an argument should not be confused with the argument's soundness.

The fact that you are on a slippery slope, by itself, does not tell you whether you are near the beginning, in the middle, or at the end. If species diversity is a matter of degree, where do we currently find ourselves—on the verge of catastrophe, well on our way in that direction, or at some distance from a global crash? Environmentalists often urge that we are fast approaching a precipice; if we are, then the reduction in diversity that every succeeding extinction engenders should be all we need to justify species preservation.

Sometimes, however, environmentalists advance a kind of argument not predicated on the idea of fast approaching doom. The goal is to show that there is something wrong with allowing a species to go extinct (or with causing it to go extinct), even if overall diversity is not affected much. I now turn to one argument of this kind.

IV. Appeals to What Is Natural

I noted earlier that environmentalists and animal liberationists disagree over the significance of the distinction between wild and domesticated animals. Since both types of organisms can experience pain, animal liberationists will think of each as meriting ethical consideration. But environmentalists will typically not put wild and domesticated organisms on a par. Environmentalists typically are interested in preserving what is natural, be it a species living in the wild or a wilderness ecosystem. If a kind of domesticated chicken were threatened with extinction, I doubt that environmental groups would be up in arms. And if certain unique types of human environments—say urban slums in the United States—were "endangered," it is similarly unlikely that environmentalists would view this process as a deplorable impoverishment of the biosphere.

The environmentalist's lack of concern for humanly created organisms and environments may be practical rather than principled. It may be that at the level of values, no such bifurcation is legitimate, but that from the point of view of practical political action, it makes sense to put one's energies into saving items that exist in the wild. This subject has not been discussed much in the literature, so it is hard to tell. But I sense that the distinction between wild and domesticated has a certain theoretical importance to many environmentalists. They perhaps think that the difference is that we created domesticated organisms which would otherwise not exist, and so are entitled to use them solely for our own interests. But we did not create wild organisms and environments, so it is the height of presumption to expropriate them for our benefit. A more fitting posture would be one of "stewardship": we have come on the scene and found a treasure not of our making. Given this, we ought to preserve this treasure in its natural state.

I do not wish to contest the appropriateness of "stewardship." It is the dichotomy between artificial (domesticated) and natural (wild) that strikes me as wrong-headed. I want to suggest that to the degree that "natural" means anything biologically, it means very little ethically. And, conversely, to the degree that "natural" is understood as a normative concept, it has very little to do with biology.

Environmentalists often express regret that we human beings find it so hard to remember that we are part of nature—one species among many others—rather than something standing outside of nature. I will not consider here whether this attitude is cause for complaint; the important point is that seeing us as part of nature rules out the environmentalist's use of the distinction between artificial-domesticated and natural-wild described above. *If we are part of nature, then everything we do is part of nature, and is natural in that primary sense.* When we domesticate organisms and bring them into a state of dependence on us, this is simply an example of one species exerting a selection pressure on another. If one calls this "unnatural," one might just as well say the same of parasitism or symbiosis (compare human domestication of animals and plants and "slave-making" in the social insects).

The concept of naturalness is subject to the same abuses as the concept of normalcy. *Normal* can mean *usual* or it can mean *desirable.*

Although only the total pessimist will think that the two concepts are mutually exclusive, it is generally recognized that the mere fact that something is common does not by itself count as a reason for thinking that it is desirable. This distinction is quite familiar now in popular discussions of mental health, for example. Yet, when it comes to environmental issues, the concept of naturalness continues to live a double life. The destruction of wilderness areas by increased industrialization is bad because it is unnatural. And it is unnatural because it involves transforming a natural into an artificial habitat. Or one might hear that although extinction is a natural process, the kind of mass extinction currently being precipitated by our species is unprecedented, and so is unnatural. Environmentalists should look elsewhere for a defense of their policies, lest conservation simply become a variant of uncritical conservatism in which the axiom "Whatever is, is right" is modified to read "Whatever is (before human beings come on the scene), is right." . . .

The idea of "natural tendency" played a decisive role in pre-Darwinian biological thinking. Aristotle's entire science—both his physics and his biology—is articulated in terms of specifying the natural tendencies of kinds of objects and the interfering forces that can prevent an object from achieving its intended state. Heavy objects in the sublunar sphere have location at the center of the earth as their natural state; each tends to go there, but is prevented from doing so. Organisms likewise are conceptualized in terms of this natural state model:

> . . . [for] any living thing that has reached its normal development and which is unmutilated, and whose mode of generation is not spontaneous, the most natural act is the production of another like itself, an animal producing an animal, a plant a plant. . . .[5]

But many interfering forces are possible, and in fact the occurrence of "monsters" is anything but uncommon. According to Aristotle, mules (sterile hybrids) count as deviations from the natural state. In fact, females are monsters as well, since the natural tendency of sexual reproduction is for the offspring to perfectly resemble the father, who, according to Aristotle, provides the "genetic instructions" (to put the idea anachronistically) while the female provides only the matter.

What has happened to the natural state model in modern science? . . . [O]ne of the most profound achievements of Darwinian biology has been the jettisoning of this kind of model. It isn't just that Aristotle was wrong in his detailed claims about mules and women;

the whole structure of the natural state model has been discarded. Population biology is not conceptualized in terms of positing some characteristic that all members of a species would have in common, were interfering forces absent. Variation is not thought of as a deflection from the natural state of uniformity. Rather, variation is taken to be a fundamental property in its own right. Nor, at the level of individual biology, does the natural state model find an application. Developmental theory is not articulated by specifying a natural tendency and a set of interfering forces. The main conceptual tool for describing the various developmental pathways open to a genotype is the norm of reaction. The norm of reaction of a genotype within a range of environments will describe what phenotype the genotype will produce in a given environment. Thus, the norm of reaction for a corn plant genotype might describe how its height is influenced by the amount of moisture in the soil. The norm of reaction is entirely silent on which phenotype is the "natural" one. The idea that a corn plant might have some "natural height," which can be augmented or diminished by "interfering forces" is entirely alien to post-Darwinian biology.

The fact that the concepts of natural state and interfering force have lapsed from biological thought does not prevent environmentalists from inventing them anew. Perhaps these concepts can be provided with some sort of normative content; after all, the normative idea of "human rights" may make sense even if it is not a theoretical underpinning of any empirical science. But environmentalists should not assume that they can rely on some previously articulated scientific conception of "natural."

V. Appeals to Needs and Interests

The version of utilitarianism considered earlier (according to which something merits ethical consideration if it can experience pleasure and/or pain) leaves the environmentalist in the lurch. But there is an alternative to Bentham's hedonistic utilitarianism that has been thought by some to be a foundation for environmentalism. Preference utilitarianism says that an object's having interests, needs, or preferences gives it ethical status. This doctrine is at the core of Stone's affirmative answer to the title question of his book *Should Trees Have Standing?*[6] "Natural objects can communicate their wants (needs) to us, and in ways that are not terribly ambiguous. . . . The lawn tells me that it wants water by a certain dryness of the blades and soil—immediately obvious to the touch—the appearance of bald spots, yellowing, and a lack of springiness after being walked on." And if plants can do this, presumably so can mountain ranges, and endangered species. Preference utilitarianism may thereby seem to grant intrinsic ethical importance to precisely the sorts of objects about which environmentalists have expressed concern.

... If one does not require of an object that it have a mind for it to have wants or needs, what is required for the possession of these ethically relevant properties? Suppose one says that an object needs something if it will cease to exist if it does not get it. Then species, plants, and mountain ranges have needs, but only in the sense that automobiles, garbage dumps, and buildings do too. If everything has needs, the advice to take needs into account in ethical deliberation is empty, unless it is supplemented by some technique for weighing and comparing the needs of different objects. A corporation will go bankrupt unless a highway is built. But the swamp will cease to exist if the highway is built. Perhaps one should take into account all relevant needs, but the question is how to do this in the event that needs conflict.

Although the concept of need can be provided with a permissive, all-inclusive definition, it is less easy to see how to do this with the concept of want. Why think that a mountain range "wants" to retain its unspoiled appearance, rather than house a new amusement park?[7] Needs are not at issue here, since in either case, the mountain continues to exist. One might be tempted to think that natural objects like mountains and species have "natural tendencies," and that the concept of want should be liberalized so as to mean that natural objects "want" to persist in their natural states. This Aristotelian view, as I argued in the previous section, simply makes no sense. Granted, a commercially undeveloped mountain will persist in this state, unless it is commercially developed. But it is equally true that a commercially untouched hill will become commercially developed, unless something causes this not to happen. I see no hope for extending the concept of wants to the full range of objects valued by environmentalists.

The same problems emerge when we try to apply the concepts of needs and wants to species. A species may need various resources, in the sense that these are necessary for its continued existence. But what do species want? Do they want to remain stable in numbers, neither growing nor shrinking? Or since most species have gone extinct, perhaps what species really want is to go extinct, and it is human meddlesomeness that frustrates this natural tendency? Preference utilitarianism is no more likely than hedonistic utilitarianism to secure autonomous ethical status for endangered species. . . .

Darwinism has not banished the idea that parts of the natural world are goal-directed systems, but has furnished this idea with a natural mechanism. We properly conceive of organisms (or genes, sometimes) as being in the business of maximizing their chances of survival and reproduction. We describe characteristics as adaptations—as devices that exist for the furtherance of these ends. Natural selection makes this perspective intelligible. But Darwinism is a profoundly individualistic doctrine. Darwinism rejects the idea that species, communities, and ecosystems have adaptations that exist for their own benefit. These higher-level entities are not conceptualized as goal-directed systems; what properties of organization they possess are viewed as artifacts of processes operating at lower levels of organization. An environmentalism based on the idea that the ecosystem is directed toward stability and diversity must find its foundation elsewhere.

VI. Granting Wholes Autonomous Value

A number of environmentalists have asserted that environmental values cannot be grounded in values based on regard for individual welfare. Aldo Leopold wrote in *A Sand County Almanac* that "a thing is right when it tends to preserve the integrity, stability, and beauty of the biotic community. It is wrong when it tends otherwise."[8] Callicott develops this idea at some length, and ascribes to ethical environmentalism the view that "the preciousness of individual deer, *as of any other specimen*, is inversely proportional to the population of the species."[9] In his *Desert Solitaire*, Edward Abbey notes that he would sooner shoot a man than a snake.[10] And Garrett Hardin asserts that human beings injured in wilderness areas ought not to be rescued: making great and spectacular efforts to save the life of an individual "makes sense only when there is a shortage of people. I have not lately heard that there is a shortage of people."[11] The point of view suggested by these quotations is quite clear. It isn't that preserving the integrity of ecosystems has autonomous value, to be taken into account just as the quite distinct value of individual human welfare is. Rather, the idea is that the only value is the holistic one of maintaining ecological balance and diversity. Here we have a view that is just as monolithic as the most single-minded individualism; the difference is that the unit of value is thought to exist at a higher level of organization.

It is hard to know what to say to someone who would save a mosquito, just because it is rare, rather than a human being, if there were a choice. In ethics, as in any other subject, rationally persuading another person requires the existence of shared assumptions. If this monolithic environmentalist view is based on the notion that ecosystems have needs and interests, and that these take total precedence over the rights and interests of individual human beings, then the discussion of the previous sections is relevant. And even supposing that these higher-level entities have needs and wants, what reason is there to suppose that these matter and that the wants and needs of individuals matter not at all? But if this source of defense is jettisoned, and it is merely asserted that only ecosystems have value, with no substantive defense being offered, one must begin by requesting an argument: *why* is ecosystem stability and diversity the only value? . . .

VII. The Demarcation Problem

Perhaps the most fundamental theoretical problem confronting an environmentalist who wishes to claim that species and ecosystems have autonomous value is what I will call the *problem of demarcation.* Every ethical theory must provide principles that describe which objects matter for their own sakes and which do not. Besides marking the boundary between these two classes by enumerating a set of ethically relevant properties, an ethical theory must say why the properties named, rather than others, are the ones that count. Thus, for example, hedonistic utilitarianism cites the capacity to experience pleasure and/or pain as the decisive criterion; preference utilitarianism cites the having of preferences (or wants, or interests) as the decisive property. And a Kantian ethical theory will include an individual in the ethical community only if it is capable of rational reflection and autonomy. Not that justifying these various proposed solutions to the demarcation problem is easy; indeed, since this issue is so fundamental, it will be very difficult to justify one proposal as opposed to another. Still, a substantive ethical theory is obliged to try.

Environmentalists, wishing to avoid the allegedly distorting perspective of individualism, frequently want to claim autonomous value for wholes. This may take the form of a monolithic doctrine according to which the only thing that matters is the stability of the ecosystem. Or it may embody a pluralistic outlook according to which ecosystem stability and species preservation have an importance additional to the welfare of individual organisms. But an environmentalist theory shares with all ethical theories an interest in not saying that everything has autonomous value. The reason this position is proscribed is that it makes the adjudication of ethical conflict very difficult indeed. . . .

Environmentalists, as we have seen, may think of natural objects, like mountains, species, and ecosystems, as mattering for their own sake, but of artificial objects, like highway systems and domesticated animals, as having only instrumental value. If a mountain and a highway are both made of rock, it seems unlikely that the difference between them arises from the fact that mountains have wants, interests, and preferences, but highway systems do not. But perhaps the place to look for the relevant difference is not in their present physical composition, but in the historical fact of how each came into existence. Mountains were created by natural processes, whereas highways are humanly constructed. But once we realize that organisms construct their environments in nature, this contrast begins to cloud. Organisms do not passively reside in an environment whose properties are independently determined. Organisms transform their environments by physically interacting with them. An anthill is an artifact just as a highway is. Granted, a difference obtains at the level of whether conscious deliberation played a role, but can one take seriously the view that artifacts produced by conscious planning are thereby *less* valuable than ones that arise without the intervention of mentality.[12] As we have noted before, although environmentalists often accuse their critics of failing to think in a biologically realistic way, their use of the distinction between "natural" and "artificial" is just the sort of idea that stands in need of a more realistic biological perspective.

My suspicion is that the distinction between natural and artificial is not the crucial one. On the contrary, certain features of environmental concerns imply that natural objects are exactly on a par with certain artificial ones. Here the intended comparison is not between mountains and highways, but between mountains and works of art. My goal in what follows is not to sketch a substantive conception of what determines the value of objects in these two domains, but to motivate an analogy.

For both natural objects and works of art, our values extend beyond the concerns we have for experiencing pleasure. Most of us value seeing an original painting more than we value seeing a copy, even when we could not tell the difference. When we experience works of art, often what we value is not just the kinds of experiences we have, but, in addition, the connections we usually have with certain real objects. . . . Nor is this fact about our valuation limited to such aesthetic and environmentalist contexts. We love various people in our lives. If a molecule-for-molecule replica of a beloved person were created, you would not love that individual, but would continue to love the individual to whom you actually were historically related. Here again, our attachments are to objects and people as they really are, and not just to the experiences that they facilitate.

Another parallel between environmentalist concerns and aesthetic values concerns the issue of context. Although environmentalists often stress the importance of preserving endangered species, they would not be completely satisfied if an endangered species were preserved by putting a number of specimens in a zoo or in a humanly constructed preserve. What is taken to be important is preserving the species in its natural habitat. This leads to the more holistic position that preserving ecosystems, and not simply preserving certain member species, is of primary importance. Aesthetic concerns often lead in the same direction. It was not merely saving a fresco or an altar piece that motivated art historians after the most recent flood in Florence. Rather, they wanted to save these works of art in their original ("natural") settings. Not just the painting, but the church that housed it; not just the church, but the city itself. The idea of objects residing in a "fitting" environment plays a powerful role in both domains.

Environmentalism and aesthetics both see value in rarity. Of two whales, why should one be more worthy of aid than another, just because one belongs to an endangered species? Here we have the $n + m$ question mentioned in Section I. As an ethical concern, rarity is difficult to understand. Perhaps this is because our ethical ideas concerning justice and equity (note the word) are saturated with individualism. But in the context of aesthetics, the concept of rarity is far from alien. A work of art may have enhanced value simply because there are very few other works by the same artist, or from the same historical period, or in the same style. It isn't that the price of the item may go up with rarity; I am talking about aesthetic value, not monetary worth. Viewed as valuable aesthetic objects, rare organisms may be valuable because they are rare.

A disanalogy may suggest itself. It may be objected that works of art are of instrumental value only, but that species and ecosystems have intrinsic value. Perhaps it is true, as claimed before, that our attachment to works of art, to nature, and to our loved ones extends beyond the experiences they allow us to have. But it may be argued that what is valuable in the aesthetic case is always the relation of a valuer to a valued object. When we experience a work of art, the value is not simply in the experience, but in the composite fact that we and the work of art are related in certain ways. This immediately suggests that if there were no valuers in the world, nothing would have value, since such relational facts could no longer obtain. So, to adapt Routley and Routley's "last man argument," it would seem that if an ecological crisis precipitated a collapse of the world system, the last human being (whom we may assume for the purposes of this example to be the last valuer) could set about destroying all works of art, and there would be nothing wrong in this.[13] That is, if aesthetic objects are valuable only in so far as valuers can stand in certain relations to them, then when valuers disappear, so does the possibility of aesthetic value. This would deny, in one sense, that aesthetic objects are intrinsically valuable: it isn't they, in themselves, but rather the relational facts that they are part of, that are valuable.

In contrast, it has been claimed that the "last man" would be wrong to destroy natural objects such as mountains, salt marshes, and species. (So as to avoid confusing the issue by bringing in the welfare of individual organisms, Routley and Routley imagine that destruction and mass extinctions can be caused painlessly, so that there would be nothing wrong about this undertaking from the point of view of the nonhuman organisms involved.) If the last man ought to preserve these natural objects, then these objects appear to have a kind of autonomous value; their value would extend beyond their possible relations to valuers. If all this were true, we would have here a contrast between aesthetic and natural objects, one that implies that natural objects are more valuable than works of art.

Routley and Routley advance the last man argument as if it were decisive in showing that environmental objects such as mountains and salt marshes have autonomous value. I find the example more puzzling than decisive. But, in the present context, we do not have to decide whether Routley and Routley are right. We only have to decide whether this imagined situation brings out any relevant difference between aesthetic and environmental values. Were the last man to look up on a certain hillside, he would see a striking rock formation next to the ruins of a Greek temple. Long ago the temple was built from some of the very rocks that still stud the slope. Both promontory and temple have a history, and both have been transformed by the biotic and the abiotic environments. I myself find it impossible to advise the last man that the peak matters more than the temple. I do not see a relevant difference. Environmentalists, if they hold that the solution to the problem of demarcation is to be found in the distinction between natural and artificial, will have to find such a distinction. But if environmental values are aesthetic, no difference need be discovered.

Environmentalists may be reluctant to classify their concern as aesthetic. Perhaps they will feel that aesthetic concerns are frivolous. Perhaps they will feel that the aesthetic regard for artifacts that has been made possible by culture is antithetical to a proper regard for wilderness. But such contrasts are illusory. Concern for environmental values does not require a stripping away of the perspective afforded by civilization; to value the wild, one does not have to "become wild" oneself (whatever that may mean). Rather, it is the material comforts of civilization that make possible a serious concern for both aesthetic and environmental values. These are concerns that can become pressing in developed nations in part because the populations of those countries now enjoy a certain substantial level of prosperity. It would be the height of condescension to expect a nation experiencing hunger and chronic disease to be inordinately concerned with the autonomous value of ecosystems or with creating and preserving works of art. Such values are not frivolous, but they can become important to us only after certain fundamental human needs are satisfied. Instead of radically jettisoning individualist ethics, environmentalists may find a more hospitable home for their values in a category of value that has existed all along.

Notes

1. Mark Sagoff, "On Preserving the Natural Environment," *Yale Law Review* 84 (1974): 205–38; J. Baird Callicott, "Animal Liberation: A Triangular Affair," *Environmental Ethics* 2 (1980): 311–38; and Bryan Norton, "Environmental Ethics and Nonhuman Rights," *Environmental Ethics* 4 (1982): 17–36.
2. Peter Singer, *Animal Liberation* (New York: Random House, 1975), has elaborated a position of this sort.
3. A parallel with a quite different moral problem will perhaps make it clearer how the environmentalist's holism conflicts with some fundamental ethical ideas. When we consider the rights of individuals to receive compensation for harm, we generally expect that the individuals compensated must be one and the same as the individuals harmed. This expectation runs counter to the way an affirmative action program might be set up, if individuals were to receive compensation simply for

being members of groups that have suffered certain kinds of discrimination, whether or not they themselves were victims of discrimination. I do not raise this example to suggest that a holistic conception according to which groups have entitlements is beyond consideration. Rather, my point is to exhibit a case in which a rather common ethical idea is individualistic rather than holistic.

4. David Ehrenfeld, "The Conservation of Non-Resources," *American Scientist* 64 (1976): 648–56. For a theoretical discussion see Robert M. May, *Stability and Complexity in Model Ecosystems* (Princeton: Princeton University Press, 1973).
5. Aristotle, *De Anima*, 415a26.
6. Christopher Stone, *Should Trees Have Standing?* (Los Altos, Calif.: William Kaufmann, 1972), p. 24.
7. The example is Sagoff's, "Natural Environment," pp. 220–24.
8. Aldo Leopold, *A Sand County Almanac* (New York: Oxford University Press, 1949), pp. 224–25.
9. Callicott, "A Triangular Affair," p. 326 (emphasis mine).
10. Edward Abbey, *Desert Solitaire* (New York: Ballantine Books, 1968), p. 20.
11. Garrett Hardin, "The Economics of Wilderness," *Natural History* 78 (1969): 176.
12. Here we would have an inversion, not just a rejection, of a familiar Marxian doctrine—the labor theory of value.
13. Routley and Routley, "Human Chauvinism," pp. 121–22.

Study Questions

1. What does Sober mean by "a holistic value system"?
2. What different meanings can be given to the term "natural"?
3. According to Sober, what is "the demarcation problem"?
4. In what ways, if any, is the extinction of a species akin to the destruction of a work of art?

The Ethics of Climate Change

John Broome

John Broome is White's Professor of Moral Philosophy at the University of Oxford. He argues that, in light of climate change, future people will suffer more, yet, given increasing wealth, will be economically advantaged compared to present people. What we do now in response to climate change depends on how we assign value to these future goods. Should we give priority to the least well-off, a view known as "prioritarianism"? If so, then the sacrifice asked of present people will be less. Broome, however, disagrees with this view. Should we treat future goods as less valuable than present ones? If so, then the goods of present people will be weighed more heavily than those of future people. Again, Broome disagrees. According to Broome, we should be temporally impartial.

What should we do about climate change? The question is an ethical one. Science, including the science of economics, can help discover the causes and effects of climate change. It can also help work out what we can do about climate change. But what we should do is an ethical question.

Not all "should" questions are ethical. "How should you hold a golf club?" is not, for instance. The climate question is ethical, however, because any thoughtful answer must weigh conflicting interests among different people. If the world is to do something about climate change, some people—chiefly the better-off among the current generation—will have to reduce their emissions of greenhouse gases to save future generations from the possibility of a bleak existence in a hotter world. When interests conflict, "should" questions are always ethical.

From John Broome, "The Ethics of Climate Change," *Scientific American*, May 2008.

Climate change raises a number of ethical questions. How should we—all of us living today—evaluate the well-being of future generations, given that they are likely to have more material goods than we do? Many people, some living, others yet to be born, will die from the effects of climate change. Is each death equally bad? How bad are those deaths collectively? Many people will die before they bear children, so climate change will prevent the existence of children who would otherwise have been born. Is their nonexistence a bad thing? By emitting greenhouse gases, are the rich perpetrating an injustice on the world's poor? How should we respond to the small but real chance that climate change could lead to worldwide catastrophe?

Many ethical questions can be settled by common sense. Sophisticated philosophy is rarely needed. All of us are to some extent equipped to face up to the ethical questions raised by climate change. For example, almost everyone recognizes (with some exceptions) the elementary moral principle that you should not do something for your own benefit if it harms another person. True, sometimes you cannot avoid harming someone, and sometimes you may do it accidentally without realizing it. But whenever you cause harm, you should normally compensate the victim.

Climate change will cause harm. Heat waves, storms and floods will kill many people and harm many others. Tropical diseases, which will increase their range as the climate warms, will exact their toll in human lives. Changing patterns of rainfall will lead to local shortages of food and safe drinking water. Large-scale human migrations in response to rising sea levels and other climate-induced stresses will impoverish many people. As yet, few experts have predicted specific numbers, but some statistics suggest the scale of the harm that climate change will cause. The European heat wave of 2003 is estimated to have killed 35,000 people. In 1998 floods in China adversely affected 240 million. The World Health Organization estimates that as long ago as 2000 the annual death toll from climate change had already reached more than 150,000.

In going about our daily lives, each of us causes greenhouse gases to be emitted. Driving a car, using electric power, buying anything whose manufacture or transport consumes energy—all those activities generate greenhouse gases that contribute to climate change. In that way, what we each do for our own benefit harms others. Perhaps at the moment we cannot help it, and in the past we did not realize we were doing it. But the elementary moral principle I mentioned tells us we should try to stop doing it and compensate the people we harm.

This same principle also tells us that what we should do about climate change is not just a matter of weighing benefits against costs—although it is partly that. Suppose you calculate that the benefit to you and your friends of partying until dawn exceeds the harm done to your neighbor by keeping her awake all night. It does not follow that you should hold your party. Similarly, think of an industrial project that brings benefits in the near future but emits greenhouse gases that will harm people decades hence. Again suppose the benefits exceed the costs. It does not follow that the project should go ahead; indeed it may be morally wrong. Those who benefit from it should not impose its costs on others who do not.

Ethics of Costs and Benefits

But even if weighing costs against benefits does not entirely answer the question of what should be done about climate change, it is an essential part of the answer. The costs of mitigating climate change are the sacrifices the present generation will have to make to reduce greenhouse gases. We will have to travel less and better insulate our homes. We will have to eat less meat. We will have to live less lavishly. The benefits are the better lives that future people will lead: they will not suffer so much from the spread of deserts, from the loss of their homes to the rising sea, or from floods, famines and the general impoverishment of nature.

Weighing benefits to some people against costs to others is an ethical matter. But many of the costs and benefits of mitigating climate change present themselves in economic terms, and economics has useful methods of weighing benefits against costs in complex cases. So here economics can work in the service of ethics.

The ethical basis of cost-benefit economics was recognized recently in a major report, the *Stern Review on the Economics of Climate Change,* by Nicholas Stern and his colleagues at the U.K. Treasury. The *Stern Review* concentrates mainly on comparing costs and benefits, and it concludes that the benefit that would be gained by reducing emissions of greenhouse gases would be far greater than the cost of reducing them. Stern's work has provoked a strong reaction from economists for two reasons. First, some economists think economic conclusions should not be based on ethical premises. Second, the review favors strong and immediate action to control emissions, whereas other economic studies, such as one by William Nordhaus of Yale University, have concluded that the need to act is not so urgent.

Those two issues are connected. Stern's conclusion differs from Nordhaus's principally because, on ethical grounds, Stern uses a lower "discount rate." Economists generally value future goods less than present ones: they discount future goods. Furthermore, the more distant the future in which goods become available, the more the goods are discounted. The discount rate measures how fast the value of goods diminishes with time. Nordhaus discounts at roughly 6 percent a year; Stern discounts at 1.4 percent. The effect is that Stern gives a present value of $247 billion for having, say, a trillion dollars' worth of goods a century from now. Nordhaus values having those same goods in 2108 at just $2.5 billion today. Thus, Stern attaches nearly 100 times as much value as Nordhaus does to having any given level of costs and benefits 100 years from now.

The difference between the two economists' discount rates is enough to explain the difference between their conclusions. Most of the costs of controlling climate change must be borne in the near future, when the present generation must sacrifice some of its consumption. The benefits will mostly come a century or two from now. Because Stern judges the present value of those benefits to be higher than Nordhaus does, Stern can justify spending more today on mitigating climate change than Nordhaus can.

The Richer Future

Why discount future goods at all? The goods in question are the material goods and services that people consume—bicycles, food, banking services, and so on. In most of the scenarios predicted for climate change, the world economy will continue to grow. Hence, future people will on average possess more goods than present people do. The more goods you already have, the less valuable are further goods, and so it is sound economic logic to discount them. To have one bathroom in your house is a huge improvement to your life; a second bathroom is nice but not so life-changing. Goods have "diminishing marginal value," as economists put it.

But there may be a second, purely ethical reason for discounting goods that come to relatively rich people. According to an ethical theory known as prioritarianism, a benefit—by which I mean an increase in an individual's well-being—that comes to a rich person should be assigned less social value than the same benefit would have if it had come to a poor person. Prioritarianism gives priority to the less well off. According to an alternative ethical theory known as utilitarianism, however, a benefit has the same value no matter who receives it. Society should simply aim to maximize the total of people's well-being, no matter how that total is distributed across the population.

What should the discount rate be? What determines how fast the value of having goods in the future diminishes as the future time in question becomes more remote? That depends, first, on some nonethical factors. Among them is the economy's rate of growth, which measures how much better off, on average, people will be in the future than they are today. Consequently, it determines how much less benefit future people will derive from additional material goods than people would derive now from those same goods. A fast growth rate makes for a high discount rate.

The discount rate also depends on an ethical factor. How should benefits to those future, richer people be valued in comparison to our own? If prioritarianism is right, the value attached to future people's benefits should be less than the value of our benefits, because future people will be better off than we are. If utilitarianism is right, future people's benefits should be valued equally with ours. Prioritarianism therefore makes for a relatively high discount rate; utilitarianism makes for a lower one.

The debate between prioritarians and utilitarians takes a curious, even poignant turn in this context. Most debates about inequality take place among the relatively rich, when they consider what sacrifices they should make for the relatively poor. But when we think about future people, we are considering what sacrifices we, the relatively poor, should make for the later relatively rich. Usually prioritarianism demands more of the developed countries than utilitarianism does. In this case, it demands less.

Temporal Distance

Another ethical consideration also affects the discount rate. Some philosophers think we should care more about people who live close to us in time than about those who live in the more distant future, just because of their temporal distance from us. If those philosophers are right, future well-being should be discounted just because it comes in the future. This position is called pure discounting. It implies we should give less importance to the death of a 10-year-old 100 years in the future than to the death of a 10-year-old now. An opposing view is that we should be temporally impartial, insisting that the mere date on which a harm occurs makes no difference to its value. Pure discounting makes for a relatively high discount rate; temporal impartiality makes for a lower one.

To determine the right discount rate, therefore, the economist must answer at least two ethical questions. Which should we accept: prioritarianism or utilitarianism? And should we adopt pure discounting or be temporally impartial?

These questions are not matters of elementary morality; they raise difficult issues in moral philosophy. Moral philosophers approach such questions by combining tight analytical argument with sensitivity to ethical intuitions. Arguments in moral philosophy are rarely conclusive, partly because we each have mutually inconsistent intuitions. All I can do as a philosopher is judge the truth as well as I can and present my best arguments in support of my judgments. Space prevents me from setting forth my arguments here, but I have concluded that prioritarianism is mistaken and that we should be temporally impartial. . . .

Market Discount Rates?

Stern reaches those same ethical conclusions. Since both tend toward low discounting, they—together with Stern's economic modeling—lead him to his 1.4 percent rate. His practical conclusion follows: the world urgently needs to take strong measures to control climate change.

Economists who oppose Stern do not deny that his practical conclusion follows from his ethical stance. They object to his ethical stance. Yet most of them decline to take any ethical position of their own, even though they favor an interest rate higher than Stern's. As I have explained, the correct discount rate depends on ethical considerations. So how can economists justify a discount rate without taking an ethical position?

They do so by taking their higher discount rate from the money market, where people exchange future money for present money, and vice versa. They adopt the money-market interest rate as their interest rate. How can that be justified?

First, some values are determined by people's tastes, which markets do reveal. The relative value of apples and oranges is determined by the tastes revealed in the fruit market. But the value that should be attached to the well-being of future generations is not determined by tastes. It is a matter of ethical judgment.

So does the money market reveal people's ethical judgments about the value of future well-being? I doubt it. The evidence shows that, when people borrow and lend, they often give less weight to their own future well-being than to their present well-being. Most of us are probably not so foolish as to judge that our own well-being is somehow less valuable in old age than in youth. Instead our behavior simply reflects our impatience to enjoy a present benefit, overwhelming whatever judgment we might make about the value of our own future. Inevitably, impatience will also overwhelm whatever high-minded arguments we might make in favor of the well-being of future generations.

But for the sake of argument, suppose people's market behavior genuinely reflected their judgments of value. How could economists then justify proclaiming an ethically neutral stance and taking the discount rate from the market? They do so, purportedly, on democratic grounds—leaving ethical judgments to the public rather than making them for themselves. The economists who criticize Stern claim the democratic high ground and accuse him of arrogantly trying to impose his own ethical beliefs on others.

They misunderstand democracy. Democracy requires debate and deliberation as well as voting. Economists—even Stern—cannot impose their beliefs on anyone. They can only make recommendations and argue for them. Determining the correct discount rate requires sophisticated theory, and we members of the public cannot do it without advice from experts. The role of economists in the democratic process is to work out that theory. They should offer their best recommendations, supported by their best arguments. They should be willing to engage in debate with one another about the ethical bases of their conclusions. Then we members of the public must reach our own decisions with the experts' help. Without their help, our choices will be uninformed and almost worthless.

Once we have made our decisions through the democratic process, society can act. That is not the job of economists. Their recommendations are inputs to the process, not the output of it. The true arrogance is imagining that you are the final arbiter of the democratic process.

Ethical considerations cannot be avoided in determining the discount rate. Climate change raises many other ethical issues, too; they will require serious work in ethics to decide what sacrifices we should make to moderate climate change. Like the science of climate change, the ethics of climate change is hard. So far it leaves much to be resolved. We face ethical as well as scientific problems, and we must work to solve them.

Study Questions

1. Should future goods be valued less than present ones?
2. What is "prioritarianism"?
3. Should we care more about present people than future people?
4. In what ways does climate change raise ethical considerations?

APPENDIX

Puzzles to Ponder

A. The Trolley Problem

Judith Jarvis Thomson

I

[L]et us imagine the situation to be as in the case I will call Bystander's Two Options. A bystander happens to be standing by the track, next to a switch that can be used to turn the tram off the straight track, on which five men are working, onto a spur of track to the right on which only one man is working. The bystander therefore has only two options:

> Bystander's Two Options: he can
> (i) do nothing, letting five die, or
> (ii) throw the switch to the right, killing one.

Most people say that he may choose option (ii). . . .

II

Here is a case that I will call Bystander's Three Options. The switch available to this bystander can be thrown in two ways. If he throws it to the right, then the trolley will turn onto the spur of track to the right, thereby killing one workman. If he throws it to the left, then the trolley will turn onto the spur of track to the left. The bystander himself stands on that left-hand spur of track, and will himself be killed if the trolley turns onto it. Or, of course, he can do nothing, letting five workmen die. In sum,

From Judith Jarvis Thomson, "Turning the Trolley," *Philosophy & Public Affairs* 36 (2008). The principles are renumbered.

Bystander's Three Options: he can
(i) do nothing, letting five die, or
(ii) throw the switch to the right, killing one, or
(iii) throw the switch to the left, killing himself.

What is your reaction to the bystander's having the following thought? "Hmm. I want to save those five workmen. I can do that by choosing option (iii), that is by throwing the switch to the left, saving the five but killing myself. I'd prefer not dying today, however, even for the sake of saving five. So I'll choose option (ii), saving the five but killing the one on the right-hand track instead."

I hope you will agree that choosing (ii) would be unacceptable on the bystander's part. If he *can* throw the switch to the left and turn the trolley onto himself, how dare he throw the switch to the right and turn the trolley onto the one workman? The bystander doesn't feel like dying today, even for the sake of saving five, but we can assume, and so let us assume, that the one workman also doesn't feel like dying today, even if the bystander would thereby save five.

Let us get a little clearer about why this bystander must not choose option (ii). He wants to save the five on the straight track ahead. That would be good for them, and his saving them would be a good deed on his part. But his doing that good deed would have a cost: his life or the life of the one workman on the right-hand track. What the bystander does if he turns the trolley onto the one workman is to make the one workman pay the cost of his good deed because he doesn't feel like paying it himself.

Compare the following possibility. I am asked for a donation to Oxfam. I want to send them some money. I am able to send money of my own, but I don't feel like it. So I steal some from someone else and send *that* money to Oxfam. That is pretty bad. But if the bystander proceeds to turn the trolley onto the one on the right-hand track in Bystander's Three Options, then what he does is markedly worse, because the cost in Bystander's Three Options isn't money, it is life.

In sum, if A wants to do a certain good deed, and can pay what doing it would cost, then—other things being equal—A may do that good deed only if A pays the cost himself. In particular, here is a . . . *ceteris paribus* principle:

First Principle: A must not kill B to save five if he can instead kill himself to save the five.

So the bystander in Bystander's Three Options must not kill the one workman on the right-hand track in furtherance of his good deed of saving the five since he can instead save the five by killing himself. Thus he must not choose option (ii).

On the other hand, morality doesn't require him to choose option (iii). If A wants to do a certain good deed, and discovers that the only permissible means he has of doing the good deed is killing himself, then he may refrain from doing the good deed. In particular, here is a second *ceteris paribus* principle:

> *Second Principle:* A may let five die if the only permissible means he has of saving them is killing himself.

So the bystander in Bystander's Three Options may choose option (i).

Let us now return to Bystander's Two Options. We may imagine that the bystander in this case can see the trolley headed for the five workmen, and wants to save them. He thinks: "Does this switch allow for me to choose option (iii), in which I turn the trolley onto myself? If it does, then I must not choose option (ii), in which I turn the trolley onto the one workman on the right-hand track, for as the *First Principle* says, I must prefer killing myself to killing him. But I don't want to kill myself, and if truth be told, I wouldn't if I could. So if the switch does allow for me to choose option (iii), then I have to forgo my good deed of saving the five: I have to choose option (i)—thus I have to let the five die. As, of course, the *Second Principle* says I may."

As you can imagine, he therefore examines the switch *very* carefully. Lo, he discovers that the switch doesn't allow him to choose option (iii). "What luck," he thinks, "I can't turn the trolley onto myself. So it's perfectly all right for me to choose option (ii)!" His thought is that since he can't himself pay the cost of his good deed, it is perfectly all right for him to make the workman on the right-hand track pay it—despite the fact that he wouldn't himself pay it if he could.

I put it to you that that thought won't do. Since he wouldn't himself pay the cost of his good deed if he could pay it, there is no way in which he can decently regard himself as entitled to make someone else pay it.

Of how many of us is it true that if we could permissibly save five only by killing ourselves, then we would? Doing so would be altruism, for as the *Second Principle* says, nobody is required to do so, and doing so would therefore be altruism; moreover, doing so would be doing something for others at a major cost to oneself, and doing so would therefore be major altruism. Very few of us would. Then very few of us could decently regard ourselves as entitled to choose option (ii) if we were in the bystander's situation in Bystander's Two Options.

B. The Altruism Puzzle

Steven M. Cahn

I

Suppose I uncover a plot to set off a bomb that would destroy a city. Only I am in position to foil the scheme. Doing so, however, would cost me my life. I may choose, of course, to sacrifice myself and thereby save thousands of others. But I am morally obligated to do so?

II

The altruism puzzle suggests a quandary that is worth attention. If in the case described I have a moral obligation to sacrifice my life, then in another situation I might be morally obligated to give up my property, my physical well-being, or my pursuit of happiness. After all, if when my life is at risk, I cannot choose self-interest over altruism, how can I do so to preserve something of lesser value than my life? Granted, in other situations the consequences of my choices might not be so calamitous, but considering the vast amount of suffering in our world, I could be obligated to abandon, if not my life, at least all my personal interests, devoting myself exclusively to providing much-needed aid to others. I would become, in the words of the subtitle of *The Pirates of Penzance,* "The Slave of Duty."

On the other hand, if in the case described I do not have a moral obligation to sacrifice my life because that price would be too great, why should I ever be morally obligated to give up my property, my physical well-being, or my pursuit of happiness? Admittedly, such values fare not as precious to me as my life, but still I may find surrendering them excessively costly. If I do, why can't I again choose self-interest over morality? Furthermore, wouldn't the justification for my doing so be even stronger in ordinary circumstances, where the consequences of my acting solely for my own advantage are far less horrific?

In sum, the altruism puzzle calls for accepting one alternative and dealing with the consequences. But which option should be chosen?

C. The Non-Identity Problem

Derek Parfit

A 14-year-old girl decides to have a child. We try to change her mind. We first try to persuade her that if she has a child now, that will be worse for her. She says that even if it will be, that is her affair. We then claim that if she has a child now, that will be worse for her child. If she waits until she is grown up, she will be a better mother and will be able to give her child a better start in life.

Suppose that this 14-year-old rejects our advice. She has a child now and gives him a poor start in life. Was our claim correct? Would it have been better for him if she had taken our advice? If she had, *he* would never have been born. So her decision was worse for him only if it is against his interests to have been born. Even if this makes sense, it would be true only if his life was so wretched as to be worse than nothing. Assume that this is not so. We must then admit that our claim was false. We may still believe that this girl should have waited. That would have been better for her, and the different child she would have had later would have received a better start in life. But we cannot claim that, in having *this* child, what she did was worse for *him*. . . .

Here is another example:

> *Depletion*: Suppose that, as a community, we must choose whether to deplete or conserve certain kinds of resources. If we choose Depletion, the quality of life over the next two centuries would be slightly higher than it would have been if we had chosen Conservation, but it may later

> be much lower. Life at this much lower level would, however, still be well worth living. . . .

This case raises the same problem. If we choose Depletion rather than Conservation, this will lower the quality of life more than two centuries from now. But the particular people who will then be living would never have existed if instead we had chosen Conservation. So our choice of Depletion is not worse for any of these people. But our choice will cause these people to be worse off than the different people who, if we had chosen Conservation, would have later lived. This seems a bad effect and an objection to our choice, even though it will be worse for no one.

D. The Divestiture Puzzle

Steven M. Cahn

I

Suppose I hold one hundred shares of stock in a company that has embarked on a policy I consider immoral. I, therefore, wish to divest myself of those one hundred shares. For me to sell them, however, someone must buy them. But the buyer would be purchasing one hundred shares of "tainted" stock, and I would have abetted the buyer in this immoral course of action. Granted, the prospective buyer might not believe the stock tainted, but that consideration would be irrelevant to me, because I am convinced that, knowingly or unknowingly, the buyer would be doing what is immoral. Surely I should not take any steps that would assist or encourage the buyer in such deplorable conduct. Nor should I try to release myself from a moral predicament by entangling someone else. How, then, is principled divestiture possible?

Reprinted from *Analysis* 47, *no.* 3 (1987); 49, no. 3 (1989); 51, no. 2 (1991). Reprinted by permission of the author.

II

Note that the question is not whether divestiture can be defended on strategic grounds. Surely it can be. Likewise, it can be opposed on strategic grounds, for by not divesting a stockholder maintains the leverage to bring internal pressure on the company to change its policy. Either strategy may succeed or fail, depending in any particular case on a variety of factors, including the percentage of total outstanding shares held, the attitudes of the board of directors, social and economic conditions, and so on. The puzzle doesn't depend on such empirical considerations but on the axiom that the only ethically proper policy is to sell tainted stock.

As for the suggestion that a possessor of tainted stock might choose to renounce ownership rather than sell, this financially fatal strategy would amount to redistributing the value of the divested shares among all other stockholders. The assets of those who had not divested would thereby be increased as would, presumably, their moral culpability.

In sum, your wish to sell your stock is logically equivalent to your wishing someone to buy it. By hypothesis, however, you believe that for anyone to buy the stock is wrong. So your wish to sell is the wish that someone else do wrong. And that desire is immoral.

Glossary

***A posteriori* proposition** A proposition whose truth-value can be known only through experience. For example, "Some swans are black" is true *a posteriori*, because we need to examine the swans in the natural world to discover if some of them are black.

***A priori* proposition** A proposition whose truth-value can be known independently of experience. For example, "triangles have three sides" is true *a priori*, because we do not need to examine any triangles in the natural world to discover that they have three sides.

Abolitionism The view that the death penalty should be abolished.

Absolutism The view that certain types of acts are impermissible no matter the consequences.

Act-consequentialism The view that you are required to perform an action if and only if (and because) of the acts now available to you, this act will uniquely bring about the most good-*simpliciter*. That is, you ought to perform the action whose outcome uniquely maximizes the good, period.

Active euthanasia Directed action taken by a physician, at the request of a terminally ill patient or the immediate family, to kill the patient.

Adultery Sex between a married person and someone other than that person's spouse.

Agency To be an agent is to have the capacity to recognize and respond to reasons.

Agent-neutral reasons Reasons that do not make essential reference to the agent to whom it applies; reasons for everyone.

Agent-relative constraint A constraint that blocks agents from promoting the good, even when violation of the constraint would minimize violations (either by other agents or at other times) of that very constraint. The reasons attached to the constraint accordingly must be agent-relative.

Agent-relative reason Reasons that make essential reference to the agent; reasons for a particular person.

Argument A series of statements, one of which (the conclusion) is claimed to be supported by the others (the premises).

Attributive goodness Good of a kind—for example, "That is a good pair of scissors."

Autonomy Having control over one's life. For Kant, autonomy is a property of the will—namely, to be a law unto oneself.

Average utilitarianism The view that, for all persons, each person is permitted to do (of the available actions) only what will bring about the maximum average utility— in other words, the total utility divided by the number of persons.

Beneficence The act of benefiting of others. (Or, conceived of as a character trait, the disposition to do so).

Consequentialist theory A theory that treats the deontic status of an act to be fully determined by the goodness of outcomes the act would bring about.

Consistency A set of claims is consistent if it is logically possible for all of the claims in the set to be true at the same time.

Constitutive value Something's having value by being a part of a larger valuable whole—for example, a piece of glass in a beautiful mosaic.

Contingent A claim that is true in the actual world, but is false in at least one possible world.

Cultural relativism The view that you are required to perform an action if and only if (and because) your performance of the act is called for by the norms of your culture.

Decisive (or conclusive) reasons Reasons to act in a certain way that outweigh any other reason (or combination of reasons) not to act in this way.

Deontic verdict A claim about the normative status of an action—for example, impermissible, permissible, required, optional, supererogatory.

Deontological theory A theory that does not treat deontic verdicts as solely a function of evaluative claims. Often such theories include at least one agent-relative constraint.

Derivative reasons Reasons that are parasitic on other reasons—in other words, reasons that are not ultimate. Derivative reasons do not supply additional justificatory weight for acting in a certain way.

Desire-satisfactionism The view that your well-being consists in having your desires satisfied. To the extent that (and because) your desires are satisfied, you are benefited. To the extent that (and because) your desires are not satisfied, you are harmed.

Determining grounds Part of an ethical theory that tells us which facts are reason providing—in other words, the facts that are relevant to the theory's deontic verdicts.

Deterrence The use of praise, blame, punishment, or reward to increase the likelihood that one will refrain from performing a certain act.

Dignity Having moral standing that makes one the appropriate object of respect.

Distributive justice The fair allocation of benefits and burdens among the members of a society.

Divine command theory The view that you are required to perform an action if and only if (and because) your performance of such acts is commanded by God.

Ecosystem The collection and interaction of living organisms and their environment.

Egalitarianism The view that justice requires equality, or perhaps the elimination of inequality.

Epiphenomenal Something that has no causal effects. (It may, however, itself be a causal effect).

Evaluative (or axiological) claims Claims about what is good or valuable.

Experience requirement Changes in your well-being must involve your experience. In order to be benefited or harmed, your experience must be affected.

Extrinsic value Something's having value because of the value some other intrinsically valuable thing bestows on it—for example, a family heirloom.

Fetus The unborn offspring of a mammal (usually taken to be in the later stages of development).

Good will A will that is able to reliably identify and carry out its duty for the sake of the duty.

Good-for Personally good. Good for some group or particular person—for example, "College was good for her."

Good-simpliciter Impersonally good. Good, period—for example, "It was good that the beautiful painting was saved from the fire."

Harm principle According to Mill, the only purpose for which power can be rightfully exercised over any member of a civilized community, against his will, is to prevent harm to others.

Hate speech Language that conveys contempt for some social (usually disadvantaged) group.

Hedonism The view that your well-being consists exclusively in facts about pleasure and pain. To the extent that (and because) your life contains experiences of pleasure, you are benefited. To the extent that (and because) your life contains experiences of pain, you are harmed. *Quantitative hedonists* hold that it is "better" the more intense the pleasure and the longer it lasts—in other words, "better" tracks the amount of pleasure. *Qualitative hedonists* hold that it is better the more intense the pleasure and the longer it lasts, but add that some kinds of pleasures are "better" than others—in other words, "better" tracks both amount and quality of pleasure.

If and only if A sentence that states both a necessary and sufficient condition—a biconditional. The "if" captures the sufficient condition. The "only if" captures the necessary condition.

Impermissible An action is impermissible if and only if refraining from the action is required.

Inference to the best explanation Tells us to infer the truth of a given hypothesis from the fact that this hypothesis explains the available evidence better than any other available hypotheses.

Instrumental value Something's having value because of what it brings about via its consequences—for example, money.

Interrogational torture Torture inflicted for the purpose of extracting information from the victim.

Intrinsic value Something's having value in and of itself, or for its own sake—for example, pleasure.

Kantianism The view that, for all persons, each person, *S*, is required to refrain from acting according to a maxim *S* could not rationally will as a universal law. Alternatively, for all persons, each person, *S*, is required to refrain from acting according to a maxim that treats humanity (rational nature), whether in *S*'s own person or in the person of another rational agent, as a mere means and not as an end.

Liberalism A view in political philosophy that takes individuals as primary, emphasizing their freedom and equality. Rawls captures the spirit of the view when he writes, "Since political power is the coercive power of free and equal citizens as a corporate body, this power should be exercised, when constitutional essentials and basic questions of justice are at stake, only in ways that all citizens can reasonably be expected to endorse in the light of their common human reason."

Libertarianism A view in political philosophy that, due to individual rights, permits only a minimal state. This meager social arrangement lacks a distributive apparatus beyond what is necessary to protect individual rights, enforce contracts, and maintain social stability.

Marginal utility The additional benefit that accrues to an agent by the acquisition of one more unit of a good or service.

Maxim A subjective principle of action that consists of the actor's intention and reason for so intending.

Moral worth The praiseworthy feature of an action associated with the motive that led the agent to perform the action. For Kant, an action has moral worth if and only if it is a dutiful action done from the motive of duty.

Necessary condition A condition p is a *necessary condition* for some q when the falsity of p guarantees the falsity of q. That is, q cannot be true unless p is true. For example, one is a mother only if one is female. That is, being female is a necessary condition for being a mother.

Negative duties A requirement to refrain from performing certain kinds of acts—for example, killing the innocent.

Normative (as opposed to descriptive) claims A claim that tells us what should, ought, or must be the case. By contrast, a descriptive claim tells us what is, was, or will be the case.

Normative reason A consideration that counts in favor of, or justifies, acting in certain ways.

Objective claim A claim that depends on how things are, independent of the speaker's psychology.

Objective list theory The view that your well-being consists in having your life contain certain objective goods and lack certain objective bads. To the extent that (and because) your life contains these goods, you are benefited. To the extent that (and because) your life contains these bads, you are harmed.

Obligatory An action is obligatory if and only if it is an action that is required.

Optimific An action is optimific if and only if (of the actions available) it is the action that makes things go best—in other words, no other action would produce a better outcome.

Optional An action is optional if and only if it is permissible to perform or not perform the action.

Passive euthanasia The withholding of treatment at the request of a terminally ill patient (or the immediate family) in order that the patient might be allowed to die.

Permissible An action is permissible if and only if it is an action that is not impermissible.

Pornography The depiction of sexually explicit material whose main purpose is the sexual arousal of the consumer. More controversially, the depiction and endorsement of degrading and abusive sexual behavior whose main purpose is the sexual arousal of the consumer.

Positive duties A requirement to perform certain kinds of acts—for example, helping those in need.

Predicate A term that tells us something about the subject of the sentence. For example, in the sentence "The cat is fat," the portion "is fat" is the predicate. The predicate here tells us that the subject (the cat) possesses a certain attribute (fatness). But predicates can also be used to tell us that there is a certain relation between two things. For instance, in the sentence "The cat is north of New York City," the portion "is north of" is the predicate.

Preferential affirmative action Programs that pay attention to group-identity criteria to increase numbers of women and minorities in the workplace.

***Pro tanto* reason** A consideration that counts in favor of acting in a certain way, but may not do so decisively.

Procedural affirmative action Measures taken to eradicate all racial, religious, ethnic, and sex discrimination from the workplace.

Psychological egoism The view that people are motivated exclusively by the promotion of their own well-being.

Racism Believing or acting on the view that certain racial groups are inherently inferior to others.

Rawls's contractualism The view that, for all persons, each person, *S*, is required to refrain from acting in ways disallowed by principles whose acceptance would be in everyone's rational self-interest to agree to behind a veil of ignorance.

Reason A consideration that counts in favor of, or justifies, acting in certain ways.

Relativism The view that ethical thought and talk is truth-apt but truth or falsity is indexed to a certain frame of reference—for example, indexed to the speaker, to the agent, or to a group. Often, an analogy is drawn to the rejection of absolute motion in physics.

Reparation A payment due, as a result of past wrongs, which restores the aggrieved party to their pre-wronged position.

Required An action is required if and only if there is decisive (or conclusive) reason to perform the action. That is, an action is required if and only it is the only permissible action available.

Resonance requirement In order for something to be good-for-you, it must resonate with you. You cannot be benefited by something that you do not endorse or that alienates you.

Rights Broadly, for *S* to have a right is for *S* to have a claim to be treated in a certain way. Narrowly, for *S* to have a right is for *S* to have a claim that corresponds to someone else's having a positive or negative duty to treat *S* in a certain way. Rights attached to a negative duty are called *negative rights*—e.g., freedom of speech. Rights attached to a positive duty are called *positive rights*—e.g., the right to be loved.

Rights infringement An action that breaches someone's rights but, given the circumstances, this breach is justified.

Rights violation An action that breaches someone's rights and, given the circumstances, this breach is unjustified.

Rule-consequentialism The view that, for all persons, each person is required to conform to the rules whose general internalization will (of the available sets of rules) bring about the most good-*simpliciter*.

Self-evident claims A claim whose truth one is justified in believing simply by virtue of adequately understanding it.

Sexism Believing or acting on the view certain members of one sex (usually female) are inherently inferior to another.

Singer's *key claim* You are obligated to prevent something bad from happening if you can do so without thereby sacrificing anything of comparable moral importance.

Soundness A valid argument that has true premises.

Speciesism A term to designate systematic discrimination based on species membership, analogous to racism or sexism.

Sufficient condition A condition p is a *sufficient condition* for q when the truth of p guarantees q. That is, p's being true is enough for q's being true. For example, if one is a mother, then one is female. Being a mother is a sufficient condition for being female.

Supererogatory An action is supererogatory if and only if it is an action that is good but not required—in other words, an action that goes beyond the call of duty.

Synthetic propositions A proposition that is not analytic. For example, "all creatures with hearts have kidneys" is true because of the way the world is, not because the predicate concept is contained within the subject concept.

Terrorism The deliberate use of force against noncombatants with the aim of spreading fear for political ends.

Terroristic torture Torture inflicted for the purpose of intimidating people other than the victim.

Total-utilitarianism The view that, for all persons, each person is permitted to do (of the available actions) only what will bring about the maximum total utility.

Universal egoism The view that you are required to perform an action if and only if (and because), of the acts now available to you, this act will uniquely bring about the most good-for-you. That is, you ought to perform the action whose outcome is uniquely best-for-you.

Universalizability The requirement that deontic verdicts must apply to all persons in relevantly similar circumstances. Put precisely, a reason to ϕ is universalizable if, for all x, were x in conditions C, then there is a reason for x to ϕ.

Utilitarianism The view that you are required to perform an action if and only if (and because) of the acts now available to you, this act will uniquely bring about the greatest sum-total of well-being. That is, you ought to perform the action whose outcome maximizes total well-being.

Validity The form of an argument is such that if all of the premises are true, then its conclusion must be true.

Vices Bad dispositions, or defects of character. Lead to negative assessments of attributive goodness.

Virtue ethics The view that you are required to perform an action if and only if (and because) this action is what a fully virtuous person (acting in character) would do in the circumstances. That is, you ought to do whatever the completely virtuous agent would characteristically do.

Virtues Good dispositions, or excellences of character. Lead to positive assessments of attributive goodness.